Dedication

To "Steb," J. Monroe Stebbins, Jr.,
and to his
outstanding Dobermans
who contributed so tremendously
to this breed.

Frontis: Ch. Galaxy's Corry Missle Belle, owned by Mr. and Mrs. N. J. Reese and Elaine Herndon, was bred by Claire Mc-Cabe and handled by Corky Vroom. Corry was the Quaker Oats Winner of Top Dog, all breeds, in 1973.

THE WORLD OF
DOBERMAN PINSCHERS

ANNA KATHERINE NICHOLAS

*With a special health section by Joseph P. Sayres, DVM,
and excerpts from the Doberman Pinscher Club of America
Judges' Educational Committee Manual*

Contents

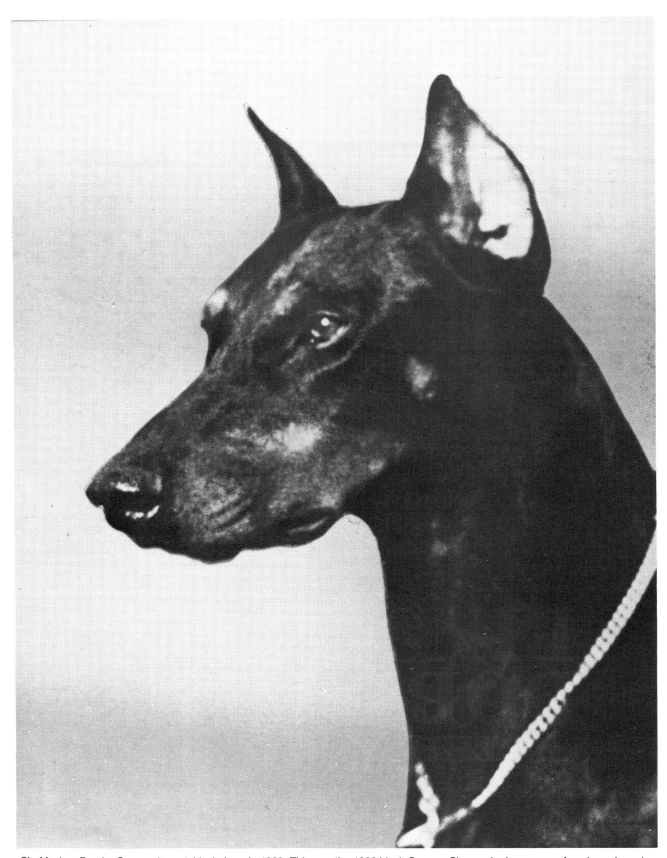

Ch. Muck v. Brunia, German import, black, born in 1929. This was the 1932 black German Sieger who became an American champion in 1932 less than a month after arrival here. Sire of six American champions, three German Siegers, and the famous Lindenhoff "F" litter. Sire of Troll v Engelsburg, who was the sire of Ch. Ferry v Rauhfelsen of Giralda. Photo courtesy of Rancho Dobe Kennels through Karen Vroom Parkhurst. Muck's progeny formed the base of many American Doberman kennels.

In Appreciation

One look at this book will tell our readers the amount of work that went into it. It also will tell of the marvelous co-operation and enthusiasm I encountered from Doberman people throughout the Fancy! For truly, so tremendous a collection of Doberman information and photographs could not possibly have been brought to you without the generosity, support and willingness to help of the great majority of Doberman people. For the endless hours devoted by those of you who have contributed searching out and collecting invaluable older photos, historical facts on some of the earlier kennels which we could not possibly have acquired entirely on our own, and all the other assistance you have so generously given to this book, my heartfelt thanks. I hope that it lives up to all your expectations, for we have really tried to make it as outstanding as this breed itself!

A special note of gratitude to the Stebbinses—Natalie and Steb—who have been so kind in answering questions, loaning us photos, and making suggestions when asked. Your support has been tremendous! The same is true of Peggy Adamson, who has taken considerable time from her already crowded schedule to go through her files and records to help us to include *all* the dogs who should be represented. Plus each and every one of you who took the trouble to hunt up your photos from early times until the present; to send us kennel story material; and to lend us your help whenever it was needed.

Marcia Foy, here at home, has really done "double duty" by sending out hundreds of letters for me and generally acting as "contact person" for a million and one details. Were it not for her help, I'm sure the book would have been much longer in reaching completion.

Then our thanks, as usual, to Dr. Joseph P. Sayres for, again, one of his outstanding Veterinarian's Corner features, this one geared to Dobermans.

There are many other people who went out of their way to be helpful, all of whom I would love to mention individually if space permitted. You will never be forgotten for the marvelous manner in which you "came through" when asked to do so!

—*Anna Katherine Nicholas*

7

About the Author

Since early childhood, Anna Katherine Nicholas has been involved with dogs. Her first pets were a Boston Terrier, an Airedale, and a German Shepherd Dog. Then, in 1925, came the first of the Pekingese—a gift from a friend who raised them. Now her home is shared with a Miniature Poodle and a dozen or so Beagles, including her noted Best in Show dog and National Specialty winner, Champion Rockaplenty's Wild Oats, a Gold Certificate sire (one of the breed's truly great stud dogs), who as a show dog was Top Beagle in the Nation in 1973. She also owns Champion Foyscroft True Blue Lou, Foyscroft Aces Are Wild, and in co-ownership with Marcia Foy, who lives with her, Champion Foyscroft Triple Mitey Migit.

Miss Nicholas is best known throughout the Dog Fancy as a writer and as a judge. Her first magazine article, published in *Dog News* magazine around 1930, was about Pekingese; and this was followed by a widely acclaimed breed column, "Peeking at the Pekingese," which appeared for at least two decades, originally in *Dogdom*, then, following the demise of that publication, in *Popular Dogs*. During the 1940's she was Boxer columnist for *Pure-Bred Dogs/American Kennel Gazette* and for *Boxer Briefs*. More recently many of her articles, geared to interest fanciers of every breed, have appeared in *Popular Dogs, Pure-Bred Dogs/American Kennel Gazette, Show Dogs, Dog Fancy,* and *The World of the Working Dog.* Currently she is a featured regular columnist in *Kennel Review, Dog World,* and *Canine Chronicle.* Her *Dog World* column, "Here, There and Everywhere," was the Dog Writers Association of America winner of the Best Series in a Dog Magazine Award for 1979.

It was during the late 1930's that Miss Nicholas' first book, *The Pekingese,* appeared, published by and written at the request of the Judy Publishing Company. This book completely sold out and is now a collector's item, as is her *The Skye Terrier Book,* which was published by the Skye Terrier Club of America during the early 1960's.

In 1970 Miss Nicholas won the Dog Writers Association of America award for the Best Technical Book of the Year with her *Nicholas Guide to Dog Judging,* published by Howell

Book House. In 1979 the revision of this book again won the Dog Writers Association of America Best Technical Book Award, the first time ever that a revision has been so honored by this association.

In the early 1970's, Miss Nicholas co-authored, with Joan Brearley, five breed books which were published by T.F.H. Publications, Inc. These were *This is the Bichon Frise, The Wonderful World of Beagles and Beagling* (winner of a Dog Writers Association of America Honorable Mention Award), *The Book of the Pekingese, The Book of the Boxer,* and *This is the Skye Terrier.*

During recent years, Miss Nicholas has been writing books consistently for T.F.H. These include *Successful Dog Show Exhibiting, The Book of the Rottweiler, The Book of the Poodle, The Book of the Labrador Retriever, The Book of the English Springer Spaniel, The Book of the Golden Retriever,* and *The Book of the German Shepherd Dog.* Most recently she has written *The Book of the Shetland Sheepdog,* another breed spectacular. In the T.F.H. "KW" series, she has done *Rottweilers, Weimaraners,* and *Norwegian Elkhounds.* She has also supplied the American chapters for two English publications, imported by T.F.H., *The Staffordshire Bull Terrier* and *The Jack Russell Terrier.*

Miss Nicholas, in addition to her four Dog Writers Association of America awards, has on two occasions been honored with the *Kennel Review* "Winkie" as Dog Writer of the Year; and in both 1977 and 1982 she was recipient of the Gaines "Fido" award as Journalist of the Year in Dogs.

Her judging career began in 1934 at the First Company Governors' Foot Guard in Hartford, Connecticut, drawing the largest Pekingese entry ever assembled to date at this event. Presently she is approved to judge all Hounds, Terriers, Toys, and Non-Sporting Dogs; all Pointers, English and Gordon Setters, Vizslas, Weimaraners, and Wirehaired Pointing Griffons in Sporting breeds and, in the Working Group, Boxers and Doberman Pinschers. In 1970 she became the third woman in history to judge Best in Show at the prestigious Westminster Kennel Club Dog Show, where she has officiated on some sixteen other occasions through the years. In addition to her numerous Westminster assignments, Miss Nicholas has judged at such other outstandingly important events as Santa Barbara, Trenton, Chicago International, the Sportsmans in Canada, the Metropolitan in Canada, and Specialty Shows in several dozen breeds both in the United States and in Canada. She has judged in almost every one of the mainland United States and in four Canadian provinces, and her services are constantly sought in other countries.

Through the years, Miss Nicholas has held important offices in a great many all-breed and Specialty clubs. She still remains an honorary member of several of them.

Ch. Dow's Cassie v Kienlesburg, bred and owned by the late Bert Dow of Davenport, Iowa. Her dam, Ch. Gretl v Kienlesburg, was a half sister of Jessy v Sonnenhohe, through their sire, and imported by Mr. Dow in the 1930's. In her one litter (she died shortly thereafter) by Ch. Kurt v d Rheinperle-Rheingold, all were lost except two who became the noted Champions Cora and Cassie, especially noted for their excellent heads. Their offspring are behind many of the best of the modern Dobermans. Photo courtesy of Peggy Adamson.

CHAPTER ONE

Origin of the Doberman Pinscher

The Doberman Pinscher came about in rather a unique manner, through the efforts principally of one man whose interest and involvement were so great that upon his death the breed of dog he had created was named for him by those carrying on his work. This man was Herr Karl Friedrich Louis Dobermann, who was born on February 2, 1823 and lived in the town of Apolda, located in the state of Thuringia, Germany. So closely associated was this man with these dogs that upon his death, on June 9, 1884, age 61 years, fellow fanciers of the breed who by then had come to share interest in it, decreed that these dogs should be known as Dobermann Pinschers in tribute to Herr Dobermann's many years spent in the perfection of his dream—that of creating a dog somewhat similar to a giant terrier (Pinscher), although actually medium in size as compared to huge. These dogs were to be fearless and aggressive, intelligent, and quick to learn. Great strength was important. Herr Dobermann had a clear and definite mental picture of his dog, and obviously the "breeder's sense" of how to go about making this dog a reality.

As a youth, Herr Dobermann was employed as an alderman, later becoming administrator of the Niederrossla-Apolda chamber of accounts, an official of the tax office—and dog catcher. Being additionally employed as night-time police officer, he needed a dog for companionship on his rounds, to give warning of the presence or approach of intruders, and for protection. As dog catcher, he was able to "pick and choose" from what was available at the pound. This is how he acquired the original Schnupp, a black and tan Pinscher, who accompanied him on his rounds and who had been carefully selected at the pound.

When Schnupp was acquired, Herr Dobermann was living in an apartment, and thus was unable to breed dogs, which had become one of his ambitions. Later he moved to larger quarters, but it was not until 1880 that he was able to move to a house in a location enabling him to both breed and train. We understand that he owned, also, pure bred Rottweilers and German Shepherd Dogs. It was during this period that Bisart was added to the family, a black bitch with tan markings and a slightly grayish tinge to her undercoat. She produced Pinko, a bitch Herr Dobermann retained for breeding as she was a natural bobtail whom he had hoped might reproduce this feature if bred to do so, but who, unfortunately, although bred to a bobtailed stud, had only one short-tailed puppy in her litter by him.

Returning to the background of our present Doberman. Obviously the ancestors of the breed were in Apolda prior to the start of Herr Dobermann's activity, or they would not have been available to him. It is felt that dogs used in his breeding program included the very popular Thuringian Shepherds, early Rottweilers (probably some of his own), the early German Pinscher, and the black and tan, quite large for the modern breed, forebears of the present Manchester Terrier. Additional theories include a bit of Great Dane, Weimaraner, and German Shorthaired Pointer, and I have read that a black Greyhound bitch also played a part, bringing with her refinement and elegance. All of the foregoing seems reasonable and to fit in with the character and appearance of the dogs which have evolved.

Germany's first dog show was held at Hamburg in 1863. Prior to that time there had taken place, at Apolda, a somewhat informal event known as "the dog market," which was a dog-show-type affair, held annually on the

Sunday following Whitsuntide. This was put on by a club dedicated to promoting the pure-bred dog and sponsored by the Apolda government in that they shared a portion of the entry fees, putting this money back into expenses for the running of the event. Groups were then divided into sets of breeds (as is the case now!), breeds, the classification being "luxury dogs," "butcher's dogs," "house dogs," "hounds," etc. Need we say that this was an affair always attended by Herr Dobermann, usually accompanied by friends who also enjoyed dog breeding? His eye was always alert for anything he might see and could buy that was of the type of dog interesting to him.

During the closing decade of the 1800's and as the 1900's began, two other breeders of importance to the Dobe's progress were Goswin Tischler and Otto Göller. Goswin Tischler owned a bitch, Tilly I von Groenland, a daughter of Lord ex Schnupine. She was bred to Lux who was a particularly splendid sire of the day, producing a litter whose members included Gelling, Greif, Krone, Lottchen, and Tilly II v Groenland. We understand that this was considered one of the finest litters of the breed until that time. Troll v Groenland was a Tilly I son, and he became the sire of Flora v Groenland, dam of Leporello v d Nidda, important in the bloodlines of Dobermans in Switzerland. Goswin Tischler's kennel name was Groenland.

Herr Otto Göller founded his Thueringen Kennels near the turn of the century. He is generally credited with having been the breeder most dedicated to carrying on Herr Dobermann's practices, beliefs and programs, and he raised many Dobermanns which included some of the very best. His famous Hellegraf von Thueringen, born in 1904, was an important force in the breed. Graf Belling von Thueringen distinguished himself by providing half of the breeding combination with Ullrich's Glocke v Thueringen that resulted in two Siegers. There was also the notable bitch Freya v Thueringen, and the popular brown dog, Junker Hans v d Ronneburg. Then there were Gerhilde v Thueringen, Ines v Thueringen, and Winfried v Thueringen. Junker Slenz v Thueringen won considerable fame when purchased by the Frankfurt Club for the use of their members as a stud dog.

The National Dobermann Pinscher Club in Germany was founded by Otto Göller in 1899, when the Standard of the Breed was also drawn up and approved for acceptance by the German Kennel Club. Herr Goller became the organization's first President.

It was in 1893 that Bosco became the first of his breed to be registered in the German Stud Book, followed the next year by a bitch Caesi born and registered during it. In 1895 these two produced Prinz Matzi v Groenland, who later gained the German title, Sieger, and who was the third breed entry in the German Stud Book.

The naming of his breed officially "The Dobermann Pinscher" is an honor well deserved in acknowledgment of Herr Dobermann's contribution in giving the world one of the most desirable breeds of dog ever to be known. And so it was that the breed identification progressed, from the original title of "Dobermann's Dogs" to the other sometimes used "Thueringia Pinschers" to, during war times, "Pliseilich Soldatenhunds," and finally to "Dobermann Pinscher." The name remained so without change ever since, except for the dropping of the second "n" in its spelling in America and the elimination of the word "Pinscher" in Germany. This latter change took place during the mid-1900's when the feeling arose that to call these dogs by a name that indicated they were terriers was actually incorrect.

We feel that Herr Dobermann would look with approval upon the manner in which his work has been carried on!

Danica Stamm's Juon at age 16 months. Born in 1978, by Guy's Hillo of Norden-Stamm (who is a champion of Norway, Sweden, Finland, Europe, and Germany; Schutzhund III; and International Champion) from Edda von Ferrolheim. Danica Stamm's Juon was a stallion recommended by the Doberman Club of France, selected first choice in 1979, 1980, 1981, 1982, and 1983. He has won 36 CACIB's and 62 CAC's in France, Germany, Italy, Belgium, Spain, Denmark, and Holland. He has 12 Bests in Show, 21 Bests in Group, and 39 Bests of Breed. Owned by Annie and Daniel Mulero, Dompierre/Mer, France,

Ch. Muck v Brunia and Ch. Ella v Graf Zeppelin. Owned by Owen A. West. Photo courtesy of Peggy Adamson.

1. D.V. Sieger Chico von Forall, bred and owned by Ernst Wilking. An important winner of the 1960's, by Odin von Forell ex Cita Germania.
2. Bdsg., Dutch and Lux. Ch. Gravin Taby van Neerlands Stam, a brown and rust bitch and a winner of the late 1960's. The post-war foundation bitch of van Neerlands Dobermans owned by Mrs. Kneif Dermont, known as the breed's greatest living breeder of Dobes in Holland. This kennel, founded in the early 1900's, has been active for some 65 years and is world famous for the excellence and quality of its Dobes.

1▲   ▼2

1. A very exciting winning bitch from Holland during the early 1980's. Ch. Gravin Aranka v. Neerlands Stam, age 10 months here, represents the kennels of Holland's foremost living breeder of Dobes, Mrs. Kneif Dermont. Aranka was Champion des Jeunes, Luxembourg 1980; Best Bitch, Champion (C.A.C.) at Eindhoven in 1980; Best Bitch, Youth Class, then Best of All Bitches (all-breeds); and finally first in Group and Best in Show, with 2,211 dogs competing, Leeunvarden Inbern Show. Numerous other important wins. Beautiful example of the type and quality in Dobes in Holland today.
2. Peggy Adamson has loaned us this interesting photo of Dobermans in Holland bred by Mrs. Kneif Dermont.
3. This photo, from 1928, is of one of the famed von Grammont Dobermans of Holland, owned by L. Kloppel. A splendid example of excellent type and quality at that time.
4. Utta of Bamby's Pride Winster, 1972, several times Best of Breed. This Japanese import needed only one championship to be Definitive Dutch Champion. Owned by Sonja von Franquemont-Freudenberg, Dordrecht, Nederland. Photo courtesy of Peggy Adamson.
5. Banglah vom Franckenhorst Weltju, Genssieger '73, owned by Sonja and David von Franquemont-Freudenberg. Photo taken at age 13 months. Courtesy of Peggy Adamson.
6. Alma von Franckenhorst, Sch.H. I, was 1973 Weltsieger at the World Dog Show. Bred by Sonja von Franquemont-Freudenberg of the Netherlands. Photo courtesy of Peggy Adamson.
7. Nederlands Schoonfeid en Workkamp. Baron Cecar v Rensloo, VH III (Schutzhund III), FH, HDTC. Dobermann Kennel v Pennolope, Rosemarie-Hennie Hartog, Holland.
8. Marta de la Morliere, owned by Annie and Daniel Mulero, France.
9. Bundessieger, 1963, Argus v. Neroberg, Sch.H. III. Photo courtesy of Peggy Adamson.

4

5

6

7

8

9

When a young puppy is to be kept for their own kennel, the Muleros will see that it is walked several times a week in the town for shopping or other errands, taking it also to the market. The puppy rides frequently in the car and is taught to not bark without reason.

Great emphasis is placed on the working qualities of their dogs, so from an early age the puppies are accustomed to work. All of the Mulero dogs participate in the working trials, which again leads to that all-important excellent character. A calm, poised dog who is never shy or aggressive is demanded. Of course good conformation is important, the Muleros' preference being a champion stud with work trial degrees. Thus all of their dogs are taken through obedience, tracking, and attack-with-biting trials. In France there are no professional handlers, and so the owners personally prepare and work the dogs in the trials and expositions.

Danica Stamm's Juon has an impressive list of titles to his credit. Owned by Annie and Daniel Mulero, this dog was Coupe de France du D.C.F. 1980; International Champion 1981; Hessen Sieger 1981; Champion de France et d'Espagne; and Meilleur Dobermann European 1980.

In 1979 Juon became Young Champion of the World at Berne, also Best Young of the Show; Young Champion of the International Dobermann Club; Young German Champion (Jugend Bunde Sieger); and Best Young Male in the National Kennel Show that year.

In 1980 he was Champion of France; Champion of Europe (winner in the Eurodog Show); Champion of the Mediterranean Week; and Vice-Champion of Germany (Bunde Siegerschan).

1981's accomplishments were International Champion; Hessen Champion (Champion of a province in Germany); Champion of Spain; and the "cup of France" of the Dobermann Club of France.

1982, again Hessen Champion (Germany); Champion of Denmark; Vice-Champion of Lux embourg; winner at Copenhagen (Denmark); Champion of Westfallen (Germany); and Best male, black, in championship of Spain.

1983 was another exciting year. Juon gained Champion of Belgium in training of

homologation, doing likewise at the German Canine Society. He earned his French work trial (Brevet de Chien de Defense), his International work trial (Schutzhund I) and Z.T.B. A excellent (German confirmation). Needless to say, the Muleros take tremendous pride in the talents and abilities of this great and handsome dog!

There are other beautiful and interesting Dobermans as well at the Muleros' kennel, such as Udine du Fief de la Garenne, born January 1983, by Juon from Anja von der Bult, first shown at the National Kennel Show in September 1982, taking third place in the Baby Show Class behind its litter sister.

Bellona von der Bult, by Juon from Yvette v Haus Junemann, was a second place winner in the Young Class at the National Kennel Show in 1983, first time out.

Anja von der Bult was born in 1979, sired by the important winner, Ero v Frankenhorst, who was a Champion of Holland, Germany, V.D.H. (Germany), D.V. (Germany, France, Luxembourg) and the German working titles Schutzhund III, National working title V.H. III, and of the International Dobermann Club. Anja's dam was Yvette v Haus Junemann, Champion of Germany, of Europe, and the holder of a Schutz hund II degree.

Anja lived up to the family quality by having won three C.A.C. certificates and three CACIB in Spain; three C.A.C., a reserve CACIB and two CACIB in France; and C.A.C. and V.D.H. in Germany. Anja's titles include Vice-Champion of Spain and Vice-Champion of France.

1980 included some notable wins for Ozzo du Fief de la Garenne's two offspring by Juon. For one, Rufus du Fief de la Garenne, having gained C.A.C. and CACIB at the Championship in Madrid was a well merited honor. For the other, Raphia du Fief de la Garenne, two C.A.C. and CACIB were added to two Bests of Breed.

Parvovirus struck this kennel during 1981, but Mr. and Mrs. Mulero did not allow themselves to be discouraged, and in 1982 they were back in the wins again with Juon offspring from Olaz du Fief de la Garenne, Tamara du Fief de la Garenne, Traycin du Fief de la Garenne, and Thor du Fief de la Garenne, the latter a C.A.C. and Best of Breed winner. Tamara is now preparing for the

Livie de La Morliere, the first of the Dobermans owned by Annie and Daniel Mulero, Dompierre/Mer, France.

working trials and will be shown in the exposition in the near future.

Several litters were planned, to be born about the time this book is being written. One is by Juon from Anja, and one by Flegon Falek v Diaspora, who was Best of Breed in the 1983 German Championship Show, from Danica Stamm's Lee, a lovely daughter of Greif v Norden Stamm, son of Guy's Hillo of Nordan Stamm and his sister, Guy's Heydy of Norden Stamm. Lee was never shown because of a tooth which was broken in a wire netting, but she is a most typical and handsome bitch who should produce quality. Also, two litters are planned by Garry v Hagenstern, one from Bellona v d Bult and one from Tamara, with the possibility that Udine du Fief de la Garenne will be another to be bred.

Now in training for the working trials, and to be shown soon, is Garry von Hagenstern. This fine young son of Juon from Chiquita v Hagenstern took third prize in the baby show at the National early in his career. He was born in 1982.

We feel that many of our readers may not be familiar with the process by which Euro-

pean championships are earned. Therefore we bring you a resume, sent us by Mr. Mulero, explaining the procedure in various European countries. CACIB is a Certificate of Aptitude to the International Championship of Beauty. A dog or bitch must have two CACIB Certificates in two different lands from two different judges within an interval of one year. Additionally the dog or bitch must also have won in an International Schutzhund Trial. CACIB is awarded to the best male or to the best female of the show in each breed, with all classes and all colors together.

C.A.C. is the certificate of aptitude to the natural championship of beauty. In France the requirements are three C.A.C. awards from three different judges with an interval of one year between the awarding of the first and the third and also a work trial. In Germany the requirements are more stringent, as they require five C.A.C. wins with four different judges in an interval of two years, and also a work trial.

C.A.C. is awarded to the best black male, all classes together. I V is one C.A.C. by color.

1. Gr. Ch. Danica Stamm's Juon winning Best in Show at the Eurodogshow with judge Avik Marshak of Israel. Owned by the Muleros, Dompierre/Mer, France.
2. Uhlann du Fief della Garenne, by Danica Stamm's Juon ex Anja v. d. Bult, at six months. Annie and Daniel Mulero, owners.
3. Danica Stamm's Lee, owned by the French breeders, Annie and Daniel Mulero.
4. Ozzo du Fief de la Garenne, daughter of Danica Stamm's Juon. Owned by Annie and Daniel Mulero.
5. Garry von Hagenstern at three months. Another young son of Danica Stamm's Juon (see pedigree). Annie and Daniel Mulero, owners.

Dobermann-Verein e.V.

Rechtssitz: 8 MÜNCHEN   im VDH und der FCI

AHNENTAFEL FÜR DEN DOBERMANN-RÜDEN

Name : Gary von Hagenstern

Wurftag : 21. Juli 1982

Eltern	Großeltern	Urgroßeltern
Danica Stamms Juon IPO I Int-Ch, Fr-Ch HD-2 DZB DKK 15114/78	Guy's Hilo v. Norden Stamm SchH III Int+D-Ch, Bdsg, Euro-Sg N-Ch HD-1 DZB 88881 Edda v. Ferrolheim DZB DK 22898/77	Bryan v. Forell N-Ch DZB 80934 Gunthersforst Burga N-Ch DZB KC 109308 Jürgen v. Hagenstern Int+D-Ch, DV-Sg, Hol+Lux-Ch, SchH I DZB 83285 Hol-Win Amanda v. Stifthub, braun SchH I, D-Ch DZB 83123
Chiquita v. Hagenstern braun HD-1 DZB 91991	Aldo v. Ferrolheim braun SchH I Int+D-Ch, Bdsg, DV-Sg Euro+VDH-Sg HD-2 DZB NHSB 714286 Uschika v. Hagenstern Welt-Sg HD-1 DZB 87139	Jürgen v. Hagenstern SchH I, Int+D-Ch, DV-Sg, Hol+Lux-Ch DZB 83285 Hol-Win Amanda v. Stifthub, braun SchH I, D-Ch DZB 83123 Anuschka Bryansdotter M: SchH III, Int+D-Ch, Bdsg, DV-Sg, DZB Reg 1/72 Welt+VDH-Sg Hol-Win Nero v. Hagenstern V: DZB 84128

Dictator and "Candy" in March 1952. Dictator was age 10½ in this picture. His daughter, Damasyn Sikhandi, and he were photographed here with their owner, Peggy Adamson, just one month before the tragic accident that led to their deaths. Candy was the dam of Ch. Damasyn The Easter Bonnet, the dam of Ch. Steb's Top Skipper.

CHAPTER THREE

Dobermans in the United States

The "key" year in early Doberman history in the United States was 1908. During that year on June 20th a black and tan dog was whelped, subsequently named Doberman Intelectus and registered with the American Kennel Club that same year, assigned #122650, thus becoming the first of his breed registered in this country. Also in 1908, the kennel prefix "Doberman" was granted by the American Kennel Club as a registered kennel prefix to Theodore F. Jaeger of Pittsford, New York—a happening which could not occur nowadays, as the A.K.C. some years ago discontinued the use of breed names as registered kennel identifications.

Doberman Intelectus, a black and tan dog, was sired by the German import, Doberman Bertel who had formerly been known as Bertel, v Hohenstein; he was from the bitch, Doberman Hertha, another from Hohenstein Kennels in Germany who in 1912 was to become the first of her breed to achieve A.K.C. championship.

It is interesting to note that a descendant of Herr Dobermann, forming a partnership with Mr. Jaeger, is credited with having brought Hertha and Bertel v Hohenstein from Germany as foundation stock for their Doberman Kennels. Certainly it was a dominant venture in the breed of that day, as when Doberman Dix became the first male and the first American-bred Doberman champion, it left these gentlemen with a "clean sweep" of firsts. First registration. First registered kennel. First Doberman Champion. First Doberman Champion Dog and Bitch. And first American-bred Dobe champion.

The appearances of these dogs did their bit to generate further interest and activity in the breed, and by the start of World War I there were active breeders of Dobermans in the mid-West, New England, New York, New Jersey and Pennsylvania, and on the Pacific Coast. There was a Doberman Pinscher Club of America founded prior to World War I, which seems to have continued through about 1919. Then there was no activity in this field until 1921, when the first steps were taken toward the formation of our present Doberman Pinscher Club of America.

With the beginning of the 1920's interest in Dobermans took on considerable growth, and some very dominant importations started to arrive in the States. During the war years owning dogs in Germany had been extremely difficult if at all possible, but by the '20's things were again on the up-swing. Servicemen are said to have brought Dobermans with them on their return home following the war. Americans were rapidly becoming aware of the many splendid features this breed had to offer. Throughout the 1920's, and most of the '30's, there was a heavy demand from American fanciers for German Siegers and Siegerins and especially for those who had proven themselves outstanding producers.

In 1921 George H. Earle, III, acquired Champion Lord v d Hortsburg, probably the best import of his time, for his Red Roof Kennels in Pennsylvania where he became a widely used stud dog. Two years later, Champion Benno v Burgholz, a 1922 German Sieger, became the first actual Sieger to reach these shores. Benno was a brown dog, born in 1929, whose coloring added to his popularity here among those with brown bitches.

Next came Champion Claus v d Spree, who proved a good investment as the sire of a dozen American champions during the 1920's, including the Best in Show winner, Champion Big Boy of White Gate, who was from Howard K. Mohr's White Gate Kennels, and one of the best of the day. Big Boy's dam was Elfrieda v d Koningstad, a Dutch-bred import. Mr. Mohr also imported Angola

1. Ch. Figaro of Pontchartrain, a Lux grandson, bred and owned by Glenn Staines, Pontchartrain Kennels, Michigan.
2. This is "Arnold," who was one of Glenn Staines's most famous Pathfinder Dogs. The harness was part of his gear which equipped him to guide the blind. Photo courtesy of Peggy Adamson.
3. Ch. Hesta of Pontchartrain in the late 1920's, bred and owned by Glenn Staines. Sired by Ch. Favoriet v Konigstad (imported).
4. Ch. Assy v Illenblick was purchased in Europe by Mrs. Rhys (Eleanor) Carpenter. Photo courtesy of Peggy Adamson.
5. A lovely head study of Ch. Westphalia's Uranus, owned by Francis F. H. Fleitmann.
6. Ch. Westphalia's Uranus, born in 1939, lived to be 10 years old and was the sire of more than 10 champions. Francis F. H. Fleitmann, owner.
7. Ch. Dow's Cassie v Kienlesberg was bred and owned by Bert Dow. Photo courtesy of Peggy Adamson.
8. Siegerin and Ch. Ora v Sandberg-Kindenhof, red daughter of Ch. Moritz v Rodeltal. This was the last great import prior to World War II and one of the most beautiful bitches ever imported. She won the Doberman Pinscher Club of America Specialty in 1939, thus becoming the third bitch to win this honor, which went to Red Roof Hilda in 1924 (the first Specialty) and to Jessy v Sonnenhohe in 1937. Photo courtesy of Peggy Adamson.
9. Ch. Echo of Marienland, litter sister to Emperor (by Domossi ex Rembla) was bred by Dick Webster and owned by Col. Lambert Caine.
10. The very famous Ch. Favoriet v Franzhuf, a red son of Uranus, owned by Westphalia Kennels, Francis F. H. Fleitmann. Photo of this famous early dog loaned to us by Peggy Adamson.
11. Ch. Lux v Blankenberg (1918-1931) pictured when he was an old dog. Owned by Glenn Staines of Pontchartrain Kennels in Detroit. A great and important sire whose influence was a strong one on the breed. Among his progeny were six with the Sieger or Siegerin titles, 19 sons and daughters who bore American championships, and 20 others with champion descendants. It has been found that more than half of the American champions completing title between 1946 and 1950 can trace their ancestry back to this highly dominant dog. Photo courtesy of Peggy Adamson.

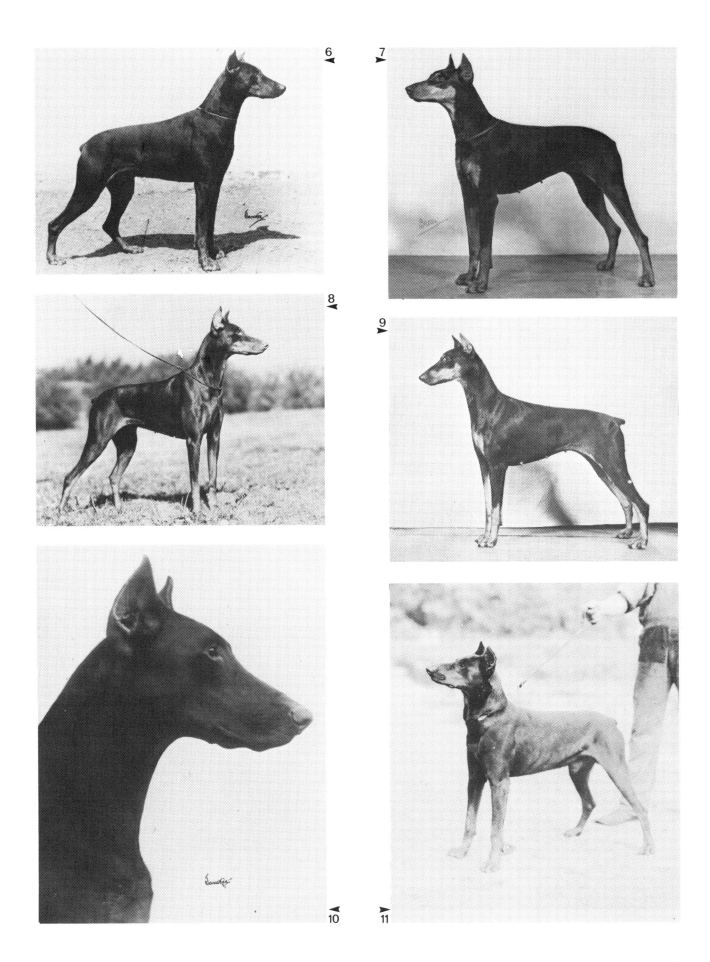

6 ◄   7 ►

8 ◄   9 ►

◄ 10   11 ►

29

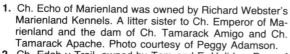

1. Ch. Echo of Marienland was owned by Richard Webster's Marienland Kennels. A litter sister to Ch. Emperor of Marienland and the dam of Ch. Tamarack Amigo and Ch. Tamarack Apache. Photo courtesy of Peggy Adamson.
2. Ch. Edah v Trail, owned by Tom and E. Holiday. Dam of three champions. Photograph courtesy of Peggy Adamson.
3. Working Dog history from the early 1940's. The great Boxer bitch, Ch. El Wendie of Rockland, in first place with her handler J. Nate Levine. The great Doberman bitch, Ch. Dow's Illena of Marienberg, in second place handled by Percy Roberts. It is interesting that this is the only Doberman Mr. Roberts ever accepted to handle, which he did in tribute to his admiration for her. Mrs. Margaret (Marge) Kilburn, owner, Pottstown, Pennsylvania.
4. Ch. Rolanna of Marienland with her handler, August R. (Gus) Hill. One of the noted winning Dobermans owned by Mr. and Mrs. Sidney A. Moss in California during the 1940's.
5. Ch. Maida von Coldod, from the 1940's, owned by Mrs. Alice Mills. The dam of Ch. Alcor v Millsdod.
6. Ch. Quo Schmerk of Marienland. Photo courtesy of Karen Vroom Parkhurst, Chino, California.
7. Mrs. Geraldine Rockefeller Dodge of Giralda Farms, Madison, New Jersey, in 1939 with her import, Ch. Ferry von Rauhfelsen of Giralda. This was one of only two Dobes to date who have won Best in Show at Westminster.

1. Ch. Kurt v d Rheinperle-Rheingold, imported in 1933 by J. C. Zimmerman, Birmingham, Michigan. Born December 1931, Dusseldorf, Germany.
2. Ch. Carla v Glenhugel, a full sister to Ch. Dictator v Glenhugel, owned by Radford Kennels, Nashville, Tennessee.
3. Ch. Beth v Glenhugel, famous bitch of the early days. Photo courtesy of Peggy Adamson. Litter sister to Champions Berta, Benchin, and Bengal v Glenhugel and Ch. Domossi of Marienland, all red Dobermans.
4. Moritz von Rodeltal, owned by Sam H. Miller, Youngstown, Ohio. Deutscher Reichseiger, 1937; Sieger von Innsbruch, 1937.
5. One of the world's most famous Dobermans, Ch. Ferry v. Rauhfelsen was imported from Germany by Mrs. M. Hartley Dodge, owner of Giralda Farms, for whom he won Best of Show at Westminster in 1939.

v Grammont and two Silberbergs from Frau Stahr. Claus had also sired a German Sieger before coming to the United States.

Champion Prinz Carlo v d Koningstad was imported during the early 1920's by Francis F. H. Fleitmann for what was to become his very famous Westphalia Kennels. Carlo was the sire of importations Champion Prinzessin Elfrieda v Koningstad, Champion Prinzessin Ilese v Koningstad, and Champion Prinz Favoriet v d Koningstad. The latter was a superlative sire who produced 15 champions, including the first American-bred Doberman to win an all-breed Best in Show here: Champion Carlo of Rhinegold. Favoriet and these two bitches produced 24 American champions in total. Prinzessin Ilese was as well the dam of Princess Ilese of Westphalia who became the first American-bred Dobe to become a German Siegerin.

It was in 1927 that Glenn S. Staines imported the great dog, Lux v d Blankenburg, for his Pontchartrain Kennels in Michigan. Lux had a truly amazing record as a sire, having produced the winners of six Sieger and Siegerin titles, nineteen American champions, and twenty other progeny who had champion descendants.

Champion Claus v Sigalsburg, who was by Lux, won thirteen Bests in Show here towards the end of the 1920's, a nice addition to his 1926 Austrian and German Sieger titles.

A very important addition to the ranks of German imported Dobermans during the 1920's was Sieger Muck v Brunia, who was three years of age when brought here. Muck was a phenomenal producer, having sired ten champions in this country and having left behind him Sieger Troll v d Engelsburg and Sieger Blitz v d Domstadt, both of which were his sons. Troll v d Engelsburg came to America in 1937 having produced the Sieger and Siegerin of 1938, Champion Ferry v Rauhfelsen and Champion Freya v Rauhfelsen, World Siegerin Alfa v Hollingen, and Siegerin Ossi v Stahlhelm. No less than thirteen Troll progeny gained American titles, five of which were American-bred.

Troll was a superlative show dog as well as sire. He earned a World Sieger title, two German Sieger titles, became both an American and a Canadian champion, and brought home 78 Working Group Firsts plus 48 Bests in

Show. Could one ask for more?

In Troll's case it could be said that he almost outdid himself with his son, Champion Ferry v Rauhfelsen of Giralda, who became the first in history (and still one of only two Dobermans) to win Best in Show at the Westminster Kennel Club event in 1939, only a matter of weeks following his arrival here. Ferry went on to an excellent career after being sold to California. A study of pedigrees will show his influence as a sire.

Completing the family's move to the United States, Champion Jessy v d Sonnenhoehe, Ferry's dam, as well as Troll, his sire, also were imported, Jessy after taking Best of Breed at two Sieger shows successively. Jessy was the dam of both Ferry and Champion Freya v Rauhfelsen. Here she produced seven champions by Champion Kurt v d Rheinperle and six champions by his son, Pericles of Westphalia. Among the latter was Champion Westphalia's Uranus, who became the sire of Champion Alcor v Millsdod and Champion Favoriet v Franzhof.

Going back to Sieger Muck v Brunia, in addition to Troll and Blitz, he also sired another son, Blank v d Domstadt, who sired thirteen American champions after gaining his own title here in 1936. The Troll daughter, Siegerin Ossi v Stahlhelm, produced eleven champions in six matings to Blank, among them two immortals in the Doberman world: Champion Dictator v Glenhugel and Champion Domossi of Marienland. The Owen Wests of Chicago were Muck's importers.

Probably the most celebrated Doberman owner in the breed's early history was Francis F. H. Fleitmann whose Westphalia Kennels became renowned for both excellent importations and outstanding homebreds. Mr. Fleitmann was a true authority on this breed. Judge, scholar, widely travelled and thus personally acquainted with the breed on both sides of the Atlantic, he was looked upon as a fountain of knowledge, and his success as a breeder almost seems to have been inevitable considering his degree of interest, time and money invested, and his natural instinct for quality. Already we have referred to his importation of Champion Jessy v d Sonnenhohe, and of her contributions as both a show bitch and as a producer, and to those dogs such as Champion Prince Carlo v d Koningstad from

1. Int. Ch. Jockel V. Berglund, the winner of 44 Bests in Show, was one of the greatest Doberman winners of all time. Owned by the Jim Randles in California, Jockel is a never to be forgotten figure in Dobe history.
2. Ch. Votan v Gruenewald, II, by Ch. Dictator v Glenhugel ex Ch. Hanschen v Gruenewald. Bred by Carl Spicer; owned by Willie Deckart, Miami, Florida, Photo loaned to us by Peggy Adamson.
3. Ch. Carlo v Bassewitz, owned by Col. Colyer P. Dodson. Photo courtesy of Peggy Adamson.
4. Ch. Ferry v. Rauhfelsen winning Best in Show at the largest California event of that time, Harbor Cities Kennel Club in 1940. Russel Zimmerman handling for Randahof Kennels.
5. The very famous and important Doberman, Ch. Dow's Dodie v Kienlesberg, owned by Bert Dow, Davenport, Iowa. By Ch. Domossi of Marienland ex Ch. Dow's Cassie v Kienlesberg. Photo courtesy of Peggy Adamson.
6. The great Tri-Int. Ch. Troll v d Engelsburg, owned by E. Bornstein, Caterpillar Tractor Co., Peoria, Illinois. Troll was renowned for his contribution both as a stud dog and in the ring. Before leaving Germany to come to America, he had produced the 1938 Sieger and Siegerin, Gerry v Rauhfelsen and Freya v Rauhfelsen respectively, plus World Siegerin Alfa v Hollingen. Thirteen American champions, of which five were American-bred, also were finished by him. His own show achievements stand at 48 times all-breed Best in Show and 78 times first in the Working Group. Troll was by Ch. Muck of Brunia ex Adda v Heek. He was from the late 1930's–early 1940's era. Photo courtesy of Peggy Adamson.
7. Ch. Bengel v Grosshugel, C.D. was owned by Mrs. George F. Harpham, Parma Heights, Ohio. This dog was born in 1939. Photo courtesy of Peggy Adamson.
8. Ch. Koenig v Heimdall, a well-known winner during 1940, owned by Mrs. Gladys Allsing. Handled by H. L. Goodrich. This dog received the nod with a consistent string of Best of Breed wins under noted judges and was the sire of Ch. Boris v Koenigsheim who finished for Mrs. Lilliam Brown in 1939–1940.
9. Ch. Kasper v. Randahof, owned by Dr. C. M. and Dr. Blanche Bobbitt of Los Angeles, California, during the early 1940's. Born February 1940, Kasper was sired by Int. Ch. Jockel v Burgund ex Iris of Randahof and was bred by Randahof Kennels.

CH. KASPER V. RANDAHOF
Owned by
DR. C. M. and DR. BLANCHE BOBBITT
Los Angeles, California

1▲

◀
2

36

1. Berta v. Glenhugel, a Best in Show winning Doberman bitch of the early 1940's, pictured taking the top award at the Riviera event under judge B. B. Berman. This beautiful bitch also was best American-bred Doberman at the Doberman Pinscher Club Specialty in Chicago that same year.
2. A very historic picture in the Doberman world depicting Col. Dodson judging the breed at Philadelphia in 1943. Dick Webster with Ch. Domossi of Marienland, older brother of Dictator; and Harold K. Mohr with his Ch. Westphalia's Ursula, black litter sister to Uranus.
3. Ch. Baptiste's War News taking Best in Show at the Interstate Kennel Association in 1948, handled by J. Nate Levine for Jean Baptiste.
4. Mr. Francis F. H. Fleitmann, famous pioneer breeder of Dobermans, with his Ch. Duvetyn of Stonecroft more than several decades back. Mr. Fleitmann owned von Westphalia Dobermans, one of the world's most illustrious kennels.

▲3

►4

1. Ch. Conayer's Onliwon, a famous Doberman of the past, has just won Best in Show, handled by Jane Kamp (now Mrs. Robert Forsyth) for owners John Carbone and Constance Ayer, the latter now an A.K.C. Field Representative, Mrs. Constance Barton. Photo courtesy of Jane Forsyth.

2. One of the "greats" in the Doberman world, Am., Can., and Cuban Ch. Borong the Warlock, C.D. Born in January 1955, by Ch. Astor von Grenzweg, C.D. ex Ch. Florowill Allure, C.D.X., he was owned by Mr. and Mrs. Henry Frampton, Miami, Florida. In 1958 he was No. 10 in the Working Group; No. 9 in 1959; No. 7 in 1960; and No. 9 in 1961. A multiple Best in Show and Group winner, his Best of Breed wins total 230 by his owner's count.

3. Ch. Storm's Donner, born April 1956, by Ch. Rancho Dobe's Storm ex Storm's Tempesta. Owned by Peter Mehlich, New York, New York; bred by M. Mark Pagano and J. R. Moore, Jr. Handled by A. Peter Knoop. Here winning Best in Show from judge John W. Cross, Jr., as Len Carey presents the trophy.

4. A very interesting historical picture taken in the Doberman ring: Peter Knoop with Ch. Dortmund Delly's Colonel Jet; Monroe Stebbins with Ch. Steb's Top Skipper; and Connie Barton with a handsome but un-named Dobe.

Facing page:
Ch. Storm's Donner, son of the famed Ch. Rancho Dobe's Storm, at Longshore–Southport in 1959. As was his sire, Donner was handled by Peter Knoop. He was owned by Peter Mehlich of New York City; bred by M. Mark Pagano and J. R. Moore, Jr. His dam was Storm's Tempesta.

Holland and several others of notable success. Looking back into pedigrees, it is interesting to note the number of famous Dobermans who trace back to the Westphalia dogs. Mr. Fleitmann's home was in Far Hills, New Jersey, over a period of many years, and his Westphalia dogs were still meeting with success through the 1950's and possibly beyond that. I believe that in later years this gentleman moved to Switzerland, or at least spent a major portion of his time there. He was the only American holding a judging license in Germany and Switzerland. Mr. Fleitmann died in the mid-1970's.

I recall that Peter Knoop handled for Mr. Fleitmann at one period, and that this gentleman recognized and admired Peter's talent and knowledge back when Peter was a very young man.

Richard Webster owned Marienland Kennels at Baltimore, Maryland, which had tremendous impact on the breed's development. Mr. Webster owned some of the Westphalia dogs, such as the littermates by Champion Kurt v d Rheinperle-Rhinegold from Jessy, who were Champions Westphalia's Rameses, C.D.X. and Champion Westphalia's Rembha (who became the dam of Champion Emperor of Marienland when bred to Domossi). Marienland were really exhibitors on a grand scale. I have catalogues from dog shows held during the 1940's which list six dogs of theirs entered for Exhibition Only and an additional seven or eight for competition. As you read the kennel stories following, you will realize the strength of this kennel and the background it provided for some of the breed's best.

Glenn Staines's Pontchartrain Kennels was one of particular interest due to some of Mr. Staines's special interests and achievements. He was the one who imported Lux v d Blankenburg during the 1920's, never hesitating to do so although Lux was already eight years old at the time. His confidence in what Lux could do for Dobes in this country was well sustained, as this dog and his progeny were what might be called phenomenal producers in both the United States and Germany.

Mr. Staines was very much interested in the training of Dobermans to work as guide dogs for blind people. He invested considerable of his time working hard for this project

in Detroit, the results of which are still in evidence. It was also Glenn Staines who drew up the Articles of Incorporation for the Doberman Pinscher Club of America and who assisted in drawing up the first version of the Doberman Standard used here in the United States.

Howard K. Mohr owned numerous famed winners at his White Gate Kennels in Philadelphia, including Champion Big Boy of White Gate who became the first American-bred Doberman Best in Show winner at Rhode Island Kennel Club in 1928.

The Doberman Pinscher Club of America was founded during the Westminster Kennel Club Dog Show in New York City in 1921. A group of Doberman fanciers, led by George H. Earle, III, of Pennsylvania (who had owned the early Red Roof Kennels) adopted the Standard for the breed in 1922, based upon the German ideas.

By 1935 it had become apparent that a Standard more explicit than the first one was needed; thus it was that the first official American Standard was drawn up by the Doberman Pinscher Club of America and approved by the American Kennel Club. Both the new Standard of 1935 and revisions of it which were made in 1938 were concerned with adjustments in height and some other small changes, after which the Standard stayed as it was until 1969 when the recognition of Isabella (fawn) Dobermans was provided for, and four or more missing teeth were made a disqualification. Further revisions were made in 1983.

1▲

◄
2

1. And again in 1953!! Ch. Rancho Dobe's Storm repeats his Best in Show victory of the previous year to become one of only *three* dogs in history ever to have gained the Westminster Best in Show on more than one occasion. Here he is gaining the nod of approval from judge James A. Farrell, Jr. as co-owner, Len Carey, accepts the award. As usual, Storm was flawlessly handled by A. Peter Knoop. This superb dog was retired after this remarkable victory, bringing to a close one of the finest show careers ever attained by a Doberman. Shown only 26 times, Storm had scored Best in Show on 19 of these occasions, with first in the Working Group on five additional occasions.

2. More nostalgia! This is Peggy (Mrs. Bob) Adamson awarding Best of Winners at the Indianapolis Specialty to Karl Straub, who is handling Kajan Brunhilde of Dell Acres. By Ch. Kilburn Cameron ex Kilburn Gay La Rose. She finished her title during 1947. Photo courtesy of Mrs. Margaret (Marge) Kilburn, Pottstown, Pennsylvania.

3. Ch. Rancho Dobe's Storm winning the Working Group at Morris and Essex Kennel Club in 1952. A. Peter Knoop handling; Joseph C. Quirk judging. Storm was owned by Mr. and Mrs. Len Carey.

4. Bordo v. d. Angelburg of Westphalia with his handler, Peter Knoop, at Ox Ridge Kennel Club in 1953. One of Francis F. H. Fleitmann's imports. Photo courtesy of Fran Knoop.

5. A moment in history! All the excitement of the moment is evident just after Ch. Rancho Dobe's Storm has been adjudged Best in Show, all-breeds, at the 1952 Westminster Show. A. Peter Knoop is handling and the judge is Joseph P. Sims. The show Chairman is John W. Cross, Jr.

1

2

42

3 ◄

4 ►

5 ►

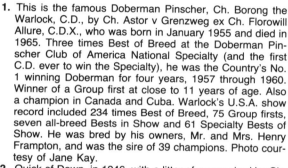

1. This is the famous Doberman Pinscher, Ch. Borong the Warlock, C.D., by Ch. Astor v Grenzweg ex Ch. Florowill Allure, C.D.X., who was born in January 1955 and died in 1965. Three times Best of Breed at the Doberman Pinscher Club of America National Specialty (and the first C.D. ever to win the Specialty), he was the Country's No. 1 winning Doberman for four years, 1957 through 1960. Winner of a Group first at close to 11 years of age. Also a champion in Canada and Cuba. Warlock's U.S.A. show record included 234 times Best of Breed, 75 Group firsts, seven all-breed Bests in Show and 61 Specialty Bests of Show. He was bred by his owners, Mr. and Mrs. Henry Frampton, and was the sire of 39 champions. Photo courtesy of Jane Kay.

2. Quick of Dawn, in 1946, with a litter of seven sired by Ch. Dictator v. Glenhugel. The owner and breeder was R. G. Allen of Vienna, Virginia.

3. Ch. Harding's Faust, born September 1951, by Ch. Rancho Dobe's Primo ex Ch. Beau Lo's Coda. Owned by Clair Stille, North Hollywood, California. Breeder, Dorothy Harding. Handler, Harry Sangster. No. 7 in the Working Group for 1956, this dog was an all-breed Best in Show winner with multiple Group wins and placements.

4. Falko von Lindenhof, prominent sire of the 1930's. Among his progeny are Sieger Muck von Brunia, who was brought to the United States and sired 10 champions, having left two Siegers behind him in his homeland. Falko also sired Cera v Rippertshaw. Photo courtesy of Peggy Adamson.

5. Ch. Westphalia's Rameses, C.D.X., was one of the first dogs bred by Dick Webster of the famed Marienland Kennels.

6. Ch. Storm's Pogo Nip of Kia Ora, born May 1954, by Ch. Rancho Dobe's Storm ex Countess Chee Chee v Huff. Owned by Mrs. Dora Sayers Caro, Bayside, New York. Bred by Mr. and Mrs. R. J. Dixon; handler, A. Peter Knoop. A Best in Show winner, multiple Group winner, and the sire of champions. No.10 in the Working Group for 1957.

6 ►

44

6▲   ▼7

1. 1958 Futurity winners, Alemaps Checkmate and Contessa of Herkules Hoehoe. Another generation of top winners, both of whom were sired by Ch. Steb's Top Skipper, whose sire in turn was Ch. Dortmund Delly's Colonel Jet. Photo courtesy of Natalie Stebbins.

2. Virginia Knauer and Peggy Adamson in 1955 at a Morris and Essex station wagon party. In the history of the Doberman Pinscher Club of America, these are the only two women to date who have held the Presidency of that organization. Mrs. Knauer later turned her attention to politics and became former President Richard M. Nixon's Director of Consumer Affairs, holding that position again under President Ronald Reagan.

3. Ch. Alemap's Checkmate, the first of close to 50 champions sired by the immortal Ch. Steb's Top Skipper. Photo of this Best in Show bitch courtesy of Natalie and Monroe Stebbins.

4. Ch. Meadowmist Elegy, from the 1950's, owned by Gwinnie Knauer. A son of Ch. Emperor of Marienland.

5. The magnificent winning Doberman of the late 1950's and early 1960's, Ch. Ebonaire's Touchdown, owned by Charles A. T. O'Neill and handled by J. Monroe Stebbins. This dog was a noted and consistent winner at prestigious shows in keenest competition.

6. Ch. Duke v. d. Ravensburg, a famous winner of the past with his handler, Jane Kamp Forsyth. The judge is the late Alva Rosenberg. Owned by Alonzo B. Reed.

7. Astrid of Lanawa taking Winners Bitch under the author at Newtown Kennel Club in 1964. Monroe Stebbins handling.

1▲  ▼2

1. This lovely bitch is Ch. Tait's Miss Scoreboard, handled by J. Monroe Stebbins to Winners Bitch at the Quaker City Doberman Pinscher Club Specialty show in December 1962.

2. Ch. Jem's Amythest v Warlock, C.D., born March 1960, by Ch. Borong the Warlock, C.D. ex Ch. Hi Dave's Korry's Kay Ingraham. Bred by Mr. and Mrs. Joe Babcock; owned by the Henry Framptons; handled by owner and Joe Gregory. No. 10 in the Working Group for 1963. No. 4 for 1964. Like her sire, Amythest was a three-time winner of the Doberman Pinscher Club of America National Specialty.

CAPTIONS FOR PLATES 1 TO 16

Plate 1
Ch. Eagle's Devil "D," a sensational puppy who matured into a very successful Best in Show and record-holding dog, pictured here in his early days with then-handler Jane Forsyth. The Forsyths have now turned from handling to judging, and Devil's career is now in the capable hands of Carlos Rojas. Owned by Dr. and Mrs. Anthony Di Nardo.

Plate 2
1. Pamelot's I'ma Traveler, owned by Mrs. Roberta (Bobbi) Brady, Westerville, Ohio.

2. Am. and Can. Ch. Pamelot's Venice, WAC, handled here, at Laurel Highlands 1977, by Pamela DeHetre for owner Roberta Brady.

3. Am. and Can. Ch. Hickory Hill's Hot Stuff, linebred on the Schauffelein bloodlines, is owned by Roberta Brady, Bra-Ner Dobermans. Handled here to Best of Breed at KARS Dog Show, 1983, by Pamela DeHetre.

4. Ch. Brown's B-Brian winning Best of Breed at the 1973 Doberman Pinscher Club of America Specialty show, Washington, D.C. Bob Wills is judging; Marjorie Brooks is handling. Photo courtesy of Peggy Adamson.

5. Ch. Brown's B-Barrett, owned by Jose Perdomo and Marjorie Brooks, Santa Rosa, California.

6. Ch. Brown's Life With Riley, shown at five years of age. He was the sire of about 10 champions and was the son of Ch. Brown's A-Amigo ex Judy's Melville. Owned by Ray and Penny Spanola. Photo courtesy of Marjorie Brooks.

Plate 3
1. Ch. Black Frog Footsteps O'Gigolo, by Ch. Edelhall's Gigolo of Amulet ex Black Frog's Bio Liberty Bell, WAC, bred and owned by Millie McCoy, Bel Air, Maryland.

2. Ch. Black Frog's Faded Jeans, linebred to Champion Elfred's The President, is a litter sister to Ch. Black Frog Footsteps O'Gigolo. Bred and owned by Millie McCoy.

3. Ch. Brandendorf's Firefly, red bitch of the early 1970's, owner-handled by Marilyn Meshirer, Massapequa, New York.

4. Ch. Peri's Prince Temujin, a Best-in-Show–winning son of Am. and Can. Ch. Brandendorf's Periwinkle. Owned and handled by Marilyn Meshirer.

5. Am. and Can. Ch. Brandendorf's Happy Hour, a black bitch owned and handled by Marilyn Meshirer, winning Best of Breed at North Country in May 1981 under judge Bob Wills.

6. Ch. Brandendorf's Summer Misty Morn, a blue bitch, with owner Marilyn Meshirer, taking Best of Winners from judge Henry Stoecker at Onondaga in 1974.

Plate 4
1. Ch. Ulrich vom Ahrtal, C.D., is owned by Avis M. Brech, New Hope, Pennsylvania. He is the 70th champion to have been bred by Tess Henseler, Ahrtal Kennels. At a celebration party for the 70th Ahrtal champion in July 1983, the pictured cake was a surprise brought by Mr. and Mrs. Charles Kalko—a masterpiece in Swiss chocolate with the names of all 70 Ahrtal champions adorning it, in the order of their finishing!

2. Ch. Ulrich vom Ahrtal, C.D., by Ch. Argus vom Ahrtal II, attained his C.D. at three consecutive shows within one week. He has sired a Canadian champion and children with points in the U.S. and Bermuda from his first litter, with his other children just beginning to reach show age. Owned by Mrs. Avis M. Brech, handled by Don Simmons. Ulrich is the 70th champion bred by Tess Henseler's Ahrtal Kennels.

3. Ch. Alisaton's Kinderwicke, WAC, after taking Winners Bitch at the National in 1973. Gwen DeMilta, owner, 17 years old at the time, was winning her first point as an exhibitor that day. Kinderwicke, doing likewise, was 12 months and one day. Gwen resides in Westbury, New York.

4. Ch. D'Mascus Sambuca v Alisaton, C.D. This is the famous "Miss Samsam" who finished her championship at one week over a year's age, along the way beating 138 Dobes on one occasion to win a Specialty Best in Show at only seven months! Thus, she took her first five points. She won the Doberman Pinscher Club of America 1982 award for the most blue ribbons won by a puppy bitch and is one of three champions in her litter. Co-breeders, Peggy Esposito and Gwen DeMilta. Owners, Charles Guardascione and Mary Manning.

5. The noted Ch. Alisaton Damascus, C.D., by Ch. Gra-Lemor's Demetrius v d Victor ex Ch. Alisaton's Kinderwicke, WAC, finished his championship at 13 months of age with a four-point and a five-point "major" from the Bred-by-Exhibitor Class. Won most puppy blue ribbons award at the 1977 Doberman Pinscher Club of America Specialty. Damascus is a Best of Breed, Specialty Show, and Group winner who has sired many champions to date including a Top Twenty placer, and he himself was in the Top Twenty for 1978. Bred by Gwen and JoAnn Satalino. Owned by Peggy Esposito and Gwen DeMilta.

6. Ch. Alisaton Q B Sneak v D'Mascus, by Ch. Alisaton's Kinsman, WAC, ex Ch. Alisaton Kinder Rose. "Sneaks" finished her championship with an exciting Best of Winners for a five-point "major" at the Quaker City Specialty. Breeders-owners, Peggy Esposito and Gwen DeMilta of Westbury, New York.

Plate 5
1. The late Ch. Alisaton Bornastar, C.D., ROM, dam of one champion and one pointed out of her only litter of two puppies. By Ch. Gra-Lemor Demetrius v d Victor ex Ch. Alisaton's Kinderwicke, WAC. Owned by Carol Wilde.

2. Alisaton Tie Score v D'Mascus, U.D.T., WAC, has 12 points towards championship. By Ch. Schauffelein's Vintage Year ex Ch. Alisaton Kinder Rose; bred by Peggy Esposito and Gwen Satalino DeMilta; and handled by Bill Harrison for owner Peggy Garic.

3. D'Mascus Mardale Alisaton, by Ch. Mardale Spirit of Malnati ex Ch. Alisaton Kinder Rose. Bred by Gwen Satalino DeMilta and Peggy Esposito. Handled by Bill Harrison for owners Jacqueline and Edward Griffin.

4. Ch. Alisaton Sean Killoran, by Ch. Marienburg's Osage ex Ch. Alisaton's Kinderwicke, WAC, is one of three American champions and a Canadian champion in his litter. He finished with a Best of Breed from the classes among his wins. Owned by Sarah Orlando and Gwen and Stephen DeMilta; bred by Gwen DeMilta, Westbury, New York.

5. Ch. Alisaton Gallorette, WAC, taking Best of Winners at Tuxedo Park in 1978. Handled by Terry Lazzaro. Owned by Janet Skidmore.

6. Ch. Alisaton The Assault, by Ch. Gra-Lemor Demetrius v d Victor ex Ch. Alisaton's Kinderwicke, WAC. Bred by Gwen and JoAnn Satalino. Owners, Rita Goodrow and Gwen DeMilta.

Plate 6
1. Brykris The Gun Runner at eight weeks of age. Bred, owned, and handled by Jo Ann James, Brykris Dobermans, Miami, Florida. Photo by Bill James.

2. Jo Ann James with her handsome litter-sister Dobes, Ch. Brykris Spirit To Win and Brykris Fight for Glory, at six months of age. Photo by Bill James.

3. Ch. Brykris Spirit To Win at nine months of age. Bred, owned, and handled by Jo Ann James. Photo by Bill James.

4. Carosel Ambush of King Hill, C.D.X., bred by Susan King and Carol Selzle Petruzzo, is the dam of Ch. Brykris Tabu, Brykris The Gun Runner, and Brykris The Masked Bandit. She is a daughter of Ch. Damasyn The Forecast, C.D., ROM ex Ch. Carosel In the Spotlight, C.D., ROM, and she is owned and handled by Jo Ann James. Photo by Bill James.

Plate 7
1. Ch. Brykris Tabu with Jo Ann James and his parrot friend, Degas. Photo by Bill James, Miami, Florida.

2. Brykris The Gun Runner, by Ch. Silent Sentry's Marauder, WAC ex Carosel Ambush of King Hill, C.D.X., going Winners Dog from the Bred-by-Exhibitor Class under judge Dr. Quentin LaHam at Venice Kennel Club 1983. Jo Ann James of Miami, Florida is the breeder-owner-handler.

3. Four generations of Brykris Dobermans with their owner Jo Ann James. These owner-handled homebreds are great-granddam, grandsire, dam, and puppy. Photo by Bill James.

4. Ch. Brykris Spirit To Win, by Ch. Dynasty's Moonshadow, C.D., ROM, ex Brykris The Moon Shadow. Jo Ann James's homebred and owner-handled bitch was the 1983 winner of the Doberman Pinscher Club of America award for Top-Winning Puppy Bitch. Pictured winning a five-point "major" in an entry of 112 bitches at the Doberman Pinscher Club of Louisiana show, host club to the 1983 National Specialty, under judge Peter Emily.

5. A highly promising Dobe puppy, future Ch. Brykris Spirit To Win, age six weeks here. Bred, owned, and handled by Jo Ann James, Brykris Dobermans.

6. Brykris The Masked Bandit, by Ch. Silent Sentry's Marauder, WAC ex Carosel Ambush of King Hill, C.D.X., is owned by Ann Gioia. A litter brother to Brykris The Gun Runner, bred by Jo Ann James, he is here winning a "major" at age 13 months under Ray Carlisle at the Florida West Coast Doberman Pinscher Club Specialty.

Plate 8
1. Ch. D'Mascus Tanguerey v Alisaton, by Ch. Mardale Spirit of Malnati ex Ch. Alisaton Kinder Rose, bred by Gwen DeMilta and Peggy Esposito. Here handled by Bill Harrison to Winners at the Lakeshore Doberman Pinscher Specialty show for owners Lynn Robley and the breeders.

2. Ch. Alisaton Carera, by Ch. Glenayr Dufferinand ex Ch. Alisaton's Kinderwicke, WAC, is the latter's 13th champion. Bred and owned by Gwen and Stephen DeMilta, Westbury, New York.

3. Ch. Alisaton Touch Down V D'Mascus, C.D., ROM, owned by Ranny Jarrelle, Richmond, Virginia. By Ch. Alisaton's Kinsman ex Ch. Alisaton Kinder Rose and bred by Peggy Esposito and Gwen DeMilta, "Touch" completed his title shown only 13 times in the Open Class. The proud holder of the Doberman Pinscher Club of America ROM title, Touch was also a finalist for the Top Twenty event in 1984. Always owner-handled by Ranny Jarrelle.

4. Ch. Alisaton Chezarain, by Ch. Alisaton Citation, WAC, ex Ch. Alisaton Raincheck, WAC. "Raini" is one of nine red bitches, the only champion to date in the litter. Owners, Sarah Orlando and Gwen and Stephen DeMilta. Bred by the DeMiltas.

Plate 9
1. On the left, 11-month-old Ch. Alisaton Hot Shot, C.D., ROM. On the right, 3-year-old Ch. Kocot Pajant de Scudamore, C.D.X., ROM. Owners, Sue Hall (Hot Shot) and Bobbie Hall (Pajant).

2. Alisaton Maserati, by Ch. Glenayr Dufferinand ex Ch. Alisaton's Kinderwicke, is one of the many fine Dobermans handled by Terry Lazzaro, Gaylordsville, Connecticut.

3. Ch. Arabar's Impertinence, by Ch. Damasyn Bo Tairic ex Kandy's Maria, foundation bitch at Alisaton Dobermans, here portrayed by famous artist Robert Hickey. Impetinence is the dam of six American champions and a Brazilian champion. Doberman Pinscher Club of America Brood Bitch, 1976. Owned by Gwen DeMilta, Westbury, New York.

4. Portrait of Alisaton Mateus, as a puppy and as a mature dog, by Leslie Hall. By Ch. Schauffelein's Vintage Year ex Ch. Alisaton Kinderwicke, WAC. This handsome Doberman died with 14 points, including both "majors." Owned by Gwen DeMilta.

Plate 10
1. This is Alberto Del Camino Real, a Chela son, owned by Carol and Miguel Chavez, Del Camino Real Dobermans, Leavenworth, Kansas.

2. Ch. Anastacio Del Camino Real, another Chela son, winning a Best of Breed handled by Miguel Chavez, co-owner with Carol Chavez.

3. Ch. and O.T.Ch. Graciela Del Camino Real, U.D.T., ROM, finishing her Obedience Trial championship by going High in Trial at Topeka Kennel Club in 1980. "Chela" is handled here by her owner, Carol Chavez.

4. Ch. and O.T.Ch. Graciela Del Camino Real, U.D.T., ROM, the very famous "Chela" owned by Carol Chavez. Handled by Miguel Chavez to a Best of Breed award from Peggy Adamson.

5. Ch. Damasyn the Forecast, C.D., ROM, is the dam of multiple champions. By Ch. Damasyn the Troycen ex Damasyn Felicity, she was bred and is owned by Carol Selzle Petruzzo, Freehold, New Jersey.

6. Ch. Damasyn the Limelight, by Ch. Damasyn the Troycen ex Damasyn the Legacy, C.D., here is winning the Veteran Bitch Class at the 1976 Quaker City Doberman Pinscher Club Specialty. She was the 1980 Top Producing Dam, and she is the dam of six champions, three ROM dogs, two C.D.X. titlsts, and three with C.D.X. degrees. Owned by Carol Selzle Petruzzo.

1

2

3

4

PLATE 3

5

6

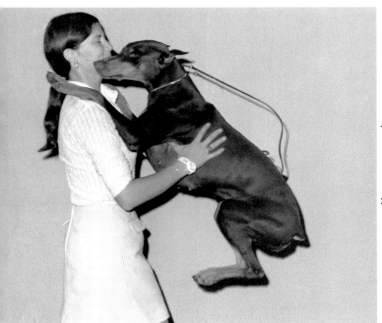

PLATE 4

1

2

3

4

PLATE 13

5

6

7

8

PLATE 14

1 ◄

2 ►

3 ◄

4 ►

7. Ch. Damasyn Wendalyn of Alisaton, WAC, by Ch. Damasyn the Troycen ex Ch. Arabar's Impertinence, was bred by Jo Ann and Gwen Satalino and is owned by Carol Selzle Petruzzo. Here she is taking points towards her title.

8. Ch. Carosel B In Charge, by Ch. Brown's B-Brian ex Ch. Damasyn the Limelight. Bred by Carol Selzle, who is handling him here to Winners Dog for a five-point "major" at the 1979 Doberman Pinscher Club of Connecticut–New York Specialty under breeder/judge Melba Stafford. Owned by Linda Ray.

Plate 11

1. Gayamon The Midnight Moon, C.D., WAC is a double grandson of Ch. Dolph Von Tannenwald. He is, as well, the sire of Ch. Brykris Tabu and grandsire of Ch. Brykris Spirit To Win. Owned by Bill & Jo Ann James, Miami, Florida. Photo by Bill James.

2. Mar-Dar's Sugar Crisp, known as "Crickett," at age nine months. Owner, Chris Hall Yamaoka, Honolulu, Hawaii, who also handles this lovely bitch.

3. A lovely photo of Carosel Starling, by Ch. Carosel B In A Hurry, C.D., ROM ex Carosel Starlight Starbright, who was imported to Hawaii by Chris Hall Yamaoka, Calliope Dobermans, from Carol Selzle back here on the mainland.

4. Ch. Carosel In The Chips of King Hill, WAC, ROM, at age two-and-a-half years, sired by Ch. Marienburg's Sun Hawk, C.D. ex Ch. Carosel In The Spotlight, C.D., ROM. Chips is a Sun Hawk son and a Demetrius grandson, and he is proving his worth as a sire and as a great show dog. Owned by Chris Hall Yamaoka, who purchased him from Carol Selzle.

Plate 12

1. Ch. Redyns High and Mighty, born November 1978, owned by Armin and Paula Hotz. By Ch. Briarwood's Yancy Jon ex Redyns Golly Gee Mom and a full litter brother to Ch. Redyns Touch of Class. Bred by Deborah and Gloria Snyder, he gained his championship breeder-handled.

2. Ch. Redyn's Touch of Class, owned by Paula Hotz, St. Peter, Illinois, here taking Best of Breed at the 1982 Doberman Pinscher Club of America National Specialty. Judge, Mrs. Margaret Kilburn; handler, Mr. Charles A. Cooper, Jr.

3. Arielle Easy Touch, a black and rust female, was born February 1983. By Ch. Silent Sentry's Marauder, WAC, ex Ch. Redyns Touch of Class. Bred and owned by Paula Hotz.

4. Ch. Aquarius Arian of Criswit and Ch. Albelarm Jessica of Aquarius both taking points on the way to their championships. Full brother and sister to Ch. Pamelot's Anthony ex Ch. Rehbar Delissa of Aquarius, Jessica was from a repeat breeding, Arian being one year older than the former. Bred by Jim Briley and Mrs. Alan Robson. The judge here is Roy L. Ayers.

5. Aquarius Anxious Andy, littermate to Arian and full brother to Jessica. This young dog needs only one "major" to finish his title. Bred by Jim Briley and Mrs. Alan Robson.

6. Ch. Aquarius Cimmaron of Celadon, bred by Jim Briley and Mrs. Alan Robson. A Best in Show winner and the No. 12 Doberman in the United States for 1983, this dog is now living in Japan.

7. Ch. Baile's Beau Rikki of Rehbar, by Ch. Devil Tree's Black Shaft ex Ch. Marks Tey Honda, was born in May 1974. Bred by Mrs. Bryce Bailes and Richard Brue; owned by Jim Briley, Aquarius Kennels, Opelousas, Louisiana. The first champion finished by Jim Briley.

8. Ch. Rehbar Delissa of Aquarius, born in March 1980. A black and rust, she is by Ch. Angil's Beau Gests ex Ch. Rehbar Anissa of Bailes (both black and rust) and is owned by Jim Briley.

Plate 13

1. Ch. Torenduf Funi-Girl of Kay Hill pictured in May 1975. Handler, Vic Blackburn; breeders, Doris and Gerry Lefkowith; owner, Donna Blackburn. By Ch. Encore's Black Rites ex Ch. Torenduf's Dago Red v Sprite.

2. Bar-Lock's Nightfire, C.D.X., WAC, going Highest Scoring Dog in Trial at the Combined Specialty shows at Miami in January 1982. This was his first time in the obedience ring. "Montauk" is currently being shown and is well on the way to his championship. He is also in training for Utility and Tracking. Handler-owner, Sharon Lockwood. Bred and co-owned by Donna Blackburn, Bar-Lock Dobermans, North Miami Beach, Florida.

3. Ch. Bar-Lock's Brown Chelsey finishing her title at Greater Miami in 1971, taking back-to-back "majors" that weekend. By Ch. Bardolf's Warlock, C.D. ex Sirius Sasha von Texan. Paul Saucier handling for breeders-owners Barbara and Fenton Taylor.

4. Am., Can. and Bah. Ch. Bar-Lock's Star Blazer finishing his title in April 1983. Jeff Brucker handling this fine young dog, by Am. and Can. Ch. Starstorm Thunderbolt, C.D. ex Ch. Bar-Lock's Star of Night, for breeder-owner Donna Blackburn, Bar-Lock Dobermans.

5. Bar-Lock's Ebony Talisman, C.D., WAC, bringing in the morning paper—one of his daily "jobs." Bred and owned by Donna Blackburn.

6. Ch. Bar-Lock's Star of Night going Best in Show at Stuart–Ft. Pierce in 1978. Judge, Phil March; handler, Paul Saucier. "Ara" had many Group wins plus this Best in Show. She was also the Doberman Pinscher Club of America Top-Winning Puppy Bitch for 1976 and got the D.P.C.A. award for most times Best of Opposite Sex in 1978. She is the dam of one champion with four others of her progeny already pointed. Bred and owned by Donna Blackburn.

7. Bar-Lock's Ketcha Star showing excellent reach and drive. By Am. and Can. Ch. Starstorm Thunderbolt, C.D. ex Ch. Bar-Lock's Star of Night. Owned by Wendy Serra. Bred and co-owned by Donna Blackburn.

8. Am., Can., and Bah. Ch. Bar-Lock's Star Blazer, by Am. and Can. Ch. Starstorm Thunderbolt, C.D. ex Ch. Bar-Lock's Star of Night. Here taking his second "major" from the 9-12 Puppy Class at Sara Bay Kennel Club, 1983. Jeff Brucker handling for breeder-owner Donna Blackburn.

Plate 14

1. Classic's Ruby Tuesday Alcher taking a four-point "major" at Oakland County, November 1983. Harvey and Bettye Carter of Knoxville, Tennessee, owners.

2. Ch. Classic's Farrah Fawcett taking Winners Bitch at the Doberman Pinscher Club of Greater Dayton Specialty, May 1981. Handled by Betty Brucker for owners Harvey and Bettye Carter.

3. Am. and Can. Ch. Classic's Eliza Doolittle, C.D. is owned by the Carters, Classic Dobermans, Knoxville, Tennessee.

4. Ch. Jaymare's Vixen of Rehbar, by Ch. Edelhall's Gigolo of Amulet ex Ch. Bishop's Circe von Rock, taking Best of Winners for a "major" en route to the title of the Doberman Pinscher Club of Charlotte Specialty. Betty Brucker handling for Harvey and Bettye Carter and Cheryl Green.

Plate 15
1. Carosel In the Clouds of King Hill needs but one point to become the fourth champion in this litter by Ch. Marienburg's Sun Hawk, C.D. ex Ch. Carosel In the Spotlight, C.D., ROM. Bred by Susan King and Carol Selzle Petruzzo. Owned by Bianca Arnold and Susan King, Freehold, New Jersey.

2. Ch. Carosel In The Clover of King Hill, by Ch. Marienburg's Sun Hawk, C.D. ex Ch. Carosel In The Spotlight, C.D., ROM, photographed with eight-year-old Kristen King. Bred and owned by Susan King and Carol Selzle Petruzzo.

3. Ch. Carosel B In A Hurry, bred and owned by Carol Selzle Petruzzo, winning Best of Opposite Sex from judge Marge Kilburn at the 1982 Doberman Pinscher Club of America Specialty. Handled by Marjorie Brooks.

4. Ch. Carosel B In Step v Thortiki, C.D., by Ch. Brown's B-Brian ex Ch. Damasyn the Limelight, is pictured going Best of Breed from the classes under judge Mary Johnston at Savannah Kennel Club in 1977. Bred and handled by Carol Selzle Petruzzo; owned by Michael and Lee Ann Rudawsky.

5. Ch. Carosel In the Spotlight, C.D., ROM, by Ch. Gra-Lemor Demetrius v d Victor ex Ch. Damasyn the Limelight. A multi-breed winner with numerous Group placements, and the dam of four champions to date. Bred by Carol Selzle Petruzzo; co-owned with Susan King.

6. Ch. Carosel Musical Light, C.D.X., ROM (April 1975—December 1979) finished with two five-point "majors" from the Bred-by-Exhibitor Class. By Ch. Damasyn the Troycen ex Ch. Damasyn the Limelight. Breeder, Carol Selzle Petruzzo, co-owner with Marjorie Hudson, Freehold, New Jersey.

7. Ch. Carosel In the Mood of King Hill, by Ch. Marienburg's Sun Hawk, C.D. ex Ch. Carosel In the Spotlight, C.D., ROM. Bred and owned by Carol Selzle Petruzzo and Susan King. Handled by Ross Petruzzo.

8. Ch. Carosel Amanda of King Hill, dam of two champions, is a daughter of Ch. Damasyn The Forecast, C.D., ROM ex Ch. Carosel In the Spotlight, C.D., ROM. Bred by Susan King and Carol Selzle Petruzzo; owned by Don and Sue Mason.

Plate 16
1. Biggin Hills Essex, handsome son of Ch. Biggin Hills Alarich ex Susan of Biggin Hill, bred and owned by Norman and Phyllis Biggin. Handled by Norman, here Essex wins the Bred-by-Exhibitor Class at the Connecticut–New York Specialty in 1973.

2. The author is among the many judges who admired Ch. Biggin Hills Alarich, Norman and Phyllis Biggin's splendid home-bred dog. Here he is winning the breed at Rockland County in 1968, handled, as usual, by Norman.

3. Am. and Can. Ch. Biggin Hills Beckett; owners-breeders, Norman and Phyllis Biggin, West Kingston, Rhode Island. Here taking points on the way to his championship, handled by Norman.

4. Ch. Billmar's B-Beau Teke, multi-breed and Group-winning bitch, finishing her title owner-handled by Captain M. E. Smith, United States Navy, retired. Owned and bred by Captain and Mrs. Smith, Cleveland, Tennessee.

5. Billmar's Crystal taking Best of Opposite Sex for two points from the 6-9 month Puppy Class under breed authority Mrs. Peggy Adamson. Handled by Captain M. E. Smith, co-owned with Billie R. Smith.

6. Ch. Billmar's CC & Co finished his title at 18 months of age from the American-bred Class. Bred and owned by Captain and Mrs. M. E. Smith. Handler, Captain Smith.

1. Ch. Dortmund Delly's Colonel Jet in June 1954 with his handler, A. Peter Knoop. Photo courtesy of the Stebbinses.
2. Ch. Gra-Lemor Plain and Fancy Lil' Eva at home. Littermate to Ch. Gra-Lemor Demetrius. By Ch. Damasyn Derringer ex Jerry Run's Boo-Sprite. Photo courtesy of Peggy Adamson.

1. Young Jeff Weiss with Damasyn The Wild Wing, foundation of Ebonaire breeding. This Dictator granddaughter, in whelp to Dictator, was leased by Judy Weiss in 1948 from Peggy Adamson. The one bitch in the litter, Damasyn The Winterwaltz, was sold to Joe Rapisardo. From her litter sired by the Dictator son, Solitaire, came Damasyn The Waltzing Raven and Ch. Damasyn The Waltzing Brook, foundation bitch of Marks-Tey. Photo courtesy of Peggy Adamson.
2. Int. Ch. Curt v d Schwarzwaldperle, Sch.H. and P. H., another of the Dobes owned by Rupprecheim Kennels in the early 1940's. Photo courtesy of Peggy Adamson.
3. The great Ch. Jet v d Ravensburg, from the 1950's. Owned by Walter and May Danker, Long Island, New York.
4. Erna v Graf Zeppelin, owned by Sidney Moss.
5. The late Glenn Staines with one of his Pathfinder Dogs. When Glenn died in the 1950's, it became known he had spent almost every penny he owned on his Pathfinder projects to aid the blind. It's no wonder his funeral was attended by a great many blind people, with their Pathfinder dogs, paying tribute to this great and selfless figure in Dobermans.

1. Ch. Jo's Brandy Alexander, by Ch. Thunder von Adelstadt ex Ch. Katrina von Vulcan. Owned by Fred and Jackie Kortwright. Sire of numerous champions and the grandsire of Ch. Marienburg's Sun Hawk.
2. Ch. Ebonaire's Touchdown winning an important Specialty in June 1962 from Miss Jane F. Kamp, now Mrs. Robert S. Forsyth, for Charles A. T. and Marie O'Neill of Philadelphia. Monroe Stebbins handling, as usual, this famous dog.
3. Ch. Mark-Tey's High Hat going Best of Breed at the Plainfield Kennel Club in May 1965. Judge, A. Peter Knoop. Handler, J. Monroe Stebbins for owners Richard and Jean Baum, Chappaqua, New York. "Rebel" was one of the famous "H" litter, whelped November 13, 1961 by Keith and Joanna Walker at Marks-Tey Kennels.
4. Ch. Rudy's Holiday Spirit, known as "The Shiek." A black and rust born December 1966 by Ch. Ru-Mar's Morgansonne, C.D. ex Rudy's Miss Samdown. One of four champions in the litter, which included Ch. Rudy's Holli-Berri Florowill, she the dam of many champions bearing the Florowill prefix. Breeder, Rudy Proffitt. Owner, Lee Wilson, Council Bluffs, Iowa. Photo courtesy of Ruth M. Edwards.
5. Ch. Ru-Mar's Tsushima, C.D., by Ch. Ranhco Dobe Cello ex Ch. Jessmyn II von Ahrtal. Breeder, Rudy Wagner; owner, Margaret Carveth. Photo courtesy of Peggy Adamson.
6. A. Peter Knoop handling Tucky Miss at Huntington Valley in June 1961. Photo courtesy of Fran Knoop.
7. Ch. Axel von Tannenwald, 1963–1973, was among the Top Ten Dobermans in America for five consecutive years. His impressive list of wins includes 105 Bests of Breed, 18 Bests in Show (five all-breed, 13 Specialty), 29 Group Firsts, and 49 additional Group placements. His most memorable win for owner Betty Moore, Houston, Texas, was Best of Breed at Westminster in 1968. Axel was owner-handled on all of these occasions.

68

5 ◄ 6 ►

7 ▼

Ch. Dolph von Tannenwald in October 1970 winning the Working Group under judge Alva Rosenberg. Dolph, truly a legend in the Doberman Fancy, was handled by Jeffrey Lynn Brucker for owners George and Sheila West.

CHAPTER FOUR

Doberman Kennels in the United States

There is no better way to describe the progress of a breed than by telling you of the individual breeders and kennels who have contributed along the way. On the following pages we are proud to present descriptions of these many breeders and their kennels, some of whom go back several or more decades, and of the many important Dobermans they own, have owned, and have produced.

We tell you not only of the long-time breeders who have played so integral a role in the progress and development of the breed, but of the newer ones as well. Each has contributed to the quality and development of these splendid dogs, and on the shoulders of the newcomers in particular squarely rests the task of carrying on and preserving what has already been accomplished, together with the responsibility for the future good ownership and progress of the breed. Study the following pages well, and you will come away with vastly increased knowledge of where the best Dobermans have been and are being produced, the care and forethought expended towards their progress, and the improvements which have taken place generation after generation. You will learn to understand which characteristics and traits are synonymous with which strains. See for yourself the exciting progress which has been made by those who have worked so hard and so selflessly to put their breed in the position of respect and admiration it demands.

Ahrtal

Ahrtal Doberman Pinschers started their exciting history in the late 1940's with the acquisition of that very remarkable bitch, Champion Meadowmist Isis of Ahrtal, a daughter of Champion Emperor of Marienland ex Dow's Ditty of Marienland. Out of thirty-five puppies in four litters, Isis produced 17 champions. All of Isis's champion progeny were sired by Champion Delegate v.d. Elbe.

Miss Henseler has the distinction of being the breeder of more than seventy Doberman champions, a Doberman record and especially remarkable when one considers that her policy has been to breed her bitches only once a year, and that they do not run to large litters. At the most, she has never kept more than ten dogs at any one time, which included the young dogs and the old ones. She has been quoted as saying, "I never turned an old dog out. They lived their lives out here." Only two litters each year have ever been bred at Ahrtal. Miss Henseler estimates that there have been about 350 to 380 puppies in total, making her average in number of champions all the more remarkable. In addition more than 50 Ahrtal Dobes have earned obedience degrees and a number have tracking degrees as well.

Tess Henseler came to the United States in 1928 from her former home, the town of Ahrweiler in Germany. She was an ardent horsewoman, and in her early days in the States managed numerous horse farms in the Pennsylvania area and in the Southwest. It was a riding accident which turned her activities from horses to dogs, which was surely a stroke of good fortune for the Doberman breed.

Her first Doberman, acquired in 1948, was intended as a farm dog and companion. Through him, Hasso vom Ahrtal, Miss Henseler became active in obedience. And Hasso, obviously talented in this regard, sailed through with flying colors first to his C.D. and then his C.D.X. Distemper cut short his obedience career, but fortunately his recovery was a complete one and he eventually participated in obedience demonstrations.

1 ◄   2 ►

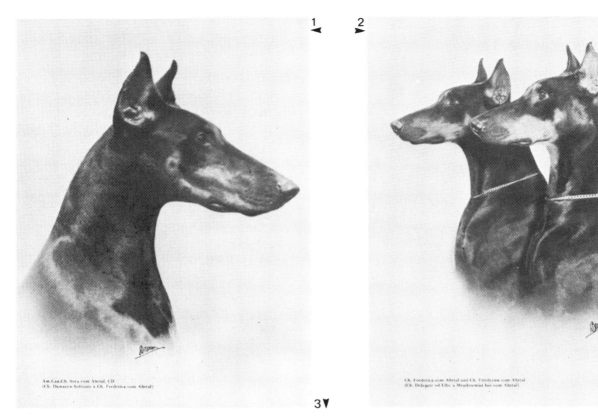

Am.Can.Ch. Nora vom Abetal, CD
(Ch. Damasyn Soldorato x Ch. Frederica vom Abetal)

Ch. Frederica vom Abetal and Ch. Frischessan vom Abetal
(Ch. Delegato vel Ufior x Meadowmist boss vom Abetal)

3 ▼

4 ◄

5 ►

6 ◄

7 ►

1. Am. and Can. Ch. Svea vom Ahrtal, C.D., by Ch. Damasyn Solitaire ex Ch. Frederica vom Ahrtal. Tess Henseler, owner, vom Ahrtal Kennels, Ottsville, Pennsylvania.
2. Ch. Frederica vom Ahrtal and Ch. Friederun vom Ahrtal, by Ch. Delegate v d Elbe ex Meadowmist Isis vom Ahrtal, were two important early dogs from Tess Henseler's vom Ahrtal Kennel.
3. Meadowmist Isis of Ahrtal (July 15, 1948–April 27, 1957). The dam of 17 champions, this daughter of Ch. Emperor of Marienland ex Dow's Ditty of Marienland was an important force in the success of vom Ahrtal Dobermans. Tess Henseler owner.
4. Ch. Felix vom Ahrtal, the sire of 29 champions, one of the "greats" from Tess Henseler's noted kennel. This is one of vom Ahrtal's handsome blue dogs.
5. Ch. Lauritz vom Ahrtal, by Ch. Felix vom Ahrtal ex Cristel vom Ahrtal. One of the many illustrious homebreds from Tess Henseler's outstanding kennel.
6. Ch. Cassio vom Ahrtal, sire of 38 champions, the progeny of Xandu vom Ahrtal and Ch. Juno vom Ahrtal. Tess Henseler, owner.
7. The Musical Doberman Drill Team was a feature of the Westminster Kennel Club Dog Show in 1959. Created and trained by Tess Henseler, vom Ahrtal Kennels, this feature was a huge success with the audience.
8. Ch. Thorvald vom Ahrtal, by Ch. Cassio vom Ahrtal ex Ilissa vom Ahrtal, with his breeder-owner, Tess Henseler.

8 ►

1. Ch. Taina vom Ahrtal, Tess Henseler's noted bitch, owner-handled to Best of Opposite Sex under the author at the Quaker City Doberman Pinscher Club Specialty, October 1962.

2. Tess Henseler with her Thane vom Ahrtal, Winners Dog, at Quaker City Doberman Pinscher Club Specialty, 1962.

Soon Miss Henseler added a second Doberman to her family, Kriemhild vom Ahrtal, who also fared well in obedience and became the dam of the first homebred vom Ahrtal show champion.

Miss Henseler's interest in obedience led her to teaching it, and she conducted classes for many years in her area. Also it is she who originated the idea of the canine drill team. This started off using a team of handlers with assorted breeds. Then she began to visualize how exciting it would be to have a team made up entirely of Dobermans. Being a lady of determination, she got busy and brought this about, the result being a team of Dobermans who performed at many events in the East, most notable of which was at the Westminster Kennel Club Show in Madison Square Garden, New York City, where they literally "brought down the house" in 1959. The team consisted of sixteen dogs with one stand-in. A note of particular interest is that only four of these dogs were actually worked by their owners; the others were "borrowed" and handled by members of Tess Henseler's classes!

While all this was taking place, Miss Henseler was breeding and starting to show her dogs in conformation. Right here let us comment that she handled her own dogs personally, and those of her breeding for other owners as well. One never found her on the circuits or travelling tremendous distances to dog shows as is the modern custom. She showed mainly in the East, and she proved to us all that owner-handlers can and do succeed. Her record as a breeder will surely long stand unchallenged.

Among the champions produced by Delegate from Isis were Dorian, the first male champion kept for the home kennel. A Group winner prior to becoming a champion, he finished his title at eleven months of age. Among his progeny were Champion Willa vom Ahrtal, who, bred to Champion Lakecrest Thunderstorm, produced an all-champion litter of six.

The leading sire from vom Ahrtal was Champion Cassio vom Ahrtal, born in February 1964, with 38 champions to his credit. He was by Xando vom Ahrtal (Champion Hagen vom Ahrtal ex Champion Fidelia vom Ahrtal, the latter from the Thunderstorm-Willa litter) and his dam was Champion Juno vom Ahrtal

(Champion Fortuna's Maestro ex Zessica, she by Alaric vom Ahrtal, C.D.X., T.D., a Delegate son, whose dam was Champion Friederun vom Ahrtal, the latter from the original Delegate-Isis combination). Cassio died in January 1974.

Close behind Cassio, with 28 champions among his progeny, was Champion Felix vom Ahrtal. He was from the Thunderstorm-Willa combination (thus had as his grandparents Champion Rancho Dobe's Storm, Champion Apache Lady of Lakecrest, Champion Dorian vom Ahrtal, C.D. and Champion Elektra v Ahrtal, C.D.).

There are numerous other outstanding producers among the vom Ahrtal Dobes, as you will note as you read this book. Tess Henseler during the 1950's and 1960's was a very outstanding breeder, and as a tremendous admirer of her dogs, I am pleased to call attention to the fact that she began with and continued to use American stock in her kennels, feeling that the dogs in the U.S. are both good quality and elegant. Certainly her breeding program has stamped vom Ahrtal dogs with distinction.

Tess Henseler is still actively involved with Dobermans, and we hope she will remain so for many years to come. Her Dobermans are her valued companions, and it seems very likely that the more than seventy champions which she has already bred will be joined by still more from vom Ahrtal!

Judging is taking much of Tess Henseler's interest these days, as her services are widely in demand both in America and abroad. Recently she has been to Australia on assignment, which she found extremely enjoyable.

Alisaton and Alisaton/D'Mascus

Alisaton began their breeding program with Champion Arabar's Impertinence, called "Bitchkin." A Best of Breed and Group-placing bitch, she was purchased by the Satalinos as a finished champion. She was bred for the first time at four years of age, with the help and guidance of Gwen Satalino's friend and mentor, Carol Selzle Petruzzo. Champion Damasyn The Troycen was chosen for the first two litters. These consisted of five puppies in each, the first litter including Champion Alisaton's Kinderwicke, WAC, Champion Alisaton's Kindman, WAC, and Alisaton's Kinbrook, C.D. The repeat breeding included

BEST OF OPPOSITE SEX

1. The noted Ch. Cassio vom Ahrtal, sire of 38 champions. A son of Xandu vom Ahrtal ex Ch. Juno vom Ahrtal, bred and owned by Tess Henseler, vom Ahrtal Kennels, Ottsville, Pennsylvania.
2. This is "Bitchkin," as she is affectionately called, or, to be more formal, Ch. Arabar's Impertinence. She was a red from Ch. Damasyn Bo-Tairic's second mating, here pictured winning under judge Margaret Kilburn. Handled by Carol Selzle.
3. Ch. Alisaton Hot Shot, C.D., ROM with a little girl. Owner, Leslie Hall, Wilton, Connecticut.
4. Ch. Alisaton Touchdown v. D'Mascus, C. D., ROM, here obeying the "sit-stay" command in the obedience ring for his C.D. title. Ranny Jarrelle, owner-handler, Richmond, Virginia.
5. Ch. Alisaton Bewitched, by Ch. Gra-Lemor Demetrius v d Victor ex Ch. Alisaton's Kinderwicke, WAC, was pointed from the Puppy Classes and is a Best of Breed and Specialty Best in Show winner, the latter from the Veterans Class over a handsome assortment of champions and Best of Breed winners. She was the Doberman Pinscher Club of America producer of most champions among bitches for 1980 and 1981 as well as the recipient of an Award of Merit in 1978 and in 1982, the latter from the Veterans Class. Bred by Gwen and JoAnn Satalino; owned by Kay and William Harrison.
6. Ch. Alisaton's Kinderwicke, WAC at age seven-and-a-half years, moving to back-to-back Best of Breed wins. By Ch. Damasyn The Troycen ex Ch. Arabar's Impertinence. Cobreeder and owner, Gwen DeMilta, Westbury, New York.
7. Am. and Can. Ch. Alemap's Checkmate, by Ch. Steb's Top Skipper ex Ch. Our Very Own Pamela, C.D., was bred by Warren Bushman and owned by Jack Hronek and Bill Haines, Birmingham, Michigan. Photo courtesy of Mr. and Mrs. J. Monroe Stebbins.

▲6

► 7

Champion Alisaton's Intrepid Lad, Champion Alisaton's Intimate Miss, and Brazilian Champion Alisaton's Infrared.

In the hope of getting a black bitch, Impertinence was then bred to Champion Damasyn The Forecast, a black Troycen son, for her third and last litter. The result of this breeding was the singleton *red* bitch, Champion Alisaton Raincheck, WAC. Of the eleven puppies that Impertinence produced, six became American Champions and Impertinence was the 1976 Doberman Pinscher Club of America Top Producing Dam; her owners, Gwen Lynn and Joann Satalino (Gwen's mother) at the same time becoming the 1976 Doberman Pinscher Club of America Breeders of the Most Champions.

1. Ch. Modern v Simmenau-Rhinegold, owned by Rheingold Kennels, Detroit, Michigan.
2. German Sieger and Am. Ch. Muck von Brunia, owned by Mr. and Mrs. Owen West of Chicago. This important and influential dog was imported by the Wests in 1933 for a reputed $3,500, at which time he was three years of age. The mighty Dictator was linebred to Muck through Muck's two most famous producing sons, Ch. Blank v. d Domstadt (imported and Dictator's sire), and his dam was the red daughter, Ch. and Siegerin Ossi v Stahlhelm (also imported) of the imported Ch. and Sieger Troll v Engelsburg. A dog who played an important role in the development of the Doberman Pinscher in the United States. Photo courtesy of Peggy Adamson.

1▲   ▼2

CAPTIONS FOR PLATES 17 TO 32

Plate 17

1. Stolz Meadow Rue v Obsidian, C.D.X., by Civetta's Bruin of Kami ex Civetta's Obsidian, U.D., WAC. Owner-handled by Kay Martin, Brooklyn, New York.

2. Kay Martin, owner of Civetta Dobermans, with her Ch. Civetta's Wolf Whistle of Kami, C.D.X., ROM.

3. Bishop's Adora's Rocker, C.D.X., WAC, Sch.H. I, TT, here is winning at the Doberman Pinscher Club of America Specialty. Kay Martin, owner.

4. Civetta's Desert Fox, by Ch. Elfred's His Excellency ex Srigo's Kase Kuchen, owned and bred by Kay Martin.

Plate 18

1. Ch. Marienburg's Lone Eagle, famous Best in Show winner and the country's No. 1 Doberman in 1980, starting his career for the DiNardos in 1977 with Jane Forsyth as handler.

2. Ch. Eagle's Devil "D" winning the Working Group at Worcester County 1982, handled, as usual, by Carlos Rojas for breeders-owners Dr. and Mrs. Anthony DiNardo, East Hartford, Connecticut.

3. Gina Marie DiNardo and Odessa, with whom she is winning first in Junior Showmanship at Elm City Kennel Club, 1980.

4. Best of Breed at Putnam Kennel Club in 1982. The mighty "Devil D," more formally known as Ch. Eagle's Devil "D," with has handler Carlos Rojas. This famed record-holding and Best in Show Doberman is owned by Dr. and Mrs. Anthony DiNardo.

5. Ch. Marienburg's Lone Eagle, the No. 1 Doberman Pinscher in 1980 and No. 2 in 1978, with his original handler (in California) Moe Miyagawa. Lone Eagle was sold by Marienburg to Dr. and Mrs. Anthony DiNardo, for whom he made an impressive show record and became an outstanding sire, the famous young Devil "D" being among his progeny.

6. Ch. Eagle's Devil "D" wins Best of Breed under Dr. Reinitz at New Castle, 1983. Carlos Rojas handling for Dr. and Mrs. Anthony DiNardo.

Plate 19

1. Jane Forsyth, who handled Dr. and Mrs. Anthony DiNardo's Ch. Marienburg's Lone Eagle to so many important victories, in an informal moment with their young Odessa.

2. Carlos Rojas and the great homebred owned by Sheila and Anthony DiNardo of East Hartford, Connecticut—Ch. Eagle's Devil "D," son of Ch. Marienburg's Lone Eagle. Carlos and Devil built up a tremendous show record together during the early 1980's.

3. Ch. Eagle's Devil "D" wins the Chattanooga Doberman Pinscher Club Specialty show for Dr. and Mrs. Anthony DiNardo, handled, as usual, by Carlos Rojas. The judge is Ray Carlisle, noted Doberman breeder and former publisher of the outstanding magazine, *The World of the Working Dog*.

4. Ch. Eagle's Devil "D," winner of more than 20 times all-breed Best in Show, many Specialties and Group Firsts. Best of Breed at the Doberman Pinscher Club of America 1984 Specialty. Pictured with his handler, Carlos Rojas. This outstanding homebred dog belongs to Mr. and Mrs. Anthony DiNardo.

Plate 20

1. Ch. Civetta's Wolf Whistle of Kami, C.D.X., ROM, had some 35 Best of Breed awards, owner-handled by Kay Martin in hottest competition during the mid-1970's.

2. Civetta's You Win Again, TT, by Bishop's Adora's Rocker, C.D.X., WAC, Sch.H. I, TT ex Ch. Civetta's Wolf Whistle of Kami, C.D.X., ROM, pictured in May 1981. Kay Martin, owner.

3. Von Stauff's Midnite Wolf, WAC, winning the Open Black Dog Class at the Doberman Pinscher Club of America Specialty in 1977. By Civetta's Big Bad Wolf of Kami. Kay Martin, Civetta Kennels, handling.

4. Ch. Civetta's Wolf Whistle of Kami, C.D.X., ROM winning the Brood Bitch Class at the Doberman Pinscher Breeders Association of Penn/Jersey Specialty in May 1980 with her "kids," Civetta's Red Hot, Civetta's Blue Suede Shoes, and Civetta's Tutti Fruitti. Kay Martin, owner, Civetta Dobes.

5. Ch. Civetta's Steel Blue of Kami, C.D.X., by Civetta's Lone Wolf of Kami, C.D ex Ch. Civetta's Shama Thrush of Kami. Photo courtesy of Kay Martin.

6. Civetta's Reynard, by Ch. Elfred's His Excellency ex Srigo's Kase Kuchen, gaining points for owner Kay Martin.

7. Head study of Ch. Knox's Carbon Copy, C.D.X., T.D., ROM, Sch.H. III, FH, AD. Owned by Bill and Susan Knox, Copyright Kennels, Cookeville, Tennessee.

8. Doberman Pinscher Club of Dallas, September 1980. Ch. Knox's Carbon Copy, C.D.X., ROM, Sch.H. III completes his U.S.A. championship by taking Winners Dog under judge Betty Moore in an entry of 125 males and 151 bitches. Handled by Ellis Arnett for owners Bill and Susan Knox.

Plate 21

1. Am. and Can. Ch. Courland Bear Hug, handled by Kathi Robinson Schoolmeyer, is a homebred belonging to Stephanie J. Taube, Alamo, California.

2. Future Ch. Courland the Blushing Bride winning Best Puppy at the Doberman Pinscher Club of Las Vegas Specialty, age six months and one day. Handler, Marjorie Brooks. Stephanie J. Taube, breeder; co-owned with Johanna Gossett.

3. Courland Fleur-De-Lis, by Ch. Inverurey's Mac Rob ex Ch. Greenlace's Heather, C.D. Bred and owned by Stephanie J. Taube.

4. Am. and Can. Ch. Courland Bear Hug at the Palace of Fine Arts, San Francisco, California. Bred and owned by Stephanie J. Taube, Courland Dobermans.

Plate 22

1. This is Am., Bda., and Can. Ch. Elfred's Stardust of Dobergal, WAC, owned by George Lightisser, West Palm Beach, Florida. Bred and handled by Ellen Hoffman, Harriman, New York. A multi-Best-of-Breed and Group winner.

2. Ch. Elfred's Larissa, owned by Ann Pacaro; bred and handled by Ellen Hoffman. By Ch. Felix von Ahrtal ex Elfred's Valura.

3. Am. and Bda. Ch. Elfred's Zarras, bred and handled to his title by Ellen Hoffman. A multi-Best-of-Breed and Group winner, "Zar" has also won three Doberman Specialty Bests in Show. Owned by Mr. S. Hamlin, for whom he currently is being handled by Bob Hastings.

4. Ch. Elfred's The President, owner-bred and handled by Ellen Hoffman, winning under judge Ted Gunderson in 1973.

5. Ch. Elfred's Raven, C.D., CACIB, ROM. Bred and handled by Ellen Hoffman. Owned by Carl Adiletti.

6. Am. and Can. Ch. Elfred's Mikki, owner-bred and handled by Ellen Hoffman. This Group-winning Doberman was the Grand Prize Futurity winner at the 1969 Doberman Pinscher Club of America show. By Ch. Brandy Alexander ex Champion Elfred's Enchanting Eloise, C.D.

Plate 23

1. Ebonaire's Rhinestone Cowboy at eight months old (Ed Weiss handling), winning the Puppy Dog Class at the Doberman Pinscher Club of the Tappan Zee Specialty in February 1977. Cowboy reigns as "top dog" at Ebonaire and is Judy Weiss's constant companion.

2. Ebonaire's Serenata now being campaigned for the title, six months of age here. Owned by Judy Weiss and Meridith McGrath, owner-handled in the ring.

3. A heretofore unpublished photo of Ch. Ebonaire's His Excellency, by Ch. Ebonaire's Entertainer ex Debbie Duchess V. Palen, being posed by a friend before the show. Owned by Judy Weiss, Ebonaire Dobermans.

4. Ebonaire's Thistledown, by Carosel's B-on-the-Move from Ch. Ebonaire's Chaldea, whose show career was cut short owing to illness in her owner's family. One of the outstanding Dobermans owned by Judy Weiss.

5. Ch. Ebonaire's Chaldea, by Ch. Ebonaire's His Excellency ex Arabar's Illizza. This red bitch was handled to her title by her owner, Robin Weiss Merlino, co-owned with Judy Weiss.

6. An unposed photo of the great Ch. Ebonaire's His Excellency as he baits in the show ring for his handler, Ellen Hoffman. A superb showman with excellent topline and forechest, this is a Dobe who seldom needed "stacking." Judy Weiss, Levittown, New York, owner.

Plate 24

1. Ch. Dabney's Shadow of Luka, black, with sire, Ch. Amulet's Luka of Sno-Glenn, C.D. Linda and John Krukar, Bethlehem, Pennsylvania, owners.

2. An ideal example of the beautiful coloring of a correct fawn (Isabella) Doberman. Ch. Amulet's Luka of Sno-Glenn, C.D. at three years. Photographed by co-owner Linda Krukar.

3. Dabney's Rootn' Tootn' Razz Berry at nine weeks. Owned by Wendy and Allen Lanoue and Linda and John Krukar.

4. Ch. Dabney's Shadow of Luka at 14 months taking Reserve Winners at the 1982 National. Linda Krukar handling; John and Linda Krukar, owners.

Plate 25

1. Ch. Damasyn The Ardon Arondi, by Ch. Damasyn The Boatswain ex Ch. Brown's Wendy, C.D. Bred by Peggy Adamson; owned by Helen F. Kamerer. Photo courtesy of Peggy Adamson.

2. In memory of Jeff De Lap and Damasyn The Czech. Czech's sire and dam died in 1984 within three months of each other. His sire, Damasyn Insider, C.D. was by Bo-Tairic ex the Jalli-Alli daughter, Damasyn The Saucy Bit. His dam, Damasyn The Jallitaire, was a singleton by Bo-Tairic ex Ch. Damasyn The Jalli-Alli, C.D. Jeff De Lap was a brilliant athlete, training for the Olympics; but an accident ended his hopes of competing. Filled with despondency and heartbroken, he killed himself shortly after this picture was taken.

3. Ch. Damasyn Bo-Tairic of Ardon (January 15, 1966—June 20, 1979) by Ch. Damasyn The Boatswain ex Ch. Brown's Wendy, C.D. Photo by Alton Anderson. Bo-Tairic was owned by Peggy Adamson and was directly linebred to Dictator's two great red sons, Ch. Damasyn the Solitaire (ex Dictator's granddaughter) on his sire's side through his Damasyn breeding, and to Brown's Eric (ex Dictator's daughter) on his dam's side through the Brown's breeding.

4. Head study of the famous Ch. Damasyn The Russian (July 1971—December 1978). Sired by Damasyn Jalli's Jaimie ex Valbrook's Pink Champagne, he was bred by Harriet Cory and owned by Fred and Terry Ferrari. A dog of importance in the breed.

Plate 26

1. Am. and Can. Ch. Tiffany's Gwynllyn of Amulet handled by Perry Phillips to first in the Working Group at Sussex Hills in 1981. Owner, Carol Nock, Gwynllyn Dobermans.

2. Tiffany's Gwynllyn of Amulet at four months, winning Best Working Puppy in Group at the Lehigh Valley Kennel Club Match Show. Owned by Carol and Bill Nock, Gwynedd Valley, Pennsylvania.

3. Ch. Amulet's Cecil v Gluckliche, the first of the Dobermans to represent Gwynllyn Kennels in the show ring, taking Best of Breed at Troy in 1981. Carol Nock, owner.

4. Ch. Highbriar Willo of Allenwood at eight years of age winning the Veteran's Class at the Doberman Pinscher Club of America show in 1972. Betsy R. Thomas, Gambier, Ohio, breeder.

5. Ch. Redjack's Robin Hood was the 1977 Doberman Pinscher Club of America Grand Futurity winner. Owned by Richard and Jeanne Goodyear, Burt, Michigan.

6. Highgate Starzafire, by Sherluck's Star Trek ex Kearney's Imprevu, was bred by Richard and Jeanne Goodyear and is owned by Richard Rodriguez. Here she is winning 6-to-9 month bitches in the Motor City Sweepstakes, November 1983.

7. This handsome young dog is Sherluck's Star Trek at 18 months, destined, we feel certain, to be a champion. Son of Ch. Sherluck's L. B. Jake ex Ch. Moraga Hill's High Fashion, WAC. Richard and Jeanne Goodyear, owners.

8. Sherluck's Star Trek, by Ch. Sherluck's L. B. Jake ex Ch. Moraga Hill's High Fashion, WAC, has 13 points including a "major." Owned by Richard and Jeanne Goodyear.

Plate 27

1. Ch. Kropka von Tontonne, bred by Richard Clayton and owned by Lynn Eggers. This lovely bitch is the dam of Mildred Bryant's beautiful Ch. Foxhall's Ann Klein.

2. Foxhall's Coral Tattoo, by Ch. Hotai Copper Tattoo ex Ch. Foxhall's Ann Klein, was bred and is owned by Lynn Eggers and Mildred Bryant of Texas.

PLATE 21

1
2
3
4

PLATE 22

1

2

3

4

PLATE 23

5

6

1 ▶

2 ▶

PLATE 24

3 ▶

4 ▶

PLATE 25

1

2

3

4

PLATE 26

5

6

7

8

1 ►

2 ►

3 ►

4 ►

BEST OF
BREED

GILBERT PHOTO

PLATE 27

5 ►

6 ►

BEST OF
OPPOSITE SEX

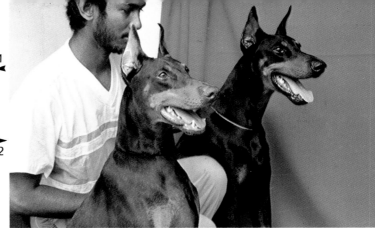

PLATE 28

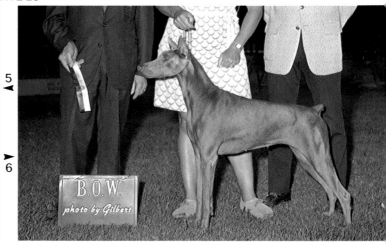

BEST IN SHOW

BEST OF
WINNERS
TRENTON
KENNEL CLUB
1980

PLATE 29

BEST OF BREED
PETRULIS

BEST OF
BREED OR VARIETY
WESTMINSTER
KENNEL CLUB
1984
LEASH 70 LENS PHOTO
BY GILBERT

BEST IN SHOW

1

2

BW
SOSA

BEST OF BREED
OR VARIETY
THRONATEESKA
KENNEL CLUB
OCTOBER 1981
PHOTO BY Graham

3

4

WINNERS

WINNERS BITCH
DPCA
NATIONAL SPECIALTY
OCT 1 1982
JAYNE LANGDON

PLATE 30

5

6

FIRST PLACE
COMB. SPECIALTY
CLUB OF MIAMI
JANUARY 1983
PHOTO BY SABRINA

BEST OF BREED
OR VARIETY
DAN EMMETT
KENNEL CLUB SHOW
AUG 12 1978

7

8

1
2

3
4

PLATE 31

5
6

7
8

1
2

3
4

PLATE 32

5
6

7
8

3. Ch. Foxhall's Ann Klein, by Ch. Georgie Porgie Dob Mann ex Ch. Kropka von Tontonne, was bred by Lynn Eggers and is owned by Mildred Bryant, Bridgeport, Texas.

4. Ch. Gemae Hanky Panky, by Ch. Gra-Lemor Hundred Proof ex Ch. Steb's Custom Maid, bred and owned by George and Mae White, Gemae Dobermans, Marlborough, Connecticut.

5. Am. and Can. Ch. Gemae Minos The Second, by Ch. Gra-Lemor Hundred Proof ex Ch. Steb's Custom Maid, bred by George and Mae White. Owned by Leon Kozikowski and G. D. Giatrakis, Vernon, Connecticut. Handled by Mike Shea.

6. Ch. Gra-Lemor Hundred Proof, by Ch. Gra-Lemor Demetrius v.d. Victor ex Gra-Lemor's Fascination Fling. Bred by Grace Moore; owned by George and Mae White.

Plate 28

1. Damasyn C'Mere, owned by Peggy Adamson and sired by Damasyn Jalli's Jaimie ex Rimar's Shalom. Bred by Edward Albano.

2. Carl Hoi Pong at the quarantine kennels in Trinidad with his two Dobermans then just imported from Peggy Adamson in February 1984. The red bitch, Damasyn The Kyrhi, and the black male, Damasyn The Kadjen, were both sired by the late Damasyn Insider, C.D. ex the German/American-bred bitch, Acsel's Princess. Mr. Hoi Pong is very active in reviving the Doberman Club in Trinidad. He visits his dogs in quarantine every day, making the trip from his home on the other side of the island. Trinidad has a strict six-month quarantine period.

3. Damasyn Incorrigible with her owner-handler Barry Pollack of Charlottesville, Virginia. "Corry" is by Damasyn Insider ex Damasyn C'Mere and was bred by Peggy Adamson. Barry's husband, James E. Pollack, is author of the best-selling book, *Mission M.I.A.* and a new title, *Centrifuge*. The latter devotes almost an entire chapter to an heroic red Doberman bitch named Jalli.

4. Ch. Galaxy's Corry Carina, littermate to Ch. Galaxy's Corry Mission Belle (sired by Ch. Tarrado's Corry) winning a Group under Jane Forsyth's handling for owners Frank and Ellen D'Amico, Glen Cove, New York.

5. Ch. Tarrado's Corry, the sire of 28 champions, owned by Frank and Ellen D'Amico. Bred by Nancy Simons.

6. Ch. Aventine's Gabrielle, finished September 1972, handled by Jane Forsyth. Owned by Frank D'Amico and Don Saslow, she is the first fawn (Isabella) Doberman champion of all time and finished in keen Eastern competition. She is a Ch. Tarrado's Corry daughter.

7. Ch. Dobergal's War Whoop, by Ch. Cardel's Renegade ex Am. and Bda. Ch. Dobergal's Princess Royal, C.D. Bred and owned by Jane Gallagher, Scarborough, New York.

8. Ch. Dobergal's Princess Royal, C.D., by Elfred's Thunder ex Dobergal's Maid of the Bramble. Bred and owned by Jane Gallagher and handled here, at Springfield in 1976, by Ellen Hoffman.

Plate 29

1. Am., Can., and Bda. Ch. Dobergal's Man of The Year, C.D. 1971—1981. Owned by Jane Gallagher, Scarborough, New York. By Ch. Elfred's The President ex Ch. Highquest Bramble.

2. Ch. Rosevale's Dark Temptation, Am. and Can. C.D., with his son, Am. and Can. Ch. Doberlyn's Kaiser v Kroysing, C.D., here are taking the first of four Best Brace in Show awards, this one at Elm City Kennel Club in February 1974. Always owner-handled, this was the only brace of male Dobermans ever shown. Equally significant, each dog was himself a Best in Show winner in his own right. Owners, Doberlyn Kennels, Robert and Bonnie Clarke.

3. Am. and Can. Ch. Doberlyn's Day Light, C.D.X. A multibreed winner from the Puppy and Bred-by-Exhibitor Classes, she acquired 13 points from them breeder-owner-handled by Bonnie Clarke. Now, just out of the whelping box, she is working on her U.D. Breeder-owners, Robert and Bonnie Clarke, Ellington, Connecticut.

4. Am. and Can. Ch. Doberlyn's Kaiser v Kroysing, C.D., the other half (with his sire) of the famous Doberlyn Best in Show Dobe Brace. Himself an all-breed Best in Show winner, "Domino" gained his title in six consecutive weekends. Sired by Ch. Rosevale's Dark Temptation, Am. and Can. C.D. Robert and Bonnie Clarke, owners.

5. Ch. Tolivar's Boo Radley Dob Mann, one of the excellent Dobermans owned by Edd and Irene Bivin, winning Best of Breed from the author.

6. Ch. Arco Dob Mann taking Best of Breed at Westminster, 1984. Owners, Len and Susan Johnson, Arlington, Texas. Handled by Teresa Nail.

7. Ch. Tolivar's Boo Radley Dob Mann at three years of age. Owned by Mr. and Mrs. Edd Bivin, Fort Worth, Texas.

8. Ch. Arco Dob Mann, owned by Len and Susan Johnson. Mr. and Mrs. Edd Bivin, breeders. By Ch. Tolivar's Boo Radley Dob Mann ex Ch. Dinah Dob Mann. A Best in Show winner at just 13 months of age, he completed championship when 10 months. In 1982 Arco was the Doberman Pinscher Club of America Grand Prize Futurity winner; and in 1983 he won the Top Twenty Competition, the youngest dog ever to achieve this honor. In 1984 he was Best Doberman and a Group placer at both Westminster and Chicago International.

Plate 30

1. Ch. Hotai Bobolink, by Ch. Hotai Sweet William ex Ch. Hotai Mercedes, was bred by Carol Clemens and Virginia Markley and is owned by Linda Zeisler. This notable *blue* dog was the Doberman Pinscher Club of America top-winning puppy dog in 1975.

2. Ch. Wyntucks Nashville Brass is an inbred grandson of Ch. Hotai Sweet William, being by his son, Ch. Hotai Willson ex his daughter Ch. Wyntucks Sweet Athena. Bred by owners, Helen Fordyce and Darlene Plicka.

3. Ch. Hotai R.E.O. Speedwagon, by Ch. Hotai Charlie ex Cin Car's Shady Lady, both Top Producers. Bred by Virginia Markley; owned by Harvey and Bettye Carter.

4. Ch. Hotai Molly Hatchet, Winners Bitch in 1982 at the D.P.C.A., was bred by Virginia Markley from Ch. Hotai Charlie ex Cin Car's Shady Lady, both Top Producers. Owned by Helen Yettaw.

5. Hotai Magic Johnson at 10 months of age. Pointed from the Puppy Class, this handsome dog belongs to his breeder, Virginia Markley, Hotai Dobermans, Marion, Ohio.

6. Ch. Hotai Willson, by Ch. Hotai Sweet William (Best in Show winner) ex Hotai Fallen Angel. Bred, owned, and loved by Virginia Markley.

7. Ch. Hotai Charlie, by Ch. Hotai Sweet William ex Hotai Fallen Angel, winning Best of Breed at the Illini Doberman Pinscher Club Specialty, June 1979.

8. Ch. Hotai Copper Tattoo, Top-Winning Doberman, 1982. Owned by David Polk. By Ch. Hotai Charlie ex Cin Car's Shady Lady, both Top Producers.

Plate 31

1. Ch. Sherluck's Fashion Designer, by Ch. Sherluck's L. B. Jake ex Ch. Moraga Hill's High Fashion, WAC. Owned by Richard and Jeanne Goodyear.

2. Ch. Hi Vale's Electric Horseman, handled by breeder-owner Sharon Tasca, taking points on the way to the title. Sharon and Jack Tasca, Hi Vale Dobermans, Danielson, Connecticut.

3. Am. and Can. Ch. Dimar's Sentinel of Hi Vale owned by Jack and Sharon Tasca.

4. Int. Ch. Hi Vale's Mahogany was No. 1 Doberman and No. 1 Working Dog in Argentina. A multi-Best-in-Show winner, pictured here following one of the latter victories. Bred by Jack and Sharon Tasca.

5. Ch. Gemae's Renegade as Grand Sweepstakes winner at the Doberman Pinscher Club of Connecticut—New York Specialty, owner-handled by Sharon Tasca.

6. Ch. Hi Vale's Santana placing in the Group under Peggy Adamson, handled by his breeder-owner, Sharon Tasca.

7. Warjo's D'Artagnon one month prior to becoming a champion, taking Best of Winners at the Maumee Valley Doberman Pinscher Club Specialty, June 1983. Handled by Colby Homer, co-owner with Joan Thompson.

8. The foundation bitch at Homer Hill, Warjo's Melodee v. Scudamore, at age 15 months. By Ch. Marwood Anubis De Scudamore, C.D., ROM, from Can. Ch. Penbar's Bonnie Belle. Owned by Colby and Patrick Homer, Wheeling, West Virginia.

Plate 32

1. Ch. Domani's Prince William, by Ch. Hotai Sweet William ex Ch. Housecarl Helene of Diversha, is the sire of 10 champions and winner of Best in Specialty Show on seven occasions. A most splendid Doberman, bred and owned by Dee Chiantella, Folsom, Louisiana.

2. Ch. Domani's Baron v Kammer and Ch. Domani's Royal Serenade making a clean sweep of the class awards by taking Winners Dog and Winners Bitch on the way to their championship. A proud day for the breeeder-owner of their sire (Ch. Domani's Prince William), Dee Chiantella.

3. Ch. Hotai Copper Tattoo relaxes in a favorite chair at the home of co-owner David M. Polk. Tattoo also belongs to Dee Chiantella and has surely done his owners proud, first in the show ring and now as a highly successful producer.

4. Ch. Domani's Royal Serenade, by Ch. Domani's Prince William ex Ch. Shaft's Symphony By Jove. A picture which depicts Doberman showmanship at it's best by Royal Serenade and her handler Gene Haupt. One of the outstanding Dobermans of Domani bred and owned by Dee Chiantella.

5. Ch. Domani's Midnight Special, by Ch. Domani's Prince William. Owned by Suzi Bickoff; bred by Dee Chiantella.

6. Toni Leigh DiNardo taking Best of Winners from the Puppy Class with the young Derek "D." Toni is one of the daughters of Sheila and Dr. Anthony DiNardo, East Hartford, Connecticut.

7. Ch. Eagle's Devil "D" with his handler, Carlos Rojas. This memorable Doberman, winner of the 1984 Doberman Pinscher Club of America National Specialty and the No. 1 Doberman Pinscher for the year (the latter for the third consecutive year), has won first in more than 70 Working Groups, has 18 Bests in Show to his credit, and has close to 200 times Best of Breed, including 10 Specialty Shows. A homebred belonging to Dr. and Mrs. Anthony DiNardo.

8. Ch. Marienburg's Lone Eagle, owned by Dr. and Mrs. Anthony DiNardo. Lone Eagle was the No. 2 Doberman in the Nation for 1978 and a 1979 Doberman Pinscher Club of America Top Twenty Winner. In 1980 he was No. 1 Doberman Pinscher in the nation. A Best in Show winner, he has 151 times Best of Breed to his credit, including 16 Specialty Shows. A sire par excellence, the best known of his sons is the great Ch. Eagle's Devil "D," No. 1 Doberman Pinscher and No. 10 Working Dog in 1982; No. 1 Doberman Pinscher, No. 2 Working Dog, and on the Top Ten all breeds list for 1983; and No. 1 Doberman Pinscher in 1984. Devil "D" was homebred by the DiNardos, handled by Carlos Rojas.

Ch. Checkmate's Beau Geste, owned by Bill Haines in Ohio, making a good win here under Peggy Adamson.

Alisaton continued breeding Dobermans that possessed a distinctive look and type through Impertinence daughter, Champion Alisaton Kinderwicke, WAC. Gwen finished Kinder from the Bred-by-Exhibitor Class, taking her first points at twelve months and one day. These were also the first points won by Kinder's 17-year-old breeder-owner-handler, Gwen, handsomely gained by a Best of Winners victory at the 1973 Doberman Pinscher Club of America National Specialty, where she was also Reserve 12-15 Month Futurity Junior. Kinder was the recipient of the 1974 Doberman Pinscher Club of America Award for most blue ribbons from the Bred-by-Exhibitor Bitch Class.

Kinder was *Kennel Review* magazine's 1978 Top Producing Doberman Bitch, winner of the 1978 Doberman Pinscher Club of America and Quaker City Specialty Brood Bitch Classes as well as the 1979 Doberman Pinscher Club of America Top Producing Bitch. She is the dam of 13 American Champions, two Canadian Champions, one Brazilian Champion, four ROM holders, seven WAC holders, and two C.D. titled Dobes. Among her champion get are two 1978 Top Twenty contenders, Champion Alisaton Damascus, C.D. and Champion Alisaton Citation, WAC. In total, nine of her progeny have won Bests of Breed with many Group placements among them, as well as Group I's. One of her daughters, Champion Alisaton Bewitched, is the dam of twelve American Champions to date. Bewitched is carrying on in the tradition of her dam and granddam, having been awarded the Doberman Pinscher Club of America Top Producing Bitch title in 1980 and 1982, making it three generations of Top Producing Bitches at Alisaton: Impertinence, her daughter Kinder, and Kinder's daughter, Bewitched. These three bitches have a total of 31 American Champions among them.

Kinder's son, Damascus, is the sire of thirteen American Champions to date.

Kinder is the granddam of at least 43 American Champions at the time of this writing, some of whom are Best of Breed, Group winners and placers, including two Top Twenty contenders, these latter being a Damascus daughter, Marienburg Wickiup v Bali-Mor and a Champion Alisaton's Kinsman son out of Champion Alisaton Kinder Rose, Champion Alisaton Touchdown v

D'Mascus, C.D., ROM (1984) whom Gwen bred with Peggy Esposito of D'Mascus.

Champion Alisaton Kinder Rose died shortly after her third litter was whelped. She was the foundation of a breeding program that involved the partnership of Gwen and the Alisatons with Peggy Esposito and the D'Mascus Dobes. Peggy and Gwen had met many years previously during a planned breeding of Peggy's bitch to an Alisaton dog. The litter never came about, but the long-term co-ownership/co-breeder relationship was born and has flourished. Peggy's address is the home of Champion Alisaton Damascus, C.D., for whom her kennel is named.

The next Alisaton-bred Dobe to arrive at Peggy's home was Kinder Rose. She took two "majors" from the Puppy Class, with a third at the Specialty held just prior to the National in 1978 and a fourth "major" en route to her title. In addition to Champion Alisaton Touchdown v D'Mascus, finished by his owner in 17 shows, Kinder Rose has produced four other American Champions for her breeders. Notably Champion D'Mascus Sambuca of Alisaton (who finished at twelve months and one week, winning a Specialty Best of Breed over 100 or more entries, and the 1982 Doberman Pinscher Club of America award for most blue ribbons in the Puppy Class which was a tie). Others are Champion Alisaton Q.B. Sneak v D'Mascus, Champion D'Mascus Tia Maria v Alisaton, and Champion D'Mascus Tanqueray v Alisaton. Sambuca has her C.D., and other titled Kinder kids include a U.D.T. and a C.D.X. There are numerous other major and minor pointed get out of Kinder, her youngest litter just eighteen months of age.

Alisaton Dobermans (Gwen and Joann Satalino or Gwen and her husband Stephen DeMilta) and Alisaton/D'Mascus (the Satalinos and Peggy Esposito) can point with pride to the success of their breeding programs and to their very real contribution to quality in modern Dobes. The original breeding stock was based on Damasyn.

The dogs to whom these bitches have been bred include Champion Damasyn's The Troycen, Champion Damasyn The Forecast, Champion Gra-Lemor Demetrius v d Victor, Champion Brown's B Brian, Champion

Schauffelein's Vintage Year, Champion Marienburg's Osage, Champion Glenayr Dufferinand, Champion Alisaton Kinsman, and Champion Mardale Spirit of Malnati.

Alisaton has produced 20 American Champions, two Canadian Champions, and two Brazilian Champions; Alisaton/D'Mascus has bred five American Champions. Additionally there are at least 23 other major pointed sons and daughters as we go to press—all this in nine litters bred by Alisaton and three litters bred by D'Mascus and Alisaton together. There are 13 Best of Breed winners included among the champions and three Top Twenty contenders.

Aquarius

Aquarius Dobermans are at Opelousas, Louisiana, where most of the dogs were bred and are co-owned by Jim Briley and Mrs. Alan Robson.

The foundation bitch is Champion Rehbar Delissa of Aquarius, who has a star-studded pedigree, being a granddaughter of Champion Tarrados Corry, Champion Angil v Alarich, Champion Highbriar Bandana and Champion Marks-Tey Waystar.

A 1978 Top Twenty contender, Delissa has four champions to her credit at the time of writing with three others just lacking a "major" for completion of their titles and several others just starting out on their show careers. Her latest litter by Champion Dubert's Rocket Cruiser is very promising, with two of the four puppies already pointed.

Champion Aquarius Cimmaron of Celadon, by Champion Thorin von Morr ex Champion Rehbar Delissa of Aquarius, both 1978 Top Twenty contenders, scored a notable career in the United States before going to Japan where it is expected his contributions to the breed will be significant. He was No. 12 Doberman in the United States for 1978 in the Doberman Pinscher Club of America ratings.

The first champion finished by Jim Briley was Champion Bailes Beau Rikki of Rehbar, who was born in 1974, bred by Mrs. Boyce Bailes and Richard Brue, a son of Champion Devil Tree's Black Shaft from Champion Marks-Tey Waystar.

Arielle

Arielle Dobermans are owned by Armin and Paula Hotz at St. Peter, Illinois, who have been highly successful with some very handsome dogs.

Champion Redyns Touch of Class and her brother, Champion Redyns High and Mighty, came to live with the Hotzes as ten-week-old puppies. After thirteen years of breeding and exhibiting purebred dogs, "Classy" was the first champion for the Hotzes and a source of tremendous pleasure to them. She was shown as a puppy by her owner, Paula, after which time her career was turned over to Charles Cooper of Louisville, Kentucky. Starting to work as a team, they won Best Puppy and Reserve Winners Bitch at the National Specialty. Then after a couple of months off during the winter weather, it only took eight times in Open Class to capture her championship. During that time, she was awarded a Grand Sweepstakes, twice was Best of Breed, received a Group II, and completed her championship with a Group I. "Classy" chalked up a show record of 91 times Best of Breed, 30 times first in the Group, 24 times Group second, and eight additional Group placements. But the real frosting was a total of 11 all-breed Bests in Show and 10 Specialty Show Bests of Breed! Events of special significance during her career include Best Puppy at the National and Reserve Winners Bitch there, in 1979; Award of Merit, Doberman Pinscher Club of America National Specialty in 1981; and Best of Breed at the Doberman Pinscher Club of America National Specialty in 1982.

With all phases and obstacles of the show ring challenged and conquered, "Classy" retired from active competition when she was chosen Best of Breed at the National in 1982. As Paula Hotz sums it up—"the ultimate complement of a Doberman's worth."

Now "Classy" continues her contribution to the breed as a producer. Her children are all still quite young, and their worth not as yet determined, but Paula and her family have great hopes for another generation with the beauty and quality of their dam.

Champion Redyns High and Mighty, "Classy's" litter-brother, was piloted to his championship by his breeder, Deborah Snyder. Now retired from active competition, he

Ch. Gra-Lemor Demetrius v d Elbe going Best of Breed over an entry of 89 Dobermans at Chicago International in April 1970. Judge, A. Peter Knoop. Photo courtesy of Peggy Adamson.

1. Ch. Emperor of Marienland sired many a famous winner and is to be found in a large number of important modern Dobe pedigrees. Pictured here, handled by Bill Rieman, winning under judge Frank Downing (Mel Downing's dad). Photo courtesy of Margaret (Marge) Kilburn.
2. Ch. Doricka v d Elbe was owned by Hans Schmidt of Downington, Pennsylvania.
3. Another of Alonzo B. Reed's famous winners of the 1950's, Ch. Dortmund's Ballerina v. d. Elbe, winning the Working Group at Great Barrington, 1954. Handled by Jane Kamp Forsyth; photo courtesy of Jane.
4. Baltimore County, 1951. Jane Kamp, now Forsyth, handling Alonzo P. Reed's famed Ch. Duke v d Ravensburg. Photo courtesy of Jane Forsyth.

3▲ ▼4

was a multi-Best of Breed, Specialty Best in Show and Group placement winner. Although many of them are still quite young, his progeny include many pointed and obedience titled "kids" of promise.

Arielle Easy Touch carries the distinction of being one of the first born from her celebrated dam, Champion Redyns Touch of Class. Her sire was Champion Silent Sentry's Marauder, WAC. Although still a youngster, "Easy" has garnered a Best Puppy at the Doberman Pinscher Club of Missouri and a Grand Sweepstakes at the Doberman Pinscher Club of Memphis.

Bar-Lock

Bar-Lock Dobermans had their inception in 1964 with the acquisition by Donna Blackburn, North Miami Beach, Florida, of Jemoel's Rosemarie, a double granddaughter of the immortal Tri-International Champion Boron The Warlock, C.D. From her first litter, whelped in 1967 and sired by Best in Show winning Champion Bardolf Von Tannenwald, came two future champions. These were Champion Bardolf's Ebony Queen and Champion Bardolf's Warlock, C.D. The latter became the sire of Champion Bar-Lock's Brown Chelsey and Champion Jo-Sin's Misty Rose.

The name Bar-Lock as a kennel identification for her dogs was coined by Donna Blackburn, a contraction of BARdolf and WarLOCK, the name of the dog who was their first champion and who really got the Blackburns into showing.

During these early days, Jane Kay and Donna Blackburn became friends, and, as Donna says, "Jane was always there when we needed help or advice." The Blackburns loved the Kay Hill dogs, and Jane was instrumental in their being able to obtain two very special bitches. The first was in 1972, a nine-and-a-half-week-old puppy who grew up to become Champion Torenduf Funi-Girl of Kay Hill, purchased from breeders Doris and Gerry Lefkowith in Pennsylvania. Funi-Girl won many breeds and Groups, two Specialty Bests in Show, and was the Blackburns' first champion bitch. She became the dam of Champion Bar-Lock's Ebony Eikon, W.A.C., Bar-Lock's Ebony Talisman, C.D., W.A.C., and Bar-Lock's Lady Alexis, C.D.X., W.A.C.

The other Kay Hill bitch who joined Bar-Lock Kennels in 1974 was Kay Hill's Letter Perfect, three years old at the time, who was co-owned with Dennis Fisher.

Letter Perfect was the Doberman Pinscher Club of America Top Producing Bitch two years consecutively. Her seven American Champions were Champion Bar-Lock's Star of Night, Champion Bar-Lock's Starbuck, U.D., R.O.M., Champion Bar-Lock's Evening Star, Champion Koven's Mystic Star of Bar-Lock, Champion Bar-Lock's Gallant Fox of Koven, Champion Koven's Black Gold, and Champion Koven's Witch Hunt, plus Canadian Champion Bar-Lock's Bounty Hunter.

Four of these above champions have themselves produced champions, including Mrs. Blackburn's Champion Bar-Lock's Star of Night, who is the dam of some winners currently being campaigned, including American, Bahamian and Canadian Champion Bar-Lock's Star Blazer, a champion in three countries by eighteen months of age and the Doberman Pinscher Club of America Top Winning Puppy Dog for 1983. Then there is Bar-Lock's Nightfire, C.D.X., W.A.C., nine points including a "major"; Bar-Lock's Angelfire, seven points including a "major", one leg on a C.D. with a High in Trial; Bar-Lock's Ketcha Star, pointed; Bar-Lock's Battlestar, pointed; and Canadian Champion Bar-Lock's Starbolt. Incidentally, a "theme" is picked for the naming of each litter, which makes it very simple to spot littermates.

Donna Blackburn does not breed many litters as she is far more interested in quality than in quantity. Each litter born has been several years in the planning. All puppies are born and raised in the house, which Donna considers of utmost importance in raising sound puppies. Her bitches are never overbred, mostly raising just two litters in their lifetime. A litter is not bred at Bar-Lock unless the Blackburns really need a new dog for themselves to show; otherwise, it is just not worth all the "blood, sweat and tears" involved. The Bar-Lock puppies are never sold outside of the United States.

Belle Reve

Belle Reve Dobermans were founded in the early 1970's, in California, on Rancho Dobe lines. The owners, the William Shatners, are

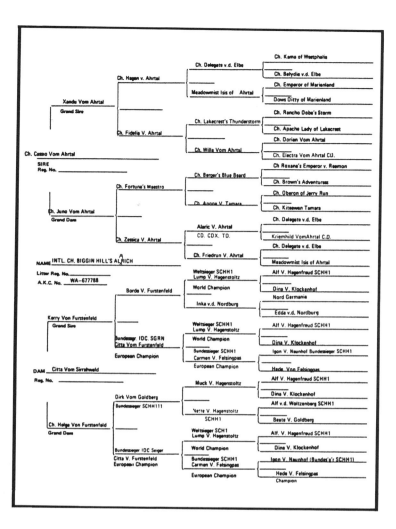

1. **Am. and Can. Ch. Biggin Hill's Alarich**, by Ch. Cassio vom Ahrtal ex Citta vom Sirrahwald, bred and owned by Phyllis and Norman Biggin. Winning here under William L. Kendrick, handled by Norman Biggin.
2. **Ch. Bardolf's Warlock, C.D.** finished his championship with all majors—five of them—under five different judges. Had ten of his points by 11 months of age. Handled by Paul Saucier for owners Vic and Donna Blackburn, Bar-Lock Kennels, North Miami Beach, Florida. Bred by Cecil Thompson, by Ch. Bardolf von Tannenwald ex Jemoel's Rosemarie.

1▲

▼2

106

3▲

▼4

1. Ch. Emperor of Marienland, by Ch. Domossi of Marienland ex Ch. Westphalia's Rembhal, was bred by Richard Webster and owned by Mrs. Wilhelm Knauer.
2. Ch. Orsova of Westphalia, owned by Francis F. H. Fleitmann, Far Hills, New Jersey. Photo courtesy of Peggy Adamson.
3. Ch. Agitator of Doberland, A red male by Ch. Dictator v Glenhugel out of Pinsch of Doberland, was bred and owned by Ivan Wolff, Forest Hills, New York.
4. Ch. Ferry von Rauhfelson of Giralda, the first Doberman to win best in Show at Westminster. Imported by Mrs. M. Hartley Dodge, Giralda Farms, Madison, New Jersey, Ferry was later sold to Randahof Kennels in California for whom he was handled to many impressive wins by Russell Zimmerman.

1. Berman Brier winning the 9-12 Month Puppy Class at Westminster in 1957, 12 in the class, at one week over nine months old. Mr. Francis Fleitmann, judge. Bill Riemann, handler. Bernard Berman, owner, New York, New York. Westminster no longer includes puppy classes at its shows, but formerly they provided some extremely exciting competition. Brier, at 17 months of age, became the Grand Victor for 1957 at the Doberman Pinscher Club of Chicagoland Specialty. The German Doberman Verein granted this club the honor of presenting Grand Victor and Grand Victrix awards annually at its Specialties. Brier was by Ch. Damasyn The Solitaire, C.D. ex Berman Armina. He was Best of Breed at the Specialty.

2. Ch. Berman Bangles, a black and tan, by Ch. Damasyn The Solitaire, C.D. ex Berman Armina, winning under judge Marge Kilburn at Queensboro Kennel Club in 1961. Bred, owned, and handled by Bernard Berman.

3. Ch. Extramiss of Snomis, born May 4, 1952, by Ch. Beltane of Tamarack ex Briget of Jan-Har. She was the dam of Berman Armina, who produced Ch. Berman Brier, Grand Victor, and Ch. Berman Bangles. Owned by Bernard Berman.

4. This handsome portrait-photo is of Ch. Berman Brier, Grand Victor at 10 months of age. Bernard Berman, breeder-owner.

dedicated enthusiasts and at present have four members of the breed, led by a fourteen-year-old Maestro granddaughter. These include Hawk's Wizard Witch, C.D., Belle Reve Royale, C.D. (soon starting in the show ring), and Belle Reve Paris.

Berman

Berman Dobermans has been a small kennel, which was started by Bernard Berman of Monroe, New York, during the 1950's. Mr. Berman owned a most excellent bitch, Berman Armina, who was royally bred, being a descendant of such Dobes as International Champion Kilburn Ideal and Champion Kilburn Jest on her sire's side and she herself a daughter of Mr. Berman's Champion Axtramiss of Snomis (International Champion Beltana of Tamarack from a Champion Saracen of Reklaw daughter).

This lovely bitch, Armina, was bred for her first litter to Peggy Adamson's Champion Damasyn The Solitaire, C.D.X. From this mating, on May 5, 1956, was born a litter of six puppies, which consisted of two red dogs, three black dogs and a black bitch. From the very beginning, one puppy, named Berman Brier, was a standout. As Bernie says, "He was a short, compact dog of great quality, an elegant appearance, proud carriage, great nobility and a wonderful temperament. Fearless and bold, while at the same time loyal and obedient, he was a dark *red* dog with good markings, almond-shaped, deep-set eyes, lovely expression." Brier became Bernie Berman's constant companion—but would go with other people *provided* his master said it would be okay.

Brier attained his Grand Victor title at seventeen months of age, handled by Peggy Adamson—an exciting occasion, as this was the very first Grand Victor title awarded in the United States at the Chicagoland Doberman Pinscher Specialty in 1957, which had been granted the honor of presenting this award and that of Grand Victrix annually at its Specialty Shows by the German Doberman Verein.

Brier was used only a few times at stud but has three worthy champions to his credit, nonetheless. One of these, owned by Betty Moore, became an all-bred Best in Show winning bitch.

Brier lived with his grandmother, Champion Axtramiss of Snomis, and his mother, Berman Armina, all as housedogs in the Bermans' home throughout their lifetimes. He was with the Bermans even before their children, Jesse and Betsy, were born in 1958 and 1960 respectively; and as Bernie says, "We never experienced anything other than good times with our children and these dogs," and they were never concerned about their children being with them.

The black bitch, Brier's litter sister, also gained her title. The Bermans have not filled us in on the others or whether any of them were shown.

Biggin Hill

Biggin Hill Dobermans, owned by Norman and Phyllis Biggin at West Kingston, Rhode Island, have long been prominent in the Doberman world, their kennel dating back several decades.

It is interesting to note that Champion Biggin Hills Alarich and Champion Biggin Hills Beckett were Best in Show winners at all-breed events, that both were in the Top Ten ratings in their day, and that both finished from the Bred-by-Exhibitor Classes.

Alarich's sister, Champion Biggin Hills Adele, was also an American and Canadian Champion.

Norman Biggin nowadays centers his dog show involvement around judging, being a popular and respected member of the panel at many of our dog shows.

Billmar

Billmar's Dobermans are owned by Captain M. E. and Billie R. Smith of Cleveland, Tennessee, who purchased their first Dobe (who was to become Champion Margrave's Armin) from Nancy Stodghill of Louisville, Kentucky when he was only eleven months of age. He was out of two Best in Show Dobes, Champion Brown's B-Brain and Champion Mattappany's Avant Garde.

Handled by Charlie Cooper, Armin gained his title in twelve weeks at eighteen months old. Then on the excellent advice of Mrs. Eleanor Brown, the breeder of his sire, he was taken home for a year in which to mature.

Meanwhile Captain Smith completed his career in the Navy and, with his wife and Armin, retired in Tennessee where they now reside. In September 1976 Charlie Cooper started Armin on his "specials" career with seven consecutive Bests of Breed. During the next eighteen months this splendid dog compiled an impressive array of awards, putting him on the Top Twenty lists for 1977 (as No. 7) and 1978 (as No. 12). Armin was known and respected by the Doberman community wherever he travelled.

In 1981, the Smiths bred their "B" and "C" litters, five years after their first litter had been born. Capturing the fine qualities of Armin's heritage, three Dobermans from these two litters gained their championships during 1983. They are from Windson's Omen of Billmar who was bred to Champion Kachina's Louisiana Man to produce the "B" litter, and from Champion Billmar's Angel of Armin who was bred to her half-brother, Keenedale's Bunker Hill, for the "C" litter.

Champion Billmar's B-Beat Tike and Champion Billmar's Belle of Beau are the two lovely "B" champion bitches. A male, Champion Billmar's CC & Co was major pointed in the puppy classes finishing at eighteen months of age. A male, Billmar's B-Burson, is also multi-pointed from the "B" litter, as is Billmar's Crystal from the "C" litter.

The Smiths do not have a kennel, preferring that the Dobes live with them in their home. They devote their efforts to all aspects of the breed; handling, limited breeding, and activities of the Doberman Pinscher Club of Greater Chattanooga keep them on the go most of the time.

Their first ten years in Dobermans have been very happy and enjoyable, and they look forward to the next ten with enthusiasm.

Black Frog

Black Frog Dobermans, owned by Millie McCoy at Bel Air, Maryland, are being line-bred on Champion Elfred's The President. Although a comparatively new breeder, Millie is off to a good start with two champions finished from her second litter. These are Champion Black Frog's Faded Jeans and Champion Black Frog Footsteps O'Gigolo, who are sired by Champion Edelhall Gigolo of Amulet ex Black Frog's Bio Liberty Bell, W.A.C.

This is Liberty Bell's only litter. A sister to these two dogs also has nine points, which include both "majors."

Bra-Ner

Bra-Ner Dobermans are owned by Mrs. Roberta (Bobbi) Brady at Westerville, Ohio.

These dogs are linebred on Joey Purdy's Schauffelein bloodlines from Canada and are also of Pamela DeHetre's Pamelot lines, as these two ladies have done some co-breeding of their Dobes.

Brown's

Brown's Dobermans, owned by Jack and Eleanor Brown of Missouri, have made a proud record in the history of this breed. The kennel was founded on the lovely bitch, Champion Dow's Dame of Kilburn, a Champion Dictator v Glenhugel daughter. Bred back to Dictator, she became the dam of the famous Champion Brown's Eric. I have frequently heard Eric referred to as the most excellent and best producer of all Dictator's sons; certainly he made his mark on the breed by siring 28 champions, among them numerous Top Producers.

Among the oustanding Eric progeny, one finds such dogs as the littermates Champion Brown's Dion (black) and his red sister, the elegant National Specialty and ten times Best in Show winning bitch Champion Brown's Bridget. Bridget was bred on numerous occasions but never conceived until, as a last attempt to get a litter from her, the Browns decided to try her with litter brother, Dion. That time it was a success, six puppies being the result. Included among them were Champion Brown's Gigi of Ar-Bel. The latter, born in 1965, eventually became the dam of Champion Brown's A-Amanda and Champion Brown's B-Brian, both of whom became Best of Breed winners at the National Specialty during their splendid show careers. Dion and Bridget were from a bitch named West Begins Dagmar, who was by Champion Patton's Ponder of Torn ex Champion Conchise's Black Magic.

A marvelous black bitch, Brown's Feegee, was sold by the Browns to the David Dows in Kansas City, for whom she became the dam of some exciting progeny by Eric. These included Champion D-Dow's Aladdin v Riecke,

CAPTIONS FOR PLATES 33 TO 48

Plate 33

1. Ch. Hotai Angel's Finale, by Ch. Hotai Sweet William ex Hotai Fallen Angel. Bred by Virginia Markley, Hotai Dobermans, Marion, Ohio.

2. Cin Car's Shady Lady is the dam of the No. 1 Doberman, Ch. Hotai Copper Tattoo, who was, as well, the youngest Dobe to gain a championship in the history of the breed. Shady belongs to Virginia Markley.

3. Ch. Ingaborge's Devil in Disguise, bred by Sue and Don Simmons, was winner of the 1982 Doberman Pinscher Club of America Award for most blue ribbons that year in the Puppy Classes. She finished at 12 months of age and is owned by Kenny Munch and Don Simmons.

4. Ch. Sherluck's Castle Rock with Don Simmons. 1983 Doberman Pinscher Club of America Best Puppy Award and Best Futurity Puppy. Grandson of Don's famous Ch. Encore's Black Rites, he is by Ch. Tolivar's Boo Radley Dob Mann ex Ch. Moraga Hill's High Fashion, she the dam of nine champions. This outstanding puppy is owned by Kenny Munch and Don Simmons, Silver Spring, Maryland.

Plate 34

1. Mardale Evil Touch v Alisaton, by Ch. Alisaton Touchdown v D'Mascus ex Ch. Alisaton Bewitched, bred by William and Kathryn Harrison and Gwen Satalino DeMilta. Owned by Charles Guardascione and Mary Manning.

2. Ch. Mardale Spirit of Alisaton, by Ch. Marienburg's Sun Hawk, C.D. ex Ch. Alisaton Bewitched, was bred by William and Kathryn Harrison and is owned by Charles Goldstine.

3. Ch. Mardale Be In The Spirit, by Ch. Marienburg's Sun Hawk, C.D. ex Ch. Alisaton Bewitched, bred by William and Kathryn Harrison, owned by Kitty Levinson. Bill Harrison, handler.

4. Ch. Mardale Spirit of Dixie, by Ch. Sherluck's L. B. Jake ex Ch. Alisaton Bewitched, bred by William and Kathryn Harrison. Owned by Pete and Diane Bretz.

5. Ch. Mardale Spirit of Malnati, by Ch. Marienburg's Sun Hawk, C.D. ex Ch. Alisaton Bewitched. Bred by the Harrisons; owned by Jacqueline and Edward Griffin. Winning Best of Breed at Warrenton in 1980, Bill Harrison handling.

6. Ch. Mardale Hell-Cat V. Marienburg, by Ch. Marienburg's Sun Hawk, C.D. ex Ch. Alisaton Bewitched, is owned by Kathryn Harrison, Mardale, Brandywine, Maryland. Handled by Bill Harrison at Maryland Kennel Club, 1981, en route to the title.

Plate 35

1. Candid photo of two of the Marienburg "greats," Sun Hawk and Mary Hartman. Mary Rodgers, owner, Marienburg Kennels, Hamilton, Montana.

2. Ch. Alisaton the Night Watchman, C.D., ROM, by Ch. Brown's B-Brian ex Ch. Alisaton's Kinderwicke. Breeders, Joanne Satalino and Gwen Satalino DeMilta. Born December 9, 1976. Photo taken at seven years. Marjorie Brooks, owner. Santa Rosa, California.

Plate 36

1. Ch. Ingaborge's Helen Patch, by Ch. Angil's Beau Geste ex Ch. Beaulane Love-Rites of Encore, is a Black Rites granddaughter. Bred by Sue and Don Simmons, she is owned by Mr. and Mrs. George Hand. Don Simmons handling.

2. The producer of 29 champions, Ch. Encore's Black Rites, son of Ch. Dolph von Tannenwald ex Ch. Ericka von Tannenwald. Bred by Mrs. Toni McMorris; owned by Don and Sue Simmons.

3. Ch. Encore's Black Rites the day he completed his title. By Ch. Dolph von Tannenwald ex Ch. Ericka von Tannenwald. Bred by Toni McMorris; owned by Don and Sue Simmons.

4. **Ch. Encore's Black Rites won the Stud Dog Class at the Pilgrim Doberman Pinscher Club Specialty with these two progeny.**

5. Ch. Kay Hill's Red Letter Day, born April 1968, by Ch. Kay Hill's Takeswon To Nowon. Handled by Jane Kay at Old Dominion in 1970.

6. Ch. Kay Hill's Red Letter Day winning the Brood Bitch Class at the Doberman Pinscher Club of America National in May 1973. Jane Kay handling.

7. The look of the line continues! Ch. Koven's Top Brass, owned by Manuel Quasada, by Ch. Triadel's High Flyer (Ch. Encore's Black Rites—Ch. Triadel's Star Route of Kay Hill) from Ch. Koven's Black Gold (Ch. Encore's Black Rites—Kay Hill's Letter Perfect). Star Route and Letter Perfect are littermates by Am. and Can. Ch. Highland Satan's Image ex Kay Hill's Red Letter Day. Bred by Rosemary and Dennis Fisher.

8. A Best in Show winner and famous bitch, Ch. Kay Hill's Witch Soubretta, is also the Top Dam record holder. Bred and owned by Jane Kay who is handling at the Doberman Pinscher Club of America Specialty, 1961.

Plate 37

1. Ch. Blackstar's Rani Jemma, WAC taken in the show ring by Kathy Yackamin. Winner of the 1982 Top Twenty, this beautiful Doberman, by Ch. Red Sun's Notorious ex My-A-Mar's Venus De Milo, was bred by Michael Seligman and belongs to Clarence Woodward, Somers, New York.

2. Ch. Fanfare's Ringmaster, owned by Theresa Lazzaro Hundt and Patricia Laurans, at the height of his career. Pictured with his handler, J. Monroe Stebbins, Jr.

3. Ch. Glenayr Dufferinand has the distinction of being a son of the great Ch. Gra-Lemor Demetrius from a Demetrius daughter, Ch. Tedell Barcarolle, and is himself the sire of many champions. An all-breed Best in Show winner and a Specialty Best of Breed dog. Bred and owned by Barbara and Richard Duklis, Barto, Pennsylvania. Handled by Terry Lazzaro Hundt.

4. Ch. Mi Bar's Clarissa of Amulet is owned by Bill MacKay and handled by Terry Lazzaro Hundt, Gaylordsville, Connecticut.

Plate 38

1. Ch. Marienburg's Mary Hartman, the No. 1 Doberman 1978 and 1979. The No. 1 of all breeds, 1978. Quaker Oats Award winner 1978 and 1979. Doberman Pinscher Club of America Best of Breed winner 1979 and 1983 from the Veterans Class. 44 all-breed Bests in Show (a breed record) and 108 Group Firsts. Top Twenty winner in 1978. Handled by Moe Miyagawa throughout her show career, and owned by Mary Rodgers, Marienburg Kennels.

2. Ch. Marienburg's Bewitched, litter sister to Ch. Marienburg's Mary Hartman. Her untimely death at three years of age cut short what would undoubtedly have been an exciting show career. Owner, Mike and Becky Pruitt. Bred by Mary Rodgers, Marienburg Kennels.

3. Ch. Hanadobe's Ryanesian, the first champion offspring of Ch. Marienburg's Sun Hawk. Dam, Ch. Gra-Lemor Princessnesian. Owners, A. and E. Hanaumi and Moe Miyagawa.

4. Ch. Marienburg's Great Spirit, by Marienburg's Red Cloud ex Marienburg's Desert Flame (dam of Sun Hawk), winning points under Charles Etner. Owner, Bill Shelton.

5. Ch. Marienburg's Discoteque, by Ch. Marienburg's Sun Hawk ex Ch. Marienburg's Only Too. Handled here by Bill Shelton. Disco is the sire of numerous champions as well as a Group and Specialty winner. Owners, Dean and Betty Jo Haugh.

6. Ch. Marienburg's Mary Hartman going Best of Breed at eight years of age from the Veterans Class at the Doberman Pinscher Club of America National Specialty, 1983, under judge Peggy Adamson. Owned by Mary Rodgers, Marienburg Kennels, Hamilton, Montana.

7. Ch. Marienburg's Only One, by Ch. Marienburg's Red Baron ex Ch. Sultana von Marienburg. Handled by Moe Miyagawa. "Only" was the dam of 15 American champions. Owned by Mary Rodgers, Marienburg Kennels.

8. Ch. Marienburg's Sun Hawk, C.D., by Marienburg's Sundancer ex Marienburg's Desert Flame, is here going Best of Breed under judge James Bennett. Handled throughout his show career by Moe Miyagawa for Marienburg Kennels.

Plate 39

1. Ch. Mardale Wings v. Marienburg, by Ch. Marienburg's Sun Hawk, C.D. ex Ch. Alisaton Bewitched, was bred by the Harrisons and Marienburg Kennels. Pam and Dale Anthony, owners.

2. Mardale Final Touch of Spirit, with 11 points in March 1984, is by Ch. Alisaton Touchdown v. D'Mascus ex Ch. Alisaton Bewitched. Bred by William and Kathryn Harrison and Gwen Satalino DeMilta. Owned by Kathryn Harrison, Mardale Kennels, Brandywine, Maryland.

3. Ch. Mardale Gentle Spirit, by Ch. Marienburg's Sun Hawk, C.D. ex Ch. Alisaton Bewitched. Owned by Joan Horak, bred by the Harrisons.

4. Ch. Mardale Sky Hawk v. Marienburg, by Ch. Marienburg's Sun Hawk, C.D. ex Ch. Alisaton Bewitched, owned by Patti and Jesse Eller. Handled by Bill Harrison to Best of Winners at the Pilgrim Doberman Pinscher Club Specialty in 1982.

5. Ch. Alisaton Bewitched receiving an Award of Merit at the National in Boston at age seven-and-a-half years. Owned by William and Kathryn Harrison.

6. Ch. Mardale Nite-Hawk v. Marienburg, by Ch. Marienburg's Sun Hawk, C.D. ex Ch. Alisaton Bewitched. Bred by William and Kathryn Harrison; owned by Kathryn Harrison and Marienburg Kennels. Handled by Bill Harrison.

Plate 40

1. Ch. Barchet Fiddler on The Roof winning the Working Group at the Kennel Club of Philadelphia, 1980. By Ch. Barchet's Maverick, C.D. ex Tigerhole's Song of The Raven. Fiddler was handled to his title by his owner at an early age; then, in Terry Lazzaro's charge, became a multiple Best in Show and multiple Specialty winner. He was a contestant in the Doberman Pinscher Club of America 1980 Top Twenty. The same year that he retired, 1982, he won the Veteran Dog Class at the National Specialty at seven years of age, then went on to receive a "Select" ribbon in the breed competition. Co-owned by Mrs. Alan Robson and Phil Bragg.

2. Ch. Alisaton Gallorette, by Ch. Gra-Lemor Demetrius v d Victor ex Ch. Alisaton Kinderwicke, finished with three "major" wins. She possesses a head, neck, shoulder, and front assembly that are truly exquisite. She is one of six in a litter who finished, earning her dam, Kinderwicke, the coveted Brood Bitch of the Year Award for 1979 from the Doberman Pinscher Club of America. Handled by Terry Lazzaro Hundt for owner Janet Skidmore.

3. Ch. Alisaton Damascus, C.D., owned by Peggy Esposito. Handled by Terry Lazzaro Hundt and Gwen DeMilta. By Ch. Gra-Lemor Demetrius v d Victor ex Ch. Alisaton Kinderwicke. Litter brother to Ch. Alisaton Gallorette and one of six champion littermates, "Mac" was a Doberman Pinscher Club of America Top Twenty contender during his career. He completed his title from the Bred-by-Exhibitor Class at the prestigious Connecticut—New York Specialty.

4. Ch. Pajant's Encore V. Rockelle has eyes only for his handler, Terry Lazzaro Hundt as he awaits his turn in the judging ring. Owned by Dot Roberts, "Cory" is a leading current "star" in the Doberman world.

5. Ch. Donneridge Charcoal Sketch, by Ch. Alisaton Damascus, C.D. ex Athena of Donneridge. His handler, Terry Lazzaro Hundt, comments on her fondness for this dog's head type, elegance and style, and true Doberman temperament. "Sharkey" is a devoted friend to his owner, Marion Whitlock.

6. Good Luck Fortune O'Liquorish (15 months of age), by Ch. Liquorish Rico's Lucky Chance, C.D., ROM ex Apollo's Good Luck Charm, C.D., is owned by S. and F. Trespalacros and G. Joffe, Ft. Lauderdale, Florida.

7. Winning Best in Show is Ch. Liquorish The Ron Rico (by Ch. Highbriar Osiris ex the Dolph daughter, Gayamon The Brandy Alexander), owned and bred by Grace and Jeff Joffe, Ft. Lauderdale, Florida. Handled by Betty Regina Brucker.

8. Ch. Liquorish Rico's Lucky Chance, WAC, winning a three-point "major" from the author at Brevard Kennel Club. Handled by his breeder-owner, Jeff Joffe.

Plate 41

1. El Jean's Liquorish Whiskey, bred by Jeff and Grace Joffe, taking Winners Bitch at Paducah.

2. Jeff Joffe with "Chance," seven months old at the time. Liquorish Dobermans, Ft. Lauderdale, Florida.

1 ◄

2 ◄

PLATE 33

3 ◄

4 ◄

1ST PLACE
IN CLASS

WALLKILL
KENNEL CLUB

JOE C   JAN 1983

BEST OF WINNERS
CAVALIER DOBERMAN
PINSCHER CLUB
KLEIN   MARCH 1982

1 ◄

2 ►

RESERVE
WINNERS

APRIL 1979
ASHBEY II

BEST OF
WINNERS
CARROLL
KENNEL CLUB
1982
GILBERT PHOTO

3 ◄

4 ►

PLATE 34

T OF
VARIETY
ENTON
L CLUB
80
RRY PHOTO

WINNERS
MARYLAND
KENNEL CLUB
1981
GILBERT PHOTO

5 ◄

6 ►

1▲   PLATE 35   ▼2

1

2

3

4

PLATE 36

5

6

7

8

PLATE 37

BEST OF BREED OR VARIETY
THE KENNEL CLUB OF PHILADELPHIA, INC.
KLEIN DEC 10 77

1 ▶

2 ▶

3 ▶

4 ▶

PLATE 38

5 ▶

6 ▶

BEST OF WINNERS

DOBERMAN
PINSCHER
CLUB OF AMERICA
OCTOBER 8 1983
BEST OF
BREED
JUDGE
MRS PEGGY ADAMSON
BOOTH
PHOTO

7 ▶

8 ▶

PLATE 39

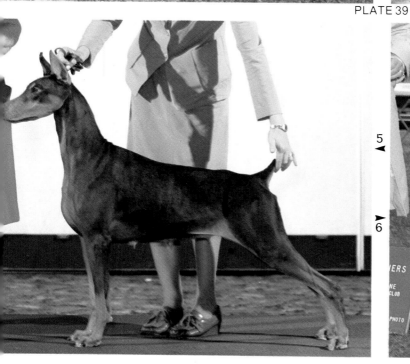

1

2

3

4

PLATE 40

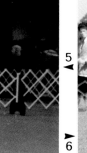

5

6

7

8

PLATE 41

1 ▶

2 ▶

PLATE 42

3 ▶

4 ▶

1

2

3

4

PLATE 43

5

6

7

8

PLATE 44

1 ▸
2 ▸

3 ▸
4 ▸

PLATE 45

5 ▸
6 ▸

1
2

3
4

PLATE 46

5
6

1

2

BITCH BLACK

MR. N. BIGGIN

BERGMAN
PHOTO

OIL CAPITAL
~RMAN PINSCHER CLUB
TULSA OKLAHOMA
MAY 16 1981
E
R P LEVI MARSMAN
BEST OF OPPOSITE SEX
PHOTO BY ESCARCEGA

3

4

BEST OF
WINNERS
HUNTINGDON VALLEY
KENNEL CLUB

PLATE 47

WINNERS BITCH
CLASSIC CITY
KENNEL CLUB SHOW
MAY 2 198
PHOTOS BY ALVERSON

5

6

BEST OF
COLUMBUS
KENNEL CLUB
DECEMBER 1980
PHOTO BY Graham

7

8

1
▶
2
▶

3
▶
4
▶

PLATE 48

5
▶

6
▶

7
▶
8
▶

3. Ch. Liquorish The Royal Salute, WAC, one of the champion sons of Am., Can., Dom., Mex., and Int. Ch. Liquorish The Ron Rico, Am., Can., and Mex. C.D., ROM. Photo courtesy of Grace and Jeff Joffe.

4. The Joffe's Liquorish Rico's Lucky Charm, WAC, with judge Frank Grover at the Tampa Specialty, 1982.

Plate 42

1. Ch. Pamelot's Garrett of Burnai, by Ch. Marienburg's Sun Hawk, C.D. ex Ch. Pamelot's Afternoon Delight, was bred by Brenda Turnley and is now owned by Moe and Mary Miyagawa. A multiple Group winner.

2. Ch. Marienburg's Mary Hartman. Photo by Alton Anderson of this famous winning Doberman bitch owned by Mary Rodgers, Marienburg Kennels, Hamilton, Montana.

3. Ch. Marienburg's Sun Hawk, C.D. at six years of age, stacked by Marjorie Brooks. Owned by Mary Rodgers.

4. Head study of Marienburg's Desert Flame, dam of Sun Hawk. Marienburg Kennels, Mary Rodgers, Hamilton, Montana.

Plate 43

1. Ch. Mardale Skyhawk v. Marienburg, by Ch. Marienburg's Sun Hawk, C.D. ex Ch. Alisaton Bewitched. Shown winning under Barbara Jarmoluk. Handled by Bill Harrison. She is one of 11 champions from two litters by Sun Hawk from Bewitched. Co-breeders, Kay Harrison and Marienburg Kennels. Owner, Jesse Eller.

2. Ch. Cyklon in April Cloud, by Ch. Marienburg's Sun Hawk, C.D. ex New Zealand Ch. Enriqueta Prima Dulce. Winner of two all-breed Bests in Show, numerous Groups and Specialties. Among the Top Ten Dobermans of 1981 and 1982. Owner-breeder, Maria Brych. Co-owner, Marienburg Kennels. Handler, Moe Miyagawa.

3. Ch. Marienburg's Mary Hartman going Best of Breed at the Doberman Pinscher Club of America National Specialty under Peggy Adamson in October 1979. By Ch. Marienburg's Sun Hawk, C.D. ex Ch. Marienburg's Only One. Owned by Marienburg Kennels, Mary Rodgers. Handled by Moe Miyagawa.

4. Ch. Marienburg's Only Too, by Marienburg's Mankato ex Ch. Marienburg's Only One. A beautiful head study of the dam of Ch. Marienburg's Discoteque. Mary Rodgers, Hamilton, Montana, owner.

5. Ch. Marienburg's Sun Hawk. A candid photo of this great dog, taken at six years of age. Marienburg Kennels, Mary Rodgers.

6. Ch. Marienburg's Angel Fire, by Ch. Marienburg's Sun Hawk ex Ch. Marienburg Apache Warbonnet. Angel is the result of Hawk's being bred to his sister; two champions having resulted in a litter of four. Winning under Dr. Carmen Battaglia; handled by Marjorie Brooks. Owned by Marienburg Kennels.

7. Ch. Sultana von Marienburg, by Ch. Steb's Gunga Din ex Farley's Princess. Mary Rodgers, owner.

8. Ch. Marienburg's Apache Firebird, by Kreck's Bourbon On-The-Rocks, C.D. ex Ch. Marienburg Apache Warbonnet. Dam of champions and beloved pet to Mary Rodgers of Marienburg Kennels. Winning points under Edgar Sellman, handled by Moe Miyagawa.

Plate 44

1. Ch. Lothlorien's High-Elven Rune, C.D.X., ROM, going Best of Opposite Sex (gaining her last point to finish) at Fox River Valley Kennel Club under judge Joseph Heine. Photo courtesy of Bunny Lanning.

2. Ch. Lothlorien's High-Elven Rune, C.D.X., ROM winning the Working Group in Nashville, March 1983. Handled by Charles A. Cooper, Jr. for owner Bunny Lanning, Lothlorien Kennels, Murray, Kentucky.

3. Ch. Lothlorien's High-Elven Rune, C.D.X., ROM, handled by Bayberry Lanning to Best of Opposite Sex en route to the title at Oak Ridge Kennel Club, 1983. Owned by Lothlorien and Cirdan Kennels; bred by Bunny Lanning, Lothlorien.

4. Bunny Lanning owns this handsome and talented Doberman, Champion Lothlorien's High-Elven Rune, C.D.X., ROM, who has won many honors in both obedience and show competition. A marvelous example of Doberman versatility, Rune slipped with ease from the show ring to Junior Showmanship to obedience to Schutzhund training for protection work and to gaining certification as a Therapy Dog. A very lovely and admirable example of the Doberman breed.

5. Doberman family portrait! Ch. Knox's Carbon Copy, C.D.X., ROM, T.D., Sch.H. III, FH and his daughter, Ch. Lothlorien's High-Elven Rune, C.D.X., ROM, in February 1984. Bunny Lanning, owner.

6. Doberman National Specialty, 1983. In second place, Stud Dog Class, is Ch. Knox's Carbon Copy, C.D.X., T.D., ROM, Sch.H. III, FH with two of his kids, Lothlorien's Dark Star, C.D. and Ch. Lothlorien's High-Elven Rune, C.D.X., ROM. Photo courtesy of Bunny Lanning.

Plate 45

1. Best of Breed at the National Specialty in 1972 at age 16 months, Ch. Lujac's Stinger investigates, and enjoys, her winnings. Owned by Lujac Dobermans, Jack and Louise Strutt, Fern Creek, Kentucky.

2. Ch. Lujac's Stinger finishing with "majors" from the Puppy Class. Owned by Lujac Dobermans, Jack and Louise Strutt.

3. Lyndobe's Show Stopper, C.D., WAC, "major"-pointed with nine points. A son of Am. and Can. Ch. Marienburg's Sun Hawk, C.D. A homebred owned by Lynne Coleman, Belleville, Michigan.

4. Ch. Sherluck's JFK V Lyndobe, C.D., ROM, co-owned by Lynne Coleman and Noreen De Palma, Belleville, Michigan. A son of Am. and Can. Ch. Marienburg's Sun Hawk, C.D.

5. Maestro's Sea Breeze, at four years of age, the dam of two litters which are currently being shown. Karen Vroom Parkhurst considers her to be the foundation bitch at Maestro, strong in Rancho Dobe breeding as a double-granddaughter of Ch. Rancho Dobe's Maestro.

6. A really neat informal snapshot of two noted Dobermans, Hawk's Wizard Witch, C.D. (red) with Augustein's Mr. Papadopolus (black). Wizard Witch is owned by William and Marcy Shatner; "Papa" by Karen Vroom Parkhurst.

Plate 46

1. Ch. Mikadobe's Paris as a puppy with his owner, Mae Downing, Marietta, Georgia.

2. Head study of Ch. Mikadobe's Paris. Mae Downing, owner.

3. Ch. Mikadobe's Serendipity, the 24th champion from this kennel, winning at Brevard in 1982 under judge Mrs. James Edward Clark. Breeder-owner, Mae Downing, Mikadobe Kennels.

4. Ch. Mikadobe's Paris on the way to his title taking Best of Winners at the Doberman Pinscher Club of America Bicentennial National Specialty in 1976. By Ch. Thorvald vom Ahrtal ex Mikadobe's Kibitzer. The sire of nine champions within his short lifetime, including Ch. Beaulane the Union Jack, Ch. Mikadobe's Valentino v Paris (now in Japan) and Ch. Moonbeam's Tango. Owned by Mae Downing.

5. Mikadobe Kennels's 24th champion, the lovely Mikadobe's Serendipity. Finished with four "majors," here taking Best of Winners at West Volusia in 1982. By Int. Ch. Mikadobe's Valentino v Paris ex Mikadobe's Lyric By Cupid. Bred and owned by Mae Downing.

6. Ch. Mikadobe's Valentino v Paris, owned by Keizo Sasada, Osaka, Japan. Taking Winners Dog at the Doberman Pinscher Club of Houston Specialty, Carlos Rojas handling.

Plate 47

1. Ch. Mi Casa's Bravo, a Top Twenty Contender. Winner of the Stud Dog Class, Doberman Pinscher Club of America, 1981. Breeder-owned and handled to his championship by Carol Luft, Tomball, Texas. Handled as a "special" by T. Owen Forbes.

2. Ch. Mi Casa's Besa Me at 20 months of age was Winners Bitch and Best of Winners at the Doberman Pinscher Club of America in 1979. A Top Twenty contender. A multi-Specialty Best in Show winner. Bred, owned, and handled by Carol Luft.

3. Ch. Mi Casa's Consuela, a multiple Best of Breed and Specialty Best in Show winner, bred and handled by Carol Luft. Owned by Connie Jo Taylor.

4. Ch. Elfred's Miss Universe II, Mi Casa's foundation bitch, was breeder-owner-handled in the show ring by Ellen Hoffman before going to Carol Luft, Mi Casa Dobermans.

5. Mikadobe's Lyric By Cupid taking Winners Bitch at the Classic City Kennel Club, May 1981. By Ch. Mikadobe's Cupid. Owned by Mae Downing, Mikadobe Kennels, Marietta, Georgia.

6. Mae Downing's two dogs who were living at home in 1962. Ch. Stormcrest Headliner, a Mikado daughter, with her young son, Yancy D. Headliner's dam was Ch. Doberman Downs Belle Blue. Mikadobe Kennels, Marietta, Georgia.

7. Ch. Mikadobe's Valentino v Paris finishing here, at Columbus Kennel Club in December 1980. Owners, Mr. Keizo Sasada of Japan and Mae Downing, U.S.A. Handled by Carlos Rojas; bred by Carlos and Kathy Rojas.

8. Ch. Mikadobe's Paris, Winners Dog at the Doberman Pinscher Club of America in 1976. Owned by Mae Downing, Mikadobe Kennels, Marietta, Georgia.

Plate 48

1. Ch. Manorie Dobe's Nutmeg, C.D., ROM, finished in a month-and-a-half of showing over three weekends. By Ch. Alisaton the Night Watchman, C.D., ROM ex Manorie Dobe's Renaissance. Bred and owned by Marjorie Brooks, Santa Rosa, California.

2. "Miss Sam Sam" (Ch. D'Mascus Sambuca v Alisaton) and "Baby Evil" (Mardale Evil Touch v Alisaton) caught by their co-owner's camera while relaxing at home. Owned by Charles Guardascione (who took the photo) and Mary Manning, Whitestone, New York.

3. Ch. D'Mascus Sambuca v Alisaton winning Best of Breed at the Pilgrim Doberman Pinscher Club in 1981. Mary Manning and Charles Guardascione, owners, March Dobermans.

4. Marel's Toast to Jack Daniels finishing his C.D. Mary Manning, owner-trainer.

5. Ch. D'Mascus Sambuca v Alisaton finishing her C.D. at Riverhead in July 1983. Mary Manning, trainer-handler and co-owner.

6. Ch. Marel's Toast to Jack Daniels completing his C.D., Mohawk Valley 1981. Mary Manning, co-owner, trainer, and handler.

7. Ch. Marel's Toast to Jack Daniels (from Mary Manning's first homebred Doberman litter) going Group four, handled by Carol Selzle, on the same day he completed his C.D. Mary Manning and Charles Guardascione, owners.

8. Ch. Mardale Dancing Spirit, by Ch. Marienburg's Sun Hawk, C.D. ex Ch. Alisaton Bewitched. Bred by William and Kathryn Harrison; owned by Esther Mae Milstead.

Champion D-Dow's Anchor v Riecke, Champion D-Dow's Anoree v Riecke, and Champion D-Dow's Erica v Riecke. Feegee completed her championship soon after becoming owned by the Dows and then proceeded to do her share for quality young Dobermans as the dam of no less than ten champions. She was royally bred, being by Champion Kilburn Cameron (Champion Alcor v Millsdod-Champion Kilburn Audacity) from Champion Brown's Belinda whose parents, Champion Emperor of Marienland and Champion Dow's Dame of Kilburn, had as their parents Champion Domossi of Marienland, Champion Westphalia's Rembha, Champion Dictator v Glenhugel, and Champion Dow's Dodie v Kienlesburg.

Brykris

Brykris Dobermans are owned by Jo Ann F. James at Miami, Florida, who named her kennel in honor of her two children, Bryan and Christine. Her interest in Dobes began in 1971 when she and her husband selected this as the breed to buy for her. Little did her husband know then what he had started—a fact of which his wife keeps reminding him today, since the number of dogs which they own has increased considerably! At the time of the original purchase, Mrs. James primarily worked her Dobes in obedience, later pointing several before finally developing the skills and ability to owner-handle successfully in the breed ring.

The Dobermans with which Brykris is breeding and showing today have resulted from a very limited breeding program of approximately five litters, these from the original Dobes which were purchased and bred. Included are Gayamon The Brave Bambino, a daughter of Champion Dolph Von Tannenwald; her son, Gayamon The Midnight Moon, C.D., W.A.C., a double grandson of Dolph; Gayamon's Chase of Brykris, a daughter of Champion Damasyn Bo-Tairic of Ardon and Champion Arjean's The Fortune Cookie; and her daugher, Brykris The Moon Shadow. Also Carosel Ambush of King Hill, C.D.X., a daughter of Champion Damasyn The Forecast, C.D., ROM and Champion Carosel In The Spotlight, C.D., ROM. Thus through her two Damasyn foundation bitches, the Tannenwald-Kay Hill male, and outside breedings to Champion Dynasty's

Moonshadow C.D., ROM (Wynterwynd and Ahrtal breeding) and Champion Silent Sentry's Marauder, W.A.C. (Marks-Tey background) they have established a true combination of the major bloodlines.

Champion Brykris Tabu (Gayamon The Midnight Moon, C.D., W.A.C. ex Carosel Ambush of King Hill, C.D.X.) is the first owner-bred and owner-handled Doberman which Jo Ann James took through to the title, this in 26 shows. She is a Best of Breed winner and Group placer at age three-and-a-half years. The second Dobe whom Jo Ann James finished is Champion Brykris Spirit To Win (Champion Dynasty's Moonshadow, C.D., ROM ex Brykris The Moon Shadow), who was the Doberman Pinscher Club of America Blue Ribbon Puppy Bitch and who won a five point "major" over 119 bitches at the Louisiana Doberman Pinscher Club Specialty, (the host club for the 1983 National Specialty). This lovely bitch is now two-and-a-half years old.

Next comes Champion Brykris The Masked Bandit, son of Champion Silent Sentry's Marauder, W.A.C. from Carosel Ambush of King Hill, C.D.X., who finished just recently as we write, before reaching two years' age and in less than thirty shows. It is hoped the next will be his brother, Brykris The Gun Runner, pointed and just starting his show career.

Jo Ann James comments, "To breed a champion is nice, and to own a champion is also nice. But to breed, own, and handle is best of all, and to do so with three within a year is a lot of points. I usually attend only the Florida shows, so my winning percentages must be pretty good. I figure about 50% of the time. Must admit I am becoming rather spoiled! Now the next challenge is to keep it in the next generation." Somehow we have confidence that Mrs. James will do exactly that!

Camino Real

It was in about 1970 that her first Doberman came into the life of Carol Chavez, who with Miguel Chavez, now owns the Camino Real Doberman Pinschers at Leavenworth, Kansas. This black male, Macho, represented Dictator, Delegate, Kuhio, and Furstenfeld (Germany) bloodlines and was the dog who

1. Am. and Can. Ch. Brandendorf's Blue Mist at Camden in 1970, owner-handled by Marilyn Meshirer, Brandendorf Dobermans, Massapequa, New York.
2. Am. and Can. Ch. Brandendorf's Periwinkle, the top-winning blue Doberman of all time and the first of Brandendorf's blue champions. By Ch. Felix v Ahrtal ex Am. and Can. Ch. Brandendorf's Sorbet, bred and owned by Marilyn Meshirer.
3. Am. and Can. Ch. Brandendorf's Bold Venture, noted black son of the blue Am. and Can. Ch. Brandendorf's Periwinkle. Marilyn Meshirer, breeder-owner.
4. Eleanor Brown with her Ch. Brown's Gigi, the dam of both Ch. Brown's A-Amanda (winner of the 1971 Doberman Pinscher Club of America Specialty), and Ch. Brown's B-Brian (winner of the 1973 and 1975 Doberman Pinscher Club of America Specialties). They are by two different sires. The triple Specialty wins for her progeny meant that the Browns retired all of the Doberman Pinscher Club of America Challenge Trophies at the Golden Anniversary Show in 1975. Photo courtesy of Peggy Adamson.
5. Ch. Brown's GiGi at 11 years of age, owned by Eleanor Brown. These photos were loaned to us by Peggy Adamson from her collection.
6. Ch. Brown's A-Amanda, owned by Eleanor Brown. Handled by Jack Brown at the Doberman Pinscher Club of America Specialty in Sacramento, 1971. Photo courtesy of Peggy Adamson.
7. Ch. Brown's Dion, son of Ch. Brown's Eric ex West Begins Dagmar (Ch. Patton's Ponder of Torn—Ch. Cochise's Black Magic). Owned by Jack and Eleanor Brown, St. Charles, Missouri. Photo courtesy of Marjorie Brooks.
8. Ch. Brown's Evangeline, 1951–1959, by Ch. Dictator v Glenhugel ex Ch. Dow's Dame of Kilburn, was bred by Eleanor Brown and owned by Peggy Adamson. She is a litter sister to Ch. Brown's Eric. Photo courtesy of Peggy Adamson.
9. Ch. Dow's Dame of Kilburn in her retirement years. Herself a Best in Show winner, she was the dam of 11 champions and granddam of at least 40 champions. Photo courtesy of Marjorie Brooks. Owners, Jack and Eleanor Brown.

4

5

6

7

8

9

134

1. Ch. Brown's Gigi of Arbel in 1966. Dam of five champions from a total of eight puppies in two litters.
2. Mrs. Rhys Carpenter owned this bitch, Ritza, which she did not crop.
3. Ch. Brown's Eric was one of the great producing champions owned by Jack and Eleanor Brown, Brown's Dobermans, St. Charles, Missouri. Eric, son of Ch. Dictator v Glenhugel ex Ch. Dow's Dame of Kilburn, carried on in the family tradition as the sire of at least 27 champions. Photo and information courtesy of Marjorie Brooks.
4. Ch. Christie's Barrier, noted Doberman dog of the 1940's. Photo courtesy of Peggy Adamson.
5. Ch. Brown's Eric finishing his title, handled by Johnny Schmitt. Owned by Jack and Eleanor Brown.
6. Ch. Westphalia's Ursula, owned by Howard Mohr.
7. Am. and Can. Ch. Brandendorf's Sorbet, black, was the dam of the first of Marilyn Meshirer's blue champion Dobes, Am. and Can. Ch. Brandendorf's Periwinkle. Owner-handled at Ox Ridge Kennel Club in 1962.
8. Charles A. T. O'Neill with his famed Ch. Ebonaire's Touchdown, one of the true "greats" in the world of Dobermans. Photo courtesy of the Stebbinses.

▲7

►8

135

led Carol Chavez into the obedience ring (becoming her first U.D.) and into the breed ring. As she comments, "He taught me a lot, and I shall always be grateful to him." Best of all, this dog turned out to be a very worthy sire.

There were three dogs in Carol's life following Macho, this first Dobe, before she finally hit the jackpot and the dream of a lifetime. The first was a German Shepherd Dog. The second, a lovely blue Dobe bitch, Sand Mark's Azul of Corry, C.D. out of the well-known Champion Sand-Mark's Joint Venture, U.D.T. (owned by Mel and Virginia Spafford of Hayward, California) whose show career ended rather abruptly when she developed a serious coat problem. The third, the red Dobe bitch, Nilee's Ramona Del Camino Real, U.D., who was a big winner as a puppy, received multiple Group wins and High in Trials on the same day at match shows, and was pointed from the 9-12 puppy class. Unfortunately she did not grow large enough to complete a show career. She did herself proud in obedience, though, obtaining all her titles through Utility Dog, with a *Dog World* award for her C.D. at eight months of age, which her owner believes to be a record for the Doberman breed.

On November 30, 1975 a very special red puppy was born out of a half-brother to half-sister breeding. Her sire was Carol Chavez's first Doberman, the black male, El Macho, U.D., W.A.C. and her dam was Sassy Beauty, a black bitch. This puppy grew up to become Champion and Obedience Trial Champion Graciela Del Camino Real, U.D.T., R.O.M., or "Chela" as she is called by friends and family, and she has earned for herself a record which will be a very hard one to beat. From the beginning, she swept the fun matches in breed and was Best Puppy in the Doberman Pinscher Club of America Show in Kansas City. She later went on to earn her C.D. and C.D.X. titles in three shows and her U.D. in five shows. Chela was always in the ribbons. Within a span of four-and-a-half years she had an outstanding record, entirely owner-handled by Carol's son, Miguel, and Carol herself. Carol handled the obedience, Miguel the breed. Chela goes down in history as the *first* and *only* Doberman to have won so many A.K.C. titles.

Chela has to her credit multiple all-breed High in Trial awards and multiple Doberman Pinscher Club of America Awards in both conformation and obedience for the years 1978, 1979, 1980 and 1981. In 1978 she won the Doberman Pinscher Club of America Award for winning the most first prizes in the American-bred Classes, and in 1979 she won DPCA Awards for High Scoring Dog in Utility and High Scoring Champion. She then received her R.O.M. Award. In 1980 she won the DPCA Awards for High Scoring Champion, Tracking, and Champion U.D.T. In 1981 the Doberman Pinscher Club of America awarded Chela, for the third time, High Scoring Champion and awards for the Greatest Number of Blue Ribbons and for her Obedience Championship.

The realization of the Chavez dream came on Easter 1980, when Chela received her Tracking Degree—making her only the eighth Doberman to attain the distinction of Champion, Utility Dog Excellent and Register of Merit. In August 1980 she went on to her own exclusive heights when she gained her Obedience Trial Championship, thus becoming the *most American Kennel Club Titled Doberman in History*. Chela was just four-and-a-half years old at the time. She is also the first Obedience Trial Champion, all-breeds, from the state of Kansas and the eleventh Dobe, nationally, to win the Obedience Trial Championship.

In the years 1980 and 1981, Chela was the only Champion in the Top Twenty Obedience events. She was also honored in the Top Ten in both the Delaney and Shuman Obedience Rating Systems for the years 1980 and 1981.

But Chela's story does not end with these accomplishments! Additionally she has proven to be a splendid producer, and in her first and, to date, only breeding, for which the sire was Champion Hotai Charlie, she presented her owners with five beautiful red puppies, four dogs and a bitch. We understand that all have matured to be of highest show quality, with one of her sons, Champion Anastacio Del Camino Real, a Group winner with multiple Group placements and numerous Bests in Breed. Another son, Alberto Del Camino Real, is pointed towards his title. Alfredo Del Camino Real will soon begin his adult show career, having a reserve to his credit when previously shown as a puppy. All of Chela's "kids" have remained with the Chavez family, excepting one male who is co-owned, and all are being owner-handled.

Camino Real wishes to be known as a kennel that produces the all-around Doberman and takes pride in the fact that although they are only just beginning, they already have earned 13 A.K.C. Obedience Title Certificates, two A.K.C. Championship Certificates, an A.K.C. Obedience Trial Championship Certificate, an A.K.C. Tracking Certificate, a *Dog World* Award, two Working Aptitude Certificates, and a Register of Merit Certificate.

Carosel

Carosel Dobermans are owned by Carol Selzle Petruzzo and located at Freehold, New Jersey. They came about as the result of Carol Selzle meeting Peggy Adamson while they both were attending obedience classes at the Suffolk Obedience Training Club, Greenlawn, New York, where Carol was training her pet Doberman. Every week she watched in awe as Peggy arrived with five or six gorgeous Dobes. Not being involved yet with dogs at this time, she had no idea who Peggy might be, but by the quality of her dogs, which was obvious even to a novice, Carol realized that she must be someone of importance. As Carol now comments, "Peggy was very patient with my novice questions and my awe."

For the next five years, an almost alter-ego relationship developed as Carol tried to learn everything she could about Dobermans. Peggy was a fantastic teacher; Carol, an eager pupil. Thus, gradually, Carol took over steadily increasing responsibility for training, whelping and raising the Damasyn Dobermans of Peggy's famed kennels.

Carol's first two Dobermans were gifts to her from Peggy Adamson. They were Damasyn Tartika, C.D.X. (litter sister to Champion Damasyn the Tartian and granddam of Champion Damasyn the Forecast, C.D., ROM) and Damasyn the Rocca Djil, U.D., who completed her U.D. before she had reached two years old. Carol's first love was obedience, and by 1964 every Doberman owned by Peggy Adamson had at least a C.D.

In 1966, as Carol became more interested in the breed ring, she suggested to Peggy that

Damasyn Bo-Tassi of Ardon (by Champion Damasyn the Boatswain ex Champion Brown's Wendy, C.D.) be bred to Champion Damasyn the Tartian, by Champion Steb's Top Skipper ex Damasyn the Strawberry Blond. Peggy agreed, and the resulting litter produced Champion Damasyn the Troycen (sire of thirteen champions), Champion Damasyn the Tadjen, and Damasyn the Tart and Sweet, a dam of champions. The latter became the foundation of Larry Clarty's Castle Land Dobermans.

Champion Damasyn the Troycen was sold at eight weeks old to Russ Meyer. Carol showed him, finishing him quickly with back to back 5-point "majors" and a Best of Breed over twelve "specials." He was shown only sparingly as a "special," with Carol still a novice handler at that time, but became a multi-Group winner and gained Group placements more than 90% of the time. The thirteen champions he has sired include Champion Alisaton Kinderwicke and Champion Damasyn the Limelight, both of them Doberman Pinscher Club of America Top Producers.

Champion Damasyn the Limelight, by Troycen ex Champion Damasyn the Legacy, was owned by Russ Meyer and Carol Selzle. Bred to Champion Gra-Lemor Demetrius v d Victor, she produced Champion Carosel In The Spotlight, C.D., ROM. Bred back to her sire, she produced Champion Carosel Musical Light, C.D.X., ROM. Bred to Champion Brown's B-Brian, she produced Champion Carosel B In a Hurry, C.D., ROM, Champion Carosel B In Step v Thortike, C.D., Champion Carosel B In Tune, Champion Carosel B In Charge, and Carosel B In A Rush, C.D.X. who died at only two years of age.

Carol considers herself very lucky to have sold Champion Carosel In the Spotlight as a young puppy to Susan King, King Hill Kennels, who at that time was a highly successful Rhodesian Ridgeback breeder. Together Carol and Susan have produced, from Spotlight, Champion Carosel Amanda of King Hill, the dam of two champions (these two sired by Champion Damasyn the Forecast, C.D., ROM) and Carosel Ambush of King Hill, C.D.X. Bred to Champion Marienburg's Sun Hawk, C.D., Spotlight became the dam, as well, of Champion Carosel In the Mood of King Hill, Champion Carosel In the

Clover of King Hill, Champion Carosel In the Chips of King Hill, W.A.C., and the nearly finished Carosel In the Clouds of King Hill (12 points as we write).

Carol Selzle Petruzzo comments, "I have always felt that the Doberman is a total dog. A dog that's beautiful to look at, has brains and thinking ability, and is strong and sound in temperament. My breeding program, although limited due to my responsibilities as a professional handler, is dedicated to producing all-around Dobermans. Towards this goal, to date, I have bred more ROM Dobermans than any other breeder."

Civetta

Civetta Dobermans are owned by Kay Martin at Brooklyn, New York. Her first Dobe was Srigo's Kase Kuchen in the mid-1960's, by Champion Felix vom Ahrtal ex Alegra von Jungsdorf, a daughter of World Champion Elfred's Spark Plug and Champion Ravensburg's Elizabeth, bred by Felicia Luburich, Srigo Kennels. Kase Kuchen finished at the age of two years, then was shown sparingly as a "special."

For her first litter, Kase Kuchen was bred to a Champion Siggeir vom Ahrtal son but unfortunately lost the entire litter. Next she was bred to Champion Elfred's His Excellency, from which litter three were successfully shown. They are Civetta's Outfox, C.D. (who, later bred to Champion Elfred's The President, in turn produced pups that bred to Champion Civetta's Black Drongo of Kami, U.D., ROM-produced champions), Civetta's Reynard (nine points, two "majors," always Best of Winners), and Civetta's Desert Fox (seven points, one "major," always Best of Winners). Outfox got her first point from Bred-by-Exhibitor at nine months of age. Kay Martin owned all three of these youngsters, but co-owners later discontinued their show careers before they could finish.

After that, Kay bred Kase Kuchen to Champion Andelane's Indigo Rock, a handsome Dobe who finished his title from the puppy class—never easy in so highly competitive a breed! Rocky was owned by Bob Bishop and handled by Jim Berger. This dog had 25 all-breed Bests in Show and was an outstanding sire as well. Kay owned Rocky's first champion daughter and his first Working

Group winner, from Kase Kuchen, who grew up to become Champion Civetta's Wolf Whistle of Kami, C.D. Following her show career, she gained a CDX and her ROM. The C.D. was earned at seven months of age, after which time she took a vacation from obedience until her conformation career had been completed. Wolf Whistle won about 35 Bests of Breed, all owner-handled in really hot competition.

From this same litter which produced Wolf Whistle also came Civetta's Lone Wolf of Kami, C.D., Civetta's Big Bad Wolf of Kami, who was owned and loved by Faye Elkin but who passed away only one point short of his title, and Civetta's Lycos of Kami—all born in the early 1970's.

Lone Wolf was used at stud only once in his lifetime. This to Civetta's Shama Thrush of Kami, and only one of the seven pups was shown. He, however, became Champion Civetta's Steel Blue of Kami, C.D.X. He was owned by Ray and Becky Sacripanti and shown by Barbara Russell.

Big Bad Wolf was bred once by Kay Martin to a blue daughter of Champion Srigo's Kimmell prior to being sold. This produced Champion Aalborg's Riel of Civetta Kami. He was owned by Joyce Howsen.

Shane was bred to a Drongo daughter and he produced Champion Motif's Sitting Bull v. Aalborg. Another Shane daughter to finish is Champion Witching Hour's Fraulein. Another son of Big Bad Wolf to be shown and pointed is the beautiful Von Stauff's Midnight Wolf, WAC, now owned by Ray Pynn. Faye Elkin bred a red champion son of Big Bad Wolf also.

When Kay Martin bred her, Wolf Whistle had three C-sections resulting in one puppy that died at eight days of age; two puppies by a vom Ahrtal dog, one that she lost and one not show quality but who earned a U.D.; and one puppy bitch by Champion Aalborg's Riel of Civetta Kami that was killed at 22 days by a Westie bitch. After so little success with three litters, Kay's heart was broken! When Bob Bishop heard about her having lost that last pup, he gave her a dog, an Indigo Rock grandson by Champion Wendorf's Dream Maker ex Champion Bishop's Mirror Image v Rock, the pick of the litter male. He is Bishop's Adora's Rocker, C.D.X., WAC,

1▲

1. Ch. Civetta's Wolf Whistle of Kami, C.D.X., ROM, owner-handled by Kay Martin, Brooklyn, New York, winning the Working Group at Westbury Kennel Club in 1973. Robert Salomon, judge.
2. Bishop's Adora's Rocker, by Ch. Wendorf's Dream Maker ex Ch. Bishop's Mirror Image v Rock, proudly carries the titles C.D.X., WAC, Sch.H. I, and TT. Owned by Kay Martin, Civetta Dobermans.

▼2

SchH.I, TT. He won the Novice class at the Doberman Pinscher Club of America Specialty in Virginia in 1979 where he also finished his C.D. He was High in Trial for his Schutzhund I, both for United Schutzhund Club of America and NASA trials. Kay bred him to Wolf Whistle. With the use of follicle stimulating hormones, she had a natural litter of five pups, surprising Kay with three colors from two black parents. The breeding was later repeated, producing two puppies by natural birth; the red male, Civetta's Great Balls of Fire, and the black bitch, Civetta's You Win Again. The latter was kept and Kay still has her, as well as the blue bitch, Tutti Frutti, from the prior breeding.

In other Civetta breedings, a littermate from the His Excellency/Kase Kuchen breeding, Civetta's Fyxen, was bred to Champion Cassio vom Ahrtal. This produced a bitch, Civetta's Obsidian, UD, WAC. Also Lisitza's Lollipop, C.D., Drongo's dam, was bred to Champion Gra-Lemor Demetrius, C.D. Kay helped the breeder, now obedience judge Vicki Riggio, place the litter. One of them won a Best in Show at fourteen months of age from the American-bred Class only three months after having been sold to Wendell and Joan Curtis.

Kay has been working her dogs in Schutzhund, feeling that they lack at this point the fine tuning needed for championship. She hopes that with the breeding of You Win Again to Carbon Copy (whose pups are winning in all aspects—show, obedience, tracking and Schutzhund) Civetta Dobes will again be in the forefront of Doberman quality. As she says, "I never wanted to produce a lot of dogs—I can't stand selling them to people who won't do right by them. I only want to produce good ones that reach their potential with a lot of love along the way."

Classic

Classic Kennels, owned by Harvey and Bettye Carter at Knoxville, Tennessee, acquired its first Doberman in 1969, which, to quote Bettye, "seems like yesterday." She vividly recalls a mahogany red puppy with almost black eyes, a Champion Singenwalds Prince Kuhio granddaughter, so quiet and well mannered while being chosen for the Carters' special puppy. It was during the three hour drive from Nashville to Knoxville that it began to dawn on the Carters that the one moment as they were choosing her was probably going to be the only quiet one in her entire life. Soon they found themselves spending 24 hours a day trying to anticipate what she might next decide to chew, taste, and investigate. In desperation the whole family enrolled in obedience school, dragging along a very reluctant and suspicious student. What fun it turned out to be! Life has never been quite the same, since, for the Carters. Two years later, their little red bitch, trained and shown by their fourteen-year-old son, Philip, was Smoky Mountain Amber, U.D. Amber was bred twice, both times to Champion Highbriar Osiris, owned by Dr. Patricia Edwards. This was strong Ahrtal and Highbriar breeding on both sides. In the first litter were three puppies, one of them a red bitch, Classic's Maxima Antares, U.D., who was bred to American and Canadian Champion Devil Tree's Black Shaft. Out of this litter, the Carters have kept two puppies: another red bitch, American and Canadian Champion Classic's Eliza Doolittle, C.D., and a black male, Classic's Damon d Shaftsohn, the latter now with eleven points.

Damon was bred to a bitch whom the Carters co-own, Champion Jaymare's Vixen of Rehbar, and this produced a red bitch, Classic's Ruby Tuesday Alcher, now being shown as we write and just short of championship. Out of Osiris and Amber's second litter, Champion Classic's Gypsy Rose was kept. She was bred to Champion Brante von Merlis, C.D.X., a Champion Tulyar vom Ahrtal son bred by Neal and Elaine Merlis and owned by Cheryl Green. This breeding produced Champion Classic's Farrah Fawcett, two other pointed youngsters, and Classic's Fancy Girl, C.D.X.

The Carters have co-owned two bitches with Cheryl Green: Champion Jaymare's Vixen of Rehbar out of Champion Edelhall Gigolo of Amulet by Champion Bishop's Circe von Rock, and Champion Lujac's Waltzing Matilda by Champion Mikadobe's Cupid from Champion Lujac's Stinger. Tilly was bred to Champion Tedell Indulto V Ri-Jan's, producing Champion Alcher's Swaps V Classic, owned by Debra Monsolino.

In 1983, the Carters finished a young black male from Mrs. Virginia Markley's kennel,

Champion Hotai REO Speedwagon Classic, a double Champion Hotai Sweet William grandson. REO was bred to Champion Classic's Farrah Fawcett and in January of 1984 produced nine puppies. And, yes, there was one red bitch, already named Classic's Voo Doo Doll, in honor of her Friday the 13th birthday.

Copyright

Copyright Kennels, the home of Champion Knox's Carbon Copy, C.D.X., T.D., ROM, SchH III, FH, AD, is at Cookeville, Tennessee and owned by William and Susan Knox.

The Knoxes had purchased their first Doberman (intended to be Susan's companion and her next obedience prospect) from the Robinsons in Atlanta. This bitch's loyalty and willingness to please introduced the Knoxes to the Doberman personality. They joined the Atlanta Doberman Pinscher Club, from whose members they received encouragement of their interest in the breed, and they followed the sensible advice they received there—to go slowly and learn—prior to starting participation in show activities.

The Knoxes were living in Carrollton, Georgia, when one day they encountered a man driving through town with a beautiful Dobe beside him on the front seat. Of course they had to meet him and inquire about his obviously excellent dog, so they followed this gentleman until they were able to pull in behind him at a parking lot. That was their introduction to Dick Hutchinson, who had just bought the dog the Knoxes had admired, Chapman's Fiero Poco Nino, as a companion to the bitch he had already owned, Hutchinson's Jo An O Warlock. Both of these Dobes were sired by International Champion Warlock's Diablo Rojo.

Soon these two would have pups, and the Knoxes wanted one of them. So when the litter arrived on February 19, 1977, a series of visits to the puppies, to check their growth and progress, began. At various stages each puppy was tested for temperament and conformation. By the eighth week the Knoxes took home two with whom to become better acquainted and from whom they would make a choice. They called them Goofus (the red one) and Rufus (the black one). The black puppy crept more closely into first place the

more the Knoxes played with and studied the two. So it was that he became Knox's Carbon Copy, named for the Grand National Walking Horse Champion.

By the time he was twelve weeks of age, Carbon Copy was ready for obedience. He and Bill Knox enrolled in the Kindergarten Puppy Training Classes offered by the Atlanta Obedience Club, this class concentrating on basic "heel" and "stay" routines, with the handler using each puppy's favorite toy as an incentive. The whole class is geared to socialization and basic training, both subjects sharing equally in importance. Two "recess periods" were part of each day's lesson; during one the pups played with each other, while during the other each pup changed handlers so that they would broaden their acquaintance with people and become accustomed to making human friends as well as canine ones. Carbon finished to graduate second in a class of twenty.

At the same time, Carbon was learning and practicing his conformation ring routine, seeming to enjoy it to the hilt! At five months of age, when for the first time he appeared before an audience, he preened and strutted, thoroughly pleased at being there.

Between age six months and just prior to reaching his second birthday, Carbon made 32 shows, at which he fared nicely and was mostly owner-handled.

When Carbon was one year old, the Knoxes met Robert Horton who introduced them to Schutzhund work, which is another way of saying tracking, obedience and protection. During the first months of training, Susan did the handling, but then Carbon started to really mature and soon was too much of a handful for Susan, so Bill took over.

Carbon earned his C.D. title at thirteen months, gained his Working Aptitude Certificate in April 1978, and garnered his first Schutzhund title during May. This one, referred to as the AD, demands that the dog trot in a show gait for twelve miles, with one rest break, and continue the test by going through a brief obedience routine upon returning. We understand that even after all that, Carbon was still "rarin' to go."

At nineteen months old, Carbon was seriously started towards his championship. During the summer of 1980, Carbon went to live,

1▲

▼2

1. Mrs. Constance Barton, known to us all as one of the American Kennel Club's most capable and respected Field Representatives, was once active in the Doberman world. Here is one of her winners, Ch. Kitchawan's Kora, C.D. Photo courtesy of Jane Forsyth.

2. Ch. Damasyn the Limelight at two years. The dam of six champions, this daughter of Ch. Damasyn the Troycen ex Damasyn the Legacy, C.D. was bred by Stephanie Meyer. Owned by Carol Selzle Petruzzo, who is handling.

142

Plate 49

1. Ch. Koven's Black Gold, by Ch. Encore's Black Rites ex Kay Hill's Letter Perfect. This bitch is a multi-Specialty and Group winner and the dam of champions. Owned by Dennis and Rosemary Fisher, Miami, Florida. Handled by Carlos Rojas.

2. Ch. Eagle's Devil "D" winning Best in Show No. 15. Owned by Dr. and Mrs. Anthony DiNardo, East Hartford, Connecticut. Handled by Carlos Rojas.

3. Ch. Barchet Fiddler On The Roof finishing at Greater Daytona in 1978, going on from the classes to take Best in Show under Thomas Gately. Carlos Rojas handling for owners Phillip and Judy Bragg, Stone Mountain, Georgia.

4. Ch. Siemhof Sabrina was the first blue bitch to take Winners Bitch at the Doberman Pinscher Club of America National Specialty, which she did in 1976 under judge Tess Henseler. Co-owned by Lain McAvoy and Carlos Rojas; handled by Mr. Rojas.

5. and 6. Ch. Barchet Fiddler On The Roof, bred by Patricia Edwards, who gave him to her friends, the Phillip Braggs, as a gift. Fiddler was shown by Phillip to gain his first few points; then, in May 1979, he was turned over to Carlos Rojas who finished him and won a Best in Show with him the same day. Carlos also won a Best in Show with Fiddler the last time he had him out; following which, leased to Mrs. Alan Robson, he was handled to an exciting career by Bobby Barlow and then by Terry Lazzaro Hundt. One of the true "greats" of the Doberman world.

Plate 50

1. Ch. Bishop's Borong v. Rock and Ch. Bishop's Dulcinea v. Rock, littermates from Ch. Andelane's Indigo Rock ex Toledobe's Generation Gap. These are the foundation sire and dam at Do Dillon's Rocado Dobermans, Barrington, Illinois.

2. Ch. Rockelle's Country Bumpkin with her handler, Jane Forsyth. Owned by Dot Roberts, New City, New York.

3. Ch. Rockelle's Butch Cassidy, WAC, by Ch. Rockelle's Sparklin' Burgandy ex Ch. Rockelle's Country Bumpkin, owned and bred by Dot Roberts. The sire of three champions out of Ch. Kocot Pajant de Scudamore, with others pointed. Butch Cassidy is a Schutzhund I dog and was among the Top Twenty for each of the three years he was being campaigned (1980, 1981, and 1982). Although used sparingly as a stud dog, Butch was a good producer and his death at only five years of age was a sad loss. As were his sire and dam, Butch was bred and owned by Dot Roberts.

4. Ch. Rockelle's Sparklin' Burgandy with owner Dot Roberts.

Plate 51

1. Ch. Red Sun's Notorious finishing his title at the Quaker City Specialty, June 1980. By Ch. Van Majer's Elijah's Red Sun ex Van Majer's Get Up and Go. Owned by John and Rita Armonia, Hopewell, New Jersey.

2. Ch. Renejade The Jazz Singer, by Ch. Bishop's Borong v. Rock ex Silent Sentry's Renaissance, C.D., was bred by Nancy Christensen. Co-owned with Do Dillon, Barrington, Illinois.

3. Ch. Bishop's Dulcinea v. Rock winning Best of Breed owner-handled by Do Dillon.

4. Ch. Bishop's Reprise v. Rocado, by Ch. Bishop's Reflection v. Rock ex Ch. Charmaron's Rockette, bred and owned by Robert Bishop and Do Dillon, Barrington, Illinois.

5. Ch. Rocado I Got You Under My Skin, by Ch. Adora's Jayhawker v. Rock ex Ch. Bishop's Dulcinea v. Rock. Bred, owned, and handled by Do Dillon.

6. Rocado My Way, by Ch. Bishop's Borong v. Rock ex Ch. Bishop's Dulcinea v. Rock, a homebred belonging to Do Dillon.

Plate 52

1. Ch. Mikadobe's Valentino v Paris, by Ch. Mikadobe's Paris ex Edinburgh Mona (by Demetrius), is owned by Keizo Sasada of Japan. Bred by Carlos and Kathy Rojas, Moonbeam Kennels, Fayetteville, North Carolina.

2. Ch. Harjo Tarahawk v. Marienburg finished in July 1978. Moonbeam Kennels, Carlos and Kathy Rojas.

3. Am. and Can. Ch. Ondega's SunDance Kid, by Ch. Domani's Royal Image ex Ch. Shady Acres Sadie, was the 1980 Doberman Pinscher Club of America Grand Prize Futurity Winner at their National competition in Dallas, Texas. The dog is pictured winning Best Puppy en route to the Grand Prize win, Eugene Haupt handling. Bred and owned by Ondega, Bruce and Kathy Lieblich, Rockleigh, New Jersey.

4. Moonraker's Satin's Hallow, by Am. and Can. Ch. Sherluck's Duke of Earl ex Moonraker's Blue Angel, pictured at four-and-a-half months. Owned by Moonraker Kennels, Morgan Hill, California.

5. Am. and Can. Ch. Ondega's SunDance Kid, by Ch. Domani's Royal Image ex Ch. Shady Acres Sadie, is a Best of Breed winner in both the United States and Canada. He is pictured here taking the breed at Carroll County Kennel Club in 1983, handled by Jeff Brucker for Bruce and Kathy Lieblich, Rockleigh, New Jersey.

6. Ch. Shady Acres Sadie, by Ch. Edelhall's Gigolo of Amulet ex Shady Acres Kim vom Thuringen, is the dam of several champions, among them Ch. Ondega's Dapper Dan, Ch. Ondega's SunDance Kid, and Ch. Domani's Private Collection, with several more pointed.

Plate 53

Ch. Pajant's Encore v Rockelle, WAC, by Ch. Rockelle's Butch Cassidy, WAC, ex Ch. Kocot Pajant de Scudamore, C.D.X., ROM, in a lovely portrait-photo with his handler Terry Lazzaro Hundt. "Cory" finished his championship at 11 months with a Best of Breed from the 9-12 month Puppy Dog Class over more than 100 Dobermans, and he was among the Top Twenty by 14 months of age. Among the Top Twenty in 1983 and 1984 (No. 2 in 1984). An all-breed Best in Show dog, his wins also include more than 10 times first in the Group plus several Specialties. Owned by Dot Roberts, New City, New York.

Plate 54

1. Ch. Pajant's Encore v Rockelle winning Best in Show at St. Hubert Kennel Club. Owned by Dot Roberts, New City, New York. Handled by Terry Lazzaro Hundt.

2. Ch. Wynterwynd's Stardust Magic, whelped September 1977, by Ch. Wynterwynd's Jesse James ex Caho Burgundy. Breeders, Wynterwynd Dobermans. Owners, Louis and Bernice Muench of Rocky Shores Dobermans, Alexander, Arkansas.

3. Rocky Shores 'Okomopila, by Ch. Wynterwynd's Spring Tornado ex Ch. Wynterwynd's Stardust Magic, whelped September 1981. Breeders-owners, Louis and Bernice Muench.

4. Ch. Rodiah's Sly-Stone Stinger, owned by Diana Stoner, Rodiah Dobermans, Conestoga, Pennsylvania.

5. Ch. Sherluck Falcon v. Marienburg taking Winners Dog at the Tucson Doberman Pinscher Club Specialty in 1981. Co-owned by Marienburg Kennels and Jane Roppolo. This is a Sun Hawk son from Ch. Morago Hills Desert Wind.

6. Ch. Ro-Jan's Crisium Coty, owned by Jane Roppolo, Ro-Jan Dobermans, Shreveport, Louisiana. Winning a Best of Breed, handled by Mike Shea.

7. Ch. Royalmead's Penny Ante making a good win. Owned by Faye Elkin, Ginanna Crouch, D.V.M., and Ann Nelson.

8. Ch. Royalmead's Jokers Wild, owned by Royalmead Dobermans, Brookshire, Texas.

Plate 55
1. In the Top Twenty Dobermans of 1983, Doberman Pinscher Club of America, the winner is Ch. Pajant's Encore v Rockelle. Handled by Terry Lazzaro Hundt for owner Dot Roberts, New City, New York.

2. Owen Forbes in an informal moment with Ch. Ro-Jan's Crisium Coty, one of the Top Ten Dobermans in 1979 and 1980. Owned by Jane Roppolo.

Plate 56
1. Ch. Pajant's Encore v Rockelle at Westminster. Owned by Dot Roberts, New City, New York. Theresa Lazzaro Hundt, handling.

2. Ch. Pajant's Encore v Rockelle, No. 2 Doberman in the country for 1983. A Doberman Pinscher Top Twenty dog, and already a successful sire with many noted bitches bred to him. Dot Roberts, owner. "Cory" is winning the Working Group at the Eastern Dog Club, 1983; Robert Forsyth judging.

3. Ch. Pajant's Encore v Rockelle, owned by Dot Roberts.

4. Ch. Kocot Pajant de Scudamore, C.D.X., ROM, by Ch. Marwood Anubis de Scudamore, C.D., ROM ex Honey-bucket's Mandy Love, the foundation bitch at Pajant Kennels. Owner-handled by Barbara Hall to her three "majors," the first from the Puppy Class. Her first litter included three champions, one of which is an all-breed multi-Group winner, No. 2 in the Doberman Pinscher Club of America Top Twenty for the second year. Richard Kocot, breeder.

5. Ch. Pajant Curtin' Call v Rockelle, by Ch. Rockelle's Butch Cassidy, WAC, ex Ch. Kocot Pajant de Scudamore, C.D.X., ROM. Bred by Barbara Hall; owned by Betty and Chester Smith and Barbara Hall. "Boy" finished in 17 shows. A multi-Best-of-Breed winner, he is one of three champions in his dam's first litter.

6. Ch. Pajant Cent'r Stage v Rockelle, WAC, by Ch. Rockelle's Butch Cassidy, WAC ex Ch. Kocot Pajant de Scudamore, C.D.X., ROM, bred by Barbara Hall and owned by Gerard Cordi. "Cowboy" finished entirely from the American-bred Class after taking his first two points from the Puppy Classes. He is one of three champions in his dam's first litter.

Plate 57
1. Pamelot's Landslide at the Chattanooga Specialty when only seven months old. Winners Dog at the Atlanta Doberman Pinscher Club Specialty, he is now on the way to his title. Sired by Ch. Cabra's Dark and Debonaire ex Ch. Pamelot's Afternoon Delight, "Slide" was bred and is handled by Pamela De Hetre, Pamelot Kennels, for owner Barbara Zahn, Marietta, Georgia.

2. Can. Ch. Pamelot's Desafinado, by Ch. Williamsburg Grand Larceny, C.D.X. from Toledobe's Never On Sunday, C.D. Owned by Marion Gutierrez and Pamela De Hetre; bred and handled by Pamela De Hetre.

3. Ch. Pamelot's Daring Dude, born April 1969, by Ch. Williamsburg Grand Larceny, C.D.X. from Toledobe's Never On Sunday, C.D. Bred, owned, and handled by Pamela De Hetre.

4. Ch. Pamelot's Scandal of Holly-Ky, owned by Pamela De Hetre.

5. Can. Ch. Pamelot's Persuasion winning four points under judge Glen Stephens. Owned by Angela De Hetre. Bred and handled by Angela's mother, Pamela De Hetre.

6. Ch. Toledobe's Unchained Melody, born November 1966, by Ch. Checkmate's Chessman ex Toledobe's Never On Sunday, C.D. Breeders, Judy Doniere and Pamela De Hetre. Owners, Patrick Doniere and Pamela De Hetre.

Plate 58
1. Ch. Royalmead's Joker's Wild taking a Best of Breed, owner-handled by Jan MacDonald, Serenade Dobermans, Houston, Texas.

2. Wynterwynd's Desiree at 13 months, taking Reserve Winners Bitch to a four-point "major" at the Dallas Specialty in 1982. Owned by Jan MacDonald.

3. Wynterwynd's Desiree, owned by Jan MacDonald.

4. Ch. Wynterwynd's Crimson Shadow, owned and handled by Debbie Keezer. Bred by Kathleen Pollock and Philip Leath. By Ch. Elexa's Final Flair of Selena ex Ch. Wynterwynd's Rusti Nail. A foundation bitch at Shartasia Kennels.

5. Ch. Wynterwynd's Crimson Shadow, age two-and-a-half years, and Wynterwynd's Indian Summer at 10 months. Both owned by Debbie Keezer, Shartasia Dobermans, Houston, Texas.

6. Wynterwynd's Indian Summer owned by Shartasia Dobermans, Debbie Keezer, Houston, Texas.

Plate 59
1. Scotsbrae's Flaming Rites, C.D., WAC, going Reserve Winners Dog under Peggy Adamson in 1980. Breeder-owner-handled by Jeanne Ratliff, Scotsbrae Kennels, Greenville, Georgia. By Ch. Triadel's High Flyer ex Am. and Can. OT Ch. Rare Ebony Wine of Scotsbrae, U.D.T., WAC, Can. U.D.

2. Ch. Scotsbrae's Fallen Angel, T.D., ROM, by Ch. Gambol-wood's Hellelujah ex Scotsbrae's Mephisto Waltz, winning Best in Show in October 1983 under judge Norton Moore. Bred, owned, and handled by Jeanne Ratliff.

1

2

3

4

PLATE 49

5

6

PLATE 50

BEST OF BREED
OR VARIETY

GOLDCOAST
KENNEL CLUB
DEC.
1983
PHOTO BY
K. BOOTH

1
2

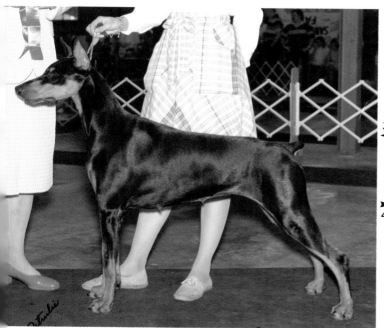

3
4

PLATE 51

5
6

NNERS
PETRULIS

1 ▶

2 ▶

BEST
OF WINNERS
DEL-OTSE-NANGO
KENNEL CLUB INC.
LEIN   JUNE 1980

3 ▶

4 ▶

BERGMAN
PHOTO

PLATE 52

5 ▶

6 ▶

PLATE 53

PLATE 54

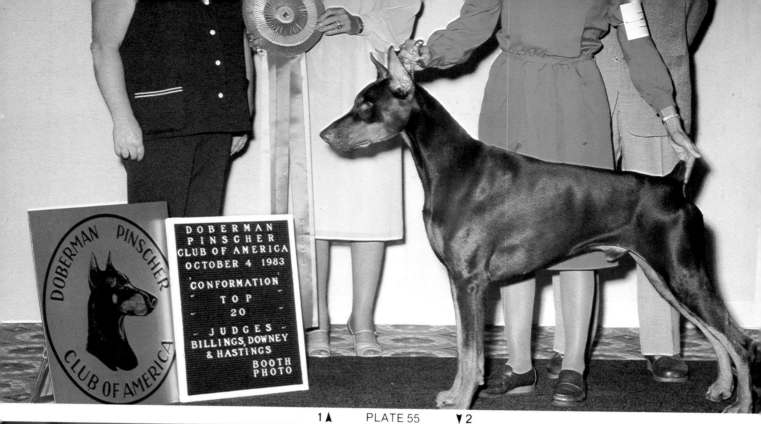

DOBERMAN PINSCHER
CLUB OF AMERICA
OCTOBER 4 1983
CONFORMATION
TOP
20
JUDGES
BILLINGS, DOWNEY
& HASTINGS
BOOTH
PHOTO

DOBERMAN PINSCHER
CLUB OF AMERICA

PLATE 56

PLATE 57

PLATE 58

B. I. S.

PHOTO BY SOSA

BEST IN SHOW

PLATE 59

BEST OF
WINNERS
BIRMINGHAM
KENNEL CLUB
NOVEMBER 1982

PHOTO BY SABRINA

1 ◄

2 ►

3 ◄

4 ►

BEST OF
WINNERS
ALAMANCE
KENNEL CLUB
OCTOBER 1979

PHOTO BY BONNIE

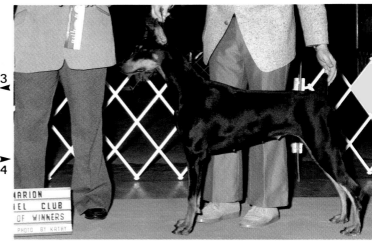

PLATE 60

JAXON
KENNEL CLUB

AUGUST 6 1978

B E S T
I N
S H O W

J U D G E
MR STANLEY WHITMORE

BOOTH
PHOTO

BEST IN SHOW

BEST OF
BREED
OR VARIETY
BOOTH PHOTO

PLATE 62

1

2

3

4

PLATE 63

5

6

1 ◄

2 ►

3 ◄

4 ►

PLATE 64

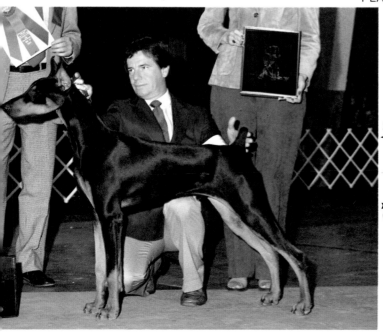

5 ◄

6 ►

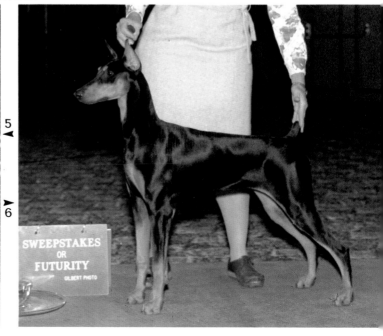

3. Scotsbrae's Silver Show, by Scotsbrae's Forty Second St., C.D.X. (black and rust) ex Scotsbrae's Kiss of Fire (red), taking Winners Dog and Best of Winners from judge Ed Bracy at age 10½ months from the Puppy Class. Bred, owned, and handled by Jeanne Ratliff, Silver Show is her first *blue* Dobe; and, interestingly, the nearest in her pedigree of this color is Ch. Felix vom Ahrtal who is five generations back.

4. Multi-pointed Scotsbrae's Kiss of Fire, by Ch. Triadel's High Flyer ex Am. and Can. OT Ch. Rare Ebony Wine of Scotsbrae, U.D.T., WAC, Can. U.D. Bred, owned, and handled by Jeanne Ratliff. Pictured taking Best of Winners under judge J. Council Parker at Alamance Kennel Club.

Plate 60

1. Pamelot's Lilly Langtree at eight months. Born April 1983, by Ch. Cabra's Dark and Debonaire ex Ch. Pamelot's Afternoon Delight. Owned by David and Ginger Snipes. Breeder-handler, Pamela De Hetre.

2. Can. Ch. Sabra Sweetheart of Sigma Chi, C.D., pictured with owner, Pamela De Hetre, in 1977—winning the largest Brood Bitch Class in Doberman Pinscher Club of America history, 21! The progeny who won the class for her are Ch. Pamelot's Velvet Veil, handled by D. Martle; Ch. Pamelot's Venice, with Charles Cooper; and Ch. Pamelot's Applause with Sherry Vert.

3. Ch. Pamelot's Anthony, WAC, at 10 months of age, bred by Pamela De Hetre. Owned while being campaigned by Maryann Caruso. Anthony now has sired four champions with other pointed get.

4. Pamelot's Loaded Pistol, by Ch. Cabra's Dark and Debonaire ex Ch. Pamelot's Afternoon Delight, owned by Larry and Brenda Proffitt and Pamela De Hetre. Handled by Larry; bred by Pamela.

5. Can. Ch. Pamelot's Hutch of Versai, by Am. and Can. Ch. Lowenbrau Magnate ex Ch. Pamelot's Applause, bred by Sherry Vert and Pamela De Hetre.

6. Am. and Can. Ch. Pamelot's Velvet Veil, C.D. finishing in July 1977 under Ed Dixon. This Canadian Best in Show winner is breeder-handled by Pamela De Hetre.

7. Ch. Pamelot's Afternoon Delight, by Am. and Can. Ch. Schauffelein's Vintage Year ex Can. Ch. Sabra Sweetheart of Sigma Chi, C.D. Born November 1976. Pictured winning the Cavalier Doberman Pinscher Club Specialty Show, March 1981. Handled by Pamela De Hetre, co-owner with Brenda Turnley.

8. Ch. Pamelot's Fantasia, born August 1978, pictured at seven months. By Alisaton Rufino ex Pamelot's Veranda. Owned by Gary Bidle and Pamela De Hetre, Loganville, Georgia.

Plate 61

1. The great winning bitch, Ch. Shinya's Better N' Popcorn, C.D., ROM. Handled here by Pamela De Hetre for Nancy Pritchard; now owned by Pamela De Hetre, Pamelot Dobermans, Loganville, Georgia.

2. One of the breed's truly great bitches. The widely admired Ch. Shinya's Better N' Popcorn, was owned during her show campaigning by Nancy Pritchard and is now owned by her handler, Pamela De Hetre. A daughter of Am. and Can. Ch. Schauffelein's Vintage Year ex Shinya's Pidgeon English. Bred by Sue Neville.

Plate 62

1. Ch. Sherluck's L. B. Jake, by Ch. Marienburg's Sun Hawk, C.D. ex Ch. Moraga Hills Desert Wind. Top Specialty Winner, Doberman Pinscher Club of America Award, 1983. Sire of 10 American champions to date. A multiple all-breed and Specialty Best in Show winner. Ranked in the Top Five, any system, for 1981 and 1982. Doberman Pinscher Club of America Top Twenty ranking for 1980, 1981, and 1982. Bred, owned, and handled by Faye Strauss, Sherluck Kennels, Kent, Washington.

2. Ch. Sherluck's Flamingo Road, by Sherluck's L. B. Jake ex Ch. Moraga Hills High Fashion, WAC. A Group winner from the classes, finishing at age one-and-a-half years. Faye and Gary Strauss, breeders-owners-handlers.

3. Ch. Wynterwynd's Sierra Shadow at two years old. By Ch. Elexa's Final Flair of Selena ex Ch. Wynterwynd's Rusti Nail. Owned by Sierra Dobes, Ann Lanier, Pacifica, California. Here winning Best of Breed at San Joaquin, November 1983. Judge, Dr. Peter Emily; handler, Gene Haupt.

4. Ch. Silent Sentry's Marauder, WAC, winning the Veterans Class at the Doberman Pinscher Club of America 1978 Specialty, judged by Mrs. Judy Doniere. Mr. and Mrs. Myron R. James, Tampa, Florida, owners.

Plate 63

1. Ch. Wynterwynd's Tax Specialist, by Ch. Wynterwynd's Wild Tempest ex Wynterwynd's Spring Breeze, is owned by Debbie Keezer of Houston, Texas; bred by Kathleen Pollock. Best Puppy in Sweepstakes at the San Antonio Doberman Specialty, owner-handled, at six months and one day old. When mature, she was handled by Teresa Nail. One of the foundation bitches at Shartasia Kennels, she completed her championship at two-and-a-half years of age, receiving both "majors" on the highly competitive Florida circuit.

2. Ch. Sherluck's Barney Miller, by Ch. Sherluck's L. B. Jake ex Moraga Hills High Fashion, WAC. A multi-Group and Specialty show winner at under two years of age. Faye Strauss is his handler, breeder, and agent. Robert and Esther Holmes, owners.

3. Ch. Sherluck's Private Benjamin, by Ch. Sherluck's L. B. Jake ex Ch. Moraga Hills High Fashion, WAC. Owned by Robert and Esther Holmes. Faye Strauss, handler, agent, and breeder. Finished her U.S.A. title at two years of age, nine of her points from the Puppy Class.

4. Ch. Sherluck's Jacqulyn Monique, by Ch. Marienburg's Sun Hawk, C.D. ex Ch. Sherluck's Moraga Hills Desert Wind, finished in the U.S. at age two years. She is pointed in Canada and is from a litter of seven American champions. Owned by Rod and Alice Meisel, Auburn, Washington.

5. A Specialty Best in Show winner, Ch. Sherluck's Anne Klein, by Ch. Sherluck's L. B. Jake ex Ch. Moraga Hills High Fashion, WAC. Bred and owned by Faye and Gary Strauss. Handled by Faye.

6. Ch. Moraga Hills High Fashion, WAC, by Ch. Encore's Black Rites ex Ch. HyLo's Joan of Arc. Owners, Faye and Gary Strauss, Sherluck Kennels, Kent, Washington. Handled by Faye. Fashion ranked in the Top Ten for 1979 and is the dam of eight American champions to date.

Plate 64

1. Ch. Van Majer's Elijah's Red Sun, for whom the Red Sun Dobermans were named, is the foundation stud owned by John and Rita Armonia, Hopewell, New Jersey.

2. Ch. Red Sun's Arabesque, owned by Gil and Lois Bohlin, Westfield, New Jersey. Full sister to Ch. Red Sun's Notorious.

3. Red Sun's Call Girl winning the Grand Prize Futurity at the 1982 Doberman Pinscher Breeders Association of Penn/Jersey and Reserve Winners Bitch in a five-point entry the same day. Owner-handled by Rita Armonia. Sired by Ch. Red Sun's Notorious.

4. Ch. Red Sun's Captain Fantastic, sired by Ch. Red Sun's Notorious and owned by the Armonias.

5. Ch. Red Sun's Captain Fantastic pictured winning Best Puppy at the Miami Specialty. Top-winning puppy on the 1981 Florida circuit, his total puppy wins included First on 21 occasions. Sired by Ch. Red Sun's Notorious. Owned by John and Rita Armonia.

6. Quaker City Futurity, 1978. Grand Sweepstakes winner, Ch. Red Sun's Amoretta, by Ch. Van Majer's Elijah's Red Sun ex Van Majer's Get Up And Go. Owned by John and Elaine Harrod. Handled by Jane Forsyth.

CAPTIONS FOR PAGES 162-163

1. Ch. Damasyn The Boatswain's beautiful daughters out of Ch. Brown's Wendy, C.D., in 1966 at one year's age. Owned by Peggy Adamson, they are Rory, Robdi, Rissi, and Raini. Rissi and Raini were never shown, but Rory became Can. Ch. Damasyn The Ardon Arori and Rondi became Ch. Damasyn The Ardon Arondi.

2. This is Peggy Adamson's favorite picture of her wonderful Ch. Dictator von Glenhugel, taken just after his West-chester Best in Show. This unforgettable Doberman, whose influence has been so tremendous on the breed, was owned by Peggy and Bob Adamson, Roslyn Heights, New York.

3. Ch. Damasyn Bo-Tai, black litter brother to Ch. Damasyn Bo-Tairic. By Ch. Damasyn The Boatswain ex Ch. Brown's Wendy, C.D. Owned by John Jeeter, of Shreve-port, Louisiana.

4. Damasyn The Saucy Bit at 10 months, owned by Mr. and Mrs. Paul Bender. Sired by Damasyn Jalli's Jaimie ex his dam, Ch. Damasyn The Jalli-Alli, C.D. Bred by Peggy Adamson. In her one litter of three, this bitch was the dam of Brazilian Ch. Damasyn Darcy, Damasyn Davni, and Damasyn Dax, sired by Bo-Tairic. The latter two of her children were never shown, nor was she.

5. The incomparably outstanding Ch. Dictator von Glenhugel.

6. One of the few pictures in existence of Damasyn The Easter Bonnet, the only bitch in Ch. Rancho Dobe's Storm's first litter and the dam of Ch. Steb's Top Skipper. Peggy Adamson, owner, pictured with Bonnet and a puppy friend.

7. Damasyn Jalli's Jing-Jing, C.D., Sch.H. I. By Damasyn Carly of Jerseystone ex Ch. Damasyn The Jalli-Alli, C.D. Breeder, Peggy Adamson; owner, Larry McKinney. Color, blue and rust. This was the first U.S.A. Doberman bitch to receive the Schutzhund title. A very beautiful blue, she was littermate of the black, Ch. Damasyn Jalli's Jaime, and the red, Ch. Damasyn Jalli's Jayna. When Larry Mc-Kinney trained her to the Schutzhund degree, Peggy was so delighted that she made a present of this bitch to him.

5▲

6◄

►7

temporarily, with Ellis and Jean Arnett in Memphis while their Dobe, Champion Alfaro's Liquorish Cutty Sark, came to live with the Knoxes. Carbon was to be shown and finished by Ellis Arnett, while their dog, known informally as "Clipper," would work with Bill Knox for a C.D.X. title. Both achieved their goals. Carbon finished his title in a blaze of glory going Winners Dog over 125 other contenders under Betty Moore at the Dallas Specialty; "Clipper" was a willing worker and returned home with the desired C.D.X.

In 1980 Carbon was shown four times as a "special." On three occasions he was Best of Opposite Sex. Under Peggy Adamson, at Birmingham, he won Best of Breed, then a Group III from Herman Fellton.

After that Carbon returned to the training field. In November 1981 he earned Schutzhund I, followed by Schutzhund II and Schutzhund III in 1982 (later repeating the latter), and his A.K.C. Tracking Dog Degree.

The Knoxes have a lovely young bitch who fits in with their plans for the future. She is by Carbon from American and Canadian Champion Kaurel Acres Savannah, C.D., SchH I, AD, the latter owned by Mike and Kellee Taylor from Oregon.

One of the special highlights of Carbon's career was his first National Specialty (and his owners' first), where he went High in Trial at the Schutzhund Trial, earning a NASA SchH II degree. At the awards banquet, Carbon was awarded the Doberman Pinscher Club of America Medallion for HIT Schutzhund.

1. A lovely head study of Ch. Damasyn Derringer, bred and owned by Peggy Adamson, Damasyn Kennels, Roslyn Heights, New York.
2. Ch. Damasyn the Flame, a red female by Dictator ex Damasyn the Flaming Sable. Breeders, Peggy Adamson and Eldon Prziborowski; Owner, E. Prziborowski, San Bruno, California.
3. Damasyn The Scarlet Scimitar, a red male by Ch. Damasyn The Solitaire, C.D.X. from Damasyn The Little Red Surrey. Owned by Ray Kramer; bred by Mrs. Bob (Peggy) Adamson. Scimitar was a full brother to the late U.S. Senator Joe McCarthy's Doberman. Photo courtesy of Peggy Adamson.

Courland

Courland Dobermans are owned by Stephanie J. Taube at Alamo, California where some very handsome Dobermans have been raised and owned.

Champion Greenlace's Heather, C.D. has been a most outstanding producing dam here, numbering among her offspring the lovely American and Canadian Champion Courland Bear Hug, born in April 1979, Champion Courland Blushing Bride, Canadian Champion Courland Blessed Event and Courland's Briquette, who is pointed. They were all sired by Bill Hitter's Champion Beaulane the Union Jack (Champion Mikado's Paris from the Champion Mikado Cupid daughter, Champion Beaulane Original Sin).

Heather brought to Courland Kennels some of the finest bloodlines in the Doberman world. Her sire, Champion Bravodob Ramses of Greenlace, was a son of American and Canadian Champion Weichardt's Rosen Cavalier, C.D. (a Champion Felix vom Ahrtal grandson), while her dam, American and Canadian Champion Sesica of Greenlace, C.D., was by Champion Kay Hill's Takeswon to Nowon from the Champion Tarra's Arin daughter, Delkamar's Na Shana Mist, C.D.

Dabney

Dabney is a fairly new Doberman kennel, owned by Linda and John Krukar, Bethlehem, Pennsylvania. The kennel was founded on the magnificent fawn dog, Champion Amulet's Luka of Sno-Glenn, C.D., who is perhaps one of the most famous modern Dobermans. In a very short time his name, due to his accomplishments and their rarity in the past for one of his coloring, has truly become a household word in the Doberman world.

Luka (meaning "light") was bred by Gail Zeravsky and Diane Downey at Cooperstown, Pennsylvania, from whom the Krukars purchased him.

The first show at which Luka competed was a Specialty, when he was just exactly eight months old. He won Best of Sweepstakes and a three-point "major" that day. As newcomers to the Fancy, the Krukars had entered him in just the one show, but excited over his success, they decided to try it a few more times. In his fifth show, at nine months old, Luka won a 5-point "major" at the

Quaker City Doberman Pinscher Club Specialty. This kind of winning is unusual for a puppy of *any* color. For a fawn Dobe, it was an unheard of event! Luka finished with a three-point "major" and Best of Opposite Sex over "specials" in less than twenty-five shows at fourteen months old, becoming the youngest fawn champion in breed history. Rather than take him home, he was "specialed" for five months, becoming the first fawn in the Top Twenty Dobermans by winning twelve Bests of Breed in those five months, at the same time defeating 600 Dobermans. He was awarded two Group seconds (in the old Working Group before it and Herding became separated) and a Group 4th. In the 1982 Doberman Pinscher Club of America Top Twenty event, Luka came in second to the winning bitch by three-tenths of a point. He was awarded the Breeders Highest score of all the Dobermans competing.

At the 1981 Doberman Pinscher Club of America Specialty, Luka was awarded the *first* Award of Merit for Superior Quality. He is the only fawn ever to have received this award. In 1983 Luka completed his C.D. title, and in the late summer he began working on his Schutzhund degree. Luka proved himself to be an excellent Schutzhund dog, with the old Doberman temperament—fearless. He loved the tracking and protection the best.

Luka was shown once or twice in 1982 and in 1983. He finished his conformation wins with fourteen times Best of Breed. At three years of age, Luka has already produced three dogs with C.D. titles, and others of his progeny are working on their Schutzhund titles. His oldest puppies are only two years of age.

Luka died very suddenly on January 18, 1984, a few weeks before his fourth birthday. The cause of death is still unknown at this time as we write, the tests having shown everything to be normal. He collapsed in his owners' arms while playing in the snow. It is a great loss to the breed, as he was showing much potential as a stud dog. Needless to say, he is sorely missed by his owners, and by them and the Fancy he will never be forgotten.

The Krukars own Luka's first champion daughter, Champion Dabney's Shadow of Luka. She was owner-handled to her title, which she completed when only sixteen

1. Ch. Damasyn the Jalli-Alli, C.D., 1962–1975, was bred and owned by Peggy Adamson, who says of her, "My red fireball, the fastest dog I've ever known running, catching, or finding anything, and her eagerness to understand my wishes is a constant source of joy. She has boundless energy, can figure out a way to unlock, get out of, jump over, or crawl under anything, and her nose would have made a wonderful tracker." She is from the only breeding of Damasyn Commander and Damasyn The Christmas Carol, U.D.

2. Damasyn The Waltzing Raven, sister of Ch. Damasyn The Waltzing Brook, C.D. and foundation of Joanna Walker's breeding. The dam of four champions, Raven was by Ch. Damasyn The Solitaire ex Damasyn The Winterwaltz, the latter by Dictator ex his granddaughter, Damasyn The Wild Wing, which Peggy leased to Judy Weiss in whelp to Dictator during the late 1940's, then later gave to Judy. Winterwaltz was the only bitch in the litter and bought by Joe Rapisarda from Judy. Meeting Peggy later, Mr. Rapisarda bred Winterwaltz to Solitaire.

3. Ch. Damasyn Liana, handled by J. Monroe Stebbins, winning under Joseph C. Quirk. By Damasyn The Commodore ex Damasyn the Classy Hassi, C.D., Liana was bred by Peggy Adamson and owned by Calvin Smith. This show in Trenton, 1964.

4. Ch. Damasyn The Tassi, C.D, a black daughter of Ch. Dictator von Glenhugel from Isolde von Gruenewald. Breeder, Mrs. Bob (Peggy) Adamson.

5. Ch. Damasyn Carly of Jerseystone, by Ch. Damasyn Derringer ex Toledobe's Misty Moonlight, owned by Peggy Adamson and Judy Doniere. This black and rust dog is the sire of 17 champions. Photo courtesy of Peggy Adamson.

6. Trinidad Ch. Damasyn the Honeybuck, owned by Frank Thompson of Trinidad, is a son of Ch. Damasyn The Boatswain and was undefeated 1969–1972. Here he is sitting with the Doberman Club's Challenge Trophy, which he retired in 1972.

7. Ch. Damasyn Derringer, by Duke of Lombardy ex Damasyn The Tcheska, 1961–1970, was bred and owned by Peggy Adamson. Red and rust, he was the sire of many champions, including Demetrius v. d. Victor, Damasyn Carly of Jerseystone, Damasyn The Boatswain, and Hollywood's Son of a Gun. J. Monroe Stebbins handling. The judge is A. Peter Knoop.

5▲

6◄

►7

167

1. Damasyn The Royal Riot at three months. Bred and owned by Peggy Adamson, Damasyn Kennels, Roslyn Heights, New York.

2. Long-time dog show enthusiasts will recall with fondness the lady presenting the trophy and the judge making the award in this picture. They are Minnie and Frank Downing, the parents of present-day popular all-breed judge Melbourne Downing, who is a second generation all-rounder. The dog receiving the trophy (The Will Judy Award for Best Imported Dog) is Damasyn Venture, a Dictator son, the first Doberman to gain championship in Cuba, taking Best in Show. This Dobe was never defeated.

3. Ch. Damasyn Tarticka, C.D., litter sister to Ch. Damasyn The Tartian. Granddam of Ch. Damasyn the Forecast. Photo courtesy of Peggy Adamson.

4. Damasyn Jalli's Jaimie at two years. This black dog had nine points when he was given antibiotics at eight months, which resulted in yellow teeth. The medicine was administered before it was realized that this might happen. He was the sire of Ch. Damasyn The Russian, and a littermate to Ch. Damasyn's Jalli's Jayna and Damasyn Jalli's Jing-Jing, Sch.H.I. Photo courtesy of Peggy Adamson.

5. Ch. Damasyn Derringer, bred and owned by Peggy Adamson, although used only occasionally at stud, produced champions and point winners from a variety of mates. Even more important, his offspring were also champion producers, such as the red Ch. Damasyn The Boatswain, and the black Ch. Gra-Lemor Demetrius and Ch. Damasyn Carly of Jerseystone. Derringer, a red, was the grandson (paternal side) and great-grandson (maternal side) of Dictator's son, Ch. Damasyn The Solitaire, C.D.X.

6. Damasyn The Christmas Carol, C.D., dam of Ch. Damasyn The Jalli-Alli, C.D., in November 1964.

7. Damasyn The Stormy Night, sired by Ch. Rancho Dobe's Storm. Owned by Selma Tucker, Manhasset, Long Island, New York.

169

1▲

2▲

3▲

4 ◀ **5** ▶

6 ▶

1. Ch. Galaxy's Corry Carina, famous winning bitch of more than 25 times Best in Show. Owned by Frank and Ellen D'Amico, Glen Cove, New York.
2. Damasyn Androcles in September 1966 with Ben Burwell at the Dog Show Dorado Beach Hotel in Puerto Rico, winning First Prize among American-bred dogs.
3. Damasyn The Rocca Djil, U.D., bred by Peggy Adamson and co-owned with Carol Selzle Petruzzo, with whom she lived.
4. Ch. Damasyn the Troycen at six years of age. By Ch. Damasyn the Tartian ex Damasyn Bo-Tassi of Ardon. Bred by Peggy Adamson, owned by Russ Meyer, and always handled by Carol Selzle Petruzzo. A multiple Group winner. The sire of 13 champions.
5. Ch. Damasyn The Boatswain, March 1962–May 1967, with his friend and handler, J. Monroe Stebbins. Bred and owned by Peggy Adamson, Boatswain was by Ch. Damasyn Derringer ex Damasyn The Li'l Red Lambchop.
6. Ch. Damasyn Liana, owned by Cal Smith of Wilmington, Delaware. By Ch. Damasyn The Boatswain ex Damasyn The Classy Hassi. Litter sister to Damasyn The Legacy and dam of Ch. Damasyn The Limelight. Handled by J. Monroe Stebbins.
7. The great Ch. Tarrado's Corry with handler Bob Forsyth. Owned by Frank and Ellen D'Amico.

▶ **7**

months old. She was the first dog ever shown by her owner and was awarded a four-point "major" in her second show at seven months. She finished with four "majors," and also took Winners Bitch at the 1982 Doberman Pinscher Club of America National Specialty in Boston, Massachusetts in 1982. Currently she is working on her Schutzhund and obedience titles.

Shadow will be the foundation bitch of Dabney Dobermans. She was Best Puppy in the Doberman Pinscher Breeders Association of New Jersey Futurity and a winner of several Sweepstakes. Luka as a puppy was the winner of two Sweepstakes and was Best Junior Puppy in the Quaker City Futurity.

Damasyn

Damasyn Dobermans were founded in the early 1940's by Peggy and Bob Adamson, Roslyn Heights, New York with the purchase of the young Dictator v Glenhugel from mid-West breeder John Cholley of Glenhugel Kennels. Dictator was a son of two German imports, Champion Blank v Domstadt and Champion Ossi v Stalhelm, and he was born in 1941. Ironically, he was second choice puppy in the litter, thus Peggy only paid $150.00 for him! Talk about a bargain—it seems almost incredible that so fabulous a dog could have been purchased for so minimal a sum.

Dictator's was truly a whirlwind show career. Short and brilliantly successful, his show debut was at Cleveland in 1944, where he took things in his stride by going from the classes to Best Dog in Show. Between Cleveland and Westminster the following February, he had accounted for 15 consecutive Bests of Breed plus five Bests in Show!

What heartbreak it must have been for Peggy Adamson when this beloved and invaluable dog died in a tragic accident in 1951 at ten years of age! During his all too short lifetime he carved an unforgettable niche in Doberman history which will continue over the generations for years to come. Dictator's influence on his breed has been second to no other dog. Doberman fanciers everywhere acknowledge and pay tribute to his greatness. This was a once in a lifetime dog of the quality and dominance that many breeds have never known. I had the pleasure of seeing him on several occasions and could never forget his excellence.

Champion Damasyn The Solitaire, C.D.X. was born in 1951, the year of Dictator's death, and quickly took over as the "heir apparent." A Dictator son, he was from a Dictator granddaughter, Champion Damasyn The Sultry Sister. Solitaire was four years old when he started his show career, doing so in style by taking the Indianapolis Specialty his first time in the ring; he gained his title with three "majors" and on each occasion went on to win the breed. It was he who became his sire's 50th champion. Solitaire sired 14 champions.

Peggy Adamson bred the beautiful bitch, Damasyn Sikhandi, who later was to die in the accident which took Dictator's life, to Champion Rancho Dobe's Storm. We understand that this bitch was Storm's first "wife," and thus produced the quality bitch, Damasyn The Easter Bonnet, who was not shown due to an eye injury. She goes down in history as the dam (leased to the Stebbins for that litter) of Champion Steb's Top Skipper.

Peggy Adamson herself is one of the most admired and outstanding ladies in all our dog show world. She is a veritable encyclopedia of knowledge of the Doberman, which she shares freely and generously. Her work for the Doberman Pinscher Club of America and the other Specialty organizations is well known, as is her willingness to assist anyone needing her to do so. She is a world respected judge and has officiated practically everywhere in the world where dog shows take place. Her schedule is so full that it is exhausting for someone with less energy to even contemplate. She has done a phenomenal job for her breed, richly deserving the title by which she is affectionately known—"Mrs. Doberman." The breed has inestimably benefitted by her interest and dedication.

Frank and Eleanor D'Amico

It was in the mid-1960's that Frank and Eleanor D'Amico, who were to become so well known in the Doberman world, purchased their first show dog, Champion Tarra's Aventina, from Nancy and Jack Simons in Pennsylvania. An "ugly duckling" as a young puppy, Aventina seemed to fairly blossom when around six months old. When Eleanor

172

1. Damasyn The Shiek at 10 months. By Ch. Dictator v Glenhugel ex Damasyn The Song. Owned by Frank Dayton, Arlington, New Jersey. This is a littermate to Sage and Sonnet.

2. Damasyn The Easter Bonnet, 1951–1953, was the only bitch in the first litter sired by Ch. Rancho Dobe's Storm, and she was the dam of Ch. Steb's Top Skipper. Bonnet's mother was Damasyn The Sikhardi, Peggy Adamson's favorite bitch who, at three years of age, was with Dictator in the tragic accident that took both their lives.

3. Damasyn The Scarlet Muff, red daughter of Ch. Damasyn The Solitaire, in 1955. Owner, Mae Schaefer, Garden City, New York.

4. Ch. Damasyn The Sonnet, C.D. and Ch. Damasyn the Sage, C.D., red son and daughter of Dictator and Damasyn The Song. Bred by Peggy Adamson. Co-owned with Agnes Johnson, who trained them to their obedience degrees and with whom they lived. Peggy handled them to their conformation titles. Sonnet's daughter, Ch. Damasyn The Pert Patrice, from Sonnet's only litter, was bred to Sage and produced the dam of Warlock.

173

1▲   ▼2

1. This lovely painting is of Ch. Damasyn The Elf, bred by
Peggy Adamson. Photo courtesy of Peggy.
2. Ch. Damasyn the Ballad, by Ch. Dictator v Glenhugel ex
Kilburn Beeline. Photo courtesy of Margaret (Marge)
Kilburn.

CAPTIONS FOR PLATES 65 TO 80

Plate 65

Ch. Tedell Key Largo winning Best in Show at Pontiac Kennel Club. By Ch. Tedell Indulto v Ri-Jan ex Tedell Connemara Castle. Bred by Ted Linck who co-owns with Mary Hawkins. A consistent Best in Show, Group, and Specialty winner and at the top of the Top Twenty for three years, including No. 1

Plate 66

1. Ch. Zeitlin's Pandora of Bolind was among the Doberman Pinscher Club of America's Top Twenty for 1978. A Group and Specialty winner, she was the dam of seven champions to date with more close to finishing. Owned by Austin B. Zeitlin, M.D. and Laura Zeitlin, Highland Park, Illinois. Handled by B. J. Orseno.

2. Ch. Zeitlin's Rogue Force v Kerri, owned by the Zeitlins. Handled by Sara Zeitlin to Best of Breed at Mahoning-Shenango Kennel Club in 1983.

3. Ch. Zenodobe's Arius, by Ch. Barricade's Adonis of Mylor ex Champion Kai Esa's Finesse, a blue and rust double grandson of Ch. Agony Acres Devotee of Zeno. Owned by Nancy Woods, Boothbay, Maine.

4. Ch. Zenodobe's Antares finishing at Boston under judge Herman Fellton. By Ch. Barricade's Adonis of Mylor ex Ch. Kai Esa Finesse. Owned and handled by Nancy Woods.

5. Ch. Zenodobe's Arius, a lovely *blue* Zeno grandson. Bred, owned, and shown by Nancy Woods.

6. Tolane's Zoe v Zenodobe, born in February 1982, a double granddaughter of Ch. Zenodobe's Arius. Owned and handled by Nancy Woods. Winning Best of Breed here under Robert S. Forsyth en route to Group Third judged by Ernest Loeb.

Plate 67

1. Ch. Wynterwynd's Crimson Shadow, by Ch. Elexa's Final Flair of Selena ex Ch. Wynterwynd's Rusti Nail. Owned by Debbie Keezer, Shartasia Doberman Pinschers, Houston, Texas.

2. Ch. Zeitlin's Panquette von Kerri is a multiple Best of Breed and Group-placing bitch. Owned and bred by Zeitlin Dobes, Highland Park, Illinois. Handled by Jim Berger. She has pointed progeny in the United States and Canadian champion to her credit.

3. Ch. Zeitlin's Panther von Kerri, owned by Dr. Austin B. and Laura Zeitlin, Highland Park, Illinois.

4. Ch. Zeitlin's Rogue Force v Kerri taking Best of Breed at Grand Rapids in May, 1982. Austin and Laura Zeitlin, owners. Handled by Jim Berger.

5. Ch. Tempesta's Rhea of Wynterwynd at 22 months. By Ch. Wynterwynd's Wild Tempest ex Wynterwynd's Tequilia Sunset. Finished her championship with three "majors," including Best of Winners at the San Antonio Doberman Specialty while under two years old. Bred by Jim and Diane Urban and Kathleen Pollock. Owned by Marilyn Johnson, Allegro Dobermans, Houston, Texas.

6. Ch. Wynterwynd's Sierra Shadow, by Ch. Elexa's Final Flair of Selena ex Ch. Wynterwynd's Rusti Nail, winning the awards for First in 9-12-Month Black Puppy (Bitch), Best 9-12-Month Puppy in Show, and Reserve Futurity Winner, 1982 Doberman Pinscher Club of America Specialty. Jane Forsyth, judging; Gene Haupt, handling. A. Lanier and D. Fouke, owners, Pacifica, California.

Plate 68

1. Ch. MiGar's Questress, by Ch. Tedell Key Largo ex Ch. MiGar's Jenne. Breeders, Gary Martin, Michael Velarde, III, and David Staddon. Owner, Ted Linck, Tedell Dobermans, Toledo, Ohio.

2. Ch. Majestyk High Sierra of Ted-L winning at Asheville in 1982. Owner, Ted Linck.

3. Ch. Tedell Vickie Bars, C.D., by Ch. Tedell Indulto v Ri-Jan ex Tedell Chateau Dresden, owned by Ted Linck and Beverly Rojems.

4. Ch. Tedell Eleventh Hour (1965–1973), by Ch. Cassio v Ahrtal ex Ch. Highbriar Valencia, owned by Ted Linck and Nancy Kibiloski.

5. Ch. Tedell Indulto v Ri-Jan (1972–1981). By Ch. Tedell Eleventh Hour ex Ch. Ri-Jan's Seneca Love Call. Bred by Janie Slayden and Kathie Priest; owned by Ted Linck.

6. "Samantha" winning the Grand Prize in Futurity, Quaker City Doberman Pinscher Club. Handled by Jeff Brucker for Jane Benfield, Westwood, New Jersey. Finished the following day, owner-handled, for a five-point "major" under judge Marilyn Meshirer.

Plate 69

1. Am., Can., and Mex. Ch. Telstar's Rachel of Bel-greg, handled by Jeff Brucker. Pictured taking Best of Breed under Stanley Saltzman at Harrisburg, 1983. Jane Benfield of Westwood, New Jersey, owner.

2. Telstar's Happy Holidays, handled by Jeff Brucker. Owned by Jane Benfield.

3. Am. and Can. Ch. Telstar's Rachel of Bel-greg winning Best in Show at the Penn/Jersey Doberman Specialty. Jeff Brucker handling for Jane Benfield.

4. Am., Can., and Mex. Ch. Telstar's Dioressence in Mexico, winning a Group Three for owner Jane Benfield.

5. Telstar's Aliage is close to finishing, here taking Best of Winners at Saratoga, 1983. Jeff Brucker handling for Jane Benfield.

6. Am., Can., and Mex. Ch. Telstar Dioressence winning Best of Breed at Greater Daytona under Mrs. Mildred Heald, January 1984. Handled by Jeff Brucker for Jane Benfield.

Plate 70

1. A lovely portrait of the noted winner Am. and Can. Ch. Star Dobe's Irish Fantasy. Owned by Don Gau, Honolulu, Hawaii.

2. Best in Show at Klamath Dog Fanciers, Inc. in 1982 awarded by Bob Wills to Am. and Can. Ch. Star Dobe's Irish Fantasy—one of two dozen or so such honors gained by this impressive bitch during her show career. Bob Hastings, handler; Don and Nora Gau, owners.

Plate 71

1. Chanda von Cort, owned by Dr. and Mrs. Joseph Day, Honolulu, Hawaii. Sired by Ch. Jager von Cort ex Triple H Kila Morgansonne. Breeders, Mary and Curtin Leser. Photo courtesy of Peggy Adamson.

2. Am. and Can. Ch. Star Dobe's Irish Fantasy out for a ride with her handler, Bob Hastings. Owned by Don Gau, Honolulu, Hawaii.

3. Early in her show career, future Am. and Can. Ch. Star Dobe's Irish Fantasy gains points towards her title here under judge Thelma von Thaden in 1979 at Sammamish Kennel Club. Bob Hastings handling for Don and Nora Gau.

4. Adding another Working Group, Am. and Can. Ch. Star Dobe's Irish Fantasy as of mid-July in 1982 had 65 Group Firsts included in her impressive show record. Roy Ayers judging. Bob Hastings handling, as usual, for owners Don and Nora Gau.

5. Derek Rayne adds Group First at Santa Barbara in 1980 to the honors brought home to Hawaii by Am. and Can. Ch. Star Dobe's Irish Fantasy. Don Hastings handling for Don and Nora Gau.

6. Again it is Best in Show for Am. and Can. Ch. Star Dobe's Irish Fantasy, Don and Nora Gau's star campaigner handled by Bob Hastings.

Plate 72

1. Ch. Toledobes Master Charge, born April 1979, by Toledobes Paisano ex Hipockets Edina v Toledobes. Owned by Judy Doniere, Toledobes, Holland, Ohio.

2. Toledobes Paisano, with nine points towards his title, is by Pamelot's Khyber of Fame (Ch. Damasyn Carly of Jerseystone ex Pamelot's Fame) from Ch. Castle Lanes Querida Miranda (Carly ex Damasyn Tart N Sweet). The sire of champions, he was bred and is owned by Patrick and Judy Doniere.

3. Pamelot's Khyber of Fame, with 12 points, was owned by Patrick and Judy Doniere, Toledobes, Holland, Ohio. By Ch. Damasyn Carly of Jerseystone ex Pamelot's Fame, the latter a Gridiron daughter.

4. Ch. Castle Lanes Querida Miranda, 1973 Grand Prize Futurity winner at the Doberman Pinscher Club of America National Specialty. Owned by K. Booher and Judy Doniere. Judy Doniere handling; Charles A. T. O'Neill, judge; Mrs. Ann Thorne, presenter of trophy. By Ch. Damasyn Carly of Jerseystone from Damasyn Tart N Sweet, this bitch is a multi-breed winner, a Group winner, and a Specialty Best in Show winner.

5. Ch. Zeitlin's v.k. Modesty Blaze, by Ch. Marienburg's Maltese Falcon ex Ch. Zeitlin's Pandora of Balind. Formerly owned and finished by Judy Doniere, now owned by M. and J. Regueiro, this bitch is now expecting a litter by Ch. Toledobes Master Charge.

6. Ch. Marienburg's Maltese Falcon, born May 1978. Bred by Mary Rodgers and Moe Miyagawa; owned by Joni Kahn, Judy Doniere, and Marienburg Kennels. By Ch. Marienburg's Sun Hawk ex Ch. Marienburg's Only One. The sire of Ch. Zeitlin's v.k. Modesty Blaze and Ch. Zeitlin's Pandette.

7. Ch. Tasso of Sylvania, C.D. owned by Dr. and Mrs. Klaus Hemsath and Judy Doniere. By Ch. Denver's Herr Rommel, C.D.X. from Ar-Lar's Misty Fire, C.D., pictured taking Best of Breed at Livonia in 1978.

8. A future winner at 12 weeks. Toledobes Jaguar v. Julmar, by Ch. Toledobes Master Charge ex Ch. Zeitlin's v.k. Modesty Blaze. Patrick and Judy Doniere, owners.

Plate 73

1. Ch. Von Shar's T & T winning a Best of Breed for owner Elaine Merlis, Valatie, New York.

2. Ch. Brante von Merlis, C.D.X., owned by Elaine Merlis.

3. Ch. Artus von Merlis (on right) and Ch. Arena von Merlis, two of the splendid Dobermans owned by Elaine Merlis.

4. Ch. Tulyar von Ahrtal, owned by Neal and Elaine Merlis, is a well-known sire and show dog. Handled by Perry Philips.

5. Ceylon von Merlis, gaining points towards her title. Owned by Elaine Merlis.

6. Can. Ch. Edinburg von Shar, owned by Elaine Merlis.

7. Am. and Can. Ch. Wen Fray's Annie Oakley, born 1981, by Ch. Brosam's Devil Mai Kare ex Solo's Pride Phi Beta Kappa, C.D.X., WAC. Handled by Jeffrey Brucker for Wendy Serra, Fort Pierce, Florida.

8. Am. and Can. Ch. Wen Fray's Annie Oakley, handled by Jeffrey Brucker for owner Wendy Serra.

Plate 74

1. Ch. Edelhall Khansort of Amulet, by Ch. Edelhall's Gigolo of Amulet ex Trademark's Zowie B, born December 1978. A. C. Martin and D. L. Downey, Kitnersville, Pennsylvania, breeders. Owned by Sidney and Marjorie Datskow, Philadelphia, Pennsylvania. Perry Phillips, handler. Finished entire title within the month of November 1980, shown six times in the Open Class. Specialed 12 times, five times Best of Breed winner, twice Best of Opposite Sex. Produced multi-breed-winning daughter and additional pointed get.

2. Am. and Can. Ch. Vondersha's Barbican Rave Revue. Owned by Sidney and Marjorie Datskow and Paul and Frances Esposito of Haverford, Pennsylvania. Handled by Perry Phillips. This lovely daughter of Am. and Can. Ch. Barbican's New Generation ex Aracrest's Hot Copy was the No. 1 Doberman Bitch in 1983. Top Ten Bitch. A Top Twenty contender, 1983–1984. Winner of an all-breed Best in Show, two Specialty Bests in Show, eight times first in the Working Group, 25 Group placements, and 50 times Best of Breed.

3. Ch. Blue Max von Hoytt, owned by Terre and Rose Naughtin, Wheaton, Illinois. Handled by Jim Dean. Photo courtesy of Phoebe Jordon Booth.

4. This lovely red bitch is Ch. Sevod's Born A Star, owned by Terre and Rose Naughtin of Wheaton, Illinois. Pictured winning the breed at the exciting "Atlanta super weekend," Columbus Kennel Club, 1980. Judged by the author, Phoebe Jordon Booth handling.

5. Ch. Devil Tree's Black Shaft, owned by Kay Smith and handled by Jeff Brucker, was an outstanding winner of the 1970's. Here he is going first in the Working Group at Sara Bay Kennel Club, January, 1977. The judge is Gerhardt Plaga.

6. Ch. Kearney's Joyeaux Noel, owned by Ellen Fetter, Lima, Ohio. Handled by her daughter, Nina Fetter Bok. Taking Best of Opposite Sex at Westminster, 1984, under Mrs. Anne Rogers Clark.

7. Ch. Dolph von Tannenwald, by Ch. Ambradobe's Choirmaster ex Ch. Kay Hill's Witch Soubretta. Selected as a young dog by Jeff Brucker for his clients, George and Sheila West of New York, Dolph started his career on the 1970 Florida circuit. Dolph was the Top Winning Doberman and Top Doberman Sire for 1971. He was bred by Charles and Kay Etner, and his total winnings stand at 28 times Best in Show (all-breeds), six Specialties, and 78 Working Groups.

176

PLATE 65

1
▶

2
▶

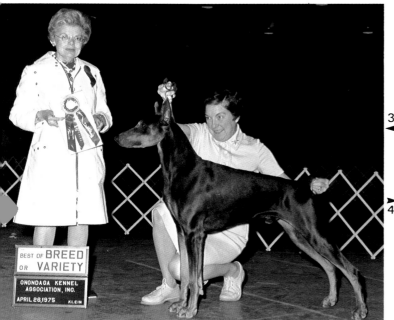

3
◀

4
▶

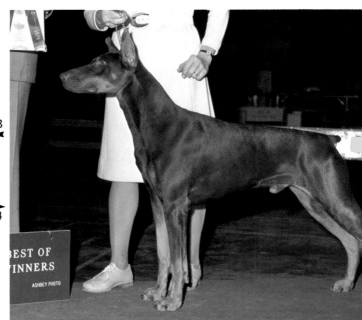

PLATE 66

5
◀

6
▶

1 ▶

2 ▶

3 ▶

4 ▶

PLATE 67

5 ▶

6 ▶

1
▶

2
▶

BEST OF BREED
OR VARIETY
NORTHEASTERN IND.
KENNEL CLUB
NOV.
1983 BOOTH PHOTO

BEST OF BREED
OR VARIETY
ASHEVILLE
KENNEL CLUB SHOW
JULY 1981
PHOTO BY ALLERTON

3
▶

4
▶

BEST OF BREED
OR VARIETY
TERRE HAUTE
KENNEL CLUB
SEPTEMBER 1978
PHOTO BY

PLATE 68

5
▶

6
▶

BEST IN
FUTURITY
QUAKER CITY
DOBERMAN PINSCHER CLUB

BEST OF
BREED OR VARIETY
HARRISBURG
KENNEL CLUB
1983
LEASH TO LENS PHOTO
BY GILBERT

BEST OF
OPPOSITE SEX
COLUMBIA
KENNEL CLUB
NOVEMBER 1981
PHOTO BY Graham

1 ►

2 ►

BEST OF
BREED
D.P.B.A. of R.J.
MAY 6, 1983
W. BUSHMAN PHOTO

FEDERACION CANOFILA MEXICANA A.C.
CIRC. INTERNACIONAL INV. 27 NOV. 83
3ª LUGAR DE
MEJOR DEL GRUPO

3 ►

4 ►

PLATE 69

BEST
OF WINNERS
SARATOGA
KENNEL CLUB INC
AUG 1983

BEST OF BREED
OR VARIETY
GREATER DAYTONA
DOG FANCIERS ASSN.
JANUARY 1984
PHOTO BY Graham

5 ►

6 ►

1 ◄

2 ◄

3 ◄

4 ◄

PLATE 71

5 ◄

6 ◄

1 ▶

2 ▶

WINNERS
BUCKS COUNTY
KENNEL CLUB
1980
ASHBEY

3 ▶

4 ▶

BEST OF
WINNERS

PLATE 72

5 ▶

6 ▶

BEST OF
WINNERS
BOOTH PHOTO

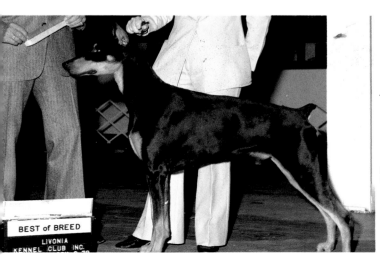

7 ▶

8 ▶

BEST of BREED
LIVONIA
KENNEL CLUB, INC.

1

2

3

4

PLATE 73

5

6

7

8

1

2

3

4

PLATE 74

5

6

7

8

PLATE 75

1 ►

2 ►

ST OF OPPOSITE SEX
PETRULIS

3 ►

4 ►

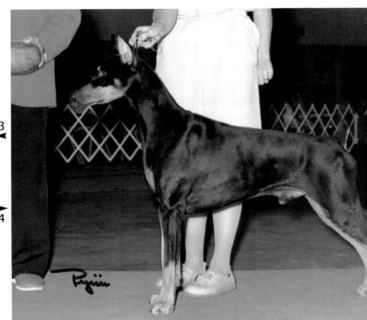

PLATE 76

5 ►

6 ►

PLATE 77

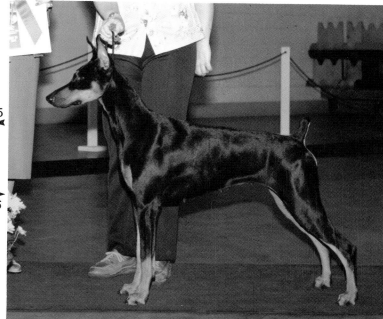

ST CHARLES KENNEL CLUB
ST CHARLES MISSOURI
JUNE 6 1983
BEST IN SHOW
JUDGE
MRS PETER GUNTERMANN
PHOTO BY
PETRULIS

BEST IN SHOW

BEST OF
BREED-VARIET

PLATE 78

BEST OF
BREED

1

2

3

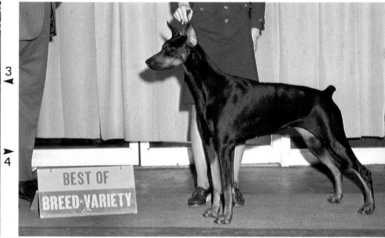

4

PLATE 79

5

6

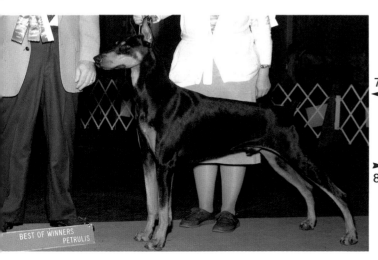

7

8

1 ◄
2 ◄

3 ◄
4 ◄

PLATE 80

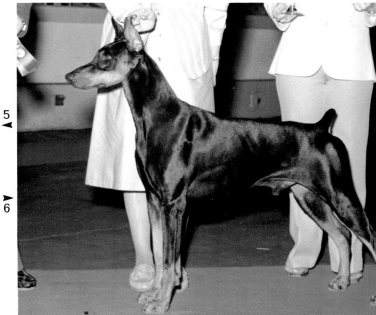

5 ◄
6 ◄

8. Ch. Deviltree's Black Shaft, important Best in Show winner of the mid-1970's, with his handler Jeff Brucker. This splendid Dobe belongs to Kay Smith.

Plate 75

1. Ch. Blue Max's Longfellow Serenade pictured with breeder-owner Rose Naughtin. Co-bred with Terre Naughton, Wheaton, Illinois. Photo courtesy of Phoebe Jordan Booth, Williamston, Michigan.

2. Ch. Kearney's Joyeaux Noel, born December 1979, finished her title in May 1981. By Ch. Briarwood's Yancy Jon ex Redlyn's Let It Be. Bred by Ruth Kearney, owned by Ellen Fetter. Pictured just after winning Best in Show at Crawford County in 1983.

3. Ch. Kearney's Joyeaux Noel is a Best in Show winner with many Working Group wins and placements. Owned by Ellen Fetter and handled for most of her career by Nina Fetter Bok.

4. Ch. Edelhall's Gigolo of Amulet was co-bred by Al Martin and owner Diane Downey. Finished by Bobby Barlow and "specialed" on a very limited basis by Jane and Bob Forsyth, Gigolo ranked among the Top Twenty Dobermans during both years in which he was campaigned. He retired just prior to his third birthday, upon winning his second Best in Show. Shown during the mid-1970's, Gigolo returned at eight years to age to win the Veterans Class at the National, going on to receive a Special Award of Merit in the Best of Breed competition. To date Gigolo has sired close to 40 champions, with an additional 20 nearing their titles. Among these are Best in Show winners and Top Twenty titlists.

Plate 76

1. Ch. Wynterwynd's Me 'N My Shadow, by Ch. Elexa's Final Flair of Selena ex Ch. Wynterwynd's Rusti Nail, is winning a four-point "major" under judge Robert S. Forsyth at the Doberman Pinscher Club of Dallas Specialty in 1983. Handled by Kathleen Pollock. Phil and Jill Leath, Albuquerque, New Mexico, owners.

2. Ch. Wynterwynd's Me 'N My Shadow, WAC, by Ch. Elexa's Final Flair of Selena ex Ch. Wynterwynd's Rusti Nail, finished at less than two years of age from the Puppy and American-bred Classes. A multi-Best-of-Breed winner and a Group winner from the classes. Now retired to maternal duties where, it is hoped, she will continue in the tradition of her great-producing dam. Bred by Kathleen Pollock and Philip Leath. Owned by Philip and Jill Leath, Shadowcrest Dobermans.

3. Ch. Wynterwynd's Stardust Dream, by Ch. Wynterwynd's Jesse James ex Caho Burgundy, finished her title in good order with wins including a five-point "major" and has now been retired to the whelping box. Bred by Donald Rooney and Kathleen Pollock; owned by Jimmy and Diane Urban, Tempesta Dobermans, Albuquerque, New Mexico.

4. Ch. Wynterwynd's Wild Tempest, by Wynterwynd's Top Candidate ex Mi Casa's Buena, finished before two years of age by winning four "majors" in six shows. A Best in Specialty show winner, a multi-Best-of-Breed winner, and a Group placement dog. Sire of six champions to date with numerous others close to finishing. Bred by Bernard and Kathleen Pollock. Owned by Jimmy and Diane Urban.

5. Ch. Wynterwynd's Rusti Nail, by Am. and Can. Ch. Amulet's Cedric v. Gluckliche ex Colombian Ch. Redlin's Always Rosy, CACIB. Finished championship with three "majors," two won from the American-bred Class, by two years of age. A Best of Breed winner. Dam of four champions by Ch. Elexa's Final Flair of Selena, with a young second litter (by this dog) now starting out. Bred by Amparo Jones and Kathleen Pollock; owned by Philip and Jill Leath. The judge is Wilfred Shute.

6. Ch. Wynterwynd's Spring Shadow, C.D., ROM, a *total* Doberman who has always been a delight to his family. "Satan" has sired one champion to date with several others close to their titles. Bred by Bernard and Kathleen Pollock. Owned by James and Judy Johnson, Houston, Texas.

Plate 77

1. Ch. Tempesta's Star of Wynterwynd, by Wynterwynd's Top Candidate ex Mi Casa's Buena, gained his title completely owner-handled at two years of age and now has won several Best of Breed awards and a Group First. Bred by Jimmy and Diane Urban. Owned by Richard and Debbie Frazee and Kathleen Pollock, Waller, Texas.

2. Ch. Wynterwynd's Spring Sunshine, by Ch. Edelhall's Gigolo of Amulet ex Ch. Wynterwynd's Irish Spring, finished championship at age 20 months with both "majors" won at Doberman Specialties. She acquired several Bests of Breed and Group placements and was the first champion offspring produced by her sire and dam. She died in April 1978, of an encephalitic virus at less than three years of age. Bred and owned by Bernard and Kathleen Pollock.

3. Ch. Wynterwynd's Irish Spring, by Ch. Tarrado's Flair ex Chance Run's Enchanted Star, C.D., finished her championship with three "majors" and several Bests of Breed from the classes. Born in 1972, Spring is the dam of three champions and granddam of five champions to date. At age 12 years, Spring is taking life easy on the sofa at Wynterwynd. Owned and bred by Bernard and Kathleen Pollock.

4. Wynterwynd's Top Candidate, by Ch. Tarrado's Flair ex Wynterwynd's Shannon, who had 16 points including a five-point "major" win at the Penn/Jersey Dobe Specialty. He died in 1981 one "major" short of his title. Sire of four champions and grandsire of six to date. Bred and owned by Bernard and Kathleen Pollock; co-owned by Nancy Pritchard.

5. Ch. Wynterwynd's Jesse James, by Ch. Tarrado's Flair ex Chance Run's Enchanted Star, C.D., is one of six champions produced by his parents. He was a Best of Breed and Group winner and has several champion daughters. Born in 1971, Jesse, at age 11, is still very much a part of the Wynterwynd family. Owned and bred by Bernard and Kathleen Pollock.

6. Ch. Wynterwynd's Summer Breeze, by Ch. Mattappanny the Fenian v. Drago ex Wynterwynd's Spring Breeze, was Grand Sweepstakes Winner at three Doberman Specialties and is a Best of Breed winner. Owned and bred by Bernard and Kathleen Pollock.

Plate 78

1. Ch. Cabra's Dark and Debonaire, WAC, a multi-Best-in-Show winner who completed his title in nine shows and won back-to-back "majors" from the Puppy Class. 1983's No. 2 Doberman and No. 10 Working Dog, January *Canine Chronicle* and winter issue of *Doberman Quarterly*. Owned by Nina McGrath, Nashville, Tennessee. Handled by Captain M. E. Smith, United States Navy, retired, Billmar's Dobermans, Cleveland, Tennessee.

2. Ch. Capital Dobe's Short Seller, C.D., still going strong at 12 years. By Ch. Brown's B-Brian ex Toria's Capital Gain, C.D.X. (Bismarck daughter). Winners Dog at the Doberman Pinscher Club of America National Specialty in 1973. Two years on the Top Twenty Dobes. Photo courtesy of Marjorie Brooks, Santa Rosa, California.

3. Ch. Warwick's Zanuck of Chalmar in motion. Carlos Rojas, handler of this noted Best in Show winner belonging to May Jacobson and Mary Jo Lewis.

4. Ch. Damasyn The Rough and Ready, by Ch. Damasyn Carly of Jerseystone ex Damasyn The Tart 'n' Sweet (litter sister to Troycen), was bred by Peggy Adamson and is owned by Dennis Clarely, St. Joseph, Missouri.

5. The consistent and famed-winning bitch, Ch. Bishop's Cassiopeia V. Rock, with her handler Jim Berger. Winning Best of Breed at Grand Rapids Kennel Club, 1977, under the author. "Cassie" chalked up an impressive record during her show career for owners Jean and Fred Meyer of Indianapolis, Indiana.

6. Ch. Nitro's Road Runner at nine years of age winning the Veterans Class at the Doberman Pinscher Club of Detroit. An all-breed Best in Show winner owned by Chuck and Judy Limbaugh, West Chicago, Illinois. Handled by Phoebe Jordan Booth.

Plate 79

1. Am. and Can. Ch. Kendobe's Zu Erica Mit Lieb. Owned by Jean Kennedy, this lovely bitch continues the winning ways of her sire, Ch. Devil Tree's Black Shaft. Handled by Jeff Brucker.

2. ElJean's Ashtar of Hotai, by Ch. Hotai Charlie from Ch. ElJean's Freya Adonica, close to championship. Proudly owned by Janet and Jim Wade and Jim and Helen Sawyers, Madison, Alabama.

3. Ch. Checkmate's Nitro, owned by Chuck and Judy Limbaugh. Handled by Stanley Flowers.

4. Ch. Nitro's Road Runner, all-breed Best in Show winner, owned by Chuck and Judy Limbaugh, West Chicago, Illinois. Handled by Phoebe Jordan Booth.

5. Ch. Van Majer's Elijah's Red Sun, owned by John and Rita Armonia, winning the breed. Handled by Jane Kamp Forsyth.

6. Darkover First Flight, sired by Ch. Edelhall Khansort of Amulet. Owned by Norman and Carol Carter, Caravista Doberman Pinschers, Hamlin, New York. "Cara" began her show career by winning a four-point "major" from the 6-9 month Puppy Class at just eight months of age. Her second "major" came at 10 months. She also has a Best of Breed over top-winning "specials" and is well on her way to the title.

7. ElJean's Ashtar of Hotai, adding to his points and now close to the title. Pamela De Hetre handling for owners Janet and Jim Wade and Jim and Helen Sawyers, Madison, Alabama.

8. Ch. Sevod's Born A Star, Group and Specialty winner. Owned by Terre and Rose Naughtin, Wheaton, Illinois. Handled by Phoebe Jordan Booth.

Plate 80

1. Wynterwynd's Centerfold, by Ch. Wynterwynd's Wild Tempest ex Ch. Kyjur's Respond Sil Vous Plait, one of four in a litter who are close to finishing. She is pointed from the Puppy Class and is a Best of Breed and Group placement winner. Bred by Kathleen Pollock and Tama Talkington. Owned by Dr. Richard and Debbie Frazee of Rochester, Minnesota and Kathleen Pollock.

2. Wynterwynd's April Breeze, by Ch. Ondega's Dapper Dan ex Wynterwynd's Spring Breeze, not yet two years old but very close to championship. Her sire was the winner of the 1983 Doberman Pinscher Club of America Stud Dog Class. Her dam has, to date, produced three champion daughters. Her handler is Cindi Huckfeldt. Bred and owned by Bernard and Kathleen Pollock, Wynterwynd Kennels, Waller, Texas.

3. Ch. Wynterwynd's Sun-Sation, by Am. and Can. Ch. Amulet's Cedric v. Gluckliche ex Colombian Ch. Redlin's Always Rosy, CACIB. From an all-red litter which produced three American champions and a Panamanian champion bitch. Following her successful show career, "Cherrie" was retired to the whelping box to follow in the footsteps of her great producing dam. Bred by Amparo Jones and Kathleen Pollock. Owned by Tina Marshall, Mariah Dobermans, Georgetown, Texas.

4. Ch. Wynterwynd's Rusti Shadow, by Ch. Elexa's Final Flair of Selena ex Ch. Wynterwynd's Rusti Nail, is the 22nd American champion produced by Wynterwynd; the 12th champion for her sire; and the 4th champion for her dam. This red bitch completed her championship completely owner-handled from the Bred-by-Exhibitor Class and is now retired to the whelping box. Bred by Kathleen Pollock and Philip Leath. Owned by Bernard and Kathleen Pollock.

5. Wynterwynd's Moonshadow, by Ch. Elexa's Final Flair of Selena ex Ch. Wynterwynd's Rusti Nail, is another winner from the litter which produced Ch. Wynterwynd's Sierra Shadow, Ch. Wynterwynd's Me 'N My Shadow, WAC, Ch. Wynterwynd's Crimson Shadow, and Ch. Wynterwynd's Rusti Shadow. Moonshadow is major-pointed. Bred by Kathleen Pollock and Philip Leath. Owned by Marilyn Johnson, Allegro Dobermans, Houston, Texas.

6. Ch. Wynterwynd's Wild Streak, C.D., ROM, by Wynterwynd's Top Candidate ex Mi Casa's Buena, is one of three champions produced from this combination. A well-known Specialty and Best of Breed winner himself, he is the sire of promising and pointed progeny. Bred by Bernard and Kathleen Pollock. Owned by Dick and Pat Westbrook, Wildfire Dobermans, Bourne, Texas.

and Frank saw her, shown for the first time at a Quaker City Specialty, it was definitely love at first sight they felt for this very pretty, showy bitch. They purchased her, showed her several times as a puppy, then decided she was destined for greater things so held her back awhile for the opportunity to mature. At a year old she was ready, completed her championship with five three-point "majors" and two Bests of Breed, plus one Reserve Winners, all within 27 days. Needless to say the D'Amicos were elated! Aventina made a superb show record, handled by the Forsyths, bringing some exciting honors home to her owners. Their first show Dobe was very definitely a success!

Aventina was from what became the "A" litter from her breeders, the Simons. They added "do" to the name Tarra, a name they had been using with which to identify their first litter, and so from then on their dogs were identified as "Tarrado." Aventina had been born in April 1964, sired by Champion Ainwick's Black Fury Bismarck ex Champion Highbriar Jasmine, the latter the Simons' foundation bitch. This litter of Jasmine's all became champions, making her the top Producing Doberman Dam for 1968.

For her third litter, Jasmine was bred to one of Ellie and Frank D'Amico's all-time favorite Dobes, Champion Felix vom Ahrtal, a most gorgeous blue dog. The D'Amicos were not really looking to take on another dog, as Aventina had been joined by Ellie's mother's Dobe male, Champion Ebonaire's TricTrac, along with various assorted other "beasties." However, they did go to see the puppies, and the rest is history! The D'Amicos thought Corry something really special—and they were surely right! He joined their family, of course, and made his show debut the day he reached six months old at Back Mountain Kennel Club under judge Peter Knoop. Peter was literally unable to take his eyes off Corry, who handily won the puppy class and Reserve Winners Dog. At his next show, in Baltimore under a German judge, Corry won a class of twelve.

The D'Amicos followed the course that had worked out so well with Aventina, holding Corry back until he was sufficiently mature. Then he came out in Open Class, gaining his first fourteen points quite handily. That final point posed a bit of a problem but was finally gained. When Corry had attained close to 30 Bests of Breed, but made little impression on the Group judges, the D'Amicos decided to retire him. They had purchased him as they felt he would make an outstanding sire, and he surely did not disappoint them! Among his progeny were two daughters who wound up among the top winning Working dogs of all time, Champion Galaxy's Corry Missile Belle, who was No. 1, and her littermate, Champion Galaxy's Corry Carina, No. 8. Corry was the sire of the first Isabella (fawn) Doberman champion, Aventina's Gabriella, and many other famous Dobes including numerous Best in Show winners, Top Twenty winners, and many others—especially outstanding when one considers that Corry's stud career was hampered by a broken blood vessel at two-and-a-half years of age.

Champion Aventina's Tamika, by Corry from Aventina, was another Best in Show winner owned by the D'Amicos, as was Champion Galaxy's Corry Carina with her impressive record of more than twenty-five times Best in Show.

DiNardos-Eagle's

Dr. and Mrs. Anthony DiNardo of East Hartford, Connecticut and their four delightful children have become familiar figures in the Doberman ring. They are owners of two of the breed's most famed and important winners, Champion Marienburg's Lone Eagle and Lone Eagle's fabulous homebred son, Champion Eagle's Devil "D."

Champion Marienburg's Lone Eagle started out for the DiNardos under Jane Forsyth's handling towards the end of the 1970's. So successful was he that he became No. 2 Doberman in America in 1978, was a Doberman Pinscher Club of America Top Twenty winner in 1979, and the Nation's No. 1 Doberman for 1980.

Eagle is a multiple Best in Show winner and a multiple Group winner, as well as 151 times Best of Breed.

Best of all, however, is Eagle's excellence as a sire. Most famous of his progeny to date is the DiNardo's young homebred son by him, Champion Eagle's Devil "D." As a puppy, Devil's success was instantaneous. From the moment he set paw in a ring he was a winner, and his points came fast and easily under Jane

1▲ ▼2

1. The red Dobermans, Ch. Brown's Evangeline, C.D. and Ch. Damasyn The Solitaire, C.D.X., the 49th and 59th champions sired by Ch. Dictator v Glenhugel. Owned and handled to their titles by Mrs. Bob (Peggy) Adamson. Evangeline was bred by Eleanor Brown and was out of Ch. Dow's Dame of Kilburn. Solitaire was bred by Peggy Adamson and out of Ch. Damasyn The Sultry Sister.

2. Ch. Damasyn The Sonnet, C.D., red daughter of Ch. Dictator von Glenhugel and Damasyn The Sond, owned by Peggy Adamson and Agnes Johnson Eathorne. Breeder Peggy Adamson handled her to her championship, at 19 months. Mr. Fleitmann, under whom she completed her title, stated, "She is truly a great one, a 'V' bitch of the highest quality." Bred only once, she produced two champions, one of which was Am., Can., and Cuban Ch. Damasyn The Pert Patrice, C.D.X., the granddam of Warlock.

3. Ch. Tarra's Aventina, the famous red bitch and winner of 78 Bests of Breed, at Ramapo Kennel Club in 1966. Owned by Frank and Ellen D'Amico, Glen Cove, New York.

4. Ch. Tara's Aventina, the Frank D'Amicos' stunning bitch, handled by Jane Kamp Forsyth to a win under Sadie Edminston.

▲3

►4

197

Forsyth's handling. When Devil finished, his owners kept him at home awhile to mature, during which time the Forsyths retired from handling. Faced with the choice of a new handler, Tony selected Carlos Rojas, who appreciated the dog's quality and what he could do with him, so off they went on what has become one of the breed's outstanding show careers. By early 1984, Devil had won a total of 18 times Best in Show and 86 times first in the Working Group, along with 180 + Bests in Breed including 10 Specialties. These figures will have grown considerably, it seems certain, by the time you are reading this, as Carlos and Devil have been making shows on a steady basis and winning at them.

In 1982, his first year out as a mature dog, Devil was No. 1 Doberman (as his sire had been two years earlier). He was also No. 10 among all Working dogs.

In 1983 he was again No. 1 Doberman, this time No. 2 Working Dog and on the Top Twenty list for all breeds.

He started out 1984 as No. 1 Doberman and a leading Group and Best in Show winner. It seems most likely that he will wind up the year this same way with still added honors!

What a thrill it must be for the DiNardos, who have a small hobby kennel in their home where the dogs are enjoyed by themselves and their children, to have bred a dog who has achieved such heights! It is the sort of success story one often has heard never happens—that one must have a huge kennel and breed on a large scale if things like this are to be accomplished. More and more this mistaken theory is being disproved, and people are finding that the small breeder and the dog who enjoys family life have just as good a chance of being successful if knowledge is there, if one works with quality stock, and if one pursues an intelligent program.

The Dobermans are very much a family project with the DiNardos. Mrs. DiNardo (Sheila) is every bit as enthusiastic as Tony over them and loves dogs dearly. As for the kids, all four are successful both in Junior Showmanship and handling—with the dogs in conformation competition as well—and have been right from the beginning. All have wins to their credit, and we feel quite certain that all will remain Doberman fans right on through the years.

Dobergal

Dobergal Dobermans are owned by Jane W. Gallagher of Scarborough, New York, who bought her first of the breed, a Halfritz bitch, in 1956 when their first child was born, since she and her husband felt that "every boy needs a dog." In 1968, twelve years later, this bitch was replaced with Highquest Bramble, a daughter of Lochinvar v. Ahrtal ex Carlatta v.d. Elbe, this one from Cora Capra. The Gallaghers made her a champion, then bred her to Champion Elfred's The President, by whom she produced three champions: Dobergal's Man of Destiny, Dobergal's Man In A Million, and American, Canadian, and Bermudian Champion Dobergal's Man Of The Year, C.D., keeping the latter for their own kennel.

After that, a bitch from the above litter, Dobergal's Maid of the Bramble, was bred to Elfred's Thunder (a double Champion Jo's Brandy Alexander grandson) from which American and Bermudian Champion Dobergal's Princess Royal, C.D. was kept. Princess Royal produced three champions by three different sires—Champion Elfred's Stardust of Dobergal when bred to Elfred's The Victor, Champion Dobergal's Something Special when bred to Champion Dobergal's Man Of The Year, and Champion Dobergal's War Whoop when bred to Champion Cardel's Renegade.

The Gallaghers bred Champion Dobergal's War Whoop to Champion Elfred's Zarras, who is a Princess Royal grandson sired by Champion Eagle's Devil "D." They also have a young bitch out of Champion Marienburg's Lone Eagle and Dobergal's Thunder N Lightnin' (by Champion Man of The Year, C.D. ex Champion Princess Royal, C.D.) waiting in the wings.

The Gallaghers' small breeding program is based on vom Ahrtal, Elfred and Marienburg. They are carefully linebreeding to maintain substance and elegance.

Doberlyn

Doberlyn Kennels are owned by Robert N. and Bonnie S. Clarke at Ellington, Connecticut. It is a kennel operated on a limited breeding program, which makes its accomplishments all the more significant. The Clarkes' policy is to breed a litter only every

1. Ch. Doberlyn's Gold Coast, a Specialty Best in Show winner, by Ch. Alisaton Citation ex Ch. RMJ's April Love. Breeders, Doberlyn Kennels, Robert and Bonnie Clarke, co-owners with Donna Bowser.
2. Ch. Rosevale's Dark Temptation, Am. and Can. C.D., an all-breed and Specialty Best in Show winner who completed his championship at Westminster at one-and-a-half years of age. With his Best in Show son, Tar was half of the only brace of male Dobermans ever shown; as a brace, they won multiple top awards. Owned by Doberlyn, Robert Linnell and Bonnie Linnell (now Clarke).

1▲ ▼2

B.O.B.
photo by Gilbert

1. Ch. Arco Dob Mann at eight months winning the Grand National Futurity, Doberman Pinscher Club of America, judged by Jane Kamp Forsyth. This stunning youngster, owned by Leonard and Susan Johnson and handled by Teresa Nail Reams, was a Best in Show winner before reaching one year's age. Winner of Top Twenty, 1983.

2. Teresa Nail, age 11 years, receiving an award for High Scoring Dog in the Obedience Trial at the 1968 National Specialty, which was earned by Ch. Azteca's Bellona, U.D. with a score of 199½. Bellona gained her first C.D.X. leg that day and finished the degree in three consecutive days with two Firsts and two High Scoring Dog Awards. Awarded a medallion as top C.D. Doberman in the nation by the Doberman Pinscher Club of America. Mrs. Edd Bivin, Teresa's mother, owner.

year or so, which is not conducive to producing large numbers of champions. Nonetheless, Doberlyn has owned three Best in Show Dobermans and a Best in Show Whippet. Currently four generations of Dobes are now in residence, ranging from twelve years down to three months of age.

Champion Rosevale's Dark Temptation, American and Canadian C.D., was born on June 21, 1969 and lived to become eleven years old. He was an all-breed and Specialty Best in Show dog who finished at Westminster at the age of a year-and-a-half. Even though he was third in seniority behind Jane Forsyth's Boxer and Great Dane, he and Jane, who was his handler, piled up an enviable breed and Group winning record together during the short period in which he was shown as a "special."

Probably to his owners, "Tar's" most memorable win was going Best in Show in the Quaker City Doberman Pinscher Club Specialty in 1975 from the Veterans Class owner-handled over 321 dogs including 21 "specials."

Tar, with his son, American and Canadian Champion Doberlyn's Kaiser v Kroysing, C.D., also a Best in Show winner, constituted a very famous Doberman brace which made history by being the only brace of male Dobermans ever shown. Handled by Bonnie Clarke, they were winners of all-breed Best Brace in Show awards and numerous Best Brace in Working Group Awards.

As an American Kennel Club licensed judge, and a Doberman Pinscher Club of America certified temperament tester, Bonnie feels a tremendous responsibility to breed, own and exhibit only the finest. As she says, "I was fortunate to start with the best, my Dark Temptation dog, and I will never be satisfied with anything less."

Dob Mann

The Dob Mann Dobermans are owned by Mr. and Mrs. Edd (Irene) Bivin and are located at Fort Worth, Texas where they are producing some very handsome dogs of exceptional merit, among them the sensational Champion Arco Dob Mann who was Best of Breed at the 1984 Westminster Show. Arco has created quite a stir in the Doberman world for his quality, type and soundness. He is beautifully presented in the ring by Irene's

daughter, Teresa Nail, and is owned by Len and Susan Johnson of Arlington, Texas.

Irene Bivin's interest in Dobermans reaches back over a number of years. Her widely admired "old dog," Champion Tolivar's Aristotle of Azteca, is still to be found behind the young stock there, as she was fortunate, following her years as an American Kennel Club Field Representative and her return to breeding Dobermans, to find a good nucleus of "Ari children" with which to work.

One of Irene's dogs whom I have especially admired is the handsome multi-Best in Show winner, Champion Tolivar's Boo Radley. Bred by Ann Platt, owner of Tolivar Dobermans, "Boo," in limited showing, amassed what Irene estimates to be about one hundred Best of Breed awards. Although used at stud on a very limited basis (A.K.C. did not approve of Irene's promoting a stud dog in any way), "Boo" sired twelve champions and is the grandsire of Arco.

Elegance, agility and medium size are among the assets which Irene Bivin especially admires in show Dobermans, and those she breeds make that fact clear.

Teresa Nail shares with enthusiasm her mother's love of Dobermans. She is the first, and Irene believes quite possibly the only, youngster to have won Best Junior Handler at Westminster with a Dobe, and her expert presentation of Dob Mann dogs is admired by us all. As Irene says, "Teresa literally grew up in the breed." She was interested in working with the dogs in obedience as well as in the show ring and gained High in Trial with one of her dogs at the National when only eleven years old.

Dob Mann is truly a family project and, as such, brings much pleasure to its participants. Theresa is now a professional handler of talent and expertise, and Irene does seem to have the instinct of a truly dedicated breeder.

Domani

Domani Dobermans belong to Dee Chiantella, who has been breeding them since the late 1960's, and she lives in Folsom, Louisiana. Dee's foundation bitch was Champion Housecarl Helene of Diversha, she was by Champion Highbriar Bandana ex Dobewick's Duress.

1▲

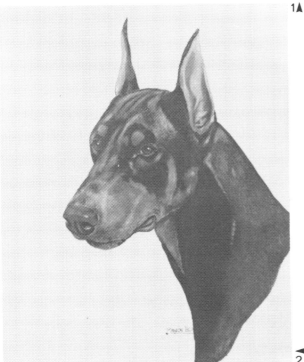

2◀

1. The foundation bitch of Domani Dobermans, Ch. House-carl Helene of Diversha. Owned by Dee Chiantella, Folsom, Louisiana. She is by Ch. Highbriar Bandana.
2. The dog responsible for "the look of Domani," Ch. Domani's Royal Image. By Ch. Domani's Prince William ex Ch. Shaft's Symphony by Jove. Bred by his owner, Dee Chiantella.
3. Ch. von Westerwald's Desert Song, an outstanding bitch bred by Judy Weiss and the late Irma Walen. By Ch. Ebonaire's Entertainer ex Ch. von Westerwald's Asta. Gained title in the mid-1960's, handled By J. Monroe Stebbins and Ellen Hoffman.
4. Ch. Ebonaire's Gridiron, By Ch. Steb's Top Skipper ex Ebonaire's Flashing Star. Bred and owned by Ed and Judy Weiss, Levittown, New York.
5. Ch. Ebonaire's Entertainer at his first show, at 18 months of age, when he went from first in American-bred to Winners Dog at the Connecticut–New York Doberman Specialty under judge Jane Kamp (now Mrs. Robert Forsyth). J. Monroe Stebbins handling in June 1962. "Thane" finished 10 months later and produced eight champions for Ed and Judy Weiss, Ebonaire Dobermans.

3 ◄

4 ►

5 ▼

DPC•CONN NY   JUNE 23 1962
JUDGE JANE KAMP
FIRST PLACE
AMERICAN BRED
PHOTO BY BUSHMAN

Helene did well at putting her owner off to a good start. Bred to Champion Hotai Sweet William, she produced Champion Domani's Prince William, who is the sire of ten champions and has himself won Best in Specialty Show on seven occasions.

Among Prince William's noted progeny are Champion Domani's Royal Image, whose magnificent head Dee credits with having given her the well-known "look of Domani" in which she takes pride. Royal Image is from Champion Shaft's Symphony by Jove. This same combination also produced another fine Doberman in Champion Domani's Royal Serenade. The latter was Winners Bitch at an important show where Prince William's son, Champion Domani's Baron v Kammer was also Winners Dog, making a very exciting day for the breeder of their sire!

Dee Chiantella has had the pleasure of co-owning with David M. Polk of the Tattoo Kennels in Columbus, Ohio a truly great winning Doberman in Champion Hotai Copper Tattoo. David Polk has kindly taken time to write up Tattoo's story for us, which follows:

"In April of 1978, a six-month-old red puppy became the object of much attention and the subject of many conversations as, owner-handled, he collected blue ribbons in the Ohio shows. By late May, Tattoo and George Rood became a team, sweeping the mid-West for "majors" as well as puppy class blue ribbons, and on July 29, 1979, Champion Hotai Copper Tattoo became an American Kennel Club Champion of Record. At 9 months and 19 days of age, he became the youngest Doberman Pinscher Champion in the history of the breed, a record still standing in 1984.

"But the best was yet to come. Given a year to mature, Tattoo re-appeared in early 1981 with Gene Haupt handling him, and for the next three years the twosome claimed the Doberman limelight.

"Never out of the Doberman Pinscher Club of America's 'Top Twenty,' Tattoo actually was never lower than third by any rating system. A breeder's Doberman, he was a two-time recipient of the Doberman Pinscher Club of America's conformation award for the Greatest Number of Specialty Bests in Show.

"Tattoo officially retired from the show ring in October of 1983. After 150 Bests of Breed, 100 Group placements, and numerous awards and records, there was little left for him to prove. At this writing, he still ranks high among the nation's top-winning Working dogs, and he hasn't set foot in the show ring for six months!

"The Tattoo puppies complement the odyssey. With two champions from his very first litter, Tattoo has emerged as a stud dog to watch. The National Specialty Grand Prize Futurity Winner in 1981 broke all records as the youngest winner in Doberman Pinscher Club of America history; he was a Tattoo son. Six champions later, all indications are that his get are "tattooed" with an indelible mark."

Tattoo is thoroughly enjoying his retirement, and his owners are basking in the pleasure of his outstanding progeny.

Ebonaire

Ebonaire Kennels came about because of Judy Weiss's great love of dogs since early childhood, because of her first visit to a Westminster Kennel Club Dog Show at the old Madison Square Garden, and because of her meeting, on the occasion, with Champion Dictator v Glenhugal. This was Judy's introduction to Dobes, and the moment she set eyes on this handsome red dog with his very approachable personality, she knew that she wanted a dog like him.

Returning home, she contacted Peggy Adamson, from whom she arranged to purchase a black Doberman bitch on breeder's terms. The rest of the story is history!

Damasyn Wild Wing gave Judy a litter of six sired by Dictator, the puppies to be divided in accordance with her "breeder's terms" agreement with Peggy Adamson. The bitch puppy in this litter was sold, reluctantly, as Judy would have liked to keep her but could not manage it with her own first baby (her son, Jeff) due at about that time. So the puppy was sold to a New Jersey fancier, bred by him in due course to Champion Damasyn the Solitaire, and Judy tells us that this bitch, Damasyn The Waltzing Brook, became the foundation bitch at Mark Tey Kennels. Wing herself remained with the Weisses throughout her good lifetime of fourteen years.

Damasyn the Flash, a Dictator daughter, was the true foundation bitch at Ebonaire.

1. Ch. Ebonaire's Balestra, owned and bred by Ed and Judy Weiss, Levittown, New York. By Ch. Steb's Top Skipper ex Ebonaire's Flashing Star, shown finishing at 20 months of age after a two-month period of showing. This is part of the renowned "football-fencing" litter which also included Champions Flying Tackle, Gridiron, Touchdown, Touche, etc. Handled by J. Monroe Stebbins for Ed and Judy Weiss, Ebonaire Dobermans.

2. Ch. Ebonaire's Entertainer and Ch. Ebonaire's Balestra, two famed winners of the late 1950's–1960's, romping in their owners' backyard. Both sired by Ch. Steb's Top Skipper, these are two of the many well-known Doberman "stars" owned and bred by Ed and Judy Weiss, Levittown, New York.

1▲

▼2

205

1▲

◀
2

1. Ch. Ebonaire's Scarlett Chutist, by Ch. Ebonaire's Entertainer ex Ebonaire's Colonel's Lady, was Winners Bitch at Westminster in 1967. She is a litter sister to Ch. Ebonaire's Ripcord. Breeder-owner, Judy Weiss. Handler, J. Monroe Stebbins.
2. Head study of Ch. Ebonaire's Laurel, by Ch. Damasyn Bo-Tairic of Ardor ex Ebonaire's Betsey Ross. Bred by Ed and Judy Weiss. Owned by the late Alton Anderson, the noted animal photographer, who did this lovely photo of his handsome bitch.
3. Ch. Ebonaire's Honor Count going Fourth in the Working Group at Westminster in 1962. Born March 31, 1960, sired by Ch. Steb's Top Skipper ex Ebonaire's Colonel's Lady. Bred by Judy Weiss; owned by Anita and Richard Ortz, Brooklyn, New York. Handled by J. Monroe Stebbins.
4. Ch. Ebonaire's Balestra, going Best of Breed under the late Ross Hamilton in 1961. By Ch. Steb's Top Skipper ex Ebonaire's Flashing Star. Owned by Ed and Judy Weiss, Ebonaire Dobermans, Levittown, New York. J. Monroe Stebbins handled this noted bitch.

206

3▲

▼4

1. Ch. Ebonaire's Mr. Esquire, sired by Ch. Ebonaire's Entertainer ex Ebonaire's Joyeuse Noel. A black male with numerous wins, including a Best in Show to his credit. Handled by J. Monroe Stebbins; bred by Ed and Judy Weiss. Lee Wagner, owner.

2. Ch. Ebonaire's Tric-Trac at seven months old. Son of Ch. Egothel's All American ex Ch. Ebonaire's Balestra and litter brother to the Weiss's Ebonaire's Charade. Pictured in 1964, his first time in the ring, at the Suffolk County Match Show. Handled by Ed Weiss under judge Lena Ludwig. Owned by Florence Robertson of Valley Stream, New York. Bred by Ed and Judy Weiss.

3. Ch. Ebonaire's Mr. Esquire, owned by Harry Wagner, winning Best in Show from Mrs. Marie B. Meyer. J. Monroe Stebbins handling.

4. Ch. Ebonaire's Touchdown, by Ch. Steb's Top Skipper ex Ebonaire's Flashing Star, was bred by Ed and Judy Weiss and owned by Charles A. T. and Marie O'Neill, Philadelphia, Pennsylvania a multiple Best in Show winner; multiple Specialty winner; one of the Nation's Top Ten Dobermans over four consecutive years. Handled by J. Monroe Stebbins.

She was purchased by Judy and Ed Weiss a few years after Wing had joined their family. The Flash was bred to Damasyn the Captain's Sabre, a Solitaire son, and this produced the excellent producing bitch Ebonaire's Flashing Star. This was a really lovely red bitch, again whom Judy would have liked to keep, but Ed Weiss felt, with some justification, that with the baby, two birds, a cat, and Wing, they really had a houseful. So Judy arranged to place Flashing Star with some people in the area on breeding terms, and when the time came, she further arranged that Star should be bred to Champion Dortmund Delly's Colonel Jet. From this came Ebonaire's Colonel's Lady, unshown, but again a top producing bitch who numbered among her progeny Champion Ebonaire's Honor Bright (a Westminster Best of Breed winner), Champion Ebonaire's Scarlett Chutist and Champion Ebonaire's Ripcord.

For Flashing Star's second litter, she was bred to the immortal Champion Steb's Top Skipper, a most dominant show and stud dog. Star and Skipper, as might have been expected, presented the Doberman breed with one of its most famous litters, the "Football and Fencing litter." This included the exquisite bitch, Champion Ebonaire's Balestra, Judy Weiss's "pride and joy," and the fantastic dog who became Champion Ebonaire's Touchdown and attained a fabulous career for the owners to whom he was sold, Mr. and Mrs. Charles A. T. O'Neill. Still another from this litter, a bitch which Judy kept and gave to her cousins (Milton and Maxine Kramer) on breeder's terms, was Ebonaire's Enguarde who, in the family tradition, became a Top Producer but was not campaigned in the ring as she hated dog shows. Champion Ebonaire's Keystone was in her first litter; in her second litter, bred back to her sire, Top Skipper, she produced Champion Ebonaire's Entertainer and Ebonaire's Bravo who went to Australia benefiting the breed there.

The "Football and Fencing" litter was one to bring joy to any breeder. Champion Ebonaire's Touchdown, known as "Spike," became a famous and consistent winner handled for the O'Neills by J. Monroe Stebbins— truly one of the "greats" of this breed. The bitch, Balestra, Judy Weiss considered, and

she is quoted as saying, "the best of them all." Champion Ebonaire's Gridiron was another extraordinary handsome dog. Ebonaire's Flying Tackle went to Sue Neville in California now but who was a resident of Utah at that time. Ebonaire's Kickoff should have finished but was sold to a Long Island fancier who, despite promises at the time of purchase, never did get him in the ring—one of the heartaches breeders face. Champion Ebonaire's Touche was sold to Ruth Ann Molnette for whom she gained her title, then re-sold to the well-known Doberman authority Alonzo P. Reed. Ebonaire's Enguarde became the dam of Champions Entertainer and Bravo (the Australian export). Of this litter of seven, five finished their titles, two bitches and three males. Judy comments, "It was a lucky litter because I found the correct people for the puppies."

One of Judy Weiss's particular favorites of her many famed homebreds was a red bitch from her "Parachute" litter, by Entertainer from Colonel's Lady, who became Champion Ebonaire's Scarlet Chutist. There was a lovely male in this litter, Champion Ebonaire's Ripcord, as well. Another great red Bitch in whom Judy takes special pride is Champion Ebonaire's Chaldea, by Champion Ebonaire's His Excellency. Robin Weiss, Ed and Judy's daughter, finished her in 1978 with five "majors" while attending college.

Of the males, Judy Weiss's favorite was very likely Champion Ebonaire's Entertainer, her inbred Top Skipper son (the only such breeding she ever has done). Yet of the two littermates, Bravo was her choice of the litter, but he has been promised to Mr. and Mrs. McNichol in Australia, so that was that. Ed Weiss, too, especially liked Entertainer, and this was the first male he had been in favor of having the family keep.

Ebonaire Kennels are really not a kennel at all. The dogs live as housedogs with their owners, and thus are thoroughly enjoyed by them. They are at Levittown, Long Island (New York) where the Weisses share their home with usually eight or so adult Dobes. All puppies have been born at home, most often with Judy in attendance.

Eikon

Eikon Dobermans, at Miami, Florida, are owned by Stuart and Nedda Vorzimer, whose

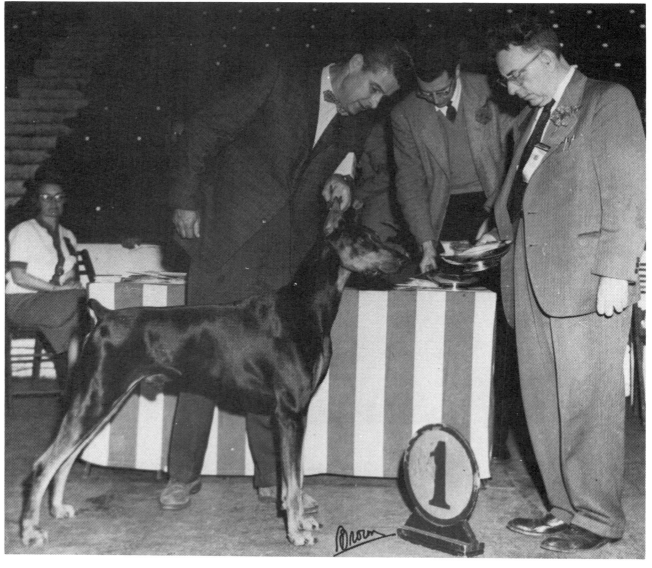

1. Ch. Ebonaire's Flying Tackle, by Ch. Steb's Top Skipper ex Ebonaire's Flashing Star, was bred by Ed and Judy Weiss; owned by Sue Neville, Shinya Dobermans, California.

2 Ebonaire's Mister Esquire winning the breed at Newtown Kennel Club in August 1964. Handled by J. Monroe Stebbins, Mister Esquire was from the Ebonaire Kennels of Ed and Judy Weiss who have produced so very many Dobermans of importance over the years.

3. From the famous "football" litter, Ch. Ebonaire's Gridiron. By Ch. Steb's Top Skipper ex Ebonaire's Flashing Star, handled by J. Monroe Stebbins. Photo courtesy of the Stebbinses.

4. The great justly famed Ch. Ebonaire's Touchdown, by Ch. Steb's Top Skipper ex Ebonaire's Flashing Star, was part of a litter that contained five champions. Bred by Judy and Ed Weiss, Touchdown was owned by Charles A. T. O'Neill and handled to many important wins, including Bests in Show, by J. Monroe Stebbins. Touchdown was the sire of nine champions. Pictured at Burlington County in June 1960.

5. Ch. Ebonaire's Touchdown taking Best of Breed at the Quaker City Doberman Pinscher Club Specialty in 1962 under the author. Handled by Monroe Stebbins for Charles A. T. O'Neill. Touchdown, by Ch. Steb's Top Skipper from Ebonaire's Flashing Star, was part of the famed "football" litter.

▲4

►5

first Dobe, Champion Bar-Lock's Ebony Eikon, WAC, is a great-grandson of Champion Dolph von Tannenwald.

This splendid young dog finished at 25 months of age, then had a brief career as a "special" handled by his owner, whose devotion to and enjoyment of Ebony would not permit of his being sent out for campaigning.

Ebony shares his owners' home with two of his daughters, Eikon's Black Eyed Susan and Eikon's Wild Flower. He himself is a son of Koven's Galant Hunter (Champion Amulet's Fortune Hunter ex Kay Hills' Letter Perfect) from Champion Torenduf Funi Girl of Kay Hill.

The Vorzimers' kennel is named for Eikon, and we hope they will enjoy a bright future.

Elfred

Elfred Doberman Pinschers are a long established and highly esteemed strain, owned and founded by Mrs. Ellen Hoffman at Harriman, New York. Many famous champions have been bred and owned here; still more have been capably handled by Mrs. Hoffman to their titles and important wins over several decades.

Champion Barlynn's Clean Sweep was the foundation bitch at Elfred, a daughter of the mighty Champion Delegate v.d. Elbe from Champion Kitchawan's Emma von Grunberg. She was a black and rust.

An important foundation stud at Elfred was a German import, Reichssieger 1949-1950 Asko von der Wolzenberg. Among other famous progeny, Asko was the sire of Canadian Champion Roger v Franconia, C.D., a Best in Show winner also owned by Mrs. Hoffman, who has remarked, "He is the foundation of all our top show dogs."

One of America's most renowned Dobermans was World Champion Elfred's Spark Plug, CACIB. This fabulous son of Champion Steb's Top Skipper from Elfred's Doretta was bred, owned, and handled by Ellen Hoffman. He completed his American championship by thirteen months of age, his Bermudian championship by winning three Working Groups there, his Canadian championship with a Best in Show victory, his Mexican championship with two Working Groups and a Best in Show, and his Colombian championship with

back to back Bests in Show the same weekend. He was the first member of the Doberman breed to have won three titles before reaching the age of two years.

A prominent bitch in the early days of Elfred was American, Canadian and Colombian Champion Belita von Tamara, C.D., who was Best of Winners at the 1956 Doberman Pinscher Club of America Specialty, to which she added the distinction of completing her C.D. at this same event. She was the producer of a number of champions.

Foxhall and Milbryan

In North Central Texas, Lynn Eggers of Foxhall fame and Mildred K. Bryant, noted for Milbryan Cairn Terriers, are working together in a small, select Doberman Pinscher breeding program.

Champion Kropka von Tontonne, bred by Richard Clayton and owned by Lynn Eggers, is one of the bitches on whom this line is based. She is the dam of Champion Foxhall's Ann Klein, an excellent bitch owned by Mrs. Bryant, sired by Champion Georgie Porgie Dob Mann.

Foxhall's Coral Tattoo, Ann Klein's daughter, is by Champion Hotai Copper Tattoo. Certainly these ladies are working with topnotch bloodlines and should be successful in their project.

Gemae

George and Mae White bought their first Doberman from a Catholic priest in Hartford, Connecticut during 1952. The priest had been in the armed services in Germany and brought back a dog and a bitch with him, the parents of this litter. The puppies had no papers (the papers had been lost in the war), but they were the result of a full German breeding. The Whites' bitch was just a pet (she was spayed) but had a lovely temperament.

Gemae Dobermans were founded by the Whites of Marlborough, Connecticut with Red Poppy of Rosevale, C.D., who was their foundation bitch. She was a daughter of Champion Mark's Tey High Hat. She had only one litter, that sired by Champion Steb's Gunga Din, but from this litter came Champion Steb's Custom Maid who was to be the Whites' first homebred champion. There were five puppies in the litter, all of which

1. Ch. Elfred's Enchanting Elaine, C.D. by Ch. Elfred's Quo Vadis ex Am. and Can. Ch. Elfred's Merri-Maker, one of the many champions bred and handled by Ellen Hoffman, Harriman, New York.
2. Am. and Can. Ch. Elfred's Merri-Maker, black and rust daughter of Ch. Steb's Top Skipper ex Ch. Barlynn's Clean Sweep, owner-handled by Ellen Hoffman.

1A

2

1. A well-known photograph of World Champion Elfred's Spark Plug, CACIB. A son of Ch. Steb's Top Skipper ex Elfred's Doretta, Sparky was bred, owned, and handled by Ellen Hoffman, Elfred's Dobermans, Harriman, New York. He completed his American championship by 13 months of age, his Bermudian championship by winning three Working Groups, his Canadian championship by taking Best in Show, his Mexican championship with two Working Groups and Best in Show, and his Colombian championship with two Bests in Show, back to back, in one weekend. One of the breed's true immortals!

2. One of the foundation studs at Elfred Kennels, imported and owned by Ellen Hoffman. Reichssieger 1949–1950, Asko von der Wolzenburg.

3. Ch. Elfred's Quo Vadis, by World Ch. Elfred's Spark Plug, CACIB, from KLS Sheba. Owned by Sherline and Hilda Norton; bred and handled by Ellen Hoffman. Here winning the Quaker City Doberman Pinscher Club Specialty, this dog was Best of Winners at the National in 1964.

4. This is the foundation bitch of the famed Elfred Kennels. Ch. Barlynn's Clean Sweep, by Ch. Delegate v. d. Elbe ex Ch. Kitchawan's Emma v Grunberg. Black and rust, bred by Peter Knoop and owned by Mrs. Ellen Hoffman. Pictured in September 1957 at Somerset Hills, handled by Mrs. Hoffman, winning under Mrs. Ruth Castellano.

214

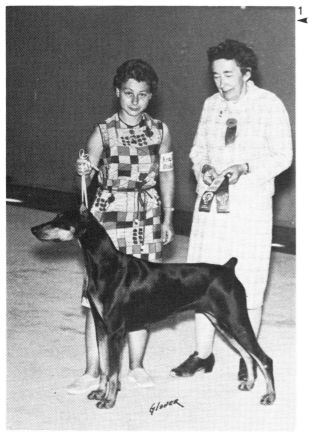

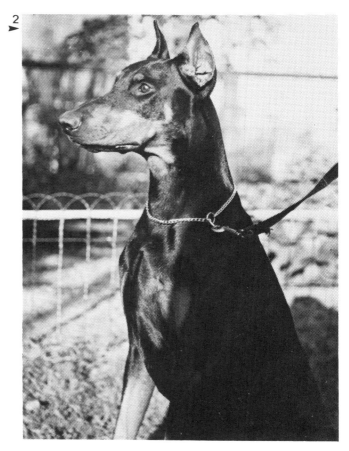

1. Ch. Elfred's Her X'Cellency, a Spark Plug daughter, owned by Jean Bremer. Bred and handled by Ellen Hoffman, Harriman, New York.

2. Can. Ch. Roger v Franconia, C.D., a Best in Show winner owned by Mrs. Ellen Hoffman, Elfred Kennels. This black and rust son of Reichssieger Asko von der Wolzenburg, Sch.H. III, is the foundation of all the Elfred top show dogs.

3. Am. and Can. Ch. Elfred's Roxie, sired by Ch. Steb's Top Skipper ex Elfred's Doretta, going best in Show at a Canadian event. Owned by Mrs. Alonzo Reed; bred and handled by Ellen Hoffman.

4. Ch. Elfred's Katrinka, owned by Mr. and Mrs. Norton Moore of Houston, Texas, was bred by Ellen Hoffman. Handled here by Mrs. Moore, winning Best in Show at Beaumont some years back under judge Dr. F. P. Miller. By Ch. Berman Briar ex Elfred's Doretta.

5 and 6. The lovely bitch, Ch. Steb's Custom Maid. By Ch. Steb's Gunga Din ex Red Poppy of Rosevale, C.D. Owned and bred by George and Mae White, Gemae Dobermans, Marlborough, Connecticut.

▲5

►6

1. Ch. Highbriar Monsoon, by Ch. Rancho Dobe's Storm ex Kilburn K. T. Owned by G. S. Forbes and bred by Mrs. Betsy R. Thomas. A versatile Doberman pictured at Beaver Run some years back taking Winners Dog for two points the same day he won first in Novice B Obedience with a score of 194½. Photo courtesy of Mrs. Marge Kilburn, Pottstown, Pennsylvania.

2. Ch. Andelane's Indigo Rock, by Ch. Ru-Mar's Morgansonne, C.D. ex Jemoel's Maui v. Cassio, was bred by Andy and Elaine Kormerny and is owned by Robert Bishop, New York, New York. Winning Best in Show at Monroe Kennel Club in 1971.

were pointed, but none finished due largely to the fact that the people to whom they had been sold lost interest in showing.

Custom Maid was a Best of Breed winner at fourteen months of age at her second show entered in the Open Class, taking the top award over nine "specials." Certainly nice going!

The Whites were not planning to breed any litters beyond just this one, which is why they used "Steb's" as the kennel prefix on this litter. Famous last words! Obviously there was a change of heart.

As they attended dog shows, the Whites decided that they preferred the Demetrius line best. Grace Moore gave them a nine-month-old black and tan male, out of Champion Gra-Lemor Demetrius v.d. Victor ex Gra-Lemor Fascination Fling. His name was Gra-Lemor Hundred Proof.

Hundred Proof was a proven stud before he became a champion. He finished at 20 months of age in a total of thirteen shows and produced four champions. He was a multi-Best of Breed winner. His first litter was with Champion Steb's Custom Maid, which was also her first litter, and this produced six puppies, three of which became champions: Champion Gemae Hanky Panky, Champion Gemae Purple Please and Champion Gemae Minos the Second. Two of these, Hanky Panky and Minos, also became Canadian Champions.

Champion Gemae Minos the Second was Best of Opposite Sex at the Connecticut-New York Specialty from the American-bred Class for five points, and the next year he returned to take Best of Breed at the Connecticut-New York Specialty over an entry of 165. He also was Best of Opposite Sex at Westminster.

Champion Steb's Custom Maid was bred a second time to Champion Gra-Lemor Demetrius v.d. Victor, and one bitch from this litter finished, Champion Gemae Brass N'Sass. The Whites kept a bitch from this litter, Gemae Royal Fantasy, whom they bred to Champion Gemae Hanky Panky, producing a dog and a bitch. The dog, Gemae's Mordecai Jones, was never shown but produced two champions, both of whom became Group placers, when bred from outside the Gemae line.

Royal Fantasy was again bred, this time to Champion Gemae Minos the Second; one dog

was finished, Champion Gemae's Renegade.

The Whites have not done any breeding lately, but as this book goes to press they are planning on going into the Ahrtal line and then back into their own.

Gwynllyn

Gwynllyn Dobermans, of Gwynedd Valley, Pennsylvania, have represented Carol Nock's interest in the showing and breeding of good Doberman Pinscher stock since the early 1970's. The kennel has been founded basically on the Amulet and Tarrado bloodlines, which of course are direct descendents from Tess Henseler's Ahrtals, so highly respected in this breed.

The first Doberman to represent Gwynllyn in the show ring was Champion Amulet's Cecil v Gluckliche. "Cecil" was purchased sight unseen for the Nocks at five months of age by Diane Downey. This dynamic red male, bred by Pamela Gordon, Melinda Gevers and Beth Smith, began his show career at the age of seven months by going Best Puppy at the Quaker City Doberman Pinscher Club Futurity his first time in the ring, then went on to finish his championship as early as two years of age, doing so owner-handled. Many judges expressed the opinion that Cecil was a true representative of the breed Standard in both conformation and especially temperament.

Unfortunately, at three years of age, Cecil was discovered to have contracted a melanoma in the roof of his mouth. At this time the Nocks found out, through the painful radiation and chemotherapy treatments, just how courageous this dog remained, making him a favorite patient of the University of Pennsylvania and Dr. Ann Jeglum, his cancer specialist.

Cecil was the first dog in the history of melanoma study and research whose melanoma was totally arrested for fifteen months by radiation treatment. Through this traumatic experience he never lost heart and continued showing successfully enough to make the Doberman Pinscher Club of America Top Twenty competition in 1982 and the No. 6 male Doberman in the country, while becoming a multi-Group and Specialty Best in Show winner. As one very close friend of Carol's has said, "Cecil will be with us forever contributing to the breed through his winning get." To date he has two American champions, one Canadian champion, and numerous others pointed on their way to finishing.

American and Canadian Champion Tiffany's Gwynllyn of Amulet, a half sister to Cecil, came to Gwynllyn Dobermans at three months of age, as cute and pert as a puppy could be. She started her show career with a bang, going Grand Prize Futurity winner and Best of Winners at the Tappan Zee Doberman Pinscher Specialty at eight months of age in 1980. She immediately went on competing successfully as a "special" under the expertise of Perry Phillips, making the Doberman Pinscher Club of America Top Twenty competition for two consecutive years, 1981 and 1982. She also was the No. 3 bitch in the United States at this time.

Upon completion of her "specials" career here, Tiffany obtained her Canadian championship and continued showing in the U.S. on a limited basis, thus capturing for herself an all-breed Best in Show again, owner-handled at Greenwich Kennel Club in 1982. Tiffany was bred in the spring of 1983 to Champion Amulet's Luka of Sno-Glenn, C.D., the top winning fawn dog of all time, and has pointed get just now one year of age. A future breeding is planned using the frozen semen collected from her half brother, Cecil, who is the Doberman to whom she was originally purchased to be bred.

A new young red male, American and Canadian Champion Gwynllyn Tom Foolery, is now standing at stud at Gwynllyn, the product of the only linebred Cecil litter. Tom finished his title in a flash, starting his career by going Winners Dog at the prestigious Westminster Kennel Club. He then went on to take a breed from the classes one month later and finished nine days after that with back-to-back five and four point "majors" and a third consecutive win on the 1984 Tar Heel Circuit, when he was just eighteen months old.

Highbriar

Highbriar Dobermans were established by Betsy Richey Thomas at Gambier, Ohio as a hobby kennel which she combined with running a home and raising three children. Its record is outstanding, for Highbriar produced 25 champions, several Best in Show dogs and many Group winners.

Betsy was raised in Ohio where she attended a private high school, then Ohio State University. For two years she studied veterinary medicine; for two years Farm Management specializing in genetics, judging and livestock management. She farmed a livestock farm south of Cleveland, Ohio for five years, breeding and marketing Hereford cattle, swine, poultry, Percheron and Belgian horses.

The first of Betsy Thomas' Dobermans was acquired in 1935, but it was in 1953 when Highbriar really got underway with the beginning of a planned twenty-five year genetic breeding program, the philosophy of which was few breedings but of quality, using genetic principles based on the Bruce-Loew theory; also accentuating the bitch as the most important part of the program. The system was developed of breeding a bitch four times, the first three times each to a different sire, then, for her fourth and final litter, returning to the sire by whom she had produced the best puppies.

The first litter Betsy Thomas bred consisted of all C.D.'s, one with a C.D.X., two champions and group winners. The most famous show bitch produced by the kennel was Champion Highbriar of Allenwood who, systematically campaigned, won a hundred Bests of Breed, 42 Groups, and eight Bests in Show between the years 1965 and 1969.

Betsy Thomas comments, "As any sincere breeder knows, their claim to fame rests on the producers they breed, not the famous show animals, and it was the luck of this kennel to breed several Top Producers, plus the fact that those who chose to use these producers improved the breed." The producers to whom she refers are Champion Highbriar Bandana, Champion Highbriar Minos, Champion Highbriar Blackbird, Champion Highbriar Jasmine, Champion Highbriar Piping Rock, and Champion Highbriar Tea for Two, U.D.

Highbriar stopped breeding in 1975, the last remaining champion from that final litter being Champion Highbriar Esquire who lives in Nova Scotia.

The complete list of Highbriar champions is as follows:

1. Ch. Highbriar Halla, C.D. 1960-1967. By Ch. Florian v Ahrtal ex Ch. Highbriar Blackbird, C.D. Co-bred and co-owned by Theodora (Ted) Linck and Betsy Thomas. Shown at four months, she later won the Grand Futurity at the DPCA, 1962.

2. Highbriar Hasty Roads pictured winning his first three-point "major" from the American-bred Class at Westminster some years back (probably during the 1960's). The judge is Robert Kerns. Owned by Betsy R. Thomas, Highbriar Dobermans.

1▲ ▼2

221

1. Ch. Highbriar Blackbird, foundation bitch at Tedell Kennels. By Ch. Jet v d Ravensburg ex Highbriar Stormette, C.D.X. Bred by Highbriar, Betsy Thomas.
2. Ch. Highbriar Piping Rock, by Ch. Ravensburg Falsta ex Ch. Highbriar Rock Sand, produced the great Ch. Tarrado's Flair. Owned by Shirley McCoy. Bred by Theodore (Ted) Linck and Betsy R. Thomas.
3. Ch. Highbriar Tea For Two, U.D., handled here by Shirley Hitter, making a good win under Maxwell Riddle in 1965. The dam of Ch. Highbriar Jasmine, she was owner-trained and handled in obedience by owner Harold Schobel, Cleveland, Ohio.
4. Ch. Highbriar American Flag, one of the better males bred by Betsy Thomas, was sold to the Phillipines.

Champion Highbriar Monsoon, C.D.
Champion Highbriar Typhoon, C.D.
Champion Highbriar Comanche
Champion Highbriar Seneca
Champion Highbriar Blackbird
Champion Highbriar Tea for Two
Champion Highbriar Jasmine
Champion Highbriar East To Love
Champion Highbriar Aphrodite
Champion Highbriar American Emblem
Champion Highbriar American Flag
Champion Highbriar Constant Comment
Champion Highbriar Hasty Roads
Champion Highbriar Rock Sand
Champion Highbriar Minos
Champion Highbriar Knossos
Champion Highbriar Oak of Allenwood
Champion Highbriar Willo of Allenwood
Champion Highbriar Valencia
Champion Highbriar Major Dare
Champion Highbriar Bandana
Champion Highbriar Osiris
Champion Highbriar Sweet Cherry
Champion Highbriar Esquire.

Tea for Two finished both championship and U.D. owner-trained, and she produced the great foundation bitch for Tarrado Kennels, Champion Jasmine.

The problem of the kennel was its part-time basis due to Betsy Thomas's other interests. Many potential top producers were bred only once because they were co-owned by people who were not interested in breeding.

Mrs. Thomas now lives in Tucson, Arizona.

Highgate

Highgate Dobermans, at Burt, Michigan, owned by Richard and Jeanne Goodyear, have been based largely on the Sherluck line as the background for their breeding program, which goes back, with a splendid record for leading winners and top producers, to the Kay Hill Dobes. The Goodyears have two dogs, full brother and sister, from the breeding of Champion Sherluck's L.B. Jake and Champion Moraga Hill's High Fashion, W.A.C., these being Champion Sherluck's Fashion Designer and Sherluck's Star Trek. The latter is also close to the title (probably a champion by now), needing only a "major" to finish. He has been entirely owner-handled to

some very nice accomplishments, including Best Puppy in Show in Canada, and, in the United States, several Specialty Grand Sweepstakes, Breeds over "specials," and a Working Group III as an eight-month-old puppy.

Champion Sherluck's Fashion Designer is pictured among our illustrations on the day she finished, with George Rood handling. She recently whelped a litter of a single puppy sired by Champion Shadow Acres Johnny Jump Up of the Tedell line.

Another lovely bitch belonging to the Goodyears is Kearney's Imprevu, a strongly linebred Champion Highland Satan's Image descendant. She is a full sister to multiple champions and Best in Show winners and is the Goodyears' foundation bitch. She is the dam of the handsome red puppy bitch Highgate Starzafire from her first litter by Sherluck's Star Trek.

The Goodyears look forward to an exciting future in the Doberman world. Their foundation stock is all linebred, and the plan is to pick up an occasional outcross for needed characteristics from complementary lines, and then bring it back again to further strengthen the present qualities.

Hi Vale

Hi Vale Kennels belong to Jack and Sharon Tasca of Danielson, Connecticut, who have owned Dobermans since about 1974 and have been showing since a few years later.

The Tascas finished their first champion in 1980, Champion Gemae's Renegade, bred by George and Mae White, Gemae Kennels. Renegade is a double Demetrius grandson.

During the time when Renegade was being shown, the Tascas bred their first litter from their foundation bitch, Brandy Ann of Hi Vale. Her bloodlines are Ahrtal, Tannewald and Kay Hill. Through the years Brandy Ann has been bred to the Demetrius line and back into the Ahrtal line, with the following results. She has produced four American champions, three Canadian champions, an International champion, and an Argentinian and Uruguayan champion. Others are close to their titles as well, some of whom will be finished by the time you are reading this.

All of the Hi Vale dogs pictured here, with the exception of Renegade, are sons or daughters of Brandy Ann of Hi Vale.

1▲

▼2

3 ◄

► 4

1. Ch. Highbriar Aphrodite, the dam of Ch. Highbriar Minos, winning in about 1960 for Betsy R. Thomas, Highbriar Dobes.
2. Ch. Highbriar Osiris, one of the many famed winners from Highbriar Kennels.
3. Ch. Highbriar Comanche, by Ch. Jet v. d. Ravensberg from the Ch. Rancho Dobe's Storm daughter, Highbriar Stormette. George Rood handling for Highbriar Kennels, Betsy Thomas. Louis Murr is the judge.
4. Ch. Highbriar Monsoon, by Ch. Rancho Dobe's Storm, winning Best of Breed at Sewickley Kennel Club during the late 1950's. Betsy R. Thomas, owner.
5. Ch. Highbriar Monsoon, C.D., was the first of Betsy R. Thomas's Highbriar champions.
6. Ch. Highbriar Monsoon taking Best of Breed at Painesville in the mid-1950's. His niece, Seneca, went Best of Opposite Sex. One of Betsy Thomas's first good show days with her Highbriar Dobes.

5 ►

► 6

1▲   ▼2

1. Can. Ch. Hi Vale's Ebony Hesh-Ke, C.D., bred by Jack and Sharon Tasca; owned by Tanya Nina Lee, Underhill, Vermont.
2. Hotai Mercedes, here taking Best of Winners for a three-point "major," going on from the Puppy Class at the Doberman Pinscher Club of Pittsburgh Specialty. Later became a champion, owned by Carol Clemens in partnership with her breeder, Virginia Markley.

Homer Hill

Homer Hill Dobermans are a small hobby kennel owned by Patrick and Colby Homer at Wheeling, West Virginia. At present six Dobes, three dogs and three bitches, are in residence there. The kennel was established in 1976 with the purchase of an uncropped red male as a pet, and after losing him, the Homers started to research the breed by reading every word that they could find in print about them.

Colby Homer soon realized that she was becoming interested in showing, and the second red male she purchased was with this thought in mind. He got her into the ring as a competitor, but she learned quite quickly that this one, too, was a pet. Finally in 1978, she did acquire one with the desired show potential, a black bitch this time, whom she was able to point towards the title herself, and also to show successfully as part of a Best in Show winning brace.

This bitch was Warjo's Melodee v Scudamore, now retired from the ring, who has proven herself as a producer, too. So far she is the dam of two litters, the younger just over a year at the time of writing, and especially noteworthy as six of its eight members are being shown successfully and another is about to tackle a tracking degree.

Colby Homer finished her first champion during 1983, Champion Warjo's D'Artagnon, who since then as a "special" has gained Best of Breed awards and a Group placement. Colby enjoys handling and someday hopes to "cross the line" to professional status. She and Patrick attempt to maintain a "quality not quantity" philosophy, so they keep their Dobe breeding activities on a limited scale.

Hotai

Hotai's first Doberman Pinscher arrived at the home of Mrs. Virginia Markley in Marion, Ohio on July 31, 1963. She was a spayed two year old black and rust bitch and was to serve as friend and protector. She was suitably named "Heller," and it was immediate love and respect for both the Doberman and Mrs. Markley. It was not long before Mrs. Markley realized that she must have another of these majestic creatures.

Within the next year, two-year-old Tamberlane Alert Abbie was purchased, and Abbie was to become foundation bitch for the very outstanding kennel which Hotai is now. Abbie was bred to the well-known Best in Show dog, International Champion Kohlen, three times before producing a litter. Then on September 24, 1965 her first puppies were born, five black and rust females and one male. This was Mrs. Markley's "god and goddess" litter, hence the kennel name of Hotai, god of good luck and happiness.

Hotai Sibyl Selene, the Doberman Pinscher Club of America Top Producing Dam of 1969 and 1970, came from this first litter. Sibyl was every thing a breeder could wish for, a beautiful lady, an excellent mother, and a joy to live with. She had a true Doberman temperament of friendliness to whomever she was properly introduced but at the same time a defender and protector of all she possessed.

Mrs. Markley bought Champion Highbriar Bandana from the Andersons after he and Sibyl had produced their first litter. From this breeding came four champions. Two—Champion Hotai Sweet William and Champion Hotai Cactus Flower—were all-breed Best in Show winners. A third, Champion Hotai Laurel, was a multiple Group winner, and the fourth, Champion Hotai Shasta Daisy, was never "specialed." From three litters sired by Bandana, Sibyl produced nine champions, of which six became Group winners. Her producing time was cut short by a very complicated surgery from which she recovered sufficiently to be bred one last time, to Champion Highland's Satan Image, from which came two puppies, a black dog and the black bitch Hotai Fallen Angel. Known as "Zsa Zsa," Fallen Angel became the dam of Champion Hotai Charlie, Champion Hotai Willson, and Champion Hotai Angel's Finale. Bandana also earned the distinction of the Doberman Pinscher Club of America Top Twenty Producing Sire Award for 1970 and 1971.

Charlie is well-known in his own right as both a Top Producer and a Top Show Dog, being awarded two of the prestigious "Award of Merit" banners presented by the D.P.C.A. from two of the matriarchs of the breed, Mrs. Peggy Adamson and Mrs. Marge Kilburn. Charlie is also the sire of the youngest champion in the history of Dobermans who became the 1982 Top Winning Doberman,

Champion Hotai Copper Tattoo, owned by David Polk.

Charlie is also the sire of other well-known top winning get. Champion Hotai Molly Hatchet, owned by Helen Yettaw, was Winners Bitch at the Doberman Pinscher Club of America Specialty in 1982. And before his death at the very young age of five-and-a-half years, Willson was the sire of six champions. These inbred brothers, Charlie and Willson, have definitely been an asset to Dobermans, having come from a line of top producers. Their sire, Champion Hotai Sweet William, Best in Show winner, was Virginia Markley's friend and companion for ten-and-a-half years, and his influence is still being seen in his grandchildren and great-grandchildren. In addition to Sweet William's other progeny, he is the sire of six Specialty Best in Show children.

To date there are twenty-two champions carrying the Hotai prefix, with Virginia Markley being the co-breeder on several more. Hotai is not a mass producer of puppies, and their stud dogs are bred selectively only to quality bitches owned by responsible people. At present Hotai is in its second year of not having a litter. They do, however, occasionally have stud puppies, and there is a champion bitch with a litter due while we are writing.

Terry Lazzaro Hundt

Terry Lazzaro is a talented and knowledgeable member of the Doberman world, known and admired throughout the United States. Although she is not a breeder, she has long been closely associated with Dobes; and, in co-ownership with Patricia W. Laurans, she has owned one of the finest, the very famous Champion Fanfare's Ringmaster.

Terry started out in Dobes as an assistant to J. Monroe Stebbins, Jr., when he was handling, prior to his resignation to take over the position of a Field Representative for the American Kennel Club. At that time, one might say "by popular demand" as Terry's expertise as a handler had already been noticed, she started out handling on her own, and she has piloted some leading winners to well-deserved success.

Champion Fanfare's Ringmaster was handled for Terry Lazzaro and Pat Laurans by

Monroe Stebbins. He was a dog with whom to reckon from the very beginning, finishing his championship with three "majors" and a Best of Breed along the way from the classes, all at the tender age of one year. "Ringer" was a Top Ten Doberman and a multiple Best in Show winner over a three year period while being campaigned only on the East Coast. He was known to the ringsiders as "Steb's wind-up toy" because of his outstanding showmanship. And, although used only sparingly at stud, he was the sire of eight champions.

Ringmaster was by Champion Lauder Fanfare (Champion Steb's Renegade ex Elblac's Doria) ex Heidi's Kriss (Damasyn The Troubleshooter ex Wilmar's Heidi). Behind him are some of the most admired and prepotent dogs in the history of the Doberman breed.

Terry herself handled "Ringer" to his first points; then Steb took over for his "specials" career. He retired in October 1971 at five years of age—marking the occasion with, of course, a Best in Show. A memorable dog!

In April 1984, Terry Lazzaro and Robert Hundt were married. Fortunately, Bob enjoys Dobermans (in fact all dogs) and the dog shows as much as Terry does.

Ingaborge

Ingaborge Dobes are owned by Donald V. Simmons, popular professional handler, of Silver Springs, Maryland, who has been involved in Dobermans over a goodly period of time.

His busy handling schedule has of necessity limited Don's activities as a breeder. Nonetheless his famous dog, Champion Encore's Black Rites, has established a line himself as the sire of twenty-nine champions to date, many of them multiple champion producers as well.

Black Rites was sired by Champion Dolph von Tannenwald ex Champion Ericka von Tannenwald and was bred by Toni McMorris and owned by Mr. and Mrs. Donald Simmons.

Champion Beaulane Love-Rites of Encore, Black Rites's daughter from Champion Beaulane the Gypsy Moth, was the foundation bitch on whom Sue and Don Simmons based their breeding program. Many other successful breeders as well have based their programs

1. Ch. Fanfare's Ringmaster, owned by Theresa A. Lazzaro and Patricia W. Laurans, on the day of his retirement at the age of five years. He went Best in Show, all-breeds, at Central New York Kennel Club, October, 1971. Handled by J. Monroe Stebbins, Jr.
2. Ch. Fanfare's Ringmaster in 1970, handled by J. Monroe Stebbins. By Ch. Laudor Fanfare ex Heide's Kriss. Born in 1966, bred by Shirley Henderson.

1▲   ▼2

NEWTON K.C.
AUGUST 30, 1975
BEST
IN
SHOW
A BUSHMAN PHOTO

1▲   ▼2

230

3 ◄

4 ►

5 ►

1. Ch. Talacon Daisy Upsala, by Ch. Tedell's Eleventh Hour ex Ch. Bansula Van Majer, won an all-breed Best in Show from the Open Class while en route to championship. Daisy's famous sire, Ch. Tedell Eleventh Hour, was the youngest Dobe ever to go Best in Show. Daisly herself was noted for her gorgeous eye, elegance, and beautiful type. She won the Quaker City Doberman Specialty in 1980 from the Veterans Class. Owned by Barbara and Joseph Micallef. Handled by Theresa A. Lazzaro, Gaylordsville, Connecticut.

2. Ch. Fanfare's Ringmaster winning his first points from the Puppy Class at age seven months; handled by his owner, Terry Lazzaro, under judge Major B. Godsel. Co-owner, Patricia W. Laurans.

3. Ch. Kay Hill's Study in Wine at Camden County in 1964. Jane Kay handling. William L. Kendrick, judge.

4. Ch. Kay Hill's The Moon Witch as Best Puppy at Norfolk in 1962. Handled by Jane Kay for owners Edna and Frank Gunn.

5. Ch. Kay Hill's The Wizard Witch in 1962. May 1960–April 1974. One of the most famed of the many important dogs from this outstanding kennel.

6. Ch. Kay Hill's Paint The Town Red in January 1957. Owned by Jane Kay, Kay Hills Kennels.

◄ 6

231

1. Ch. Kay Hill's The Wizard Witch taking one of her Best in Show wins at Talbot Kennel Club in June 1962. Jane Kay, owner-handler.
2. Ch. Kay Hill's The Merrye Witch, owned by Frank Amsden, taking a nice win at the Doberman Pinshcer Club of Florida, January 1982. Jane Kay handling.
3. Ch. Kay Hill's Witch Sprite taking Best of Breed and first in the Working Group, Harrisburg, March 1962. Jane Kay handling.
4. The Doberman bitch behind Kay Hill. Ch. Westerholz Elita completing her title at the Florida Doberman Specialty, early 1950s' George Rood handling for Jane Kay, Harrisburg, Pennsylvania.
5. Ch. Kay Hill's Witch Power, from the first breeding of Ch. Kay Hill's Paint The Town Red to Ch. Borong The Warlock. Bred and handled by Jane Kay, Kay Hill Dobermans.

on Black Rites and his progeny. In 1969 Rites and his sister, Champion Encore's Mystic Melody, scored a clean sweep in the puppy competition at the Doberman Pinscher Club of America National Specialty, Rites taking Best Puppy in the Specialty while Melody was the Futurity winner. Sad to say, Rites died in his prime at only six years of age.

As a handler, Don's current "superstar" and young hopeful as this book is being written is a Rites grandson, Sherluck's Castle Rock, who was the 1983 Doberman Pinscher Club of America Futurity Puppy and Best Puppy at the National Specialty. He took both of his "majors" from the puppy classes, so he should be sporting the title "champion" by the time you are reading this.

Jemstar

New recruits to the Doberman world, but ones we feel sure are here to remain, are Dr. and Mrs. Clarence E. Woodward of Somers, New York, and Holly Woodward.

It was in June 1979 that the Woodwards, who had previously owned Beagles, a Dachshund and a Poodle, set out to find a Doberman for their family, since this was a breed whose beauty and elegance they had long admired. They wanted one combining these assets along with good sound temperament, so they very wisely proceeded to shop carefully to see what might be available among the breeders. They found their dog in a most appealing puppy, eight weeks old when they took her home after five visits to make absolutely certain that *she* was the one. She was bred by Michael Seligman, sired by Champion Red Sun's Notorious (Champion Van Major's Elijah's Red Sun-Van Major's Get Up and Go) from My-A-Mar's Venus De Milo (Ki Jan's Jason ex Ms. My-A of Marko, C.D.), representing Tarrado, Steb's, Gra-Lemor and Highbriar lines on the sire's side and Marks Tey, Dolph von Tannenwald and Ahrtal on the dam's.

Pointing out that the puppies had long since been nominated, and thus it was foolish not to do so, Mr. Seligman persuaded the Woodwards to bring their puppy, when the time arrived, to the Quaker City Doberman Pinscher Club Futurity in December 1979. She took second in her class of fourteen, her very first time in the ring, judged by Gwen DeMilta.

With a bit of urging from friends, the Woodwards turned their Blackstar's Rani Jemma over to Jane Forsyth to be shown, under whose handling she promptly accounted for nine points, including Best of Winners at the 1980 Quaker City Specialty a year later. When the Forsyths retired from handling, Terry Lazzaro took over Jemma for her second "major."

In July 1981 Jemma became Champion Blackstar's Rani Jemma. Terry had previous commitments so could not handle her as a "special" and Gwen DeMilta took over the bitch. It was under her handling that Jemma made it to the Top Twenty in five months of limited showing, winning the breed eighteen times, Group I three times, Group II twice, Group II once and A Group fourth.

She won the 1982 Top Twenty, then, on February 6, 1983, had a litter of three red males sired by Champion Pajant's Encore v Rockelle, all show prospects. One, Jemstar The Bard v Rockelle, earned two "majors" as a puppy. Another, Jemstar Oberon v Alisaton, was pointed as a puppy and received a "major" from the American-bred Class at 13 months. Jemma has earned the W.A.C. and has one leg on the C.D. The Woodwards are expecting that she will be named to the Register of Merit at the next National.

Kay Hill

Kay Hill Dobermans are a legend within their own time in the Doberman Pinscher world, and I doubt that there is a Doberman fancier alive who does not know and respect the outstanding dogs and bitches with whom Jane Kay attained so many significant honors.

It all began in the early 1950's when Jane (Mrs. Harold) Kay acquired future Champion Westerholz Elita, a daughter of International Champion Beltane of Tamarac (Champion Ximines of Elblac, C.D.-Zita of Elblac) from Champion Erika of Damhof (Champion Kama of Westphalia-Topaz of Westphalia). Elita started her match show career at an early age and did well, then was shown a bit in conformation competition at the point shows. But it was through the whelping box that her greatest contribution was made, and that was very notable.

For her first litter (and Jane's own first Dobe litter) Elita was bred to Champion Gaylord of Westphalia by Champion Delegate

234

1. Ch. Kay Hill's Paint The Town Red and Kay Hill's Slightly Scarlet winning Best Working Group Brace with their breed-owner-handler, Jane Kay, under Len Carey at Westminster 1958. This was the first time in history that a pair of *red* Dobermans accounted for this honor at the Garden!

2. Kay Hill's Kat On A Hot Tin Roof pictured at a few days past six months old. Winning The Puppy Class at the Quaker City Specialty in 1966, handled by breeder Jane Kay.

3. The great bitch, Ch. Kay Hill's Paint The Town Red, pictured in 1957. Bred and owned by Jane Kay.

4. A lovely portrait-photo of Ch. Kay Hill's Takeswon to Nowon at eight years and three months. A multiple Best in Show and Group winner and sire of many champions. Owned by Jane Kay.

5. Ch. Beaulane Love-Rites of Encore, by Ch. Encore's Black Rites ex Ch. Beaulane the Gypsy Moth. Love was Don and Sue Simmons's foundation bitch and was the dam of champions.

6. Ch. Kay Hill's Takeswon to Nowon going Grand Prize Futurity Dog at the Doberman Pinscher Club of America Futurity Stakes in October 1965. This is the only dog in the history of the Doberman Pinscher Club of America to be an all-breed Best in Show *before* becoming Grand Prize Futurity Winner. Jane Kay, breeder-owner-handler.

7. Ch. Encore's Black Rites, 1970 Doberman Pinscher Club of America Best Puppy and Best Futurity Puppy, pictured with Black Rites's litter sister, Ch. Encore's Mystic Melody, Grand Prize Futurity winner. Both became Best in Show winners. Photo courtesy of Don Simmons, Silver Spring, Maryland.

8. Ch. Kay Hill's Black Enchantress, by Ch. Defender of Jan Har ex Ch. Westerholz Elite, born August 15, 1955, taking Best Puppy at the New York–Connecticut Specialty in 1955. Judge, Jane Kamp (now Forsyth).

9. Kay Hill's The Conjure Witch, 10 months old, taking Reserve Winners Dog at Harrisburg, March 1962. Jane Kay handling.

10. Ch. Kay Hill's Red Letter Day in September 1970. Charles Hamilton, judge; Jane Kay handling.

v.d. Elbe ex Champion Adithkin O'Lon. Although on paper, as she studied in preparation for it, the plans for these puppies would strike one as being the creation of something spectacular, when the litter arrived Jane found them to be disappointing. So a different approach was taken next time.

Although he was still little more than a puppy, and not yet even a champion, Jane selected Dr. Wilfred Shute's young dog, Defender of Jan-Har, to be the sire of Elita's second litter. This time she produced three champions, including the great bitch Champion Kay Hill's Paint The Town Red and littermates Champion Kay Hill's Black Enchantress and Champion Kay Hill's Ebonetta. The latter was sold to Canada where she was highly successful as a show bitch and as a producer.

Needless to say, with a bitch of "Red's" excellence among the progeny in the first litter, Jane could hardly wait to try the same combination a second time, and so Elita was sent back to Defender. This time they produced Champion Kay Hill's Something Special and Kay Hill's Slightly Scarlet, the latter being the bitch who made up half the brace (with Paint The Town Red) which won Best Working Dog Brace at Westminster in 1958—the first such honor for red Dobermans. Scarlet became the dam of Champion Kay Hill's Seigfried v Hagen, who was to become the sire of Jane's first Grand Prize Futurity winner, Champion Kay Hill's Study in Wine.

It was then decided to try Elita with Champion Dobe Acres Cinnamon. Champion Kay Hill's Rubietta, Champion Kay Hill's Fiddler's Folly, Champion Kay Hill's Mandarin Red, C.D.X. and Champion Kay Hill's Amador Allegre were the results.

The winning which Paint The Town Red might have done had it not been for two missing teeth probably would have been very spectacular; as it was, she finished her title under George Rood's handling, then was shown a bit as a "special" by Jane. She won the Pittsburgh Specialty one year in very hot competition and had multiple Groups to her credit but never a Best in Show. Her "children," however, took care of that for her.

Jane did not get all that excited over the two missing teeth. She never made any effort to conceal the fact, and when asked her own feelings in the matter she replied (saying "you can quote me") that she considered this merely a fault—to her not as serious as a sloppy topline or poor fore and aft angulation, giving as an example that it takes two or three generations to breed out excess length, but only one generation to correct missing teeth.

Dr. E. S. Montgomery predicted that Paint The Town Red, before she had even been bred, would become the most prepotent bitch the Doberman Fancy had seen in many a year. How correct a prediction this turned out to be!

Champion Kay Hill's Paint The Town Red was bred for her first litter to Champion Patton's Ponder of Torn, bringing forth an all-champion litter consisting of Champion Kay Hill's Caroletta, Champion Kay Hill's Gold Braid and Champion Kay Hill's Painted Coquette. Jane had planned to repeat the breeding, but Ponder's death caused a change of plans. Tri-International Champion Borong The Warlock, C.D. (Champion Astor v Grensweg, C.D. ex Champion Florowill Allure, C.D.X.) was selected and that was the start of the "Witch" litters that have gained such fame.

The breedings to Warlock were repeated three times with champions in each and three Best in Show winners in the second one. "Red" produced eleven champions during her lifetime, including a daughter, Champion Kay Hill's Witch Soubretta, who broke the record as a brood bitch (which had previously been held by Meadowmist Isis vom Ahrtal) and who is the Top Producing Dobe bitch of all time.

Speaking further of the missing teeth, Jane states that only a small percentage of "Red" puppies were born with this fault, and that the factor jumped a generation and then died out. Occasionally she would get a puppy with two missing teeth in the same spot as had been the case with "Red," but never more than one puppy in a litter, and usually none.

Would our readers believe that, prior to owning the breed, Jane was deathly afraid of Dobermans? Because she was, and that's the truth! It was her cousin, Frank Laventhal, who owned Beltara Dobermans, who finally "cured" her. It was done by a quite innocent-sounding invitation to meet Frank halfway (at Philadelphia, between Harrisburg, Pennsylvania and New York), for lunch. After some

1. Ch. Kay Hill's Majorette v Heiko, Ch. Dobermar's Fabian, and Ch. Kay Hill's Caroletta in Florida during 1960. Fabian belonged to the Martins, the others to Jane Kay.
2. Ch. Ambradobe's Cantatrice, litter sister to Choirmaster, with Jane Kay handling for owners F. T. Amsden and E. W. Broderick.

1. Ch. Rubigold's Deutuda, by Ch. Kay Hill's Gold Braid ex Ch. Kay Hill's Rubietta, winning the Working Group. Jane Kay handling at Warren, Ohio, in 1961.
2. Ch. Kay Hill's Dealers Choice, by Ch. Dolph von Tannenwald ex Ch. Kay Hill's Kat-A-Maron, winning Best in Show for owner Mrs. Bruce Moray. Photo courtesy of Jane Kay.
3. Ch. Kay Hill's Luck Is A Lady. Photo courtesy of Jane Kay.
4. Ch. Kay Hill's Mandarin Red, born May 1957, By Ch. Dobe Acres Cinnamon ex Ch. Westerholz Elita. With Jane Kay at Danville Kennel Club in 1959.
5. Kay Hill's Luck Is A Lady, by Ch. Dolph von Tannenwald ex Kay Hill's Kay-A-Marow, in April 1970 in Iowa. Photo courtesy of Jane Kay.
6. The noted Dobe bitch, Ch. Kay Hill's The Wizard Witch, in March 1962. Jane Kay, Kay Hill Dobermans.
7. Ch. Sheck of Wilmaur, by Kilburn Monk ex Ch. Kilburn Busybody, was bred by Margaret (Marge) Kilburn and owner-handled by Frances Walker. In 11 times shown, this lovely Dobe accounted for eight all-breed Bests in Show.
8. Future Ch. Kay Hill's Red Letter Day at seven months, one week old. Winning under Isidore Schoenberg. Jane Kay handling.

▲7

► 8

239

1. This gorgeous Doberman is the Best-in-Show-winning Ch. Kilburn's Allure, by Ch. Emperor of Marienland ex Ch. Dow's Illena of Marienland. Mrs. Margaret (Marge) Kilburn, Pottstown, Pennsylvania. From the Kilburn "A" litter, which included three who won Best in Show.
2. Ch. Kilburn Ballerina was born on June 16, 1944. She was a Best in Show winner by Ch. Domossi of Marienland (Dictator's full brother) from Ch. Dow's Illena of Marienland. From the Kilburn Dobermans, Mrs. Margaret (Marge) Kilburn.
3. Ch. Dow's Cassie v Kienlesberg and Ch. Dow's Cora v Kienlesberg, two magnificent bitches who stand behind the Kilburn Dobermans. Photo courtesy of Mrs. Margaret (Marge) Kilburn.
4. Ch. Dow's Dame of Kilburn in March 1948. Owned by Mrs. Eleanor M. Brown; handled by Larry Downey. Judge, Alva Rosenberg; breeder Margaret (Marge) Kilburn. Mrs. Brown herself became a noted Doberman breeder, and Dame was her foundation bitch. By Dictator from Ch. Dow's Dodie of Kienlesberg.

conversations regarding the state of Frank's sanity, Jane agreed. Following a pleasant luncheon filled with family news and conversation, Frank asked Jane to stop by his car for a second—and there it was—a black Doberman puppy which Frank insisted Jane must take, as he had stolen—or to be more accurate *PUPNAPPED* her. She was a puppy belonging to Ted Nintzel by Champion Beltane of Tamarack (owned by Frank Laventhal) from Champion Erica of Damhoff. The "pup-napped" part refers to the fact that Frank had stopped at Ted Nintzel's kennel early that morning where he grabbed one of the two puppies which he knew were by his stud. He telephoned the Nintzels before they got out to the kennel to let them know where she was. Anyway, Jane continued to protest that she wanted nothing to do with that "thing" until finally Frank succeeded in wearing her down with his continued insistence. So she took the puppy, only with the understanding that she would call and explain the situation to Ted and let him know she wanted no part of his puppy and that she would return it to him.

The puppy never went back, though. After nestling in her lap throughout the drive, and kissing her face periodically, it had Jane pretty thoroughly won over by the time they reached Harrisburg. So when she made the call to Ted to explain, the question was not, "How soon can I return her?" but rather, "How much do you want for her? You know you're not getting her back." This little puppy was Westerholz Elita. She gained her championship, and this story opened with her accomplishments as a producer.

Jane Kay's breeding program was not a large one. She bred a total of 22 litters, from which thirty gained their titles. Jane was strictly a "for quality" breeder. I have read, and it seems very likely the case, that Jane Kay from the standpoint of percentages holds the record for having bred more champions from the number of litters produced than any other breeder in the United States.

The famous names at Kay Hill have included some of the best known in the American Dog Show world, such as Champion Kay Hill's Takeswon to Nowon, who was sold to Mrs. Michael Pym as a puppy but then came back to Jane when Mrs. Pym retired from dogs. Takeswon to Nowon was sired by Champion Kay Hill's The Wizard Witch from Champion Rubigold's Harmony of Kay Hill. He won multiple Bests in Show and Groups and has sired Best in Show and Group winning champions. The last bitch she bred at Kay Hill was Red Letter Day by Champion Highland Satan's Image.

Kilburn

The foundation for Kilburn Dobermans was laid back in 1941 when Marge and Paul Kilburn purchased Bock of Kernia, partly as a show dog and partly to learn more about the breed. Shown a few times, Bock soon took his place as being of mediocre quality, but he taught the Kilburns a great deal about what to look for in acquiring a second Doberman. This was done at Dick Webster's Marienland Kennels in Baltimore, Maryland, to which Marge and Paul made a visit, selecting a gorgeous bitch puppy who was available "only to someone interested in breeding" for the then quite huge price of $150.00.

The choice was a good one, as the puppy selected became, quickly and easily, Champion Dow's Illena of Marienland.

Illena was bred first to Champion Emperor of Marienland, by whom she produced three Best in Show winners: International Champion Kilburn Avenger, Champion Kilburn Award, and Champion Kilburn Allure, plus Champion Kilburn Audacity. Later she was bred to Dictator's full brother, Champion Domossi of Marienland, which brought forth the Best in Show winning Champion Kilburn Ballerina, the Group winner Kilburn Bushranger, Champion Kilburn Busybody and Champion Kilburn Blaze. Champion Kilburn Audacity, from the Emperor-Illena litter, bred to Champion Alcor v Milsdod produced Best in Show winning Champion Kilburn Conqueror, Champion Kilburn Cameron, and Champion Kilburn Celebrity. The latter finished with all requirements, then lost one point when a bitch she had defeated was disqualified. Losing the point so angered the owners that they refused to show again.

Illena was bred to Emperor a second time, producing the foundation for Von Cort Kennel in Champion Kilburn Escort. Then twice to Champion Dow's Dusty of Kienlesberg, the first time producing Champion Kilburn Gamin and Champion Kilburn Glenna of Carwin, and the second time producing Best in

242

5

6

7

1. Ch. Kilburn Ideal at his first match show winning Best in Match, handled by owner Marge Kilburn under judge Richard Kerns. By Ch. Dow's Dusty v. Kienlesberg ex Ch. Dow's Illena of Marienland. A Best in Show winner, one of the many bred and/or owned by Margaret (Marge) Kilburn.

2. The Kilburn "B" litter, by Ch. Domossi of Marienland (Dictator's full brother) from Ch. Dow's Illena of Marienland. Pictured are Ch. Kilburn Ballerina (Best in Show winner), Ch. Kilburn Bushranger (Group winner), Ch. Kilburn Blaze, and Ch. Kilburn Busybody. Margaret Kilburn, breeder-owner, Kilburn Dobermans, Pottstown, Pennsylvania.

3. Ch. Kilburn's Escort, son of Ch. Emperor of Marienland ex Ch. Dow's Illena v Marienland. The foundation dog for Von Cort Kennels, Honolulu, Hawaii. Photo courtesy of Marge Kilburn.

4. Twelve little Dobermans, eight weeks old, by Fair Glory of Marienland ex Ch. Dow's Dodie of Marienland, bred by Margaret (Marge) Kilburn, then at Shanesville, Pennsylvania. This was the "F" litter with Flair, Fancy, and Fettish.

5. Ch. Kilburn's Audacity, member of the Emperor–Illena "A" litter, bred and owned by Mrs. Margaret (Marge) Kilburn. Another of the Kilburn numerous Best in Show Dobes!

6. Ch. Kilburn's Escort, C.D. bred by Mrs. Margaret Kilburn. By Ch. Emperor of Marienland ex Ch. Dow's Illena of Marienland. Photo courtesy of Peggy Adamson.

7. This is the great Ch. Dow's Illena of Marienland, by Ch. Westphalia's Rameses, U.D.T. ex Ch. Dow's Cora v. Kienlesberg. Bred by Richard C. Webster and owned by Margaret (Marge) Kilburn, Illena produced 12 champions by three sires. Five of her progeny were all-breed Best in Show winners.

8. Ch. Kilburn Allure, black and rust bitch by Ch. Emperor v Marienland ex Ch. Dow's Illena v Marienland. Photo courtesy of Marge Kilburn.

8

1 ◄   2 ►

3 ▼

1. Ch. Kilburn Jingo, owned by Mr. and Mrs. Richard Robinson, was bred by Margaret (Marge) Kilburn. A famous winner of the 1940's.
2. Ch. Dow's Illena of Marienland, the dam of 12 champions, was owned by Marge Kilburn, for whose kennel she was foundation bitch back in the early 1940's. Illena was by Ch. Westphalia's Rameses, U.D.T. ex Ch. Dow's Cora of Kienlesberg.
3. The multiple Best-in-Show-winning Ch. Kilburn's Award, bred by Mrs. Margaret (Marge) Kilburn. Owned by Albert Meyer.
4. A fabulous historical photo depicts the late Alva Rosenberg, dean of all dog-show judges, awarding Best in Group to Ch. Kilburn Jingo, who went on to Best in Show later that day at Baton Rouge, Louisiana in 1948. Jingo was by Ch. Alcor v. Millsdod ex Ch. Kilburn Audacity. One of the famed Kilburn Dobes belonging to Margaret (Marge) Kilburn of Pottstown, Pennsylvania, his breeder. Jingo was sold to Mr. and Mrs. Richard Robinson.
5. Ch. Kilburn's Conqueror, handled by Nicky Finn, taking Best of Breed at Golden Gate Kennel Club January 1950 for breeder-owner Mrs. Marge Kilburn. Conqueror was by Ch. Alcor v Millsdod ex Ch. Kilburn Audacity.

▲4

► 5

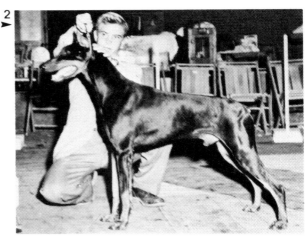

1. Ch. Kilburn's Conqueror, Best in Show winner by Ch. Alcor v Millsdod ex Ch. Kilburn Audacity, handled here by Nicky Finn for breeder-owner Mrs. Margaret (Marge) Kilburn, Pottstown, Pennsylvania.
2. Ch. Kilburn Jingo, by Ch. Alcor v Millsdod ex Ch. Kilburn Audacity, winning Best in Show at Baton Rouge, Louisiana in 1948. Bred by Margaret (Marge) Kilburn. Owned by Mr. and Mrs. Richard Robinson.
3. Bock of Kernia, linebred from Ch. Muck of Brunia, was the first of the Kilburn Dobermans. With him here is Ch. Dow's Illena of Marienland.
4. A photo filled with nostalgia! Ch. Kilburn Blaze, handled by John Cholley, with Frank Grant judging, making a good win for breeder-owner Margaret (Marge) Kilburn. One from the famous "B" litter, by Ch. Domossi of Marienland ex Ch. Dow's Illena of Marienland.
5. The Group-winning Ch. Kilburn Jest is one of the important members of the "J" litter, by Ch. Alcor v Milsdod ex Ch. Kilburn Audacity, from the Kilburn Dobermans.
6. Ch. Kilburn Cameron, by Ch. Alcor v Millsdod ex Ch. Kilburn Audacity. Bred by Mrs. M. Kilburn; owned by Edward Ackerman, Louisville, Kentucky.
7. Ch. Dow's Dame of Kilburn, the Best-in-Show-winning foundation bitch of Brown's Dobermans, owned by Eleanor and Jack Brown. By Ch. Dictator v Glenhugel ex Ch. Dow's Dodie v Kienlesberg. Kilburn Dobes have provided foundation stock for a good number of highly prestigious breeders.
8. The classic head of Ch. Dow's Illena v Marienland, foundation bitch behind the Kilburn Dobes.
9. Ch. Dow's Deedo of Kilburn, litter sister to Dame, was the only black in the litter. Margaret K. Kilburn, owner.
10. Ch. Kitchawan's Cara Mia, by Ch. Dacki v d Elbe ex Kitchawan's Kilburn Mia, from the Kilburn Kennels.

Show winning International Champion Kilburn Ideal.

Champion Dow's Dodie of Kienlesberg was acquired by the Kilburns, bred to Champion Dictator v Glenhugel, and made a very significant contribution to the breed in the form of Champion Dow's Dame of Kilburn (a Best in Show winner and the foundation bitch for Brown's Dobermans), Dow's Ditty of Marienland (who became the foundation for Ahrtal Kennels and was the dam of Isis of Ahrtal), Group winning Champion Dow's Departure of Marienland, and other champions.

The Emperor-Illena daughter, Champion Kilburn Audacity, was bred twice to the Dusty-Illena son, International Champion Kilburn Ideal. Some excellent producers came in the first of these litters: Kilburn Mia, who was dam of the Best in Show winning Champion Kitchewan's Cara Mia, and Kilburn Monk, who was the sire of three Best in Show dogs, plus several champions. The second litter also "hit the jackpot" with Champion Kilburn Nudge, foundation for Westwind Kennels and a Best in Show winner.

Audacity's early breeding to Champion Victor v Milsdod was later repeated, too, this time giving two Best in Show winners, Champion Kilburn X-tra and Champion Kilburn Jingo, and the Group winning Champion Kilburn Jest.

Marge Kilburn never really had the heart of a breeder. She found it more than she could bear when tragedies occurred, and so her entire breeding program was limited to about five years' activity. What a credit to its success when one considers that in that length of time she produced probably fewer than one hundred puppies; but these puppies grew into dogs who contributed inestimably to the quality of Dobermans in the United States, and they had far more beneficial impact than many a far broader breeding program!

Liquorish

Liquorish Dobermans are owned by Grace and Jeff Joffe who live in Fort Lauderdale, Florida, and they have earned a position of tremendous respect among fanciers of the Doberman breed.

When Grace was a child she wanted to be a veterinarian. Her parents allowed her to bring in stray animals and nurse them back to health. The turkey her mother had bought to fatten up for a family Thanksgiving dinner became a pet, and some other form of dinner was served instead. However, Grace's desire to become a veterinarian ended abruptly when she learned that one of their duties was putting animals to sleep. After that she contented herself with nursing the strays.

During her fifth year of teaching school, a group of her students gave Grace a beautiful coal-black kitten for her birthday. The Joffes were living in a second floor apartment at that time, where animals were not allowed. The floors were wooden, and every time Mohammed ran across the floor, the downstairs neighbor would yell up to Grace to stop her dancing. Mohammed grew into an eighteen pound beauty who resembled a baby panther.

Mohammed was the Joffes' "dog substitute." He walked on lead, pounced on Jeff's chest when he came home from work, and licked Jeff's beard.

Both of the Joffes wanted a dog, but dogs require time and that was a luxury the Joffes could not arrange. They received a gift from a friend—another cat, also male, with gorgeous aqua eyes. His name was Cleopatra until Grace discovered he was a male. Consequently Cleopatra became "Stinky." Mohammed and Stinky got along famously and were really quite a team. Still something was missing!

Grace's hunger for a dog was growing stronger, and when she and Jeff had been married for ten years, she became adamant about it. Her mother-in-law lent her support to Grace's cause in favor of a dog. Jeff finally conceded. Two women working on one man would weaken even the strongest willed! Collectively they decided that it is not the amount of time one spends with an animal—it is the quality of time.

Jeff wanted a pure bred. They bought books, visited the local obedience club, and consulted vets regarding the hardiest breeds to have in south Florida. At the top of each list was the Doberman Pinscher.

Grace Joffe was then afraid of Dobermans—never had known one, just had heard that they turn on their masters. Now, fourteen years after the purchase of their first Dobe, who is still with them, the Joffes cannot imagine life without this handsome and

1▲

▼2

1. Ch. Kilburn Bushranger, Group-winning sire of several champions and a son of Ch. Domossi of Marienland ex Ch. Dow's Illena of Marienland. One of the Kilburn Dobes.
2. Ch. Kilburn Avenger winning Best in Show, handled by Nicky Finn for breeder-owner Mrs. Margaret (Marge) Kilburn.

1. Alice Mills with Ch. Alcor v Millsdod; Margaret (Marge) Kilburn with Ch. Kilburn Conqueror. Two great Dobermans snapped informally while waiting for the judging at a dog show.
2. Ch. Alfaro's Liquorish Cutty Sark, C.D.X., ROM, sire of Ch. El Jean's Bit of Clipper, Ch. El Jean's Freya Adonica and, pointed, El Jean's Bit of Liquorish, C.D., WAC. Grace and Jeff Joffe, Liquorish Dobermans, Ft. Lauderdale, Florida. This is the Joffes's well-known "Clipper."
3. The excellent bitch, "Lucky," is Ch. Kay Hill's Luck Be A Lady. Owned by Grace and Jeff Joffe.
4. Am., Can., Dom., Mex., and Int. Ch. Liquorish Ron Rico, Am., Can., and Mex. C.D., ROM at age seven-and-a-half years winning his last Best of Breed in 1979. Jeff Brucker handling here for owners Jeff and Grace Joffe.

loving breed. They have very definite ideas about the Doberman. It's the greatest breed going. The full potential of an individual can be reached when working people have no more than two Dobes living with them at a time. The ultimate is for the dog to be a complete Doberman—beauty, brains and good temperament. This can be reached only when the dog lives in the home and people make the commitment to work with each aspect.

For their first Doberman, the Joffes selected in 1970 Gayamon The Brandy Alexander, C.D.X., Canadian C.D., American and Canadian pointed, who is still with them. Two weeks after they brought their four-month doe-like "Brandy" home, breeder Liz Fraizer called them to be ready at 6:30 A.M. Saturday to go to their first fun match. After two hours of driving to their destination, she placed Brandy on the tailgate of her station wagon, took her ears down, cut a few hairs, placed a contraption (martengale collar) on Brandy's neck, presented Grace with a piece of leather (actually liver) and showed her what to do when she entered the ring. A few moments later a first place ribbon was in Grace's hand. Still later she and Brandy returned to the ring—another first place ribbon! And so it continued until Brandy had won Best Puppy in the match. Need I add that they were "hooked"?

Brandy, handled by Jeff Joffe, took points, and Best of Opposite Sex from Dr. Boshell, at a local show. At this point there was a lack of guidance from anyone, and being novices, the Joffes just "did their thing" in obedience and let the breed ring wait. Brandy learned quickly, and in south Miami he was known as "Brandy the Wonder Dog."

The Joffes are interested in creating better dogs in each succeeding generation—not just more dogs. At the Doberman Pinscher Club of America National Specialty for 1980, Grace Joffe was presented with the first Cope-Rescue Committee Award for her contribution in curbing the overpopulation of Dobermans. Thirteen bitches in the state of Florida, who were brought to be bred to the Joffe's champion stud dog, were spayed and the Joffes are happy to have been able to convince the people that their bitches should not be bred.

Brandy's half sister was next acquired, Gayamon The Sheri K' Joffa, C.D. (1971-1982). She was lovely but hated the breed and

obedience rings. The thrill of having these two "girls" was like watching two living bookends. Where one was, the other was close behind, and Sheri quickly became Brandy's pal.

Sheri was bred to the Joffes' Champion Liquorish the Ron Rico, C.D., ROM and produced Liquorish The Sheri Mateus, C.D.X., AD., who was the Doberman Pinscher Club of America Obedience Award winner for highest score in Open in 1977.

The Joffes shipped Brandy to Champion Highbriar Osiris, W.A.C., for her first and only breeding. They were hoping for more bone from "Baron" and wanted to keep the elegance that Brandy had inherited from Dolph. Out of that breeding came Rico—American, Canadian, Dominican, Mexican, International Champion Liquorish The Ron Rico, C.D., ROM (1972-1981). Grace Joffe remarks, "Had we been more knowledgeable at that point, we would have kept another pup or two from that litter. Each one enjoyed a good home, but none of the owners followed through on their promises to show."

Rico made quite a record for himself as a class dog, taking 25 Reserve Winners in five months. It was Marge Kilburn who advised the Joffes, after she had given Rico his 25th Reserve, to take him home and let him mature, and the Joffes had the good sense to do as this very knowledgeable lady had suggested.

Three months later, under Maxwell Riddle, Rico went from the Bred-by-Exhibitor Class to a three point "major" and on to Best of Breed—which made the Joffes realize that Mrs. Kilburn really knew what she was talking about!

A few months later, Jeff Brucker handled Rico to second in the Open Black Class at the National Specialty in San Diego under judge Derek Rayne. In December, just a few shows after the National, he finished his championship with an all-breed Best in Show. Rico started his "specials" career in January on the tough Florida circuit, winning one Best of Breed toward the end. From there it was uphill for his nine months of showing, during which he amassed five Bests in Show, No. 2 Doberman, and Doberman Pinscher Club of America Awards for Most Bests of Breed, Most Group Firsts and Placements, and Best in Show. Rico also took a Best in Show on the way to his Canadian title.

His C.D. was quickly earned by Rico, who enjoyed his W.A.C. test, loved tracking, and couldn't wait to get to Schutzhund practice. He was a working Doberman who did anything and everything asked of him.

Jeff Joffe took Rico to the foreign countries for his CACIB, and finally both the Joffes put him through his tracking and man-work to pass his CACIB, thus making him the only International Champion in the Top Twenty in Canada.

Rico was truly a dog of a lifetime and emulated all that a Doberman Pinscher should be!

Because of their experience with people reneging on their promises to show the puppies they had bought, the Joffes were afraid to let "Clipper" go until he was a champion. They knew full well they would not be able to keep two males in their home, but for three years they succeeded in warding off any tragedies until the Ft. Lauderdale show, where Clipper gained his championship points and Rico took Best of Breed. It should have been one of the happiest days in the Joffes' dog- show lives! Rico was having his picture taken. Clipper was waiting ringside for his. There were many males around, but Rico pulled out of his handler's hand and made a dash for Clipper's neck. Rico allowed Grace Joffe to put her fingers in his mouth to release his fang from Clipper's neck. However, to quote Mrs. Joffe, "Some nut kept kicking Rico in his rear, damaging a lumbar vertebra for the rest of his life."

Clipper, now Champion Alfaro's Liquorish Cutty Sark, C.D.X., ROM (1974-1983), was fine and had to leave the Joffes' home three days later. But he left with his titles and took a big portion of the Joffes' hearts with him. Living for three years with an animal who was the clown of the house and possessed such a loving personality is not conducive to a final farewell. Many trips were made to Memphis, Tennessee to visit Clipper during the remainder of his lifetime!

El Jean's Bit of Liquorish, C.D., WAC, pointed, joined the Joffe family in 1978 and is still with them. She was obtained from Clipper's co-owners when she was four months old, a gorgeous bitch who moved like a dream. Some of the best hands in the country were on the other end of her lead. Many dollars and only eight points to her championship at four years of age convinced the Joffes that they should breed her. They did so, to Champion Duberet's Rocket Cruiser. Three of these pups are on their way, having championship points, and several others are almost ready for obedience. "Liqi" has brought a bit of her sire, Clipper, back to the Joffes in many ways.

Champion Kay Hills Luck Be A Lady, born in 1972, is still with the Joffes, who acquired her in September 1978. She was bred to Rico and produced Liquorish The New Year Joy and Liquorish The New Year Wishes, both lovely bitches and both "major" pointed.

The second and last breeding of Rico and Luck Be A Lady produced Liquorish Lucky Charm, W.A.C., whose life was snuffed out by a poisonous frog, and Champion Liquorish Rico's Lucky Chance, C.D., ROM, who is the product of a Top Twenty sire and dam. Because they do not plan to campaign him as they did Rico, nor as his dam was campaigned, Lucky Chance must be content with his local wins, which include a Group I and a Group III. He took a 3-point "major" under Robert Salomon, at nine months of age on the tough Florida circuit, and won his other "major" under the author in a big Florida Dobe entry when just over a year old, owner-breeder handled. He took another four-point "major" on the next Florida circuit one year after his first win, under Nick Apollony, and finished his championship by two years of age despite such limited showing.

Lucky Chance has been the *Dog World* magazine standard bearer and is known as being the possessor of many important good qualities. He is an easy dog to live with and tries to please his owners in every possible way. He is a constant reminder of his sire in the love that he spreads, while his clown-like antics are a reminder of his dam. He has been used very sparingly at stud but now has a few show pups who are making their mark in the ring.

All of the Joffes' dogs in the future will be owner-handled. As Grace Joffe comments, "Chance's kids might take longer to reach their championships because of this, but quality dogs will be found by quality judges no

1. Gayamon The Sheri K'Joffe, C.D., the dam of one litter which included the winner of the Doberman Pinscher Club of America award winner of Highest Scoring in Open, 1977. Sheri is quick to recognize a familiar voice over the phone. Jeff and Grace Joffe, owners, Ft. Lauderdale, Florida.

2. Pictured are Am., Can., Dom., Mex., and Int. Ch. Liquorish The Ron Rico, C.D. ROM; his dam, Gayamon The Brandy Alexander, C.D.X., Can. C.D., American and Canadian pointed; and Sheri. All are owned by Jeff and Grace Joffe, Liquorish Dobermans.

1▲   ▼2

matter who handles the dogs."

"Chance" is now being worked for his Open title in obedience, while, for the show ring in the immediate future, the Joffes' hopes are concentrated on the Chance son, Good Luck Fortune O'Liquorish and the little bitch, T.J.'s Liquorish the Rum Runner, and her sister, T.J. Liquorish Liquer. The next breeding under consideration is of Liqu, Rico's granddaughter, to Chance, Rico's son.

Lothlorien

Lothlorien Dobermans are the result of Bunny Lanning's interest in and involvement with the breed, which dates back to about 1957 when, as Bunny says, "At that time there must have been about 4,000 Dobermans in the United States, which is the number there now seems to be in Western Kentucky alone." Bunny's first Doberman's only claim to fame was that of being the oldest Dobe ever recorded. Quoting from *The Doberman Quarterly*, Summer 1976, we find the following notation: "OLDEST DOBERMAN. Fraulein Rakshe, C.D., owned by Bunny Lanning, lived to 16 years, 1 month and 8 days. She caught a squirrel in her 15th year, and slowed down in her last year, dying in her sleep." A very worthwhile accomplishment, actually, comments her owner, as for the entire span of her lifetime she taught her all the things a Doberman should and could be. When Bunny was 16, she put a C.D. on Fraulein Rakshe, and was introduced to the dog show world. Though Rakshe had been spayed, Bunny sent for her pedigree and studied the dogs that had produced her. Essentially just a pet, she nonetheless had some of the "greats" in her background—
Dictator, Domessi and Emperor. Bunny was then determined that she would some day breed Dobermans with the same background to reproduce this fiery, hard, devoted red bitch.

A thirteen-year-old girl living nearby shared Bunny's youthful interest in this project and together they planned their imaginary Doberman kennel. After they had grown up, and Bunny had been to college, married, had children, and her beloved Rakshe had finally died, that same girl with whom she had planned the imaginary kennel years before

found the dog who would become the foundation bitch for Lothlorien and (from California) sent her to Bunny in Kentucky. As Raksha had been, essentially, the result of Peggy Adamson's early Damasyn breeding, so was Smaug. She was a Demetrius granddaughter with a touch of Kay Hill for elegance. Demetrius was the one sire, again quoting Bunny, "...that could give the fire and hardness I felt a Doberman should always have. Anyone who had ever had a Demetrius bitch would know what I mean. Their enormous pride and firm belief in their own superiority to all other dogs gives them a quality all their own."

Having found this prepotent trait, Bunny decided to set it with a linebred Demetrius dog, Champion Karlo von Forsthaus. He was in the Top Twenty at the time, although he was not extensively "specialed." By then Smaug had her C.D. and had done some winning in conformation classes. Karlo seemed to Bunny exactly the right stud for her.

It was at the time of whelping this litter that Bunny Lanning's daughter, Bayberry, became a full partner in Lothlorien Kennels. Bunny had been through surgery at that time, which resulted in her not being able to even bend over the whelping box. And so, at six years of age, Bayberry delivered her first litter with the cool, calm attitude of an obstetrician. She has been whelping Lothlorien litters, and those of friends, ever since.

Bunny kept the littlest bitch from this litter. Her temperament was exactly what was wanted. Eventually she got her C.D., then her C.D.X. and her Schutzhund I degree. Unfortunately, she turned out to be a disappointment as she did not have sufficient breadth of chest. The veterinarian assured Bunny that breeding her would improve the condition; however, after a litter of twelve, she was unshowable. And the puppies were inconsistent, so that breeding direction was dropped from Bunny's plans.

Bunny selected a major-pointed very masculine dog with obedience and Schutzhund degrees to be the sire of her next litter. He finished his show title by going Winners Dog at the National just prior to the breeding and is now Champion Knox's Carbon Copy C.D.X., T.D., ROM, SchH. III, FH. He was of double Diablo Roho linebreeding, thus he would give the tighter pedigree Bunny felt she needed, though he is an outcross. Commenting on this dog, Bunny remarks that when she really got to know him, she easily understood his reputation for outstanding Doberman temperament. As she says, "A regal and courteous gentleman at home, a gentle love with the babies in his family, and the hardest, most courageous Doberman on the Schutzhund field."

This litter produced nine puppies and the consistency Bunny had hoped would be there. The pick bitch was kept for breeding. This one grew up to become Champion Lothlorien's High-Elven Rune. In showing this bitch in the beginning in the puppy classes (handled by Bayberry), the Lannings travelled with the couple who had purchased the show male from the previous litter and who had a young bitch of good breeding. They, too, fell in love with Rune's beauty and personality, helped with her training, and when she was two years old worked with the Lannings to put Rune in the hands of a professional handler to give her the opportunity of reaching full potential as a show bitch. Previous to this she had won three Bests in Match and a High in Trial. It was agreed to co-lease Rune for her first breeding, and a dual kennel began under the name Lothlorien/Cirdan, the latter owned by Sandra and Danny King of Martin, Tennessee.

On Rune's first big weekend out with Charlie Cooper, she came home with a 5-point "major" and Best of Winners. The next weekend it was Best of Breed over six "specials," three of which were Best in Show winners. She went on to take Group I. Over the next twenty shows she garnered the rest of her points (and lots of reserves), always going Best of Winners when she took the purple. Bayberry, at ten, had the thrill of putting a point on her and Best of Opposite Sex. She had put a lot of points on various breeds, even a Group II on a Terrier. But she knows how hard it is to point a Dobe!

While all this was taking place, Rune also earned her C.D. with all scores over 190, and she was being shown in Junior Showmanship, where she helped her young handler qualify for Westminster. The ease with which Rune slipped from one type of competition to another, and her great stamina, proved her to be the working dog she was bred to be. Additionally she was trained in tracking and

Schutzhund work, and in her spare time she became certified as a Therapy Dog. Her favorite task of all is to work with children's groups.

Though the "show homes" of Rune's littermates did not work out, several of the dogs have changed hands and now will be shown. The pick male came back to Carbon Copy's owner, who is grooming him as a replacement for his sire and who plans to make him an Obedience Trial Champion as well. Since Darkstar got his C.D. in three tries after only two months of training, he should make it. The early puppy obedience training that Bunny Lanning gives all her dogs, at six to eight weeks old, makes them easier to train later.

Because Rune is an outcross, Bunny felt that she needed a stud dog with a very tight pedigree. Her selection was a linebred Ahrtal/Hotai dog, Champion Ondega's Dapper Dan, as they seemed properly complementary to one another. It certainly proved to be a good choice, as at the National Specialty Rune and her litter brother won for their sire second place in the strongly contested Stud Dog Class, and Dapper Dan with their Rune kids won first! Also at the National, Rune got her ROM and Bayberry got Best Junior Handler. In addition the male offspring who helped win the Stud Dog Class for Dapper belonged to Danny and Sandra King, owner of Cirdan, Lothlorien's "dual kennel." On July 6, 1985, Champion Lothlorien's High-Elven Rune, C.D.X., ROM became the first ever second-generation champion, Schutzhund-titled Doberman in the USA. Rune did it in style with a V rating in all phases, a 98 in tracking, a 95 in obedience, and a 97 in protection, for High in Trail.

The Kings will keep a bitch from the Rune/Dapper breeding which will be co-owned. Bunny Lanning will keep a male, and both are keeping a red bitch out of their young Dapper son and their Demetrius bitch. She will be named Raksha in honor of the red bitch who started all this.

Bunny Lanning is firm in her belief that among serious breeders and Dobe lovers there has been developing an increasing desire for the breed to be an all 'round working dog, with which she sincerely agrees. She feels that for awhile there was an inclination for a split

1. Gayamon's The Brandy Alexander, C.D.X., American and Canadian pointed, is the foundation bitch at Liquorish Dobermans.
2. Ch. Lujac's Stinger, by Ch. Highland Satan's Image ex Highbriar Willow's Wand. Bred and owned by Jack and Louise Strutt. Judge, A. Peter Knoop. Handler, Charles Cooper. Photo courtesy of Peggy Adamson who is presenting the trophy.
3. Marjorie Brooks's magnificent winner, Ch. Alnwick's Black Fury Bismark, C.D., sired a total of 28 champions. By Ch. Felix vom Ahrtal ex Mikadobe's Flambeau, he was bred by Jeanne M. Borger. Here taking Best of Breed at Des Moines in 1962 under Peggy Adamson who was judging an entry of 60.
4. Ch. Manorie Dobe's Im Pavon v Du Rel, dam of two champions, by Ch. Weichardt's Rosen Cavalier, C.D. ex Ch. Annheim's Dark Imp, C.D. Bred by Marjorie Brooks; owned by Lynn Woods.

to be developing in the breed, which has happened in too many other instances, where one set of dogs has won in conformation with an entirely different group competing in the obedience and working areas. This, in the minds of the public, can lead to a suspicion that breed champions are not mentally or physically as capable as those competing in the obedience and working areas. Now the tendency would seem to be for people seeking show dogs and breeding stock to prefer both conformation and working backgrounds. There are some of the latter to be found, and it appears from the interest lately that their numbers will be increasing in the future. You will note that both Lothlorien and Cirdan Kennels own dogs active in Schutzhund and obedience.

Bunny's husband, Adam Lanning, is a college professor who provides much support for her interest in the Dobes. He is a long time marathoner who runs every day. Each of the dogs, thus, has had the benefit of graduated training which keeps them hard and fit. They also learn the rules of the road, mainly when autos approach: **GET OFF THE ROAD.** Smaug, the Lannings' foundation bitch, once completed the Smoky Mountain Marathon, in 1978 at Oak Ridge, Tennessee, and was awarded a "Finisher's" ribbon which now hangs proudly in the Lannings' trophy room.

Lujac

Lujac Dobermans, at Fern Creek, Kentucky, is the home of the very famous Dobe bitch, Champion Lujac's Stinger. Owners of this establishment are Jack and Louise Strutt, keen enthusiasts of the Doberman breed.

Lujac's Stinger, a black and rust female, was born on May 14, 1971. Her breeding was the very finest, since she is a daughter of American and Canadian Champion Highland's Satan Image (Champion Caesar My Love ex Barryten's C.P. Twink, the latter a daughter of Champion Singendwal's Prince Kuhio and Champion Kay Hills Rubietta). On the dam's side, Stinger is from Highbriar Willow's Wand (by Champion Tarrado's Banque and Champion Highbriar Willo of Allenwood, the latter a Champion Florian vom Ahrtal and Champion Steb's Top Skipper descendant.

Stinger started her show career at nine months of age in December 1972, finishing in 18 shows with wins including a Best of Breed and Group placement while still in the puppy classes. Upon her retirement, following Best of Breed at the Quaker City Doberman Pinscher Club Specialty after one year and ten months of active competition, Stinger had a total record of four all-breed Bests in Show, seven Specialty Bests in Show, 14 times first in the Working Group, ten times Group 2nd, three times Group 3rd, and twice Group 4th. Her Best of Breed wins totalled 46. She was Best of Opposite Sex 31 times. Shown only a total of 112 times, including in the classes and as a "special," this is surely very good going in a breed as competitive as the Doberman!

In 1974, Stinger came out of retirement briefly—just long enough to win Best in the Top Twenty Tournament, which was certainly a very exciting occasion for her owners.

Lyndobe

Lyndobe Kennels are owned by Lynne A. Coleman of Belleville, Michigan, who purchased Champion Sherluck's JFK V Lyndobe, C.D., ROM from Faye and Gary Strauss, Sherluck Dobermans. Lynne put all his titles on him and now owns him in partnership with Noreen De Palma, as she is busy working on the championship title for her Lyndobe's Show Stopper, C.D., W.A.C., who is "major" pointed with a present total of nine points. Both of these dogs are sons of Champion Marienburg Sun Hawk, C.D., the Top Producing Doberman of All Time. Ms. Coleman is keeping her own breeding program, following closely on the Sun Hawk lines.

She also has a Sun Hawk daughter, Lyndobe's Eighty's Lady, C.D., W.A.C., with six points on her championship, and a daughter of Eighty's Lady by Champion Sherluck's JFK V Lyndobe who will be shown this year, as well as Lyndobe's Pack O'Passion, a sister to this youngster who is already pointed at ten months. These were sired by Champion Sherluck's JFK V Lyndobe, C.D., ROM.

Lyndobe's Smoochin' Pooch (black), Lyndobe's Eighty's Lady, C.D., W.A.C., and Lyndobe's Show Stopper, C.D., W.A.C., the latter two red, are littermates.

The original bitch which Lynne crossed on Sun Hawk, Lyndobe's Fancy Free, C.D., W.A.C., was a daughter of Champion Alisaton's Damascus, C.D., by Demetrius. This

1▲

2◄

1. Ch. Maestro's Madchen, C.D., owned by Tony and Janet Sherg, in May 1969 with handler Bob Hastings. This daughter of Ch. Rancho Dobe's Maestro ex J.B.'s Shadow Dorr of Shaytana finished in 1970. Photo courtesy of Karen Vroom Parkhurst, Chino, California.

2. Ch. Rancho Dobe's Maestro with his handler, Corky Vroom, here illustrates the form which caused Vivian Edwards to say of him, "That is the way a Dobe is supposed to move in rear and topline" and Beatrice Godsol to comment, "One of the finest moving dogs I have judged and one of the greatest rear ends." Maestro was owned by Karen Vroom Parkhurst.

3. Stud Dog Class, Doberman Pinscher Club of America, 1967. Ch. Haydenhill's Hurrah, sire, with his progeny, Ch. Rancho Dobe's Maestro and Hurrado's Onyx. The latter was co-owned by Karen Vroom Parkhurst and Hilda and Jose Feleciano. Photo courtesy of Karen.

4. Ch. Rancho Dobe's Maestro, age five years, at the Los Angeles Doberman Pinscher Club Specialty, 1969. This was an exciting occasion for "Mo," as Maestro was called. His progeny won Winners Dog from the American-bred Class, Reserve Dog from the Open Class, Reserve Bitch from the Open Class, Best Puppy, and Top Obedience Dog. He was winner of the Stud Dog Class and, with Ch. Vollis Cascade of Cognac, won first prize in the Brace competition (also No. 2 Working Brace at Westminster in 1970). Karen Vroom Parkhurst, owner.

3▲

▼4

has proven to be an excellent cross for her, and she is now doing a double Sun Hawk and double Demetrius cross. She hopes for some spectacular pups from this for showing in the future.

Maestro

Karen Vroom Parkhurst, owner of the Maestro Dobermans at Chino, California, purchased the first of her Dobes in 1950, a well-bred bitch named Dixie Queen von Weinhardt, who had been bred to Champion Kilburn Avenger prior to Karen's purchase and produced a champion. Karen, as an eighteen-year-old, was not financially able at the time to show this bitch, but she did make friends with other Dobe owners, from whom she learned much about the breed and became increasingly enthusiastic. Particularly she mentions Doc and Clare Davis (who were showing and finished a dog named Champion Toezie Boi Gonzolos A Michael during this period) and with whom she spent long hours discussing Dobermans.

Karen's next Doberman was the great Rancho Dobes Maestro, in honor of whom her kennel is named. She was living in Boise, Idaho, when she decided that she needed a second Dobe, and this one she would be able to show. Looking in the Boise area for a dog to please her proved futile so she contacted professional handler C. D. Lawrence and also a Sheltie breeder with whom she was acquainted. These two put her in touch with R. E. Souders, making it possible for her to own Maestro.

This magnificent dog completed his title in Oregon, taking his first Best in Show with C. D. Lawrence handling him for Karen. The dog aroused immediate interest among knowledgeable fanciers, and when Karen moved to California in 1966, Corky Vroom was able to handle him for her. Maestro and Corky chalked up quite a record, despite the fact that the dog was heavily shown during only one year of his career, 1970, when he completed the year No. 2 among all-breeds.

Maestro was a prepotent sire who can still be recognized in young stock bred from his line. He sired only 34 litters which averaged about six puppies each, yet he produced sixteen champions and a lot of C.D. dogs—at least thirteen of them, and he was the sire of

two Schutzhund II dogs of which Karen is aware. As a canine personality, Maestro was a very proud gentleman of the type and temperament Karen wishes to retain in her dogs. She describes him as having been "a pleasure to live with and a pleasure to own"—which comes through in his progeny very strongly.

While she was married to Corky Vroom, Karen attended dog shows on a very steady basis but after that she lost interest for ten years or so, although her enthusiasm for Dobermans never lagged. As she says, "During my handling days I did not have time for litters, so it was a great joy for me to be able to stay home and enjoy the puppies." The last of the Dobes Karen showed prior to this period was Dorr's Son of Maestro, whom she owned and on whom she put a 5-point "major" at 19 months of age. Since Karen did not show the dogs herself over those years, she did not sell them to show homes, but just to good homes where the dogs would have a proper family to love. She was not perturbed if the new owners had the bitches spayed, or the dogs neutered, if that was what they preferred to do. If, however, they wanted to have puppies, she was always ready to be helpful. For herself, she has consistently kept a bitch with which to continue her line and a male that can be used as sire of her litters.

Now Maestro Dobermans have returned to showing again, since about 1983. Karen saw a head-study picture of a bitch who attracted her to the extent that she called the phone number which was listed. It turned out to belong to William and Marcy Shatner, who brought their dogs for her to see and fell in love with Karen's dogs, convincing her that she really should return to the show ring. As a result, she now has two in competition: Kieboko and Rain. When the Shatners brought their dogs for her to see, Karen most admired their Belle Reve Paris, breeding a bitch of hers to him. There are four show puppies from this breeding.

The Shatners used Karen's Augustein's Mr. Papadopolus on one of their bitches, from which came Belle Reve Royale, a recently completed C.D. who will now be starting in the conformation ring. She is about a year-and-a-half old as we write. Her dam is Hawk's Wizard Witch, a daughter of the Shatner's Champion Dobedell's Danny Boy.

1. The great Ch. Rancho Dobe's Maestro's first champion from his first litter—Ch. Mein Tauchen v Maestro. Photo courtesy of Karen Vroom Parkhurst.
2. Ch. Rancho Dobe's Maestro, the No. 2 Dog in the Nation (all breeds) for that year, on his last ring appearance, winning the Working Group at Antelope Valley in December 1970. It is interesting to note that in the same year, Maestro tied with another Dobe for the Doberman Pinscher Club of America Award for most Specialties won. The other Dobe?? His son, Ch. Maestro's Reflection. Karen Vroom Parkhurst, owner. Maestro retired at the height of his career, his owner wishing him at home as a stud dog. Corky Vroom, handler.

1▲

▼2

ANTELOPE VALLEY
KENNEL CLUB
WORKING
GROUP

1▲

▲2

1. Ch. Maestro's Georgie Girl, by Ch. Rancho Dobe's Maestro ex Rancho Dobe's Trey O'Hearts, at the Northern California Doberman Pinscher Club Specialty in 1968, winning Best Puppy in Show under judge Joe Gregory. Owned by Sharlene Hanson, Delroy, Ohio; handled by Corky Vroom. Georgie Girl was the only puppy in this litter, so a return breeding was given, which produced Ch. Maestro's Reflection. Photo courtesy of Karen Vroom Parkhurst.

2. Doberman puppies at Maestro Kennels in 1969. By Ch. Rancho Dobe's Maestro ex Hurrado's Serenata. Karen Parkhusrt, owner, Chino, California.

3. Ch. Rancho Dobe's Maestro in 1969, age five years. From a head study by Joan Ludwig, this pencil drawing was done by Steve Hubble. Maestro was owned by Karen Vroom Parkhurst.

4. Ch. Rancho Dobe's Maestro with his litter. These puppies were hand raised, with Maestro "playing mother," taking care of them from three days of age. Karen Vroom Parkhurst, owner.

5. Ch. The Maestro's Reflection, sire of two champions, a son of Ch. Rancho Dobe's Maestro ex Rancho Dobe's Trey O'Hearts. Owner Sharlene Hanson. Photo courtesy of Karen Vroom Parkhurst.

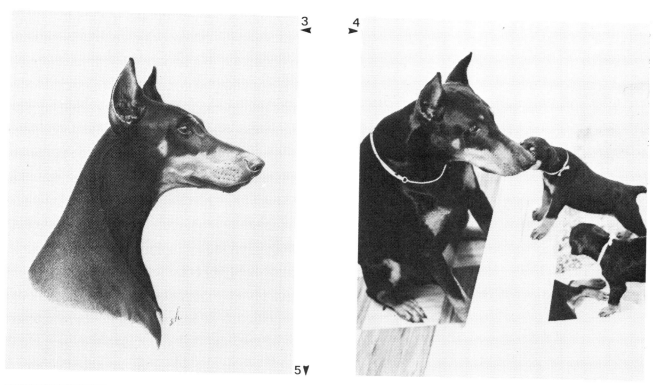

3 ◄   4 ◄

5 ▼

1. Dixie Queen von Weinhardt in 1953 at two years of age. The very first Doberman owned by Karen Vroom Parkhurst, Chino, California, whom she had purchased in 1950. Dixie Queen was the dam of a champion from her one breeding to Kilburn Avenger.
2. Ch. Rancho Dobe's Maestro winning the Working Group under Mr. Herman Cox. Went on to Best in Show at the Kennel Club of Beverly Hills. Maestro was the 32nd Winning Dog, all breeds, and the Top Working Dog in 1970. Corky Vroom handler.

1▲   ▼2

A note of interest is that Karen Vroom's dogs are about as close in bloodlines to the old Rancho Dobe dogs as can be found in the breed today, with Hurrah and Maestro in her fourth generation. She still has descendants of Riff, Roulette, Primo, Presto, and Storm in her pedigrees, and she is linebreeding on them. They will be in the sixth generation of the puppies bred at Maestro as we write.

Karen is very strong in the belief that Dobermans should not be bred for beauty alone, nor for trainability alone. She wants the *whole* dog, one with beauty and brains. This was one of the reasons that the Forell line from Germany was introduced into her Maestro line. She felt that a little more sharpness might be desirable, combined with the brains to handle it.

Karen Parkhurst at present has a two-year-old male, Maestro's Rocky Road, that is in training now. He will be trained to do anything he is capable of doing, and Karen has great hopes that he will learn everything. One of her dogs, back in about 1974, was trained for Seeing Eye, guard dog, and police work and was also a Dobe "sniffer" dog (used to detect drugs). He was called "Sneakers." The school which Rocky is attending does all that type of training also. It is located in Alabama, and Karen is pleased with the information that Rocky is showing particular aptitude for trailing.

The current dogs at Maestro include: Maestro's Sea Breeze by Maestro's Keno ex Maestro's Satin Navigator. She is listed first because she is Karen's foundation bitch and the dam of two litters (none pointed yet but five puppies getting ready for winning). Sea Breeze is a double Maestro granddaughter with linebreeding. Maestro's Keno, by Dorr's Son of Maestro ex Farrell's Miss Bardahl, was bred by Jessie Farrell and is linebreeding to an outcross. The already mentioned Maestro's Kieboko is heavily linebred to Maestro. Maestro's Stormy Weather is the littermate to Kieboko. Maestro's Rain, by Belle Reve Paris ex Maestro's Sea Breeze is now being shown and is tightly linebred for outbreeding. Belle Reve Fade to Black, by Augustein's Mr. Papadopolus ex Hawks Wizard Witch is inbred to outbred. Karen also is co-owner of Maestro's Rocky Road and Maestro's Summer Wind.

Returning to the accomplishments of Champion Rancho Dobe's Maestro, this wonderful dog was bred by Rancho Dobe Kennels, born on April 16, 1964, died on February 18, 1972, a son of Champion Haydenhill's Hurrah with this breeding. R. E. Souders, owner of Hurrah, was visiting Rancho Dobe Kennel with his dog, to whom one of their top bitches was being bred. He spotted Lotto and fell for her immediately and was anxious that she be bred to Hurrah when the time came. She was, the resulting litter producing not only Maestro but the famous Champion Rancho Dobe's Primo Donna, along with some other good ones in the litter of eight. When Mr. Souders was contacted about a show-quality male for Karen, Maestro was the one which he immediately thought of, leading to Karen's purchase of the young dog. He won his first Best in Show, handled by C. D. Lawrence, at the Lizard Butte Kennel Club All-Breed Match two weeks after Karen acquired him. A prophetic start for his show career.

Maestro's total show record included 17 all-breed Bests in Show, four Specialty Bests of Breed, 68 Working Group Firsts; and 128 times Best of Breed.

During the first half of 1970, Maestro chalked up 14,866 rating points in a six-month period, making him Number One among all-breeds—a position he held until late November. When the year's final statistics were totalled, Maestro was Number One Working Dog (at nearly seven years of age), Number Two all-breeds, and Number One Doberman.

Maestro retired, as we like to see any truly great winner do, "in a blaze of glory," winning the Working Group the last four times he was shown. Sad to relate, just two months before his eighth birthday, he succumbed to cancer—an inestimable loss to his breed and to those who loved him.

Survivors of Maestro include eight champions and many champion grandchildren. An unforgettable dog. A true "great" in the history of this breed.

Manorie

Manorie Dobermans are located at Santa Rosa, California and owned by Marjorie Brooks who has been an active, highly successful Doberman fancier over a good many

Dorr's Son of Maestro, 1972–1979, by Ch. Rancho Dobe's Maestro ex Regal Brandy Regina v Dorr, was shown three times when around 16 months, had a five-point "major," but never tried to complete his title as his owner stopped going to dog shows around that time. He did, however, become one of the leading sires behind the present-day Maestro Dobes.

years as a Doberman breeder, owner, and as a professional handler.

Among the most famous of Marj's winners is the wonderful Champion Alnwick's Black Fury Bismarck, C.D. who sired a total of 28 champions among his other accomplishments. This splendid dog was a son of Champion Felix vom Ahrtal ex Mikado's Flambeau, and he was bred by Jeanne M. Borger. He was an important winner of the 1960's.

Another who is a tremendous credit to the quality Dobes at Manorie is the handsome Champion Alisaton the Night Watchman, C.D., ROM, who was born December 9, 1976. At eight years old, he is as lovely as ever and a true credit to his sire, Champion Brown's B-Brian and to his dam, Champion Alisaton's Kinderwicke. He was bred by Joanne Satalino and Gwen Satalino DeMilta.

Yet another distinguished Dobe, from Manorie's earlier days, was Imprevu, a Rosen Cavalier daughter, bred by Marj Brooks who co-owned her with George Anagnost. This bitch really attracted attention when she swept through from the Open Class to Best in Show, gaining the approval of three different judges along the way at Oakland Kennel Club in 1969. The dam of this very worthy champion was Annheim's Dark Imp. Another bitch from these same parents is Champion Manorie Dobe's Im Pavon Du Rel owned by Lynn Woods.

A young champion who gained title with spectacular success over three weekends is Champion Manorie Dobe's Nutmeg, C.D., who gained the title in only a month-and-a-half's time—a homebred owned by Marj Brooks, sired by Night Watchman from Manorie Dobe's Renaissance.

Marj maintains a very busy dog show schedule with the Dobes in her charge and deserves much credit for the quality of her dogs and for their always flawless presentation.

March Dobermans

March Dobermans came into existence in 1975 when Mary Manning's dogs were better known as Marel Dobes. She acquired her first bitch of the breed, Fraulein Sonnya, by Champion Olympus Marcus Brutus out of Seuvins Satan. She got her, in whelp, from a gentleman who could not keep her. One

month later Mary had her first Doberman litter—eleven puppies, one of which became her first show dog, a male puppy named Marel's Jack Daniels. He was shown over a period of several years, then in 1978 was bred to his cousin, Brandy Dobe, producing Mary's first homebred litter from which she kept pick male, Marel's Toast to Jack Daniels.

While she was showing Jack Daniels, Mary became acquainted with Charles Guardascione, who was looking for a nice Doberman to purchase. She told him about her young male, Toast to Jack Daniels, and it was agreed that they would arrange a co-ownership for this dog. "Justin," as the dog was called, completed his title during 1981 in fifteen shows—Mary's first homebred champion. Both Mary and Charlie were thrilled with Justin's success and decided that they would purchase a good bitch to show and eventually start a breeding program. They were introduced to Peggy Esposito and Gwen Satalino by their handler, Terry Lazzaro. They had a litter of puppies by Champion Mardale Spirit of Malnati from Champion Alisaton Kinder Rose, C.D.

Mary and Charles went to see the pups and chose a "fiesty little redhead with a mouth that wouldn't quit" to be the one they would like to own. She became D'Mascus Sambuca v. Alisaton. At six months old she started her show career by going Reserve Winners Bitch and the next day she took Winners Bitch for two points. At seven months she was Best Puppy in Sweepstakes and on to Best in Show over top Best in Show winning "specials" at the 1981 Pilgrim Specialty. What a fabulous day! She continued her career in Terry Lazzaro's capable hands and gained an early championship. At the 1982 National she was recipient of the award for most Blue Ribbons in the Puppy Classes. Entered at the 1982 National Specialty, she was the youngest Dobe in the ring and remained there through all the various cuts right until the very end. Her owners were practically bursting with pride!

While all of the March Dobermans were shown, they also were expected to work. In August of 1981, "Justin" completed his obedience degree in three shows, and in September he received his ROM without problem. In November 1981 Jack Daniels gained Highest Scoring Dobe and finished his obedience title. In the summer of 1983 Sambuca attained her

1. Ch. Mardale The Spirit Hawk, by Ch. Marienburg's Sun Hawk, C.D. ex Ch. Alisaton Bewitched. Bred by Kathryn and William Harrison. Handled by Don Simmons for owner, Joyce Lee.
2. Ch. Mardale Beguiling Spirit, by Ch. Marienburg's Sun Hawk, C.D. ex Ch. Alisaton Bewitched. Breeders, William and Kathryn Harrison. Bill Harrison handling for owners Dr. James and Dyanne Ratliff.

obedience degree under judge Doris Miller.

The kennel name "March" was selected by Mary and Charlie, coined from a combination of their two names: MAR from Mary and CH from Charles. They have a pretty young red bitch now named Mardale Evil Touch V. Alisaton, by Champion Alisaton Touch Down V. D'Mascus out of Champion Alisaton Bewitched, with which they won many blues while she was shown as a puppy. Now she is waiting to grow up. Kay and Bill Harrison were her breeders.

It is planned that March Kennels will be the home of quality Dobermans for a long time to come. In the future, Charlie would like to become a judge. But Mary prefers staying home to condition and continue showing their dogs.

Mardale

Mardale Kennels, at Brandywine, Maryland, are owned by Kathryn (Kay) and William (Bill) Harrison who purchased their first Doberman in 1969, a black male named Jarvis. This dog was 90% Kay Hill breeding and was shown only a few times (never used at stud) and remained with the Harrisons until his death at age ten years.

Their second Doberman, a lovely red bitch named Scarlett, is still with the Harrisons at age fourteen. She was purchased in 1970 and is a Demetrius granddaughter.

The Harrisons started actively showing in 1972, and Bill became a licensed professional handler six years later.

In 1975 the Harrisons purchased their beautiful red bitch, Champion Alisaton Bewitched, who is a Champion Alisaton Kinderwicke ex Champion Gra-Lemor Demetrius V.D. Victor daughter, this one from Gwen Satalino DeMilta. "Spirit" went on to prove herself both as a show bitch and as a producer and was the Top Producing Working Dam in the years 1979 and 1980. She was awarded recognition by the Doberman Pinscher Club of America as the bitch producing the most champions in 1982, and she would have also been awarded the same honor in 1981 according to the figures had Kay not forgotten to nominate her. She also has been awarded several certificates of distinction by H.I.S. Publications.

Bill and Kay were awarded Breeders of the Year in 1981 by the Doberman Pinscher Club of America.

Spirit was bred twice to Champion Marienburg's Sun Hawk, C.D. which produced a total of eleven champions. On this Kay comments, "More would have finished; however, because of personal reasons in some of the show homes, the additional three that were pointed did not."

For Spirit's second litter she was bred to Champion Sherluck's L. B. Jake, producing one champion from that breeding.

Her final litter was by Champion Alisaton Touchdown V. D'Mascus, her nephew, and in that litter one male, Mardale the Final Touch of Spirit, the last puppy Spirit every had, is nearing the championship title. His brother, Mardale Touch and Go Alisaton, has a four-point "major," and two of the littermates have died. This litter was born in 1982.

Spirit at present has six champion grandchildren, with many more pointed.

Kay and Bill at this writing own five Dobermans and one Whippet.

Marienburg

Marienburg Doberman Pinschers, owned by Mary M. Rodgers, formerly of El Cajon, California but now located at Hamilton, Montana, has become one of the most famous kennels of show dogs in the United States.

Mary obtained her first of the breed back in 1961 from a little-known breeder in Kansas, knowing nothing of dog shows in those days. A year later, following her move to California, she became acquainted with Richard Sufficool, a handler of show dogs, who sold her another Doberman and offered to handle him at the next dog show. This was the Glendale Kennel Club in March 1962. It was Mary Rodgers' very first dog show and obviously the start of a dedicated hobby for her, as it is doubtful that she missed more than an occasional show in southern California from that time on until her move to Montana in 1980.

Richard Sufficool took Reserve at this first show for Mrs. Rodgers, who was greatly impressed—and not a little excited over it all!

Marienburg's first two champions were purchased as youngsters in 1962. They were a bitch, Champion Zigeuner's Fiesta, who was entirely of Rancho Dobe breeding (being a

1. Ch. Sultana von Marienburg, Best of Breed at the Doberman Pinscher Club of America National Specialty in 1967. Judge, Major Godsol; handler, Rex Vandeventer. Dr. William Shute presenting the trophy. Sultana is by Ch. Steb's Gunga Din ex Farley's Princess. Mary Rodgers, Marienburg Kennels, Hamilton, Montana.
2. Ch. Zigeuner's Fiesta, the first champion bitch there, and the foundation for Marienburg Kennels. By Ch. Rancho Dobe's Bach ex Ch. Zigeuner's Conga. Handled throughout her show career by Bob Hastings. Owned by Mary Rodgers. Shown winning Best of Opposite Sex over "specials" at San Fernando in 1963.
3. Ch. Marienburg's Copy of Sultana. By Ch. Marienburg's Maximilian ex Ch. Sultana von Marienburg. Breeder-owner, Marienburg Kennels.
4. Ch. Marienburg Apache Warbonnet, by Ch. Marienburg's Sundancer ex Marienburg's Desert Flame. Full sister to Sun Hawk. Dam of several champions. Handled by Moe Miyagawa for Mary Rodgers.
5. Ch. Gretchen von Marienburg, by De Crescent's Fugue ex Ch. Zigeuner's Fiesta. Finished by Jane Kamp Forsyth from the first litter bred by Marienburg Kennels. Gretchen's background was almost entirely Rancho Dobe. Mary Rodgers, owner.
6. Ch. Sultana von Marienburg, No. 1 Doberman for 1966 and 1967; No. 2 of all-breeds, 1967. Quaker Oats Award winner, 1967. Doberman Pinscher Club of America Best of Breed, 1967 and 1968. Championship finished by Jane Kamp Forsyth. Handled for two years as a "special" exclusively by Rex and Leota Vandeventer. Mary Rodgers, owner.
7. Ch. Sultana von Marienburg going Best in Show at Mississippi Valley in 1967 under judge F. Rutherford. Handled by Leota Vandeventer for Marienburg Kennels.
8. Ch. Marienburg's Sun Hawk, C.D. at two years of age. Owned by Marienburg Kennels.

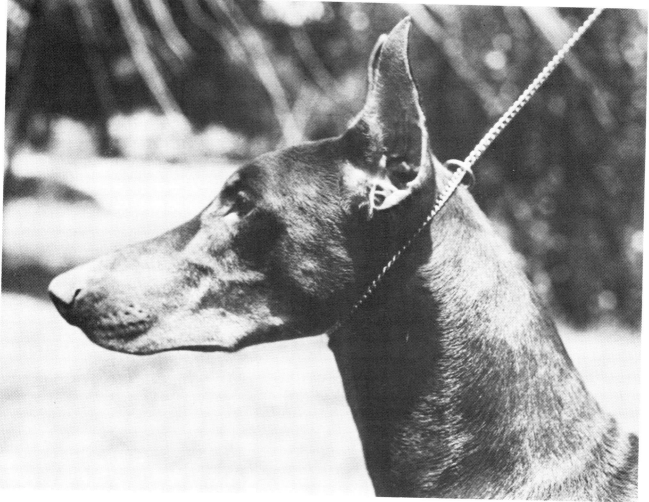

granddaughter of Riff, Roulette and Primo) and a male, Champion Westwind's Gunsmoke. He was Elblac breeding which was basically Delegate.

Fiesta was the dam of the first homebred Marienburg litter, whelped in January 1963, which produced two champions sired by Fiesta's half-brother. Mary never bred anything from Gunsmoke and placed him in a good home soon after he finished.

In mid-1963 two six-week-old puppies were purchased from a man anxious to sell a litter he had bred. The breeding was Top Skipper and Ponder background and Mary felt it quite a bargain when she was able to obtain both puppies for a mere $125.00 for the two of them! Indeed they proved to be, for the dog became Champion Wilhelm von Marienburg and the bitch, Champion Sultana of Marienburg.

Sultana's accomplishments were amazing. She ended her career with 36 all-breed Bests in Show, over 90 Group Firsts, two National Specialties, the 1967 Quaker Oats Award and No. 2 of All-Breeds! Sultana was not prolific and had a total of only ten puppies from four breedings. Four of them finished and one became the spectacular producer, Champion Marienburg's Only One, the dam of fifteen American Champions, two Best in Show winners, among them the fabulous Champion Marienburg's Mary Hartman.

In 1964, Mary Rodgers arranged for a breeding to take place in the Midwest on the condition that she purchase the resulting puppies. This breeding was for the most part Brown's, Damasyn through Dictator, background on the dam's side with a very strong Alcor line through the sire, Champion Jo's Brandy Alexander. Mary kept two of these puppies, neither of which finished, but the male, Marienburg's Sundancer, sired Champion Marienburg Sun Hawk. The bitch, Marienburg's Topaz, was the granddam of Hawk's dam, Marienburg's Desert Flame.

In the late 1960's, Mary introduced Champion Gra-Lemor Demetrius into her line through Sultana and those of her bitches who were direct descendants of Fiesta, the original of her bitches, with the Rancho Dobe background. Several champions resulted from these breedings, including Champion Marienburg's Red Baron, the sire of Only One.

Mary comments, "My dogs seemed like they were going in two different directions for many years. The two biggest successes I had were Only, who was descended from my original Fiesta and crossed with Sultana and Demetrius, and Sun Hawk, who was Brown's, Dictator and Alcor background." Thus, after much careful thought and study, Mary decided to try an experiment and combine these lines. The result made history, and Mary Hartman was from this first combination of Hawk and Only. Eleven champions came from this breeding, which was repeated three times.

Her greatest breeding accomplishment, Mary feels, has been Sun Hawk. He did well as a show dog in spite of his dislike for the show ring. His two year career included five Bests in Show, 34 times first in the Working Group, and 24 Specialties of which two were the Doberman Pinscher Club of America Nationals. He has sired 76 American champions thus far. The previous record was held by Delegate with 55. Sun Hawk died at nine years of age and was used at stud only over a seven year period.

Mary Rodgers has bred 62 American champion Dobermans to date, which she "believes is second only to Tess Henseler at this time." Since Sultana was No. 1 Doberman in 1966, Marienburg Dobermans have been in the Number One position during eight years. In tabulating this, Mary is including the current No. 1 Champion Eagle's Devil D, who "is Marienburg." During this time, Marienburg Dobermans have gone Best of Breed at the National six times, which is a record. They have won the Quaker Oats Award three years. Hawk has been the Doberman Pinscher Club of America Sire of the Year for five consecutive years. Marienburg has been Doberman Pinscher Club of America Breeder of the Year on five occasions.

Moe Miyagawa handled many of the Marienburg champions, including Hawk and Mary Hartman, throughout their show careers. Rex Vandeventer handled Sultana and finished numerous champions for the kennel during the 1960's.

We are happy to note that Mary Rodgers seems as enthusiastic and full of plans for her Dobermans as ever and that there are some

1. Ch. Dorian von Marienburg, by De Crescent's Fugue ex Ch. Zigeuner's Fiesta, owned by Howard Sullenberger. Dorian is from the first litter bred at Marienburg Kennels.

2. Ch. Marienburg's Sun Hawk at the Garden in 1977. No. 1 Doberman for 1975 and 1976. Doberman Pinscher Club of America Best of Breed winner, 1976 and 1978. Sire of 76 American champions as of May 1984. Top Twenty winner in 1975. Five Bests in Show, 34 Group Firsts, 24 Specialty Bests of Breed. Handled by Moe Miyagawa throughout his show career. Owned by Mary Rodgers, Marienburg Kennels.

3. Ch. Mikadobe's Honey Bun, by Ch. Steb's Top Skipper ex Ch. Mikadobe's Cinnamon Bun, finishing her title in May 1963. Owned by Mae Downing, Marietta, Georgia.

4. Mae Downing, with her first litter in 1948 in Kansas City, Missouri.

1. Ch. Mikadobe's Calamity Jane, by Ch. Highland Satan's Image ex Mikadobe's Flamingo, taking Best of Winners en route to the title. Mae Downing, Marietta, Georgia.
2. Ch. Mikadobe's Kiss of Fire finishing with her fourth "major" at Chattanooga in 1965 under judge Hollis Wilson. Michele Leathers (now the noted judge, Michele Billings) handling for breeder-owner Mae Downing. By Ch. Singenwald's Prince Kuhio ex Ch. Mikadobe's Honey Bun.
3. Ch. Mikadobe's Kismet, finished during the early 1960's at 13 months of age, a Group winner owned by Mrs. Mae Downing. Handled by Michele L. Billings.
4. Ch. Mikadobe's Kantata, by Ch. Hollyhigh's Damon ex Ch. Mikadobe's Kismet, owned by Mae Downing.

splendid ones now in competition who will keep the banner high.

Mi Casa

Mi Casa Dobermans started their breeding program when, in the mid-1970's, Carol Luft of Tomball, Texas had the good fortune to acquire a lovely black bitch with nine points including both her "majors." With the help of her breeder-handler, Ellen Hoffman, she was to become Champion Elfred's Miss Universe II.

Carol Luft has not done a great deal of breeding, perhaps one litter a year. But from Miss Universe she has Champion Mi Casa's Besa Me, who was owner-handled to her title as well as having gained the glorious distinction of being Winners Bitch and Best of Winners at the Doberman Pinscher Club of America in 1978. This lovely granddaughter of Champion Elfred's Nikki is a multi-Specialty Best in Show winner and Group placement winner, and during her short but glowing "specials" career she was ranked in the Top Twenty.

Next comes Champion Mi Casa's Bravo, who Carol Luft showed to all but four of his championship points. "Toby" is a Group winner, winner of the Stud Dog Class at the Doberman Pinscher Club of America, Seattle in 1981 and was also a Top Twenty Contender during most of his "specials" career, through which he was handled by T. Owen Forbes.

Mi Casa's Buena, although she did not finish her title, produced several champions who brought honors to the kennel. They are Champion Wynterwynd's Wild Tempest, Champion Wynterwynd's Wild Streak, C.D., ROM, and Champion Tempestra's Star of Wynterwynd. She was leased to a friend and later sold to Jim and Diane Urban, the owners of Wild Tempest, thus the "children" do not carry the Mi Casa prefix but all own a piece of Carol Luft's heart.

In this litter also was Mexican Champion Mi Casa's Belinda, who finished her title as a puppy, handled by her twelve-year-old owner, Patrick Cohen. As Carol comments, "They both made us very proud."

From the repeat of the "B litter" came Champion Mi Casa's Consuela who was handled to her title by Carol Luft and who, although shown but a few times as a "special,"

is a multi-Best of Breed and Specialty Best in Show winner. She is owned by Connie Jo Taylor of Elk City, Oklahoma.

Currently being campaigned, in 1984, is Mi Casa's Fiadora, a daughter of Besa Me sired by Wild Streak. "Fia" took her first points by going Best of Breed and Group I over multi-Best in Show winners, breeder-owner-handled. Then there is Destry's Wildcat of Mi Casa, a daughter of Cabriole, owned by her co-breeder, Connie Jo Taylor, who is just a few points from her title. Through these lovely young bitches, the future of Mi Casa looks bright.

Mi Casa will continue breeding on a small scale, as Carol really likes only having a litter when she needs something to show for herself. None of her bitches to date has ever been bred more than three times before being spayed and becoming house pets.

Carol's husband, Tom, and son, Thomas, are great supporters of her interest in the Dobermans, adding to her pleasure in Mi Casa Dobermans.

Mikadobe

Mikadobe Kennels have produced twenty or more champions since being founded by Mae Downing of Marietta, Georgia.

Mae received her first Doberman as a gift from her father in 1934, following his attendance of the Doberman Pinscher Club of America Specialty Show in Chicago where he had taken some of his 4-H Club boys and his steer to compete in the Grand Championship Livestock Show also taking place there at that time. Mae's father was County Agent and livestock judge.

She was in high school at the time the Doberman joined the family. But the dog came along with her when she married, and she has never been without a member of the breed since that time.

The Mikadobe breeding program was founded on Damasyn The Bat, a daughter of Champion Dictator v Glenhugel from Kilburn Beeline. For awhile the Downings were residents of Japan, where they were accompanied by their Champion Mikado v. d. Elbe, a son of Bat sired by Champion Dacki v. d. Elbe. The latter was by Champion Kama of Westphalis from Champion Belydia v. d. Elbe. Mikado was born October 21, 1949. He

1▲

2◀

1. Mikadobe's Chocolate Kiss and Ch. Mikadobe's Choco-late Soldier, puppies by Ch. Axel von Tannenwald ex Ch. Mikadobe's Kiss of Fire. Mae Downing, owner, Mikadobe Kennels, Marietta, Georgia.
2. Ch. Mikadobe's Riptide, by Ch. Steb's Top Skipper ex Mikadobe's Cinnamon Bun, owned by the noted A.K.C. judge Virgil Johnson. Photo courtesy of Mae Downing.
3. Ch. Mikadobe's Chocolate Soldier.
4. Ch. Mikado's Cupid, by Ch. Highland Satan's Image, is what Mae Downing considers to be the most influential of all the Dobes carrying her Mikadobe prefix . . . a Top 20 Dog; the sire of many, many champions; and a noted win-ner in his own right. Photo courtesy of Mae Downing. Cupid was owned by Linda Duff, Oregonia, Ohio. George Rood handling; Dr. Shute judging.
5. Mikadobe's Lyric By Cupid with her litter, the sire of which is Ch. Mikadobe's Valentino v Paris. Mae Downing, owner.
6. Ch. Mikadobe's Kismet, Ch. Mikadobe's Kiss of Fire, and Ch. Mikadobe's Honey Bun (their dam), with their owner, Mae Downing.

3▲

4▲

▶5

▶6

277

was twice Grand Champion in Japan, where he had a host of admirers and a highly beneficial influence on the breed.

During the early 1950's, the Downings returned to the United States where Mae continued her breeding program. While in Japan she had been asked by the Japanese to endeavor to trace Mikado's pedigree back to Germany and its original dogs. This she did with the help of Hans Schmidt, the breeder of Champion Delegate, Champion Dacki v. d. Elbe, and a number of others of note. She was able to connect with those in Grunig's book on the origins of the Doberman. The only connection she could find in the Japanese line was the import, Caesar V Rauhfelsen, litter brother to International Champion Cherloc V Rauhfelsen. He was a BLUE! Mikado produced three blues in Japan, but when bred to a blue in the U.S., he produced all black. Also one "blue" was actually a brindle. In Japan Mikado sired a litter of bob-tail puppies, which never happened again. A study of Mikado's pedigree is very interesting, as one finds all the old "famous names"—Jessy, Kurt, Troll, Muck, Blank, Helios, etc.

Minoo Yasuda kept Mikado's line going until he died, and it was then that his friend, Keizo Sasada of Osaka, Japan, contacted Mae Downing and eventually purchased from her the now Champion Mikadobe's Valentino v Paris.

Valentino, by Champion Mikadobe's Paris, was bred by Carlos and Kathy Rojas and given to Mae Downing as a puppy. He was a very loving and caring male and easy to live with. In Japan he is doing an excellent job of producing and has a son and a daughter, both of whom are Best in Show winners.

Champion Mikadobe's Paris, by Champion Thorvald vom Ahrtal ex Mikadobe's Kibitzer, represents something of a tragedy for his adoring owner, as she had but three short years with him prior to his death. During his lifetime Paris sired nine champions. He finished his championship at the 1976 Doberman Pinscher Club of America Bicentennial National Specialty, taking Winners Dog and Best of Winners to have gained the title under three judges. His life was terminated by a ruptured aneurysm soon after his "specials" career had begun.

Mae Downing tells us that of all the dogs carrying her kennel prefix Champion Mikado's Cupid has been probably the most influential on the breed. A prolific sire, he has produced a goodly number of excellent progeny. He is owned by Linda Dubb of Briarwood Kennels, Oregonia, Ohio. Cupid is by Champion Highland Satan's Image ex Mikado's Athena.

Then there is Champion Black Fury Bismarck owned by Marjorie Brooks, to whom Mae Downing also pays tribute; he is by the Mikado's Flambeau and out of Champion Mikadobe's Kismet, a daughter of Champion Singenwald's Prince Kuhio, through whom came Champion Mikadobe's Paris.

Mae Downing now has just the Paris granddaughter, Champion Mikadobe's Serendipity, and the pointed Cupid daughter, Mikadobe's Lyric. She is hoping to breed "Sierra" to the Cupid son, Champion Highbriar Esquire.

Moonbeam

Moonbeam Kennels are at Fayetteville, North Carolina, where they are owned by Kathy and Carlos Rojas. Doberman breeders themselves, they have produced some excellent ones, but nowadays the emphasis is more on Carlos as a handler, as his profession keeps him very much on the go.

Among the great Dobes with whose show careers Carlos has been involved are Champion Barchet Fiddler On The Roof and Champion Eagle's Devil "D." There have been numerous others as well, and many, many champions made up by Carlos, but these two have been very special to him and have certainly earned a place in history.

Moonraker

Moonraker Dobermans, at Morgan Hill, California, are owned by Mr. and Mrs. D. P. Fulkerson who started in the early 1970's with a pet-quality Doberman. The Fulkersons loved their female but wanted to have something for show as well. They felt most fortunate in knowing that their pet would turn out to be a top-notch producer, if properly bred.

This bitch was descended from Champion Borong The Warlock. Having a high interest

278

1. Ch. Mikadobe's Maxamilian, by Ch. Kama of Westphalia ex Damasyn The Bat. Early members of the Mikadobe Kennels owned by Mae Downing.
2. Ch. Mikadobe's Sharpshooter had nine points when his rear leg was injured by a car, so he never finished. Outstanding son of Ch. Steb's Top Skipper ex Mikadobe's Cinnamon Bun, born June 1959. Bred by Mae Downing. Owned by Mrs. Kay Goguen.

1. Ch. Ru-Mar's Morgansonne, C.D., black and rust, born May 1962. By Ch. Rancho Dobe's Cello ex Ch. Jessamyn II vom Ahrtal. The sire of 26 champions. Top Sire for three years, Doberman Pinscher Club of America, during the 1960's. Owned and handled by Ruth Morgan Edwards, Monterey, California.

2. Ch. Morgansonne's Rembrandt, black and rust, born February 2, 1971. By Ch. Azteca's Bret Morgansonne, C.D. ex Windyhill's Jill Morgansonne. Best of Breed and Group two at Montgomery, Alabama, November 1972, on the way to his title. Breeder, Ruth M. Morgan. Owner, Toni Robison, Doraville, Georgia.

in breeding quality Dobermans, the Fulkersons gave much thought and study to her pedigree, then selected Champion Montwoods Aquarius as the stud to whom she should be bred. From this litter Moonraker's Blue Angel was produced. The Fulkersons love the look of the breed's older "greats," and the goal at Moonraker is to maintain a higher than average quality in their breeding program.

The Fulkersons breed only one litter every eighteen months to two years and thus are able to keep their puppies until all can be placed in the perfect home most suitable for buyer and puppy. All are sold with a lifetime guarantee for health and temperament. Another goal of theirs is that no dog or bitch from their kennel now or in the future will wind up in a dog pound or rescue center.

Morgansonne

Morgansonne Dobermans are owned by Mrs. Ruth M. Morgan Edwards, and located at Monterey, California. Top dog here has been the very famous and notable Champion Ru-Mar's Morgansonne, C.D., who under the Phillips System, was a Top Producer, producing some splendid champions during the 1960's and early 1970's. He was born May 13, 1962 by Champion Rancho Dobe's Cello ex Champion Jessamyn II vom Ahrtal. He was bred by Rudy and Marie Ann Wagner.

Mrs. Edwards comments, with satisfaction, that of all "Sonny's" champions, only one was co-bred by her, Champion Retrac's Jody Morgansonne. She notes, "I was proud of the fact that I wasn't the one touting him as a good sire—others were doing that for me."

Mrs. Edwards' kennel was a small one when she had "Sonny," and he was the family housedog. He was handled to his title solely by Mrs. Edwards, who was a novice at the time. Later Ruth applied for and was granted a handler's license and showed some of "Sonny's" progeny to their titles.

Ondega

Ondega Doberman Pinschers are owned by Bruce and Kathy Lieblich and are located at Rockleigh, New Jersey.

The Lieblichs are owners of an excellent bitch, Champion Shady Acres Sadie, whose sire is Champion Edelhall's Gigolo of Amulet (Champion Tarrado's Flair-Amulet's Careless Heart) and whose dam is Shady Acres Kim vom Thuringen (Champion Lauritz vom Ahrtal-Jessica vom Thuringen).

Sadie is the dam of Champion Ondega's Dapper Dan, Champion Ondega's SunDance Kid, and Champion Domani's Private Collection, along with two others who should be finished when you are reading this book: Ondega's Danny Boy and Amulet's Corry v Clemmwood. She herself has also been successful in the show ring under Jeff Brucker's handling.

Sadie's son, American and Canadian Champion Ondega's SunDance Kid, who is by Champion Domani's Royal Image, was the 1980 Doberman Pinscher Club of America Grand Prize Futurity winner at their National Competition that year in Dallas, Texas. The Futurity judge was Mr. Charles Cooper, and SunDance was handled by Eugene Haupt. This dog is also a multiple Best of Breed winner in the United States and Canada and is handled usually by Jeff Brucker.

SunDance Kid was born March 20, 1980. He has behind him many of the breed's "greats," so his success both as stud dog and in the ring himself would seem assured.

Pajant

Pajant Dobermans are owned by Barbara Hall of Wilton, Connecticut, where Champion Kocot Pajant de Scudamore, C.D.X., ROM, bred by Richard Kocot, is the foundation. Finishing with three owner-handled "majors," the first from the Puppy Class, Pajant is her owner's first champion. Barbara has been involved with Dobermans, primarily in obedience, since the early 1970's, breeding her first litter in 1981.

Sired by the late Top Twenty Doberman, Champion Rockelle's Butch Cassidy, WAC, Pajant has produced three champions to date from this, her first, litter. This splendid bitch, in whose honor the kennel was named, numbers among her champion progeny the current (as we write) No. 2 Doberman in the country, Champion Pajant's Encore v Rockelle, WAC, who is an all-breed Best in Show winner and a multi-Group and Specialty winner. Cory finished at eleven months of age, winning 24 of the 26 classes in which he competed, plus Best of Breed over a 105 Doberman entries along the way.

Pedigree

American Kennel Club

WE562485
Individual Reg. No.

Ralph
Call Name

Litter Reg. No.
American Kennel Club

Registered With

Am. & Can. Ch. Ondega's Sundance Kid
Registered Name Of Dog

Breed. __Doberman Pinscher__   Date Whelped __3/20/80__   Sex __Male__

Breeder __Bruce & Kathy Lieblich__   Address __7 Piermont Road, Rockleigh, NJ   07647__

Owner __Bruce & Kathy Lieblich & Pat Hall__   Address __7 Piermont Road, Rockleigh, NJ   07647__

General Description __Black and Rust__   (201)-767-6915

Sire

Reg. No. _____

Ch. Domani's Prince William
- Ch. Hotai Sweet William
  - Ch. Highbriar Bandana
    - Ch. Felix vom Ahrtal
    - Ch. Highbriar Constant Comment
  - Hotai Syble Selene
    - Int. Ch. Koylen
    - Tamerlane Alert Abbie
- Ch. Housecarl Helene of Diversha
  - Ch. Highbriar Bandana
    - Ch. Felix vom Ahrtal
    - Ch. Highbriar Constant Comment
  - Dobereich's Duress
    - Ch. Felix vom Ahrtal
    - Dobereich's Going Jessie

Ch. Domani's Royal Image
- Am. Can. Ch. Deviltree's Black Shaft
  - Ch. Mattappany The Anchor Man
    - Ch. Highbriar Bandana
    - Ch. Marks-Tey Shay
  - Moorwood's Wild Thing
    - Ch. Tevrac's Top of the Mark
    - Ch. Dobereich's Dawn
- Ch. Shaft's Symphony by Jove
  - Ch. Tarrado's Corry
    - Ch. Felix vom Ahrtal
    - Ch. Highbriar Jasmine
  - De Bella's Krystal Kai Ya
    - Ch. Ares of Highquest
    - Doblens Set. Storm
  - De Bella's Aethalia

Dam

Reg. No. _____

Ch. Edelhall's Gigolo of Amulet
- Ch. Tarrado's Flair
  - Ch. Tarrado's Corry
    - Ch. Felix vom Ahrtal
    - Ch. Highbriar Jasmine
  - Ch. Highbriar Piping Rock
    - Ch. Ravensburg's Falsta
    - Ch. Highbriar Rock Sand
- Amulet's Careless Heart
  - Ch. Rockland J.E.T.
    - Ch. Siggier vom Ahrtal
    - Ch. Rockland's Cordovan's Terrafire
  - Amulet's Antigo
    - Ch. Tarrado's Flair
    - Chance Run's Enchanted Star C.D.

Ch. Shady Acres Sadie
- Ch. Lauritz vom Ahrtal
  - Ch. Felix vom Ahrtal
    - Ch. Lakecrest Thunderstorm
    - Ch. Willa vom Ahrtal
  - Christel vom Ahrtal
    - Xandu vom Ahrtal
    - Ch. Juno vom Ahrtal
- Shady Acres Kim vom Thuringen
  - Ch. Cassio vom Ahrtal
    - Xandu vom Ahrtal
    - Ch. Juno vom Ahrtal
  - Jessica vom Thuringen
    - Ch. Siggier vom Ahrtal
    - Bagatelles Pamela
    - Bagatelles Nancy of the Hills

I hereby certify that this pedigree is true and correct to the best of my knowledge and belief

Signed _____

Date _____ 19 ____

1. Ch. Pamelot's Applause, by Am. and Can. Ch. Schauffelein's Vintage Year ex Can. Ch. Sabra Sweetheart of Sigma Chi, C.D., at four months of age. Bred by Pamela De Hetre.
2. Am. and Can. Ch. Pamelot's Black Knight, born November 1967. By Ch. Walire's Bollo II ex Toledobe's Never On Sunday, C.D. Bred and handled by Pamela De Hetre, co-owner with John Connolly.

1▲ ▼2

Among the Top Twenty at fourteen months, Cory was the Reserve twelve-to-fifteen-month Futurity winner at the 1982 Doberman Pinscher Club of America National Specialty, returning to receive an Award of Merit from Peggy Adamson at the 1983 National. He also was the 1982 Doberman Pinscher Club of America Most Puppy Dog Blue Ribbons award winner.

As a sire, Cory has already made his presence felt with five pointed puppies from the puppy classes to date.

Pajant's other two champions, with another on the way, are the multi-Best of Breed winner and Group placer, Champion Pajant Curtin' Call v Rockelle, who finished in seventeen shows and Champion Pajant Cent's Stage v Rockelle, WAC, who finished his championship entirely from the American-bred class. Pajant's second litter is just reaching show age as this is written.

Pamelot

Pamelot Dobermans are owned by Pamela De Hetre of Loganville, Georgia, who acquired her first of the breed in 1965 from Patrick and Judy Doniere, Toledobes Kennels. In 1966 Pam co-bred her first litter of Dobes with the Donieres, from which came her first champion.

Pamelot's foundation bitch was Toledobe's Never On Sunday, C.D., who was sired by the great Champion Ebonaire's Touchdown, owned by Charles O'Neill, out of a Champion Brown's Dion daughter. Never on Sunday (call name "Misty") produced a total of four champions who were Champion Toledobe's Unchained Melody by Champion Checkmate's Chessman and co-owned by Pamela with Patrick Doniere, American and Canadian Champion Pamelot's Black Knight sired by Champion Walire's Rollo II and co-owned by Pam with John Connolly, Champion Pamelot's Daring Dude sired by Champion Williamsburg Grand Larceny, C.D.X. owned by Pam, and Champion Pamelot's Desafinado sired by Champion Williamsburg Grand Larceny C.D.X. owned by Pam with Marion Gutierrez. Pam pauses here to comment, "I must mention one of Misty's 'great-grand-kids,' who was my daughter, Angela's, first personal pet. This was the red bitch, Canadian Champion Pamelot's Persuasion, the dog

Angela handled the very first time she was ever in a ring."

In 1972 Pamela became an American Kennel Club licensed handler. At that point she cut back on breeding Dobes, keeping only Misty, Dude, Karma, and some of her Toys in order to pursue her handling career and support her daughter; her marriage had dissolved.

In November 1974 a bitch whom Pam had handled became available, and with that bitch, who was one of her favorites, Pamela De Hetre plunged into breeding Dobermans again. The bitch was Champion Sabra Sweetheart of Sigma Chi, C.D., who was bred by Eunice Plotkin Ciaccio, sired by Champion Checkmate's Chessman, the sire of Pamela's first champion. "Gilda" gave Pam five champions. She won the Brood Bitch Class at the Doberman Pinscher Club of America in 1977 over the largest entry (21) for this class in its history. This was the same year that Pam piloted American and Canadian Champion Schauffelein's Vintage Year to his Top Twenty victory.

Gilda was bred to American and Canadian Champion Schauffelein's Troll Arabasque. From this litter came American and Canadian Champion Pamelot's Venice, W.A.C., a multiple Best of Breed winner and Group placer in the United States and a Canadian Best in Show winner. Gilda was also bred to American and Canadian Champion Schauffelein's Vintage Year which produced three champions. These were Champion Pamelot's Applause owned by Sherry Vert, Champion Pamelot's Afternoon Delight owned by Pam with Brenda Turnley, and Pam's favorite dog, Champion Pamelot's Anthony, W.A.C. owned by Marion Caruso, while being finished, after which he belonged to Pam. Anthony lived with Pamela for his entire life and was definitely her dog, right up until his death in September 1982. There are four champions to date among his progeny, with about three others extremely close at this time. Anthony had the ideal Dobe temperament: fiery when anyone approached his pen, or Pam's van or house; playful and silly, always carrying things around, but never, never chewing anything that he shouldn't. He was happy all of the time; wherever he was put he could cope. All of Pam's friends handled him, taking him at ringside and off he would go with them, eager to please. Perry Phillips liked him so well that he used to come to the van and take him out for walks just to play with him.

Champion Pamelot's Applause produced one Canadian champion, Pamelot's Hutch of Versai, who was bred by Sherry Vert and sired by American and Canadian Champion Lowenbrau Magnate. His litter sister, Pamelot's Headliner, was Pam's daughter's Junior Showmanship dog and also has ten points. Champion Pamelot's Afternoon Delight was bred to Champion Marienburg's Sun Hawk, C.D., producing Champion Pamelot's Garrett of Tournal, a multiple Group winner who is now owned by Mary Pistol. There were others as well in that litter who were pointed.

For her second litter, Afternoon Delight was bred to Champion Tedell Key Largo, resulting in Pamelot's Kissimmee of Ted-L who is "major" pointed and should finish. Lastly, Afternoon Delight was bred to Champion Cabra's Dark and Debonaire, from which has come Pamelot's Loaded Pistol (owned by Larry and Brenda Proffitt and Pamela De Hetre), already having seven points at one year old, handled by Larry; Pamelot's Legal Tender, owner-handled by Marcia Wolkerstorfer to several points and a Best of Breed from the puppy classes; Pamelot's Landslide, owned by Barbara and Ben Zahn; and Pamelot's Lilly Langtry, owned by David and Ginger Snipes. The latter two are both not far behind. The first two of these litters were bred by Pam with Brenda Turnley; of the third one, Pamela De Hetre alone was the breeder.

Another of Pamela's Troll daughters, Pamelot's Verenda, was leased back to her for breeding to Alisaton Rufino, a son of American and Canadian Champion Schauffelein's Vintage Year and Champion Alisaton Kinderwicke. This produced Champion Pamelot's Fantasia, whom Pam considers to be one of the best that she has bred. Later Fantasia was bred to Champion Tedell Key Largo, producing a very promising bitch, Pamelot's Make Mine Albelarm, owned by Mrs. Alan R. Robson. Fantasia was co-owned by Gary Bidle and Pamela De Hetre.

Rufino's litter sister, Canadian Champion Alisaton Kinder Vintage, bred to Champion Pamelot's Anthony produced Champion Pamelot's Scandal of Holly-Ky. Scandal was

bred by Marilyn Brush and is owned by Pamela De Hetre and Nancy Wilckens. This black bitch will be handled by Gwen DeMilta and it is expected that her show future will be an exciting one.

Scandal was Anthony's first champion. His others to date are American and Canadian Champion Hickory Hills Hot Stuff, from American and Canadian Champion Loyalist Amiga Hugelhof, W.A.C., bred by Richard Ronevitch and owned by Roberta K. Brady; Champion Aquarius Arian of Criswit owned by Jim Briley, J. Withers and B. Hering; and, from a repeat breeding, Champion Albelarm Jessica of Aquarius owned by Jim Briley and Mrs. Alan Robson. These are out of the Group winning Champion Rehbar Delissa of Aquarius and were bred by Mr. Briley and Mrs. Robson. Two others from this same combination are within a few points of their titles. Another close to the title by Anthony is Hollywood's Grasshopper owned by Beverly Nelson. All told, four champions to date and several others close behind them are on Anthony's record as a sire, which is surely not bad for a dog who only lived to six years.

Behind the bloodlines with which Pam has been so successful stand the great Dobermans of Damasyn and Ahrtal. Each are the producers of outstandingly excellent dogs, and, as Pam points out, it is probably that every successful Doberman bloodline today traces back to one or both of these.

When Nancy Pritchard purchased the gorgeous Popcorn from Sue Neville of Shinya fame, Pamela De Hetre was chosen to be her handler, having already successfully campaigned her illustrious sire, American and Canadian Champion Schauffelein's Vintage Year, owned and bred by Mr. and Mrs. Ron Purdy. The feeling was that what Pam had accomplished with the sire she could do with the daughter, and certainly she and Popcorn made history together. American and Canadian Champion Shinya's Better N'Popcorn, C.D., ROM won four all-breed Bests in Show, numerous Specialties, and many Groups under Pam's handling. She, like her sire, won the Doberman Pinscher Club of America Top Twenty competition. In every way, Popcorn is an incredible bitch! Shown until five years of age, she was then bred, and after having one litter she went out to win the Top Twenty. Following this victory she was given to Pam, the handler with whom she had gained such acclaim. She won the first leg on her C.D. the same day that she won the Veterans Bitch Class at the Lakeshore Doberman Pinscher Club Specialty. Then she had two more litters before again reentering the ring at the Quaker City Doberman Pinscher Club Specialty to capture Best of Breed there. Popcorn was born on June 1, 1975. So far she has produced one champion, bred by Pam, sired by American and Canadian Champion Starstorm's Thunderbolt. As a Doberman judge, the author of this book considers Popcorn to be one of the breed's truly memorable bitches.

Rancho Dobe

Rancho Dobe is one of the most esteemed and successful kennel names in all Doberman history. The owners, Brint and Vivian Edwards, were dedicated breeders who achieved a well-deserved place of honor in our Fancy and who will never be forgotten by the Doberman world.

Vivian Edwards, as she has been quoted as saying, loved Doberman Pinschers way before she knew how to spell the breed's name. Her first approach to owning one was in the form of a cross-bred puppy, Doberman and Shephard combination, a gift from a friend when the Edwardses felt they needed a watchdog. The puppy was killed by a car at six months of age, and Vivian was inconsolable. This was in 1939, and Vivian Edwards was appearing in a radio performance before a live studio audience. The director was not appreciative of her tears during the shows so against her protests presented her with a purebred registered Doberman puppy to help ease the pain of her loss. Right then Dobermans made a new friend and in no time at all both the Edwardses were converts to this wonderful breed.

In 1940 the Edwardses moved from California to St. Louis, Missouri, where Brint was well occupied with his work but Vivian had time to spare on her hands. They decided to join the Greater St. Louis Training Club, with Vivian becoming this newly organized group's first secretary. When Gretchen, their Doberman, had earned her C.D. degree it was decided to breed her, and this produced a litter of eleven puppies sired by a dog with

seven points towards his title. A bitch of quality was acquired from a Chicago breeder. This bitch was bred to Sieger and American Champion Ferry v Rauhfelson of Giralda. In this litter were included two future champion dogs and a bitch, Juno of Moorpark, C.D. (the Edwardses had started out with Moorpark as their kennel name), who turned out to be a great producer and is to be found behind every Rancho Dobe Doberman. This litter represented a linebreeding of a double granddaughter of Sieger Champion Muck v Brunia to a grandson of Muck.

In the year-and-a-half she lived in Missouri, during which her interest in purebred Dobermans was budding, Vivian Edwards spent much time studying Doberman bloodlines, poring over those very worthy works on the breed, the Schmidt and the Gruenig books. Through these she was able to work out a fourteen generation pedigree on her original bitch. It was from this pedigree and from noting the circumstances under which some breedings had been highly successful, others not, that she came to realize the importance of linebreeding which led to breeding the Chicago-purchased bitch to Ferry.

As already noted, the earliest of the Edwardses homebreds bear the kennel identification "of Moorpark." The name Rancho Dobe first appeared as a prefix for them in 1943, used on those Dobermans bred by the Edwardses alone.

Some of the unforgettable Rancho Dobe dogs have included the Best in Show winner Champion Rancho Dobe's Riff and his littermates Goth and Kashmir, all of whom in their turn produced other champions. Riff completed his American and Canadian titles in six consecutive shows, three in each country—certainly a noteworthy accomplishment.

Then there were Champion Rancho Dobe's Primo and Champion Rancho Dobe's Presto, part of a litter from the above-mentioned Kashmir as the result of her being bred to Champion Alcor v Millsdod. Primo sired at least thirty-two American champions and three who made title in foreign countries, which included the Harding litter of eight champions. Presto was a Best in Show winner who also made his American and Canadian championships in six consecutive shows, three in each country. He sired the famed

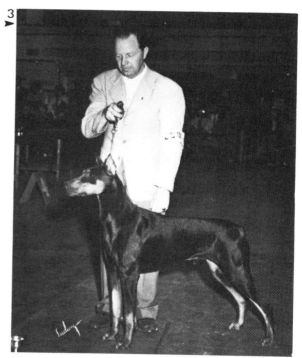

1. Ch. Rancho Dobe's Primo sired 32 champions. Here he is pictured with George Sangster, handling him to win the Stud Dog Class judged by Robert Walters at the Sierra Doberman Pinscher Club Specialty show in March 1955. Pictured with him are seven champions from Mrs. Harding's record-making "Opera" litter. Left to right, all champions are Ch. Harding's Faust, with Claire Steele; Ch. Harding's Rigoletto; Ch. Harding's La Traviata (finished that day); Ch. Harding's Mignon; Ch. Harding's Thais, Ch. Harding's Oberon (also finished that day); and Ch. Harding's La Boheme. The dam of this litter was Ch. BeauLo's Coda; the breeder, Dorothy M. Harding. Ch. Harding's Tosca, missing from this picture, brought the total to eight, which was advertised at the time as the "world's record Doberman litter for champions." Photo courtesy of Rancho Dobe Kennels through Karen Vroom Parkhurst.

2. Ch. Rancho Robe's Roulette, half sister to Ch. Rancho Dobe's Storm. Owned by the Edwardses, Rancho Dobe Kennels. Photo courtesy of Peggy Adamson.

3. Ch. Rancho Dobe's Presto with handler Russell Zimmerman. Sire of the "gambling" litter, which included Ch. Rancho Dobe's Roulette, Fan Tan, Pangingi, and Chuck A'Luck. Photo courtesy of Rancho Dobe Kennels through Karen Vroom Parkhurst.

4. Ch. Alcor v Millsdod, the sire of 33 champions and one of the "greats" of the 1940's. Best of Breed at Westminster on two occasions and sire of Ch. Rancho Dobe's Presto. Photo courtesy of Karen Vroom Parkhurst.

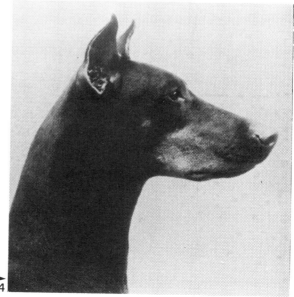

3 ◄

4 ◄

5 ◄

1. A portrait photo by William Brown of Ch. Rancho Dobe's Storm owned by Mr. and Mrs. Len Carey, Greenwich, Connecticut. Photo courtesy of Fran Knoop.
2. Juno of Moorpark, C.D. was Rancho Dobe's foundation bitch and was to be found behind every Rancho Dobe champion. She was the dam of two champions and is to be found behind all of the Rancho Dobes, according to their co-owner, Vivian Edwards.
3. Rancho Dobe's Primo, at 10 years, was Best of Breed the first time shown. The sire of Ch. Rancho Dobe's Storm, Primo gained his title in short order. Here with his handler, Russell Zimmerman. Photo courtesy of Peggy Adamson.
4. The great Ch. Rancho Dobe's Storm in 1952 with his handler, Peter Knoop. This fantastic dog was highly influential in the present-day breeding programs of both England and Australia and was, as well, a dog of importance in the United States.
5. Ch. Haydenhill's Hurrah at nine years with R. E. Souders, competing in the "specials" class that day at Beverly Hills Kennel Club. As the photo clearly shows, quality Dobes hold their excellence to a good age! This dog was the sire of Ch. Rancho Dobe's Maestro, among his 17 champions. An important winner himself who contributed well to his breed. Photo courtesy of Karen Vroom Parkhurst.
6. A youthful informal photo of the renowned Ch. Rancho Dobe's Primo, loaned to us by Karen Vroom Parkhurst.

► 6

1. Ch. Rancho Dobe's Riff, sire of 14 champions. Picture from Karen Vroom Parkhurst. Courtesy of Rancho Dobe Kennels.
2. Rancho Dobe's Cointreau, foundation bitch of Haydenhill Kennels, handled here by Henry "Red" Vroom, Corky Vroom's father. Cointreau was the dam of seven champions, including Ch. Haydenhill's Diana. Photo courtesy of Karen Vroom Parkhurst.

1▲   ▼2

"gambling litter" when only 11½ months old—his first stud service. This litter included Champion Rancho Dobe's Roulette, Fan Tan, Pangingi and Chuck a Luck. Roulette was the first Doberman bitch ever to win more than three all-breed Bests in Show, her record of nine standing unchallenged over about a ten-year period. During this time she produced three litters, two of them sired by Riff, the other by Primo. Fan Tan also attracted considerable notice with her eight Working Groups and four Bests in Show prior to her untimely death when only four years old.

Along with her success as a show bitch, Roulette achieved still further fame as a producing dam. Among her daughters was Champion Rancho Dobe's Cointreau, sired by Riff, who was the foundation bitch at Haydenhill Kennels.

Champion Rancho Dobe's Storm was born in December 1949 at the Rancho Dobe Kennels. He was sired by Champion Rancho Dobe's Primo from Champion Maedel v Randahof, the latter a Ferry and Muck granddaughter. There were thirteen puppies born in this litter, of which four survived. Storm was the only one of them to reach the show ring.

Storm was sold, at three months of age, to advertising executive Len Carey, who came East to divide his time between the Careys' home in Greenwich, Connecticut and New York City. Storm seemed to make the entire world Doberman-conscious, with his beauty, his type, his showmanship and his exciting personality. Peter Knoop handled this magnificent dog through one of the most spectacular careers in dog show history. Shown only on twenty-six occasions, Storm chalked up a total of 17 times Best in Show, two Specialty Bests of Breed, and 22 times first in the Working Group. Included among his Bests in Show were two at Westminster Kennel Club, 1952 and 1953 (only three dogs in all history have ever won Westminster's Best in Show more than once). Storm was retired from further competition following his second Westminster victory. He was the dearly loved housepet of the Carey family until his death in 1960.

Storm was the fifth generation of the Edwardses' Rancho Dobe breeding program.

Storm produced twenty champions. He was defeated in the breed only once, this while a puppy. It is noteworthy that his accomplishments were gained at probably one of the keenest competitive periods in Working Group history, as the also very great Boxer, Champion Bang Away of Sirrah Crest, was being campaigned at that same time.

Vivian Edwards passed away before work on this book was started. Karen Vroom Parkhurst, knowing of my anxiety to cover the kennel with full justice here, very kindly contacted Brint Edwards for me, received his permission to write about the dogs and the loan of a number of valued pictures for reproduction. We are deeply grateful to her, and to Mr. Edwards, for his section of the book. Karen, as we all know, owned one of the greatest of the Rancho Dobes, Champion Maestro, who was descended from Storm, Cointreau, Bach, Bongo, and others. The esteem and friendship Karen felt for the Edwardses is very evident in her remarks which I quote as follows: "I do not know how many champions they (the Edwardses) produced, but when Maestro got his title they sent a card of congratulations saying that he was their 34th. I could go on and on about the Edwardses, and all I feel that they did for the Doberman. If we look back on most of our well-known lines we will find that Rancho Dobe had a large hand in their getting started, and I doubt that there are many lines which do not trace back to Rancho Dobe. Of course most of them would be back seven or eight generations now (in the mid 1980's)."

Rancho Dobe Kennels were voted Breeders of the Year in 1971 by *Kennel Review* Magazine. At the time, *Kennel Review* carried the following notation: "The Edwardses' outstanding contributions to the sport of dogs stem from approximately 300 puppies whelped since 1941, many of which were record holders for Group and Best in Show wins, along with the numerous Champions and Top Producers bred by Rancho Dobe." The winners of this award, known in the Fancy as "The Winkie," are selected by secret ballot of more than 1,800 licensed Variety Group and All-Breed judges, licensed handlers, and members of The Dog Writers Association of America.

1. Ch. Rancho Dobe's Presto, litter brother of Primo, Storm's sire. Owned by the Edwardses, Rancho Dobe Kennels.
2. Ch. Maedel v Randahof, the dam of Ch. Rancho Dobe's Storm, was by Mr. Butch of Rittenhouse (son of Ch. Ferry v Rauhfelsen of Giralda ex Kara v Randahof) ex Ch. Indra v Lindenhof (by Sieger and Ch. Muck v Brunia ex Mitzi of Lawnwood). Photo courtesy of Peggy Adamson.
3. Ch. Rancho Dobe's Primo, sire of Ch. Rancho Dobe's Storm, by Ch. Alcor v Millsdod ex Ch. Rancho Dobe's Kashmir. Bred and owned by Brint and Vivian Edwards.
4. Ch. Domossi of Marienland, red older brother of Dictator, was from the second litter of Ch. Blank v d Domstadt ex Ch. Sgn. Ossi v Stalhelm. Bred by John Cholley; owned by Richard Webster.
5. Int. Ch. Roxanna's Emperor v Reemon produced 17 champions, among them Ch. Rancho Dobe's Riff. Photos and information courtesy of Rancho Dobe Kennels through Karen Vroom Parkhurst.
6. Ch. Ebonaire's Laurel, owned by Dot Roberts, Rockelle Kennels, New City, New York.
7. Ch. Red Sun's Friendly Persuasion, owned by John Writer, Chicago, Illinois. A full sister to Ch. Red Sun's Notorious.

5 ◄   6 ►

7 ▼

293

Red Sun

Red Sun Dobermans are owned by John and Rita Armonia at Hopewell, New Jersey, breeders who have met with considerable success with their Dobes right from the beginning. For their first Dobe they had the good fortune to own the marvelous red dog, Champion Van Majer's Elijah's Red Sun, for whom they have named their kennel. "J. R." scored almost instant success, shown from start to finish by Jane Forsyth, finishing his title in a month-and-a-half's time. He was a member of the Top Twenty Dobermans in the Nation for three consecutive years and has sired eight American champions with seventeen others of his progeny pointed.

Behind J. R. one finds some of the most noted and respected names in the Doberman world. His paternal grandsire, Champion Tarrado's D'Artagnon, was a son of Champion Steb's Gunga Din (he by Champion Steb's Top Skipper), while on the maternal side, his grandsire was Champion Gra-Lemor Demetrius v d Victor and his granddam a daughter of Champion Mark's Tey Shawn. Champion Red Sun's Notorious finished before the age of three and was a multi-Best of Breed and Group placing dog. But most noteworthy is his record as a top producing sire, as he has multiple Group winners together, including the 1982 Top Twenty winner, Champion Black Star's Rani Gemma, WAC.

Champion Red Sun's Captain Fantastic finished his title in eleven starts from the Open Class with four "majors" and breed and Group placements from the classes. He is now just embarking on his "specials" career, and his owners have high hopes for him.

Rocado

Rocado Dobermans are founded on a combination of Indigo Rock and Toledobe bloodlines by Do Dillon at Barrington, Illinois late in the 1960's. All of the breeding there has been based upon Champion Andelane's Indigo Rock whose sire, Champion Ru-Mar's Morgansonne, C.D., was by Champion Rancho Dobe's Cello ex Champion Jessamyn II vom Ahrtal and whose dam, Jemoel's Maui v. Cassio, was by Champion Cassio vom Ahrtal ex Champion Jemoel's Elaine (a granddaughter of Champion Borong the Warlock, C.D.).

"Rocky" was born in June 1969 and died in November 1977. He was bred by Andy and Elaine Komorby and owned by Robert Bishop of New York.

Rocky had been purchased by Mr. Bishop as a pet. He finished from the puppy classes when he was eleven months old, going on to a short but brilliant career as a special. When he retired, at age three years, he had to his credit 189 times Best of Breed plus 21 all-breed Bests in Show. This dog was a breeder's dream come true, Do Dillon points out, having that special ability to pass on his quality and type to his offspring. Bred very sparingly, he nonetheless produced 22 American champions and many others close to finishing. Two of his daughters were Best in Show winners as were countless grandchildren. His sons, daughters and grandchildren have proven themselves capable of consistently producing "the Rocky type."

Do Dillon selected Rocky progeny on which to found her kennel and states that she now is "really the only one carrying on the Rocky line at present, as Bob Bishop no longer has the time to devote to doing so since moving East to New York." Since 1978 Do has consistently linebred from Rocky, and both she and Bob Bishop are well pleased with the results.

The kennel identification "Rocado" was coined from a combination of Do's first name and Rock. She purchased her foundation bitch as a eight- week-old puppy who became Champion Bishop's Dulcinea v. Rock and a year later acquired the litter brother who was to become Champion Bishop's Borong v. Rock. Both finished owner-handled before reaching two years of age. Dulcinea culminated a short "specials" career with a Best in Show and retired to the whelping box. Borong then was "specialed" for two years, doing very well with numerous Bests of Breed and Group placements. His greatest value, however, was as a sire. Like his father he was bred sparingly (Do's philosophy is "quality, not quantity"), siring only a total of 42 puppies, eight of them in Japan. As of this writing, six of his progeny have become champions with five others close to finishing. Unfortunately his stud career was cut short by his untimely death of cardiomyopathy in 1982.

1. Ch. High Tor's Arabella winning Best of Breed in 1972 for Dot Roberts. Ellen Hoffman handling.
2. Ch. Adora's Jayhawker v. Rock, by Ch. Andelane's Indigo Rock ex Adora's Angel Sunshine. Bred by Gerald Brewer; owned and handled by Do Dillon, Barrington, Illinois.

1▲   ▼2

Do also owned and finished another Rock son, Champion Adora's Jayhawker v. Rock. Bred to two of Rock's daughters, Champion Bishop's Dulcinea v. Rock and Champion Bishop's Mirror Image v. Rock, Jayhawker has sired three champions.

Bob Bishop and Do Dillon co-owned Champion Charmaron's Rockette from whom they co-bred several litters. Among the progeny was Bishop's Reprise v. Rocado, who became Do's first homebred champion, finishing entirely from the Bred-by-Exhibitor Class.

Champion Rocado I Got You Under My Skin was Dulcinea's first champion, and Champion Rocado My Way is Do's newest one. He completed his title in September 1984 and is a double Rock grandson from the brother-sister breeding of Borong and Dulcinea. As of the time of this writing, his puppies are very young, but he is passing on the same qualities his father did before him. Do has high hopes for him as a sire.

In 1983 Do Dillon acquired ownership of Champion Renejade the Jazz Singer from his breeder, Nancy Christensen. He is currently being campaigned by Roger Thompson and is Borong's biggest winning son to date. He is the No. 3 Doberman for 1984 and a third generation Best in Show winner. Puppies from his first litter are already pointed, and his owners are hopeful that he will carry on the Rock tradition of quality type Dobermans.

Speaking of Renejade the Jazz Singer, his breeder-co-owner Nancy Christensen relates an incident involving him which we feel should be included here as an example of the true temperament of Doberman show dogs. Nancy and her friend Marilyn Heiden were driving home to Nebraska from Boston accompanied by Jazz Singer and Marilyn's young bitch, Silent Sentry's Sandcastle. Stopping to exercise the dogs at a rest area in Iowa, the two had their Dobermans on lead at the designated "pet exercise area," keeping each at an opposite end of this space as Marilyn's bitch was in season. First thing she knew, Nancy heard a dog barking wildly and turned to see a man actually "siccing" a medium-sized spotted mongrel on herself and her dog. Nancy pulled Jazz Singer in close to her, and as the mutt reached about two feet from

her in its attack, she aimed and kicked it under the jaw, sending it yelping back to its owners. As Nancy says, "I hated doing that, but I sure wasn't going to stand there and allow my dog or me to be bitten." At this point harsh words were exchanged between Nancy and these people, with the result that the man who, quoting Nancy, "was six feet tall and looked like a gorilla" started advancing on her, and Nancy realized to her horror that he was carrying a knife. And that is when her happy, friendly Doberman took action! This seventeen-month-old show dog swelled up with every hackle on end and took his stand about two feet from his owner, straining on his lead and growling loudly. The "gorilla" stopped dead in his tracks; then he and his friend got their dog and left. Another example of the true Doberman devotion and spirit coming to the fore! Jazz Singer, incidentally, is a great grandson of the legendary Champion Marks Tey the Maverick who died of a bullet wound sustained while protecting his loved ones.

Rockelle

Dot Roberts acquired her first Doberman from Alton Anderson, the noted animal photographer, in September 1970. She was out of Champion Damasyn the Troycen and Champion Ebonaire's Laurel, one of ten puppies in the litter. Six of the puppies had been graded as show quality, and the one Dot acquired was number six. Knowing nothing about showing, and really looking for just a pet, Dot was delighted when told that she could have her.

At Alton Anderson's urging, the Robertses took their new puppy to some match shows, and after a few placement ribbons, they were hooked! The puppy finished her championship at two years of age, becoming Champion High Tor's Arabella and the foundation bitch for Dot's Rockelle Kennels which have put New City, New York on the Doberman map. It is interesting to note that "Belle" was the only puppy from that litter who finished, although several of her litter mates were pointed. Only out briefly as a "special," she had several Bests of Breed and a Group I to her credit.

While Belle was doing all this, the Robertses acquired their second Doberman, this one purchased from Ellen Hoffman. He was Elfred's Rock & Rye by Champion Elfred's The President ex Champion Elfred's Nikki.

Belle was bred to Rock & Rye to produce the Robertses first Dobe litter, and they fell in love with a red puppy dog among them whom they took to Florida for the January circuit (just for the ride, really, as they were showing "Rocky" at that time). On the circuit, the Robertses met George Rood who liked their pup and agreed to take another look at him that summer. When he did so, he promptly agreed to show him the following October at the National. Meanwhile, Terry Lazzaro had taken him to a couple of shows in the local area and had put his first point on him. The Robertses went to Houston for the Specialty and took Reserve Winners Dog at 14 months of age. George Rood said that he would take the dog on the Florida circuit, so off the Robertses went and their puppy came home with Winners Dog from the first three shows, Reserve Winners Dog in the fourth show, and Winners Dog the fifth time to finish. No small accomplishment, with which I am certain anyone familiar with the huge and highly competitive entries on the Florida circuit in Dobes will agree! This dog is Champion Rockelle's Sparklin Burgundy, who finished at 17 months of age. He was shown sporadically and he did his share of winning as a "special," but he really did not enjoy the ring and was much happier at home.

Belle had been bred again by now, this time to Champion Tamarak's Rampage V Flores, a dog owned at that time by Ray Carlisle. Among the puppies was a red bitch that the Robertses particularly liked, so she was kept to try her luck in the ring. In December when she was 18 months old Bob Forsyth was asked if he would handle her at the Quaker City Specialty; he agreed, and she went Winners Bitch there for a five-point "major." In January, again it was off to Florida with George Rood, where three "majors" were added, and then, one point short of title, Jane Forsyth took over, finishing her in April with a Best of Breed from the classes. This bitch thus became Champion Rockelle's Country Bumpkin.

Country Bumpkin was bred to Sparklin Burgundy and again there was a red male

puppy the Robertses really liked. At seventeen months old he followed the by now familiar pattern of "off to Florida" with George Rood, and he returned with two "majors." The Robertses took him to Ohio, where George picked up a few more points with him, and then finally only two points were needed. Again Jane Forsyth took over, and on the first show out with him two points were won and Champion Rochelle's Butch Cassidy, W.A.C. was finished. At that time, George, Jane and Terry all had "specials" dogs so Richard Bauer took Butch for a couple of months until Jane's "special" dog retired. Then Jane took Butch and specialed him for a year, which was her last year of handling. When Jane retired, Carlos Rojas took Butch and showed him for about seven months. In his time out as a "special," Butch took about 65 Bests of Breed, many Group placements and was in the Doberman Pinscher Club of America Top Twenty for three consecutive years—the last year, to Dot Roberts's great sorrow, posthumously, as Butch died quite suddenly at four years of age. Prior to his death he had been used sparingly at stud.

Fortunately, Butch had been bred to Champion Kocot Pajant de Scudamore, C.D.X., ROM, who was owned by Dot's friend Bobbie Hall. This breeding produced eight red males and one red bitch. Dot told Bobbie she would take a puppy in lieu of a stud fee. She waited for Dot to make her choice, which she did when the pups were three months old, selecting one of the males. This puppy turned out to be Champion Pajant's Encore V Rockelle, W.A.C., known to his friends as "Cory." When George Rood looked at this puppy, his comment was, "I'm ready when he is." He graded him as an excellent puppy, something we understand he has done on fewer than a dozen such occasions to date. Come January it was, as usual, down to Florida for the Robertses. Cory was now in the 9-12-month puppy class. He took Winners Dog for 5-points under Betty Moore and another 5-point "major," going through to Best of Breed under Frank McCarthy. Needing one point to finish, the Robertses took him back to Ohio to finish, making him a champion at eleven months!

1. Rocky Shores Mokuaha by Ch. Wynterwynd's Spring Tornado ex Ch. Wynterwynd's Stardust Magic, born September 1981. Breeders, Louis F. and Bernice M. Muench. Mrs. Muench is co-owner with Linda K. Chance.
2. Ro-Jan's Good Time Charlie takes Best of Breed from the American-bred Class, handled by Samuel Shelton under judge Theodore Wurmser for owner Carlo P. Roppolo, Jr., Shreveport, Louisiana.

Now the Robertses started travelling to Ohio every weekend. George did very well with Cory, making good wins in both breed and Group competition. However, the weekly roundtrip to Ohio was taking its toll on the Robertses, and when they found that Terry Lazzaro was available, they decided to try Cory out locally with her. Dot Roberts's comment on this now is, "It turned out to be a match made in heaven. Seeing them in the ring together is a joy to watch." Terry has piloted Cory to No. 2 Dobe in the country, Doberman Pinscher Club of America Top Twenty standing. For 1983 alone, Cory had 50 Bests of Breed, 11 times first in the Group, 22 Group placements, and an all-breed Best in Show, at only two-and-a-half years old. He was already in the Doberman Pinscher Club of America Top Twenty in 1983 and will be in this year (as we write) as well.

Among the beautiful top-quality bitches who have been bred to Cory thus far are Champion Dawn-Ri's Desperada, Canadian Champion Jagermeister's Lady Be Good, Champion Blackstar's Rani Jemma (Top Twenty winner 1982), Champion Vormunds Priceless Gem, Champion D'Mascus Tia Maria, Champion Aquarius Cirabria of Celadon, Canadian Champion Vondersha's Hot Copy, Champion Warwick's Zanessa De Valehr, Cara's Dallas Cow Girl, and Daramar's Howling Success. His oldest progeny are still only a year-and-a-half old but almost every one of them that has been shown consistently in puppy classes is pointed, including several with "majors." Cory is now being shown by Jeff Brucker and has added many Bests in Show.

Rocky Shores

The owners of the Rocky Shores Dobermans, Bernice and Louis Muench of Alexander, Arkansas, got into Dobermans by way of obedience. They bred several litters of companion dogs that have made excellent pets and obedience winners. Betsy Adams, of Largo, Florida, owns the best trained of the Rocky Shores obedience workers–Kentucky's Jana of Rocky Shores, who earned her C.D. in three shows and thus won a *Dog World* Award. She also had the C.D.X. and U.D. degrees, along with a tracking title, and she was awarded a W.A.C. Temperament Test. She participated in the Gaines Regionals one

year (1980), earning sixth place in her class and being the only Dobe. She has been listed several times in the Top Ten Working lists in magazines. Since Betsy has worked professionally as a dog trainer, Mr. and Mrs. Muench are very proud when she says that Jana is the smartest dog with which she ever has worked.

Mr. and Mrs. Muench purchased their champion show bitch from Wynterwynd Kennels when she was five-and-a-half months old. After almost three years of showing her, with some blues and some reserves, Mr. and Mrs. Muench felt they were too old to personally handle a working dog competitively in the ring. For awhile the Muenches tried having a handler take her, but in this way she moved from handler to handler; thus no one got to know and understand how to bring out the best in her, as no one had her as his or her own bitch. Jeffrey Brucker took her on, but mostly wound up supervising another handler for her because of conflicts with prior clients' entries; he did get a five-point "major" on her along the way. Finally, with fourteen points on their bitch, the Muenches felt that they really must breed her if they ever intended to do so. They had long anticipated that she would do well for them as a producer. She gave them four puppies, the result of a linebreeding, and two of them are already pointed. Linda Chance, co-owner of one, is learning to handle and doing very well at it. Her fourth time in the ring, at the Memphis Specialty under Edd Bivin, her dog was awarded Winners, which was very exciting for a novice handler with a fourteen-month-old young Doberman!

As for Wyndy herself, she finished at five-and-a-half years of age after having her four sons, so she is now Champion Wynterwynd's Stardust Magic.

Rodiah

Rodiah Dobermans, Conestoga, Pennsylvania, is a fairly new kennel owned by a most enthusiastic fancier, Diana Stoner, who bred her first bitch, Kayza von Stetton, to a Fortune Hunter son. She kept the "pick" puppy from this litter, who was to become her first homebred champion, Rodiah's Sly-Stone Stinger. From the time Stinger entered the ring he was a hit and at ten months of age was in the Open Class, completing his title at 16 months. Very nice going in so highly competitive a breed as Dobermans!

Shown as a "special," Stinger continued making his presence felt by taking Best of Breed on twenty occasions and several Group placements, and he is already proving himself an excellent stud dog.

The breeding program at Rodiah is based mainly on Amulet and Edelhall lines, especially those related to Edelhall Gigolo of Amulet. At present there is a Stinger son with "major" points and several promising puppies are also coming along.

Ro-Jan

Ro-Jan Dobermans are owned by Jane Roppolo at Shreveport, Louisiana who has some very excellent Dobes in which to take pride.

Champion Ro-Jan's Crisium Coty was bred by Jane Roppolo, who co-owns him with Irwin J. Rice, M.D. This handsome dog finished his championship by winning three "majors" on the highly competitive Texas circuit, finishing in seven shows. Then his first time out as a "special," handled by Mike Shea under judge Betty Moore, he went Best of Breed over fourteen other titled contenders. Coty was among the Top Ten Dobermans in 1979 and in 1980. He is of Gra-Lemor breeding, being a grandson of Champion Gra-Lemor Plain N' Fancy Lil Eva (Champion Damasyn Derringer ex Jerry Run's Boo Sprite), and a descendant of Champion Gra-Lemor Demetrius v. d. Victor (also by Champion Damasyn Derringer ex Jerry Run's Boo Sprite), and Champion Gra-Lemor v. Brandywine (by Champion Egothels All American).

Ro-Jan Good Time Charlie is a full brother to Coty from a repeat breeding of the sire and dam. He was Best of Breed at the Doberman Pinscher Club of Louisiana Specialty from the American-bred Class to retire the Champion Dolph von Tannenwald Trophy (Coty had been Best of Breed at this event the two preceding years), a very exciting honor for his breeder-owner Jane Roppolo.

Champion Sherluck Falcon v Marienburg was bred by Gary and Fay Strauss and is owned by Jane Roppolo and Marienburg Kennels. He is a son of Champion Marienburg Sun Hawk, C.D. from Champion Morago Hills Desert Wind (both Top Producers). He has many nice wins to his credit, including Best of Breed in California from the American-bred Class over one hundred Dobes.

Royalmead

Royalmead Dobermans, owned by Ginanna Crouch, D.V.M. and Ann E. Nelson at Brookshire, Texas, are currently crossing the Wynterwynd and Tolivar bloodlines.

Their foundation bitch, Tolivar's Belle of the Ball, WAC, known as "Gaby," is a daughter of Champion Tolivar's Aristotle of Azteca and was bred to Champion Wynterwynd's Spring Meadow, son of Champion Mikadobe's Cupid ex Champion Wynterwynd's Irish Spring. Later, on two occasions, she was bred to Champion Wynterwynd's Wild Tempest, son of Wynterwynd's Top Candidate ex Mi Casa's Buena. Two from the first breeding gained championships at a very early age, becoming Champion Royalmead's Penny Ante and Champion Royalmead's Jokers Wild. Two of their littermates are currently pointed, Royalmead's Black Jack and Royalmead's Pat Hand. One bitch puppy, Royalmead's Wheel of Fortune, out of the repeat breeding, has distinguished herself with a Best in Match win, a Best Puppy Specialty win, and several reserves in good competition. Penny Ante is now owned by Faye Elkin, A. Nelson, and G. Crouch, D.V.M. and is being shown in the East by Bob Stebbins where she has already won one Best in Show.

Royalmead's Night Editor, a son of Champion Royalmead's Jokers Wild, is already major pointed at ten months of age. And there are a number of other promising youngsters also coming along.

The owners of Royalmead Kennels describe themselves as "the new kid on the block." They are anticipating weaving their breeding program back and forth between the two lines they have selected. Their goal is to produce new prospects which can exemplify that excellence required for success in the show ring today.

Scotsbrae

Scotsbrae Dobermans are owned by Jeanne A. Ratcliff and are located at Greenville, Georgia. Jeanne has been a "horse and dog" person since the day she was born and has never deviated from this interest. Her first Doberman Pinscher was the first of the Champion Rancho Dobe Storm grandsons whelped in the early 1950's, although when she registered Scotsbrae with the American Kennel Club as her kennel name in 1953, it was intended as an identification for her Collie breeding operations. It was not until 1966, when she purchased a Champion Bailes Bronz Baron Nordo son and a triple Top Skipper bitch, that she started breeding a few litters of Dobermans.

From her early breeding program in Dobes, the bitches have pretty well disappeared from her current pedigrees. But Ebony Baron of Scotsbrae, known as "Dog," is the great-grandsire of her current American and Canadian Obedience Trial Champion Rare Ebony Wine of Scotsbrae, U.D.T., WAC, Canadian U.D. Ebony Baron himself was never shown as Jeanne was "trying to stay away from dog shows in order to appease her anti-show husband." When their marriage finally split up, however, in 1979, she put the Obedience Trial Championship on "Sherry," as Rare Ebony Wine is known, giving this first priority as Sherry was already six years old at the time.

Sherry finished her Obedience Trial Championship as a seven year old, competing mostly in local shows in stiff competition. Earlier she had gained a U.D. at two years old when Jeanne had taken her on a New England circuit. Later a trip was made to Canada where Sherry picked up titles too. As Jeanne comments, "It is a measure of the dog's reliability that we were able to enter five and six show circuits 1,500 miles away and come home with two titles. On her last Canadian trip Sherry demonstrated Utility exercises for Canadian television at the request of the judges. She was such a quick one to learn. Show her something once and she usually had it, unlike some dogs who have to be schooled constantly to stay up on things. She went months, at one point years, without practice; then I'd enter a show and we'd do a little brushing up and she'd go out there and look great." Certainly indicative of a high degree of both intelligence and willingness!

Sherry was bred one time to Champion Triadel's High Flyer. He and she are both

Champion Dolph von Tannenwald grandchildren, and it was a good "nick." Had she been able to show as she would have like to do or had access to show homes for the puppies, Jeanne feels certain that quite a few of them would have finished. She took three of the males through the Doberman Pinscher Club of America Temperament Test (TT) and got WAC degrees on them. She also put tracking titles on two, and a third was certified to track. That third son was also a High in Trial dog and Jeanne had him trained through C.D.X. but was never sure when he'd be available to compete in a trial, so he never had the opportunity to earn the titles. He was also shown occasionally in breed and won some nice classes. He is Scotsbrae's Flaming Rites, C.D., WAC. Scotsbrae's Kiss of Fire, a red daughter from the same breeding, also earned several points. And, "the best candidate for everything, breed and obedience, Scotsbrae's Mephisto Waltz," was never shown at all. The latter elegant black bitch when bred to Champion Gambolwood's Hellelujah gave her owner Champion Scotsbrae's Fallen Angel, T.D., ROM, an all-breed Best in Show and Specialty Best of Breed winner. Hopes for the future as we go to press center around a planned breeding of Angel to Champion Toliver's Boo Radley Dob Mann.

We feel that Jeanne Ratcliff has some accomplishments with her Dobes in which to take justifiable pride. Sherry has been in the Obedience Top Twenty during both of the years when she was in competition, once to get the scores she needed to compete in the Gaines Obedience Classic (only scores of 195 or higher qualify) and the year she was working for her Obedience Trial Championship. Again quoting Jeanne, "The Doberman Pinscher Club of America has changed the requirements for the Top Twenty, and had they then been as they are now, Sherry would never have been out of it. She earned many thirds, for example, over 195 points, which in past years did not count for anything although it does now since the change. We had our own Atlanta Obedience Club, in which at least three Golden Retrievers were having a bad day as they averaged below 197, so Sherry earned her OTCH points the hard way."

In the United States and in Canada, Sherry was a Super Dog Contender in the Gaines Classic at the same time that her High in Trial son was a Classic competitor as a Novice.

Angel, Sherry's granddaughter, has been breeder-owner-handled entirely throughout her show career. She was always very competitive and finished quite rapidly when seriously campaigned. She is now an all-breed Best in Show winner in addition to her obedience successes.

As a breeder-owner-handler, and one not too widely known in Dobes, Jeanne surely has many credits due her based on the fact that her "family" includes an all-breed Best in Show winner, an Obedience Trial Champion, a Specialty Best of Breed winner, a Canadian Obedience Trial Champion, an ROM, five WAC's, five T.D. titlists, Top Twenty Obedience competitors two years, and multiple other obedience honors and dogs pointed in conformation competition.

Serenade

Serenade Dobermans are a product of the early 1980's, a very new kennel and a very ambitious one. The owner is Jan MacDonald of Houston, Texas who purchased her first show puppy in 1981.

Now her Dobes include Champion Royalmead's Joker's Wild, by Champion Wynterwynd's Wild Tempest ex Tolivar's Belle of the Ball, W.A.C., who is her first champion, having finished at fourteen months, owner-handled all the way. Very nice going in a breed as competitive as this one! At 20 months of age he is a multi-Best of Breed winner, again owner-handled.

There are two excellent bitches on whom the breeding program is being founded: Wynterwynd's Fox of Tempesta, daughter of Wynterwynd's Wild Tempest ex Wynterwynd's Tequila Sunset, who has ten points with one "major" and is currently being shown as we write, and Wynterwynd's Desiree, by Champion Wynterwynd's Wild Tempest ex Champion Kyjur's Respond Sil Vous Plait, who has seven points and is also currently being shown. Ms. MacDonald has personally pointed all three of these Dobes and looks forward to the two bitch winners being finished by the time this appears in print.

Serenade Dobermans recently bred their first litter, by Joker's Wild ex Wynterwynd's Lady O'The Nite, and their owner is anticipating one of these lovely puppies becoming her first homebred champion.

Shartasia

Shartasia Dobermans are among the newer kennels and are owned by Debbie Keezer at Houston, Texas who has started out with some excellent foundation bitches all bred by Kathleen Pollack.

Champion Wynterwynd's Crimson Shadow is a daughter of Champion Elexa's Final Flair of Selena ex Champion Wynterwynd's Rusti Nail. She earned her first points at only seven months of age, owner-handled, and was the winner of the 9-12 month Any Other Allowed Color Class at the 1982 National Specialty, also winning her Futurity Class there.

At 13 months, Shadow went Best of Breed from the American-bred Class over "specials," and on to Group II. She finished at 20 months, owner-handled by Debbie Keezer all the way. Now she is a multi-Best of Breed and multi-Group placement winner at age 20 months, still proudly owner-handled.

Champion Wynterwynd's Tax Specialist, by Champion Wynterwynd's Wild Tempest ex Wynterwynd's Spring Breeze, was Best Puppy in Sweepstakes at the San Antonio Specialty, owner-handled, when only one day over six months of age. As a mature bitch, she was handled by Teresa Nail, gaining her title at two years and three months old after receiving both her "majors" in the huge Dobe entries of the 1984 Florida circuit.

Wynterwynd's Indian Summer is the baby of the family, just starting out on her show career. She is by Champion Wynterwynd's Wild Tempest ex Champion Wynterwynd's Summer Breeze.

Sherluck

Sherluck Dobermans are owned by Faye Strauss at Kent, Washington who has met with considerable and well-deserved success in the Doberman Pinscher world. Since she believes in holding breeding to a limited basis, there have been only six litters bred at Sherluck as we are writing. Yet the number of champions raised there (which should have risen considerably by now, as several are but

1. Ch. Silent Sentry's Bikini, by Ch. Tedell's Eleventh Hour ex High Hale's Camelot. Bred by Betty Brockman James; owned by Mr. and Mrs. Myron R. James, Tampa, Florida.

2. Ch. Moraga Hills Desert Wind, the dam of 10 American champions and one Obedience Trial champion to date, with more on the way. Top Producer, Doberman Pinscher Club of America Award, 1980 and 1983. A Specialty and Group winner. Bred by Ray and Joan Frank; owned by Faye and Gary Strauss.

3. Ch. Azteca's Bellona finishing her title under judge Herman Cox. This lovely bitch, the great granddam of Ch. Arco Dob Mann, gained her championship between September 1967 and March 1969. Her wins included Best of Breed from the classes and Group 2nd at Tampa Bay under Dr. Shute and Best of Winners at Westminster under Mrs. Augustus Riggs, II. Owned by Mrs. Edd Bivin, Fort Worth, Texas.

1▲

▼2

1. Ch. Steb's Point of Order taking Best of Opposite Sex at the 1957 Connecticut–New York Specialty. Handled by J. Monroe Stebbins. Bred by Natalie Stebbins, she was sired by Delegate v d Elbe from Tauzieher Lady Ambercrest, who was the dam, as well, of Ch. Dortmund Delly's Colonel Jet.
2. Ch. Steb's Point of Order with J. Monroe Stebbins.

a few points short of their titles) stands at eighteen. Certainly an imposing accomplishment which speaks well for the breeding talents of the owner!

Among the Sherluck Dobes one finds numerous breed, Group and Specialty show winners and some Top Twenty Dobes. Currently the young Sherluck's Desert Gypsy is nationally ranked in obedience.

From their pictures you will note the splendid quality of the Sherluck dogs.

Sierra

Sierra Dobermans are owned by Ann Lanier and located at Pacifica, California.

The current "star" here is Bambi, more formally known as Champion Wynterwynd's Sierra Shadow who is by Champion Elexa's Final Flair of Selena (Champion Tarrados Flair ex American and Canadian Champion Vivians Selena) from Champion Wynterwynd's Rusti Nail (American and Canadian Champion Amulet's Cedric v. Gluckliche ex Colombian Champion Redlich's Always Rosy, CACIB).

Bambi is the Laniers' third Doberman, purchased after the death of their first one and the purchase of a second one, Tracker, the original dog's grandson, who turned out to be less than showable but is a splendid working dog. It took about a year of careful study and research into kennels, bloodlines, and what it takes to make an outstanding show dog after Tracer joined the family before the selection of Bambi was made—time well spent as Bambi has proven a delight in every way.

Bambi started right out winning 75% of the classes in which she was entered. She delighted her owner when she was selected Grand Prize Futurity Reserve at the Doberman Pinscher Club of America Specialty in 1982, as well as Best nine-to-twelve-month puppy. In twenty months she had become Champion Wynterwynd's Sierra Shadow, and except for two single points, her wins were all in California. Bambi defeated the No. 1 and No. 2 Dobermans in the United States at ten months of age. The Laniers indeed consider themselves to have been very fortunate in this purchase! Bambi was bred and purchased from Kathy Pollack.

As we are preparing to send this book to press, Champion Wynterwynd's Sierra Shadow stands Top Doberman Bitch (Routledge Group System, May 1984), Top Doberman Bitch (Canine Chronicle System), Top 25 Working Group (Routledge Group System), Top Twenty Doberman—Doberman Pinscher Club of America (in four months as a "special"), and a Top Ten Doberman (Routledge Breed System).

Silent Sentry

Silent Sentry Dobermans, established in 1961, is owned by Betty Brockman James and Myron James of Tampa, Florida. This kennel has never believed in quantity but has produced some top quality dogs from just a few litters.

Their first puppy was a bitch sired by Champion Damasyn the Gambler. She was bred to Champion Derek of Marks-Tey and produced one black male. This puppy won the Best Futurity Puppy Award at the 1964 Doberman Pinscher Club of America National Specialty, as well as Best Puppy in Show, and finished his championship to become Champion Solo Sentry of Marks-Tey, C.D. at 14 months of age. He, in turn, produced three champions. This breeding was repeated and produced three puppies of which one male, Silent Sentry's Samurai, gathered eight points prior to his untimely death at a young age.

In 1965 Betty purchased another bitch, from the Melvin Dolds in Kansas, named High Halo's Camelot sired by Champion Marks-Tey's Hanover out of Champion High Halo's Brooke of Kondo. Camelot was bred to Champion Tedell Eleventh Hour and produced a lovely blue bitch puppy who also went Best Puppy in Show at the 1968 Doberman Pinscher Club of America National Specialty and went on to become Champion Silent Sentry Bikino, finishing with five "majors."

This breeding was also repeated, resulting in one black bitch, Silent Sentry's Dojoji San. Joji was bred to Champion Marks-Tey The Maverick and produced Mexican Champion Silent Sentry's Mi Rajas and Champion Silent Sentry's Marauder, W.A.C. Marauder finished his championship with four "majors" and two smaller pointed shows at 21 months of age. He was shown on a limited basis the following year and was No. 8 in the Top

Twenty in 1979. He did not win the Top Twenty but was only one-and-a-half points below the winner on the total tally.

In August 1983, Maraurder was old enough for the Veterans' Class at the Florida West Coast Doberman Pinscher Club Specialty and went on to Best of Breed there from that class. In October 1983 he also won the Veterans' Class at the Doberman Pinscher Club of America National Specialty and was one of four dogs still under consideration until the very end.

Silent Sentry Jubilee, also a daughter of Joji by Marks-Tey Dust Commander, was bred to Marauder and produced Silent Sentry's Renaissance, who in turn was bred to Champion Bishop's Borong v Rock and produced Best in Show Champion Renejade the Jazz Singer.

At Silent Sentry, as previously stated, quantity has never been the goal, and Mauraurder was allowed to breed only what the Jameses felt were compatible bitches. Even so, with few breedings, he has produced two champions with four others very close to the title, including Silent Sentry's Sand Castle, some other outstanding get are just beginning.

Silent Sentry Dobermans all live in their home with Betty and Myron James, as family members, which is the way their owners prefer it, as do the dogs.

Stafford

Stafford Dobermans are owned by Jack and Melba Stafford of California who first acquired one of the breed in 1948. In 1955 they bred their first litter under the kennel prefix Wallire. This produced Champion Wallire's Rupert, a Best in Show winner who formed the foundation for the later Stafford Dobes.

The first breeding, with Stafford for the kennel prefix, was the one which produced Stafford Sparkle, who became the true foundation bitch for this kennel. Bred to Steb's Blazing Raven she became the dam of three champions, Stafford's Sparkling Moselle and Sparkling Toddy from the first litter and Champion Stafford's Spitfire from the repeat breeding in 1964. The latter, Spitfire, eventually was bred to Champion Rancho Dobe's Maestro with a resulting four champions, the progeny of which are still producing well.

Mr. and Mrs. Stafford have bred very few litters and permit use of their stud dog only when they feel it is for the betterment of the breed. Nonetheless, some twelve champions have been bred at this kennel.

Steb's

Steb's Doberman Pinschers, owned by Mr. and Mrs. J. Monroe Stebbins, are known throughout the Dobe world for exciting quality and some of the breed's truly greatest winners. As a professional handler, "Stebbie" had the lead on many an important and memorable member of the breed, while Natalie took pleasure in breeding some of the best. The Stebbinses formerly lived on Long Island (New York) which was a lively center of Doberman activity in those days (and still is). Now they are located at Kent in the beautiful hills of Connecticut. Since his retirement from professional handling at the beginning of the 1970's, Steb has been a very excellent Field Representative of the American Kennel Club, having "hung up his lead" in favor of this position.

When one thinks of Steb's outstanding dogs, immediately one's thoughts turn to Top Skipper, for Champion Steb's Top Skipper has earned a position of prominence and respect in the U.S.A. history of this breed for his own quality, his show winning, and his dominance as a sire. A product of the 1950's, Top Skipper was by Champion Dortmund Delly's Colonel Jet (Champion Delegate v d Elbe-Tazieher Lady Ambassador) from Damasyn the Easter Bonnet (Champion Rancho Dobe's Storm-Damasyn Sikhandi, a Champion Dictator v Glenhugel daughter), leased by the Stebbinses from Peggy Adamson specifically for breeding to Natalie's favorite, Colonel Jet. Jet spent his last years with the Stebbinses.

Skipper's start in life was inauspicious, but what a superb animal he became! He was a stud-fee puppy to the then owner of his sire, Bob Mullen, who did not keep him but sold him to other fanciers who never returned, as promised, for ear taping. It is not surprising therefore that in time the puppy became available for re-sale, discouragement having set in when the owner was unable to get the ears to stand correctly. The Stebbinses went to see him and were hardly impressed with

1. Ch. Stafford's Spitfire, by Steb's Blazing Raven ex Stafford's Sparkle, August 1964—June 1971, was the dam of four champions. Handled by Corky Vroom for breeder-owner Melba Stafford. Photo courtesy of Karen Vroom Parkhurst.

2. Ch. Stafford's Cairo, by Ch. Rancho Dobe's Maestro ex Ch. Stafford's Spitfire, owned by Melba Stafford and handled by Corky Vroom. A winning sire of champions.

3. Another by Ch. Rancho Dobe's Maestro ex Ch. Stafford's Spitfire, this is Ch. Stafford's Peppertree. Handled by Corky Vroom for Melba Stafford.

4. Ch. Stafford's Calgary, by Ch. Rancho Dobe's Maestro ex Ch. Stafford's Spitfire, was bred by Melba Stafford and handled by Corky Vroom. Photo, taken March 1970, courtesy of Karen Vroom Parkhurst.

1. Ch. Dortmund Delly's Colonel Jet, one of Natalie Stebbins's favorites, was the sire of Ch. Steb's Top Skipper, who made so tremendous a contribution to the Doberman breed. Colonel Jet was by Ch. Delegate v d Elbe from Tazieher Lady Alexander. Top Skipper's dam was Damasyn The Easter Bonnet, by Ch. Rancho Dobe's Storm ex Damasyn Sikhandi. Photo courtesy of Mr. and Mrs. Monroe Stebbins.
2. Ch. Stafford's Heather, by Ch. Rancho Dobe's Maestro ex Ch. Stafford's Spitfire, is still another excellent Doberman produced by these two. Bred by Melba Stafford; handled by Corky Vroom.
3. Ch. Steb's Point of Order back in 1956 winning a Specialty show in Connecticut. J. Monroe Stebbins handling. The judge is Jane Forsyth, who was still a professional handler in those days, which were during the period when handlers were granted permission to judge at Specialty shows when invited to do so.
4. Ch. The Stebbins Campaigner in May 1959 at Plainfield Kennel Club. J. Monroe Stebbins handling.
5. Ch. Rancho Dobe's Roulette taking best in Show at Sun Maid Kennel Club under Anton Korbel, handled by Russell Zimmerman. The fifth generation of Rancho Dobe breeding and the tenth homebred from there to finish. Roulette was the dam of Ch. Rancho Dobe's Cointreau, foundation bitch of Haydenhill Kennels, and she was the only Rancho Dobe Doberman to be campaigned by this kennel for any length of time. She held the record for Best in Show bitches for ten years. Photo courtesy of Karen Vroom Parkhurst.

1. Ch. Steb's Gunga Din, son of Ch. Steb's Top Skipper ex Ch. Ebonaire's Flashing Star, was owned by the J. Monroe Stebbinses. This dog was the sire of Mary Rodgers's Ch. Sultana von Marienburg, who was from Farley's Princess.

2. Ch. Steb's Country Boy in 1962, winning with J. Monroe Stebbins.

3. In June 1959, Ch. Stebbins Campaignor with J. Monroe Stebbins.

4. The very great and highly influential bitch, Ch. Jessy v d Sonnenhoehe, born in 1934. A Best of Breed winner at two German Sieger events and the dam of Sieger Ferry v Rauhfelsen and Siegerin Freya v Rauhfelsen (before leaving Germany). She then produced two litters in the United States, including, among others, Champion Westphalia's Uranus. Photo courtesy of Peggy Adamson.

5. Ch. Steb's Captain Treble, litter brother to Ch. Steb's Top Skipper, died soon after completing his title. In his one litter, he sired the dam of Ch. Damasyn Derringer.

his looks at the time. Skipper sensed the way to Natalie's heart, however, coming to her and licking her face, and so he joined the Stebbinses' household.

It took five operations, performed by an expert, to turn the trick with Top Skipper's ears. But finally this was accomplished, and George Rood, who had brought this about, entered him in a dog show in order to show the Stebbinses how their young dog looked with his ears up. He still was not what would be considered ready for winning, so he went back home with Natalie to put on a bit of weight and maturity.

Top Skipper's second ring appearance was under no less an expert than Francis F. H. Fleitmann, who was sufficiently impressed to take this youngster clear through from the classes to Best of Breed. In 1957, Skipper won the Top Ten in Chicago and the Chicagoland Specialty under another great Doberman authority, Fred Curnow, over from England for the occasion. But the most exciting thing about Top Skipper was the smashingly handsome puppies he was siring. For three consecutive years he held the position of Top Doberman Sire, and he produced in the neighborhood of fifty champions despite his brief lifetime. Champion Steb's Top Skipper died suddenly of a heart attack at only six years of age. What sadness for the Stebbinses as Skipper was a beloved family companion with so many other splendid qualities! And what a loss to the Doberman breed, as it is difficult to contemplate the additional quality dogs he would undoubtedly have produced had his lifetime been longer.

Top Skipper's first breeding produced a Best in Show winner, Champion Alemap's Checkmate, owned by Mr. Bushman. But his second litter is undoubtedly the one which had the most striking impact on the Doberman world, as it was the famed "football" litter, from the Weiss's bitch Ebonaire's Flashing Star, (a granddaughter of both Champion Damasyn The Solitaire, C.D.X. and Champion Dictator v Glenhugel). This litter included Champion Ebonaire's Touchdown, the sire of nine champions and winner of numerous all-breed and Specialty Bests in Show for Charles A. T. O'Neill; Champion Ebonaire's Gridiron, owned by Mr. and Mrs. Al Lefkowitz of New York, for whom he was a

noted winner; Champion Ebonaire's Touche; the noted and successful winning bitch Champion Ebonaire's Balastra; and Champion Ebonaire's Flying Cloud.

Needless to say, the Stebbinses could hardly wait for a repeat of this breeding, from which was acquired Champion Steb's Gunga Din. This dog sired the famous Champion Sultana v Marienburg who had so fantastic a show career for Mary Rodgers.

Over the years Natalie Stebbins bred a number of excellent Dobermans who have done her credit in the show ring. It is she who so tremendously admired Top Skipper's sire, Colonel Jet, that she purchased his dam even at the age of ten years, breeding her back to Delegate, Colonel's sire. From this came a well-known bitch, Champion Steb's Point of Order, and a smashing good black male for whom hopes were high, which they named Stebbin's Investigator. The accidental death of this young dog at less than a year's age was hard to bear. It was a few months after that had happened when the opportunity arose for them to own Top Skipper, which possibly might not have interested them had Investigator lived. Certainly Top Skipper must have done a great deal towards easing the loss of this other young dog.

In the following paragraphs, Natalie Stebbins talks about Top Skipper:

"Champion Steb's Top Skipper, Champion Steb's Diablo of the Seven Seas, Champion Steb's Captain Treble, and Champion Steb's Sea Mist were all offspring of the breeding of Champion Dortmund Delly's Colonel Jet to Damasyn The Easter Bonnet. The greatest sires and showmen of the breed (Delegate, Dictator, and Storm) lay within their first two generations. Their sire, Colonel Jet, was a multi-Best in Show winner. Their dam, Bonnet, unable to be shown because of an eye injury, was of superb quality and temperament.

"Top Skipper fulfilled this rich heritage as a dominant sire, an outstanding show dog, and, above all, as an endearing personality. Shown a total of twenty-three times, he finished his championship with four straight "major" wins. He was Best of Breed from the classes at Westminster under world-famous breed authority Herman Fleitmann (Francis F. H. Fleitmann) of Westphalia Kennels. A multi-breed and Group winner, Skipper retired from the ring by going Best in Show at Chicagoland. His selection as winner of the Top Ten Show Winning Dobermans of 1957 was a fitting climax to his show career.

"At 28 inches tall at the withers, with a sleek black coat and proud carriage, he was noble and aristocratic. He had a beautiful head and neck with an expressive dark, almond-shaped eye. His front assembly was excellent with well-laid-back shoulders, good elbows and pasterns. However, he was somewhat straight in stifle. A good moving dog, he was rated best by the judges in the Top Ten Competition. Alert and gregarious, he liked to pose. When doing so he had, as Sue Neville so aptly put it, 'The look of eagles.'

"A truly prepotent sire, a dominant black, he stamped his get with his outstanding temperament, personality, quality and type. He produced many outstanding sires and dams, breed and obedience champions, multi-Best in Show, Group and breed winners. Today many of his great- and great-great-grandchildren are among our top producers and show specimens, not only in the United States but in Canada, England, Australia and Japan.

"Skipper was such a very special dog! Intelligent, instinctively knowing the difference between friend and foe—yet always hoping to meet a friend. Mentally and emotionally sound. Completely trustworthy in any situation. Abounding in love. Surely his outer beauty was a delight to the eye, but it was his nobility of spirit that enchanted all who knew him. An unforgettable dog in every way."

Tedell

Tedell Dobermans belong to Theodora (Ted) Linck of Toledo, Ohio, who, like the majority of people involved with dogs, grew up with them. One of her aunts raised Boston Terriers; another raised smooth Collies. And a third took in strays!

Ted's husband, on the other hand, had never been permitted to have a dog, although he had always wanted one. So, when the son of Otis McClure, who was one of the family's employees, went into the armed services and was looking for a home in which to leave his grown male Doberman, Mr. Linck volunteered to take him. At that time the Lincks'

baby daughter was just learning to toddle, and Ted therefore wanted nothing to do with a large Doberman just then. After all, she had heard all the horrid stories about them.

However, "Champ" began following the baby around the house, literally purring at her and sleeping under her crib. Naturally, that sold the Lincks on the breed and taught Ted that her previous fears of the breed had been quite pointless.

Later, in 1951, with their second Dobe, Ted went into obedience training, putting a C.D. and a C.D.X. on him and training him for U.D. Then it was that she joined the Toledo Kennel Club, becoming one of their obedience instructors and holding various offices, including President—the only woman to hold this office in the sixty-year history of the club. At the time of writing, she is Vice President and American Kennel Club Delegate. She is also a founding member of the Maumee Valley Doberman Pinscher Club.

It was not until their fourth Dobe that the Lincks had a champion. This was a vivacious little black bitch that Ted got from Betsy Thomas of Highbriar at the suggestion of George Rood. Champion Highbriar Blackbird, 1957-1970, was by Champion Jet of Ravensburg ex Highbriar Stormette, C.D.X., bred by Walter and May Dencker, owned by Theodora (Ted) Linck and Betsy Thomas.

Blackbird's sire, Jet, was twice the Best of Breed at Westminster and twice topped the Doberman Pinscher Club of America. Her dam, Stormette, was a National top-scoring obedience Dobe and became the dam of five champions.

Blackbird was energetic, intelligent, inventive, and fond of children. Originally Ted had bought her from Betsy but in return for Betsy's guidance offered co-ownership when Blackbird finished her championship. Ted took Blackbird into obedience and earned her C.D. in four shows. She was bred twice to Champion Florian v Ahrtal, C.D. and once to Champion Singenwald's Prince Kuhio, both Best in Show winners. She produced five champions. Between them, Betsy and Ted produced eight champions in eight years.

From the first mating of Blackbird to Florian (and the first co-breeding with Betsy Thomas) came the red male Champion Highbriar Halla, C.D. At ten months of age she

1. Ch. Checkmate's Flower Girl (1964-1972), by Ch. Checkmate's Beau Geste ex Ch. Alemap's Glamour Girl, C.D. Bred by Bill Haines. Owned by Ted Linck, Toledo, Ohio. Of her, Ted Linck says, "She was one of the loveliest bitches it ever has been my pleasure to see, and she was a privilege to own. Even now, more than 10 years after she died, many dog people, even in other breeds, still talk about her." Handled by George Rood.
2. Ch. Tedell Private Label, Best in Show brother to Eleventh Hour, owned by Stuart Rogell. Handled by Bob Hastings.

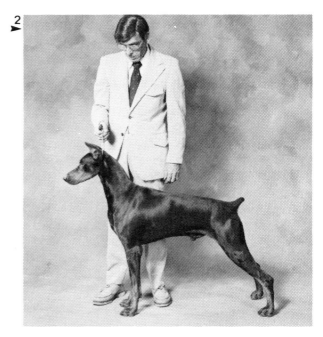

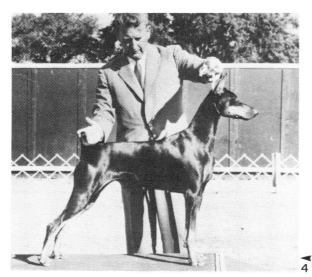

1. Ch. Tedell Red Carpet, litter brother to Eleventh Hour. A Specialty and Best of Breed winner owned by Barbara Shourt Hendley.
2. Ch. Tedell Nottingham Palace was the first of 15 champions by Ch. Tedell Indulto v Ri-Jan's. Owned by George Streeter and handled by Bill Haines.
3. Ch. Tedell Barcarolle (1972–1975), by Ch. Gra-Lemor Demetrius v d Victor ex Ch. Triadel's Honey B. Bred by Ted Linck, Tedell Kennels, Toledo, Ohio. Owned by Dick and Barbara Duklis. Winning Best of Breed under judge Arnold Woolfe in 1974. Handled by Robert J. Stebbins.
4. Ch. Highbriar Blackbird, C.D., one of the many fine Doberman winners owned by Theodora (Ted) Linck.
5. Ch. Tedell Balmoral Castle taking the breed at Lima, Ohio. Bill Haines handling. By Silvae Sidus v Ted-L ex Ch. Balmoral Bonnet of Norloch. Ted Linck, owner.
6. Ch. Highbriar Valencia (1963–1974), by Ch. Felix v Ahrtal ex Ch. Highbriar Halla, C.D. Bred by Ted Linck and Betsy Thomas. Owned by Joe Worman.
7. Ch. Aventina's Tamika, Aventina's daughter sired by Corry, died of cancer two weeks after her first Best in Show. Owned by Frank and Ellen D'Amico, Glen Cove, New York. Handled by Jane Forsyth. A most beautiful bitch whose loss was a sad one for her owners.

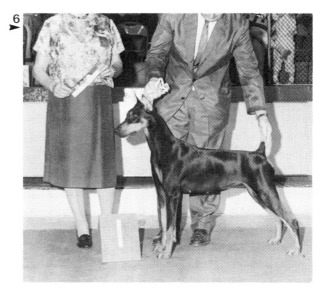

became the Doberman Pinscher Club of America 1961 Grand Futurity winner and Best Puppy in the Specialty. After that she finished quickly, going Best of Breed along the way. Shown a few times as a "special," she placed regularly in the Groups. Ted earned the C.D. on her in four shows before she was bred, first to Champion Felix vom Ahrtal and then to Champion Highbriar Minos, producing one champion in each litter. Halla spent the last several years of her life as the beloved companion of Ted Linck's daughter.

Blackbird and Florian produced, in 1962, Champion Highbriar Rock Sand. Although Rocky produced only one champion, this one proved to be of great importance to the breed, as his little red daughter, Champion Highbriar Piping Hot, became the dam of the great producer Champion Tarrado's Flair when she was bred to Champion Tarrado's Corry. After her retirement from showing and breeding, Rocky went to live with Betsy's friend, Peggy Schambaugh, for whom she earned all her obedience degrees.

In 1963 the red bitch Halla was bred to the blue dog Felix, producing a litter of black puppies. Of these a small, vivacious black bitch was sold to Joe Worman of Columbus, Ohio, who was a theatrical projectionist and lighting expert. Every night when the theater closed, Valencia accompanied the guard to the bank depository. One time she made her unexpected appearance on the stage where Joe was supervising the lighting effects. He had not missed her from her place in his cubicle until he heard a voice from below exclaim "I thought I just saw a Doberman cross the stage."

Since Joe's busy schedule precluded any puppy tending, he leased Valencia to Ted Linck for two litters. Ted chose as her mate the young Cassio vom Ahrtal whom she had first seen as a puppy and determined then to breed a bitch to him. This was the first litter to be registered in Ted Linck's now so very famous Tedell kennel prefix, and from it came her first homebred Best in Show winning champion. From these two litters, Valencia produced three champion sons: the red Champion Tedell Red Carpet, and the black Best in Show boys, Champion Tedell's Eleventh Hour and Champion Tedell's Private Label.

Eleventh Hour, co-owned by Ted Linck and Nancy Kibiloski, was a powerful but very elegant black male of superb temperament. At the tender age of eight months and eleven days he topped an all-breed event as Best in Show—a record that still stands as the youngest Dobe ever to win Best in Show. This was at Hodgensville, Kentucky in 1966. Three prominent judges passed on him there: the late Leona Sykes Sharpley for the breed, the late Virgil Johnson for the Group, and Charles Kellogg, doing his first Best in Show assignment, for Best.

Eleventh Hour, called "Shad" at home, was originally sold to Jim and Nancy Kibiloski of Fort Wayne, Indiana, registered in Nancy's name. When his potential was realized, they concluded also that they could not handle his career alone, and Ted became co-owner. Bill Haines handled Shad during his run to the title; then he went to Jane Kay for "the woman's touch," and it was Jane who took him to many Specialty and Group victories.

Three other champions came from the mating of Cassio and Valencia. The male, Champion Tedell Red Carpet, was sold to Barbara Shourt Hendley as a young puppy. Because of his potential and not having been previously acquainted with her, Ted insisted on being co-owner until such time as Barbara had proven herself as a handler. This she did by taking Winners Dog with him right off from the puppy class.

Champion Tedell Private Label went to Stuart Rogell, who is now a handler of some note, when he was a youngster. Stu did much of the handling himself, but it was Ruth (Rusty) Fahrion who took Best in Show.

CACIB Champion Tedell Midas Touch, a red male, was owned by Jack Goldberg.

Returning to Champion Eleventh Hour, he accounted for seven all-breed Bests in Show and six Specialties. For his adult years he was campaigned by George Rood. During his show career, he became No. 1 Doberman and also became a top stud. Eleventh Hour's numerous champion offspring included two Best in Show daughters, Champion Angil's Eleventh Melody (from Champion Angil v Alarich, who was owned by the Pillsburys) and Champion Talacon Daisy Upsala, who took her Best in Show from the classes. Daisy was owned by the Micalifs and became an excellent producer for them.

In addition to Daisy, another good producing Eleventh Hour daughter was Champion Triadel's Honey B, which Ted Linck had the good fortune of leasing for a litter by Champion Gra-Lemor's Demetrius. This produced the lovely Champion Tedell Barcarolle, purchased by Dick and Barbara Dukalis. Bred back to her sire, she became the dam of their Champion Glenayr Dufferinand, the foundation of their many champions.

Ted Linck considers her own Champion Tedell Indulto v Ri-Jane to be "probably Eleventh Hour's best son." This dog is from the final litter of Champion Ri-Jane's Seneca Love Call, and she was overjoyed when Seneca's owner, Janie Slayden, approached her about breeding Seneca to Eleventh Hour. Janie asked to take a stud fee puppy instead of cash, as she had always admired Senna.

In character and temperament, Indulto was much like his great-great-grandmother, Blackbird. He was a happy, busy dog, always inventing little stunts to help him get his way. Although not the great winner his sire was, Indulto took an impressive number of Groups and Specialties, thus keeping himself high on the Top Twenty for three years.

Indulto produced fifteen champions, among them three all-breed Best in Show dogs, these all black: Champion Tedell Nottingham Palace, owned by Gerry Streeter and handled by Bill Haines; Champion MiGar's Good Greef, bred and owned by Gary Martin and Michael Velarde III, handled by Mike; and Ted's own Champion Tedell's Key Largo. Also among his noteworthy offspring were the notable producers Champion Indulto's Ebony Ace v Rasmus; Champion Kyjer's Enforcer; Champion Royalton's Timberline; and the littermates Champion Jim-Mar's Dandy Jack and Champion Jim-Mar's Morning Star. All but one of his champions was a Best of Breed winner and most of them had Groups and Group placements.

Key Largo was shown only a few times in puppy classes, as Ted was travelling extensively with his sire. When he was ten months old, she entered him at the Doberman Pinscher Club of Indiana Specialty where he went Best in Sweepstakes. After that he was held back to gain more maturity until the

Gainesville Show the following July. He went Best of Winners from the American-bred Class under Charles Wiler. In December at Western Reserve he finished his title under Nick Appolony and started on a whirlwind "specials" career. In August of 1978 he took his first all-breed Best in Show, and from there on he gained a whole series of them, along with Specialties and Group wins which kept him at the top of the Top Twenty for three years, including No. 1.

Because his sire was a popular stud, Largo was late getting started, so it will be awhile yet before his importance as a stud can be appraised; because of an infection he has already been retired. To date he has one champion son and three titled daughters, every one able to account for Bests of Breed and Group wins and placements.

It is interesting that when Key Largo was at his peak, Eriko Sasada of Osaka, Japan, was in this country studying American handling methods with George Rood. She fell in love with Largo and urged her family to buy him. Of course the Lincks would not dream of parting with him, however. Right after Largo was retired from showing, Ted obtained his handsome son, Majestyk High Sierra of Ted-L and turned him over for handling to Pam DeHetre. He finished with ease, then went out to take some breeds and Group placings. The Sasada family then asked to buy Sierra, and Ted said that she would let him go only if Eriko, personally, flew to Japan with him. She agreed to this. Ted has now heard from Eriko that Sierra has placed Best in Show in Japan and that they are delighted with the quality puppies he is producing.

Back in 1964, when Bill Haines lived down the road from the Lincks, he and Ted used to visit back and forth to exchange show news, discuss breeding, appraise each other's puppies. When Bill had a small litter from his Champion Checkmate's Beau Geste and Champion Alemap's Glamour Girl born in 1964, Ted particularly admired one of the puppies, Flower Girl. One day Bill suggested that Ted take the puppy. When the puppy was six months old, they started showing her, and she took her first points, a "major" in September. In October she was Best nine-to-twelve-month puppy at the Doberman Pinscher Club of America, then took her second "major" in November, later that month completing her title. From there she went immediately on to win breeds, Groups, Specialties, and an all-breed Best in Show.

Ted Linck describes this bitch as "one of the loveliest it has been my pleasure to see, and a privilege to own. Even now, more than ten years after she died, many dog people, including those in other breeds, still continue to talk of her."

Champion Tedell Black Chiffon and Champion Tedell Black Walnut were littermates by Champion Ru-Mar's Morgansonne ex Highbriar Ionia. Their dam was a littermate to Highbriar Valencia, the dam of Eleventh Hour.

Both Chiffon and Wally were black. Ted owned Wally herself and co-owned Chiffon with Andrea Ray, whose co-ownership was Andrea's wedding present from her husband.

Bill Haines took Chiffon to three shows in Ohio, one all-breed and two Specialties. He brought her home with a 5-point "major" from each of the Specialties and Reserve at the all-breed. The following October Jane Kay took Wally to two Specialties and an all-breed in Texas. Again the pattern was the same, and this littermate came home with 5-point "majors" from the Specialties (one of which was the Doberman Pinscher Club of America) and Reserve from the all-breed. Strange that both littermates should have started their careers in exactly the same pattern!

In the early 1970's a great stroke of luck enabled Ted to lease the Eleventh Hour daughter, Champion Triadel's Honey B, which she herself had bred, from owners Dick and Barbara Duklis for a litter by Champion Gra-Lemor Demetrius v d Victor. This was the first complete outcross breeding Ted had ever attempted. It produced the black Canadian Champion Tedell Fandango, owned by Canadian handler John Griffith, and the lovely little red Champion Tedell Barcarolle, who was purchased by Dick and Barbara Duklis, then turned over by them to Jeff Brucker for handling. Her trip to the title was a short one, after which she went to Bobby Stebbins as a "special," accounting for Bests of Breed and Group placements. Bred back to her sire, she produced a handsome red dog

that became foundation for the Duklis's successful breeding program, Champion Glenayr Dufferinand.

Bill Haines was interested in breeding his lovely Champion Balmoral Bonnet of Norloch to the good-winning Eleventh Hour son in California, Champion Silvae Sidus v Ted-L, owned by the Stebeltons, but his activities as a handler made caring for a litter difficult. Ted Linck, thus, leased Bonnie and raised the litter for him as her own. From this came her Champion Balmoral Castle and two non-champions who proved valuable, Tedell Limerick Castle and Tedell Connemara Castle. Margi Morrison bought Limerick Castle as a young puppy, later breeding him to her Checkmate's Edeldame and producing several champions, one of whom became a Best in Show winner and sire of champions in his own right. Connemara Castle stayed with Ted, was bred to Indulta and produced two champions—Tedell Key Largo and Key Biscayne. Her sister, Champion Balmoral Castle, strangled on an apple while running in the orchard.

A young bitch with both parents Best in Show winners, Champion MiGar's Questress, born in 1981 by Champion Tedell Key Largo ex Champion MiGar's Jenne, is Ted Linck's current "star." One would naturally expect Questress to be the talented show girl that she is, and her wins are adding up in a very satisfactory manner, George Murray handling.

Telstar

Telstar Dobermans are owned by Jane N. Benfield of Westwood, New Jersey.

Currently being shown from here are dogs sired by Champion Edelhall Gigolo of Amulet out of different bitches. One of the dams is Telstar's Happy Holidays who is a Champion Devil Tree's Black Shaft daughter from a linebred Elfred bitch, which was bred by Mrs. Benfield. She in turn was bred to Gigolo, doubling up on the Ahrtal line, which gave Mrs. Benfield a litter including Dioressence, Aliage, and The Flea-Flicker, all finished or pointed. Of the total of five puppies in the litter, one bitch is in Mexico and another was never shown.

A repeat of the same breeding produced Telstar's Blackgama, Grand Prize Winner at the Penn Jersey Doberman Futurity before her untimely death at twelve-and-a-half months.

American and Canadian Champion Telstar's Rachel of Bekgreg is a red Gigolo daughter out of a bitch carrying Kay Hill-Brown's B-Brian bloodlines. Rachel was bred to "The Flea-Flicker" and her puppies are just being shown as we write.

Rachel finished her American and Canadian championships by sixteen months of age. Dioressence did likewise, before fifteen months, and gained her Mexican title at twenty months.

Toledobes

Toledobes Dobermans, owned by Patrick and Judy Doniere at Holland, Ohio, began in 1955, although actually Judy had owned a Dobe since the age of six. What Judy wanted most of all from her husband as a wedding gift was a Doberman puppy, so on the day that they returned from their honeymoon they immediately bought one. Of her Judy says, "Although she was a sweet bitch, I wanted a show dog" and so two years later the Donieres bought a lively red bitch puppy from Robert Wahl. Her name was Wahlmars Baroness, and she later became a champion—Judy's first champion and finished by husband Pat, as Judy was at that time eight months pregnant. Otherwise, she herself handled Baroness all the way.

Baroness was bred twice to Champion Alemaps Checkmate, producing five champions. She had another champion from a breeding to Champion Browns Dion. Sad to relate she had two litters which were almost completely wiped out by "hard pad," and all but one of those who lived gained the title. Baroness had the distinction of being the first champion in Toledo and was No. 1 Doberman Dam in the U.S. for 1962 and 1963. Two of her daughters followed in her pawprints, so to speak, by themselves becoming leading dams: Champion Toledobes Barbiturate and Champion Toledobes Classic Cameo. A grandson out of Champion Toledobes Covergirl produced Champion Toledobes Linebacker who was a Best in Show winner and Best of Breed at the Doberman Pinscher Club of America National Specialty in 1966. Another grandson, out of Champion Toledobes Classic Cameo, was Grand Prize Futurity winner at the same National. He was

Champion Toledobes Quarterback. Both Linebacker and Quarterback were sired by Charles O'Neill's great Champion Ebonaire's Touchdown, and Mr. O'Neill co-owned Quarterback with Judy.

Baroness also produced Champion Checkmates Chessman, sire of eight champions; Champion Checkmates Chancellor, sire of two champions; and Champion Toledobes Filibuster, sire of seven champions.

Champion Toledobes Barbiturate produced six champions; Champion Toledobes Classic Cameo produced four champions; and Champion Toledobes Covergirl produced two champions. Most of these champions themselves produced multiple champions and were the foundation of numerous kennels, principally in the Midwest.

The Donieres handled their own dogs in the show ring, those they had bred themselves and owned or co-owned. Between them they finished the very impressive total of about a hundred or more Dobermans.

One of their dogs in whom they took particular pride was Champion Damasyn Carly of Jerseystone. In less than three years of being offered at public stud, he sired seventeen champions in three litters, plus three Canadian champions. Pat and Judy acquired him at age four-and-a-half years, unshown, from Peggy Adamson and finished him at the age of five. Interestingly, the Donieres had bred his dam.

Pat Doniere is now a judge of Working and most of the Herding Group, having started to officiate in 1969. He is the first American judge to have officiated in Japan, and he has as well judged in Australia, Canada, and most of the Specialties for Dobermans in the United States, among them the National three times. He is a member of the Doberman Pinscher Club of America Judges Educational Committee.

Judy Doniere has also turned her interest towards judging, and currently she is approved for the Hound Group in addition to Dobermans and has recently applied for some Sporting breeds. She has officiated in Australia and Canada and for numerous Specialty Clubs in the United States along with her all-breed show assignments. Judy's sister, incidentally, is Mrs. Michael (Joni) Kahn, owner of Kahn-Tex Kennels. She, too, is becoming

ROCADO DOBERMANS
Do Dillon
Rt. 5 • Box 144 • Algonquin Road
Barrington, Illinois 60010
(312) 428-7155

WE 877167
INDIVIDUAL REG. NO.

LITTER REG. NO.

AKC
REGISTERED WITH

Jesse
CALL NAME

Ch. Renejade The Jazz Singer
REGISTERED NAME OF DOG

BREED Doberman Pinscher   DATE WHELPED 4-21-81   SEX Male

BREEDER Nancy Christensen   ADDRESS 5500 Old Cheney Rd., Lincoln, Nebraska 68516

OWNER Do Dillon & Nancy Christensen   ADDRESS Rt. 5 Box 144, Barrington, Illinois 60010

GENERAL DESCRIPTION Black & Rust

SIRE

Ch. Andelane's Indigo Rock

- Ch. Ru-Mar's Morgansonne CD
  - Ch. Rancho Dobe's Cello
    - Ch. Rancho Dobe's Bach
    - Hannah of Adobe Hill
  - Ch. Jessamyn II vom Ahrtal
    - Ch. Fortuna's Maestro
    - Ch. Zessica vom Ahrtal
- Jemoels Maui v. Cassio
  - Ch. Cassio vom Ahrtal
    - Xandu vom Ahrtal
    - Ch. Juno vom Ahrtal
  - Ch. Jemoels Elaine
    - Ch. Borong the Warlock's Lancer C.D.
    - Ch. Hi Dave's Korry's Kay of Ingral

Ch. Bishop's Borong v. Rock

REG. NO. ....

Toledobes Generation Gap

- Ch. Damasyn Carly of Jerseystone
  - Ch. Damasyn Derringer
    - Duke of Lombardi
    - Damasyn the Tcheska
  - Toledobes Misty Moonlight
    - Ch. Toledobes Filibuster
    - Ch. Toledobes Classic Cameo
- Toledobes Zock It to Me
  - Ch. Ebonaires Touchdown
    - Ch. Steb's Top Skipper
    - Ebonaire's Flashing Star
  - Ch. Toledobes Jail Bait
    - Ch. Toledobes Filibuster
    - Ch. Toledobes Classic Cameo

Certified Pedigree

DAM

Ch. Silent Sentry's Marauder WAC

- Am. Can. Ch. Marks-Tey The Maverick
  - Ch. Marks-Tey Alfie of Rads
    - Walkaways Ablaze of Marks-Tey
    - Ch. Marks-Tey Vale
  - Ch. Marks-Tey Yasmine
    - Ch. Gra-Lemor Demetrius vd Victor
    - Marks-Tey Stacy
- Silent Sentry's Dojoji San
  - Ch. Tedell Eleventh Hour
    - Ch. Cassio vom Ahrtal
    - Ch. Highbriar Valencia
  - High Halo's Camelot
    - Ch. Marks-Tey Hanover
    - Ch. High Halo's Brooke of Kondo

Silent Sentry's Renaissance CD WAC

REG. NO. ....

Silent Sentry's Jubilee

- Marks-Tey Dust Commander
  - Ch. Marks-Tey Shawn CD
    - Ch. Derek of Marks-Tey
    - Ch. Marks-Tey Melanie
  - Ch. Marks-Tey Vale
    - Ch. Gra-Lemor Demetrius vd Victor
    - Ch. Marks-Tey Melanie
- Silent Sentry's Dojoji San
  - Ch. Tedell Eleventh Hour
    - Ch. Cassio vom Ahrtal
    - Ch. Highbriar Valencia
  - High Halo's Camelot
    - Ch. Marks-Tey Hanover
    - Ch. High Halo's Brooke of Kondo

I HEREBY CERTIFY THAT THIS PEDIGREE IS TRUE AND CORRECT
TO THE BEST OF MY KNOWLEDGE AND BELIEF.

SIGNED _____

DATE _____ , 19 ____

320

1. Ch. Toledobe's Line Backer, black male, born in 1964 by Ch. Ebonaire's Touchdown ex Toledobe's Cover Girl. Best of Breed at the Doberman Pinscher Club of America National Specialty in 1966 and a multi Group and Best in Show winner. Bred by the Donieres; owned by Loren Nichols.

2. Ch. Toledobes Classic Cameo, bred and owned by Patrick and Judy Doniere, Holland, Ohio. The No. 1 Doberman Dam of 1965, she was a daughter of Ch. Alemaps Checkmate (by Ch. Stebs Top Skipper from Ch. Our Very Own Pamela) ex Ch. Wahlmars Baroness, C.D. (by Ch. Brown's Hobgoblin from Barbarosa v. Siegerstadt.

1▲

▼2

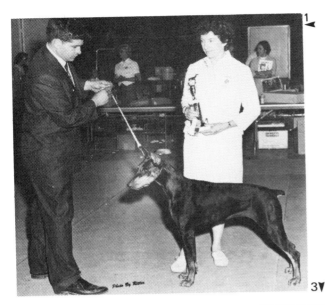

1. Ch. Toledobes Jailbait was born in 1963 by Ch. Toledobes Filibuster ex Ch. Toledobes Classic Cameo. Owned by Patrick and Judy Doniere, Toledobes, Holland, Ohio.
2. Nearing a decision! Charles A. T. O'Neill taking one last look at future champion Castle Lanes Querida Miranda prior to making her the winner. This is in the 6–9–month class, from which she went on to Grand Prize Futurity Winner. Judy Doniere, co-owner, is handling.
3. Ch. Damasyn Carly of Jerseystone, by Ch. Damasyn Derringer ex Toledobes Misty Moonlight, is the sire of 17 American champions in 17 litters and of three Canadian champions. Owned by Patrick and Judy Doniere.
4. What a lot of history this photo covers! Ch. Toledobes Quarterback winning the Grand Prize Futurity Award at the Doberman Pinscher Club of America in 1966. Bred by Patrick and Judy Doniere; owned by Charles A. T. O'Neill and Judy Doniere. The judge is Mrs. Marge Kilburn, with Pat Doniere handling the winner. Quarterback was sired by Ch. Ebonaire's Touchdown (Top Skipper son) from Ch. Toledobe's Classic Cameo.
5. Norwegian Ch. Toledobes Keepsake, owned by Maida Johnnson, Oslo, Norway. Bred by Patrick and Judy Doniere, this is a daughter of Ch. The Sundance Kid ex Toledobe's Team Mascot.
6. Ch. Toledobes Barbiturate, owned by W. T. Haines and bred by the Donieres. Born May 1960, by Ch. Alemaps Checkmate ex Ch. Wahlmar's Baroness, C.D. The dam of seven champions and the No. 1 Doberman Dam for 1976.
7. Ch. Checkmates Chessman, bred, owned, and handled by Pat and Judy Doniere.

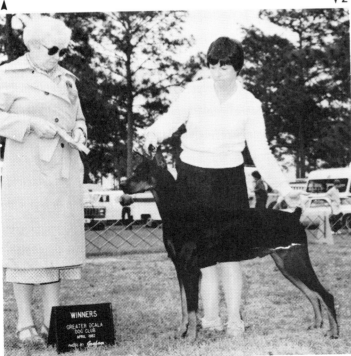

1. The foundation bitch from Von Merlis Kennels, Hillview's Shante' Sheeba, the dam of several champions owned by Elaine Merlis, Valatie, New York.
2. Wen Fray's Baby Face Nelson, littermate to Am. and Can. Ch. Wen Fray's Annie Oakley, has points and was winner of the DPCA most Bred-by-Exhibitor Classes in 1982. Bred, owned, and handled by Wendy F. Serra, Fort Pierce, Florida.

active as a judge, having recently been approved as a provisional. She co-bred many Dobe champions with the Donieres and has herself bred several who have finished. She is, with Marienburg Kennels, co-owner of Champion Marienburgs Maltese Falcon, WAC, already a sire of two champions.

Judy Doniere is currently Chairman of the White Doberman Research Committee, and together with Mrs. Nancy Heitzman, she purchased two white Dobermans which were bought by the Doberman Pinscher Club of America as part of a breeding research project.

While they are judging frequently, the Donieres still have several dogs at home. These include Champion Toledobes Master Charge, age four-and-a-half; his sire, Toledobes Paisano, age seven-and-a-half; Toledobes Editorial, age six; and their new Dobe baby, Toledobes Jaguar of Julmar, age four months; the white Doberman, Clorox; and two Whippets, ages ten and six years respectively.

The Donieres have bred about 46 champions and they would like someday to bring the total to 50.

Von Merlis

Von Merlis Dobermans, at Valatie, New York, are owned by Elaine Merlis whose first bitch, she tells us, although of excellent breeding, lacked the elegance with which to win. Her many virtues were quick to catch the eyes of the judges, but only for the blue ribbons, not for the purples. Those same high qualities, however, stood Shante' Sheeba in good stead in the whelping box, as she became the dam of three champions with two more each needing just one "major" to finish.

Whatever Sheeba was lacking, Elaine Merlis's splendid dog, Champion Tulyar von Ahrtal definitely was not. His owner describes him as, "Fire and ice. Elegant and noble. All Doberman, and he was our pal." "Tully" in the show ring was a difficult dog to overlook. He finished quickly in tough competition and as a sire also distinguished himself as having been used at stud just over a dozen times. In spite of this, however, he managed to produce four champions, a multi-Best in Show dog, and two Top Twenty dogs.

Von Merlis Kennels have tried to breed for style and elegance, and Elaine feels that lovely heads and elegance were their contribution to Dobermans.

Although the results are extremely satisfying, the time, effort and hard work that goes into breeding and exhibiting dogs to their championship is very taxing. As time goes on, interests change and new challenges come along, causing the thought of breeding to diminish. Elaine Merlis has found this new interest in judging and hopes that she will thus be able to fulfill what she loves doing.

Wen Fray

Wen Fray Dobermans at Fort Pierce, Florida belong to Wendy F. Serra, who is working to establish a line of her own in Dobermans.

Her foundation bitch, Solo's Pride Phi Beta Kappa, C.D.X., W.A.C. is a daughter of Bar-Lock's Starhawk, C.D. (Champion Encore's Black Rites-Kay Hill's Letter Perfect) from Shana's Solo Fancy. She has produced well as the dam of the littermates (Champion Brosam's Devil Mai Kare, their sire) American and Canadian Champion Wen Fray's Annie Oakley, who finished in stiff competition, handled by Jeffrey Brucker; and Wen Fray's Baby Face Nelson, with points and numerous Reserves from the Bred-by-Exhibitor Class, who was the Doberman Pinscher Club of America's winner of the most Bred-by-Exhibitor Classes during 1982. The maternal granddam of these two, Kay Hill's Letter Perfect, was the breed's Top Producing Dam in 1976-1977.

Wynterwynd

Wynterwynd Dobermans have been actively breeding since 1972, although the owners, Bernard and Kathleen Pollock of Waller, Texas, have owned and shown the breed since 1963. To date the kennel has produced twenty-two American champions, in addition to one Panamanian champion, and one Mexican champion. In 1983, Wynterwynd was honored by the Doberman Pinscher Club of America for breeding eight champions in one year and received the coveted Breeder of the Year Award.

Tracing back to the beginning of Wynterwynd, it was in the summer of 1963 that a black puppy dog from the Stormson Kennels joined the Pollock family, later to become

Champion Stormson's Jet Gallant Thane, C.D. Thane was a linebred son of Champion Stormson's Crashing Baron Jet, the 1963 Best of Breed winner at Westminster, and he was a grandson of the famous Champion Rancho Dobe's Storm. He was finished completely owner-handled and won Best of Breed honors on many occasions. In 1968 Thane was bred to his half sister, producing Chance Run's Enchanted Star, C.D., who was to become the foundation bitch for both Wynterwynd and Amulet Dobermans. Enchanted Star was bred four times, each time by Champion Tarrado's Flair. She produced Champion Amulet's Angelique, Champion Amulet's Star Attraction, Champion Wynterwynd's Irish Fling, Champion Wynterwynd's Irish Spring, Champion Wynterwynd's Jesse James, and Champion Wynterwynd's Johnny Ringo.

Enchanted Star also produced Wynterwynd's Shannon, a spayed bitch lacking three single points towards her title. Shannon was bred to her sire, Champion Tarrado's Flair, and produced a singleton puppy, the beautiful red male Wynterwynd's Top Candidate, who died needing a "major" to finish. In his short lifetime, "Tops" sired Champion Wynterwynd's Wild Streak, C.D., R.O.M., Champion Wynterwynd's Wild Tempest, Champion Tempesta's Star of Wynterwynd (these three from Mi Casa's Buena), and Champion Vendar's Blazing Kristi (from Shadow v. Hartfiel).

Zeitlin

Zeitlin Dobermans are owned by Laura P. Zeitlin and Austin B. Zeitlin, M.D. and are located at Highland Park, Illinois.

To date this kennel has finished ten Dobe champions, and they have bred seven who have finished, with numerous others either just starting out or close to completion of their titles.

The Zeitlins are proud of being the owners of two Doberman Pinscher Club of America Top Twenty contenders: Champion Zeitlin's Pandora of Bolind in 1978 and Champion Zeitlin's Rogue Force in 1982 and 1983. Of course they take particular pleasure in being the breeders of an all-breed Best in Show winner.

Their Rogue Force dog, currently being handled by Sara Zeitlin, has an all-breed Best in Show and is a Specialty and multiple Group winner.

The principle bitch in the Zeitlin breeding program is Champion Zeitlin's Pandora of Bolind, who is the dam of Rogue Force. She has been on the Doberman Pinscher Club of America Top Twenty in 1978, as mentioned above, and she is a Group and Specialty winner. Pandora is a daughter of Champion Green Lakes Fortunato (Champion Tedell Nottingham Palace-Champion Redjack's Rain Flower) from Hollywills Kismet of Pandora (Champion Lisitza's Gilligan-Hollywills Penny Candy), and reaches back in her pedigree to Demetrius and the Tarrado and Damasyn dogs.

Rogue Force and Champion Zeitlin's Panquette von Kerri are littermates from Pandora and were born in June 1980, bred and owned by the Zeitlins. Their sire is Champion Marienburg's Maltese Falcon, he by American and Canadian Champion Marienburg's Sun Hawk ex Marienburg's Only One. In the tradition of her forebears, she is proving to be a notable producer.

Champion Zeitlin's Panther von Kerri, another homebred female, was born in August 1979. Champion Beaulane The Union Jack (Champion Mikadobe's Paris-Champion Beaulane Original Sin) is her sire; Champion Zeitlin's Pandora of Bolind, her dam.

Zenodobe

Zenodobe Dobermans, at Boothbay, Maine, were founded in the mid-1960's, the result of many years' admiration for this marvelous breed on the part of Nancy Woods and her husband.

It was not just by accident that the Woodses selected dogs from the bloodlines with which they have worked. During the 1950's they were frequent spectators at dog shows in the East, including Westminster. It was here, in 1962, that their future in the Doberman world was decided when Champion Singenwald's Prince Kuhio came to New York. There, for them, was the correct Doberman, and their decision took place. Four years had passed, however, by the time the Woodses were free to act upon it, during which period Prince Kuhio became the leading American Doberman sire. In 1966 a letter to his owner, Bea Rickert, led Nancy Woods

1. Ch. Zeitlin's Rogue Force v. Kerri winning Best of Breed and Group First at Palm Beach in January 1983. Jim Berger handling here for owners, Laura P. and Austin B. Zeitlin, M.D.
2. Ch. Zeitlin's Rogue Force v. Kerri, handled by Sara Zeitlin. Best of Breed in Nebraska, 1983.
3. Ch. Kai Esa's Finesse, by Ch. Agony Acres Devotee of Zeno ex Ch. Dobedach's Kai Esa. Owned and handled by Nancy H. Woods. Here taking a "major" towards her title at Bucks County Kennel Club in 1970.
4. Ch. Agony Acres Devotee of Zeno, 1966–1971, by Singenwald's Prince Kuhio ex Ch. Agony Acres Allegro, owned by Mr. and Mrs. James F. Woods, Boothbay, Maine.
5. Ch. Stormson's Jet Gallant Thane, C.D., by Ch. Stormson's Crashing Baron Jet ex Stormson's Star of Stars. A grandson of Ch. Rancho Dobe's Storm, Thane is the first Doberman owned by Wynterwynd Kennels. Finished his championship owner-handled and was a multi-Best-of-Breed winner. Bred by Betty Louise van B. Ueltzen, Stormson Dobermans. Owned by Bernard and Kathleen Pollock.

to the Herbert Davidsons in Pennsylvania, who had bred their Champion Agony Acres Allegro to Prince. The litter, which included seven black males, was eight weeks old when the Woodses saw the puppies, and from them they selected Zeno.

This strikingly look-alike Prince son became Champion Agony Acres Devotee of Zeno at 21 months, and a couple of years later he was tied in fourth place among top-producing sires. He had inherited not only his sire's phenotype but his genotype as well, with a prepotent ability to pass on the good things. One propitious early mating was to a half sister, Tommie Jones's Prince Kuhio daughter, Champion Dobedach's Kai Esa. This linebreeding produced three champions in the first litter: the dog, Champion Kai Esa's Foxfire, owned by Herman Rierson in Connecticut; and two bitches, Fantasy, owned by Erven Boles in North Carolina, and Finesse who came to the Woods at five months, took her first points at six months, and finished at sixteen months.

There was a strong infusion of Kay Hill in Zeno's dam. Thus it seemed to the Woodses that the combination of Kuhio and Kay Hill worked well, as Zeno turned out to look so like his sire, and Kay Hill bitches bred to him produced very well indeed. So, when Finesse was three years old, Nancy bred her to a half brother with a good bit of Kay Hill on his dam's side. This dog was the red Zeno son, Champion Barricade's Adonis of Mylor, owned by the Robert Tolvos in Massachusetts. This linebreeding produced three champions which Nancy Woods refers to as her "rainbow litter," since they were a black, a red and a blue.

The black, Champion Zenodobe's Anton, was owned and finished by the Jeffry Briggs in Wisconsin. Nancy herself kept and finished both the blue, who became Champion Zenodobe's Arius, and the red Champion Zenodobe's Antares.

Straight down from Alcor and Delegate and the wonderful Ravensburg dogs and Prince Kuhio, Zeno, his daughter Finesse, and his double grandson Arius were all multi-breed winners with Group wins for both dogs as well. What a sad and tragic loss that, at the age of five years, at the height of his fame and producing power, Zeno dropped dead. In

two-and-a-half years he had produced eleven champions. Finesse lived happily into her fourteenth year. Ari died at eleven, having added a fascinating facet to Nancy Woods's experience. He had proved that a blue coat *can* be trouble free, and for life.

Zeno made a name for himself abroad as well as in the United States, being behind the top-winning breeding in Norway today. Champion Honor Guard's Vesta, owned by Ingrid Strawser of Herrenhof Kennels in Virginia, was bred to Zeno and shipped in whelp to that country in 1970. Their descendants star in Maida Johnson's "Dogs in Europe" report on the IDC Sieger Scandinavia in the autumn of 1983 *Doberman Quarterly*.

A study of the pedigrees of Zeno and Arius list an unbroken line of champion sires for eight generations, back to Westphalia's Uranus, and include most of the great producers in American Doberman history. As Nancy comments, "The miracle to me of all such pedigrees is that over the years and over the miles so many people who would never meet did something right." Nancy goes on to remark that she never met Bea Rickert, who owned Prince Kuhio, but they have been fast friends since Nancy's first letter to her back in the 1960's. The Christmas notes continue to be exchanged, and this year Bea Rickert wrote, "The fact that you still enjoy showing Prince descendants is music to my heart." And to her own, adds Nancy.

Dobermans in Hawaii

It is not only on the mainland of the United States that Dobermans are a popular breed; they are also very much appreciated in Hawaii, and there are some excellent dogs representing the finest bloodlines there, in the hands of a very enthusiastic group of owners.

The Doberman Pinscher Club of Hawaii, Incorporated, is a Doberman Pinscher Club of America Chapter Club, holding three Specialty Shows during 1983, two Temperament Tests, and obedience match, and it conducts an active rescue program. Truly a very busy and constructive organization.

Chris Hall Yamaoka of Honolulu, who is secretary of this club, owns the *Calliope Dobermans* there, having been involved with the breed since 1977. Her enthusiasm was sparked that year when she attended the

Quaker City Doberman Pinscher Club Specialty on the mainland and for the first time met Carol Selzle (now Petruzzo) who was most cordial and helpful. After Chris returned to Hawaii, she and Carol corresponded for a year, which led to Chris's importing the bitch Carosel Starling, daughter of Champion Carosel In A Hurry, C.D., ROM ex Carosel Starlight Starbrite, purchased from Carol. "Ling" won her first Best of Breed at the age of a year-and-a-half under judge Frank Grover shortly after being released from the quarantine station in Hawaii. Chris describes Ling as having been "the true Dobe, physically and mentally, being fearless yet gentle and aware." Sad to report, Ling was lost to cancer at four years, having nine points and both her "majors."

Currently Chris has Champion Carosel In The Chips King Hill, W.A.C., who is three-and-a-half years of age. This dog has just completed his C.D. title and his ROM as we go to press, and he was the winner of two of the 1983 Doberman Pinscher Club of Hawaii Specialty Shows. Sired by Champion Marienburg Sun Hawk, C.D. from the late Champion Carosel In The Spotlight, ROM, Chip is thus a Sun Hawk son and a Demetrius grandson, a rare and desirable combination. He has, just before we are writing this, sired a litter of thirteen puppies out of Carosel There Goes My Baby, a black bitch by Champion Red Sun's Notorious ex Mah'L's Carillon, who is Chris's latest import. Chip was shown in Hawaii to his title, which he completed before reaching three years of age.

Mar Dar's Sugar Crisp, or Crickett as she is called, owing to her pep and energy, is the Dobe whom Chris Hall describes as "the light of my life." She was Winners Bitch at eleven months old under judge Mrs. Mildred Heald and also Best of Opposite Sex and Best of Winners under judge Judy Doniere for a fine Specialty win only shortly after turning one year of age. She was sired by Champion Mardale Spirit of Malnati ex Mar Dar's Spring Fling.

Fantasy Island Dobermans are owned by Don and Nora Gau at Honolulu, Hawaii and have become very famous throughout the dog show world due to their tremendously successful bitch, American and Canadian Champion Star Dobe's Irish Fantasy.

Fantasy was bred by Jay and Jackie Freitas, by Champion Irish Jig of Aramis ex Brandy Morning Star. Irish Jig, by Champion Ridgecrest's Bit O'Irish ex Champion Keresme's Eireanne, has as his grandparents those four very distinguished Dobes, Champion Brandendorf's Periwinkle, Champion Dobereich's Top of the Morning, Champion Tarrado's Corry, and Champion Lolani vom Ahrtal, C.D. Brandy Morning Star is by Warrick's Thunderbolt (Champion Ru Mar's Morgansonne, C.D. ex Champion Hamil's Buff Phoenix) from Victoria Melody Lady, the latter a granddaughter of Champion Haydenhill's Hurrah, Champion Hyvale Acres Ilysa, C.D., Champion Alnwick's Black Fury Bismarck, C.D. and, again, Champion Hyvale Acres Ilysa, C.D.

"Poppins," as Irish Fantasy is known to her friends, gained her championship during 1979. In 1980 she first entered the Top Twenty as Number Twenty, from which she rose to Number Two her second time, in 1981, and then to Number One for her third and final time, in 1982.

As of mid-July in 1982, Poppins had won Best of Breed on 159 occasions; Best in Specialty Show at eight independent Specialty events; 65 times First in the Working Group; 25 additional Group placements; and 24 times Best in Show. Impressive to say the least!

We know that puppies were planned as a part of Poppins's future, so we hope that they will carry on in her own great tradition.

1944 Doberman Pinscher Club of America Specialty show. Best of Breed, Ch. Dictator v Glenhugel. Handled by John Cholley for owners Mr. and Mrs. Bob Adamson. Judged by Anton Rost.

CHAPTER FIVE

The Doberman Pinscher Club of America

The day you acquire your first Doberman, you owe it to yourself to start to plan on becoming a member of the Doberman Pinscher Club of America and/or an affiliate club for Dobes in your area. The benefits to you will be tremendous. There is no finer, more involved and helpful organization to be found anywhere than the Doberman Pinscher Club of America, parent club for this breed. In addition, of course, belonging to a local club as well permits one to participate conveniently, attend meetings, etc., which may not always be possible if one is, for instance, at the extreme opposite end of this country from where DPCA is headquartered. Despite this fact, one *should* belong to DPCA as I am sure each and every reader will agree when becoming aware of the advantages.

The membership of the Doberman Pinscher Club of America, as we are writing this, consists of more than two thousand individuals from nearly every one of the fifty states. It is a non-profit organization formed in 1922 for the encouragement and promotion of the breeding of purebred Dobermans, and its affiliates include 59 "Chapter Clubs" spread throughout the United States. DPCA is a member club of the American Kennel Club. It is also a founding member of the North American Working Dog Association which works for the betterment of Working Dogs.

As well, it is a member of the American Dog Owners Association, which was formed for the protection of those who breed and exhibit dogs as a non-commercial venture and for the purpose of involving itself in legislative and educational activities for the protection and promotion of better welfare for dogs.

Membership in the Doberman Pinscher Club of America offers the opportunity to participate in the process of revising the breed Standard, if and when any changes may be contemplated; an opportunity to vote on proposed changes in the Club Constitution whenever such might be contemplated; a vote in the election of judges for the Annual Specialty Show, Obedience Trial and Futurity Stakes; a chance to participate in the Annual Election of Officers and Directors; and an opportunity to purchase a listing in the Doberman Pinscher Club of America Breeders Directory, providing stipulated requirements are fulfilled. It affords to you as a breeder the opportunity to nominate your bitches and compete in the Futurity which offers substantial sums of prize money; the opportunity to participate in the program of Annual Conformation and Obedience Awards to be competed for throughout the year and awarded at the Awards Banquet in conjunction with each Annual Specialty Show; and membership entitles you to receive a free copy of each issue of the Doberman Pinscher Club of America's publication *Pipeline*, and of each new edition of the Yearbook and Breeders Directory, plus free copies of the DPCA Constitution, breed Standard, color chart, and Doberman Pinscher Club of America decals. Additionally there is a special reduced rate available on the numerous Doberman Pinscher Club of America's excellent educational materials.

Membership in the Doberman Pinscher Club of America costs $15.00 annually. Applicants must be over 18 years of age and sponsored by two active DPCA members. Membership pins are available to members at a cost of $6.00 including packaging and mailing. The secretary of the Membership Committee is Marjorie Hudson, P.O. Box 76, Clarksburg, New Jersey, 08510. The Club's Delegate to the American Kennel Club is Charles A. T. O'Neill, 425 Roumfort Road, Philadelphia, Pennsylvania.

One of the most sought-after and respected honors to be attained by any Doberman breeder is recognition of one's dog by the Doberman Pinscher Club of America in its Register of Merit Awards Program. In order to earn the right to use ROM following a Doberman's name, that dog must have earned an American Kennel Club championship, one or more A.K.C. Obedience Titles, and a Working Aptitude Certificate. These titles may have been earned in any order. Upon the completion of all three, photocopies of the notification of titles must be sent to the co-ordinator (Adelaide Combs, 6302 Memorial Highway, Tampa, Florida 33615). The ROM title holders for that year are announced at the Annual Awards Dinner each October.

The Working Aptitude Certificate, or WAC, mentioned in the above ROM requirements is earned by a Doberman passing the Doberman Pinscher Club of America Working Aptitude Evaluation. For this any A.K.C. registered Doberman who is over 18 months of age is eligible for testing. These Working Aptitude Evaluations are sponsored by the various chapter Doberman Pinscher Clubs throughout the country, conducted by Doberman Pinscher Club of America approved evaluators. This Evaluation is designed to measure an individual Doberman's response to people, footing, visual and acoustic stimuli, and to threat situations. Upon passing this series of tests, a Working Aptitude Certificate will be sent by mail to the owner of each Doberman who has qualified.

Each year the Doberman Pinscher Club of America holds a National Convention and Specialty Show and Obedience Trial in a different area of the country, with one of the Chapter Clubs acting as host. This is generally referred to as "Doberman Week," as the events and those associated with them run for about six days, in addition to the National Specialty.

The Doberman Pinscher Club of America Symposium Programs serve as outstanding educational "happenings" for those interested in learning correct evaluation and the fine points of this breed. The Club is to be highly commended on the outstanding job it is doing in this regard! Having decided that the best way to deal with the many new fanciers joining the ranks during the 1970's was by making information on the breed understandable

and readily available, DPCA decided to sponsor a series of workshops, seminars or symposiums, holding up to three annually, each sponsored by the DPCA itself and one or more of the Chapter Clubs. Gerald D. Gaines is Chairman of this Committee. He can be reached at 8921 NE 190th Street, Bothel, Washington and invites the interest, co-operation and inquiries for assistance from breeders and owners. The Educational Committee has prepared a marvelous series of articles, which are available in sets, on many important subjects relating to the breed.

Then there is the COPE/Rescue program. COPE stands for Committee On Population Explosion, which is headed by Mrs. Judith Fellton of 219 Johnson Ferry Road, Marietta, Georgia 30067. This Committee was established during the population explosion in Dobermans during the 1970's and is a National Rescue Committee for the breed. Judith Fellton has written an excellent booklet entitled *The Beginner's Doberman Pinscher*, with the assistance of illustrator Tom Pollack. Mervy Hampton is in charge of production; and Barbara Fleischaker, Kay Martin, and Marjorie Veerkamp are co-writers. New goals of COPE/Rescue are headed by the wider education of all Doberman owners to the perils of overpopulation in the breed. Many Club Constitutions within the breed have been changed to include the words "preserve and protect the Doberman." Every effort is being made by all of these clubs to hold down surplus breeding and the overpopulation of unwanted Dobes who wind up homeless, in laboratories, or in shelters—fates which I am certain none of us wish to have befall our beloved dogs! Surveys have revealed that much "backyard" breeding of Dobermans takes place, done by people who are not even aware of the existing population problem. An attempt is being made at every opportunity to reach these people and to educate them on the cruelty of breeding animals carelessly. Also COPE endeavors to rescue as many Dobermans as possible who are abandoned, in shelters, or in need of homes; but the true importance of their work is the effort to educate people on the harm they are doing in creating surplus puppies.

One of the most exciting events in the world of Doberman Pinscher Dog Show competition is the Top Twenty Event, part of the

Doberman Pinscher Club of America's National Convention since 1974. This became an actual DPCA program in 1979; and in 1980 the Top Twenty Obedience Event was introduced, offering those attending these events the thrilling opportunity of seeing the most outstanding of that year's winners in both conformation and obedience areas. A panel of three judges officiates at each of these events, and the final winners announced at the Annual Awards. Films of past events, available for Chapter Club meetings are extremely popular.

The judging procedure for the Top Twenty competition is both interesting and exciting. Each of the Dobermans competing will be scored by each judge individually, using the Scale of Points from the Standard with which to work. The winner will be determined on the basis of the total score of each dog. We bring you herewith one of the scoring sheets from a Top Twenty Judges' Book, on which you will note that the original scale of points has been combined into four categories rather than eight, the point system remaining the same.

Three dogs will enter the ring at the same time, each one being completely scored independently by each judge, the dogs being rotated until each has been scored. The dogs next will be moved individually, then be scored by each of the judges for movement, and the process will be repeated until each of the twenty dogs has been examined and scored. Not until the day the winner is announced, and then by an impartial panel, will the results be tabulated and the winning selection named.

Selection of the Top Twenty Obedience Winner will be made as each dog performs the basic exercises and one optional exercise. The former are those expected of any well-trained Doberman, with, however, the patterns varied and more difficult than usually seen in the obedience ring. Optional exercises are selected from the Open and Utility classes. Point values are assigned to each. Again three judges will score each dog, with performance order drawn by lot at least one hour prior to the scheduled time of the event. The first steward will call commands for all dogs, and preplanned patterns will be used, not necessarily in the same order for each of the dogs. Included are all of the basics, and

the format will have been approved by the judges prior to beginning the event. The scores will be totalled by the Auditing Committee and announced at the Annual Awards Dinner. We include a page from the judges' book outlining the exercises used.

Competitors for the Top Twenty Conformation are selected on the basis of number of breed wins and of dogs defeated in making them. As an example, following is the list from which the 1982 Top Twenty winner came:

	Breed Wins	Points
1. Ch. Star Dobe's Irish Fantasy	82	4527
2. Ch. Hotai Copper Tattoo	57	3759
3. Ch. Redyn's Touch of Class	40	2076
4. Ch. Sherluck's L.B. Jake	26	1273
5. Ch. Grandobe's Mighty Convoy	25	1193
6. Ch. Tiffany's Gwynllyn of Amulet	25	1136
7. Ch. Eagle's Devil D	16	1134
8. Ch. TedellKey Largo	25	1111
9. Ch. Cyklon in April Cloud	14	950
10. Ch. Rockelle's Butch Cassidy	22	875
11. Ch. Blackstar's Rani Jemma	16	829
12. Ch. Zeitlin's Rogue Force v Kerri	19	808
13. Ch. Amulet's Cecil v Gluckliche	11	792
14. Ch. Tolivar's Boo Radley Dob Mann	25	778
15. Ch. Laurenwald's Never Delay	19	745
16. Ch. Fra Mar Optimist's Daughter	16	719
17. Ch. Dynasty's Moonshadow, C.D.	14	691
18. Ch. Triadel's On Stage, C.D.	11	612
19. Ch. Amulet's Luka of Sno-Glenn, C.D.	12	599
20. Ch. Tregua's Breakaway	11	514
21. Ch. Kendobe's Zu Erica Mit Lieb	10	502

You will note that there are actually 21 names as Champion Redlyn's Touch of Class had won first in the Top Twenty competition previously, therefore was no longer eligible to compete. Thus the addition of another name to bring the list to twenty actually competing.

The list from the catalogue for the Top Twenty Obedience Competition of 1982 follows:

		Total
1. OT Ch. Duchess Danielle II	820 (8)	6750
2. Larwyck's Czarina, U.D.	147 (3)	3105
3. Tucari's Racime Razzmatass, C.D.X.	200 (3)	2760
4. OT Ch. Warwick's Prelude to Winter	201 (2)	2760
5. OT Ch. Dawn's Never So Lucky		2162.5
6. Acadia's Black Swan, U.D.	325 (3)	1901.5
7. Scorpio's Ms. Rita, C.D.X.	268 (5)	1854.5
8. Tucari's Topaz Tallulah, C.D.X.	95 (1)	1671
9. Lisa's Diligent Derringer, U.D.T.	189 (2)	1570
10. Spinner "D", C.D.X.	272 (2)	1457.5
11. Mindemoya's Triple Crown, C.D.X.	122 (3)	1306
12. OT Ch. Vanessa von Heink		1178
12. Wichwind's Rasen of Davidsburg, U.D.		1178
14. Charla of Paradise, C.D.X.		1177.5
15. Connoisseur's Premiere, C.D.	13 (1)	998
16. OT Ch. Rare Ebony Wine of Scotsbrae	172 (2)	961
16. Loriens Ebony's Helgar, C.D.X.	17 (1)	800.5
18. Ling II		787
18. Largo's Sidekick, C.D.		787
20. Lulberg's Candy Barr, C.D.X.		786
20. Tayon Hell Hath No Fury		886

NOTE: A tie for #20 resulted in 21 dogs listed.

The purpose of these Top Twenty events is to encourage the showing of Doberman Pinschers in both conformation classes and obedience trials. Each event, being part of a Doberman Pinscher Club of America National Convention, makes them highly useful in the education of judges, exhibitors, breeders, and the Fancy, generally, and gives special recognition, so well deserved, to the dogs whose records are outstanding, their breeders, owners, trainers and handlers.

The first Top Twenty Conformation Event was held in conjunction with the Doberman Pinscher Club of America in 1974, as already mentioned. It is further interesting that it was sponsored by Ray Carlisle and *Top Dobe* magazine, with the DPCA Judging Committee working out the system to be used by judges for these events. The panel of three judges consists of a breeder/judge, a multi-breed judge, and a professional handler. The ring is

arranged with three judging stations, each judge scoring the dogs one at a time until each has been judged by all three of them. The dog whose score is highest based on combined score average is the winner. It was in 1979 that the Conformation Top Twenty event became a Doberman Pinscher Club of America program—one of the leading highlights of convention week.

The Top Twenty Obedience Event started out in 1980, meeting with instant popularity and success. Basically it works the same way, judged by a panel of three people. In this case those officiating are a trainer closely identified with Dobermans; an exhibitor-trainer identified with Dobermans and successful in obedience; and a judge approved by A.K.C. to judge all obedience through Utility who is *not* identified with Dobermans. Scores are on performance, but with a strong emphasis on attitude and teamwork as well as precision. The dog with the highest combined average score becomes the winner. The name is announced at the Awards Banquet.

Eligibility for these events is compiled on standings information as collected each year through the June and July issues of the American Kennel *Gazette*. For conformation competition, the points are allotted based on the number of dogs defeated in winning each Best of Breed. For obedience, all points of 195 or better, earned in regular Obedience classes, are used. The awarded points equal the total of the score. Bonus points equal to the number of dogs defeated are issued to High in Trial Dobermans.

Thus the Dobermans who have scored in the Top Twenty of the breed in each of these areas are invited to attend and be honored at the very exciting official judging for Number One position in each category.

Following are sample sheets from Doberman Pinscher Club of America Top Twenty Conformation and Obedience. Additionally, in the appendices of this book, you will find lists of all Top Twenty winners in both conformation and obedience competition and complete lists of Highest Scoring Dog in Trial (1937-1985) and Best of Breed winners (1924-1985) from the Doberman Pinscher Club of America Specialty shows.

CAPTIONS FOR PLATES 81 TO 96

Plate 81

1. Mamiya Negra De Mico Y Tormak, by Glenayr Jamison ex Laica de Mico y Tormak, at age six months taking Best of Opposite Sex for five points. Bred and owned by Max Toro. Handled by Ceci Martinez de Santana, Jay-Mee's Dobbies.

2. Dynasty's Midnite at the Oasis, by Ch. Wynterwynd's Spring Tornado ex Wynterwynd's Peace On Earth, taking Best in Show at the Seventh International Dog Show in Venezuela, November 1980. This is the first Puerto-Rican–owned dog to go Best in Show at one of these events. The judge was Herman Cox from the U.S.A. The next day this splendid dog went Reserve Best in Show under judge Robert Waters of Canada. Israel Torres, owner; Mike Masferrer, handler.

3. Redenau Lucifer, by Am. and Can. Ch. Lindenau Arrowsmith ex Redlin's Countess Cleopatra. Bred by Diane Tharp. Owned by Herman Hauss and Jay-Mee's Dobbies, San Juan, Puerto Rico.

4. Tjara's Shades of Times, bred by Betty Stoudts. Owned by Jay-Mee's Dobbies, Jaime and Ceci Martinez de Santana, San Juan, Puerto Rico. "Angel" is by Destiny's Royal Star of Futura ex Lady's Little Rose, and she is a granddaughter of Ch. Edehall's Gigolo of Amulet.

5. P.R., Dom., and Ven. Ch. Magesil's Black Octopus, C.D., a Best in Show winner with many titles to his credit, owned by Madeline George, Carolina, Puerto Rico. Pictured on one of his visits to the mainland taking Reserve Winners at Westminster in 1982.

6. Glenayr Jamison, bred by Richard and Barbara Duklis. Owned by Jay-Mee's Dobbies.

7. The well-known winner, Glenayr Jamison. By Ch. Glenayr Dufferinand (Ch. Gra-Lemor Demetrius—Ch. Tedell Barcarolle) ex Tedell Taras Harp (Ch. Tedell Key Largo—Tedell Mirabelle Palace). Bred by Richard and Barbara Duklis; owned by Jay-Mee's Dobbies. Best of Breed in the Venezuela International, 1982, under judge Richard Guevera.

8. Rubicon's Anasazi, by Ch. Marienburg's Sun Hawk ex Rubicon's Little Ginger, at four months. Owned by Jam-Mee's Dobbies, San Juan, Puerto Rico.

Plate 82

1. Moondancer's Easter Bonnet, a one-year-old bitch by Can. Ch. Vondersha's Chapter One ex Klauswalts Foxey Lady (a Ch. Vince daughter, "Rollie's" dam). Owned by Bob and Sally Robson, Cargill, Ontario, Canada.

2. Bob Robson taking Best of Breed with a one-year-old Moondancer bitch, "Heritage." A daughter of Can. Ch. Moondancer's Rolls Royce and granddaughter of the German import Gladiator's Tara. Owned by Bob and Sally Robson.

3. The second leading winner among Canadian Doberman bitches at the present time, Ch. Dobermien's Virgo, is owned by Michel Plamondon of Lac Beauport, Quebec, Canada and has been handled to her ring achievements by Harold Butler. By Ch. Shingo's War Admiral.

4. Ch. Dobermien's Virgo, owned by Michel Plamondon and handled by Harold Butler, winning the Working Group at Bellville District Kennel Club in 1983.

Plate 83

1. Can. and Bda. Ch. Shauffelein's Shady Lady, C.D.X., owned by Fred Heal, Ontario, Canada. Handled by Harold Butler.

2. Ch. Jagermeister's Renown, shown as a puppy, winning at the Doberman Pinscher Club of Canada Specialty. Mrs. Peggy Adamson judging. Bred, owned, and handled by Fred Heal, Jagermeister Kennels.

3. Can. Ch. Moondancer's Rocky Road taking Best of Winners at Belleville for owners Bob and Sally Robson, Cargill, Ontario, Canada.

4. Can. Ch. Moondancer's Rolls Royce won a Best in Match the first time shown, as a puppy, at Barrie Kennel Club. Bob Robson handling. Moondancer Dobermans belong to Bob and Sally Robson.

5. Moondancer's Imperial Dragon at four months. A son of Can. Ch. Moondancer's Rolls Royce. Owned by Bob and Sally Robson.

6. Gladiator's Tara in 1980. The foundation dam at Moondancer Dobermans, owned by Bob and Sally Robson.

Plate 84

1. Ch. Valentino at Carbourg, owned by Christianne Carbonneau, winning Best of Breed at the Doberman Pinscher Club of Quebec in May 1983. May Jacobson (of the United States), judge. Handled by John Griffith.

2. Can. Ch. Trollhattan's High Voltage Tye, by Ch. Tarrado's Chaos ex Ch. Warlock Witch v Trollhattan. Finished his title in hottest western Canadian competition, then returned to Trollhattan as a stud dog. His son is still being used there and is also the sire of champions.

3. Can. Ch. Tarrado's Chaos, by Ch. Felix vom Ahrtal ex Ch. Highbriar Jasmine, the only sibling of the famous Tarrado "C" litter to come to Canada. Chaos was an excellent sire for Trollhattan, producing over 21 champions, most of whom were homebreds.

4. Ch. Doberdamen's War Eagle, born in May 1977, by Ch. Gambolwood's Hellelujah ex Ch. Aldebaron Taurus Alrescha. Owned by Mary Spinelli, Alderheim Dobermans, Dartmouth, Nova Scotia, Canada.

Plate 85

1. Ch. Carvon's Sweet Sara, by Ch. Starstorm Santana ex Ch. Fairest Nymph Echo, C.D., pictured at Mission Kennel Club under judge Eileen Fraser in June 1983. This bitch won the Northern Alberta Doberman Pinscher Club Specialty show in August 1983. Bred, owned, and shown by Carmen Haller of Carvon Kennels, Coquitlam, British Columbia, Canada.

2. Ch. Carvon's Mai Tai, at 10 months, winning Best Puppy in Show at Cranbrook Kennel Club, August 1983, L. T. Haverstock judging. Bred, owned, and handled by Carmen Haller. By Am. and Can. Ch. Starstorm Thunderbolt, Can. and Am. C.D. ex Ch. Fairest Nymph Echo, C.D.

3. Ch. Fairest Nymph Echo, Susan Hillman handling, winning at Vernon Kennel Club in 1979 under judge Mrs. Danielle-Jenkins. Owned by Carmen Haller.

4. Ch. Lady's Jaguar, C.D. It is believed that this is the first natural-eared (uncropped) Dobe to finish a championship in Canada. He completed his title in 1975 with a Group 3rd and Canadian-bred in Group under judge Heywood Hartley. Owned by Carmen Haller, Carvon Dobes.

5. Ch. Carvon's Spiderman, age eight months, by Ch. Starstorm Thunderbolt, C.D. ex Ch. Fairest Nymph Echo, C.D. Pictured at Vernon Kennel Club, July 1983. Judge Tom Quilley awarding Best Puppy in Group. Carmen Haller, breeder-owner-handler.

6. Ch. Dawnaquinn's Damn Yankee, by Am. and Can. Ch. Starstorm Thunderbolt Can. and Am. C.D. ex Ch. Dawnaquinn's Galina Petrova, owned by A. E. (Bud) and Wendy Beck, Dawnaquinn Dobermans, Calgary, Alberta, Canada.

7. A handsome study of the lovely Doberman, Ch. Dobestar's Seventh Saturn, C.D.X., ROM, born March 1981. By Ch. Carbourg's Herr Ansel ex Darklords' Jaded Shadow. Owned by Mary Spinelli, Alderheim Dobermans, Dartmouth, Nova Scotia, Canada.

8. Ch. Dobestar's Seventh Saturn, C.D.X., ROM. By Ch. Carbourg's Herr Ansel ex Darklords' Jaded Shadow. Owned by Mary Spinelli, Alderheim Dobermans.

Plate 86
1. Ch. Ryas Applause ("Missy"), owned by Mr. and Mrs. Davis of Nebraska, was from the first litter of Troll and Rya. She was Best of Opposite Sex to her famous half-brother, Ch. Schauffelein's Vintage Year, at the Doberman Pinscher Club of Canada Specialty in 1977, judge J. D. Jones, judging. "Missy" was bred by Dave and Pat Cunningham, Ryas Dobes, Vinemount, Ontario, Canada.

2. Ch. Ryas Applause, photographed by Bixler at Chatham, Ontario, in 1977 following the Specialty. Bred by Dave and Pat Cunningham. Owned by Mr. and Mrs. Davis of Nebraska.

3. A very handsome Doberman from Canada, Ch. Ryas Anticipation at two-and-a-half years of age. Owned by Pat Cunningham.

4. Ch. Ryas Anticipation, C.D., ROM with his granddaughter, Rhonnie. Dave and Pat Cunningham, Ryas Dobermans, Vinemount, Ontario.

Plate 87
1. Ch. Dobermien's Virgo, owned by Michel Plamondon of Lac Beauport, Quebec, Canada, handled here by Harold Butler to a Group First under Mrs. Danielle-Jenkins.

2. Can. Ch. Tamarak's Brigadoon, by Am. Ch. Tamarak's Hot Off The Press ex Tamarak's Whirlwind, was bred by Doris Nemeth. Owned by Sherry George and Shirrel DeBaie, Eastern Passage, Nova Scotia, Canada.

3. Can. Ch. Regnancy's Wildfire, C.D., by Can. Ch. Tamarak's Brigadoon ex Can. Ch. Trollhattan's Special Edition. Owned and bred by Sherry George and Shirrel DeBaie.

4. Pastel head study of Ch. Ryas Anticipation, C.D., ROM by his owner, Pat Cunningham.

Plate 88
1. Ch. Dawnaquinn's Day Dream Rose, by Am. and Can. Ch. Starstorm Thunderbolt ex Dawnaquinn's Kira Arganova. Owned by A. E. (Bud) and Wendy Beck, Dawnaquinn Dobermans, Calgary, Alberta, Canada.

2. Am. and Can. Ch. Dawnaquinn's John Galt, by Am. Ch. Tamarak's Fire Blaze ex Ch. Free Spirits Quinnella. Handled in the U.S. by Larry Sinclair. Owned by A. E. (Bud) and Wendy Beck.

3. Am. and Can. Ch. Defender's Xerxes, by Am. and Can. Ch. Starstorm Thunderbolt ex Ch. Starstorm Sunni The Defendre. Owner, Gary Lee.

4. Ch. Dobenhaus The Slipstitch, by Ch. Jagermeister's Five Card Stud ex Tanya's Cassandra, in 1983 at age five-and-a-half years. Winning an Award of Merit under judge Judy Doniere at the Doberman Pinscher Club of Canada Specialty. Slipstitch is the dam of four champions to date from two litters, and she is the granddam of champions. Bred and owned by Joe and Janet Lobb, Brucefield, Ontario, Canada.

5. Ch. Dobenhaus Darn 'Knit Pearl, by Ch. Jagermeister's Blackmail ex Ch. Dobenhaus The Slipstitch. Bred by Joe and Janet Lobb. Owned by Mike and Cheryl Greenhill.

6. Ch. Dobenhaus The Daquari, by Ch. Jagermeister's Blackmail ex Ch. Dobenhaus The Slipstitch. Finished at three consecutive shows with five-point wins, including Best of Winners and an Award of Merit at the Doberman Pinscher Club of Canada Specialty in 1981. Handled by Joe Lobb, co-breeder with Janet Lobb. Owners, Mr. and Mrs. G. Tieman.

Plate 89
1. Can. Ch. Dobenhaus Full Impact, a black dog finishing at 12 months. By Ch. Lowenbrau Magnate ex Ch. Dobenhaus The Slipstitch. Owners, Mr. and Mrs. Scott Beamish. Breeders, Joe Lobb (handling) and Janet Lobb, Brucefield, Ontario, Canada.

2. Tanya's Cassandra and Kerri Lobb, Winter 1983. Joe and Janet Lobb, owners.

3. Ch. Dobenhaus The Slipstitch at four years. By Ch. Jagermeister's Five Card Stud ex Tanya's Cassandra. Bred and owned by Joe and Janet Lobb.

4. Esquire's Amoretta, by Ch. Highbriar Esquire ex Ch. Erivan R. Tucky Miss, was Best of Breed and Group 3rd in June 1983 over Specialty and Best in Show winners at the South Shore Kennel Club. Ken and Sheila Valentine, Windsor Junction, Nova Scotia, Canada.

5. Ch. Edelmar's Bold Venture, by Ch. Highbriar Esquire. Owned by Ken and Sheila Valentine.

6. Ch. Esquire's B.R.T. of Annarbe, by Am. Ch. Eric von Alpindobe ex Am. Ch. Haltbar Titian Barque, winning under Mae Jacobson for five points at the Doberman Pinscher Club of Canada Specialty in 1983. Handled by Ken Valentine, co-owner with Sheila Valentine, Esquire Dobermans.

Plate 90
A great and famous mother-son brace of Dobermans: Ch. Schauffelein's Vintage Year and his dam, Ch. Lowenbrau Aloha Schauffelein, winning the Brace Class at a Doberman Pinscher Club of Canada National Specialty judged by Peggy Adamson. Ron and Joey Purdy, owners, Cheltenham, Ontario, Canada.

PLATE 81

PLATE 82

1 ►

2 ►

3 ►

4 ►

PLATE 83

5 ►

6 ►

1 ◄

2 ►

PLATE 84

3 ◄

4 ►

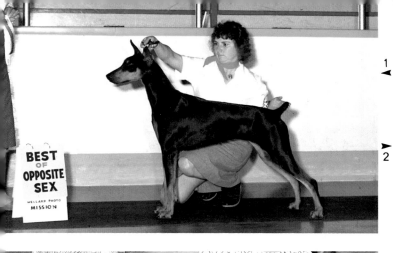

1
2

3
4

PLATE 85

5
6

7
8

BEST OPPOSITE SEX

DOBE SPEC. '77

1 ◄

2 ►

PLATE 86

3 ◄

4 ►

1 ►

2 ►

PLATE 87

3 ►

4 ►

1 ►

2 ►

3 ►

4 ►

PLATE 88

5 ►

6 ►

PLATE 89

PLATE 90

1 ▶

2 ▶

3 ▶

4 ▶

PLATE 91

5 ▶

6 ▶

7 ▶

8 ▶

PLATE 92

1▲   PLATE 93   ▼2

MONROE
KENNEL CLUB
NOVEMBER 23 1974

1 ▶

2 ▶

3 ◀

4 ▶

PLATE 94

5 ◀

6 ▶

1 ▶

2 ▶

3 ▶

4 ▶

PLATE 95

5 ▶

6 ▶

1

2

3

4

PLATE 96

5

6

Plate 91

1. Ch. Ryas Legacy, born April 1982, finishing at 14 months owner-handled in eight shows. "Viper" was the seventh champion for her sire, Ch. Ryas Anticipation, C.D., ROM, and the second for her dam, Ryas Effervescence. Owned by Dave and Pat Cunningham, Ryas Kennels, Vinemount, Ontario, Canada.

2. Ryas Keynote, with four points, by the Anticipation son, Ch. Wrath's Cannonball Run ex Ch. Ryas Curtain Call. Born April 1982. Shown only once at six months and 10 days old, "Magnum" garnered Best of Winners (pictured) under John Connolly. Dave and Pat Cunningham, Ryas Dobermans, breeders.

3. Ch. Ryas Anticipation showing his excellent reach and drive in motion. Ryas Dobermans, the Cunninghams, Vinemount, Ontario, Canada.

4. Ch. Ryas Hot To Trot, born April 1981, by Ch. Warcrick's Achilles (a Troll grandson) ex Ryas Effervescence. "Samba" finished in only four shows on consecutive weekends, including Winners Bitch at a Doberman Pinscher Club of Canada National Specialty. Owned by Dave and Pat Cunningham. Pictured at two years of age on the day she finished. Handled by Scott McNair.

5. Ch. Schauffelein's Superior Odds, born in 1980, pictured at two-and-a-half years of age winning the Doberman Pinscher Club of Canada National Specialty. Finished in one week, three shows, with two Group placements (a First and a Second) from the classes plus a Best of Winners at age 15 months. He is one of the current stud dogs at Schauffelein Kennels, Ron and Joey Purdy, Cheltenham, Ontario, Canada. This dog is by Schauffelein's Pierce Arrow (by Champion Schauffelein's Vintage Year—Schauffelein's Red Knickers) from Schauffelein's Twelfth of Never (Vintage Year—Schauffelein's Reflections).

6. Am. and Can. Ch. Schauffelein's Wild Country winning the first of the five "majors" in three outings, during which his title in the States was gained. Jeff Brucker handling for Ron and Joey Purdy.

7. Am. and Can. Ch. Schauffelein's Wild Country finishing with his fifth "major" in three trips to the U.S.A. "T-Bone," winning here under judge Muriel Freeman, is the current "star" at Schauffelein Kennels. By Ch. Grindlewald's Connoisseur, C.D. (Vintage Year—Ch. Jagermeister's Strawberry Tart) ex Ch. Schauffelein's Elderberry Wine (Vintage Year—Schauffelein's Red Knickers). Jeff Brucker handling for owners Ron and Joey Purdy.

8. Am. and Can. Ch. Schauffelein's Vintage Year, known as "Goober." Pictured winning his last Best in Show during a drenching storm with everyone thoroughly soaked. Ron and Joey Purdy, owners, Schauffelein Dobermans, Cheltenham, Ontario, Canada.

Plate 92

1. Kronen's Special Edition at 12 weeks. Born September 1983, by Ch. Highbriar Esquire ex Ch. Starstorm Sister Sara. Bred by J. Healy; owned by Ken and Sheila Valentine, Esquire Dobes, Windsor Junction, Nova Scotia, Canada.

2. Ch. Esquire's B.R.T. of Annarbe, by Ch. Eric von Alpindobe ex Ch. Haltbar Titian Barque, pictured as a puppy with her handler Gene Haupt at the National Specialty in Boston. Bred and owned by Ken and Sheila Valentine.

3. Ch. Haltbar Titian Barque, a daughter of Ch. Highbriar Esquire, born in June 1976. Owned and loved by Ken and Sheila Valentine.

4. Ch. Istvanhazi's Fantasy Miss Rigo at age 16 months going Winners Bitch at the Canadian National Sportsmen's Dog Show in 1978 with a large "booster" entry. Jerry Rozinka, Pickering, Ontario, Canada, breeder.

5. Istvanhazi's Hop-te Zsiga, bred by Steve Rozinka and owned by Jerry Cudahy, Canada.

6. Ch. Huncut Betyar of Istvanhazi taking a five-point "major" at Credit Valley under Mrs. Danielle-Jenkins for Steve Rozinka, Pickering, Ontario, Canada.

Plate 93

1. Am. and Can. Ch. Free Spirits Blackgammon, a multi-Best-in-Show winner and the sire of U.S. and Canadian champions. Owned by Free Spirits Dobermans, Surrey, British Columbia, Canada.

2. Am. and Can. Ch. Schauffelein's Vintage Year pictured winning the Working Group under renowned judge and Doberman authority A. Peter Knoop at the Monroe show, November 1974. A thrilling climax to his 1974 American show season. Owned by Ron and Joey Purdy, Schauffelein Dobermans, Cheltenham, Ontario, Canada.

Plate 94

1. Am. and Can. Ch. Sherluck's Crimson N' Clover, foundation bitch, winning the Brood Bitch Class at the Doberman Pinscher Club of Canada National Specialty in 1983. Lana Sniderman and Bob Krol, Simca Dobermans, owners.

2. Can. Ch. Simca's Almost Like Flying taking Best of Winners on the 1984 Florida circuit for his first "major" in the United States. Judge, Virginia Markley. Don Simmons handling for Simca Kennels, Lana Sniderman and Bob Krol.

3. Am. and Can. Ch. Sherluck's Crimson N' Clover, all-breed Best in Show and Specialty winner. Foundation bitch at Simca Dobermans.

4. Can. Ch. Simca's April Wine, handled by Teresa Nail. Judge, Carol Selzle Petruzzo. First Canadian-bred Doberman to be judged Grand Prize Futurity Winner at the Doberman Pinscher Club of America National, October 1983.

5. Can. Ch. Simca's April Wine, Doberman Pinscher Club of America 1983 Grand Prize Futurity Winner, taking Best of Winners for her second "major" on the 1984 Florida circuit. Judge, Terry Temple. Owned by Simca Kennels, Nobleton, Ontario, Canada.

6. Am. and Can. Ch. Sherluck's Crimson N' Clover winning Best in Show. Owner-handled by Lana Sniderman.

Plate 95

1. Am. and Can. Ch. Simca's Amanda Trees, owner-handled by Bob Krol, taking Winners Bitch (when only 18 months of age) under Thomas Gately. Simca Dobermans, Nobleton, Ontario, Canada.

2. Can. Ch. Simca's April Wine, owner-handled by Lana Sniderman of Simca Kennels, to a Group placement.

3. Can. Ch. Simca's Asleep At The Wheel, handled by co-owner Lana Sniderman to Best of Opposite Sex under Mrs. Phyllis Wolfish, judge.

4. Can. Ch. Simca's Almost Like Flying with handler Shirley DeBoer. Lana Sniderman and Bob Krol, owners, Simca Kennels.

5. Can. Ch. Simca's April Wine taking Winners Dog at Guelph. Dr. Richard Meen handling for Lana Sniderman and Bob Krol.

6. Am. and Can. Ch. Sherluck's Crimson N' Clover winning the Group at Sault Ste. Marie. Richard Meen handling for Simca Dobermans.

Plate 96

1. Am. and Can. Ch. Free Spirits Apollo, U.D., ROM, a multi-Best-in-Show winner and Canada's No. 1 Working Dog for 1981. Free Spirits Dobermans, Surrey, British Columbia, Canada.

2. Ch. Istvanhazi's High Spirits, owned by Steve Rozinka of Pickering, Ontario, Canada.

3. Istvanhazi's Almos Zsu-Zsa at nine months. Here taking Winners Bitch over 23 Open Bitches from the Puppy Class. Steve Rozinka, owner.

4. Istvanhazi's Fantasy Miss Gigi winning the breed her second time out. Steve Rozinka, owner.

5. Istvanhazi's Csini Baba, sister to Rigo, taking Reserve Winners Bitch under judge Doris Wilson at her only show to date. Steve Rozinka, owner.

6. Can. and Bda. Ch. Jagermeister's Seven Come Eleven. Bred, owned, and handled by Fred Heal; here winning one of his 22 Bests in Show. The judge is Mrs. Yan Paul.

CAPTIONS FOR PAGE 354

1. Ch. Christie v Klosterholz, dam of Ch. Christie's Barrier. Famous bitch from the 1940's.
2. Breite v Rupprechtheim in November 1942, owned by Jim Roberts. Photo courtesy of Peggy Adamson.
3. Ch. Kasper v Lobenstein, Sch.H., owned by Mrs. C. W. Harris, Winston-Salem, North Carolina.

BASIC EXERCISES

	Maximum points
1. Heeling	
A. Maintaining of heel position at different speeds (from slow walk to fast jog) while moving in straight lines, large curves, small curves, medium curves — (6 foot diameter), right, left, and about turns, in and among obstacles (both animate and inanimate)	50
B. Automatic sits when stopped	25
2. Stands, sits, and downs	
The dog may be stood or commanded to stand.	25
From the stand, the dog shall sit on command with the handler at the dog's side.	
From the stand, the dog shall down on command with the handler directly in front of the dog; with the handler ten feet in front of the dog.	
From a sit, the dog shall down on command with the handler at the side. The dog shall down on command from a sit with the handler at a distance of ten feet.	
3. Recall	
The dog shall perform recalls from a short distance (eight feet), medium distance (fifteen feet), and a long distance (forty feet).	50
Return to heel.	10
4. Stays	40
TOTAL SCORE	200

OPTIONAL EXERCISES

	Maximum points
1. Directed jumping	50
2. Signals	40
3. Retrieve over the jump	35
4. Retrieve on flat	30
5. Scent discrimination	40
6. Directed retrieve	35
7. Drop on recall	35
8. Broad jump	30

1▲   ▼2

1. Ch. Amulet's Luka of Sno-Glenn, C.D., the *first fawn ever in the Top 20,* pictured with Top Twenty judges Joey Purdy, Muriel Freeman, and Terry Lazzaro. Owned by Linda and John Krukar, Bethlehem Pennsylvania.
2. Ch. Zeitlin's Rogue Force v Kerri owned by A. B. Zeitlin, Highland Park, Illinois. Bob Wills judging; Jim Berger handling.

SCALE OF POINTS
For Evaluation of Individual Specimen
on the Basis of the Standard

1. General conformation and appearance	Maximum points	Points assigned
Proportions 8		_____
Bone, substance 8		_____
Temperament, expression, nobility 8		_____
Condition 5		_____
Coat, color, markings 5		_____
34		_____

2. Head	Maximum points	Points assigned
Shape 6		_____
Teeth 5		_____
Eyes 3		_____
Ears 1		_____
Neck 3		_____
Body		
Backline, withers, loins, tail placement 8		_____
Chest, brisket, rib spring, tuck-up 8		_____
Shape and proportions 4		_____
38		_____

3. Forequarters	Maximum points	Points assigned
Shoulders, upper arms, legs, pasterns 5		_____
Angulation 4		_____
Paws 2		_____
Hindquarters		
Upper thigh, stifles, hocks 5		_____
Angulation 4		_____
Paws 2		_____
22		_____

4. Gait	Maximum points	Points assigned
	6	_____
	6	_____
TOTAL SCORE	100	_____

PLEASE NOTE: Final score is *not* to be tabulated by judges or stewards.

Glenayr Jamison and friend Christian. Owned by Jay-Mee's Dobbies, San Juan, Puerto Rico.

Doberman Pinschers in Puerto Rico

Although it is not known exactly when Dobermans started to appear in Puerto Rico, it is established that the breed began appearing in dog shows there in 1958. The first member of the breed appearing in the show ring there was Dobeking Allure, owned by Mrs. Aurora A. Lugo Lopez. The occasion was the first American Kennel Club Licensed point show which took place during that year.

The following year, in 1959, a Doberman bitch owned by William L. Artau was handled to Best of Breed and Group Fourth by Mrs. Artau at the second A.K.C. Puerto Rican Dog Show under judge Forest Hall.

In 1960, Wong Dai, owned by Laurian B. and Dr. Ralph J. Lum, Jr., became the first Doberman to win a Working Group in Puerto Rico. And in 1962, Thor Chiman of Greenbriar, owned by Mrs. Charles W. Gable, won Best of Breed and Group Second there.

Early Doberman Pinschers in Puerto Rico included Marienburg Amaya de Granada, owned by Cristobel and Josefina del Pulgar, who finished her title but sad to report died of pneumonia; she did leave, however, a beautiful litter of puppies who were successfully hand raised by Mrs. del Pulgar.

Mr. and Mrs. Alexis Rodriquez Pou were among the most diligent of breeders who helped develop the Puerto Rican Dobe, continuously striving for improvement through their breeding program. One of their first Dobermans, Champion Muscor Atilla, was sent to the Florida circuit to gain the title in good order. And it was in 1964 that these breeders purchased Champion Kay Hill's Witch Hunt from Mrs. Jane Kay, a significant event for the breed. Among Witch Hunt's important show successes were nine Bests of Breed, Best of Opposite Sex at the Chicago International Specialty, and some half-dozen Group placements including a first. In Puerto Rico, during 1964, she was awarded Best Local Dog and another Group Second at the Puerto Rico Kennel Club.

Champion Jem's Diamond von Warlock was imported to the island by Theodore and Rita Fajardo in 1964. This couple also owned Muscor D'Artagnan. He was usually handled in the show ring by Mrs. Alexis Rodriquez Pou, who in 1965 imported Ce-Ce Dobe's Allegro—handled by Jane Kay to her championship. Her victories included Winners Bitch at the Chicago International, and she was the first Doberman to attain a Best in Show in Puerto Rico, handled on the latter occasion by Mr. Pou. She completed her title at Charleston, South Carolina when only twenty-two months of age.

The second Doberman to win Best in Show in Puerto Rico (owned by Mr. Pou) was Champion Arjean's Half Time under Mr. Kenneth Given in September 1970, handled by Arthur Conwell.

Mr. Pou now lives in Florida and has retired from the show dog world, or at least from active involvement with it.

Other major personalities responsible for the development and improvement of the Doberman in Puerto Rico include Mr. Cesar Sierra and Mr. and Mrs. Luis Puig Schumann. Mr. Sierra was the first President of the Doberman Pinscher Club of Puerto Rico, an organization which was founded in 1974 by him, Mr. and Mrs. Puig, and Mr. and Mrs. Jorge Casanova.

Mr. Sierra at that time owned Puerto Rican and Dominican Champion Black Jack Ace O'Spades, a Thorval son, who was a multi-Group and Best in Show winner. Unfortunately this splendid dog only lived to be nine years old, 1974-1983. Mr. Sierra has always

1 ▲

◄ 2

◄ 3

1. Ch. Ce-Ce Dobe's Allegro, the first Doberman ever to go Best in Show in Puerto Rico, this in 1965. Judge, Maxwell Riddle. Owned by Alexis Rodriquez Pou.
2. Jay-Mee's Latin Dandy, owned by Tony and Hilda Morales. Bred by Jay-Mee's Dobbies, by Glenayr Jamison ex Taina Red Poison.
3. Pictured are Jaime and Ceci Martinez de Santana with Glenayr Jamison, Jay-Mee's Latin Dandy, and Mamiya Negra de Mico y Tormak. These owners of Jay-Mee's Dobbies claim, "Versatility is what we breed for, striving for perfection." The Santanas live in San Juan, Puerto Rico.

been recognized as a devoted fancier of the breed, and his influential personality assisted greatly in the understanding and breeding of quality Dobermans. Now a resident of Venezuela, he steadily maintains his active interest in Dobes, and two of his young imports are just starting their show careers as we write.

The Puigs became active with Kaiser von Schumann in 1964, making him the first homebred Puerto Rican Doberman champion. In 1967 he was on the Florida circuit with professional handler Ben Burwell, scoring good wins there, and in 1969 he completed his title.

When Kaiser died some years later of heart failure, his owners imported Marienburg Schroder von Shumann from Mary Rodgers's Marienburg Kennels in California. He finished title in short order and, like Kaiser, gained a local C.D. as well. Two of Schroder's offspring, a dog and a bitch, have been carrying on well for their owners. The male, Von Schumann Babalu, went Best in Show at only 16 months of age in 1979 under judge Mrs. Virginia Hampton at the Puerto Rico Federation Show. This dog has points towards his championship but is shown only on a limited basis due to the current work of Mrs. Puig.

Mr. Puig has always been the trainer and handler of his Dobermans. No longer as active as formerly, he is nonetheless always interested in the breed and ready to be of help to anyone asking his advice or opinions.

These people above are the "pillars" responsible for the development of the Doberman in Puerto Rico. The breed is now considered one of the most popular on this island—as a show dog, a family and personal protector, a companion dog, or simply as a "most important friend," they fit well into any kind of situation.

Today's currently active Doberman breeders and owners are living up to the standards set for them by those who preceded them in these activities. The awareness of the importance of quality and its development are very evident, and many of the breeders habitually send their best bitches to the mainland United States to stud dogs carefully selected for their bloodlines and their excellence when the time for breeding them arrives. At the same time, outstanding new imports are constantly being brought to Puerto Rico for the purpose of strengthening the bloodlines already represented there, which is beneficial to the breed as a whole. Breeders are placing tremendous emphasis on temperament. Protection of the Doberman's versatility is never overlooked, for it is of prime importance in protecting the future of this wonderful breed.

Most of the bloodlines being used in Puerto Rico have been brought there from the mainland United States. Some dogs who are distinguishing themselves in current breeding programs include Glenayr Jamison, bred by Mr. and Mrs. Richard Duklis from Barto, Pennsylvania. He is a Champion Glenayr Dufferinand-Tedell Tara's Harp son, and he has become a Best in Show dog, a Specialty winner, and a Top Producer. He is owned by Jamie Santana and Ceci Martinez de Santana, Jay-Mee's Dobbies. He is known for the consistency with which he produces excellent temperament and type, and his dominance as a producer enables him to pass on his fine qualities and temperament. Ironically, he has not himself been tremendously successful in the show ring, although he was Best of Breed under Richard Guevera in the Venezuela International 1972 and has some other good placements at American and International shows; but he is a disinterested showman in the ring which has placed him at a disadvantage despite his quality.

Taina Red Poison was bred by Mike and Melinda Guffey and is a daughter of Champion Warlock's Diablo Caballero out of Downey's Flaming Brook daughter. She is a Champion Henlon's Martial Music granddaughter and great-granddaughter and has been used mostly for breeding, producing lovely conformation and temperament. The highly successful show and Schutzhund dog, Jay-Mee's Latin Dandy, is one of her sons.

Rubicon's Anasazi, bred by Mrs. Billye Stephens of New Mexico, is a daughter of Champion Marienburg's Sun Hawk ex Rubicon's Little Ginger (a Sun Hawk granddaughter). This is the only sire-to-granddaughter breeding so far at Jay-Mee's Dobbies kennel, and it has proven quite successful, producing several champions plus a Best in Show winner. Anasazi is the only Hawk daughter in Puerto Rico, and she is from his final litter. As we write, she is sitting at home awaiting maturity before she is shown.

Shadows of Lisitzas Sasche is owned by Mrs. Annie Hauss and Ceci Martinez de Santana and is a Lisitza's Bucaneer granddaughter. Redenau Lucifer, bred by Mrs. Dianne Tharp, is owned by Mr. Herman Hau and Mrs. Ceci Martinez de Santana. Lucifer is out of a breeding by American and Canadian Champion Lindenau Arrowsmith ex Redlin's Countess Cleopatra, a Champion Gambolwood's Cleopatra daughter. Used as a stud, he is producing well, and he is being trained for Schutzhund work. Unfortunately, too short an ear crop proved detrimental to his show career; but it is expected that his will become a famous name due to the outstanding quality of his descendants.

Jay-Mee's Dobbies, the owners or co-owners of these last several dogs mentioned above, are owned by Jaime Santana and Ceci Martinez de Santana. Ceci has always been a Doberman fancier who, as she says, "had a Doberman leg to grab onto" before she herself could even walk and who has always considered Dobermans to be an important part of her life. Jaime Santana was a Labrador Retriever field trial trainer who came to love Dobermans just as greatly as does his wife. Their dogs are worked in all possible phases, as the belief of these fanciers is that the versatility of the breed, balanced temperament along with conformation, is a "must" in their breeding program. The breeding program is based on linebreeding with an occasional judiciously selected outcross. Glenayr Jamison is their greatest pride and joy among their Dobes.

Other current Doberman breeders in Puerto Rico who should be included in this resume are Max Toro who owns Tormak Kennels (headed by Mamiya Negra de Mico y Tormak, a Jamison daughter who currently is being worked in Schutzhund training) and Tony and Nilda Morales, also strong believers in the "dual" Doberman and whose Jay-Mee's Latin Dandy is another now undergoing Schutzhund training.

In Madeline George's story here, it is interesting to note that many Dobermans in Puerto Rico are being worked for their C.D. titles in obedience, for to become an International Champion, Dobermans must take an obedience and working test—a point which has motivated breeders to develop the potential of their dogs to the maximum.

The Schutzhund movement was introduced into Puerto Rico during June 1983 by a gentleman named Mr. Monsanto who became strongly attracted to the sport while travelling through Florida. Taking into consideration the large amount of good temperament among the Dobermans in Puerto Rico, he felt that this would be a marvelous area in which to found a Schutzhund club. He did so, becoming the first President of the Puerto Rican Schutzhund Club, which became recognized in the United States in November 1983 and in Germany one month later.

Mr. Monsanto imported two Schutzhund-bred Dobes from Florida, who have been used successfully for breeding purposes. Others active in the Schutzhund movement include the aforementioned Max Toro; Luis Solis, who is the actual Vice-President and Training Director (formerly a professional handler in the conformation ring since 1973), who in 1977 switched his interest to Schutzhund work and titled his first Schutzhund dog during 1979, Baron Von Odin Second to None—Damasyn breeding—who has obtained his C.D. and Schutzhund A); Mr. and Mrs. Sergio Casein and Mr. and Mrs. Morales, who have already been written of earlier in this chapter. The Schutzhund Club has had visits from Mr. Ken Howe, who came to give a seminar and help for the development of the club; and Mr. and Mrs. Deer, who brought dogs and gave a demonstration with them.

It has been said, quite truthfully, that Puerto Rico offers the dog fancier "the best of two worlds," as it holds the distinction of being the only place in the world where one can compete for and gain championship titles under both the Federation Canofila International and the American Kennel Club regulations. Both organizations are recognized there. Thus the F.C.I. titles of National Champion and International Champion are recognized and attainable there, while the American Kennel Club, represented by the Puerto Rican Kennel Club, runs a dog show annually in Puerto Rico at which dogs can earn points towards A.K.C. championship.

Each year a large representation from various countries, particularly South America, Mexico, the Dominican Republic, the mainland United States, and elsewhere can be found in Puerto Rican dog shows, sharpening

Mamiya Negra de Mico y Tormak, by Glenayr Jamison. Bred and owned by Mr. Max Toro, San Juan, Puerto Rico.

the competition and making winning prestigious. There is no need to go through customs, nor is a passport required when entering Puerto Rico for a dog show. Dogs must be fully vaccinated and have a health certificate in order to be allowed on the show premises.

To become a Puerto Rican (national) Champion, ten points are required. The dog must be a minimum of fifteen months of age, and these ten points must be acquired during a circuit; if such is not the case, and ten points are NOT won during a circuit, then the dog is required to obtain a total of fifteen points for the Puerto Rican championship, these awarded by three different judges and being entirely "major" points. All Winners Males and Winners Bitches may receive a total each time of three points or more and the Best in Group up to five points, at the judge's discretion.

To obtain International CACIB points, the minimum age limit is fifteen months and four CACIB certificates must be awarded by four different judges. A CACIB is a point awarded, by a judge recognized by the F.C.I., to a dog or bitch that the judge feels conforms to the breed standard and whose quality he feels merits this honor. Every breed may be awarded a CACIB each for the top dog and the top bitch competing. CACIB awards are made on the International circuits, which means your dog can become a South American Champion under similar regulations of the F.C.I. South American championship requires four CACIB awards under three different judges.

To gain the title of International championship, working breeds must pass temperament, working, and obedience tests and earn the four CACIB awards.

Kaukauna's Hi-Mark and Tanya's Cassandra, two of the earliest Dobermans owned by Joe and Janet Lobb, Dobenhaus Kennels, Ontario, Canada.

CHAPTER SEVEN

The Doberman Pinscher in Canada

Doberman Pinscher interest in Canada began to stir earlier but it was not until around the late 1930's that really significant action took place, in the form of two distinguished breeders, Mr. Harvey Gratton of Trollhattan Kennels at Truro, Nova Scotia, and Dr. Wilfred Shute of Mannerheim Kennels, also located in the eastern portion of Canada.

While he was at the time a resident of Grand Bend, Ontario, Mr. Gratton acquired his first Doberman when there were only fourteen representatives of the breed in all of Canada. Along with Dr. Shute, he worked toward getting quality Dobermans off to a good start in his country. The two men worked hard to enhance the image of the breed to both novices and established dog people. It is interesting to note that perhaps Canada's foremost kennel of the present day, Schauffelein (Joey and Ron Purdy—see kennel story further along), got started with a bitch bred by Harvey M. Gratton although she did not bear his kennel name. She was Trinka Von Edelweissen.

Through the late 1940's and early 1950's, Trollhattan produced many winners across the country. Several Trollhattan dogs were acquired by J. P. McGinnis of Prince Edward Island, who was a hobbyist and dog fancier rather than a breeder. His main interest was in acquiring good dogs and having them shown by his handler, who at this time was Phyllis Fulton, a professional handler and Smooth Fox Terrier breeder. She later became Mrs. Gratton in 1955.

As a result of the marriage, Mr. Gratton moved his kennel to his wife's hometown which is the present location, Truro, Nova Scotia. The 40-plus acres of the new kennel allowed plenty of space for kennel area and training and exercise.

Nova Scotia had gotten off to a bad start with Dobermans in the pre-1955 years Miss Gratton tells us. A careless breeder had produced and sold many half-cross—half-shy specimens. By the time the Grattons were setting up in their kennel, Maritimers were scared to death of Dobes. Thus it was necessary for Mr. Gratton to launch a public awareness campaign to tell people more about *good* Dobes and about purebred dogs in general.

He started his campaign about dogs in an expanding society with speaking engagements at service clubs, tours of schools for the blind and deaf, and appearances on regional T.V. At the same time, Mr. Gratton was serving as the Canadian Kennel Club's Director for Nova Scotia and Newfoundland. It was in this capacity that he helped arrange the first dog shows ever to be held in Newfoundland.

After retiring as Canadian Kennel Club Director, Mr. Gratton devoted himself to all-breed judging across Canada and in Bermuda, and to breeding Dobermans. The Maritimers were coming around to the idea that well-bred Dobermans properly raised were safe with children and did make good family dogs. Many were convinced of this by seeing the Grattons' little daughter, Emily, asleep on the benches with a Dobe at the shows. At first many people seemed to think it was closely akin to child abuse to "put that little child in with *that* dog."

While Trollhattan dogs of the 1960's had dated back to his original lines, the 1970's saw new lines brought in with the purchase of Canadian Champion Tarrado's Chaos from Nancy Jo Simmons. Chaos easily finished his Canadian title and while offered at stud on a very limited basis, he produced more than twenty champions, the majority of whom were homebreds.

The combination of Chaos and Warlock Witch v Trollhattan was highly successful. "Missy" was also a Canadian champion. Numerous Dobermans of today date back to these two, and a Chaos grandson is still being used at stud at Trollhattan.

The Grattons had been experimenting with the lines from Champion Arylawn's Nemo and Champion Tamarack's Fireblaze before Mr. Gratton's death in 1977.

Along with the Dobermans over the years, the Grattons had bred and exhibited German Shepherd Dogs, Dachshunds, Wire Fox Terriers, Poodles, Beagles, Lhasas and Labrador Retrievers. The Dobes and the Smooth Fox Terriers, however, consistently remained their favorites.

Early in 1978, the Trollhattan Kennels was passed along to the Grattons' daughter, Emily. Born into the Dog Fancy so to speak, she has since childhood been active as a trainer and breeder of Dobes and Smooths. Since 1978 Emily and her mother, Phyllis Gratton, have owned and managed the kennel. Together they have kept Trollhattan Dobes in the winner's circle with dogs like Champion Trollhattan Amos Moses, Champion Trollhattan's Serica, and several Smooth champions as well.

Due to career commitments and Mrs. Gratton's judging assignments, the kennel operates on a somewhat reduced basis from the pre-1977 years. Two or three selective breedings each year are the present "order of the day."

Emily Gratton's feeling about Trollhattan and the work done by her father comes forth clearly from the following in which we quote her exact words:

"We're proud to be entering our sixth decade of breeding, selecting and showing quality Doberman Pinschers. It's been our goal to continue the best dogs from the best bloodlines to conform to 'standard' type rather than chasing fads. As well as being show calibre, our dogs have had to meet our standards for sound temperament as family companions.

"We're proud of our achievements but we're not satisfied to rest on our accomplishments. There's still so much we can do.

"It is with great enthusiasm that we meet this challenge of breeding dogs of excellence."

What a fortunate gentleman Mr. Gratton was in having the family so strongly share his interest in the Dobes! One of the sad things one sees happen, and far too frequently, is the immediate disbanding of a kennel into which years of work, thought and love have been invested, owing to lack of interest on the part of the survivors and heirs when a famous breeder passes on. This obviously has not happened at Trollhattan, nor does it seem likely to do so in the foreseeable future!

Now a bit of background on the best known of the Trollhattan dogs.

Canadian Champion Tarrado's Chaos was by Champion Felix v Ahrtal ex Champion Highbriar Jasmine. He was the only sibling to come to Canada of the famous Tarrado "C" litter.

Canadian Champion Warlock Witch v Trollhattan, by American and Canadian Champion Bruno v Tannenwald ex Kay Hills The Tribal Witch, was bred by A. K. and Mary Bara and owned by Trollhattan Kennels, who imported her as a youngster. She easily won her Canadian championship and certainly proved herself a superb mate to Chaos. Their daughter, American and Canadian Champion Trollhattan Toni Tigra, was sent back to the Baras where she later produced Champion Warlock's Diablo Elegante, and her name is found in many a present-day pedigree.

Another Chaos-Witch offspring, Canadian Champion Trollhattan's High Voltage Tye, went to Western Canada where he finished his title in tough competition, then returned to the Grattons as a stud dog. His son is still being used at Trollhattan and is himself the sire of champions.

Canadian Champion Trollhattan's Serica is a homebred by Trollhattan's Lanson Solitaire ex Cormac's Spirit of the Czar. She is a granddaughter of High Voltage Tye and was a multiple breed winner while still in the classes. She will be trying for her American title as we are writing.

Trollhattan Fast Forward was also bred by Trollhattan, by Canadian Champion Buster Bartok Von Breck ex Trollhattan's Belle Gretchen, and is starting out at this same time. She and Serica represent a new era of Trollhattan, as they are a combination of the old bloodlines with some exciting new lines.

CAPTIONS FOR PLATES 97 TO 112

Plate 97

1. Am. and Can. Ch. Starstorm Thunderbolt, Am. and Can. C.D., at age two years. Cec Ringstrom, owner, St. Albert, Alberta, Canada.

2. Am. and Can. Ch. Starstorm Thunderbolt, Am. and Can. C.D., winning Best in Show. Cec Ringstrom, owner.

3. Portrait of Am. and Can. Ch. Starstrom Thunderbolt, Am. and Can. C.D., a magnificent Doberman owned by Cec Ringstrom.

4. Am. and Can. Ch. Starstorm Thunderbolt, Am. and Can. C.D., April 8, 1978—November 12, 1983. The Top Stud Dog in Canada from the years 1980–1983 with more than 60 Canadian champion offspring; five U.S. champions; and a South African champion to his credit. Doug Ringstrom, owner, Starstorm Kennels, Calgary, Canada.

5. Allan Marshall, Solar Kennels, winning Best Puppy in Show at the Doberman Pinscher Club of Canada Specialty under U.S. judge Donald Booxbaum with Can. Ch. Star Wars Solar Thunderstorm, September 1982. Owners, Allan, Jane, and Maureen Marshall, Woodstock, Ontario, Canada.

6. Can. and OT Ch. Daphne the Defender, U.D., is proudly owned by Cec Ringstrom, St. Albert, Alberta, Canada.

Plate 98

1. Ch. Taure's Gilda v Marienburg winning Best Female and Best of Breed in Specialty under breeder-judges Mr. A. Reis and Mr. Marcos Hotz. Owner-handled by Jamie Martinelli, Pent Kennels, Brazil.

2. High Hope of Pent Kennels, owned by Jamie and Evalina Martinelli, Brazil.

3. Ch. Brazil v Marienburg pictured winning the Stud Dog Class under noted U.S.A. breeder-judge Mrs. Marge Kilburn. Jamie Martinelli, owner/handler.

4. Am. and Braz. Ch. Di Jadobe's Chelsea winning Second in Group under Canadian judge Mrs. Heather Logan. Owned and handled by Jamie Martinelli.

Plate 99

1. Int. Ch. Marienburg's Sunbonnet, handled by Mr. Sergio Capps, co-owner with Ana Maria Capps, Goiania, Brazil.

2. Ch. S.C. Mama's Corleone, one of the many splendid Dobermans at S.C. Kennels belonging to Ana Maria and Sergio Capps.

3. Ch. Damasyn Darcy, handled by Sergio Capps, co-owned with Ana Maria Capps.

4. Int. Ch. S.C. Mama's Mariella, owned by S.C. Kennels, Ana Maria and Sergio Capps.

5. Geba Goldjim von Diaspora, owned by Mrs. Suzanne Blum, Haus Viking Kennels, San Paulo, Brazil.

6. Geba Goldjim von Diaspora, owned by Mrs. Suzanne Blum.

Plate 100

1. Am. and Can. Ch. Starstorm Thunderbolt, Am. and Can. C.D., belonging to Cec Ringstrom, St. Albert, Alberta, Canada.

2. Can. Ch. Starstorm Chivas Regal, C.D., a young Group-winning son of the late Am. and Can. Ch. Starstorm Thunderbolt, C.D. Owned by Doug Ringstrom, Starstorm Dobermans, Calgary, Canada.

3. Ch. Starstorm Chivas Regal, C.D., owned by Cec Ringstrom, St. Albert, Alberta, Canada.

4. Ch. Starstorm Chivas Regal, C.D., a very well-known Doberman owned by Cec Ringstrom.

Plate 101

1. Ch. Wrath's Irish Cream, a Best of Breed winner by Ch. Karalynn's Black Liberator, T.T., ex Ch. Wrath's Honour Bound, C.D. Owned by Carla Kowalchuck, Thunder Bay, Canada. Handled by Pat Blenkey.

2. September 1980 at the Doberman Pinscher Club of Canada Specialty show. Ch. Karalynn's Black Liberator, T.T., "Luger" to friends, winning Best of Breed under judge Dr. Peter Emily. Handled by Brian Casey, owner with Pat Blenkey.

3. Ch. Wrath's Pleasure Seeker at five months of age. By Ch. Karalynn's Black Liberator, T.T., ex Ch. Wrath's Honest Pleasure. The Doberman Pinscher Club of Canada Puppy of the Year, 1981. Pat Blenkey, owner, Wrath-Liberator Kennels, Harley, Ontario, Canada.

4. Ch. Tennessee Tailgunner, T.T., a multi-breed winner, was bred by Larralyn and Dave McKay and is owned by Larralyn with Frank Jones of Toronto. Tailgunner is a son of Ch. Karalynn's Black Liberator, T.T., ex Ch. Hugelhof Wishing Ring. Handler, Brian Casey.

5. Ch. Wrath's Cannonball Run, by Ch. Ryas Anticipation, ROM ex Ch. Wrath's Lively Action. A multi-breed and Group winner. Award of Merit at the Doberman Pinscher Club of Canada 1982 Specialty. Pat Blenkey, owner.

6. Ch. Ambermark Accolade For Pip at 18 months winning the Working Group at Brantford in 1983 under judge Helen Miller Fisher. A multi-breed, Group, and Best in Show winner; and a U.S. breed winner when only 11½ months old. Owned by Pat Blenkey and Brian Casey; handled by Mr. Casey. Bred by Larralyn and Dave McKay.

7. Ch. Wrath's Judge Advocate, U.S. breed winner, by Ch. Schauffelein's Outrigger ex Ch. Wrath's Good Vibrations. Handler, Brian Casey. Owner, Pat Blenkey.

8. Ch. Karalynn's Black Liberator, T.T., multi-breed and Group winner, and Best of Breed at the 1980 Doberman Pinscher Club of Canada Specialty show. By Ch. Schauffelein's Outrigger ex OT Ch. Karalynn's Black Amanda, U.D., handled by owner, Brian Casey. Pat Blenkey says of this Dobe, "our all-time favorite dog."

Plate 102

1. Stevemor's Bannerman of Bellmarsh relaxing in the garden. Mrs. B. Rowland, Dorking, Surrey, England, owner.

2. Bellmarsh Gaspard, Rebecca of Bellmarsh, and Bellmarsh Gaucho—age four months. Owned by Mrs. B. Rowland.

3. Bellmarsh Florimond, age 11 months, by Stevemor's Bannerman of Bellmarsh. Owned by Mrs. B. Rowland.

4. Harcox Lincoln, age 12 months, by Stevemor's Bannerman of Bellmarsh. Owned by Lesley Wright. Photo courtesy of Mrs. B. Rowland, Dorking, Surrey, England.

5. Stevemor's Bannerman of Bellmarsh, in 1983, at three years of age. By Eng. Ch. Olderhill Sheboygen ex Treasurequest Pearl. Owned by Mrs. B. Rowland.

6. Sasha Belladonna of Bellmarsh, 1976–1983, was the first of the Dobermans owned by Mrs. B. Rowland of Dorking, Surrey, England. By Eng. Ch. Studbriar Chieftain (Eng. Ch. Iceberg of Tavey—Eikon Jest's Amazon) from the Australian import Lynmara Solitaire (Aust. Ch. Ritten Romulus—Lynmara Odetta).

Plate 103

1. Head study of Sasha Belladonna of Bellmarsh, Mrs. B. Rowland's first Doberman. By Eng. Ch. Studbriar Chieftain ex Australian import, Lynmara Solitaire.

2. Jorob's Sweet Sherry, owned by Mr. N. Hughan, Liverpool, England. Winner of many first prizes, four Bests of Breed, and a Working Group. Pictured here, informally, with Rita Hughan.

3. Bellmarsh Florinda, at age eight months, by Stevemor's Bannerman of Bellmarsh. Owned by Mrs. B. Rowland, Surrey, England.

4. Harcox Lincoln at 18 months. A double grandson of Eng. Ch. Olderhill Sheboygen, his wins have included a Reserve Best Puppy in Show when eight-and-a-half months of age. Lesley Wright of Margate, Kent, England, owner.

Plate 104

1. Judgar's High Esteem, a handsome young Doberman, winning Best Puppy in Show at the Thousand Islands Kennel Club in 1980. By Ch. Jagermeister High Noon ex Judgar's Lady Amazon, High Esteem was bred by G. and J. Kauffeldt. Owned by Wayne Hedges of Orleans, Ontario, Canada; handled by Donna Fraser.

2. Ch. Amulet's Cedric v Gluckliche winning Best of Breed at the Doberman Pinscher Club of Canada Specialty show in 1983. Judge, Judy Doniere. Handler, John Griffith. Owner, Pam Gordon, Ft. Wayne, Indiana.

3. Ch. Sandford's Yucatan, owned and bred by Jerry Cudahy, Ontario, Canada. Sired by Ch. Schauffelein's Limited Edition ex Istvanhazi's Kishedyes.

4. An informal photo of two famous Canadian Dobermans, Ch. Trouble Times Two, C.D.X. and Ch. Wrath's Power Play, C.D. Owned by Pat Blenkey, Harley, Ontario, Canada.

5. Here are the two-dog sled team, owned by Gary and Mary Lovie of Waterloo, Ontario, Canada, and the four-dog sled team, owned by John and Joy Leiskau of Baden, Ontario, out sledding. These Dobermans are often not permitted to participate in the sled-dog races, which were originated by the northern breed fanciers to promote their own breeds. But when they are, they make their presence felt with some notable wins and placements.

6. This outstanding show bitch, Hill Street Blue Yasha, owned by Gary and Mary Lovie of Waterloo, Ontario, is a highly successful winner at Canadian dog shows as well as being a member of their noted sled-dog team. Here she is taking a strongly contested Best of Breed over numerous "specials" from the classes at the Limestone City Kennel Club in July 1984. Handled by John Griffith.

Plate 105

1. Arg. Gr. Ch. Mandinga's Farah Roja, by Ch. Altar's Midas (by Demetrius) ex Mandinga's Ornella. Breeder, Arminda San Martin. Owner, Javier Farina.

2. Arg. Gr. Ch. Black Shadow Henry Theral, by Ch. Bismarck v Euequoz ex Ch. Hi Vales Mahogany. Top Doberman of 1983. Judge, Anne Benson Wanner from the U.S.A.; handler, Hector A. Iriarte; breeder, C. Marchesi y Munoz; owner, Roberto Pestile.

3. Arg. Ch. Flash de Doblado Grande, by Arg. Ch. Alexander Bririsc of Mikater ex Arg. Ch. Andrea de Doblado Grande. Top Doberman, Argentina, 1982. Bred by Teresa y Eduardo Ustariz, owned by R. Lisi y Sra.

4. Texas v Haus Viking, at four months, winning the Futurity at Clube Bandeirante Doberman Show in San Paulo, Brazil. Sired by the U.S.A. import, Alisaton's Infrared out of Naja v Haus Viking.

5. Ch. Mardale Nite Hawk v Marienburg, by Ch. Marienburg's Sun Hawk ex Alisaton Bewitched, owned by Luis Roberto Zini, San Paulo, Brazil.

6. Braz. Ch. Arabelle v Schloss, by Ch. Brazil v Marienburg ex Ch. Graca de Belafonte. Breeder, V. Palumbo. Raul Lis Boa, owner.

Plate 106

1. Geifang Cash and Courage winning Best Puppy in Breed for owner James Glover, St. Helen's, Merseyside, England.

2. Omega Royal Rhythm at Geifang, winner of numerous awards. Mr. and Mrs. James Glover, owners.

3. Doberman puppies from Milperra Kennels. Vicki Cuthbertson of Huntingdon, Cambs, England, owner.

4. Jorob's King of Spring, bred by R. McDonald and owned by N. Hughan, Liverpool, England, ended his career with four Reserve Bests of Breed, three Bests of Breed, one Best Working, two Bests Puppy in Show, and many firsts. Put to sleep at 21 months of age after a long illness.

5. Show training at the Syrinx Kennel in England. From left to right, Syrinx Carina, owned by Mr. J. Holden; Syrinx Calisto, owned by Mrs. A. Sowter; and Syrinx Major Ursa, owned by Mrs. R. Hughan.

6. Jorob's Sweet Sherry was bred by R. McDonald of Liverpool, England and is owned by H. Hughan, also of Liverpool. She is the winner of four Best of Breed awards, a Best Working, and numerous first prizes.

7. Jorob's Sweet Sherry being examined by the judge at a Welsh show, handled by Mr. Hughan, where she took Best of Breed.

8. Syrinx Rough Diamond owned by the Hughans.

1
2

GROUP
1ST

BEST
IN
SHOW

3
4

PLATE 97

5
6

CLUBE
BANDEIRANTE
DO DOBERMANN

1
LUGAR

MELHOR
FÊMEA
DA EXPOSIÇÃO

EXPOSIÇÃO
ESPECIALIZADA
14 DE OUTUBRO DE 1979

FOTO: JEAN-JACQUES

1 ◄

2 ◄

PLATE 98

CLUBE
BANDEIRANTE
DO DOBERMANN

IÇÃO ESPECIALIZADA
VEMBRO DE 1980

M.K.KILBURN
(U.S.A)

MELHOR
ADREADOR

1
LUGAR

JEAN-JACQUES

3 ◄

4 ◄

1 ▸

2 ▸

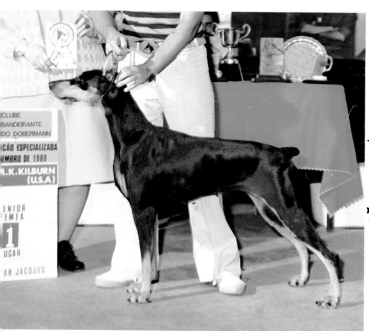

3 ◂

4 ▸

PLATE 99

5 ◂

6 ▸

1 ▸

2 ▸

PLATE 100

3 ▸

4 ▸

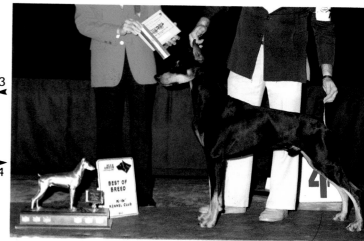

PLATE 101

1 ◄

2 ►

3 ◄

4 ►

PLATE 102

5 ►

6 ►

PLATE 103

PLATE 104

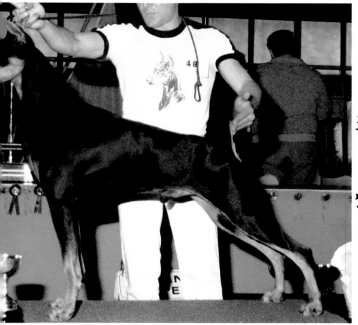

PLATE 105

1 ◄
2 ►

3 ◄
4 ◄

5 ◄
6 ►

PLATE 106

7 ◄
8 ►

1
▶

2
▶

3
▶

4
▶

PLATE 107

5
▶

6
▶

1 ◄

2 ►

3 ◄

4 ►

PLATE 108

5 ◄

6 ►

1

2

3

4

5

6

PLATE 110

1▲　　PLATE 111　　▼2

1 ►

2 ►

3 ►

4 ►

PLATE 112

5 ►

6 ►

Plate 107

1. A homebred bitch from Mrs. B. Rowland's first litter of Dobes. Antoa Loretta of Bellmarsh, by Phileen's Duty Free of Tavey ex Sasha Belladonna of Bellmarsh.

2. Stevemor's Bannerman of Bellmarsh, a handsome Doberman dog owned by Mrs. B. Rowland, Dorking, Surrey, England.

3. Bellmarsh Fernando at 14 weeks of age. By Stevemor's Bannerman of Bellmarsh ex Simron's Black Diamond (a Duty Free granddaughter). Mrs. B. Rowland, owner, Bellmarsh Dobermans.

4. Omega Royal Rhythm at five months. Owned by Mr. and Mrs. James Glover, St. Helens, Merseyside, England.

5. Omega Royal Rhythm at Geifang going Best Puppy and Reserve Best in Show. Owned by Geifang Dobermans, Mr. and Mrs. James Glover.

6. Birmingham championship show, 1983. Geifang Cash and Courage was among the winning Dobermans there. Mr. and Mrs. James Glover, owners.

Plate 108

1. Ch. Piu Bella de Mantua, with breeder Marcio Massari of Brazil. This lovely red bitch was sired by the Damasyn Bo-Tairie son, Damasyn Justa Blast, ex the Bo-Tairie daughter, Damasyn Remarkable. Photo courtesy of Peggy Adamson.

2. Canela de Mantina, litter sister to Cara Mia de Mantina, by Alisaton's Infrared ex Damasyn the Cullie, with breeder-owner Marcio Massari, San Paulo, Brazil.

3. Cara Mia de Mantua, owned by Marcos Hotz of Brazil and bred by Marcio Massari. By Ch. Alisaton's Infrared ex Damasyn the Cullie.

4. Savannah de Mantua, owned by Marcio Massari of Brazil, is by Damasyn Justa Blast ex Carmen von Haus Viking. Photo courtesy of Peggy Adamson.

5. Damasyn The Kahshi, born March 1980, by Damasyn Insider, C.D. ex Ansel's Princess. Imported by Marcio Massari. Pictured with Gwen DeMilta, March 1983. Brother of Damasyn The Kadjen and Damasyn The Kyrhi in Trinidad and Damasyn The Gypsy Jewel in Venezuela. Photo courtesy of Peggy Adamson.

6. Savannah de Mantua, by Damasyn Justa Blast ex Carmen von Haus Viking, born in October 1976. Photo at age three years. Owned by Marcio Massari, San Paulo, Brazil.

Plate 109

1. and 2. In Brazil, they have ingenious ways of training Doberman ears prior to trimming them. Marcos Hotz's trained birds are admiring the headgear of their owner's puppy, S.C. Soc's Track, bred by Sergio Capps and sired by Damasyn Justa Blast ex Ch. Marienburg's Sunbonnet.

Plate 110

1. Harcox Lincoln at 18 months. Owned by Lesley Wright, Margate, Kent, England. This dog is a son of Stevemor's Bannerman (Ch. Olderhill Sheboygen—Treasurequest Pearl) from Tinkazan Marsala (Sheboygen—Tinkazon Serenora). Born November 1981, he has placed at most shows attended and his wins include a Reserve Best Puppy in Show at eight-and-a-half months.

2. Ganna's Something Special of Tavey is from Tavey Dobermans, Kirdford, West Sussex, England.

3. Phileen's Duty Free of Tavey, one of the present day Tavey winners, owned by Reg and Mary Barton, Tavey Dobermans, West Sussex, England.

4. Tavey's Diploma, a very handsome dog owned by Tavey Dobermans.

5. Tavey's Emulation and Pirouette of Tavey, two modern representatives of England's most famous Doberman kennels, which are now owned by Reg and Mary Barton.

6. Dancaway's Miss Muffet of Tavey, one of the current bitches at this most famous of British kennels. Owned by Reg and Mary Barton.

Plate 111

1. Jorob's Sweet Sherry and Syrinx Rough Diamond, with their owner, Mr. N. Hughan, Liverpool, England.

2. Front view of Harcox Lincoln. Lesley Wright owns this handsome dog who has been winning well for her at the English shows.

Plate 112

1. Ch. Arabelle von Schloss, one of the outstanding Dobermans owned by Umberto and Sonia Palumbo, Brazil. By Ch. Brazil v Marienburg ex Ch. Graca de Belafonte.

2. Int. Ch. Graca de Belafonte, foundation bitch at Von Schloss Kennels, Brazil. Umberto and Sonia Palumbo, owners.

3. Int. Ch. Max von Schloss, by Ch. Koven's Westminster ex Ch. Graca de Belafonte. Breeder, Umberto Palumbo. Owner, Oswaldo Macedo, Brazil. Al Maurer, U.S.A., is judging.

4. Ch. Barbarella von Schloss, by Ch. Aleph von Schloss ex A-One v Heiss. Breeder and owner, Umberto Palumbo, Brazil. Peggy Adamson, judge.

5. Males in the Working Class. Von Henik Kennels, Brazil.

6. Oakford Celina at 10 years of age. The foundation bitch of Von Henik's Dobermans, Alice and Juan Carlos Di Lucca, Curitiba, Brazil.

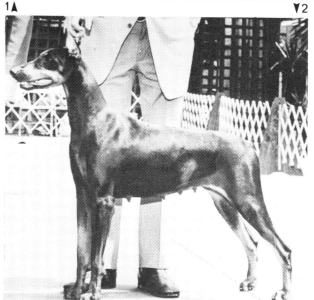

1. Ch. Damasyn The Ember in 1953, winning at Detroit. By Dictator ex Damasyn The April Rain. Bred by Helen F. Kamerer, Ember was owned by the famous fancier, Dr. Wilfred Shute, Mannerheim Kennels, Canada.

2. Am. and Can. Ch. Trollhattan Toni Tygra, by Ch. Tarrado's Chaos ex Ch. Warlock Witch v Trollhattan. The dam of Ch. Warlock's Diablo Elegante. She was bred by Trollhattan Kennels; owned by A. K. and Mary Bara. A famous winner and producer of the early 1970's.

It is anticipated that they will do well in show competition and as producers. Special interest is centered, too, around one of Serica's puppies sired by Canadian and American Champion Schauffelein's Wild Country.

Dr. Wilfred Shute was a widely respected and renowned heart specialist whose very great love and hobby was the Doberman Pinscher. To his Mannerheim Kennels he brought a goodly number of excellent Dobes, from whom he bred some memorable ones.

American and Canadian Champion Defender of Jan-Har was among the finest Dr. Shute purchased. A red son of Champion Saracen of Reklaw (Champion Dictator v Glenhugel-Kay of Reklaw, the latter by Champion Emperor of Marienland ex Champion Nana of Rhinegold). Defender's dam was Champion Cissi of Jan-Har, by the Saracen son, Champion Brigum of Jan Har from Kilburn Jiffy, daughter of Champion Alcor v Milsdod and Champion Kilburn Audacity. He was bred by Jane McDonald, and he sired a total of 21 champions.

An older brother of Dictator was also owned by Dr. Shute, Champion Cognac von Glenhugel, and the Damasyn bitch, Champion Damasyn The Ember. Champion Dietrich of Dawn and Champion Judy of Navigator are two others, and there were a number more.

Like most of us, however, I am sure that Dr. Shute took tremendous and particular pride in his homebreds. His first Group winner was Champion Adam of Mannerheim, which, it is believed, was one from his first homebred litter. One of his famous and widely admired bitches was Champion Dixie of Mannerheim, a Cognac daughter, who gained fame both as a Best in Show bitch and as a Top Producer. Another was American and Canadian Champion Renco of Mannerheim, who was Reserve Dog to Dictator the year the latter was Winners at the Doberman Pinscher Club of America Specialty in Chicago. Two other youngsters from Mannerheim who were in the classes at this same period as Dictator were future champions Flora and Figaro of Mannerheim, both Junior Puppy Class winners at one of the Nationals when Dictator was out in Senior Puppy.

Others from that period keeping the Mannerheim banner high were two owned by

Bonnie Moon, Lendvay Kennels in Alberta: Champion Goethe of Mannerheim and Champion Presto of Mannerheim.

With the arrival of the 1960's, Dr. Shute added further history to Dobermans with the acquisition of American and Canadian Champion Sabre of Mannerheim, the Top Winning Doberman of 1964. This handsome Best in Show winner truly made it for himself as a sire when it turned out that the Top Dobermans of 1965, 1966, 1967 and 1968 were all Sabre progeny: Champion Kaukauna's Hi Star in 1965, repeating in 1967; Champion Konigshausen Inspiration in 1966; and Champion Bonnie v Mannerheim Nagidrac in 1968.

Champion Von Usher's Aurora, daughter of Champion Highbriar Bandana, won well for Dr. Shute later in the 1960's, after which she was bred to American and Canadian Champion Highland Satan's Image. This produced Dr. Shute's "Z" litter, which is the last he is known to have bred in the East, although we understand that after he moved to Vancouver a bit later, he became very friendly with some Doberman people in that area, and it is said that he did some co-breeding with them.

Dr. Shute became close friends with Fred and Eleanor Lapp while still in eastern Canada; they looked after his dogs and became co-owners with him, so we are told.

The last of Mannerheim's great Best in Show winners, Champion Schauffelein's Solar Wind, won the 1971 Doberman Pinscher Club of Canada Specialty under Tess Henseler, plus the annual award from that club for "Puppy of the Year." This was at the start of his show career. He is the 47th champion for Mannerheim and Dr. Shute.

Even after his semi-retirement from breeding, Dr. Shute retained his involvement and interest in the Doberman world as a judge, lecturer, and noted authority on the breed. His death a few years ago (early '80's) was a sad loss to humanity as well as to the Fancy.

As a judge, Dr. Shute was absolutely without compromise. I still recall my feeling of awe the time he fulfilled an important engagement, I believe at a Specialty in Washington, D.C., and shocked both exhibitors and onlookers no end when he withheld all ribbons in the puppy classes for "lack of merit." It was like a bolt from the blue, particularly as some of these puppies were "major pointed." But that was Dr. Shute's opinion of them, so that is what the people got. Whether in agreement or not, one must admire a man so completely in command of the courage of his convictions, not for a moment hesitating to do as he felt was right. As a tribute to their seniority, and to the major roles their owners have played in advancement of the Doberman Pinscher in Canada, we have started this Canadian resume not in alphabetical order as is our custom in telling kennel histories, but in the order of seniority, as both Trollhattan and Mannerheim kennels are an integral part of the history of the entire Doberman breed in Canada.

Before going on to the stories of the currently active kennels, which will follow—in alphabetical order—I do want to mention someone who has been a very long-time professional handler and Doberman breeder there and who has surely contributed a great deal in knowledge, encouragement, and quality to the Dobe fanciers of Canada. This is Harold Butler, a resident of Quebec, who is apt to turn up at shows with some good ones almost anywhere in the United States or Canada. Mr. Butler owned and bred a litter or two with Dr. Shute at one time, including one from Bonnie von Mannerheim Nagidrac to Champion Highbriar Minos, which produced the successful winner Champion Ashuniong's Heidi.

Among the famous dogs handled to successful show careers by Harold Butler have been some of the most noted from Mrs. Bea England's Kaukauna Kennel, where more than 50 Dobes have gained titular honors. Harold and Champion Kaukauna's Hi-Star made history together for Mrs. England, as Hi-Star was Top Doberman in Canada in 1965, 1966 and 1967, retiring in 1968.

The steady procession of winners continues for Harold Butler. Year after year, as we visit Canadian shows, we note that he is always busy and that he invariably has an exciting Dobe or two in his string.

The Doberman Pinscher Club of Canada conducts a full schedule of activity for the breed, and there are numerous regional Doberman Clubs there, too, all working for the further advancement of Dobermans. Canadian breeders also take an active (and successful) part in obedience and Schutzhund training, you will note in the following kennel resumes, as well as in their conformation showing.

1▲ ▼2

1. Four-and-a-half-month-old Free Freespirit's High Sierra, by Ch. Freespirit's Damascus ex Ch. Freespirit's Winter Witch, owned by Sherry George, Eastern Passage, Nova Scotia.
2. Am. and Can. Ch. Schauffelein's Vintage Year, "Goober," as he appeared on the cover of the Christmas issue, 1978 of *Top Dobe* magazine. Owned by Ron and Joey Purdy, Cheltenham, Ontario.

Adlerheim

Adlerheim is a small kennel of Doberman Pinschers located in Dartmouth, Nova Scotia, owned by Mary Spinelli with bloodlines based on American and Canadian Champion Highland Satan's Image.

Adlerheim is home to Canadian Champion Doberdamen's War Eagle and Canadian Champion Dobestar's Seventh Saturn, C.D.X., ROM, both of whom completed their titles owner-handled. Saturn additionally had the distinction of earning all three legs of her C.D.X. with High in Class awards.

A carefully planned linebreeding has resulted in Saturn's first litter by Koven's Patrick of Bowcrest, he by American and Canadian Champion Koven's Mischief ex Champion Koven's Black Gold.

Carvon

Carvon Dobermans are owned by Carmen Haller of Coquitlam, British Columbia, who has been involved with the breed in both obedience and conformation since 1973.

Carmen's start in Dobes came with natural-eared (uncropped) dogs. She felt very strongly that pedigree, structure, temperament and movement were the foundation for breeding stock. For these reasons she also felt than an uncropped dog should not be valued less simply because an owner chose not to be involved with the work and expense of cropping. Carmen therefore became interested in altering the standard for the Doberman to include ear cropping as optional. She lobbied strongly, both on her own and through her club affiliations, and was elated when, in 1980, her ambition in the matter was fulfilled and she was instrumental in having the Canadian Kennel Club adopt a new Standard for the Doberman Pinscher which stated "EARS—Either cropped or uncropped."

Carmen's first Doberman was an uncropped male, Champion Lady's Jaguar, C.D. She believes he was the first natural-eared Dobe to complete a Canadian championship, which he accomplished in 1975 with a Group 3 and Best Canadian Bred in Group under judge Heywood Hartley.

The next of Carmen's Dobes was a bitch, Champion Fairest Nymph Echo, C.D. This one was the first uncropped bitch in Canada to finish with a Group placement (Group 2nd). In 1979 she was the Top Winning Doberman bitch in British Columbia.

Under the Carvon kennel name, this lovely bitch, Nymph Echo, has produced twelve champions in three litters, one of which, the cropped Carvon's Sweet Sara by Champion Starstorm Santana ex Echo, won the Northern Alberta Doberman Pinscher Specialty in 1983. Six of the nine puppies from this litter were shown and have finished their championships. A seventh was shown once, on that occasion taking Reserve Winners.

In 1983 an uncropped bitch owned by Carmen, Champion Carvon's Mai Tai (Thunderbolt ex Nymph Echo), won three Best Puppy in Group awards and one Best Puppy in Show, two all-breed Puppy Sweepstakes, four Firsts in all-breed Sweepstakes competition, and Best of Breed over "specials" from the puppy class. Her championship was complete at the age of ten months. Carmen feels that this is a record for an uncropped Doberman pup. Her litter brother, who is cropped, gained his championship, won three Best Puppy in Groups, a Best Puppy in Show, two all-breed Puppy Sweepstakes, Best of Breed and a Group 4th also by ten months of age. He is Champion Carvon's Spiderman.

Dawnaquinn

Dawnaquinn Dobermans, owned by A. E. (Bud) and Wendy Beck, were founded on the lovely bitch Champion Free Spirits Quinnella, C.D. The bloodlines used here are primarily Kay Hill and Satan.

The Becks have owner-handled dogs to all-breed Bests in Show, two of them to date being American and Canadian Champion Dawnaquinn's John Galt and Champion Dawnaquinn's Day Dream Rose, the latter only eleven months of age at the time.

The Becks breed on a very small scale, usually only one litter annually. Despite this they have produced more than thirty champions, which is surely a very imposing record.

They express their gratitude to Mary White, of Free Spirits Dobermans, from whom they purchased Champion Free Spirits Quinnella. While Quinn was certainly not their first Doberman, she was the foundation from which all of their success has come in the many generations to follow her.

Defender

Defender Dobermans, bred and shown primarily by Lynell Korella, Calgary, Alberta, have made their mark in western Canada over the last two decades.

While not actually breeding now, the last of the Defender "greats" was American and Canadian Champion Defender's Xerxes, a multi-Best in Show winner, culminating his American stint by going Best of Winners at the Doberman Club of America National Specialty held in Seattle, handled by Larry Sinclair.

Dobenhaus

Dobenhaus Kennels are owned by Joe and Janet Lobb at Brucefield, Ontario, Canada, who purchased their first Doberman as a pet back in 1973. He was of Kaukauna and Highbriar breeding. Mrs. Bea England of Kaukauna Kennels convinced the Lobbs to show this dog, and they became instantly "hooked" on the Fancy.

The Lobbs' second dog came from Kaukauna breeding, and she became the foundation for their Dobenhaus breeding program. This female, Tanya's Cassandra, was bred to the Best in Show winning Champion Jagermeister's Five Card Stud, which resulted in two champions, Dobenhaus The Solicitor and, more notable, Dobenhaus The Slipstitch. Stitch was the recipient of a coveted Award of Merit at the 1980 and 1983 Doberman Pinscher Club of Canada National Specialties. From her first litter, by the Lobbs' Champion Jagermeister's Blackmail, she produced three champions: the lovely bitches Champion Dobenhaus The Daquari, Champion Dobenhaus Darn 'Knit Pearl, and Champion Dobenhaus Touch of Class. Daquari attended the 1981 Doberman Pinscher Club of Canada Specialty where she took Best of Winners and an Award of Merit. Touch of Class is now the dam of champion offspring.

Stitch's second litter was by Best in Show winning Champion Lowenbrau Magnate, and these youngsters hold great promise for the future. Already one of the males has finished, becoming Champion Dobenhaus Full Impact at only twelve months of age. It is interesting to note that all but one of these dogs mentioned above were breeder/owner-handled.

With ten years in the Fancy already behind them, and youth still on their side, the Lobbs

plan for Dobenhaus to continue as a small, select kennel producing the champions of tomorrow.

Esquire

Esquire Dobermans are home raised, being very dearly loved family members of the household of Ken and Sheila Valentine at Windsor Junction, Nova Scotia. Breeding therefore is held to a limited basis.

Esquire is founded on the Highbriar line and named after the lovely Champion Highbriar Esquire whom the Valentines acquired in 1977. This dog, incidentally, is the last of the Highbriars bred by Betsy Thomas of Gambler, Ohio. Prior to his retirement from the show ring, at age six years, Esquire was a multiple breed winner and Group placer in limited showing. In 1983 this great dog appeared at the Lakeshore Doberman Pinscher Club Specialty at Ravenna, Ohio, where he proudly took home the Veteran Dog win at eight-and-a-half years of age. A very treasured day in the Valentines' Doberman memories. Added to the win was the pleasure of having Betsy Thomas (who had not seen Esquire since he was a youngster) present. What joy it was for the Valentines to meet her and reintroduce her to Esquire as an adult Dobe!

Esquire has been at stud on a limited basis. While with Betsy Thomas, he sired Champion Haltbar Titian Barque, a champion who placed in the ratings in the 1978 *Doberman Quarterly*. She earned her title in good style and is now a multiple breed and Specialty Show winner. As well, she is the dam of some lovely winning progeny including a Grand Prize Futurity winner and the Valentines' newest addition, Champion Esquire's B.R.T. of Annarbe, sired by the late Champion Eric von Alpindobe. B.R.T. was shown at the Doberman Pinscher Club of America Specialty in Boston and at the Louisiana Specialty, both times by her special friend Mr. Eugene Haupt. She placed at both. Shown in Canada as a 6-9 month puppy, she was Best Puppy and Best of Breed over "specials" at the Montreal Specialty.

The Valentines' 1984 breeding, as we write, will be of B.R.T. back to her grandsire, Esquire. Needless to say, hopes are high for something exciting from these puppies.

In 1979, Champion Erivan R. Tucky Miss came to Esquire Kennels, a daughter of

1A **▼2**

1. Dr. Wilfred Shute, famous Doberman authority and owner of the Mannerheim Kennels in Canada, here is handling his noted winner, Ch. Schauffelein's Solar Wind, to Best Puppy in Breed, Best of Breed, Best Canadian-bred, and Best Canadian-bred Puppy at a Doberman Pinscher Club of Canada Specialty show in 1971. Tess Henseler judging. This was Mannerheim Kennels's 47th champion. Photo courtesy of Pat Blenkey.
2. Ch. Highbriar Esquire, by Ch. Mikadobe's Cupid ex Highbriar Tangerine, bred by Betsy Thomas. Owners, Ken and Sheila Valentine, Esquire Dobermans, Windsor Junction, Nova Scotia.

1. Ch. Haltbar Titian Barque, by Ch. Highbriar Esquire ex Ch. Martingdale's Moon Shadow, bred by Barbara and Carl Pew. Owned by Ken and Sheila Valentine, Windsor Junction, Nova Scotia.
2. Can. Ch. Schauffelein's Trendmaker, C.D., by Ch. Schauffelein's Troll Arabasque, finished with a Group First and his C.D. at the same show. Also pictured is Can. Ch. Schauffelein's Westward Bound, many times Group and Best of Breed winner. Gord and Shirl Bracey, owners, Gorshir's Dobermans, Mission, British Columbia.
3. Can. Ch. Schauffelein's Westward Bound, handled by Shirl Bracey who co-owns with her husband Gord. Gorshir's Country Kennels.
4. Can. Ch. Unies Debonaire Trish Chic, a Ch. Schauffelein's Vintage Wine daughter, owned and handled to the title by Gord and Shirl Bracey, Gorshir's Country Kennels.
5. Can. Ch. Gorshir's Honest Pleasure, a homebred by Gord and Shirl Bracey. He is a grandson of Ch. Schauffelein's Vintage Wine. Handled by Chuck Jordan, this young dog gained his championship in three shows, each a five-point "major." He took Best of Winners on all three occasions.

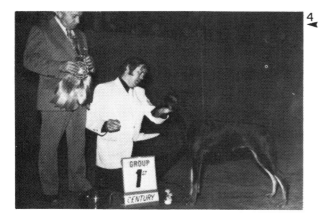

Champion Edelhall Gigolo of Amulet from Highbriar Nantucket. She was bred to Esquire in 1981, producing five puppies, three of which are close to finishing as we write.

Esquire as a producer is felt to retain the quality of his dam adding his own in a constant and dominant fashion. His puppies possess good bone and substance with a touch of elegance and splendid movement. His list of champions should continue to grow as an increasing number of his progeny, who are presently pointed and others to follow, come along.

Free Spirits

The Free Spirits Dobermans of Mary B. White and Dave Hayden at Surrey in British Columbia are of strong Kay Hill and Ahrtal background.

From the first litter, whelped in 1974, came consistently high-quality dogs, which were used as a nucleus for the kennel's further breedings.

Free Spirits have produced or owned well over forty Canadian and seven American Champions, with many other Canadian owned dogs from there "major" pointed in the United States at this
time. Several Free Spirits Dobermans are Group winners, three of them also being Best in Show winners.

American and Canadian Champion Free Spirits Apollo, U.D., ROM, was Canada's Top Winning Doberman in 1980, 1981 and 1982. "Rocky," as he is affectionately called, won a total of 166 times Best of Breed, 70 Group Firsts, a total of 143 Group placements, and 22 Bests in Show. He was Canada's No. 2 Dog, all breeds, in 1980 and Canada's No. 3 Dog, plus No. 1 Working Dog, in 1981. After retirement at four-and-a-half years of age, Rocky has achieved his Canadian U.D. and American C.D.X., shown by his owner Dave Lim. He was the first Dobe in Canada to achieve the Doberman Pinscher Club of America ROM award.

American and Canadian Champion Free Spirits Blackgammon is also a multi-Best in Show winner, placing No. 3 Doberman in Canada in 1983 with only four months of limited showing. A Tamarak's Fire Blaze son, "Khyber" at three-and-a-half years has produced exceptionally well with many Canadian

champions and three American champions to his credit.

The owners of Free Spirits are proud to say that their dogs are found to be strongly influencing the pedigrees of several other current top Canadian Doberman kennels. Their foundation bitch, Champion Free Spirits Electra, C.D.X. is the dam of two group winners and has six Best in Show winning grandchildren and great-grandchildren.

Free Spirits has won, in 1982 and 1983, the Doberman Pinscher Club of Canada Top Conformation Breeder of the Year Award. Our congratulations!

Gorshir

Gorshir Kennels started out in eastern Canada, in Ontario, but are now situated at Mission, British Columbia where owners Gord and Shirl Bracey are winning well and breeding some extremely high quality Dobes.

The Braceys purchased their first Doberman in 1968 from Schauffelein Kennels. This bitch was purchased as a pet and what a delight she turned out to be, according to Shirl Bracey, who describes the entire family as having been thrilled with her. They had never experienced so entirely satisfactory a dog. Needless to say, from then on life without a Doberman would be unthinkable for these folks. Thus when they lost her, they returned to Schauffelein for their next one.

A lovely male show puppy, out of the famous Troll Arabasque, was the selection on this second occasion. He finished his title in the grand manner taking a First in Group to do so; in addition he gained his C.D. that same day with Highest Score in Trial.

Then the Braceys decided that the time had come for them to acquire an outstanding show bitch, for the ring and to breed. Thus they selected the bitch who became Champion Schauffelein's Westward Bound, daughter of Champion Schauffelein's Troll Arabasque and Lowenbrau Aloha Schauffelein. She was named Westward Bound, as the Braceys were then just moving from Ontario to Western Canada, and she really has "done them proud" having finished her championship in short order in three shows. She then went on to a good career of breed and Group wins as a "special," handled by Shirl Bracey.

In 1974 the Braceys registered their kennel name, Gorshir's Country Kennels. Since then

1. Can. Ch. Gorshir's Royal Reserve taking Best Puppy in Show. Gorshir Dobermans, Gord and Shirl Bracey, Mission, British Columbia.
2. Can. Ch. Schauffelein's Westward Bound, Gord and Shirl Bracey's lovely bitch, so named as they were just moving from Ontario to western Canada.
3. This Best in Show and multiple Group placing Canadian Doberman is Ch. Dobermien's Virgo, proudly owned and enjoyed by the Michael Plamondons, Lac Beauport, Quebec. Here winning a Working Group in 1983 with noted professional handler Harold Butler.
4. Can. and Bda. Ch. Jagermeister's Seven Come Eleven, "as he looked upon retirement at six years of age." Fred Heal, owner, Jagermeister Dobermans, Spencerville, Ontario.
5. Dr. Wilfred Shute's famed dog, Am. and Can. Ch. Defender of Jan-Har, was bred by J. MacDonald of Pontiac, Michigan. Born in 1951 by Ch. Saracen of Reklaw (Ch. Dictator v Glenhugel—Kay of Reklaw) ex Ch. Cissie of Jan-Har (Int. Ch. Brigum of Jan-Har—Kilburn Jiffy), this dog figures prominently in the background of Kay Hill Dobermans and in Dr. Shute's own dogs. Photo courtesy of Jane Kay.

▲4

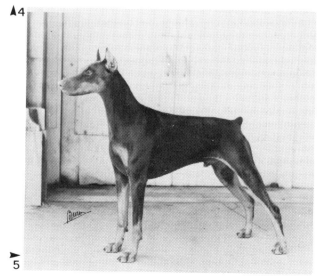

► 5

395

they have had a Vintage Year daughter which was shown and finished owner-handled, then bred, and for them she produced three champions, including a very excellent bitch who became Champion Gorshir's Royal Velvet—another who finished for them in three shows, then did well in "specials" competition. She, too, proved a worthy producer with another beautiful bitch, Gorshir's Touch of Tiffany, who, the first time in the ring, won Junior Puppy and a Reserve Winners.

Over the years, the Braceys have bred ten owner-handled champions who have accounted for many Group wins as well as honors for Best Puppy in Show.

Istvanhazi's

Istvanhazi Dobermans belong to Steve Rozinka of Pickering, Ontario who had owned dogs all his life but did not become involved with Dobermans until about 1973 when he purchased a black bitch from Countrygate Dobermans. This was Countrygate's Darling Victoria, or "Vicky" as she is known at home, who became the mother of the first champion for Mr. Rozinka, Istvanhazi's High Spirit. The latter in turn sired the current stud dog at the kennel, Champion Huncut Betyar of Istvanhazi who is the sire of the newest champion, a red male named Champion Istvanhazi's Prophesy. There are in total seven champion Dobes carrying the Istvanhazi identification, including among them Champion Istvanhazi's Fantasy Miss Rigo, Fantasy Miss Gigi and Hop-te Zisga.

At the Canadian Specialty in 1981, Champion Huncut Betyar of Istvanhazi won Best Puppy. In 1982 a Huncut pup, Champion Virgon Betyar of Istvanhazi, took Winners Dog as well as an Award of Merit. Mr. Rozinka feels that his most important litter to date was one sired by Champion Sandaraska's Love Stud, a Vintage Year son. When bred to Istvanhazi's Black Beauty, fifteen healthy pups were the result, these including Champions Rego and Zsiga. The best of this litter, Mr. Rozinka regrets, never made it to the show ring. She is Istvanhazi's Kishedyes, and, bred to Champion Schauffelein's Limited Edition, she produced for F. Cudahy and Sandford Hill Dobes a striking red dog who became a Best in Show winner from the classes, defeating many of Canada's top dogs to gain this honor.

Jagermeister

Jagermeister Dobermans were established in 1961 by Fred Heal, who had acquired his first Dobe in 1944 as a birthday gift. Although not registered and with uncropped ears, the Doberman temperament and loyalty were unforgettable. It was these characteristics that caused Fred to start his own kennel after leaving military service.

The Jagermeister bloodline of today is based on the popular Schauffelein breeding through a bitch purchased from Joey Purdy in Toronto. The bitch, Canadian and Bermudian Champion Schauffelein's Shady Lady, C.D.X., later became Canada's Top Winning female of all time. Shady was bred back to her sire, Canadian and American Champion Schauffelein's Troll Arabasque, to set type, and she produced one of Fred's finest producing bitches, Champion Jagermeister's Renown. The two bitches, Shady and her daughter Renown, became the cornerstone of the prominent Jagermeister Dobermans. Both bitches were later bred to Champion Andelane's Indigo Rock, this combination proving very successful. In particular, from Shady and Indigo Rock, came the stunning Canadian and Bermudian Champion Jagermeister's Seven Come Eleven.

Renown was also bred, on two occasions, to American Champion Highland Satan's Image. These two prominent American stud dogs played a large part in establishing the style and type of the Jagermeister line. In fact, at one point Jagermeister had three Best in Show producing dogs in residence: Shady, Renown, and Seven Come Eleven. Other noted American stud dogs who have added their mark directly to Jagermeister are Champion Tarrado's Flair and Champion Gambolwood's Hellalujah. More recently, American Champion Pajant's Encore v Rochelle produced a fine litter at Jagermeister. While these dogs, out of a linebred Jagermeister bitch, are still young, one black male, Champion Jagermeister's Easy Rider, shows a lot of promise.

The Jagermeister dog who was by far the most successful, however, was the previously mentioned Canadian and Bermudian Champion Jagermeister's Seven Come Eleven. "Sunny," as he is called, when only eighteen months old in 1974, won the prestigious

PEDIGREE CERTIFICATE

Name of Dog Ch.Dobestar's Seventh Saturn,CDX,ROM   Tattoo No. H4W 7N

Breed of Dog ....Doberman Pinscher........   CKC Registration No. NE 232676

Sex Female.... Colour & or Markings Black & Tan........   Date Whelped March 12, 1981

Breeder Gerry & Louise Stark........   Address of Breeder Belleville, Ontario........

Reg. Name Dobestar's Seventh Saturn   Address of Owner Dartmouth, Nova Scotia

AKC # WF049607
Black Type #1 or #3
Clear VWD
Clear CVI
OFA clear HD
Clear Thyroid problems

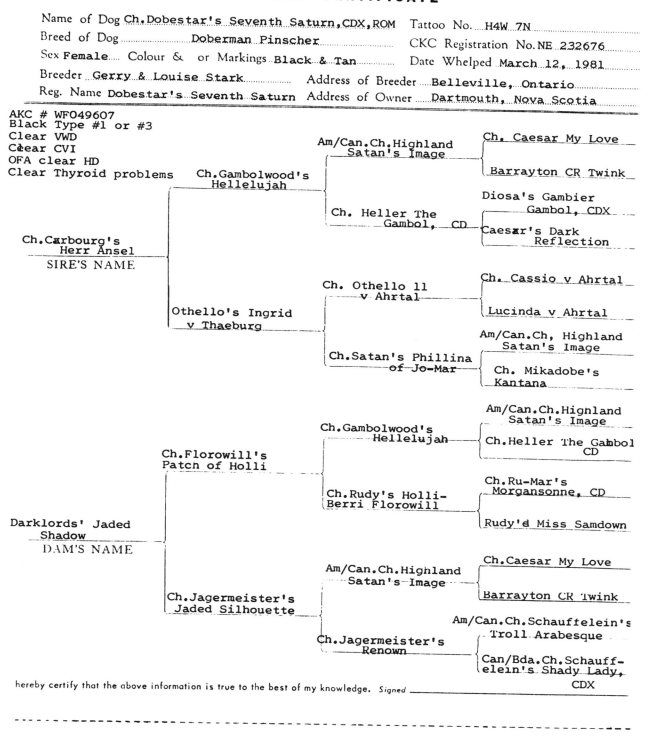

SIRE'S NAME
Ch.Carbourg's Herr Ansel

- Ch.Gambolwood's Hellelujah
  - Am/Can.Ch.Highland Satan's Image
    - Ch. Caesar My Love
    - Barrayton CR Twink
  - Ch. Heller The Gambol, CD
    - Diosa's Gambier Gambol, CDX
    - Caesar's Dark Reflection
- Othello's Ingrid v Thaeburg
  - Ch. Othello ll v Ahrtal
    - Ch. Cassio v Ahrtal
    - Lucinda v Ahrtal
  - Ch.Satan's Phillina of Jo-Mar
    - Am/Can.Ch. Highland Satan's Image
    - Ch. Mikadobe's Kantana

DAM'S NAME
Darklords' Jaded Shadow

- Ch.Florowill's Patch of Holli
  - Ch.Gambolwood's Hellelujah
    - Am/Can.Ch.Highland Satan's Image
    - Ch.Heller The Gambol CD
  - Ch.Rudy's Holli-Berri Florowill
    - Ch.Ru-Mar's Morgansonne, CD
    - Rudy's Miss Samdown
- Ch.Jagermeister's Jaded Silhouette
  - Am/Can.Ch.Highland Satan's Image
    - Ch.Caesar My Love
    - Barrayton CR Twink
  - Ch.Jagermeister's Renown
    - Am/Can.Ch.Schauffelein's Troll Arabesque
    - Can/Bda.Ch.Schauffelein's Shady Lady, CDX

hereby certify that the above information is true to the best of my knowledge. Signed _____

- -

1. Ch. Amulet's Aspen v Bluckliche, owned by Jo Ann Jewell and Diane Downey, is a noted winner in keenest Canadian competition.
2. Can. Ch. Kurtzhaus Golden Notes, owned by George Treschak and handled by John Griffith, here is taking Best of Breed under judge Robert Slay at the Doberman Pinscher Club of Canada Specialty Show, 1979.

1▲   ▼2

CAPTIONS FOR PLATES 113 TO 128

Plate 113

1. Silvan Glen J.R., a handsome puppy owned by Silvan Glen Kennels, Kemps Creek, New South Wales, Australia. Mick and Lauris Parrish.

2. Silvan Glen Hot Choklat, by Elmora Morning Breeze ex Olderhill Pandora (U.K. import), owned by Silvan Glen Kennels, Mick and Lauris Parrish.

3. Silvan Glen The Star, by Elmaro Morning Breeze ex Olderhill Pandora (imported from U.K.). A handsome puppy at Silvan Glen Kennels, owned by Mick and Lauris Parrish.

4. Aust. Ch. Stehle von Wickens at two-and-a-half years. D. Eschbach, owner, Stehle Dobermans, North Wagga, New South Wales, Australia.

5. Aust. Ch. Maharighi King Cobra, Best Puppy in Breed and Best Puppy in Group at the Spring Fair, 1983, Sydney. Judges, Robert Forsyth, U.S.A., and Dr. J. Nesvadba of Switzerland. Also Best Puppy in Group and Best Exhibit in Parade, Doberman Club of Melbourne, 1983. D. Eschbach, owner.

6. A lovely Doberman from Australia, Ch. Tanunda Sportsaction, owned by Mae Hart, Kellyville, New South Wales. Pictured at the Doberman Specialty show in 1980.

Plate 114

1. Cecar's Eddo van Belling Home and Cecar's Aida v.d. Vollerswaal are excellent examples of the correct type Dobermans in the Netherlands. Photo courtesy of J. Theunissen, Saeva-Dobe Kennels, Curacao, Netherlands Antilles.

2. Cecar's Eddo van Belling Home, son of Baron Cecar van Rensloo, VH III, Sch.H. III, Sp.H., FH. Owned by J. Theunissen.

3. Cecar's Aida v.d. Vollerswaal, sister of multiple show winner in Holland at the moment and daughter of Cecar van Rensloo, VH III, Sch.H. III, Sp.H., FH. Owned by J. Theunissen.

4. In Trinidad, Ch. Damasyn The Honeybuck takes a mud bath to escape the heat. Owned by Frank Thompson, Trinidad; bred by Peggy Adamson. Best in Show and never defeated in Trinidad.

5. Japanese Ch. Benares of M-Greatriver, by Japanese Ch. I-Elite of EC Sasada ex Japanese Ch. Olga of EC Sasada. Owner, Motoko Amatsuji. Winner of Best of Breed at the Japanese National Specialty in 1981, judged by Frank Grover (U.S.A.). Best of Breed at the Japanese National Specialty in 1982, judged by Walter Hensel (Germany).

6. Hollyhigh's Kan Kan, a daughter of Ch. Mikadobe's Paris, is now in Japan. Photo courtesy of Mae Downing, Mikadobe Kennels.

Plate 115

1. Rufus du Fief de la Garenne, at Valencia, Spain, winning the Young Class. A son of Danica's Stamm Juon. Owned by Annie and Daniel Mulero, Dompierre/Mer, France.

2. Danica's Stamm Juon, Westfallen champion (Germany) Best in Show. Owners, Annie and Daniel Mulero.

3. Danica's Stamm Juon, Best in Show at the show in Caen (France). Judge, Sir Wiblishauser, President of the German Doberman Club and of the International Doberman Club. Juon is owned by Annie and Daniel Mulero.

4. Trayon du Fief de la Garenne at 10 months. A son of Danica's Stamm Juon. Owned by Annie and Daniel Mulero.

5. Danica's Stamm Juon going Best in Show from the Youth Class, Essen, Germany.

6. Afra von Bavaria, DV Sieger, 1973. International champion. Schweizer Sieger. Sch.H. III. Owned by Hans Wiblishauser, West Germany. Photo courtesy of Peggy Adamson.

Plate 116

1. This handsome uncropped Doberman is Aust. Ch. Stehle von Wickens at nine months of age. A splendid representative of the noted Australian kennel whose name he carries. D. Eschbach, owner.

2. Aust. Ch. Silvan Glen Centrefold, by Eng., Irish, and Aust. Ch. Kenstaff Tornado of Achenburg, owned by Silvan Glen Kennels, Mick and Lauris Parrish, Kemps Creek, New South Wales, Australia.

3. Aust. Ch. Stehle King, C.D. and Aust. Ch. Summer Sky Eliza are the foundation dog and bitch of Stehle Dobermans, they being the sire and dam of Aust. Chs. Stehle von Wickens, Stehle Victoria, Stehle Mia, and Stehle Binda. Owner, D. Eschbach, Stehle Dobermans, North Wagga, New South Wales, Australia.

4. Aust. Ch. Stehle Binda at nine months. Owned, bred, and shown by D. Eschbach.

Plate 117

1. Aust. Ch. Maharighi King Cobra, bred by F. S. L. Price. Owned by D. Eschbach, Stehle Kennels, North Wagga, New South Wales, Australia.

2. Aust. Ch. Stehle Binda, bred, owned, and exhibited by D. Eschbach of Stehle Kennels, is a multi-Best-in-Show and Group winner. She was Challenge Certificate winning bitch and Best of Breed at the 1983 Spring Fair Dog Show judged by Robert Forsyth from the United States.

3. Father and son. Aust. Ch. Ardries The Auctioneer at four-and-a-half years of age, handled by the gentleman. Aust. Ch. Stehle King at 14 months, handled by the woman. D. Eschbach, owner.

4. Aust. Ch. Stehle Binda, bred, owned, and shown by D. Eschbach. A multi-Best-in-Show and Group winner, Challenge Certificate winning bitch, and Best of Breed at the 1983 Spring Fair judged by Robert Forsyth.

5. Ch. Tanunda Beau Brummel, owned by Mae Hart of Tanunda Kennels, Kellyville, New South Wales, Australia.

6. Aust. Ch. Tanunda Fiery Spirit, C.D., owned by Mae Hart. Best Bitch in Show, Melbourne Doberman Pinscher Club Specialty; Kitty Drury, of the United States, judge.

Plate 118

1. Ch. Amulet's Luka of Sno-Glenn, C.D. at home. Three years old, this splendid Dobe belongs to Linda and John Krukar, Dabney Kennels, Bethlehem, Pennsylvania.

2. Gayamon The Midnight Moon, C.D., WAC imparting some grandfatherly advice to his grandson. Both owned by Jo Ann James, Brykris Dobermans, Miami, Florida. Bill James, photographer.

Plate 119

1. Akitsu vom Walden, by U.S.-imported Bellhans Dr. Pepper ex Japanese Ch. Benares of M-Greatriver. Owner, Niriko Hirakawa. Breeder, Motoko Amatsuji. Best Puppy under judge Frank Grover (U.S.A.) at the 1984 Tokyo FCI International Show.

2. Ch. Mikadobe's Valentino v Paris, completing his championship at Columbus Kennel Club just prior to being shipped to Keizo Sasada's well-known kennels in Osaka, Japan. Carlos Rojas handling.

Plate 120

1. Aust. Ch. Shato Norwegian Wood, by Aust. Ch. Tanunda Royal Bacchus ex Vredenburg Czarina, is primarily Australian and New Zealand breeding; although the paternal grandsire is Tavey's Stormy Perfection. Mae Hart, owner, Kellyville, New South Wales, Australia.

2. Aust. Ch. Tanunda Thorgerda at seven months. One of the many outstanding Dobermans belonging to Mae Hart.

3. Carosel B A Friend, by Ch. Brown's B-Brian ex Ch. Damasyn the Limelight, handled by his breeder, Carol Selzle Petruzzo, to a good win at the Quaker City Doberman Pinscher Club 1976 Futurity under judge Robert Slay. This handsome Dobe now resides in Australia, owned by Wayne and Sharon Brown.

4. Aust. Ch. Tanunda Sportsaction at the Doberman Specialty show in 1980. Mae Hart, owner, Tanunda Kennels.

Plate 121

1. Ch. Tanunda Thorgerda asks that we forgive her false pregnancy. A lovely bitch belonging to Mae Hart, Kellyville, New South Wales, Australia. By Aust. Ch. Shato Norwegian Wood ex Tanunda Funny Girl.

2. Approach with caution! This is a trained guard dog at Windswept Kennels, Mr. and Mrs. Pausey, New South Wales, Australia.

3. The lovely Best-in-Show-winning bitch, Pansy, at 12½ years of age. A great favorite with Mrs. Pausey, Windswept Kennels.

4. Kimbertal's Prima Donna is owned by Windswept Kennels, New South Wales, Australia.

5. Aust. Ch. Windswept Baby Doll as a 10-month-old puppy. Sheridan Pausey, owner.

6. Windswept Baby Bunting at 10 years, the sire of five champions. Owned, bred, and loved by Sheridan Pausey, Windswept Dobermans.

Plate 122

1. Ch. Carosel In the Spotlight, C.D., ROM, with Kristen Marie King in 1975.

2. Can. Ch. Tamarak's Brigadoon, owned by Sherry George and Shirrel De Baie, Eastern Passage, Nova Scotia, Canada.

3. Dobermans and kids get along just great together! Pamelot's Legal Tender helping to prove this point. Pamela De Hetre, Loganville, Georgia.

4. Two six-month-old puppies of quality. Liquorish Lucky Charm and Ch. Liquorish Lucky Chance, littermates, bred and owned by Grace and Jeff Joffe, Ft. Lauderdale, Florida.

Plate 123

1. Wynterwynd's Fox of Tempesta, owned by Serenade Dobermans, Jan MacDonald, Houston, Texas.

2. Ch. Billmar's Angel of Armin and Billmar's Crystal, the latter pointed from the Puppy Class and now maturing at home for a "specials" career. Captain M. E. (United States Navy, retired) and Mrs. Smith, owners, Cleveland, Tennessee.

3. Ch. Tolivar's Aristotle of Azteca at 10½ years of age. Owner, Mrs. Edd Bivin, Fort Worth, Texas.

4. Ch. RMJ's April Love, by Cardel's Dudley-Do-Right, C.D. ex Cardel's Amy v Berghof, is the dam of two champions, one of them a Best in Show winner. Owner, Doberlyn Kennels, Robert Clarke and Bonnie Clarke.

Plate 124

1. A young puppy sent to Hong Kong from Australia. Bred by Windswept Kennels, Sheridan Pausey, Australia. Owned by Mr. Wong Wing On.

2. An Australian Doberman, Windswept Black Prince, at eight months old. From Windswept Kennels, Mr. and Mrs. Pausey, New South Wales.

3. This Windswept puppy, Windswept God Saturn, was sent to the U.S.A. for ear cropping. Owned by Mr. and Mrs. Pausey, Windswept Kennels.

4. Ch. Ecquen Bengazi at age one year when he went Best in Show at the first National Doberman Show in Australia. Born in 1973 by Ch. Elmaro All Fire ex Ecquen Moon Mist.

5. Ebonstorm's The Honey Buck, red and rust, age 11 months. This lovely Damasyn-bred dog belongs to the Andersons in Sidney, Australia. Photo courtesy of Peggy Adamson.

6. Aust. Ch. Maharighi Panach, Challenge Certificate Winner and Best of Breed, Sydney Royal, 1983. Owner and breeder, F. S. L. and Mrs. Price, Maharighi Kennels, Sydney, Australia. Sire of Aust. Ch. Maharighi King Cobra.

Plate 125

1. Uhlan du Fief de la Garenne, handsome young son of Gr. Ch. Danica's Stamm Juon, at 10 months. Owned by Annie and Daniel Mulero, famous Doberman breeders in France.

2. Reine, daughter of Danica's Stamm Juon, is Champion of Work (Sch.H. III) and Champion of Beauty in France. Annie and Daniel Mulero, Dompierre/Mer, France, owners.

3. Bellona von der Bult, owned by Annie and Daniel Mulero.

4. Anja von der Bult, owned by the Muleros.

5. Gr. Ch. Juon with three of his children. Annie and Daniel Mulero.

6. Miranda v Ferrolheim, Sch.H. I, HD I, by Danica's Stamm Juon. Owned by the Muleros.

1 ◄

2 ►

3 ◄

4 ►

PLATE 113

5 ◄

6 ►

1 ◄

2 ►

3 ◄

4 ►

PLATE 114

5 ◄

6 ►

1 ▶

2 ▶

3 ▶

4 ▶

PLATE 115

5 ▶

6 ▶

1 ◄

2 ►

PLATE 116

3 ◄

4 ►

1 ◄
2 ◄

3 ◄
4 ◄

PLATE 117

5 ◄
6 ◄

BEST OF
WINNERS
COLUMBUS
KENNEL CLUB
DECEMBER 1980

PHOTO BY *Graham*

1 ◄

2 ►

PLATE 120

3 ◄

4 ►

1 ►
2 ►

3 ►
4 ►

PLATE 121

5 ►
6 ►

1

2

PLATE 122

3

4

1
2

PLATE 123

3

4

1 ▶
2 ▶

3 ▶
4 ▶

PLATE 124

5 ▶
6 ▶

1 ▶
2 ▶

3 ▶
4 ▶

PLATE 125

5 ▶
6 ▶

1 ◄

2 ◄

3 ◄

4 ◄

PLATE 126

5 ◄

6 ►

1▲   PLATE 127   ▼2

1 ◄

2 ◄

PLATE 128

3 ◄

4 ◄

Plate 126
1. Left to right are Ch. Arabar's Impertinence, Ch. Alisaton's Raincheck, WAC, and Ch. Alisaton's Kinderwicke, WAC. Owner, Gwen DeMilta, Westbury, New York.

2. Koven's Sweet Charity of Kay Hill relaxing in her favorite spot. Jane Kay, Kay Hill Dobermans, owner.

3. Ch. Carosel B In A Hurry, C.D., ROM, at seven years. By Ch. Brown's B-Brian ex Ch. Damasyn the Limelight. Breeder-owner, Carol Selzle Petruzzo, Freehold, New Jersey.

4. Gayamon The Bravo Bambino, pictured at 11 years of age, and Gayamon The Midnight Moon, C.D., WAC, pictured at nine years, are owned by Bill and JoAnn James, Miami, Florida. Bill James caught them with his camera in this playful mood.

5. A *white* Doberman related to the two acquired for breeding research by the Doberman Pinscher Club of America. This color is a breed disqualification. Photo courtesy of Pat and Judy Doniere.

6. Glenayr Jamison, bred by Richard and Barbara Duklis. Owned by Jaime and Ceci Martinez de Santana, San Juan, Puerto Rico.

Plate 127
1. Bobby Robson holding future Can. Ch. Moondancer's Imperial Dragon when the latter was eight weeks old. Note littermates clustered around! Bob and Sally Robson, Moondancer Dobermans, Cargill, Ontario, Canada.

2. Ch. Marienburg's Lone Eagle, owned by Dr. and Mrs. Anthony DiNardo of East Hartford, Connecticut, with the DiNardo's four youngsters, Toni Leigh, Anthony III, Cheri, and Gina. All share their parent's love of and enthusiasm for the Doberman breed.

Plate 128
1. The Muleros take their famous winning Dobermans for a walk in the snow—obviously being enjoyed by all. The Mulero family are leading French breeders of Dobermans.

2. Stone, daughter of Danica's Stamm Juon, shown here by Marilyn Meshirer, owner of the Brandendorf Kennel in the United States. Stone, at 16 months of age, has three CACIB's and two Bests in Show. Annie and Daniel Mulero, owners, Dompierre/Mer, France.

3. A son of Juon, Babur, who is a chmapion in Brazil. Annie and Daniel Mulero, breeders.

4. Ramses, a lovely two-year-old son of Danica's Stamm Juon. Annie and Daniel Mulero, owners.

Informally at home, Ch. Highbriar Esquire, born March 1975, at age nine years. Bred by Betsy R. Thomas. Owned and loved by Ken and Sheila Valentine, Esquire Dobermans, Windsor Junction, Nova Scotia.

1. Am. and Can. Ch. Schauffelein's Troll Arabasque, by Ch. Schauffelein's Extra Special ex Ch. Midnight Glow of Arabasque. Famous as "Canada's outstanding producer of champions," he has earned that title well, with well over 100 Canadian champion sons and daughters to his credit and about 30 American champions. Joey and Ron Purdy, owners, Schauffelein Dobermans, Cheltenham, Ontario.
2. Ryas Accolade at one-and-a-half years. Owned by Nancy Butterfield, Fort Leavenworth. Bred by the Cunninghams, Ryas Dobes, Vinemount, Ontario.

"Show of Shows." This show is Canada's premier event, restricted to dogs of any country who have won a Best in Show somewhere in Canada during the current year. The cream of North American dogdom competes at this event. Jagermeister's Seven Come Eleven is the only Doberman ever to have won the top honor there! Sunny followed this win by becoming Canada's Top Working Dog in 1975 and second Top Dog, all breeds. In all, Sunny accumulated 22 all-breed Bests in Show and holds the Canadian record for the most points accumulated by a Doberman in a single year of competition. Sunny died in 1982. Truly the end of an era.

Fred Heal is still an active breeder and shows his own dogs when time allows. In total, dogs that he has owned or bred have accounted for 37 Best in Show awards. Fred is now an accredited conformation judge of all Sporting, Hound and Working Dog breeds and Groups. He finds that judging Dobes all over North America provides him an excellent opportunity to see, at close range, the dogs that may one day add their genes to the Jagermeister line.

Michael Plamondon's

Michael Plamondon's Doberman Pinschers are located at Lac-Beauport in Quebec and have been active in the dog show world since the early 1980's when he started to show his first male, Canadian Champion Doebet's First Satan.

Soon after this he had the good fortune to become acquainted with Doug and Donna Fraser, to whom Mr. Plamondon pays sincere tribute for their guidance and counsel which so greatly helped him to get off to a good start in the breed.

A few months after meeting the Frasers, Mr. Plamondon purchased his now very famous female Doberman from them. This was "Casey," or, to be more formal, Canadian Champion Dobermein's Virgo, who at the time of this writing has become the No. 2 winning Doberman female in Canada.

Casey is a daughter of Champion Shingo's War Admiral ex Champion Northwoods Ebony Rose. The Plamondons felt themselves especially fortunate in having acquired this bitch, as her sire is by American and Canadian Champion Schauffelein's Vintage Year and out of Champion Jagermeister's Santana, thus combining the lines of two very outstanding kennels.

Casey won so many Best of Breed and Group placements that Mr. Plamondon was asked by many professionals to show her at both Canadian and American dog shows. Then it was arranged that she be placed in Harold Butler's charge, of which Mr. Plamondon says, "Harold became our favorite handler. This man has done quite a remarkable task by sparing no trouble on his animals' well being and on the welfare of their owners."

Canadian Champion Dobermein's Virgo is a Best in Show winner with more than 40 Bests of Breed and 30 Working Groups to her credit. She is now the No. 2 Doberman bitch in Canada according to a message we have received from her owner, and she was graded First Doberman at the Ralston Purina International Show of Shows in 1982. Also she has visited the United States, where she has attained one "major" and five points.

At present, the Plamondons have three dogs at home: Casey, of course, who is four years old as we write; a male Doberman, Canadian Champion Ashumong's Mumm's Cordon Rouge; and a Best in Show winning German Shorthaired Pointer bitch.

Moondancer

Moondancer Dobermans are owned by Bob and Sally Robson at Cargill in Ontario. The parents of three small children, they usually have around ten adult Dobermans. Around 1975 Sally bought her first Dobe, never knowing then what lay in the future for her and her family as Dobe owners and breeders.

After Sally met and married Bob Robson, they decided to get a companion for Sally's original bitch, and so they purchased not one but *two* lovely Vince von Avery daughters. One of them, as a puppy, won the Sweepstakes at the Doberman Pinscher Club of Canada Specialty. The other, bred to Champion Schauffelein's Limited Edition, gave her owners an outstanding litter of puppies from which they kept a dog who became Champion Moondancer's Rolls Royce and who has now become their most important and successful sire.

Sally's first bitch, Tanya, is out of the famous German bloodline known as Furstenfeld, which in Germany has produced World Siegers and Siegerins. After years of experimenting, the Robsons discovered that the best temperament and the most outgoing and intelligent dogs were coming from this German bitch who was never shown and was not as stylish as what was in the ring at the time.

By then, the Robsons had many bitches of different bloodlines, but they never produced with the same consistency that outgoing temperament which was so outstanding in all of Tanya's puppies no matter what stud was the sire. So, to make a long story short, the Robsons have combined Tanya's bloodline with those of Rolls Royce, who also has a super temperament, and they are now getting both style and brains in their young homebreds.

The Robsons feel that since the Doberman is a working dog he should be capable of performing the jobs for which he was created and that nervous, shy or high-strung dogs cannot do this successfully, nor can such a Doberman make a successful show dog. Thus they plan to continue working along the bloodlines which are now producing so satisfactorily for them, and they hope that the dogs will continue to be successful in the future.

Regency

Regency Dobermans are the result of Sherry George's having purchased her first of the breed in 1975 from Harvey Gratton of Trollhattan Kennels. However, it was not until she purchased her linebred Kay Hills male, Canadian Champion Tamarak's Brigadoon, from Doris Nemeth in 1980 that her serious interest in showing started to take shape.

Brigadoon finished his championship from the Junior Puppy Class in three consecutive days, which was certainly an exciting start of the type which usually *does* completely sell a new exhibitor on the sport of showing dogs!

Sherry's first homebred, Champion Regency Wildfire, C.D. was sired by Brigadoon and earned her C.D. from the Novice A Class in three consecutive trials.

Being impressed with the Kay Hills breeding, Sherry has recently purchased, from Mary White, a Kay Hill linebred bitch, Freespirits High Sierra, and hopes to establish her own line from this bitch and Brigadoon.

Ryas

Ryas Dobermans are owned by Pat and Dave Cunningham and are located at Vinemount, Ontario. Following their marriage in 1968 the Cunninghams purchased their first dog, a Labrador of somewhat uncertain descent. Although Pat carefully trained her, "Bess," not being pure-bred, was never eligible to compete in formal obedience.

Dave had always loved Dobermans; in fact, he had grown up with them. So in 1971 the step was taken and the first of what was to become a long series of Dobermans came to live with the Cunninghams. This was Lord Spartacus von Weissenfelz, C.D., who, although never bred, did his share for the breed as his owners learned a good deal about Dobermans from him.

Next to join the family was future champion Lowenbrau Huntress, acquired in 1973. Known as "Rya," she provided the kennel name under which the Cunninghams since have operated, and Ryas was registered by them with the Canadian Kennel Club in 1975.

Huntress was handled by Pat, who was still very much a novice at that time, to complete her championship in only a dozen shows. She then went on to produce five champions sired by multi-Best in Show winning Champion Schauffelein's Troll Arabasque, Canada's all-time Top Producing Doberman. She also has three "major" pointed progeny sired by Champion Karalynn's Black Liberator, T.T., along with a couple who are "major" pointed by Troll, and several with obedience titles.

Another Troll daughter, who was out of a Troll daughter, Comfetanya Rima von Ryan, was purchased for the purpose of breeding back to Champion Vince von Avery, sire of twenty or more champions and who was Best of Breed from the classes at the 1972 Doberman Pinscher Club of Canada Specialty Show. She produced Champion Ryas Bowery Boy, but had she lived longer, more champions undoubtedly would have come from this beautiful bitch. Unfortunately she died in 1981 after ingesting a foreign object.

Rya's breeding to Troll was repeated in 1977, this time producing that great sire's last litter. The progeny included Champion Ryas Curtain Call for Troll, who was the dam of pointed progeny; Champion Ryas Schauffelein Cartel, a champion producer co-owned by

1. Ch. Ryas Legacy at three months. Pat Cunningham, owner, Vinemount, Ontario.
2. Ch. Lowenbrau Huntress, a daughter of Ch. Vince von Avery, was the first by this dog to finish. She is, as well, the foundation bitch for Ryas Dobermans, Dave and Pat Cunningham. Vince became the sire of more than 20 champions during his career.
3. Comfetanya Rima von Ryas joined Ryas Kennels in the summer of 1975. A Troll daughter out of a Troll daughter, she produced a champion, Ryas Bowery Boy, and a nine-pointer who was spayed before having the opportunity to finish. This bitch died in 1981, before finishing, after ingesting a foreign object. A great loss both for her quality and her bloodlines! Dave and Pat Cunningham, owners.
4. Ch. Lowenbrau Huntress at 16 months. Known as "Rya," she provided the Cunninghams with their kennel name, which became *Ryas* and was registered in 1975. This handsome bitch became the dam of six champions. Owned by Dave and Pat Cunningham.

```
                                                    Ch. Delegate vd Elbe
                                  Ch. Iago vom Ahrtal
                                                    Meadowmist Isis v. Ahrtal
              Ch. Schauffelein's Blackberry Brandy
                                                    Ch. Delegate vd Elbe
                                  Ch. Schauffelein's Silhouette
                                                    Ch. Schauffelein's Allegro
    Ch. Schauffelein's Extra Special (9)
                                                    Ch. Schauffelein's Blackberry Brandy
                                  Ch. Bramalea's Argonaut
                                                    Allangail's Heidi
              Schauffelein's Specially Fancy
                                                    Ch. Elfred's Spark Plug Cacib
                                  Schauffelein's Starfire
                                                    Ch. Schauffelein's Silk Tassel
Ch. Schauffelein's Troll Arabesque (60+)
                                                    Ch. Rancho Dobe's Storm
                                  Ch. Storm's Donner
                                                    Storm's Tempestra
              Ch. Kurtzhaus Thunder
                                                    Ch. Iago v. Ahrtal
                                  Ch. Schauffelein's Soliloquoy
                                                    Ch. Schauffelein's Silhouette
    Ch. Midnight Glow of Arabesque
                                                    Ch. Sabre v. Mannerheim
                                  Ch. Bar-Jak's Caesar
                                                    Ch. Kaukana's Golden Sceptre
              Quinesta's Twilight Fantasy
                                                    Ch. Kay-Jon's Commander
                                  Jessica
                                                    Brandia Roxanne

CH. RYAS ANTICIPATION (7)
        "CANNON"
                                                    Ch. Brown's Dion
                                  Ch. Checkmate's Count von Glam
                                                    Ch. Alemap's Glamor Girl
              Ch. Checkmate's Erik Rudolph
                                                    Ch. Alemap's Checkmate
                                  Ch. Toledobe's Barbiturate
                                                    Ch. Wahlmar's Baroness
    Ch. Vince von Avery (20+)
                                                    Ch. Schauffelein's Blackberry Brandy
                                  Ch. Saracen of Dachurst
                                                    Ch. Konigshausen Inspiration
              Angelia von Hallberg
                                                    Ch. Bramalea's Argonaut C.D.
                                  Schauffelein's Sabrina
                                                    Schauffelein's Starfire
Ch. Lowenbrau Huntress (5)
                                                    Ch. Schauffelein's Blackberry Brandy
                                  Ch. Schauffelein's Extra Special
                                                    Schauffelein's Specially Fancy
              Ch. Lowenbrau's Artful Dodger CDX
                                                    Ch. Sabre v. Mannerheim
                                  Ch. Konigshausen Honor C.D.
                                                    Ch. Konigshausen Dedication
    Ch. Lowenbrau Destiny CDX
                                                    Ch. Iago vom Ahrtal
                                  Ch. Schauffelein's Blackberry Brandy
                                                    Ch. Schauffelein's Silhouette
              Ch. Konigshausen Jade
                                                    Ch. Dobe Acre's Cinnamon
                                  Ch. Konigshausen Destiny C.D.
                                                    Ch. Kay Hil's Ebonetta
```

Ryas Dobermans Reg'd.

PAT & DAVE CUNNINGHAM
1156 Ridge Road
Vinemount, Ont.
Vinemount, Ont. L0R 2G0
1-(416) 643-3628

Joey Purdy and the Johnsons; and Ryas Chablis Toast To Troll, C.D.X., T.T. The latter has made the Cunninghams especially proud not only for her working achievements in obedience, which led to her gaining U.D., but for her contribution to the Hamilton Dog Obedience Club Flyball Team in garnering top honors at the Detroit-Windsor World Series in July 1983 over seven American teams. The next breeding of Rya, Champion Lowenbrau Huntress, was to Champion Karalynn's Black Liberator in 1978. One puppy resulted, Ryas Destiny C.D., so the breeding was repeated in 1978, this time producing five puppies. Of these, Ryas Eager Leader, C.D., has five points towards conformation title, as does Ryas Easy Rider. Ryas Nantom Entertainer, C.D. has four conformation points and is the dam of "major" pointed progeny; and Ryas Effervescence, still to be shown herself, is the dam of two champions. Pat Cunningham notes that she believes Rya was the first champion bitch to be bred to "Luger" (Black Liberator), who went on to become a leading producer and Specialty winner.

Champion Ryas Hot To Trot was whelped in April 1981 from Ryas Effervescence by Champion Warcrick's Achilles, a Troll grandson. She finished with Scott McNair handling in four shows on two consecutive weekends, including Winners Bitch at a Doberman Pinscher Club of Canada booster show.

Champion Ryas Legacy, born in April 1982, was owner/breeder-handled to finish in eight shows at age fourteen months. "Viper," as she is known, was the seventh champion for her sire, Champion Ryas Anticipation, C.D., ROM, and the second for her dam, Ryas Effervescence.

In 1982 the Cunninghams leased Best in Show bitch Champion Hugelhof Wishful Thinking, C.D. from the Hilliards in Manitoba. On New Year's Day in 1983 a litter was born to her, sired by Ryas Accolade.

Ryas is known, and admired, as a small, professional breeding kennel which has built up a solid reputation among the members of the dog fancy. Dave Cunningham is a Sales Manager for an international chemical company, and Pat Cunningham is a part-time artist with considerable talent. Both have been extensively involved with all-breed and specialty clubs for some years, are active members of obedience clubs, and are long-time members of the Canadian Kennel Club. Pat studied canine anatomy and movement and also canine behavior and breeding practices at Mohawk College in Hamilton during the early days of Ryas' inception. Both she and Dave enjoy attendance at lectures and seminars regarding dogs in general and the Doberman Pinscher in particular.

Schauffelein

It would be impossible to write a section on Doberman Pinschers in Canada without becoming increasingly (almost with every page, it has seemed) impressed with the impact Schauffelein dogs have had on this breed there. Kennel after kennel, famous winner after famous winner, one finds Schauffelein behind an impressive number of the best—in itself a tribute to the folks who own this kennel and to the magnificent type and quality of the dogs that they have bred.

Schauffelein is owned by Ron and Joey Purdy and is located at Cheltenham in Ontario. Love of Dobermans is something with which Joey Wright Purdy was obviously born, or that developed within a very short time thereafter, as we have read that she wanted nothing more, as a child, than to own a Dobe of her own; and that she had friends who were Dobermans whom she never missed an opportunity to visit with as a child.

Joey started pressuring her Dad for one of these dogs when she was just a little girl. This was shortly after World War II, and Mr. Wright was uneasy over some of the tales he had heard regarding the viciousness of these dogs; thus he hesitated to get one for his daughter. No other breed would do—that became increasingly obvious. So finally, on St. Patrick's Day in 1947 when Mr. Wright agreed to look at a litter of Dobe puppies, Joey was ecstatic, even though these puppies were not the black bitch which was secretly her first choice. However, among them only two red males were available. Joey reasoned, probably quite sensibly, that even a Doberman of the wrong color and sex to be her *real* preference was better than *no* Doberman, and so the visit to look at the puppies was made. Joey came away with the red dog whom she called "Troll" after his grandfather, Troll v d Engelsburg. The puppy was officially Belshazzar of Jarwat.

Since one of the breed now had actually joined the family, Joey's father started to become increasingly interested in Dobermans, a fact which delighted Joey as it permitted her to finally get that black bitch when she persuaded Mr. Wright to purchase Trinka von Edelwesen, who was a Goethe v Mannerheim daughter. This bitch was a considerably better specimen of the breed, as they soon found out when they started to show her. Showing was one of the interests Joey had developed through the first dog, Troll, even though he was not quite up to Dobe quality to be truly competitive.

Fate would seem to have been behind the beginning of Schauffelein as a kennel. Somehow when the bitch was in heat, the two dogs got out together and the accidental breeding took place in the lake—which was surely a unique place for the big event to happen! In due time two puppies resulted.

With the arrival of the young homebreds, a kennel name became important. Joey spent a great deal of time and study on its selection, as she wanted it to be a German name—pleasant sounding but not too hard or gutteral. Many trips to the library followed before her decision was reached. Then one day Joey's attention hit upon the name of a European artist. She liked the sound of it, and thus it was that Schauffelein was adopted and has now become a watchword in the Doberman Fancy.

The Troll-Trinka breeding was repeated three times (but planned on each of these occasions). From this combination the first two Schauffelein champions were produced. Joey was becoming a very knowledgeable young lady about Dobermans, availing herself of every opportunity to learn everything she could about her chosen breed.

The first seriously planned breeding at Schauffelein was to Champion Meadowmist Elegy, belonging to Virginia Knauer. Joey had a "feeling" about this dog and he sired five champions for her in that litter, including her first Best in Show dog, Champion Schauffelein's Black Gold, who subsequently was owned by Roy Harper. Champion Schauffelein's Allegro was kept at home, finished her title, then was bred to Champion Delegate v d Elbe. Joey hoped she would produce a blue, which she did! This young dog, Schauffelein's Steeldust, became the first Canadian

blue champion Doberman. He made his presence strongly felt in the show ring, despite the presence of an almost invincible German Shepherd who was out at this very same time; he gave Joey great satisfaction when Dr. Wilfred Shute, who had warned her not to keep a blue, himself paid tribute to her dog by awarding him a Group 2nd in keen competition.

Joey and Ron Purdy were married in 1952. Joey had the foresight to fall in love with a young man who also likes dogs and horses, although he prefers horse shows to dog shows, and who has a natural "eye" for both the horses and the dogs. As a pharmacist with a highly successful business, Ron finds his time quite busy, and since in his work weekends are full for him, he does not object to Joey's hobby of going to dog shows.

Schauffelein's Silhouette, from the Allegro-Delegate litter, was the next from whom Joey bred. She had finished her title at three straight shows, and for her Joey selected as a stud Champion Iago v Ahrtal, one of Delegate's best sons. So well did the Silhouette-Iago breeding work that it was repeated three times, producing nine champions, among which four were Best in Show dogs.

Silhouette and Iago produced the Purdys' first truly outstanding sire, Schauffelein's Bl'Kberry Brandy, who sired twelve champions and who became a multiple Best in Show winner. Also a sister from the same litter, Champion Schauffelein's Silk Tassel, added her share to the list of homebred champions which has made the Purdys so famous in the Doberman world when she was sent to be bred to International Champion Elfred's Spark Plug.

Occasionally the Purdys went outside for a breeding, although they usually remained within their own line. They felt, however, that if one sees a dog which really makes an impression, is of good bloodlines and should complement one's own stock, by all means breed to it. They did so on several occasions, to such sires of greatness as Champion Steb's Top Skipper, Sparkplug, Periwinkle, and of course Felix.

As seems to happen to most of us at one time or another, the Purdys ran into a spell of bad breaks at one period around the mid-60's. They handled it by leasing a bitch named

Ch. Schauffelein's Outrigger, by Ch. Schauffelein's Troll Arabasque ex Ch. Lowenbrau Aloha Schauffelein. Bred by Joey and Ron Purdy. Owned by Pat Blenkey, Harley, Ontario.

Starfire, from the Spark Plug-Silk Tassel litter, with which they turned luck back into their corner again.

A lovely bitch named Champion Schauffelein's Specially was bred back to her grandsire, Champion Schauffelein's Bl'Kberry Brandy, from which combination another of the superb Schauffelein studs was born. He was named Schauffelein's Extra Special because that is what he was. He was called Troll, in honor of Joey's original Troll. He sired nine champions in three litters produced prior to his sudden death at only three-and-a-half years of age. Troll's death was a shocking tragedy in its suddenness. We understand that he seemed to be in the best of health and was "helping" the Purdys' son put the horses up for the night when—suddenly and without warning—Troll died. The autopsy revealed no cause, and he had never known a single day of sickness.

Having been bred only three times, Troll's puppies were not numerous. There was, however, a litter at Arabasque Kennels by him from Champion Midnight Glow of Arabasque. One of these puppies, a black male, excited Joey Purdy very greatly. There was a red male, too, whom everyone else felt was "pick of the litter," but Joey was not quite certain about this, as she still inclined towards the black. Eventually Joey decided to have them both: the red puppy as pick of litter as everyone agreed; the black one just for herself as it would soon be her birthday and that was the one she *really* favored. The red dog became Champion Schauffelein's Beau Arabasque. The black, however, grew up to be Champion Schauffelein's Troll Arabasque. Need we say more? The two of them are credited with having set a whole new standard of excellence for Dobermans in Canada, to quote Pat Blenkey in a story she wrote about them, with Troll's records outstanding. For three years he was Top Doberman Pinscher in Canada. He was winner of the Doberman Pinscher Club of Canada Specialty in 1972. For three years he was a multiple Best in Show dog and listed in the Top Ten Dogs in Canada for three years. Additionally he received the Doberman Pinscher Club of Canada award for Dog of the Year for two years and has been Sire of the Year for at least three years. Dr. Shute, himself the owner of a Troll

son, once predicted that Troll Arabasque would become the Top Producing Doberman Canada has known and the most influential sire of the breed. This prediction has certainly come true, with more than 58 champions on Troll's record, at least, as we write a decade later.

At thirteen months of age, Troll Arabasque had completed his championship and was starting off on his career as a "special."

Canadian and American Champion Schauffelein's Troll Arabasque was the sire of Champion Schauffelein's Vintage Year, who was born in the Purdys' kitchen from Champion Lowenbrau Aloha Schauffelein, one of twenty-two champions produced by this combination, six of them in "Goober's" own litter, including several others that became Group and Best in Show winners. Even at earliest puppyhood, Goober stood out, and everyone who came to see the puppies spotted him instantly. In deference to the others in the litter, Goober's show career did not begin until he was eleven months of age, by which time one brother had become a champion at eight months, another at ten months. Even despite the handicap of waiting until the others were on the way, Goober was a champion by thirteen months, including an important win at the Greenwood show.

Goober competed three times in the Top Twenty. He had four consecutive Best in Show wins at the Doberman Pinscher Club of Canada Specialties, the last time at seven years of age! The standout show experience for him in his owners' memories, however, was Atlanta, when J. D. Jones made intersex judging at that Specialty so thrilling for exhibitors and spectators. Goober's win there was unforgettable! So too was his taking the Stud Dog Class later in the week at the National; the success which his "kids" met there; his three consecutive Bests in Show in Quebec straight there from the Specialty; and his winning the Quaker City Specialty under judge Marilyn Meshirer—what a time of triumph in the life of a truly great dog!

The Purdys did not really keep full count of Goober's show record. He had two dozen or more all-breed Bests in Show, four large Specialties, and the Doberman Pinscher Club of Canada Specialty, as mentioned above, four consecutive times. He won the Stud Dog

Class at the American National and Quaker City Specialties in 1976. The Purdys consider his ultimate honor to be winning the Top Ten in 1977 at seven years of age. He had at least one hundred champions to his credit as a sire, and at the time of his death two of them were in the Top Twenty. Pam DeHetre handled Goober in the United States.

Schauffelein Dobermans have made impressive records in the obedience ring too. It is thought that Schauffelein's Salutation, who came to the United States to Carol Silverman, may well have been the most titled of *any* Doberman, certainly of that day if not right until the present, as she was an American and Canadian Champion, American U.D. and Canadian C.D.X. She was from Troll and Lolly. Then Schauffelein's Dilemma was the first Doberman ever to earn a perfect score at the Doberman Pinscher Club of America National Specialty, in 1972 in Toledo.

The Schauffelein story would not be complete without a salute to the great and magnificent bitch Champion Lowenbrau Aloha Schauffelein. In five litters she produced 22 champions. Little wonder that she won the Brood Bitch Class at the Canadian Specialty at least three years consecutively. Truly a producer to be regarded with awe, she certainly has done a tremendous amount of good for the Doberman breed.

The Purdys' achievements have been reached through a small kennel (never more than eight dogs are at the kennel at any one time, with about another four out on co-ownership). Just one more example of the fact that quantity does not necessarily go with quality. The latter comes through "dog sense," knowing one's dogs and their bloodlines, and the ability to understand and recognize the fact that quality comes from quality!

Simca

Simca Doberman Pinschers became a kennel in 1980, founded by Lana Sniderman and Bob Krol at Nobleton, Ontario. Previous to this, in 1977, these fanciers had purchased a Samoyed who, because of stubbornness, led them to obedience training classes where they became acquainted with the Doberman breed on a one to one basis, as the instructor bred Dobermans and used her own dogs in class.

In 1978 Lana and Bob bought their first Doberman, a red and tan male whom they

named Shane. They began training Shane in obedience, going from there to dog shows in which they started to compete. Soon Lana had a C.D. on Shane, and it was decided, after watching the conformation classes at the shows, that they wanted to get involved in this area of dog showing, too.

In the autumn of 1978, Lana and Bob purchased Roblan's Dallas, a black and tan bitch, their first "show dog." At this time both of them became members of the Canadian Kennel Club and the Doberman Pinscher Club of Canada, and they started to learn more about their breed as they increased their attendance at dog shows. Their new veterinarian, Dr. John Reeve-Newson, was formerly a Doberman breeder and helped to encourage Lana and Bob although he himself had since switched to Borzois, becoming, with Dr. Richard Meen, owner of Kishniga Borzois, famous around the world for excellence.

In the summer of 1979, Lana and Bob started showing Dallas on a regular basis with a professional handler. She always placed in her class but never made it to a blue ribbon, causing her owners to feel that something must be lacking. So they discussed their feelings with Dr. Reeve-Newson and his partner Dr. Meen. After considerable discussion and soul searching, the decision was reached to spay Dallas and train her to compete in obedience rather than conformation. It was during this same conversation that it was pointed out to Lana and Bob that they needed to think and plan about what their goals of accomplishment and contribution to their breed might be. Their decision was reached to establish Simca Kennels, their goals and priorities being to breed Dobermans of the finest quality and conformation, emphasizing temperament, substance and good bone. At the same time it was decided that the breeding program would be held within close limits, litters being produced only when it was necessary to further the best interests of their own lines.

In June 1980, Lana and Bob met Hans Brunotte. Upon learning that they were in search of a really high quality Doberman bitch on which to found their kennel, he told them of a red bitch he had judged and admired in the United States. Faye and Gary Strauss were her owners; her name, Sherluck's Crimson N'Clover. As a novice at the time, Bob did not quite realize that this particular bitch would definitely not be for sale and that what Mr. Brunotte undoubtedly must have meant was that perhaps Mrs. Strauss would have some puppies or have some available soon. The next morning he was on the phone. Call it beginner's luck, being in the right place at the right time, or whatever you like! As fate would have it, Bob's call came on the morning after the Strausses had been discussing the fact that they did not really need Clover as a "special" since they wanted to give priority to campaigning their dog, Sherluck's L.B. Jake and felt that they could do him more justice if they were not campaigning a bitch, too. So, it seemed a sensible decision to let her go to a good show home where she would receive top priority. It took three weeks of daily telephone conversations between the four individuals involved for a decision to be reached, and that was that Faye Strauss would visit Toronto for a few days to see if she thought Crimson would be happy living with Lana and Bob. One week later, Clover obviously decided that life in Canada looked pretty good and since the two couples had developed a strong bond of friendship, Faye Strauss returned home, leaving Simca Kennels with their foundation bitch, Champion Sherluck's Crimson N'Clover, who was a daughter of Champion Wessyngtons Molock, C.D. (Champion Kay Hills Takeswon to Nowon-Sky-Raider's Misty Nite, she by Champion Marks-Tey's Hondo ex Damasyn The Sky Maiden) from Champion Moraga Hills Desert Wind (Champion Von Lieb's London-Champion Hy-Lo's Joan of Arc).

The only drawback to Lana and Bob's having purchased Clover at the time they did was that she was in the Top Twenty in the United States along with having Best in Specialty Show and Group placements; thus they could not compete with her in any more shows in the States that year, which dropped her just out of the Top Twenty. But, as Lana and Bob point out, her Canadian show career was to far more than make up for that!

Clover was entered in four shows where she became a Canadian champion during the autumn of 1980. At the same period, Roblan's Dallas completed her C.D. That was when

Lana and Bob became members of the Doberman Pinscher Club of America.

Clover was seriously campaigned in Canada during 1981, but on a limited basis, handled by Dr. Richard Meen. She wound up the year with numerous Group wins and was owner-handled to an All-Breed Best in Show. She became No. 6 Doberman in Canada.

Lana's and Bob's association with John Reeve-Newson and Dick Meen had created in them a liking for Borzois as well as Dobes, and soon Simca became the home of a lovely black and white male. This fact did not lessen the intensity of their Doberman interest, however, and their major thoughts of that period centered around finding the right mate for Clover, who would be bred in 1982.

Combining the thoughts of the Strausses and Lana and Bob, the choice was finally settled, and the dog for Clover was to be Champion Tolivar's Boo Radley Dob Mann, belonging to Irene and Edd Bivin.

Many changes took place at Simca during 1982, starting with Lana's and Bob's move from downtown Toronto to a farm with 125 acres just north of the city, where they have recently completed building their lovely new home. Clover's first litter of seven puppies was born in May of that year, the entire litter kept on the advice of John Reeve-Newson. The logic behind this is that when you are trying to establish a new line, the best way to learn about breeding is to watch the puppies as they grow and be able to see and note the changes they go through as they develop. Simca also added a third breed in 1982, a black Standard Poodle bitch puppy.

1983 saw the completion of the main kennel building, which is the last word in comfort and convenience. Also Clover's second litter arrived during April—ten this time, again sired by Boo Radley. Her first litter began Bob's and Lana's show careers, and by the end of the year, Simca had four new homebred Canadian champions. Two of these were owner-handled to their championships, plus two Best Puppy in Show and breed wins from the puppy classes over "specials." In September at the Doberman Pinscher Club of Canada National Specialty, Clover was third in the class of eleven brood bitches. The highlight of 1983 was when Champion Simca April Wine, a bitch from the first litter, won the Grand Prize Futurity over 165 puppies,

1▲   ▼2

1. Istvanhazi's Fantasy Miss Rigo at eight months old on her first day out in the ring, winning Best Puppy In Group at Trio Kennel Club. Never out before, not even in fun matches! Owned by Steve Rozinka, Pickering, Ontario.
2. Trollhattan's Fast Forward. "Billie" at eight months. Stunning young dog from Trollhattan Kennels, Phyllis and Emily Gratton, Truro, Nova Scotia.

becoming the first Canadian-bred to achieve this honor at the Doberman Pinscher Club of America National. April Wine was handled by Teresa Nail.

Solar

Solar Dobermans at Woodstock, Ontario are a family project belonging to Allan Marshall, his wife, Jane, and their daughter Maureen. The Marshalls, who have no grown dogs that are not champions, started raising Dobermans in about 1972 with the assistance of Dr. Wilfred Shute who guided them to the purchase of a male dog sired by Canadian Champion Schauffelein's Solar Wind, owned by Dr. Shute. When this dog completed his championship in three shows at less than twelve months of age, the Marshalls returned to the same kennel where they next purchased a black and tan bitch sired by Canadian Champion Schauffelein's Vintage Year. This elegant bitch soon finished her championship and the Marshalls bred her to Canadian Champion Jagermeister's Five Card Stud who was sired by Canadian Champion Seven Come Eleven, Canada's Top Dog in 1975. From the breeding of Canadian Champion Bar-Jak's Appolo Dawn to Jagermeister's Five Card Stud came three puppies, two females and one male. The Marshalls selected the female black and tan and registered her as Solar's Toronado. This young black beauty went to shows and won Best of Breed over "specials" on several occasions under American judges, such as Dr. Booth, and English judge Joe Braddon while she was still under nine months of age, becoming Doberman Pinscher Puppy of the Year in 1977.

During the following four years, Toronado was Top Doberman Bitch in Canada. Her winning continued at a steady rate and in 1980 she was selected Dog of the Year by the Doberman Pinscher Club of Canada. During 1983, she won four Bests in Show and many, many Groups and placements, attaining a total of close to 7,000 rating points. Thus she is Top Doberman Pinscher in Canada for '83 and very possibly No. 2 Working Dog with a high place among the all-breed winners as well. Allan Marshall comments, "I do not know of another Doberman Pinscher bitch who has acquired such a record at the shows as this one has done." Especially nice considering that "Tory" was raised by the Marshalls

and owner-handled in the ring.

The grandparents of "Tory" are Champion Schauffelein's Vintage Year who was Top Dog of the Top Twenty dogs in the U.S. and Jagermeister's Seven Come Eleven who was Canada's Top Dog in 1975.

The Marshalls also have in their kennel additional champions with excellent bloodlines, such as Champion Solar's Star Wars who was sired by Seven Come Eleven, and a two-year-old male sired by Canadian and American Champion Star Storm's Thunderbolt. This youngster won Best Puppy in Specialty at the Doberman Pinscher Club of Canada event judged by Donald Booxbaum.

Prior to the Dobermans, the Marshalls raised Boxers for 18 years, Mrs Marshall having presented one to her husband as a birthday gift early in their marriage. But from 1971 onward, it has been Dobermans only, so far as dog breeds are concerned, for this family.

Starstorm

Starstorm Dobermans, at St. Alberts, Alberta, began in 1973 with the purchase by Cec Ringstrom of a six-month-old Dobe bitch from Defender Kennels in Alberta. This was Daphne the Defender; the breeder from whom she was purchased was Lynell Korella. Cec and her ex-husband had decided on Dobes as their breed (after previous ownership of Toy Poodles) and very sensibly purchased the best bitch they could find from the top breeder in their area.

Daphne finished her championship quickly, and Doug Ringstrom put a U.D. on her even more quickly. She got her C.D., C.D.X. and U.D in a ten-month period with quite a number of Highs in Trial. She was also a Best in Show winner, but where Daphne really excelled was in the whelping box.

In her first litter, Daphne produced a Best in Show bitch, Champion Sunni the Defendress, and an excellent male who has also produced well, Champion Starstorm Santana. For Daphne's next litter it was decided to go back to her grandfather, American and Canadian Champion Highland Satan's Image, because of his producing record. This litter gave the Ringstroms American and Canadian Champion Starstorm Thunderbolt, American

CAPTIONS FOR PLATES 129 TO 144

Plate 129

1. Ch. Hotai Charlie, a top producer owned and bred by Virginia Markley, Hotai Kennels, Marion, Ohio, is dressed and ready for his "Lunar Patrol" duty.

2. Liberator's Casablanca at three weeks with friend. Pat Blenkey, owner, Harley, Ontario, Canada.

3. Dobe El Macho and his friend, Gus, catching forty winks. Both owned by Carol Chavez, Leavenworth, Kansas.

4. Champion Hotai Charlie always enjoys his cup of milk. Famous winner owned by Mrs. Virginia Markley, Marion, Ohio.

5. Bar-Lock's Ebony Talisman, C.D., WAC with owner Donna Blackburn, North Miami Beach, Florida. A typical loving Doberman.

6. Ch. Alfaro's Liquorish Cutty Sark, C.D.X., ROM at seven weeks old in the arms of his owner, Grace Joffe.

Plate 130

Ch. Gold Grove's Solitaire, daughter of Lone Eagle, handled by Cheri DiNardo, co-owner with her brother, Anthony D. DiNardo, III. Solitaire here is taking Best of Winners at the Albany Kennel Club, 1983. The DiNardos live in East Hartford, Connecticut.

Plate 131

1. At five weeks and six days of age, Homer Hill's First Page already is accustomed to being "stacked" in show pose. Bred and owned by Patrick and Colby Homer, Wheeling, West Virginia.

2. Courland Flashdance, by Am. and Can. Ch. Courland Bear Hug ex Todeldof Damasyn Gretchen, bred by Lorie J. Breazeale. Owned by Stephanie Taube, Alamo, California.

3. Ch. Liberator's Key Largo at six weeks, "learning to show." The earlier you start show training your promising puppy, the more easily he will learn! Pat Blenkey, owner, Wrath-Liberator Dobermans, Harley, Ontario, Canada.

4. This gorgeous 11-week-old puppy, with owner Dr. Anthony DiNardo, grew up to become Ch. Devil "D's Krista. Note the elegance of this youngster and the manner in which she sets up, despite her extreme youthfulness.

5. Caravista's Erin V. Datelis, pictured at four months of age, is owned by breeders Norman and Carol Carter, Hamlin, New York. Even though not yet of show age, this handsome puppy is already trained to stack and pose to best advantage. Sired by Ch. Edelhall Khansort of Amulet.

6. This is how promising baby Dobes should be taught to stack correctly in the show ring. Future Ch. Courland The Blushing Bride, at 10 weeks, is every inch the show dog as she poses with Jim Williams, owner of Ch. Greenlace's Pumpkin Patch. Owner, Johanna Gossett. Breeder and co-owner, Stephanie Taube, Alamo, California.

Plate 132

1. Enjoying one of the thrills of visiting New York City, Ch. Star Dobe's Irish Fantasy shares a buggy ride in Central Park with her handler, Bob Hastings. Don and Nora Gau, Honolulu, Hawaii, own this noted winning bitch.

2. Ryas Hugelhof Meridian at one year, in costume on Halloween night for his obedience class. Dave and Pat Cunningham, Vinemount, Ontario, Canada.

3. Mi Casa's Fiadora, snapped informally with her owner, Carol Luft, Tomball, Texas.

4. A loving send-off to a new home. Grace Joffe exchanging a kiss with four-month-old Liquorish Sheri's Velvet.

Plate 133

1. Ch. Wynterwynd's Rusti Nail (red) and daughter, Ch. Wynterwynd's Sierra Shadow. Photo by Ann Lanier.

2. Ch. Ro-Jan's Crisium Coty, owned by Jane Roppolo, Shreveport, Louisiana. By Gra-Lemor Copper Qualode (pointed) ex Gra-Lemor News Item. Photo by Skipworth Studios.

3. Ch. Brykris Tabu at two-and-a-half years of age with his breeder-owner-handler, Jo Ann James, Brykris Dobermans, Miami, Florida. Photo by Bill James.

4. June 21, 1975. Joe and Janet Lobb, Brucefield, Ontario, Canada, on their wedding day. With them is "Dobie," their first Doberman.

Plate 134

1. Bar-Lock's Angelfire going Highest Scoring in Trial at the Florida West Coast Doberman Pinscher Club Specialty, February 1984. Judge, Lena Danner. "Angel's" first time in the obedience ring. Currently being shown, with half her championship points already to her credit. Breeder-owner-handler, Donna Blackburn, Bar-Lock Dobermans, North Miami Beach, Florida.

2. Can. Ch. Mikadobe's Paris Polka, C.D.X., U.D.T. Sired by Ch. Mikadobe's Paris, Polka was 1980's No. 1 Doberman Pinscher, No. 1 Working Group, and No. 6 all-breed among Canadian obedience winners. A High in Trial winner. Owned and handled by Gertrude Payant, Montreal, Quebec, Canada. Photo courtesy of Mae Downing, Mikadobe Kennels.

3. Ch. Alisaton Damascus, C.D., by Ch. Gra-Lemor Demetrius v d Victor ex Ch. Alisaton's Kinderwicke, WAC. Note the beautiful head and expression of this gorgeous bitch as she holds her dumbbell. Bred by Gwen and JoAnn Satalino. Owned by Peggy Esposito and Gwen DeMilta.

4. Am. and Can. OT Ch. Duchess Danielle, II, WAC, famous obedience winner, owned by Richard Simmet, Eden Prairie, Minnesota.

Plate 135

1. Toni Leigh DiNardo, daughter of Dr. and Mrs. Anthony DiNardo, with a handsome Lone Eagle daughter. All of the DiNardo kids are great dog-show enthusiasts; all have competed successfully in Junior Showmanship.

2. Bayberry Lanning winning Best Junior Handler at the Doberman Pinscher Club of America Specialty, October 1983, with Ch. Lothlorien's High-Elven Rune, C.D.X., ROM. Owned by Bunny Lanning, Murray, Kentucky.

3. Ch. Carosel In the Mood of King Hill, by Ch. Marienburg's Sun Hawk ex Ch. Carosel In the Spotlight, C.D., ROM, handled here by 13-year-old Kelly Marquis who is winning Best Junior Handler at the Pilgrim Doberman Pinscher Club Specialty. Kelly won the 1983 Doberman Pinscher Club of America Award for Junior Showmanship with a total of 25 wins. She co-owns this lovely Dobe bitch with Susan King and Carol Selzle Petruzzo.

4. Angela De Hetre, age 14 years, winning Best Junior Handler at Nashville with Pamelot's Headliner of Versai. By Am. and Can. Ch. Lowenbrau Magnate ex Ch. Pamelot's Applause. Bred by Sherry Vert and Pamela De Hetre. Owners, Jim Sawyers and Angela De Hetre.

431

Plate 136

1. Civetta's You Win Again at five months old. Kay Martin, of Civetta Dobermans, owner.

2. Simca Doberman puppies, age three weeks. Lana Sniderman and Bob Krol, owners, Nobleton, Ontario, Canada.

3. A future champion from Serenade Kennels, by Ch. Royalmead's Joker's Wild ex Wynterwynd's Lady O'The Nite.

4. A Saeva-Dobe puppy from J. Theunissen's noted kennels in the Netherlands Antilles.

Plate 137

1. Doberman puppies of all four allowed colors. Sired by Beverly Capstick's Am. and Can. Ch. Misti Morn's Stormy Knight.

2. Teresa Thomas with two puppies from Ch. Damasyn The Russian ex Damasyn Remarkable. Teresa's mother, Terry Ferrari, was Terry Thomas, a famous model in the 1940's.

3. Lana Sniderman, co-owner of Simca Dobermans, with three-week-old Simca's Box Car Willie. Simca Kennels, Nobleton, Ontario, Canada.

4. Doberlyn's Scarlet Dream and Doberlyn's Mood Indigo at seven weeks. By Ch. Brown's B-Brian ex Am. and Can. Ch. Rosevale's Ebony Temptress, C.D. Breeder, Doberlyn Kennels, Robert and Bonnie Clarke, Ellington, Connecticut.

Plate 138

1. Ch. and OT Ch. Daphne The Defender and Ch. Defender's Raider, C.D. Both owned by Cec Ringstrom, St. Albert, Alberta, Canada.

2. Classic's Maxima Antares, U.D., showing fine form on a jump. Owned by Classic Dobermans, Harvey and Bettye Carter, Knoxville, Tennessee.

3. Ch. Carosel Musical Light, C.D.X., ROM, taking a jump with ease to show the form which gained C.D.X. honors. Carol Selzle Petruzzo, Carosel Dobes, Freehold, New Jersey.

4. Am. and Can. Ch. Classic's Eliza Doolittle, C.D. at five years of age. Owned by Harvey and Bettye Carter, Classic Kennels, Knoxville, Tennessee.

5. Am. and Can. OT Ch. Duchess Danielle II, WAC, in training. Richard Simmet, owner, Eden Prairie, Minnesota.

6. Gayamon The Brandy Alexander, C.D.X., Can. C.D., is being an Olympic Champion as she enjoys a swim. The first Doberman, owned by Jeff and Grace Joffe, who was so very instrumental in teaching them to love the breed. She is still part of their family.

Plate 139

1. Eric, owned by William and Charlene Benner, Rochester, New York, going over the high jump during a training session.

2. OT Ch. Duchess Danielle II, WAC, with owner-handler Richard Simmet of Eden Prairie, Minnesota.

3. Ch. Amulet's Luka of Sno-Glenn, C.D. completing his C.D. title. Pictured with owner Linda Krukar and judge Geraldine Sullivan. Luka is a fawn, or Isabella, Doberman.

4. Solo's Pride Phi Beta Kappa, C.D.X., WAC, born in 1977, by Bar-Lock's Starhawk, C.D. Owned by Wen Fray Dobermans, Wendy Serra, Fort Pierce, Florida.

Plate 140

1. Ch. Sherluck's Crimson N'Clover nursing her second litter, age two weeks. Simca Dobermans, Lana Sniderman and Bob Krol, Nobleton, Ontario, Canada.

2. First outing of Stehle von Wickens and Stehle Victoria at Stehle Kennels. D. Eschbach, owner, North Wagga, New South Wales, Australia.

3. Litter of 12 puppies bred and owned by England's famous Tavey Kennels, owned by Reg and Mary Barton.

4. "We want dinner, please!" is what these Dobe puppies seem to be saying. Owned by Grace and Jeff Joffe, Ft. Lauderdale, Florida.

5. Seven-week-old Dobe puppies at Maestro Kennels enjoying a bit of roughhousing. This 1982 snapshot is from Karen Vroom Parkhurst, Chino, California.

6. With never a thought of his future greatness, pictured at eight week's age is Ch. Encore's Black Rites, before it all became a reality. He became the sire of 29 champions and established a line all his own. A Dolph son, Rites was bred by Toni McMorris and owned by Mr. and Mrs. Donald V. Simmons.

Plate 141

1. Billmar's "B" litter in November 1981. Two have already finished and are multi-breed and Group winners. A third is pointed. By Ch. Kachina's Louisiana Man ex Windsong's Omen of Billmar. Bred by Captain M. E. (United States Navy, retired) and Mrs. Smith, Cleveland, Tennessee.

2. "Angel" seems a very appropriate call-name for this darling six-week-old puppy. Officially Bar-Lock's Angelfire, owned by Donna Blackburn, North Miami Beach, Florida.

3. With her litter, and her squeaky toy, this lovely Dobe bitch looks quite contented. Karen Vroom Parkhurst, owner, Maestro Kennels, Chino, California.

4. Littermates of the famous "Rico" at three weeks old. Courtesy of Jeff and Grace Joffe, Liquorish Dobermans, Ft. Lauderdale, Florida.

5. Doberman puppies outside for the first time survey the world through their fence. This is the first litter produced by Can. and Am. Ch. Sherluck's Crimson N'Clover. Owned by Simca Kennels, Lana Sniderman and Bob Krol, Nobleton, Ontario, Canada.

6. This adorable Dobe puppy is Simca's Blind Faith owned by the Simca Dobermans, Nobleton, Ontario, Canada.

Plate 142

Ch. Tarsha's Sir Mark, by Mark of Satans (Ch. Marks Tey Oliver—Corb's First Mate) ex Tarsha's Lady Bug (Ch. Schauffelein's Vintage Year—Can. Ch. Valkyries Charm of Windriver), during 1983 was an important winner, leading the breed at the state of Washington's most important shows. Adding a note of special interest to this is the fact that Mark's sire is a Doberman used by the police department for work on finding drugs and other contraband. Who says that show dogs do not have brains? Behind Mark and his sire are some of the finest, most successful show dogs in the country. Mark belongs to Robert Paynter, Mountlake Terrace, Washington.

1 ▶

2 ▶

3 ◀

4 ▶

PLATE 129

5 ◀

6 ▶

BEST OF
WINNERS

ALBANY
KENNEL CLUB

1983

ASHBEY

PLATE 130

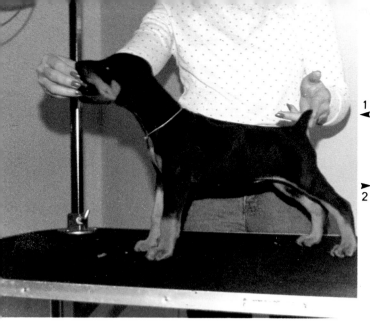

1 ▶

2 ▶

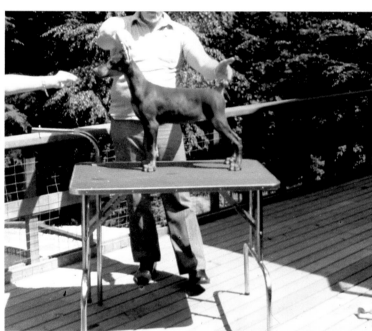

3 ▶

4 ▶

PLATE 131

5 ▶

6 ▶

1 ►

2 ►

PLATE 132

3 ►

4 ►

1
►

2
►

PLATE 133

3
►

4
►

PLATE 134

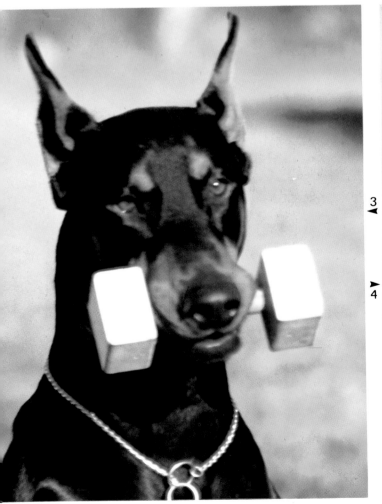

1

2

3

4

1 ▶
2 ▶

PLATE 139

3 ▶
4 ▶

1

2

3

4

PLATE 140

5

6

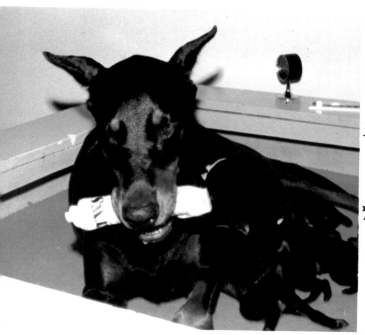

PLATE 141

PLATE 142

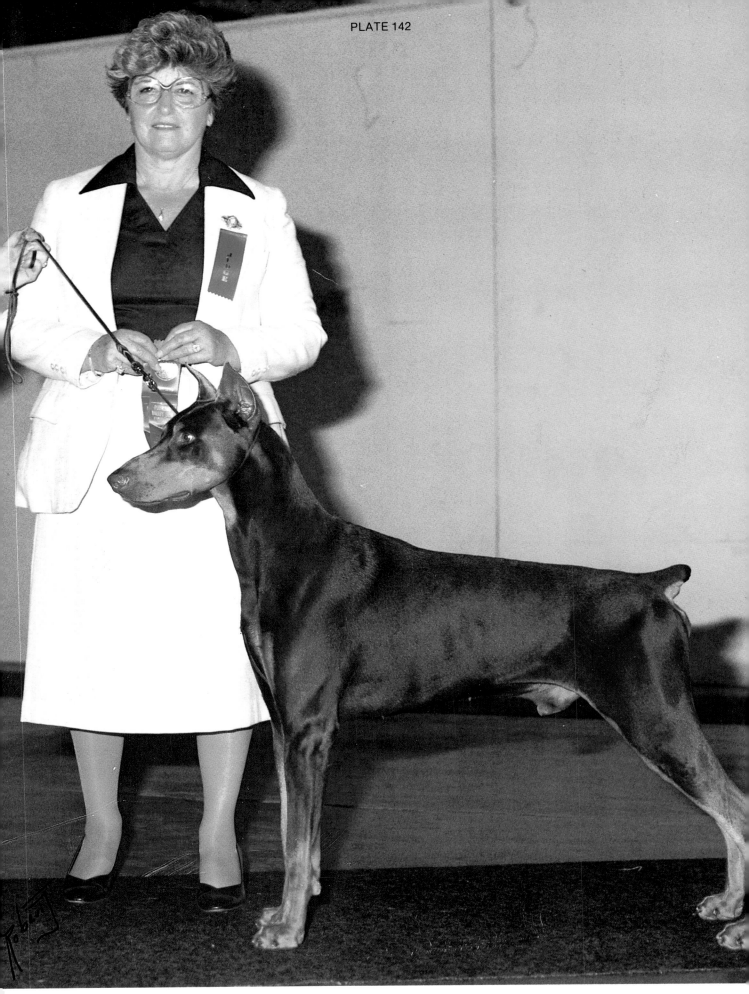

PLATE 144

1
2
3
4

Plate 143

1. Am. and Can. OT Ch. Duchess Danielle II, WAC. Owned by Richard Simmet, Eden Prairie, Minnesota, she is a very remarkable and talented member of this breed. Among her honors have been a "clean sweep" of the first three Doberman Pinscher Club of America Top Twenty in Obedience competitions! Here she is at the National in Dallas, scene of one of these triumphs.

2. Ch. Carosel Musical Light, C.D.X., ROM, the result of a father-to-daughter breeding (Ch. Damasyn the Troycen—Ch. Damasyn the Limelight), demonstrates brains as well as beauty. Bred by Carol Selzle Petruzzo, co-owner with Marjorie Hudson, Freehold, New Jersey.

Plate 144

1. Future Am., Can., Dom., Mex., and Int. Ch. Liquorish The Ron Rico, Am., Can., and Mex. C.D., ROM, having his first bath. It is quite safe to bathe puppies, when necessary, if it is done carefully and if the pups are completely dried. Grace and Jeff Joffe own Rico.

2. Bar-Lock's Angelfire at nine weeks with her ears done. Breeder-owner, Donna Blackburn, North Miami Beach, Florida.

3. Toria's Old Fashion Love Song at about three months. Stephanie J. Taube, Alamo, California. Photo taken in December, 1975.

4. Ch. Liberator's Key Largo at three months. A typical Wrath-Liberator puppy and a beautifully fronted one! By Ch. Schauffelein's Superior Odds ex Ch. Liberator's Breezy Spirit. Pat Blenkey, owner, Wrath-Liberator Dobermans, Canada.

1. Ch. Chassevente Deja Vu, in May 1979, winning a Best of Breed from judge Eleanor Evers. Owned by Don Clarke. Photo courtesy of John Griffith.
2. Alou Bo Brummel de Baviere, owned by Diane and Robert Dubois, winning first in the Puppy Working Group and Second in the regular Working Group under Robert S. Forsyth at eight months of age in 1983. A nice representative of Canadian Dobermans.
3. Can. Ch. Shinya's Scarlett Petticoat had 11 points including both "majors" as of May 1982. Handled here under judge Robert S. Forsyth for owner Kathleen Dailey. A quality bitch.

449

1▲   ▼2

1. Ch. Schauffelein's Vintage
   Year at two years of age.
   The famous "Goober," an
   American and Canadian
   champion and a dog of
   tremendous importance to
   the breed. Owned by Joey
   and Ron Purdy,
   Cheltenham, Ontario.
2. Five-day-old puppies by
   Ch. Schauffelein's Superior
   Odds ex Ch. Liberator's
   Breezy Spirit. Owned by
   Pat Blenkey, Harley,
   Ontario.

and Canadian C.D. Thunder did some nice winning for his owners, handled mostly by Larry Sinclair of Spokane, including multi-Best in Show wins, both all-breed and Specialty. He became a U.S. Top Twenty Dog and a Top Dog in Canada. But most important of all to his owners was his being a top producer. He died of cardiomyopathy in November 1981 at six years of age, leaving at least 70 champions in three countries with quite a few more still to finish. He was just being recognized for his excellence as a producer at the time of his death. Despite the considerable distance involved in traveling to Alberta, Cec Ringstrom was impressed with the number of breeders from the far south and from the east coast of the United States who did go to all that trouble, worry and expense of shipping all the way to western Canada!

At the time of this writing, Daphne is still alive and well. All told she gave her owners a total of nine champions and numerous obedience-titled children. Her pedigree was a combination of Ahrtal and Satan, and through the years that same combination has been kept going at Starstorm since it has proven so highly successful.

To date, Starstorm has produced 30 conformation champions, two obedience trial champions, and many C.D.X. and C.D. titled Dobes in nine litters. Even though just one litter a year is bred there, Starstorm is working to retain the quality Daphne brought them.

The Ringstroms together accomplished many honors with their dogs. Their marriage broke up during the 1980's, with Cec keeping the kennel and her interest in it very much alive.

Wrath-Liberator

Wrath Dobermans (named in honor of the top English Dobe, Champion Tavey's Stormy Wrath) came into being in Canada during 1963, although owners Pat and John Blenkey had been active in Dobermans in England since 1958.

On leaving England for Canada, they unfortunately had to part with their three English Dobes, but finding, after three weeks in their new homeland, that they simply could not live without a dog, they purchased a

Champion Alemap's Checkmate granddaughter. "Wrath," as she was called, turned out to be an exceptional obedience worker and chalked up many fine scores, quite quickly becoming Obedience Trial Champion Wrath's Stormy Rebel, U.D. Trained and handled by John Blenkey, she was the Top Obedience Doberman in Canada for 1966, '67 and '68 and could well have been top all-breeds had the official Canadian points system for obedience come into effect at that time. She did, however, receive the Ontario Obedience Association award for Top Utility Dog, all-breeds, with an average score of 198½. She also became the foundation bitch for Wrath Dobermans, providing both working ability and outstanding temperament.

Bred to Champion Bramalea's Argonaut, C.D., she produced another obedience great, Obedience Trial Champion Wrath's Apolda Blunderbuss, U.D., Bermudian C.D. "Asta" took over from her dam as Top Obedience Doberman for the next three years and was a very fast, exuberant worker. Trained and handled by John Blenkey, the two worked together as a perfect team, drawing considerable interest from the obedience fancy.

Bred just once to Champion Schauffelein's Extra Special, Asta produced Champion and Obedience Trial Champion Wrath's Cabanuela, U.D. and Champion Wrath's Campeador, C.D. Cabanuela in turn produced three champions from Champion Schauffelein's Troll Arabasque (her half-brother), which included Champion Wrath's Elegancia, C.D., named Doberman Pinscher Club of Canada 1971 Puppy of the Year, and the foundation bitch for Karalynn Kennels.

While many dogs in those early years did not reach show homes, others did make a significant impact on the obedience ring. From 1966-1976, in a very limited breeding program, twelve champions were produced out of thirty-eight puppies, with eighteen earning obedience degrees, including five Obedience Trial Champions!

The purchase of Champion Schauffelein's Outrigger, a younger brother to the famed Vintage Year, exerted a great influence on the kennel, and Pat will always be indebted to Joey and Ron Purdy for the opportunity of owning such a truly lovable dog. "Dax" produced a number of fine champions, the best known of which is Champion Karalynn's Black Liberator, T.T. (ex Obedience Trial Champion Karalynn's Black Amanda, U.D.), a multi-breed and Group winner and winner, under Dr. Peter Emily, of the 1980 Doberman Pinscher Club of Canada Specialty, the largest to date. Owned by Brian Casey, Liberator Dobermans, "Luger" has since proven to be one of the area's leading sires. Used at stud on a limited basis, he has to date twenty-two champions (including two U.S. breed winners) with a number of other progeny needing only points to finish.

Among Luger's leading youngsters, bred by Larralyn and Dave McKay (Ambermark) out of their lovely Champion Hugelhof Wishing Ring are Champion Tennessee Tailgunner, T.T., owned by the McKays and Frank Jones, a multi-breed winner and Group placer; Champion Ambermark Accolade for Pip, multi-breed, Group and Best in Show winner; and Champion Trouble Times Two, C.D.X., T.T., a super obedience worker owned by Barb and Doug Lane.

The amalgamation in 1977 of Wrath Dobermans, by this time operated exclusively by Pat Blenkey, and Brian Casey's Liberator Dobermans has resulted in more involvement in conformation shows. Since that time, of thirty-two puppies born, two dozen have earned their championship, the majority of them handled to their wins by Brian. In addition, Wrath-Liberator Dobes are competing in obedience and two are beginning to work on Schutzhund I.

Temperament, soundness and health are of prime importance to these breeders, and while Pat and Brian are pleased with the percentage of champions produced, they are even prouder of the fact that all of their dogs have made stable and loving family companions.

With a maximum of two litters a year, linebreeding (and very occasional inbreeding) has continued from the original foundation bitch, "Wrath," using such prominent sires as Champion Schauffelein's Vintage Year, Champion Vince von Avery, Champion Amulet's Cedric v Glucklicke (their first outcross), and of course their own Champion Karalynn's Black Liberator, T.T.

Among the notables here are Champion Wrath's Grand Slam, foundation bitch for Liberator and the 1978 Doberman Pinscher Club of Canada Dam of the Year. Bred once to Champion Vince von Avery she produced an all-champion litter of five including Champion Liberator's Brigantine, C.D.X., T.T., 1978 Doberman Pinscher Club of Canada Puppy of the Year; and Champion Liberator's Brass n Sass, Best of Breed Winner and foundation bitch for Sterling Kennels.

Champion Wrath's Honest Pleasure has produced all champions from three litters, including Champion Wrath's Pleasure Seeker, Doberman Pinscher Club of Canada 1981 Puppy of the Year; and Champion Wrath's Knight of Liberty, now working towards Schutzhund I. These both were sired by Black Liberator.

Champion Wrath's Honour Bound, C.D., produced from two litters, both of which were sired by Black Liberator, and all but one of the youngsters grew up to become champions. These include Champion Wrath's Major Leaguer, Doberman Pinscher Club of Canada Best Opposite Sex Puppy of the Year; Champion Wrath's Irish Cream, a Best of Breed winner owned by Carla Kowalchuk of Thunder Bay; and Champion Wrath's Power Play, C.D., T.T., an excellent obedience worker.

Champion Wrath's Lively Action has produced Champion Wrath's Cannonball Run, T.T., a multi-breed and Group winner and Award of Merit winner at the Doberman Pinscher Club of Canada Specialty 1982; also Champion Wrath's Ragtime, Doberman Pinscher Club of Canada 1982 Puppy of the Year. These both were sired by Champion Ryas Anticipation, C.D., T.T.

The newest future stars are Champion Ambermark Accolade for Pip, a Best in Show winner at 14 months and a U.S. Best of Breed winner at 11½ months "Cola," still not yet two years old, will be campaigned starting in 1984 as we write, and Champion Wrath's Midas Touch who recently completed his title at seven-and-a-half months of age with three Best Puppy in Show along the way.

One of Canada's leading Doberman kennels, Wrath-Liberator had the distinction of being named Doberman Pinscher Club of Canada Breeder of the Year in 1972, 1978, 1979 and 1980. And No. 2 Kennel in 1981 and 1982.

1. Can. Ch. Trollhattan's Servica, "Serrah" to her friends, one of Trollhattan's current winners. Phyllis and Emily Gratton, Nova Scotia.

2. Can. Ch. Solar's Toronado ("Tory" to her friends) is by Can. Ch. Jagermeister's Five Card Stud ex Can. Ch. Bar-Jak's Appolo Dawn. During 1983 she won four all-breed Bests in Show and many Group placements, attaining a total of nearly 7,000 rating points, making her Top Doberman in Canada well up in the Working Dog and all-breed ratings as well. Owned by Solar Dobermans, the Marshalls, Woodstock, Ontario.

453

1▲ ▼2

1. Ch. Dixie von Mannerheim, one of Dr. Wilfred Shute's famous early homebred Best in Show winners.
2. A four-dog sled team consisting of Joy's Blue Lady Tu, C.D.X., TT and her offspring, Ch. Joy's Doctor Cassio, C.D., TT, Cassio's Tar Baby, and Cassio's Prinz. These dogs are owned and were bred by John and Joy Leiskau of Baden, Ontario.

454

This two-dog sled team, comprised of Can. Ch. Hill Street Blue Yasha, C.D., TT and Joy's Victory Chimes, C.D., TT, is owned by Gary and Mary Lovie of Waterloo, Ontario.

Doberman Sled Dog Racing in Canada

Recently judging at a Canadian dog show, I was intrigued to have one of the exhibitors tell me, later in the day, that the excellent show bitch I had taken from the classes to Best of Breed over a strong turn-out of "specials" is part of a highly successful sled dog team of Dobermans as well.

These fanciers, Gary and Mary Lovie of Waterloo, Ontario, along with another couple, John and Joy Leiskau of Baden, Ontario, are active participants in this sport along with being Doberman owners. They start out with their dogs each year as soon as snow is settled on the ground.

Usually, in one session, the teams cover distances of from seven to ten miles during the week, with longer runs from between ten and fifteen miles on weekends. The Dobermans themselves seem unaffected by the cold; the humans prefer not going out when the temperature falls below -20.

Most of the formal races, Mary Lovie tells us, are originated by the fanciers of the northern breeds designed to promote those breeds. Thus the Dobermans are not always welcome participants. However, when permitted to compete, they make their presence strongly felt and do Dobermans proud, as evidenced by some of the racing they were able to enter during the 1983-84 season.

For example, one race consisted of three dogs for three miles and five dogs for five miles. In the three-dog race, two of the Dobes were participants in one team, all three in another. These two teams came in second and first respectively.

For the second part of the event, the Dobe folks had one team consisting of four Dobermans. This four-dog team not only came in first, but did so very well ahead of the other eight teams also in competition.

Mary Lovie speaks of the fact that these dogs often all work together in obedience as well as in the sledding, and that they spend free time romping and playing together. She feels this to be among the reasons the dogs perform so smoothly together as a team.

Ch. Ebonaire's Laurel, by Ch. Damasyn Bo-Tairic of Ardon ex Ebonaire's Betsy Ross, C.D. was from Bo-Tairic's first litter. She was owned by the late famous dog photographer, Alton Anderson, who took this picture.

CHAPTER EIGHT

The Doberman in Argentina

It was during the 1950's that the first Dobermans imported to Argentina arrived from Europe brought over by some families well established in Buenos Aires. One of the pioneers of the breed was Mr. Mendez Chavarria, and this small new animal population was the start of Doberman breeding in this area. The rise to popularity of the Doberman there was underway at the beginning of the 1960's when Mr. Jorge Hess, Haus Thuring Kennels, imported from Germany the blue male, Arthur V. Forrell, followed later by the red male, Haldo v Furstenfeld, to help the betterment of the breed already living in Argentina.

At the beginning of the 1970's, Mr. Jorge Galdiz imported from the United States the black male, Sunset's Johaan of Manorie, a descendant of both Champion Emperor of Marienland and Champion Dictator v Glenhugel. Also from the United States came the red bitch, Sunset's Rhiengold, to Von Duc Kennel.

At this same time more importations were arriving from Germany to Mr. Tabieze's Lupay Kennel: the black male Ulino v. Furstenfeld and Una v. Furstenfeld. Then from Norway came the black bitch Zandra v Nordem Stamm. In 1974, Tereza and Eduardo Ustariz, Doblado Grande Kennels, decided to try with the English bloodlines purchasing the

black female Tavey's Etoil. She was undoubtedly the foundation bitch of the modern Doberman in Argentina which soon surpassed the German type there in popularity.

Argentina's Golden Era of Dobermans began about 1973. Mr. Jayme Broitmann Valdez decided to import from the United States, his choice being the black male Marienburg's Genghis Khan, a son of Demetrius. This male was then sold by Mr. Valdez to Arminda and Ricardo Cavalli, owners of the Mandinga Kennels. Better heads started to appear, better size, excellent angulation and really beautiful style. The importations to Mandinga continue, with the next one a red female, Marienburg's Red Mary, a daughter of Red Baron.

In 1978, Dr. Hector A. Iriarte also imported from the United States, in this case Altar's Nemesis v Amulet, a black male sired by Edelhall Gigolo of Amulet. He was by Tarrado's Flair.

In 1979 Mr. Victor Dalessandro imported Altar's Nemo v Amulet, and the importations have continued without interruption since then. Favored especially among Argentinian breeders are descendants of the magnificent Sun Hawk.

Mr. and Mrs. Ustariz brought to Argentina the black male Alexander Brirics of Mikater. Mr. C. Marchese imported the black male Marienburg's Tyron (by Champion Marienburg's Lone Eagle), followed by Titian Barque Sun Shade (by Champion Marienburg Sun Hawk), and still later the red bitch Marienburg Sunlit Sherry, again by Sun Hawk, this one from Marienburg's Only One.

Mr. Tashiro, owner of the Samurai Kennel, brought to Argentina the handsome Marienburg's Cannon, a full brother to Marienburg's Mary Hartman. He brought also the black female Echonan's Athena v Exodus.

In 1979 Mr. Genoud, owner of the La Promesa Kennel, brought to Argentina the red male, Damasyn The Russian Redbill; and Argentina's most recent import as we write was to the Dannydobes Kennel, owned by Mr. Daniel Garcia and Mr. D. Riccio—Gold Groves Only Mold, a red son of Champion Marienburg's Lone Eagle.

At the moment the Doberman is the most popular breed in Argentina, with about three thousand dogs yearly recorded in their stud book.

Hawk's Wizard Witch, C.D., owned by William and Marcy L. Shatner. The head that got the Shatners' Belle Reve Kennels and Karen Parkhurst's Maestro Dobes together! This lovely bitch was bred to Augustein's Mr. Papadopolus, owned by Karen Vroom Parkhurst, bringing Karen back into active participation in the Dobe world after more than 10 years of just enjoying her dogs at home.

CHAPTER NINE

Doberman Pinschers in Brazil

Haus Viking Dobermans came into being during 1956 when their owner, Mrs. Suzanne Blum of San Paulo, Brazil, imported her first male from France, Flip de la Moliere, immediately followed by a foundation bitch from Recifand (north of Brazil), her name If Tabajara Do Norte. From these two were born the first Haus Viking litter.

Many importations from Europe have been made over the years. From Germany in 1958 came the first of several German Dobes purchased by Mrs. Blum: the male, Toxi Germania; another male, Arko v Muhleneck; Reby and Sonny von Forell; Juanita von Frankenhorse; Cherie von Heurocke; Don Juan von Heurocke; Sjarai von Frankenhorst; and, from Holland in 1983 Geba Goldjim von Diaspora.

Even with so many European importations, Mrs. Blum always has bred her bitches to the best American imports. The number of her homebred champions is now past eighty, and many are the thrilling victories these homebreds have earned!

Mrs. Blum was Number One Doberman Breeder for the years 1970, 1971, 1972 and 1973, which speaks well for her success.

Pent

Pent Kennels in Brazil are owned by two of the most dedicated dog fanciers one could possibly know. They are Evaline and Jaime Martinelli, and their love for all breeds is well known as they have been highly successful with Lhasa Apsos, Borzoi, Springer Spaniels, Kerry Blue Terriers, Norwegian Elkhounds, Poodles, and others. Mr. Martinelli is an exhibitor and excellent handler of all breeds, but as a breeder he specializes in Doberman Pinschers and Boxers.

The Martinellis' involvement with Dobes began in 1976 when they visited the Marienburg Kennels in the United States. From this friendship many importations began, the first of which to arrive in Brazil was named Marienburg's Brazil, a top sire and a top winner as well. He was soon followed by Marienburg's Star Streak, Mary Hartman's litter sister, who tragically died at only nine months of age. Immediately after this loss, Mr. Martinelli replaced her with "Missy," more formally known as Champion Tanre's Gilda von Marienburg, who had an exciting show career winning in all-breed and Specialty competition and who is now enjoying retirement.

The Martinellis really liked working with the Marienburg bloodlines, and so two more Dobes from there were purchased: Champion Marienburg Council of Fire and Marienburg's Ebony Charm. Council of Fire was a highly successful stud in Brazil, then was later sold to Mr. Ramon Podesta in Chile, where, after gaining his Chilean title, he became an outstanding producer.

Next the Martinellis, with help from Mrs. Chris Baum in the United States, selected the outstanding bitch Champion DiJadobe's Chelsea. She has become a Best in Show winner and recently has been bred to Champion Koven's Westminster, producing a highly promising black girl, High Hopes of Pent Kennels.

Mr. Martinelli's background as a Doberman breeder goes all the way to 1956 when he and his father imported a couple of them from Holland, during which period they bred more than thirty litters. The change in type has been radical by now, however, with the American bloodlines becoming increasingly dominant in the breed and in Pent Kennels.

S. C. Kennels

S. C. Kennels are owned by Ana Maria and Sergio Capps and located at Goiania (Goia's State) in Brazil's midwest. Numerous other

1. At an important show in Brazil, Frank Grover from the U.S.A. is judging. Best of Breed, Ch. Pancho Red Midas von Henik; Best of Opposite Sex, Ch. Bruma von Henik. Both owned by Von Henik Dobermans, Alice and Juan Carlos Di Lucca, Curitiba.

2. The exciting 1983 breeding! Ch. Bruma von Henik, sent to the U.S. by Von Henik Kennels especially for breeding to Ch. Hotai Copper Tattoo, pictured together here.

Doberman breeders and their kennels are to be found here, whose interest has been generated by Mr. Capps's enthusiasm for the breed.

Sergio Capps acquired his first dog in 1967. Soon thereafter he had decided that Doberman Pinschers would be his show breed, and he became increasingly involved with it. Having acquired a well-known German-bred male, Champion Bodo von Olderburg, the winner of nineteen all-breed Bests in Show, Mr. Capps's name was from then on kept before the public as one of the most prominent breeders and exhibitors in his country.

In 1969 Mr. Capps started to judge, an occupation which he enjoys, and he is very active now as a Working Group judge and as a breeder.

1974 was the year in which Mr. Capps founded the Doberman Department of the Kennel Club Paulista (San Paulo State Kennel Club), and immediately thereafter he and some fellow breeders founded the Club Bandeirante Do Doberman (San Paulo State's Doberman Club), one of the most important clubs in Brazil.

Having moved his household to Goias, in spite of his already active schedule he founded the Doberman Club of Goias State (D.C.G.S.) and the Goias State Kennel Club (G.S.K.C.). He is President of the Board of the D.C.G.S. and the President of the G.S.K.C. Mr. Capps also is President of the Board of the Doberman Club of Brazil.

In 1973 Mr. Capps made a trip to the United States, spending three months visiting kennels and people, becoming acquainted personally with many Doberman people, and helping to arrange the importation of some outstanding dogs to Brazil and other parts of South America. Soon after that he became a member of the Doberman Pinscher Club of America. Since then he has never missed a National Specialty and the opportunity to represent his country at these events.

Mr. Capps has imported, for his own kennel, a number of handsome Dobes from the United States. Outstanding among them have been Champion Marienburg Sun Bonnet, Champion Damasyn Darcy, and Alisaton Time Out v. Damascus. For three consecutive years he won Best in Show at the National Specialty in Brazil, working only with

bloodlines from the above three outstanding kennels. He never breeds more than two litters a year and is proud that his homebreds have included Best in Show and Specialty Best of Breed winners. Mr. and Mrs. Capps were honored this year at the National where they were ranked as Number One breeders, all breeds, for 1983; and a female of their breeding, Champion S. C. Mama's Mariella, won the trophies offered for No. 1 Working Dog and No. 4 All Breed for 1983.

Undoubtedly Ana Maria and Sergio Capps are two of the most serious, competent, and interested breeders and exhibitors in their country.

Von Henik

Von Henik Kennels are owned by Alice and Juan Carlos Di Lucca, located in Curitiba-Parana, and are undoubtedly among the most important of the Brazilian kennels breeding Doberman Pinschers. Involvement with the breed for this couple began in 1969, and the first litter at Von Henik arrived in 1970. Since then many champions have been bred by this very charming couple.

In 1974 these folks imported from Germany (Mr. Di Lucca's homeland) the Doberman female Champion Kenia von Zulligain, who was bred to Champion Altar's Midas, son of Demetrius. This produced one of the leading Brazilian winners, Champion Pancho Red Midas von Henik, who is also a Top Producer and winner of 23 times Best in Show.

In 1980 Carlos Rojas, from the United States, sent to von Henik the lovely Champion Zeitlin Calypso von Kerry, who arrived bred to Champion Barchet Fiddler On The Roof. In 1983, Champion Bruna von Henik was sent to the United States to be bred to Champion Hotai Copper Tattoo, and, as might be expected, the Brazilian Doberman Fancy is all astir to see the results of this par excellence breeding.

In eleven years of work, the Di Luccas have produced an impressive 33 champions at von Henik, of which five are all-breed Best in Show winners.

As might be expected, the von Henik dogs are always to be found in the National Rankings. Mr. Di Lucca's main pride, though, is undoubtedly the record held with the C.D.R.D. (Brazilian Doberman Club) with their wins as Number Two Breeder and No. 3 Stud Dog. From the 10 Best Dams, Mr. Di Lucca was breeder of No. 2, No. 4 and No. 5. From the 10 Top Winning Males, he bred No. 1, No. 9 and No. 10. From the ten Top Winning Females, he bred No. 10. Very nice going indeed for 1983's National Ranking of the Doberman in Brazil!

The kennel accommodates fourteen adult dogs, of which eleven are brood bitches—one an eleven-year-old veteran dog, one a ten-year-old veteran bitch, and a stud dog.

Von Schloss

Von Schloss Kennels, owned by Umberto and Sonia Palumbo, began with the acquisition in 1974 of their foundation bitch, Champion Graca De Belafonte, from Mrs. Suzanne Blum. She was an excellent dam, and she now lives her happy retirement in the Palumbo household as a very respected family member. She was also a winner who has to her credit 17 Specialty Bests of Breed, 15 Group Firsts, and two all-breed Bests in Show. Her breeding to the Martinelli's Champion Brazil von Marienburg, son of the great Champion Marienburg Sun Hawk, produced a litter of ten, six males and four females. Six of these puppies became champions, which is certainly nice going. Two of this litter deserve very special acclaim. They are Champion Arabelle von Schloss, who won an all-breed Best in Show from Joe Brandon of England, and Champion Arko von Schloss, who was undoubtedly the best male bred by the Palumbos. He was the only Dobe recorded to win three times consecutively the great National Specialty, first under Mr. Walter Hensel (Germany), second under Mrs. Margaret Kilburn (U.S.A.), and third under Mrs. Ilona Ostenk-Schenk (Holland). Arko was No. 1 all-breed male in 1980 and again in 1981, having competed in only eight shows.

In 1979, with Mrs. Jane Kay's help, the Palumbos imported from the U.S.A. Champion Koven's Westminster, by Lieb's London ex Champion Bar-Lok's Evening Star. They bred their foundation bitch Graca to him and from her litter of ten—eight males and two females,—six completed their titles, all of them Specialty winners, Best of Breed and Group winners.

From these Champion Max von Schloss was the most successful, his winnings alone

keeping the Palumbos for three consecutive years among the ten best breeders of the year according to the breed's National Ranking.

Champion Graca De Belafonte was bred twice more for a total of four litters in her lifetime. In addition to the above two litters she was bred once to her son, Champion Arko von Schloss, which produced seven puppies; one of which, a very special female, was kept to take over for her dam in the von Schloss breeding program. This is Fabiola von Schloss, who gives every indication of being one who will follow in the footsteps of her illustrious mother!

The fourth breeding of Graca was to Champion Koven's Westminster again, eight puppies the result this time. Two already have become champions and some of the others are on their way.

With so many happy memories, the Palumbos will always feel deep gratitude to this wonderful bitch, Graca, for all she did and still is doing to keep this kennel in a position of such prominence.

Braz. Ch. Damasyn Darcy, owned by Sergio de Souse Capps, Goiania.

CAPTIONS FOR PLATES 145 TO 160

Plate 145

1. Shady Acres Hurrahcaine, Sch.H. III, FH, AD, giving an excellent display of courage and fearlessness during Schutzhund work with owner-trainer Ken Howe, Ft. Lauderdale, Florida.

2. Shady Acres Destiny's Bliss, C.D., Sch.H. III, VB at Dallas DVG Championship in November 1983. Nanci Little, owner-breeder. Bliss placed third in Sch.H. II championship competition.

3. Schutzhund Club practice, featuring Ch. Lothlorien's High-Elven Rune, C.D.X., ROM, working towards earning her degree. Bunny Lanning, Murray, Kentucky, owner.

4. Shady Acres Endless Summer, C.D., Sch.H. III, VB, WH, AD; pictured with Phil Hoelcher, decoy, and Anita Chandler, owner, Miami, Florida.

Plate 146

1. Ch. Queensover Pearl's Retort, a Black Rites daughter, is a champion-producing bitch owned by Lynn Phillips. Don Simmons handling her to Winners at Old Dominion in 1978.

2. Warjo's D'Lite taking Winners Bitch under judge Lynette Saltzman, handled by Colby Homer at Penobscot Valley Kennel Club, 1983. Breeders-owners, Joan and Warren Thompson, Warjo's Dobermans, Gorham, Maine.

3. Ch. Charalane' Black Sabbath, by Ch. Tedell's Black Walnut ex Kay Hill's Monetta, owned by C. N. Waterfield. Pictured at Plainfield in 1973. Photo courtesy of Jane Kay.

4. Ch. Maple Meadow's Fancy Pants belongs to Linda Willhoit and was shown to the title by Jane Forsyth.

5. Ch. Beauland Naturally Rites, a champion-producing Black Rites daughter, owned by Mr. and Mrs. Roy Shulman. Photo courtesy of Don Simmons, handling.

6. Chicago International, 1982. Ch. Elysian's Brielle, handled by Nancy Sheehan Martin, winning Best of Breed under judge Robert Forsyth for owner Leslie Leddo. Photo courtesy of the Forsyths.

Plate 147

1. Ch. B.J.'s Gift of Joy, handled by Monroe Stebbins for owner Bill Farnum.

2. Ch. Morwyn The Velvet Lady, owned by Frema Kennels, Fred and Alma Stewart, Hickory, North Carolina. Handled by Betty Brucker.

3. Ch. Regulus of Marks-Tey with J. Monroe Stebbins.

4. Ch. Brierpatch's Christmas Dream, owned by Tonja J. Chiles, is by Ch. Briarwood's Yancy Jon ex Ch. Kearney's Joyeaux Noel. Litter sister to Ch. Brierpatch's Feliz Navidad. This bloodline goes back to the great bitch, Ch. Redlyn's Touch of Class.

5. Ch. Beaulane The Union Jack, a Paris son ex Ch. Beaulane Touch of Sin. A Group-winning producer of champions owned by Shirley Hitter. Photo courtesy of Mae Downing.

6. Ch. Briarwood's Yancy Jon, by Mikadobe's Cupid ex Bremon's Cracklin' Rosie, is the sire of seven champions. Owned by Tonja and Jocelyn Chiles.

Plate 148

1. Passing the courage test with flying colors is Shady Acres Persuasion, U.D.T., WAC, Sch.H. III, FH, VB, WH, AD, at the Schutzhund Trial in Miami, Florida, April 1981. Nancy Little, owner-trainer, Miami.

2. Shady Acres Endless Summer, C.D., Sch.H. III, VB, WH, AD, displaying excellent form working with Phil Hoelcher. Owned by Anita Chandler; bred by Nanci Little.

3. Ziegfried v. Stoberhai, Sch.H. I, owned by Bob and Jonni Dear, Vero Beach, Florida. Photo by Fred Adams.

4. Ch. Lothlorien's High-Elven Rune, C.D.X., ROM, preparing to follow in the paw-prints of her sire and dam as she works towards her Schutzhund degree. Lothlorien and Cirdan Kennels; photo courtesy of Bunny Lanning.

Plate 149

1. Jonni Dear, Vero Beach, Florida, with Nero v. Stoberhai, C.D., Sch.H. II and her husband, Bob Dear, with Nero's son, Ziegfried v. Stoberhai, Sch.H. I. The Dears are active and very enthused over Schutzhund training and work with their Dobes. Photo by Fred Adams.

2. Some of the Shady Acres Dobermans owned by Anita Chandler, Miami, Florida.

Plate 150

1. Array Exclusive, C.D. at Greater Clark County dog show judged by Robert Forsyth. Owned by Beth Wilhite and Judith Bingham.

2. Ch. Jaymar's Vixen of Rehbar, owned by Cheryl Green and Dr. Harvey and Bettye Carter, Knoxville, Tennessee. Handled by Betty Brucker to Best of Breed at Kennesaw Kennel Club, May 1979.

3. Ch. Elexa's Final Flair of Selena, owned by Shirley McCoy, taking Best of Winners at Old Dominion in 1978. Handled by Jane Forsyth.

4. Ch. Wynterwynd's Stardust Dream, owned by Jim and Diane Urban, Brazoria, Texas. Handled by Betty Brucker.

Plate 151

1. Ch. Rosecroft The Victorian finished her title in September 1978. Handled by Jane Forsyth for owners Sam and Pat Glunt, Carlisle, Pennsylvania.

2. Cara's Mandi de Scudamore, handled by Terry Lazzaro Hundt, taking Best of Winners at Long Island Kennel Club in 1979.

3. Am. and Can. Ch. Wyntuck Sweet Athena, owned by Helen Fordyce, Okolona, Mississippi. Handled by Betty Brucker and here taking the points at the Illini Doberman Pinscher Club Specialty in June 1979.

4. Ch. Kearney's Joyeaux Noel winning the Working Group at Muncie Kennel Club, 1983, for owners Ruth Kearney and Ellen Fetter, Lima, Ohio.

5. Ch. Triadel's High Flyer, by Ch. Encore's Black Rites ex Ch. Triadel's Star Route of Kay Hill. This Black Rites son was many times a champion producer. Don Simmons handling.

6. Ch. Beauland the Legacy, one of Black Rites's champion children, out of Beaulane the Gypsy Moth. Two finished from her litter. Photo courtesy of Don Simmons, Silver Spring, Maryland.

Plate 152

1. Ch. Knox's Carbon Copy, C.D.X., TD, ROM, Sch.H. III, FH, AD locates the agitator during Schutzhund trials after searching five other blinds. Bill and Susan Knox, owners.

2. Shady Acres Persuasion, U.D.T., WAC, Sch.H. III, FH, VB, WH, AD during Schutzhund trials. Nanci Little, owner-trainer, Miami, Florida.

3. "Justin" (Marel's Toast to Jack Daniels) "hangs out" at co-owner Charles Guardascione's service station during the day, considering himself to be a guard dog.

4. Ch. Red Sun's Notorious showing his stuff as a working dog. Owned by John and Rita Armonia, Red Sun Dobermans, Hopewell, New Jersey.

Plate 153

1. Good form displayed by "Caine" (Shady Acres Hurrah-caine, Sch.H. III, FH, AD) for owner-trainer Ken Howe during Schutzhund workout.

2. The very famous Schutzhund bitch, Shady Acres Persuasion, U.D.T., WAC, Sch.H. III, FH, VB, WH, AD, bred by Anita Chandler. By Amerbrit's Valient ex Chandler's Second Chance, C.D. Owned by Nanci Little, Miami, Florida.

3. Shady Acres Hurrahcaine, Sch.H. III, FH, AD, by Ch. Dobe's Reward of Maestro, C.D.X., Sch.H. II ex Shady Acres Persuasion, U.D.T., WAC, Sch.H. III, FH, VB, WH, AD. Owned and trained by Ken Howe, Ft. Lauderdale, Florida.

4. Lothlorien's Galadriel II, C.D.X., Sch.H. I, at the Bluff City Schutzhund Trial, Memphis, Tennessee. Bunny Lanning, owner.

Plate 154

1. Tasha of Talacon with her handler, Robert Forsyth.

2. Pamelot's Fast Eddie is the dog who introduced Marilyn Sabat of Santa Barbara, California to Dobermans! A son of Alisaton's Rufino (Am. and Can. Ch. Schauffelein's Vintage Year—Ch. Alisaton's Kinderwicke) ex Pamelot's Verenda (Am. and Can. Ch. Schauffelein's Troll Arabasque—Can. Ch. Sabra Sweetheart of Sigma Chi, C.D.), he has been shown only three times since coming to California, and twice in Michigan before that.

3. Elysian's Brio taking Best of Winners at Danville Kennel Club, 1982. Owned by Wally and Tom Pollock, Hoboken, New Jersey.

4. Ch. Henlon's Martial Music, a multi-Best-in-Show winner and the sire of many champions. Also a Top Twenty winner. By Ch. Brown's B-Brian ex New Era's Cinnamon Hexe. Bred by Warren and Rita Henlan. Owned by Mr. and Mrs. Boyd. Photo courtesy of Marjorie Brooks.

Plate 155

This beautiful head study is of Ch. Warwick's Zanuk of Chalmar, owned by May Jacobson and Mary Jo Lewis, Boston, Massachusetts. Handled by Carlos Rojas, he became a multi-all-breed Best in Show winner and a Specialty winner.

Plate 156

1. Shady taking first place at Miami with her owner-trainer, Nanci Little.

2. Nero v. Stoberhai, C.D., Sch.H. II relaxing at home. Owned by Bob and Jonni Dear of Vero Beach, Florida.

3. Hi-Hope's Josie Holly, owned by Cirdan Kennels. Photo courtesy of Bunny Lanning. Both Cirdan and Lothlorien are firm believers in Schutzhund training for their dogs, believing in the "all-purpose Doberman."

4. Shady Acres Endless Summer, C.D., Sch.H. III, VB, WH, AD, pictured at two-and-a-half years of age. By Sandy's Derringer Dirk, U.D.T., Sch.H. II ex Shady Acres Foxfire, C.D. Owned by Anita Chandler, Miami, Florida.

5. Ch. Amulet's Luka of Sno-Glenn, C.D. working with owner, Linda Krukar, and Schutzhund trainer, Ron Heist. The photo shows how hard Luka is biting. Both people are pulling the dog in opposite directions, and he is holding firm.

6. Cornering the decoy, "Caine" during a Schutzhund trial. Ken Howe owner.

Plate 157

1. Ch. Warwick's Zanuck of Chalmar, Specialty Best in Show winner and multi-Best-in-Show winner. Bred and owned by May Jacobson and Mary Jo Lewis of Boston, Massachusetts. Handled by Carlos Rojas. Here winning Best of Breed under Ed Bracy at Asheville in July 1980.

2. Ch. Moonbeam's Tango, by Ch. Mikadobe's Paris, is a litter brother to Ch. Mikadobe's Valentino v Paris. Carlos Rojas handling. Photo courtesy of Mae Downing, Mikadobe Kennels.

3. Ch. Dapper Alemeda, owned by Betty J. and Edgar O. Elberts, Atlanta, Georgia. Handled by Betty Brucker.

4. Ch. Kachina's Louisiana Man taking Winners at Furniture City in 1980 handled by Betty Brucker for Jerry and Debbie Davis, Dayton, Tennessee.

5. Dexter of Sic-Amour, handled by George Murray. Owned by Roger and Kimberly Stoops. Here he is taking Best of Winners at Crawford County Kennel Club in January 1984. Robert Forsyth, judge.

6. Ch. Chalmar's Shannon de Valehr, handled by Mae Jacobson. Co-owned with Mary Asbell and M. Lewis. Pictured taking Best of Winners at Cape Cod in 1982 under judge Robert Forsyth.

Plate 158

Am. and Can. Ch. Sherluck's Duke of Earl, owned by Linda Villasenor, is a grandson of Ch. Kay Hill's Takeswon to Nowon. By Ch. Wessynton's Moloch, C.D. from Ch. Morago Hill's Desert Wind (Ch. Von Lieb's London—Ch. Hy-Lo's Joan of Arc). Photo courtesy of Roseann Fulkerson, Moonraker Dobermans.

Plate 159

1. Ch. Vormund's Candy Spots, belonging to Howard Aubin. Shown to his title by Jane Forsyth.

2. Ch. Cabra's Dark and Debonaire, winner of four all-breed Bests in Show, three Specialty show Bests of Breed, and 40 Best of Breed wins. Owned by Nina McGrath, Nashville, Tennessee. Handler-agent, Captain M. E. Smith, United States Navy, retired, Cleveland, Tennessee.

3. Ch. Brierpatch's Feliz Navidad, by Ch. Briarwood's Yancy Jon, taking Best of Breed at Dayton Kennel Club in 1982. Owned by Tonya Chiles.

1 ▶
2 ▶

PLATE 145

3 ▶
4 ▶

1
2

3
4

PLATE 146

5
6

PLATE 147

1 ▶

2 ▶

PLATE 148

3 ▶

4 ▶

PLATE 150

BEST OF
WINNERS
BERKS COUNTY
KENNEL CLUB
SEPTEMBER 1978
ASHBEY

BEST OF
WINNERS
LONG ISLAND
KENNEL CLUB
1978
GILBERT PHOTO

1
2

RMAN
CLUB
Y
1979

3
4

WORKING GROUP
MUNCIE
KENNEL CLUB SHOW
AUG 1983
PHOTO BY ASHBERGER

WORKING GROUP

PLATE 151

BEST OF
BREED
ASHBEY PHOTO

22

5
6

BEST OF
OPPOSITE SEX
RICHLAND COUNTY
KENNEL CLUB, INC.
DEC. 14, 1974
KLEIN

1 ◄

2 ◄

PLATE 152

3 ◄

4 ◄

PLATE 153

PLATE 154

PLATE 155

1

2

3

4

PLATE 156

5

6

1 ◄

2 ◄

Best of Breed or Variety
Asheville Kennel Club
July 1980
Photo by Sabrina

3 ◄

4 ◄

Best of Winners
Greater Gainesville Dog Fanciers Assn.
April 1979
Photo by Bonnie

Winners
Furniture City Kennel Club
May 1980

PLATE 157

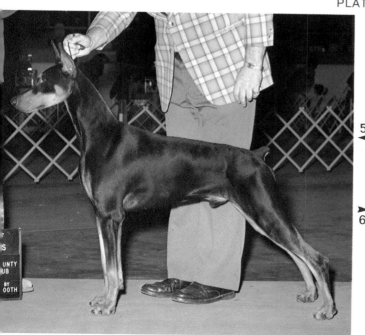

5 ◄

6 ◄

Best of Winners
Cape Cod Kennel Club
1982
Gilbert Photo

PLATE 158

BEST OF WINNERS
MID-HUDSON
KENNEL CLUB
JUNE 1979
ASHBEY

BEST IN SHOW
ANDERSON
KENNEL CLUB SHOW
AUG 1983
PHOTOS BY ALVERSON

BEST IN SHOW

PLATE 159

BEST OF BREED
DAYTON
KENNEL CLUB
1982
ASHBEY

1 ▸

2 ▸

BEST IN SHOW

BEST OF
OPPOSITE SEX

PHOTO K. BOOTH

3 ▸

4 ▸

MICHIANA
KENNEL CLUB
DECEMBER 3 1972
WORKING
GROUP
JUDGE
MRS SALLY KEYES
PHOTO BY BOOTH

WINNERS
GREATER OCALA
DOG CLUB
APRIL 1980

PLATE 160

5 ▸

6 ▸

BEST OF
WINNERS
BREVARD
KENNEL CLUB
DECEMBER 1981
PHOTO BY Graham

BEST OF BREED
OR VARIETY
GREATER DAYTONA
DOG FANCIERS ASSN.
MAY 1980
PHOTO BY Graham

4. Ch. Kay Hill's Torrid Zone, a Ch. Kay Hill's Takeswon to Nowon littermate, by Wizard ex Harmony. Jane Kay, handling.

Plate 160

1. Ch. Stolz Larkspur v Obsidian, owned by Wendell and Joan Curtis, taking Best in Show (age 11 months) at Nolan River Kennel Club, 1976. By Civetta's Bruin of Kami ex Civetta's Obsidian, UD, WAC. Photo courtesy of Kay Martin.

2. Ch. Shiloh Secretariat Wyntuck, owned by Norman and Sue McCall, Memphis, Tennessee. Handled by Betty Brucker.

3. The outstanding Ch. Andelone's Indigo Rock, a widely admired and highly successful winner owned by Bob Bishop winning the Working Group at Michiana in 1972 with his handler Jim Berger.

4. Ch. Wynterwynd Spring Tornado, owned by Gretchen and Cindy Stephens, Waham, North Carolina. Handled by Betty Brucker.

5. This lovely bitch is Ch. Tara's Scarlet Prima Donna, taking Winners Bitch, Best of Winners, and Best of Opposite Sex at Brevard Kennel Club in 1981. Carol Kepler, owner-handler, Sarasota, Florida.

6. Ch. Dynasty's Moonshadow, handled by Betty Brucker to a win under Max Riddle at Greater Daytona, May 1980. Owned by Grace Appollony Black and Elizabeth C. Estrumsa, Miami, Florida.

Ch. Pancho Red Midas von Henik, Top Doberman of 1982 in Brazil. Owned by Alice and Juan Carlos Di Lucca, Curitiba.

1. Best in Show at the 1966 Japanese Kennel Club Specialty show for Dobermans was the two-year-old red male, Break of South Dobes, one of the few occasions on which a red has won in Japan. Japanese-bred, he was owned by H. Stani. Breeder, M. Minami; handler, K. Kasumi. Peggy Adamson was the first woman Doberman judge permitted to officiate in Japan.

2. Damasyn The Bat with her son, Japanese Grand Champion 1951 and 1952 and Am. Ch. Mikadobe v d Elbe, by Ch. Dacki v d Elbe. Handler, Mr. Tashichiro Matsumoto. Owned by Mrs. Earl (Mae) Downing of Georgia. Photo courtesy of Peggy Adamson.

3. Minoo Yasuda, N.P.D.A. judge, with Mikado. A notable judge in Japan who was a great admirer of Mikado.

4. Mizuko v. d. Elbe, litter brother to Mikado, in Japan in the early 1950's.

5. Int. Ch. Mikado v. d. Elbe, ZPR, after winning his American championship. Photo courtesy of Mae Downing, Mikadobe Kennels.

6. At a Japanese dog show in 1952, Grand Champion Mikado v d Elbe and brother Mizuko v.d. Elbe (with back turned) are among the competitors being shown.

7. Japanese Ch. Erene of Grepon, by Am. Ch. Sherluck's Ring of Fire ex Japanese Ch. Black Beauty of Targetdobes. Owned by Sadeo Tsuzuki; bred by Takayuki Suzuki.

8. The very famous and influential Ch. Galaxy's Corry Missile Belle, owned by Elaine Herndon.

9. Gr. Ch. Mikadobe's Mikado v d Elbe. Photo, taken in 1952 by Aoki, was loaned to us by Mae Downing.

 7

 8

9

483

Syrinx Rough Dimond taking Best in Show at age six months and one day. Mr. and Mrs. N. Hughan of Liverpool, England, owners.

484

CHAPTER TEN

The Doberman Pinscher in Great Britain

Dobermans were not popular in Great Britain until the period following World War II, with the Doberman Club of England founded in 1948 by Mr. and Mrs. Fred Curnow and a rather small but very keen group of fanciers anxious to promote the breed there. The foundation stock at that period was principally from Holland and Germany. In keeping with the German thinking at that period, this new club dropped the word "Pinscher" from the breed name, and adopted the German spelling of Doberman, which was with a double "n" or Dobermann.

In due time other clubs devoted to the breed were formed, such as the Midlands Dobermann Club, the North of England Dobermann Club, and also Dobermann Clubs in Scotland and Wales.

The original club's membership enjoyed steady growth, and by now must reach well on towards a thousand, with members representing all parts of the world. The annual registration of Dobermans in England is in the area of over two thousand.

British Doberman fanciers have a tremendous appreciation of the working qualities of their dogs, and many leading winners are also highly successful in working and obedience areas as well. This is encouraged by the Dobermann Club of England which provides working tests and whose Working Dog members support several dog shows annually, including a Championship event.

Probably the best known of all English Doberman breeders world-wide are the late Fred and Julia Curnow, who traveled far and wide fulfilling judging engagements in many countries, becoming acquainted with the fanciers in each of them, and leaving very warm friendship as they were respected, popular and well liked. It was probably in the '50's that I had the pleasure of meeting them at one of our American shows, Westchester, I believe, and one could not help but admire their very sincere devotion to their breed. It was largely through them and their Tavey Kennels that the Rancho Dobe bloodlines went to England from the United States, with highly successful results, we might add. Tavey Kennels is still being carried on, and one notes the many countries in the Dobe world where they are represented.

Dobermans are still going strong in Great Britain in the mid-1980's. The entries are excellent, we are told, with more than two hundred Dobes competing at some of the big championship events. In answer to my inquiry, a British breeder has told me that there is not really any *one* dominant kennel in the breed there, dominating the awards so to speak. There are extremely *good* dogs in many of the leading kennels, sometimes making very little difference between them as the judges make their decisions, especially for the high awards. We understand also that a number of the exhibitors have had the good fortune to win well with their first Dobe, making up championship on it, which is a good thing for the breed, strengthening the opinion that a worthy dog can reach the top regardless of whether or not there is a "face" on the other end of the lead. Contrary to the situation in the States, and many other places, there are really not many true professional handlers involved with the breed in Great Britain. Sometimes, though, the breeders will take in a dog of their breeding, but owned by another fancier who is a novice, just to get the dog properly handled in the ring.

Dobes at Crufts in 1984 were judged by Alan Barnard, starting at about 9:30 a.m. and winding up around 5:30 p.m. The eventual Best of Breed was Pompie Dutch Leivlir, a bitch bred by Hilary Partridge of the Pompie

1. Graaf Carlos v d Edele Stam, son of Dutch and Int. Ch. Graaf Aristo v Neerland Stam and Elsa v Het Rapenland. Unfortunately this fine young dog sustained back and leg injuries while in quarantine, to the deep distress of his new owner, Mrs. Vicki Cuthbertson, Milperra Dobes, Huntingdon, Cambridgeshire.
2. Tamar's Red Baron of Milperra, multiple Best of Breed winner, is a popular stud dog by Ch. Kirnvar's Athos. Mrs. Vicki Cuthbertson, owner.
3. Milperra The Misdemeanor is a C.C. and Reserve C.C. winner. Sired by Ch. Hillmora the Corsair. Owner, Mrs. Vicki Cuthbertson.

Kennels. The dog Challenge Certificate went to Champion Torjet Colonial Boy, who is by a Malaysian import, Champion Von Kleborgs Solar Encore of Achenburg, owned by Margaret and Henry Woodward of the Achenburg prefix.

We have contacted a number of current British Doberman fanciers, asking for information about their kennels and dogs. Stories on them follow.

Gerfang

Gerfang Dobermans are owned by James Glover at St. Helens, Merseyside, England, where the foundation bitch is Omega Royal Rhythm at Gerfang. Maternal duties have kept this good bitch from being shown recently, but when younger she won three Best Puppy in Show (All-Breeds) awards, one Best in Show, two Reserve Bests in Show, many first prizes, and she is a multiple Best of Breed winner. A puppy kept by the Glovers from her first litter, a brown called Gerfang Cash and Courage, had a successful puppy career, winning many first prizes: Best Puppy in Breed, reserve Best of Breed, Best Puppy in Show, etc. She was the product of a half brother/sister breeding, the dominant line being their sire, Zalphas Treble Top, litter brother to English Champion Zalphas Spirit and Champion Zalphas Midland Miss, Best of Breed at Crufts two years.

The Glovers have bred both of the above bitches to a new stud which they recently acquired from the very famous British kennel, Dixown, owned by Di Patience. His name is Dixown Johnny Be Good, and he is a son of the highly successful sire, English Champion Dixown The Hustler (who has many successful offspring in the rings) from Champion Olderhill Seattle, sister to Champion Olderhill Sheboygen. These puppies are starting out in the ring at the time of this writing and look very promising. Johnnie is principally of American bloodlines, with a few English Champions in the second and third generations.

Johnnie's puppies have gone mostly to show homes, and their new owners are filled with enthusiasm over them.

Gerfang is a young kennel, having been showing Dobes only over a few years. They also breed Manchester Terriers and in the past have shown Irish Setters and owned Beagles and German Shepherd Dogs.

The next year or so will see the Glovers in the ring with increasing frequency, hopefully winning but above all enjoying their showing and being amongst their beloved Dobes.

Milperra

Milperra Dobermans are a very successful kennel belonging to Mrs. Vicki Cuthbertson, Huntingdon, Cambs, England. At present an imported dog and bitch are being used there for breeding, with excellent results. The dog is Graaf Carlos v d Edele Stam, the bitch Gravin Cita v Neerlands Stam.

Carlos is by Dutch and International Champion Graaf Aristo v Neerlands Stam, SchH. (Norwegian and International Champion Guy's Hilo v Norden Stam, SchH. III—Dutch and International Champion Gravin Wietske v Neerlands Stam, SchH. I) from Elsa van het Rapenland (Dutch and International Champion Jurgan von Hagernstern, SchH I—Anja van het Rapenland).

Cita is a daughter of Dutch and International Champion Ero v Frankenhorst, Work and Beauty Champion, SchH. II (German Champion Chico v Dorell—Amarilda v d Wachenburg) from Dutch and International Champion Gravin Wietske v Neerlands Stam, SchH. 1 (Dutch and International Champion Graaf Questor van Neerlands Stam, SchH. 1—Dutch and Canadian Champion Gravin Jorinda v Neerlands Stam).

Cita whelped a most excellent litter by Carlos in 1983, which is hopefully scheduled to be repeated in 1984. Cita is a full litter sister to Graaf Cuno v Neerlands Stam, by now a French Champion.

Mrs. Cuthbertson has handsome young stock by Carlos from Milperra The Misdemeanour, a Challenge Certificate and Reserve Challenge winner, which mating she intends to repeat. Milperra Serendipity, with two Reserve Certificates, and Milperra Sin T'late, a first prize winner at championship and open shows, are two from the first litter doing nicely.

Mrs. Cuthbertson also owns Tamars Red Baron of Milperra, a brown male sired by English Champion Kirnvars Athos, noted for producing his bone and substance, who is a multiple Best of Breed winner.

Miss Lesley Wright

Miss Lesley Wright is a very new addition to the British Doberman Fancy but one filled with love for and enthusiasm over the breed. She lives at Margate in Kent.

At present Miss Wright owns only two Dobes, but there are plans for more in her future. She has been showing Harcox Lincoln with pleasing success, and in his first eighteen months he has garnered a number of exciting victories. Miss Wright is planning, now, to give him a respite from the shows while she starts out her bitch. She tells us that Lincoln has now won 35 first prizes, 40 seconds, 47 third prizes, and 50 fourths, which is certainly very nice going indeed!

We wish Miss Wright equal success in campaigning her bitch, and hope that there will be some quality puppies later on in the future.

Syrinx

Syrinx Dobermans, at Liverpool, are owned by Mr. and Mrs. N. Hughan who breed on a small scale, producing up-and-coming quality dogs of the old type.

Having a fairly outcrossed bitch, Jorob's Sweet Sherry, the Hughans' breeding program started out with a stud of a very dominant line. Their choice was a full Tumlow dog, Kaufman's Assassinator, to produce the older type of dogs they wanted. This mating is now proving to have been very successful, and the Hughans are doing well with their young homebred, Syrinx Rough Dimond. Their bitch was retired, on a winning note, shortly after the pups started making their debuts.

Since then, Sweet Sherry has had another litter to the Hughans' own dog, Jupiter's Manxman, and it is hoped that these will be even more successful than the earlier litter.

The Hughans owned another lovely dog, Jorob's King of Spring, who unfortunately had to be put to sleep at an early age. But his short career really made their name winning just about everything in which he was entered. It is through all of this that Mr. Hughan now does some handling for other people and is soon starting a judging career.

Bellmarsh

Bellmarsh Dobermans, owned by Mrs. B. Rowland of Dorking, Surrey, England, started just past the mid-1970's and are based primarily on American lines through Phileen's Duty Free of Tavey (American Champion Tarrado's Corry ex Kay Hills Outrigger), Champion Iceberg of Tavey (an American Champion Steb's Top Skipper grandson), and the American import, Vanessa's Little Dictator of Tavey.

Stevemor's Bannerman of Bellmarsh is by English Champion Olderhill Sheboygen, son of Phileens Duty Free of Tavey ex Olderhill Dhobi. Bannerman's dam is Treasurequest Pearl, by English Champion Davelogs Crusader ex Findjan's Armetis.

Rebecca of Bellmarsh is by Brazilian Champion Cadmus de Fazenda Inglesa of Studbriar (Brazilian Champion Puma de Itaipava-Champion Studbriar Fortune Cookie) from Bellmarsh Bedazzle (Champion Studbriar The Red ex Sasha Bella Donna of Bellmarsh). Most of the puppies, and there are some for which Mrs. Rowland has high hopes as future show dogs and for breeding stock, are by Stevemor's Bannerman of Bellmarsh ex Simron's Black Diamond (Champion Studbriar the Red ex Ikos Tecknika at Simron).

The Kennel Club Breed Standard

Below is a variation to the American Kennel Club breed standard for anyone interested in registering and showing their Dobermans in Great Britain. For more information we suggest you write directly to: The Kennel Club, 1-5 Clarges Street, Piccadilly, London WIY 8AB England.

EARS: Should be small, neat, and set high on the head. Erect or dropped, but erect preferred. [Cropping is illegal in Great Britain.] BODY: Should be square, height measured vertically from the ground to the highest point of the withers, equalling the length measured horizontally, from the forechest to rear projection of the upper thigh. The back should be short and firm with the topline sloping slightly from the withers to the croup; the bitch, needing room to carry litters, may be slightly longer to loin. The belly should be fairly well tucked up. Ribs should be deep and well-sprung, reaching to elbow. Long,

weak, or roach backs to be discouraged. FEET: All dewclaws to be removed. Long, flat deviating paws and weak pasterns should be penalised. WEIGHT AND SIZE: Ideal height at withers: dogs 27 inches; bitches 25½ inches. Considerable deviation from this ideal to be discouraged. FAULTS: Shyness or visciousness must be heavily penalised. Head out of balance in proportion to body, dish-faced, snipy or cheeky should be penalised. Light eyes in black dogs to be discouraged. Overshot or undershot mouths, badly arranged or decayed teeth to be penalised. Dewlap and loose skin are undesirable. Long, weak, or roach backs to be discouraged. White markings of any kind are highly undesirable. Hair forming a ridge on the back of the neck and/or along the spine should be classed as a serious fault. NOTE: In Great Britain this breed is known simply as the Dobermann.

1. Doberman puppy from the kennels of Mrs. V. T. Cuthbertson, Cottage Farm, Huntington, Cambridgeshire.
2. Bellmarsh Fernando winning his first Best Puppy in Breed award at just seven months age at an open show in Sussex, England.
3. Stevemor's Bannerman of Bellmarsh, age two-and-a-half years, by Eng. Ch. Olderhill Sheboygen ex Treasurequest Pearl. Mrs. B. Rowland, Woodmancote, Dorking, Surrey.
4. Eng., Irish, and Aust. Ch. Kenstaff Tornado of Achenbury was one of England's leading winners and a Crufts Best of Breed winner (1976) when purchased for the Australian kennel Silvan Glen. This dog became the first English-bred international champion Dobe. Mick and Lauris Parrish, Silvan Glen, owners.

July 1974 in Melbourne, Australia. "Jedda," the great performing Doberman owned by S. Catania, made a 2,000 mile trip from his home in Perth to greet Peggy Adamson, the arriving judge, with a bouquet of Australian wild flowers. The occasion was the first National Doberman Show in Australia.

CHAPTER ELEVEN

Dobermans in Australia

Silvan Glen Kennels was founded during the mid-1960's, when Mick and Lauris Parrish purchased their first Doberman. The breed was quite new in Australia, where this couple lived, and the kennel had previously been well-known producers of Australian Silky Terriers.

In 1970 the Parrishes purchased a beautiful property on the outskirts of Sydney with five acres of land, and then their activity in Dobermans got underway. Notable dogs owned by this couple back at that time were Australian Champion Silvan Glen Red Rufus, a Challenge Certificate winner at the Sydney Royal Easter Show in 1974 and victor of many other "major" wins; his litter sister, Australian Champion Silvan Glen Samantha, also a notable winner; Australian Champion Silvan Glen Sinbad; Australian Champion Silvan Glen Typesetter; Australian Champion Silvan Glen Red Supreme; and Australian Champion Silvan Glen Dazzler.

In 1976 it was decided to import some new blood for this kennel. After months of negotiations with people in the U.K., the decision was reached to purchase one of England's top Dobes, English and Irish Champion Kenstaff Tornado of Achenburg. Kenny, as he is known, was one of England's greatest winners and was also Best of Breed at Crufts in 1976. This dog was England's first International Champion. Upon his arrival in Australia and subsequent release from quarantine, Kenny obtained his Australian Championship, making him an English, Irish and Australian title-holder. In Australia he also won a Best in Show with nearly 1700 dogs entered. He has sired many champions and now at age twelve years lives a life of luxury in his owners' home.

The next import for Mr. and Mrs. Parrish was a bitch, Achenburg Nola, from the same kennels as Kenny. She was purchased for breeding back to Kenny. Nola turned out to be a not successful brood bitch, as she had trouble whelping and required Caesareans, so she also is a pet in the home.

In 1979 Mr. and Mrs. Parrish travelled to the United Kingdom where they purchased Olderhill Paladin and Olderhill Pandora, littermates by English Champion Olderhill Sheboygan out of Olderhill Olga. Olderhill Paladin obtained his Australian Championship and also won Best in Show at the Doberman Parade in 1981. These two dogs carry some of the old English lines and the Kay Hill American bloodlines.

At present the current bitch is Australian Champion Silvan Glen Centrefold, and hopes are high for the success in the future of the lovely puppy, Silvan Glen The Star.

Aust. Ch. Olderhill Paladin, U.K. import. By Eng. Ch. Olderhill Sheboygen from Olderhill Olga and imported to Silvan Glen Kennels in Australia by Mick and Lauris Parrish, Kemps Creek, New South Wales.

1. Aust. Ch. Tanunda Royal Nemesis, Best Puppy in Show, Sydney Royal 1972; Challenge Certificate Bitch, Sydney Royal 1973 and 1974. This great bitch won more than 3,000 Challenge points and produced 12 champions. Owned by Mrs. M. Hart, Kellyville, New South Wales. She is a daughter of Tavey's Stormy Princess, imported from the U.K., whose grandsire was Am. Ch. Rancho Dobe's Storm.

2. Aust. Ch. Windswept Blue Bootees, a Best in Show winner owned by Windswept Kennels, Blackton, New South Wales. Sheridan Pausey, owner.

3. Windswept Babyface at 10 weeks is already into obedience training. Owned by Windswept Kennels.

4. Windswept Baby Bunting at 11 months. Owned by Windswept Kennels.

5. Aust Ch. Stehle Victoria, bred by Stehle Kennels, D.A. Eschbach. Owned by Mr. and Mrs. M. D. Arapovic. Multiple Best in Show and Group winner. 1980, 1981, and 1982 Top Winning Doberman Bitch, Doberman Club of Queensland, Brisbane. Litter sister to Aust. Ch. Stehle Von Wickens. Dam of Kharissma Kamaro.

6. Aust. Ch. Stehle Binda at 14 months after winning at Victoria in 1982. Owned by A. Ecshbach, North Wagga.

7. Aust. Ch. Maharighi King Cobra as a 10½-month-old puppy. Bred by Stehle Kennels, this lovely dog has brought many honors and victories to his owners through his highly successful show career.

8. Damasyn Bo-Tandy, by Ch. Damasyn The Boatswain ex Ch. Brown's Wendy, C.D., was sold at the age of three by Peggy Adamson to Joan Anderson of Sydney, Australia. Littermate of Ch. Damasyn Bo-Tairic, Ch. Damasyn Bo-Tai, and Damasyn Bo-Tassi (dam of Ch. Damasyn The Troycen). Also full sister to Ch. Damasyn The Ardon Arondi and Can. Ch. Damasyn The Ardon Arori.

1. Ch. Windswept Love Game, owned by Windswept Kennels. Photo taken June 1980 at seven months. Sheridan Pausey, New South Wales, owner.
2. Windswept P-for-Passion, winning baby puppy. Bred by Windswept Kennels.

494

Tanunda Dobermans are owned by Mrs. Mae Hart at Kellyville in New South Wales. She is a breeder-owner-handler of her dogs and a Doberman specialist judge.

The kennels were established in 1969 with the purchase of a puppy bitch from Equina Kennels. This puppy, who became Australian Champion Equina The Panade and whose sire and grandsire was Jemoel's Michael von Warlock (imported from the U.S.A.), made up her title at age thirteen months. She also won Challenge Bitch at Sydney Royal under Canadian judge Bob Waters. She was subsequently mated to Tavey's Stormy Perfection (imported from the U.K.) and produced three champions, Australian Champion Tanunda Royal Bacchus, Australian Champion Tanunda Royal Nike, and the widely acclaimed Australian Champion Tanunda Royal Nemesis.

Nemesis did very well in the show ring, gaining Puppy Bitch in Show at the Sydney Royal in 1972 under J. G. Plunkett from Ireland, Challenge Bitch at the Sydney Royal 1973 under Hans Lehtinen from Finland, and Best of Breed at the Sydney Royal 1974 under noted Australian authority Dr. H. Spira. She had many Best in Group and Best in Show awards under both local and international judges and completed her show career at six years of age with Challenge Bitch and Best of Breed at the Spring Fair under Frans Thyssen of Holland.

Not only was Nemesis a good show bitch, but she was also a most excellent producer. She was mated to Marks-Tey Yancey, imported from the United States; Australian Champion Jelthom Black Otto, C.D.; Australian Champion Elmaro All Flame (these latter two both sons of Champion Chaquen Chevalier; and Australian Champion Shato Norwegian Wood (his nephew). She produced twelve champions, which included Australian Champions Tanunda Laras, Intrigue, Fiery Spirit, C.D., Anastasia, and Beau Brummel, all of which went on to produce well. At the age of thirteen years, she is still happy, healthy and very, very active.

Australian Champion Tanunda Royal Bacchus, who is a brother of Nemesis, sired some very good champions including the late Australian Champion Dobeherr Thunder Sue, Australian Champion Tanunda Autumn

Wonder (Challenge Bitch, Sydney Royal, 1980), Australian Champion Silvengren Super Star, and one of the top winning dogs of today in Australia, Champion Shato Norwegian Wood, the latter owned by Mrs. L. Kann. This dog's major wins include Puppy in Show, Spring Fair 1977; Runner-up Best in Show, Doberman Club of New South Wales 1980; Best in Show, Doberman Club of Victoria, 1980; Best in Show, Doberman Club of New South Wales, 1982; and Reserve Challenge dog, Sydney Royal 1982. He has sired some of the best animals in the New South Wales show rings today.

In 1976 the Doberman Club of New South Wales introduced the Futurity Sweepstakes for breeders. It is of interest to note that Tanunda Kennels won it in 1976 with Australian Champion Tanunda Fiery Spirit, C.D.; in 1977 with Tanunda Alcor; in 1978 with Australian Champion Tanunda Excalibur; (in 1979 the event was not held); in 1981 with Australian Champion Tanunda Sportsaction; in 1982 with Australian Champion Tanunda Thorgerda; and in 1983 with Tanunda The Ecstatica.

Windswept, owned by Sheridan Pausey at Blacktown, New South Wales, is probably one of that country's largest kennels. Mrs. Pausey has approximately twenty-five Dobermans and has had four imports, hopefully with more to come. She breeds very tightly within her chosen line. In fact, as she comments, "I should really head any piece that I write about my dogs 'all roads lead to Rancho Dobe's Storm,'" as everything of hers goes back to this super dog. Interestingly, Mrs. Pausey has no German lines at all, breeding only to American bloodlines as she considers those to be the best in the world.

Both Mrs. Pauley and her husband (who is a Pekingese breeder) are dog-show judges, in Mrs. Pausey's case for more than 25 years. As she says, she likes judging dogs; the dogs themselves and her dog breeding are everything to her, and overseas invitations, although received, cannot be accepted due to this fact.

Windswept has housed nearly two hundred champions, including Cocker Spaniels, Dachshunds (all varieties), Beagles, Miniature Pinschers, Miniature Poodles and Pekingese—and, of course, her beloved Dobermans.

1. Windswept Kennels, New South Wales, are owners of Ch. Windswept May King. Sheridan Pausey, owner.
2. Ch. Barrage of Tavey, a Best-in-Show-winning sire of champions, was imported from the United Kingdom by Windswept Kennels.
3. Ch. Tanunda Royal Bacchus, owned by Mrs. M. Hart, Kellyville, New South Wales.
4. Ch. Elmaro All Fire in 1974 at the first National Doberman Specialty in Australia. The first three placements, under judge Peggy Adamson, included Best in Show and Reserve Best in Show. Owned by Hedi Wetherall of Melbourne.
5. Jemoel's Michael von Warlock at four years, the famous American import who produced many champions in Australia. He was littermate to the outstanding bitch, Ch. Jem's Amethyst v Warlock, sired by Ch. Borong The Warlock from Ch. Hi Dave's Korry's Kay of Ingraham.
6. Ch. Elmaro's Sugar and Spice, dam of All Fire. Both are owned by Hedi Wetherall, Melbourne.
7. Ch. Windswept A for Amour, Reserve C.C. at the Sydney Royal under Mr. Waters, is one of the many famous Dobermans owned by the Pauseys in New South Wales.

Mr. Pausey has been heard to remark that his wife is the world's worst "dobermaniac," to which she comments, "Maybe I am." At the moment there are three house Dobermans in residence, a sixteen-year-old Pekingese, and about twenty-five tanks of goldfish, as the Pauseys breed and judge aquarium fish as well as the dogs. At the present time, the kennel has six Doberman champions with more on the way.

The Pauseys allow their Dobermans contact with the smaller breeds, finding them completely safe together. In fact the very old house Pekingese bullies them all, which I, as a former Pekingese owner, completely believe! There are but two rules in the Pausey family for any dog of any breed crowding their kitchen: the first is to get on well with the others; the second, that they be house-clean. This resulted in Mrs. Pausey's getting a small folding table for meals, as it is not unusual to find five or six Dobermans, their champion Rottweiler, and a couple of Pekingese all sitting down together in the kitchen.

6▲   ▼7

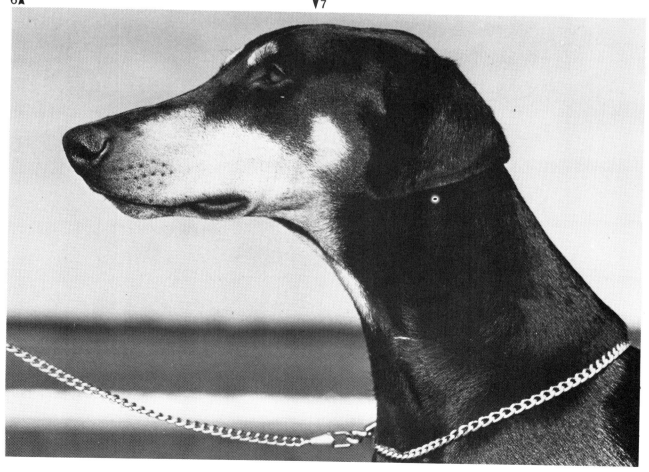

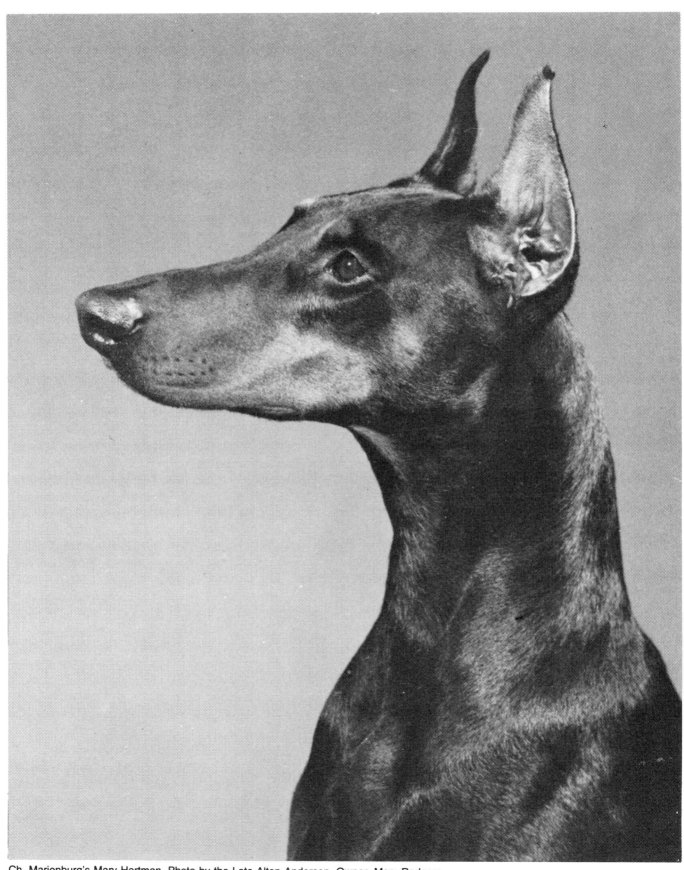

Ch. Marienburg's Mary Hartman. Photo by the Late Alton Anderson. Owner, Mary Rodgers.

CHAPTER TWELVE

The Standard of the Breed

The "standard of the breed," to which one sees and hears such frequent references whenever purebred dogs are written of or discussed, is the word picture of what is considered to be the ideal specimen of the breed in question. It outlines, in minute detail, each and every feature of this breed both in physical characteristics and in temperament, accurately describing the dog from whisker to tail, creating a clear impression of what is to be considered correct or incorrect, the features comprising "breed type," and the probable temperament and behavior patterns of typical members of this breed.

The standard is the guide for breeders endeavoring to produce quality dogs and for fanciers wishing to learn what is considered beautiful in the breed, and it is the tool with which judges evaluate and make their decisions in the ring. The dog it describes is the one which we seek and to which we compare in making our evaluations. It is the result of endless hours spent in dedicated work by knowledgeable members of each parent specialty club, resulting from the combined efforts of the club itself, its individual members, and finally the American Kennel Club by whom official approval must be granted prior to each standard's acceptance, or that of any amendments or changes to it, in the United States. Breed standards are based on intensive study of breed history, earlier standards in the United States, and the purposes for which the breed was originally created and developed. All such factors have played their part in the drawing up of our current standards.

General Conformation and Appearance:
The appearance is that of a dog of medium size, with a body that is square; the height, measured vertically from the ground to the highest point of the withers, equalling the length measured horizontally from the forechest to the rear projection of the upper thigh.

Height at the withers: Dogs—26 to 28 inches, ideal about 27½ inches; *Bitches*—24 to 26 inches, ideal about 25½ inches. Length of head, neck and legs in proportion to length and depth of body. Compactly built, muscular and powerful, for great endurance and speed. Elegant in appearance, of proud carriage, reflecting great nobility and temperament. Energetic, watchful, determined, alert, fearless, loyal and obedient.

The judge shall dismiss from the ring any shy or vicious Doberman.

Shyness: A dog shall be judged fundamentally shy if, refusing to stand for examination, it shrinks away from the judge; if it fears an approach from the rear; if it shies at sudden and unusual noises to a marked degree.

Viciousness: A dog that attacks or attempts to attack either the judge or its handler is definitely vicious. An aggressive or belligerent attitude towards other dogs shall not be deemed viciousness.

Head: Long and dry, resembling a blunt wedge in both frontal and profile views. When seen from the front, the head widens gradually toward the base of the ears in a practially unbroken line. Top of skull flat, turning with slight stop to bridge of muzzle, with muzzle line extending parallel to top line of skull. Cheeks flat and muscular. Lips lying close to jaws. Jaws full and powerful, well filled under the eyes.

Eyes: Almond shaped, moderately deep set, with vigorous, energetic expression. Iris, of uniform color, ranging from medium to darkest brown in black dogs; in reds, blues, and fawns the color of the iris blends with that of the markings, the darkest shade being preferable in every case.

1. Ch. Baptiste's War News winning Best in Show with her handler, J. Nate Levine. Owned by Mrs. Albert C. Lanshaw and bred by Jean L. Baptiste, War News was sired by Ch. Favoriet v Franzhof ex Ch. Fidelia v Tauzieher.

2. Ch. Galaxy's Corry's Missle Belle, owned by Mr. and Mrs. N. J. Reese and Elaine Herndon, was Top Dog, all breeds, 1973. Breeder, Claire McCabe; handler, Corky Vroom.

1▲   ▼2

Teeth: Strongly developed and white. Lower incisors upright and touching inside of upper incisors—a true scissors bite. 42 *correctly placed teeth*, 22 in the lower, 20 in the upper jaw. Distemper teeth shall not be penalized. *Disqualifying faults*—Overshot more than 3/16 of an inch. Undershot more than 1/8 of an inch. Four or more missing teeth.

Ears: Normally cropped and carried erect. The upper attachment of the ear, when held erect, is on a level with the top of the skull.

Neck: Proudly carried, well muscled and dry. Well arched, with nape of neck widening gradually toward body. Length of neck proportioned to body and head.

Body: Back short, firm, of sufficient width, and muscular at the loins, extending in a straight line from withers to the *slightly* rounded croup. *Withers*—pronounced and forming the highest point of the body. *Brisket*—reaching deep to the elbow. *Chest*—broad with forechest well defined. *Ribs*—well sprung from the spine, but flattened in lower end to permit elbow clearance. *Belly*—well tucked up, extending in a curved line from the brisket. *Loins*—wide and muscled. *Hips*—broad and in proportion to body, breadth of hips being approximately equal to breadth of body at rib cage and shoulders.

Tail: Docked at approximately second joint, appears to be a continuation of the spine, and is carried only slightly above the horizontal when the dog is alert.

Forequarters: *Shoulder blade*—sloping forward and downward at a 45-degree angle to the ground meets the upper arm at an angle of 90 degrees. Length of shoulder blade and upper arm are equal. Height from elbow to withers approximately equals height from ground to elbow. *Legs*—seen from front and side, perfectly straight and parallel to each other from elbow to pastern; muscled and sinewy, with heavy bone. In normal pose and when gaiting, the elbows lie close to the brisket. *Pasterns*—firm and almost perpendicular to the ground. *Feet*—well arched, compact, and catlike, turning neither in nor out. Dewclaws may be removed.

Hindquarters: The angulation of the hindquarters balances that of the forequarters. *Hip bone*—falls away from spinal column at an angle of about 30 degrees, producing a slightly rounded, well-filled-out croup. *Upper shanks*—at right angles to the hip bones, are long, wide, and well muscled on both sides of thigh, with clearly defined stifles. Upper and lower shanks are of equal length. While the dog is at rest, hock to heel is perpendicular to the ground. Viewed from the rear, the legs are straight, parallel to each other, and wide enough apart to fit in with a properly build body. *Cat feet*—as on front legs, turning neither in nor out. Dewclaws, if any, are generally removed.

Gait: Free, balanced, and vigorous, with good reach in the forequarters and good driving power in the hindquarters. When trotting, there is strong rear-action drive. Each rear leg moves in line with the foreleg on the same side. Rear and front legs are thrown neither in nor out. Back remains strong and firm. When moving at a fast trot, a properly built dog will single-track.

Coat, Color, Markings: *Coat*—smooth-haired, short, hard, thick and close lying. Invisible gray undercoat on neck permissible. *Allowed colors*—Black, red, blue, and fawn (Isabella). *Markings*—Rust, sharply defined, appearing above each eye and on muzzle, throat and forechest, on all legs and feet, and below tail. *Nose*—Solid black on black dogs, dark brown on red ones, dark gray on blue ones, dark tan on fawns. White patch on chest, not exceeding 1/2 square inch, permissible. *Disqualifying fault*—Dogs not of an allowed color.

Faults: The foregoing description is that of the ideal Doberman Pinscher. Any deviation from the above described dog must be penalized to the extent of the deviation.

Disqualification: Overshot more than 3/16 of an inch; undershot more than 1/8 of an inch. Four or more missing teeth. Dogs not of an allowed color.

Approved February 6, 1982

Ch. Van Majer's Elijah's Red Sun, owned by John and Rita Armonia, Pennington, New Jersey. Photo courtesy of the Forsyths.

CHAPTER THIRTEEN

Selection of a Doberman Pinscher

Once you have made the decision that the Doberman Pinscher is the breed of dog you wish to own, the next important step for you is to determine the right Doberman to best satisfy your needs. Do you prefer to start out with a puppy, with an adult dog, or with one partially mature? Do you prefer a male or a female? What type of dog do you wish—one for show or for competition in obedience? Are you looking for a Doberman for breeding, possibly as the foundation for a kennel? Do you simply want one for companionship, to be a family pet?

A decision should be reached about these matters prior to your contacting breeders; then you can accurately describe your requirements and the breeder can offer you the most suitable dog for your purposes. Remember that with any breed of dog, as with any other major purchase, the more care and forethought you invest when planning, the greater the pleasure and satisfaction likely to result.

Referring to a dog as a "major investment" may possibly seem strange to you; however, it is an accurate description. Generally speaking, a sizable sum of money is involved and you are assuming responsibility for a living creature, taking on all the moral obligations this involves. Assuming that everything goes

well, your Doberman will be a member of your family for a dozen or more years, sharing your home, your daily routine, and your interests. The happiness and success of these years depend largely on the knowledge and intelligence with which you start the relationship.

Certain ground rules apply to the purchase of a dog, regardless of your intentions for its future. Foremost among these is the fact that no matter what you will be doing with the dog, the best and most acceptable place at which to purchase a Dobe is a kennel specializing in that breed. Even though pet shops occasionally have Doberman puppies for sale, they are primarily concerned with *pet* stock, puppies without recognizable pedigrees. When you buy from a breeder you are getting a dog that has been the result of parents very carefully selected as individuals and as to pedigree and ancestry. For such a breeding, a dog and a bitch are chosen from whom the breeder hopes to achieve show type dogs that upgrade both his own kennel's quality and that of the breed generally. Much thought has been given to the conformation and temperament likely to result from the combination of parents and bloodlines involved, for the breeder wants to produce sound, outstanding dogs that will further the respect with which he is regarded in the Doberman Pinscher world. A specialist of this sort is interested in raising *better* dogs. Since it is seldom possible to keep all the puppies from every litter, fine young stock becomes available for sale. These puppies have flaws so slight in appearance as to be unrecognizable as such by other than the trained eye of a judge or a specialist on Dobermans. These flaws in no way affect the strength or future good health of these Dobermans; they simply preclude success in the show ring. The conscientious breeder will point them out to you when explaining why the puppy is being offered for sale at "pet price." When you buy a Doberman like this, from a knowledgeable, reliable breeder, you get all the advantages of good bloodlines with proper temperament, careful rearing, and the happy, well-adjusted environment needed by puppies who are to become satisfactory, enjoyable adults. Although you are not buying a show dog or show prospect, puppies raised in the same

1. Dobes at play, depicted in a photo by the late Alton Anderson. Owned by Leslie Hall, Wilton, Connecticut.
2. The Morales family with Jay-Mee's Latin Dandy, who is a show dog, a Schutzhund-trained dog, and a family protector and friend. Dandy is by Glenayr Jamison ex Taina Red Poison. Dobes have gained considerable popularity in Puerto Rico where this family lives.

1▲ ▼2

manner have all the odds in their favor to become dogs of excellence in the home and in obedience.

If you are looking for a show dog, obviously everything I have said about buying only from a specialized Doberman breeder applies with even greater emphasis. Show-type dogs are bred from dogs of proven producing lines and are the result of serious study, thought, and planning. They do *not* just happen.

Throughout the pages of this book are the names and locations of dozens of reliable Doberman breeders. Should it so happen that no one has puppies or young stock available to go at the moment you inquire, it would be far wiser to place your name on the waiting list and see what happens when the next litter is born than to rush off and buy a puppy from some less desirable source. After all, you do not want to repent at leisure.

Another source of information regarding Doberman breeders is the American Kennel Club, 51 Madison Avenue, New York, NY 10010. A note or phone call will bring you a list of breeders in your area.

Information can also be obtained from professional handlers. They have many contacts and might be able to put you in touch with a breeder and/or help you choose a dog.

The moment you even start to think about purchasing a Doberman, it makes sense to look at, observe, and study as many members of the breed as possible prior to taking the step. Acquaint yourself with correct type, soundness, and beauty before making any commitments. Since you are reading this book, you have already started on that route. Now add to your learning by visiting some dog shows if you can. Even if you are not looking for a show dog, it never hurts to become aware of how such a dog appears and behaves. Perhaps at the shows you will meet some breeders from your area with whom you can discuss the breed and whom you can visit.

If you wish your Doberman to be a family dog, the most satisfactory choice often is a bitch (female). Females make gentle, delightful companions and usually are quieter and more inclined not to roam than males. Often, too, they make neater house dogs, being easier to train. And they are of at least equal intelligence to the males. In the eyes of many

pet owners, the principal objection to having a bitch is the periodic "coming in season." Sprays and chlorophyll tablets that can help to cut down on the nuisance of visiting canine swains stampeding your front door are available; and, of course, I advocate spaying bitches who will not be used for show or breeding, with even the bitches who are shown or bred being spayed when their careers in competition or in the whelping box have come to a close. Bitches who have been spayed, preferably before four years old, remain in better health later on in life because spaying almost entirely eliminates the dangers of breast cancer. Spaying also eliminates the messiness of spotting on rugs and furniture, which can be considerable during her periods with a member of a medium-sized or large breed and which is annoying in a household companion.

To many, however, a dog (male) is preferable. The males do seem to be more strongly endowed with true breed character. But do consider the advantages and disadvantages of both males and females prior to deciding which to purchase.

If you are buying your Doberman as a pet, a puppy is usually preferable, as you can teach it right from the beginning the ways of your household and your own schedule. Two months is an ideal age at which to introduce the puppy into your home. Older puppies may already have established habits of which you will not approve and which you may find difficult to change. Besides, puppies are such fun that it is great to share and enjoy every possible moment of their growing up process.

When you are ready to buy, make appointments with as many Doberman breeders as you have been able to locate in your area for the purpose of seeing what they have available and discussing the breed with them. This is a marvelous learning experience, and you will find the majority of breeders are willing and happy to spend time with you, provided that you have arranged the visit in advance. Kennel owners are busy folks with full schedules, so do be considerate about this courtesy and call on the telephone before you appear.

If you have a choice of more than one kennel where you can go to see the dogs, take advantage of that opportunity instead of just settling for and buying the first puppy you see. You may return to your first choice in the long run, but you will do so with greater satisfaction and authority if you have seen the others before making the selection. When you look at puppies, be aware that the one you buy should look sturdy and big-boned, bright-eyed and alert, with an inquisitive, friendly attitude. The puppy's coat should look clean and glossy. Do not buy a puppy that seems listless or dull, is strangely hyperactive, or looks half sick. The condition of the premises where the puppies are raised is also important, as you want your puppy to be free of parasites; don't buy a puppy whose surroundings are dirty and ill kept.

One of the advantages of buying at a kennel you can visit is that you are thereby afforded the opportunity of seeing the dam of the puppies and possibly also the sire, if he, too, belongs to the breeder. Sometimes you can even see one or more of the grandparents. Be sure to note the temperament of these Dobermans as well as their conformation.

If there are no Doberman breeders within your travelling range, or if you have not liked what you have seen at those you've visited, do not hesitate to contact other breeders who are recommended to you even if their kennels are at a distance and to purchase from one of them if you are favorably impressed with what is offered. Shipping dogs is done with regularity nowadays and is reasonably safe, so this should not present a problem. If you are contacting a well-known, recognized breeder and buying a puppy sight unseen, the puppy should be fairly described and represented to you. Breeders of this caliber want you to be satisfied, both for the puppy's sake and for yours. They take pride in their kennel's reputation, and they make every effort to see that their customers are pleased. In this way you are deprived of the opportunity of seeing your dog's parents, but even so you can buy with confidence when dealing with a specialized breeder.

Every word about careful selection of your pet puppy and where it should be purchased applies twofold when you set out to select a show dog or the foundation stock for a breeding kennel of your own. You look for all the things already mentioned but on a far more sophisticated level, with many more factors to be taken into consideration. The standard of the Doberman must now become your guide,

and it is essential that you know and understand not only the words of this standard but also their application to actual dogs before you are in a position to make a wise selection. Even then, if this is your first venture with a show-type Doberman, listen well and heed the advice of the breeder. If you have clearly and honestly stated your ambitions and plans for the dog, you will find that the breeders will cooperate by offering you something with which you will be successful.

There are several different degrees of show-dog quality. There are dogs that should become top-flight winners which can be campaigned for Specials (Best of Breed competitions) and with which you can hope to attain Working Group placements and possibly even hit the heights with a Best in Show win. There are dogs of championship quality which should gain their titles for you but are lacking in that "extra something" to make them potential Specials. There are dogs that perhaps may never finish their championships but which should do a bit of winning for you in the classes: a blue ribbon here and there, perhaps Winners or Reserve occasionally, but probably nothing truly spectacular. Obviously the hardest to obtain, and the most expensive, are dogs in the first category, the truly top-grade dogs. These are never plentiful, as they are what most breeders are working to produce for their own kennels and personal enjoyment and with which they are loathe to part.

A dog of championship quality is easier to find and less expensive, although it still will bring a good price. The least difficult to obtain is a fair show dog that may pick up some points here and there but will mostly remain in class placements. Incidentally, one of the reasons that breeders are sometimes reluctant to part with a truly excellent show prospect is that in the past people have bought this type of dog with the promise it will be shown, but then the buyer has changed his mind after owning the dog awhile, and thus the dog becomes lost to the breed. It is really not fair to a breeder to buy a dog with the understanding that it will be shown and then renege on the agreement. Please, if you select a dog that is available only to a show home, think it over carefully prior to making a decision; then buy the dog only if you will be willing to give it

1. Ch. Von Mac's Rustuy, an Axel daughter, handled by Norton Moore for Evelyn Callier. By Ch. Axel von Tannenwald.
2. A memorable Best in Show Doberman bitch, Ch. Tarra's Aventina, winning one of her Specialty show Bests of Breed for Mr. and Mrs. Frank D'Amico, handled by Jane Kamp Forsyth.

1▲   ▼2

WESTCHESTER KENNEL CLUB
D.P.C. CONN. N.Y. SPECIALTY
SEPTEMBER 11, 1966
JUDGE MISS ANNA K. NICHOLAS
BEST
OF
BREED
★ A BUSHMAN PHOTO ★

the opportunity to prove itself in the show ring as the breeder expects.

If you want a show dog, obviously you are a person in the habit of attending dog shows. Now this becomes a form of schooling rather than just a pleasant pastime. Much can be learned at the Doberman ringside if one truly concentrates on what one sees. Become acquainted with the various winning exhibitors. Thoughtfully watch the judging. Try to understand what it is that causes some dogs to win and others to lose. Note well the attributes of the dogs, deciding for yourself which ones you like, giving full attention to attitude and temperament as well as conformation. Close your ears to the ringside "know-it-alls" who have only derogatory remarks to make about each animal in the ring and all that takes place there. You need to develop independent thinking at this stage and should not be influenced by the often entirely uneducated comment of the ringside spoilsports. Especially make careful note of which exhibitors are campaigning winning homebreds—not just an occasional "star" but a series of consistent quality dogs. All this takes time and patience. This is the period to "make haste slowly"; mistakes can be expensive, and the more you have studied the breed, the better equipped you will be to avoid them.

As you make inquiries among various breeders regarding the purchase of a show dog or a show prospect, keep these things in mind. Show-prospect puppies are less expensive than fully mature show dogs. The reason for this is that with a puppy there is the element of chance, for one never can be absolutely certain exactly how the puppy will develop, while the mature dog stands before you as the finished product—"what you see is what you get"—all set to step out and win.

There is always the risk factor involved with the purchase of a show-type puppy. Sometimes all goes well and that is great. But many a swan has turned into an ugly duckling as time passes, and it is far less likely that the opposite will occur. So weigh this well and balance all the odds before you decide whether a puppy or a mature dog would be your better buy. There are times, of course, when one actually has no choice in the matter; no mature show dogs may be available for sale. Then one must either wait awhile or gamble on a puppy, but please *be aware that*

gambling is what you are doing.

If you do take a show-prospect puppy, be guided by the breeder's advice when choosing from among what is offered. The person used to working with a bloodline has the best chance of predicting how the puppies will develop. Do not trust your own guess on this; rely on the experience of the breeder.

Although initally more expensive, a grown show dog in the long run often proves to be the far better bargain. His appearance is unlikely to change beyond weight and condition, which depend on the care you give him. Also to your advantage, if you are a novice about to become an exhibitor, is that a grown dog of show quality almost certainly will have been trained for the ring; thus, an inexperienced handler will find such a dog easier to present properly and in winning form in the ring.

If you plan to have your dog campaigned by a professional handler, have the handler help you locate and select a future winner. Through their numerous clients, handlers usually have access to a variety of interesting show dogs; and the usual arrangement is that the handler buys the dog, resells it to you for the price he paid, and at the same time makes a contract with you that the dog shall be campaigned by this handler throughout the dog's career.

If the foundation of a future kennel is what you have in mind as you contemplate the purchase of a Doberman, concentrate on one or two really excellent bitches, not necessarily top show bitches but those representing the finest producing Doberman lines. A proven matron who has already produced show-type puppies is, of course, the ideal answer here; but, as with a mature show dog, a proven matron is more difficult to obtain and more expensive since no one really wants to part with so valuable an asset. You just might strike it lucky, though, in which case you will be off to a flying start. If you do not find such a matron available, do the next best thing and select a young bitch of outstanding background representing a noted producing strain, one that is herself of excellent type and free of glaring faults.

Great attention should be paid to the background of the bitch from whom you intend to breed. If the information is not already known to you, find out all you can about the

1. Ch. Jemoel's Easy Temptation, owned by Wally and Tom Pollock, Elysian Kennels, Hoboken, New Jersey.
2. Ch. Damasyn The Flame, A red Dictator daughter ex the Dictator granddaughter, Damasyn The Flaming Sable. Co-breeders, Peggy Adamson and Eldon Prziborowski, owned by the latter. Photo courtesy of Peggy Adamson.

temperament, character, and conformation of the sire and dam. A person just starting in dogs is wise to concentrate on a fine collection of bitches and to raise a few litters sired by leading *producing* studs. The practice of buying a stud dog and then breeding everything you have to that dog does not always work out. It is better to take advantage of the availability of splendid stud dogs for your first few litters.

In summation, if you want a family dog, buy it young and raise it to the habits of your household. If you are buying a show dog, the more mature it is the more certain you can be of the future. If you are buying a foundation stock for a breeding program, bitches are better than dogs, but they must be from the finest *producing* bloodlines.

Regarding price, you should expect to pay up to a few hundred dollars for a healthy pet Doberman puppy and more than that for a show-type puppy with the price rising accordingly as the dog gets older. A grown show dog can run well into four figures if of finest quality, and a proven brood matron will be priced according to the owner's valuation and can also run into four figures.

When you buy a purebred Doberman dog or puppy that you are told is eligible for registration with the American Kennel Club, you are entitled to receive, from the seller, an application form that will enable you to register your dog. If the seller cannot give you the application, you should demand and receive an identification of your dog consisting of the breed, the registered names and numbers of the sire and dam, the name of the breeder, and the dog's date of birth. If the litter of which your Doberman is part has been recorded with the American Kennel Club, then the litter number is sufficient identification.

Do not accept a verbal promise that registration papers will be mailed to you. Demand a registration application form or proper identification. If neither is supplied, do not buy the dog. These words are to be especially heeded if you are buying show dogs or breeding stock.

Ch. Liquorish Rico's Lucky Chance, C.D., ROM, doing guard duty at his owner's gate. Jeff and Grace Joffe, Liquorish Dobermans, Ft. Lauderdale, Florida.

CHAPTER FOURTEEN

You and Your Doberman Pinscher

The popularity of Dobermans is great all over the world, and in the United States the number of yearly A.K.C. registrations of the breed indicates that the Doberman continues to remain near the top of the list of the most popular dog breeds—a tribute to the versatility, talents, and intelligence of these very worthy dogs. Sadly, many of them are not well cared for; and through neglect, lack of understanding, and sometimes downright disinterest on the part of their owners, the dogs become less than satisfactory as companions or pets. This is a pity, because there is no breed with more potential for outstanding loyalty and service than a properly managed Doberman.

Versatility of Dobermans

It should be remembered that the Doberman is a true *working dog,* happiest when serving mankind. Such a dog deserves an understanding owner, one who appreciates him and his potential, one who is interested in developing the dog's intelligence. No Doberman should ever be left without at least basic obedience training. No Doberman, no matter what your reasons for owning him, should be ignored and treated as a machine rather than as a living creature. No Doberman should be turned loose to fend for himself by an owner

who likes to have him "enjoy his freedom."

Because of the Doberman superior intelligence, working with this breed can be exceedingly rewarding. The police have found this to be true, as has the military. All sorts of specialized tasks are now being performed by members of this breed, from bomb and drug detection and scenting out criminals to locating and rescuing lost persons and working as true Police Dogs, accompanying human "partners" in squad cars as they make their rounds (particularly in what are known as "high risk" areas), adding considerably to the safety of these men by their presence, courage, and alertness. If Dobermans have ever received adverse publicity in the press, the tables are surely turned now. With consistent regularity New York and Connecticut newspapers, and I am certain those in other areas of the United States as well, carry accounts of incidents of heroism on the part of Dobermans as they assist in law enforcement and in the apprehension of criminals. The Doberman is proving himself to have the keen nose of a scent hound, plus the size, strength, stamina, courage, and keen intelligence to make his results outstanding.

Countless Dobermans serve their masters as guard dogs on commercial property or at home. Somehow just the appearance of one of these impressive canines gives a would-be burglar, or any other person with less than honorable intentions, pause. And I am certain that many times a crime is averted by the protective presence of such a dog.

I do not believe in guard-dog training for an animal who will live as a family member, and I am particularly against this being done by an amateur or uninformed owner. Should you determine that you wish such training for your dog, carefully investigate until you find a competent and reliable trainer who, through experience, really knows what he is doing. In the hands of an amateur, a partially or badly trained guard dog can become a real menace—a risk which should not be taken with a dog who will be part of your family, coming into contact with children, strangers, or people unaware of how to handle such a situation. The Doberman is instinctively protective of his home and people. That natural instinct, plus normal obedience training, should be all that is necessary to equip your dog for general family living and for watch-dog duty.

While it is possible for them to manage in a limited area, Dobermans really need more space in which to exercise than is generally supplied by apartment living. However, if it is the only breed for you and you are willing to provide the time and energy required for walking your dog a decent distance daily, it can be worked out. And certainly nothing could give a greater feeling of safety on city streets than a Doberman at one's side.

As a dog for companionship, nothing quite matches a Doberman. Their intelligence makes them almost seem to know what you are thinking. They are clean dogs in the house, are easily trained, and bask in personal attention. They are splendid dogs with children if both are raised together, strong enough to withstand the long hours of play which a youngster enjoys with his dog; and they are alert companions for a child, quick to sense danger should it arise and intelligent in their reaction.

A Doberman is at his best when treated as a family member, permitted to share the daily routine, to live in the house, and to be a true companion to his owner. His brains and train-ability make him fill this role admirably, which is one of the prime reasons why the breed has earned such enormous popularity with people wishing a dog for this purpose.

Responsbilities of Breeders and Owners

Whether you are a one-dog owner, the owner of a show kennel, one involved in obe-dience, or a breeder, there are definite re-sponsibilities—to your dog or dogs, to your breed, and to the general public—involved which should never be overlooked or taken lightly.

It is inexcusable for anyone to breed dogs promiscuously, producing unneeded litters. The only time a responsible breeder plans a litter is when it is *needed* to carry on a blood-line or to provide dogs for which this breeder has very definite plans, including orders for at least half the number of puppies which will probably be born. Every healthy puppy de-serves a good and loving home, assuring its future well-being. No puppy should be born to an uncertain future on someone's assump-tion that there will be no problem selling or otherwise finding a home for it, as very defi-nitely this is not always easy. Overpopulation is the dog world's most heartbreaking trag-edy. Those of us who love dogs should not add to canine overpopulation by carelessly producing more. If you have any reason to feel that the puppies may not be assured of homes, don't breed the bitch; wait for a more propitious time. Certainly no Doberman breeder likes the thought of running around frantically trying to find someone who will take puppies off his hands, even if they must be given away. The latter usually is not a good idea anyway, as many people cannot re-sist saying "yes" to something which costs nothing, regardless of whether or not they re-ally want it. As the Doberman grows larger and demands more care, their enthusiasm wanes to the point that the dog soon is left to roam the streets where he is subject to all sorts of dangers, and the owner simply could not care less. If one pays for something, one seems to respect it more.

One litter at a time is all that any breeder should produce, making sure that all those puppies are well provided for prior to the breeding of another litter. Breeders should do all in their power to ascertain that the home to which each of his puppies goes is a *good* home, one that offers proper care, a fenced-in area, and a really enthusiastic owner. I have tremendous respect for those breeders who make it a point to check carefully the creden-tials of prospective purchasers, and I firmly believe that all breeders should do likewise on this important point. I am certain that no breeder wants any Doberman puppies to wind up in an animal shelter, in an experi-mental laboratory, or as a victim of a speeding car. While complete control of such situations may not be possible, it is at least our responsi-bility to make every effort to turn our puppies over to people who have the same outlook as our own where love of dogs and responsibility toward them are concerned and who realize that the ownership of a dog involves care, not neglect.

It is the breeder's responsibility to sell ev-ery puppy with the understanding that should the new owner find it necessary to place the dog elsewhere, you, the breeder, must be contacted immediately and given the opportu-nity to take back the dog or to help in finding

512

it a new home. Many a dog starting out in what has seemed a good home has, under unforeseen circumstances, been passed along to others, only to wind up in exactly the sort of situation we most want to avoid. Keep in touch with what is happening to your dogs after they are sold.

The final obligation every dog owner shares, be there just one dog or many, is that of leaving detailed and up-to-date instructions in our wills about what is to become of our animals in the event of our death. Far too many of us are apt to procrastinate and leave this matter unattended to, feeling that everything will work out all right or that "someone will see to them." The latter is not too likely to happen, at least not to the benefit of the dogs, unless the owner makes absolutely certain that all will be well for them in the future.

If you have not already done so, please get together with your lawyer and set up a clause in your will specifying what is to be done with each and every dog you own and to whom each will be entrusted (after first ascertaining that this person is willing and able to assume the responsibility); also include details about the location of all registration papers, pedigrees, and kennel records, along with ways of identifying each dog. Just think of the possibilities of what might happen otherwise!

It is not wise to count on family members, unless they share your involvement with the dogs. In many cases our relatives are not the least bit "dog- oriented" (perhaps they think we're a trifle crazy for being such enthusiasts) and they might absolutely panic at the thought of suddenly having even *one* dog thrust upon them. They might mean well, and they might try; but it is unfair to them and to the dogs to leave the one stuck with the other!

If you travel a great deal with your dogs, another wise idea is to post prominently in your vehicle and carry in your wallet the name, address, and telephone number of someone to be called to take charge of them in case of an accident. Of course, this should be done by prearrangement with the person named. We have such a friend, and she has a signed check of ours to be used in case of an emergency or accident when we are travelling with our dogs; this check will be used to cover her expenses to come and take over the care of our dogs should anything happen to make it impossible for us to do so.

The registration certificates of all our dogs are enclosed in an envelope with our wills, and the person who will be in charge knows each of the dogs, and one from the other, so there will be no identification problem. These are all points to be considered, for which provision should be made.

We also owe an obligation to our older dogs who too often are disregarded. It disgusts me that so many supposedly great dog lovers think nothing of getting an older dog (even though it is well, happy, and enjoying life) out of the way to make room for younger show prospects or additional puppies. The people I consider to be genuine dog lovers are the ones who permit their dogs to live out their lives in comfort as loved, respected members of the household or kennel. How quickly some of us seem to forget the pleasures these dogs have brought us with exciting wins and the devotion they have shown to us and our families!

So much for our responsibility to our dogs, but we also owe a responsibility to our breed: to keep up its quality and to protect its image. Every Doberman breeder should breed only from and for high-grade stock and should guard against the market being flooded with excess puppies. We should display good sportsmanship and concern for the dogs at all times, and we should involve ourselves whenever possible in activities beneficial to the breed.

To the general public we owe the consideration of good dog ownership. Our dogs should not be permitted to run at large and annoy others. Dogs should not be left barking endlessly, tied outside or closed in the house. We should pick up after our dogs, as required in most cities, when we exercise them where people must walk. We should, in other words, enjoy our dogs without allowing them to infringe on those who may be less enthusiastic.

Traveling With Your Doberman

When you travel with a dog, you must always remember that everyone does not necessarily share your love of dogs and that those who do not, strange creatures though they

513

may seem, have their rights too. These rights, on which we should not encroach, include not being disturbed, annoyed, or made uncomfortable by the presence and behavior of other people's pets. Doberman owners, since theirs is an intelligent and easily trained breed, should have the dog well schooled in proper canine behavior by the time maturity is reached. You dog should not jump enthusiastically on strangers, no matter how playful or friendly the dog's intentions. We may love having them do this to us, but it is unlikely that someone else will share our enthusiasm, especially in the case of muddy paws on delicate or light-colored clothes which may be soiled or damaged. A sharp "Down" from you should be promptly obeyed, as should be "Sit," "Stay," and "Come."

If you expect to take your Doberman on many trips, he should have, for your sake and for his, a crate of appropriate size for him to relax in comfortably. In cases of emergency or accident, a crated dog is far more likely to escape injury. Left in a parked car, a crated dog should have the car windows fully open in hot weather, thus being assured sufficient ventilation. For your own comfort, a dog in a crate does not hang from the car window, climb over you and your passengers, and shed hair on the upholstery. Dogs quickly become accustomed to their crates, especially when started with one, as they should be, from puppyhood. Both you and the dog will have a more enjoyable trip when you provide him with this safeguard.

If you do permit your dog to ride uncrated in the car, see to it that he does not hang from the windows. He could become overly excited by something he sees and jump out; he could lose his balance and fall out, should you stop short or swerve unexpectedly; he could suffer an eye injury induced by a strong wind generated by the moving car. All of these unnecessary risks can so easily be avoided by crating!

Never, ever, under any circumstances, should a dog be permitted to ride uncrated in the back end of an open pick-up truck. I have noted, with disgust and horror, that some people do transport their dogs in this manner, and I think it cruel and shocking. How easily such a dog can be thrown out of the car by sudden jolts or an impact! And I am sure that many dogs have jumped out at the sight of

something exciting along the way, quite possibly into the path of an oncoming car. Some unthinking individuals tie the dog, probably not realizing that if he were to jump under those circumstances, his neck could be broken, he could be dragged alongside the vehicle or get under its wheels, or he could be hit by another vehicle. If you are for any reason taking your dog *anywhere* in an open back truck, *please* have sufficient regard for that dog to provide a crate to protect him. Also please remember that with or without a crate, a dog riding exposed to the sun in hot weather can really suffer and have his life endangered by the heat.

If you are staying in a hotel or motel with your dog, please exercise him somewhere other than in the parking lot, along the walkways, or in the flower beds of the property. People walking to and from their rooms or cars really are not thrilled at "stepping in something" left by your dog and should not be subjected to the annoyance. Should an accident occur, pick it up with tissues or a paper towel and deposit it in a proper receptacle; don't just let it remain there. Usually there are grassy areas on the sides or behind motels where dogs can be exercised with no bother to anyone. Use those places rather than the busy, more conspicuous, carefully tended areas. If you are becoming a dog-show enthusiast, you will eventually need an exercise pen to take with you to the show. They are ideal to use when staying at motels, too, as they permit you to limit the dog's roaming space and to pick up after him easily. Should you have two or more dogs, such a convenience is truly a "must!"

Never leave your dog unattended in a room at a motel unless you are absolutely, positively, sure that he will stay quiet and not destroy anything. You do not want a long list of complaints from irate fellow-guests, caused by the annoying barking or whining of a lonesome dog in strange surroundings or an overzealous watchdog barking furiously each time a footstep passes the door. And you certainly do not want to return to torn curtains or bedspreads, soiled rugs, or other embarrassing (and sometimes expensive) evidence of the fact that your dog is not really house-reliable.

If yours is a dog accustomed to travelling with you and you are positive that his behavior will be acceptable when left alone, that is

1. Int. Ch. Mikado v. d. Elbe, ZPR, by Ch. Dacki v. d. Elbe ex Damasyn The Bat. Grand Champion of Japan for 1951. Photo courtesy of Mae Downing, Mikadobe Kennels, Marietta, Georgia.
2. Ch. Kay Hill's Living Fire, by Choirmaster from Swan Song, at age two and three-quarter years finishing championship. Judge, Isidore Schoenberg; handler, Bob McPherson. Photo courtesy of Jane Kay.

fine. But if the slightest uncertainty exists, the wise course is to leave him in the car while you go to dinner or elsewhere and then bring him into the room when you are ready to retire for the night.

When you travel with a dog, it is sometimes simpler to take along his food and water from home rather than to buy food and to look for water while you travel. In this way he will have the rations to which he is accustomed and which you know agree with him, and there will be no problems due to different drinking water. Feeding on the road is quite easy now, at least for short trips, with all the splendid dry prepared foods and high quality canned meats available, not to mention the "just remove it from the packet" convenience foods. And many types of lightweight, refillable water containers can be bought at many types of stores.

If you are going to another country, you will need a health certificate from your veterinarian for each dog you are taking with you, certifying that each has had rabies shots within the required length of time preceding your visit.

Remember that during the summer, the sun's rays can make an inferno of a closed-up car in a matter of minutes, so always leave windows open enough that there is sufficient ventilation for the dog. Again, if your dog is in a crate, this can be done easily and with safety. Remember, too, that leaving the car in a shady spot does not mean that it will remain shaded. The position of the sun changes quickly, and the car you left nicely shaded half an hour earlier may be in the full glare of the sun upon your return. Be alert and be cautious.

When you travel with your dog, be sure to take a lead and use it, unless he is completely and thoroughly obedience trained. Even if the dog is trained, however, using a lead is a wise precaution against his getting lost in strange territory. I am sure that all of us have seen in the "Lost and Found" columns the sad little messages about dogs who have gotten away or been lost during a trip, so why take chances?

Ch. Amberdobe's Choirmaster, by Ch. Rubigold's Denbuda ex Ch. Kay Hill's Caroletta. Jane Kay, owner, Kay Hill Kennels.

CHAPTER FIFTEEN

The Doberman as a Family Dog

There is a tendency on the part of the general public to think of the Doberman as a guard dog, an attack dog, or a dog to be used only for working purposes. This is by no means a correct evaluation. For while Dobermans are without equal for these purposes when *raised and trained specifically for them*, our average Doberman is an affectionate, gentle, devoted animal, adoring of his humans, reliable and trustworthy with children (whose lives have been saved by their pets of this breed on countless occasions).

The Doberman is second to none as a family companion. Quiet, sensible, devoted, these dogs are ideal members of the household and seem happiest and thrive well under such circumstances. The Doberman to be at his best definitely should be permitted the privilege of sharing the family life. This applies to show dogs as well as to those purchased as family dogs. Many of the country's most famous Dobermans live, or have lived during their lifetime, with their owners or handlers, and it has been my observation that such dogs always excel in personality and self-confidence.

The majority of American Dobermans are raised and owned for pleasure—they make excellent family dogs. Handsome and very satisfactory show dogs, they are intelligent, easily-taught obedience dogs, and they are instinctively protectors of their home, family and

property. Serious Doberman breeders put a great deal into the raising of their puppies. Socialization is of utmost importance, and conscientious breeders see to it that this is provided from an early age. Puppies so raised should mature free of shyness or sharpness—poised, well- adjusted canine characters.

Not every one should own a Doberman, in this writer's opinion. This definitely is *not* a dog that is happy spending his life in a kennel, or being kept outside the house day and night with no more than an occasional pat on the head by way of human companionship. It is not enough, as I am sure everyone acquainted with them will agree, to just provide these dogs with the bare necessities of staying alive. They are too intelligent to thrive tied to a dog house which is their so-called "home." Also, they are not endowed with coats which would equip them to "rough it" in extreme heat or bitter cold. What a waste it is to fail to provide the opportunity for one of these dogs to develop its potential!

To own a Doberman, one should truly love dogs and enjoy having them around—at home and abroad; sharing your activities indoors and out; minding the baby, or playing with the older kids; snoozing by your side as you read or watch television; sharing at least your room (if not your bed); going with you in the car or for walks on a lead in the city or in the suburbs, or going for a run through the woods in the country. All of the pleasures of dog ownership can be thoroughly enjoyed if one's dog is a Dobe!

Let me tell you the story of Champion Hotai Sweet William, Best in Show winning show dog, as an example of true Doberman-owner rapport, and of the very deep devotion which can and usually does develop.

Sweet William was bred, owned and loved by Virginia K. Markley of Marion, Ohio, owner of the world famous kennel "Hotai." He was one of a litter of ten puppies bred by Mrs. Markley from her Champion Highbriar Bandanna and sired by a well-known dog whom she was negotiating to purchase. These puppies were born in February 1968. It would seen that "Willie" was destined to remain with Mrs. Markley, for the new owners to whom he had been promised were unable to take him when the time came. Mrs. Markley at that time was a relatively unknown

1. Alamaps Glamour Girl, bred by Warren Bushman, by Ch. Steb's Top Skipper ex Ch. Our Very Own Pamela. At the Kennel Club of Northern New Jersey in 1960. Photo courtesy of Natalie and J. Monroe Stebbins.
2. Taking Best of Breed at Philadelphia in 1971 under the incomparable judge, Alva Rosenberg, is Ch. Tranell's Maxwell Smart. Handled by J. Monroe Stebbins for Raymond Carlisle, Suffern, New York.

breeder from whom puppies were not yet sought with frequency; so Willie stayed at home where he had been born.

Sweet William was a show dog in the greatest sense of the word. He loved to "ham it up" whether at a show or at home. The world was his arena. When the Markleys neglected to include him in any conversation, especially if company was present, Willie would think of every trick he knew in order to be noticed. Like pushing a kitchen chair across the floor with his nose, or putting his head through the cafe doors and over the baby gate; then when someone would notice him, he would appear to "slam the door in your face" by quickly pulling his head back and disappearing. Or another trick that he and his sire both used when a Doberman lady friend came for breeding to one or the other was for the one not being used to run to the switches in the kitchen, turning off the light in the garage where the breeding was taking place!

Even though Willie was a clown, he was also a true Doberman. He was discriminating and thoughtful about when to defend, like the night he and his handler Gene Haupt were asleep in a motel room when someone opened their bedroom door. Willie took off down the hall after the intruder with Gene in close pursuit.

True to the breed, Willie disliked other male dogs. Once when Mrs. Markley was trying to get him through the crowd at a show, some woman with a small white dog in her arms started to really come down hard on her. Mrs. Markley had no idea why until she glanced at Sweet William who was standing there looking innocent with a whole mouthful of white hair. He loved waiting at the Group ring, where he had a choice of easily accessible furry ones. We might note that he never did the damage his powerful jaws were capable of inflicting had he been so inclined. It was by way of being a sort of prank with him. Once through the gates and in the ring, Willie was the true gentleman, never threatening another dog. He definitely knew that this was business, not the time for jokes. It did become a real challenge, though, trying to get him to ringside and back without having him get hold of at least one other dog.

At the same time, Willie adored most people. When a guest whom he considered a friend came to visit, he would back up to the couch and sit beside that person; or if a chair were used he would make every attempt to sit on the person's lap. He never could understand that his 98 pounds did not go well with being a lap dog. Willie always slept with overnight guests whether he was invited to do so or not. He always felt he was doing them the favor.

Willie was definitely an ambassador for the Doberman breed. He was also Mrs. Markley's salesman when a prospective buyer came. One day a couple arrived with their five-year-old granddaughter. They were interested in a puppy but had heard all the usual stories about Dobermans "eating" their owners. They were naturally concerned for the welfare of their grandchildren and did not want to jeopardize the kids' safety in order to indulge their own admiration for the breed. Mrs. Markley invited them to come in, and after they had chatted for a few minutes they looked down to see the granddaughter rolling around the floor with Sweet William who was having a grand time becoming acquainted with his newly discovered friends. Please remember, dear reader, that this was a full grown male Doberman who *had not been raised with or was accustomed to children;* in addition, he was a stud dog. Needless to say, these people left with one of William's puppies. They came back about a year ago (at the time this book is going to press) for a second one, as the original Dobe is now getting along in years.

Virginia Markley and Willie were so attuned to each other that he could read her thoughts almost before she knew them, to quote her very words. She adds, "We held long conversations with one another. He also sang on command, and like most Dobermans he thrived on attention. He never knew but what he was a people."

Sweet William was a dog of commanding appearance, with great bone and substance. His topline was hard as iron, and straight, with a super tail-set. He had a lovely headpiece with nice expression. Mrs. Markley notes, "Willie was a grinner and would show you a full set of teeth when he was talked to."

Willie attended only one National Specialty, when it was held in San Diego. Again quoting Mrs. Markley, "He enjoyed himself

Am., Can., Dom., and Int. Ch. Liquorish The Ron Rico, Am., Can., and Mex. C.D., ROM looking over the fence. Grace and Jeff Joffe, Ft. Lauderdale, Florida, are owners of this famous dog.

more than anyone there. He had his own private balcony overlooking the beach where he sat each morning watching the birds, and the joggers running. Some would stop and talk with him. He particularly enjoyed his friends coming to the room to visit with him," says Mrs. Markley, "and he gladly sang for all who requested that he do so."

That is the story of Willie, a very typical representative of Doberman breed character, and the devotion between these dogs and the owners who love them. In the kennel stories section you will read about Champion Hotai Sweet William, the famous Best in Show winning show dog. A great Doberman in both areas!

Then there is a story given us by Peggy Adamson of another Doberman, this one in Australia, telling of Jet, age three years at the time, and a baby named Adam, age then 15 months. The parents, Mr. and Mrs. Olney, tell about the day when Adam was left out alone to play, just for a moment until his mother's return from inside the house. Jet was still a bit too big to really play with Adam, but Mrs. Olney had devised a game by which she would ask Jet, "Where's Adam?" and the dog would immediately find him. That is what she did that day, when she came outside to find her son missing. Jet went immediately to the old well close to the house, whimpering. Mrs. Olney followed, but seeing nothing there, walked away. Yet Jet remained whimpering by the well. Noting the dog's persistence, she returned for a second look, this time seeing her baby face down in the water. Without a second thought she went to get him and finally succeeded in reviving the baby, after which time she had no alternative but to stand there 12 feet down the well in cold water to her waist with the baby in her arms and *hope* that help would come. When her mother finally arrived, Jet was on the job to show the way, and after eight hours in the well, Mrs. Olney and Adam were brought up with the help of her mother and a neighbor. Thanks to the alertness and intelligence of this Doberman, the baby was saved from what would surely have been fatal.

There are people who feel that a Doberman is an inappropriate breed for city dwellers. Not at all. In fact I would heartily recommend them for the safety factor as well as the pleasure their companionship can bring. If you provide a couple of daily walks on lead, with a quick trip to the curb between times, your Doberman can be as well and happy in an apartment as in a mansion. In fact he will probably prefer it, since this way he'll be closer to you and thus better situated for sharing in all of your activities.

The fact that a Doberman needs exercise in order to stay in good health should not deter anyone loving the breed from keeping one in the city. All dogs need exercise, so a city dog owner must provide daily walks anyway, and surely it is safer to do so through city streets when accompanied by an imposing looking dog of a breed considered by the general public to be guardians and protectors. It is hard to imagine that anyone would be mugged or otherwise molested or robbed when under the watchful eye of a Doberman walking or standing alongside! Anyone so imprudent as to try would very definitely be sorry! A Doberman is excellent burglar insurance, as one would hesitate to break into premises where a member of this breed is on duty.

Dobermans are equally at home in the suburbs or country. They grace your premises with style and elegance. They have a strong sense of protection bred into them, so they make sensible and reliable guardians of the premises.

Along with his many other assets, the Doberman also excels in style and beauty. His clean lines and attractive coloring, plus his intelligent expression and overall style make him a dog definitely "easy on the eyes" who graces your home in every way.

While collecting material for this book, I have repeatedly been impressed by the very deep satisfaction and appreciation expressed by Doberman owners for their dogs. It would seem to be rare when anyone who has owned a Dobe can be satisfied with another breed— a fact which speaks for itself when considering the Doberman's attributes as a family dog and companion.

"Mandy as a puppy." From the Elysian Kennels, Wally and Tom Pollock, Hoboken, New Jersey.

522

CHAPTER SIXTEEN

Caring for a Doberman Puppy

Ownership of a dog entails a great deal of responsibility. You must be willing and prepared to provide your pet with shelter, food, training, and affection. With proper attention and care, your pet will become a loving member of the family and a sociable companion to be enjoyed for many years to come.

Advance Preparation

The moment you decide to become the owner of a Doberman puppy is not one second too soon to start planning for the new family member in order to make the transition period more pleasant for yourself, your household, and the puppy.

The first step in preparation is a bed for that puppy and a place where you can pen him up for rest periods. I am a firm believer that every dog should have a crate of its own right from the very beginning. This will fill both of the previously mentioned requirements, and the puppy will come to know and love this crate as his special haven. Crates are ideal, for when you want the puppy to be free, the crate door stays open. At other times, you securely latch it and know that the puppy is safe from harm, comfortable, and out of mischief. If you plan to travel with your dog, his crate comes along in the car; and, of course, to travel by plane, the dog must be put in a crate. If you show your dog, or take him to obedience trials, what better place to keep him when you are not working with him than in his crate? No matter how you look at it, a crate is a very sensible, sound investment in your puppy's comfort, well being, and safety—not to mention your own peace of mind.

The crates we prefer are the sturdy wooden ones with removeable side panels. These wooden crates are excellent for cold weather, with the panels in place, and they work equally well for hot weather when the solid panels are removed, leaving just the wire sides for better ventilation. Crates made entirely of wire are all right in the summer, but they provide no protection from drafts or winter chills. I intensely dislike solid aluminum crates due to the manner in which aluminum reflects surrounding temperatures. If it is cold, so is the metal of the crate. If it is hot, that too is reflected, sometimes to the point that one's fingers can be burnt when handling it. For this reason I consider them unsuitable.

When you choose the puppy's crate, be certain that it is roomy enough not to be outgrown as your Doberman matures. He should have sufficient height in which to stand up comfortably and sufficient area to stretch out full length when relaxed. When the puppy is young, give him shredded newspapers as his first bed. In time, the newspapers can be replaced with a mat or turkish towels. Carpet remnants are great for the bottom of the crate, as they are inexpensive and in case of accidents can be easily replaced. Once the dog has matured past the chewing stage, a pillow or a blanket for something soft and comfortable is an appreciated luxury in the crate.

Sharing importance with the crate is a safe area where the puppy can exercise and play. If you are an apartment-dweller, a baby's playpen works well for a young puppy and a portable exercise pen (which will come in handy if you show your dog) is good for a mature dog. If you have a yard of your own, then the fenced area in which he can stay outdoors safely should be ready and waiting upon his arrival. It does not need to be a vast area, but it should have shade and be secure. Do have the fenced area planned and installed *before* bringing the puppy home if you possibly can do so; this is far more sensible than putting it off until a tragedy occurs. If you have close neighbors, stockade fencing works out well, as then the neighbors are less aware of the dog and the dog cannot see and bark at everything that passes near the area. If you live in the country, then regular chain-link fencing is fine. To eliminate the possibility of your Doberman jumping the fence when he matures, the fence should be six feet high. As an absolute guarantee that a dog cannot dig his way out under the fence, an edging of cinder blocks tight against the inside bottom of it is very practical protection. If there is an outside gate, a key and padlock are a *must* and should be *used at all times*. You do not want to have the puppy or dog set free in your absence either purposely or through carelessness. I have seen people go through a fence and then just leave the gate ajar. So for safety's sake, keep the gate locked so that only someone responsible has access to its opening.

The ultimate convenience, of course, is if there is a door in your house situated so that the fence can be installed around it, thereby doing away with the necessity for an outside gate. This arrangement is ideal, because then you need never be worried about the gate being left unlatched. This arrangement will be particularly appreciated during bad weather when instead of escorting the dog to wherever his fenced yard is, you simply open the house door and he exits directly into his safe yard.

If you have only one dog, however, do not feel that he will get sufficient exercise in the fenced area; most dogs just sit there when they're alone. Two or more dogs will play and move themselves around; but from my own experience, one dog by himself does little more than make a leisurely tour once around the area and then lie down. You must include a daily walk or two in your plans if your puppy is to be rugged and well.

When you go to pick up your Doberman, you should take a collar and lead with you. Both of these should be appropriate for the breed and age of the dog, and the collar should be one that fits him now, not one he has to grow into. Your new Doberman also needs a water dish (or two, one for the house and one for outside) and a food dish. These should be made preferably of an unbreakable material. You will have fun shopping at your local pet shop for these things, and I am sure you will be tempted to add some luxury items of which you will find a fascinating array. For chew things, either Nylabone® or real beef

bones (leg or knuckle cut to an appropriate size, the latter found as soup bones at most butcher shops or supermarkets) are safe and provide many hours of happy entertainment, at the same time being great exercise during the teething period. Rawhide chews can be safe, too, if manufactured under the proper conditions. There was a problem, however, several years back owing to the chemicals with which some of the rawhide chew products had been treated, so in order to take no chances, avoid them. Also avoid plastic and rubber toys, *particularly* toys with squeakers. If you want to play ball with your Doberman, select a ball that has been made of very tough construction; Dobermans have very strong jaws. Even then do not leave the puppy alone with the ball; take it with you when you finish the game. There are also some nice "tug of war" toys which are fun when you play with the dog. But again, do not go off and leave these playthings to be chewed in privacy.

Too many changes all at once can be difficult for a puppy. Therefore, no matter how you eventually wind up doing it, for the first few days keep him as nearly as you can on the routine to which he is accustomed. Find out what brand of food the breeder used, how frequently and when the puppies were fed, and start out by doing it that way yourself, gradually over a period of a week or two making whatever changes suit you better.

Of utmost precedence in planning for your puppy is the selection of a good veterinarian whom you feel you can trust. Make an appointment to bring the puppy in to be checked over on your way home from the breeder's. Be sure to obtain the puppy's health certificate from the breeder, along with information regarding worming, shots, and so on.

With all of these things in order, you should be nicely prepared for a smooth, happy start when your puppy actually joins the family.

Joining the Family

Remember that as exciting and happy as the occasion may be for you, the puppy's move from his place of birth to your home can be a traumatic experience for him. His mother and littermates will be missed. He will perhaps be slightly frightened or awed by the change of surroundings. The person he trusted and depended on will be gone. Everything, thus, should be planned to make the move easy for him, to give him confidence, to make him realize that yours is a pretty nice place to be after all.

Never bring a puppy home on a holiday. There just is too much going on, with people and gifts and excitement. If he is honoring "an occasion" (a birthday, for example), work it out so that his arrival will be a few days before or, better still, a few days after the big occasion. Then he will be greeted by a normal routine and will have your undivided attention. Try not to bring the puppy home during the evening. Early morning is the ideal time, as then he has the opportunity of getting acquainted, and the first strangeness wears off before bedtime. You will find it a more peaceful night that way, I am sure. Allow the puppy to investigate his surroundings under your watchful eye. If you already have a pet in the household, carefully watch that things are going smoothly between them, so that the relationship gets off to a friendly start; otherwise, you may quickly have a lasting problem. Be careful not to let your older pet become jealous by paying more attention to the newcomer than to him. You want a friendly start. Much of the future attitude of each toward the other depends on what takes place that first day.

If you have children, again, it is important that the relationship start out well. Should the puppy be their first pet, it is assumed that you have prepared them for it with a firm explanation that puppies are living creatures to be treated with gentle consideration, not playthings to be abused and hurt. One of my friends raised her children with the household rule that should a dog or puppy belonging to one of the children bite one of the children, the child would be punished, not the dog, as mother would know that the child had in some way hurt the dog. I must say that this strategy worked out very well, as no child was ever bitten in that household and both daughters grew up to remain great animal lovers. Anyway, on whatever terms you do it, please bring your children up not only to *love* but also to *respect* their pet, with the realization that dogs have rights, too. These same ground rules should apply to visiting children. I have seen youngsters who are fine with their own pets unmercifully tease and harass pets belonging to other people. Children do not always realize how rough is too rough, and without intending to, they may inflict considerable pain or injury if permitted to ride herd on a puppy.

If you start out by spoiling your new puppy, your puppy will expect and even demand that you continue to spoil it in the future. So think it out carefully before you invite the puppy to come spend its first night at your home in bed with you, unless you wish to continue the practice. What you have considered to be a one-night stand may be accepted as just great and expected for the future. It is better not to start what you may consider to be bad habits which you may find difficult to overcome later. Be firm with the puppy, strike a routine, and stick to it. The puppy will learn more quickly this way, and everyone will be happier as a result.

Socialization and Training

Socialization and training of your new baby Doberman actually starts the second you walk in the door with him, for every move you make should be geared toward teaching the puppy what is expected of him and, at the same time, building up his confidence and feeling of being at home.

The first step is to teach the puppy his name and to come when called by it. No matter how flowery or long or impressive the actually registered name may be, the puppy should also have a short, easily understood "call name" which can be learned quickly and to which he will respond. Start using this call name immediately, and use it in exactly the same way each time that you address the puppy, refraining from the temptation to alternate various forms of endearment, pet names, or substitutes which will only be confusing to him.

Using his name clearly, call the puppy over to you when you see him awake and looking about for something to do. Just a few times of this, with a lot of praise over what a "good dog" he is when he responds, and you will have taught him to come to you when he hears his name; he knows that he will be warmly greeted, petted, and possibly even given a small snack.

As soon as the puppy has spent a few hours getting acquainted with his new surroundings, you can put a light collar on the puppy's neck so that he will become accustomed to having it on. He may hardly notice it, or he may make a great fuss at first, rolling over, struggling, and trying to rub it off. Have a tasty tidbit or two on hand with which to divert his attention at this period, or try to divert his attention by playing with him. Soon he no longer will be concerned about that strange new thing around his neck.

The next step in training is to have the puppy become accustomed to the lead. Use a lightweight lead, attached to the collar. Carry him outdoors where there will be things of interest to investigate; then set him down and see what happens. Again, he may appear hardly to notice the lead dangling behind him, or he may make a fuss about it. If the latter occurs, repeat the diversion attempts with food or a toy. As soon as the puppy has accepted the presence of the lead, pick up the end of it and follow after him. He may react by trying to free himself, struggling to slip his head through the collar, or trying to bite at the lead. Coax him, if you can, with kind words and petting. In a few moments, curiosity regarding his surroundings and an interesting smell or two should start diverting him. When this takes place, do not try to pull on him or guide his direction at first. Just be glad that he is walking with the lead on and let him decide where to go. When he no longer seems to resent the lead, try gently to direct him with short little tugs in the direction you would like him to travel. Never jerk him roughly, as then he will become frightened and fight harder; and never pull steadily or attempt to drag him, as this immediately triggers a battle of wills with each of you pulling in an opposite direction. The best method is a short, quick, gentle jerk, which, repeated a few times, should get him started off with you. Of course, continue to talk encouragingly to him and offer him "goodies" until he gets started. Repetition of the command "Come" should accompany all of this.

Once this step has been mastered and walks are taken on the lead pleasantly and companionably, the next step is to teach him to remain on your left-hand side. Use the same process as you used to teach him to respond correctly while on the lead, this time repeating the word "Heel." Of course, all of this is not accomplished in one day; it should be done gradually, with short work periods each time, letting the puppy know when he pleases you. The exact length of time required for each puppy varies and depends on the aptitude of each individual puppy.

Housebreaking a puppy is more easily accomplished by the prevention method than by the cure. Try to avoid "accidents" whenever you can rather than punishing the puppy once these have occured. Common sense helps a great deal. A puppy will need to be taken out at regularly spaced intervals: first thing in the morning directly from his bed, immediately after meals, after he has napped, or whenever you notice that he is "looking for a spot." Choose roughly the same place outdoors each time that you take the puppy out for this purpose, so that a pattern will be established. If he does not go immediately, do not just return him to the house, as chances are that he will go the moment he is back inside. Try to be patient and remain out with him until you get results; then praise him enthusiastically and both of you can return indoors. If you catch the puppy having an "accident," pick him up firmly, sharply say, "No!" and rush him outside. If you do not see the accident occur, there is little point of doing anything beyond cleaning it up, as once it has happended and been forgotten, the puppy will likely not even realize why you are angry with him.

Your Doberman puppy should form the habit of spending a certain amount of time each day in his crate, even when you are home. Sometimes the puppy will do this voluntarily, but if not, he should be taught to do so. Lead the puppy by the collar over to the crate, and then gently push him inside firmly saying "Down" or "Stay" as you fasten the door. Whatever command you use, always make it the same word for each act every time. Repetition is the big thing in training, and the dog must learn to associate a specific word or phrase with each different thing he is expected to do. When you mean "Sit," always say exactly that. "Stay" should mean that the dog should remain where he was when you gave the command. "Down" means something else again. Do not confuse the dog by shuffling the commands, as you will create confusion for him and a problem for yourself by having done so.

As soon as he has received his immunization shots, take your Doberman puppy with you wherever and whenever possible. Nothing else can equal this close association for building up self-confidence and stability in a young dog. It is extremely important that you spend the time necessary for socialization, particularly if you are planning on the puppy becoming a show dog.

Take your Doberman in the car so that he will learn to enjoy riding without becoming carsick, as can happen to a dog unused to the car's motion. Take him everywhere you go, provided you are certain he will not be unwelcome or create any difficulties by his presence: visiting friends and relatives (if they like dogs and do not have house pets of their own who will consider your puppy an intruder), to busy shopping centers (always keeping him on his lead), or just walking around the street of your town. If someone admires him, as always seems to happen under these circumstances, encourage that person to pet or talk with him; becoming accustomed to people in this manner always seems especially beneficial in instilling self-confidence in your dog. You want your puppy to develop a relaxed, happy canine personality and like the world and its inhabitants. The most debilitating thing for a puppy's self-confidence is excessive sheltering and pampering. Keeping a growing puppy away from strange people and strange dogs may well turn him into a nervous, neurotic dog—surely the last thing anyone can enjoy as a pet.

Make obedience training a game with your puppy while he is extremely young. Try to teach him to meaning of and expected responses to the basic terms such as "Come," Stay," "Sit," "Down," and "Heel," along with the meaning of "No" even while he is still too young for formal training, and you will be pleased and proud of the good manners that he will exhibit.

Feeding

There was a time when providing good, nourishing food for our dogs involved a far more complicated routine and time-consuming process than people now feel is necessary.

The old belief was that the daily rations should consist of fresh beef, vegetables, cereal, egg yolks, and cottage cheese as basics, with such additions as brewer's yeast and other vitamin supplements.

During recent years, however, many attitudes have been changed regarding the necessity, or even the desirability, of this procedure. We still give eggs, cottage cheese, and supplements to the diet, but the basic methods of feeding dogs have changed; and the changes are definitely for the better in the opinion of many an authority. The school of thought now is that you are doing your dogs a definite service when you feed them some of the fine commercially prepared dog foods in preference to your own home-cooked concoctions.

The reasoning behind this new outlook is easy to understand. The production of dog food has grown to be a major industry, participated in by some of the best known, most highly respected names in the dog fancy. These trusted firms do turn out excellent products. People are feeding their dogs these preparations with confidence, and the dogs are thriving, prospering, and keeping in top condition. What more could we want or ask?

There are at least a half dozen absolutely splendid dry foods which can be mixed with water or broth and served to your dog, either "as is" or with the addition of fresh or canned meat. There is a variety of canned meat preparations for your dog, either 100% meat to be mixed with kibble or complete prepared dinners, a combination of meat and cereal. There are several kinds of "convenience foods," these in packets which you open and dump out into the dog's dish. It is just that simple. The "convenience foods" are neat and easy for you when travelling, but generally speaking we prefer to feed a dry food mixed with hot water, to which we usually add canned meat (although leftover meat scraps or ground beef are sometimes added instead of the canned meat.) Actually we feel that the canned meat, with its added fortifiers, is more beneficial to the dogs than the fresh meat. However, the two can be used alternately or, if you prefer and your dogs do well on it, by all means use ground beef.

Dogs enjoy variety in the meat part of their diet, which is easy to provide with the canned

1. Am., Bda., Can., and Col. Ch. Elfred's Spark Plug was truly a fun dog—pictured here in his favorite position. Bred, owned, and handled by Mrs. Ellen Hoffman, Elfred Kennels, Harriman, New York.
2. Nylabone® is the safest chew toy to give your Doberman: it helps cut the puppy teeth, it massages the gums, and it provides an outlet for doggie tension.
3. The great Ch. Muck v Brunia at the age of 12 years. Photo courtesy of Peggy Adamson.
4. Ch. Ru-Mar's Morgansonne, C.D. at age seven years. Born May 1962. Photo courtesy of Mrs. Ruth M. Edwards, Monterey, California.

meat. The canned meats available include all sorts of beef (chunk, ground, stewed, and so on), lamb, chicken, liver, and numerous concoctions of several of these blended together.

There also is prepared food geared to every age bracket of your dog's life, from puppyhood on through old age, with special additions or modifications to make it especially nourishing and beneficial. The dogs of yesteryear never had it so good during the canine dinner hour because these foods are tasty and geared to meet the dog's gastronomical approval.

Additionally, contents and nutritional values are clearly listed on the labels, and careful instructions for feeding exactly the right amount for the size and weight of each dog are also given.

With the great choice of dog foods available today, we do not feel that the addition of vitamins is necessary; but if you do, there are several highly satisfactory vitamin products available at pet shops. These products serve as tasty treats along with being beneficial.

Of course there is no reason not to cook up something for your Doberman's dinner if you feel happier doing so, but it seems to us superfluous when such truly satisfying rations are available at so much less expense and trouble.

How often you feed is a matter of how a schedule works out best for you and for your dog or dogs. Many owners prefer to feed their dogs once a day. Others feel that twice daily is better for the digestion and more satisfying to the dog, particularly if he is a family member who stands around and watches the preparation of family meals. The important thing is that you *do not overfeed*, as overfeeding can bring on many canine problems.

From the time your puppy is fully weaned until he reaches about twelve weeks of age, he should be fed four times daily. His breakfast and his dinner should consist of about two to two-and-a-half cups of moistened puppy kibble to which about one cup (slightly more if necessary to soften) of hot water or broth has been added, mixed with either a quarter-pound of fresh ground beef or a quarter-can of canned beef (these amounts are approximate as there is no harm in slightly more of the beef and a bit less kibble if you prefer). At noontime and at bedtime the puppy

should be given one can of evaporated milk mixed with one can of slightly warmed water.

As the puppy grows older, from three to six months of age, cut back to three meals daily, substituting the milk meals with a meal of meat and kibble. If the puppy cleans his dish with gusto and is not putting on too much weight, you will know the amount of food is right for him. If he is starting to look chubby, cut back a bit on the amount; you do not want your puppy to be fat. Too much weight can be overburdening on growing limbs and muscles and can also result in a sagging topline. So do guard against it. If the puppy is eating up everything but looking thin, slightly increase the amount of food, as he may not be getting all he needs. At six months of age, the pup should be fed twice daily, and at twelve months, if you wish, you may cut back to one daily feeding with a biscuit or two morning and evening. If you do feed just once daily, the meal should be given by early afternoon.

Remember that fresh, cool water should always be available for your Doberman. This is of utmost importance to his good health throughout his lifetime.

Don't forget to have the puppy checked regularly for worms and to keep a watchful eye. Each puppy is an individual and needs to be treated as such.

4
▶

529

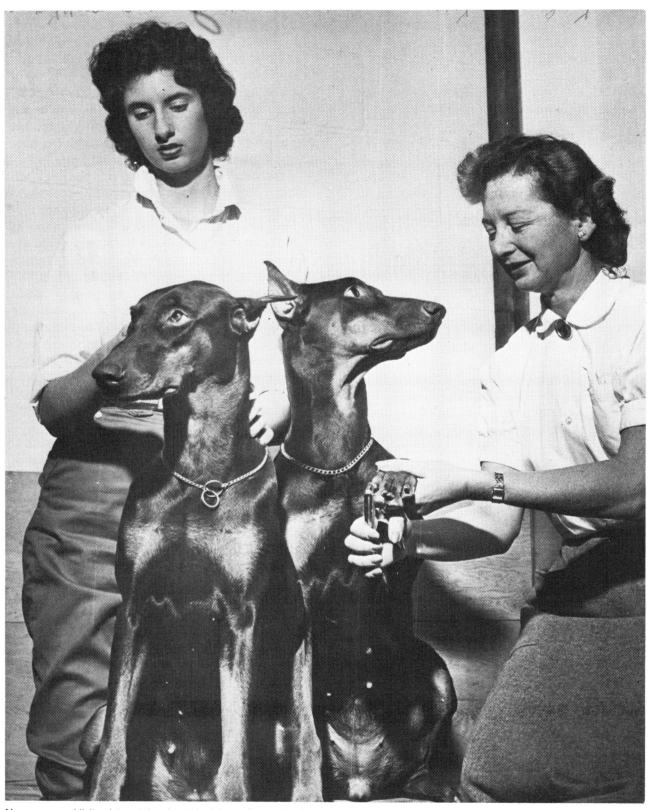

Newspaper publicity picture taken by a Harrisburg, Pennsylvania newspaper after Jane Kay won Best Brace of Working Dogs at Westminster 1958 with Ch. Kay Hill's Paint The Town Red and Kay Hill's Slightly Scarlet.

CHAPTER SEVENTEEN

Grooming the Doberman

Doberman owners are fortunate since theirs is one of the easiest breeds of dog to keep looking at their sleek, well groomed best. They require only a minimum amount of bathing (if at all) and can be completely groomed in a short period of time. A good brushing daily, or even every few days; a weekly shortening of nails and a check of the ears; and a monthly check on and scaling of the teeth should keep him handsome. Added to this, when he comes in wet from inclement weather, dry him briskly with a soft turkish towel, which will clean his coat and which, coupled with the frequent brushing, should keep the need of baths to a minimum. Should there be an emergency leading to the necessity for a bath, you will find complete instructions further along in this book.

Arrange your Doberman's grooming supplies together in one place (a tack box, if you plan on showing him, keeps everything in place and ready to go, whether at home or "on the road"). Included should be a correct grooming tool with which to remove loose, dead hair from the coat and encourage the fresh new growth to come through more quickly. The most popular item for this purpose is the rubber curry groomer, which has V-shaped teeth and is inexpensive, readily available at your pet supply headquarters. You will find it just great for keeping ahead of coat changes, and it encourages the new

growth while removing that which is loose and ready to fall, thus controlling shedding all over the house and furniture.

Cotton swabs and peroxide should be used to clean out the ears on a weekly basis. Remember especially that uncropped ears are prone to problems, as ear mites and infection can more readily develop beneath the concealment provided by the earflaps. So if your Doberman is uncropped, keep a check on the ears with special diligence. There are numerous excellent products on the market designed to keep ears clean and healthy and to assist in clearing up any problems. Ask your veterinarian for a recommendation. Also we think Panelog ointment, available by prescription or from your veterinarian, is like magic in cases of ear infections. Signs of ear discomfort are vigorous head shaking, head carried slightly to either side, and of course scratching an ear with the hind foot.

Proper nail care is important, for if nails are neglected and permitted to just grow, they can become painful, cause the dog to move gingerly, help break down pasterns, and turn a neat, clean, compact looking foot into one just the opposite. Nails should be kept close to the quick (if you cut into the quick it will bleed, so have Kwik Stop handy for immediate application should this occur). Either nail clippers or electric nail grinders can be used, each method having its followers. The grinders leave a nice smooth finish but should be used with caution so as not to take the nail back too far. Neglect of the nails can cause additional problems, as the quick grows right along with the nail, so when it is overgrown it is practically impossible to take the nail back to its proper length without pain to the dog.

There is no breed of dog where greater emphasis is placed on teeth than the Doberman, so these should be guarded carefully. Check them every month diligently, and if tartar is accumulating, remove it carefully with a tooth scaler. These handy gadgets are available at the pet supplier's and your veterinarian will show you how it is to be used.

For cleaning the Doberman's coat and at the same time keeping it glossy, spray him lightly with a grooming product (many are available) before going over him with the rubber curry groomer, and finish by polishing

531

with a dry towel. Try a few until you find the preparation you like best, as there is a wide range of choices. These are usually pleasantly scented, which keep any trace of "doggy odor" under control.

There you have the necessary routine for grooming a family Doberman. The same applies to a show dog, with the following additions.

You will need to have some additional tools for your show Doberman and it will be very much to your advantage if you immediately purchase a rubber-topped grooming table, complete with arm and "noose" (the latter slips around the dog's neck and the former holds him in place while being groomed). Your dog should be taught to stand and lie on this table from his earliest grooming sessions, as it is so much easier this way. The table is useful both at home and at the dog shows (they are equipped with collapsible legs, and thus fold easily for transportation) so plan on taking it with you when you travel to shows. Your Dobe will come to be very relaxed and comfortable on this table once he has learned what is expected of him. You will also need a show lead (choke-chain type is best for a Doberman), a pair of high quality blunt tipped (or curved at the tip) scissors for trimming, as pointed scissors should never be used when working on any dog. Thinning shears are also part of the equipment, as are hair clippers, the latter either electric or manually operated. Perhaps at first the latter would be your best choice, as they work more slowly and one is less liable to carry "mistakes" too far before realizing what is happening. Electric clippers in inexperienced hands can create considerable havoc. Before using any hair clippers on your Doberman, watch how the experienced groomers, handlers and breeder-exhibitors are doing it. If possible, have one of them do your dog the first time.

The clipping and trimming work done on a Doberman is not a great deal; but having it done smoothly and correctly will make all the difference in the appearance of your dog. Work in good light, and start by removing the whiskers and eyebrows with the curved scissors, taking them close and checking an hour or so before you show the dog to ascertain that none are starting to re-appear. Any long hair along the jaw or on the sides of the face should likewise be removed. Ears should

be "neatened" by using a fine blade in your clippers, going along the edges of each ear for a nice smooth finish. Hair inside the ear should also be cleared away, working from the tip to the base, and the hair surrounding the base of the ear should be smoothed by cutting it short.

Cowlicks, wherever they appear, should be trimmed out with the thinning shears, then blended in carefully to be smooth with the rest of the coat, using the careful thinning and blending method. Generally these appear mostly on the forechest or seat of the dog but may do so almost anywhere on an individual. If left they "stand out like a sore thumb," so it is important that this be attended to nicely. In the same category is the ridge which runs along the sides of the neck from the base of the ear, and which can ruin the appearance of a clean, correct neckline. This also can appear on the shanks, so check the dog over carefully for these as you work.

Clippers should be used where long or scraggly hairs appear on the stomach or in the loin area, as the underline of the dog in silhouette should look neat and clean.

Finish the job by doing the feet, removing surplus hair from between the pads and around the edges of the feet, so that they look compact and catlike, as they should.

Complete your grooming by making certain that the eyes are clear and clean. A dab of petroleum jelly on the nose leather will make it look moistly shining. And a light touch of coat dressing (but *very* light, as judges will not appreciate having the coat feel greasy) and/or a quick "shine" with a "hound glove" (again from your pet supplier) as this will have the dog elegantly prepared to take on the world of competition.

Ear Cropping

If you live where ear cropping is legal, and are planning to show your Doberman, you almost certainly will want to have him cropped as it does add enormously to a stylish appearance. There are many who truly like the uncropped look, but to receive recognition among a large number of cropped dogs is extremely difficult if not impossible.

Ear cropping age is usually around six to eight weeks and cropping should *never be attempted by an amateur*. I will agree that there

1. Courland Inherit the Wind and Courland Gone with the Wind at nine weeks. By Ch. Beaulane Windfall ex Courland All That Glitters, WAC. Bred and owned by Stephanie J. Taube, Alamo, California. These babies have had their ears cropped and they are in the process of healing. Correct care of the ears at this period is of utmost importance if they are to heal and stand properly.
2. Doberman puppies, their ears lately done, at Diana Stoner's Rodiah Kennels, Conestoga, Pennsylvania.
3. A Brykris Dobe puppy photographed by Bill James; owned by Jo Ann James, Miami, Florida.

▲1
2
►

►
3

are some veterinarians who do not do ears well, so you will need to make inquiry prior to the arrival of that time for your puppies. By the time you have your first litter, you will also have friends in the breed in your area. Discuss this subject at length with them, note how dogs whose ears were cropped (by the person recommended) have turned out, and select very carefully as the style and smart appearance of your dog can be entirely ruined by an inept or crude job. Sometimes ears can be re-done when the dog is mature; but if this correction can possibly be avoided it should be, as what for a young puppy can be comparatively quick healing and painless can be a far more traumatic experience for an older dog.

The closer to six weeks the puppies can be done, the easier it will be on them, as the ears are thinner and more easily cut at that time than even a couple of weeks later. Of course it goes without saying that the puppy should be in top physical condition when this is done. Never attempt to crop ears on a sickly or weak puppy until that puppy is back to bouncing normal health.

I am not even going to make suggestions here as to how the cropping should be done, as I feel very strongly that it should be attempted only by a qualified expert. Plan ahead and try to see the finished results on some of your friends' dogs *before* you make arrangements. Suggested sources of information are the person from whom you purchased your puppy; the owner of the stud dog or bitch; or other folks who are showing (and winning with) Dobermans which were raised in your area. Most breeders are very glad to help a newcomer with this information, so if you see some nice, smart, handsomely shaped and well-carried ears on any young stock in your area, do not hesitate to ask for a recommendation.

When you are having the ears done, perhaps you could get a breeder-friend (with winning dogs) to come with you, one who might be able to make suggestions as to the length and shaping of the ear, should you be unable to find a veterinarian who already has this knowledge of Dobermans. Obviously the matter of ear cropping is extremely important as the entire appearance of the dog, and his possible show career, can be ruined if the ears

are botched up, cut too short, or otherwise not done *expertly*.

Sharing the importance, and usually of even greater concern, is the healing of the ears. All sorts of problems can arise if they do not heal promptly and cleanly. Therefore every effort should be made to avoid infections. In discussing the various methods of after-care with Doberman breeders, I find three which are well recommended and each has proven easy to handle and successful for many people.

The first of these is the traditional taping method, which has worked out well for many hundreds of young Dobermans. The following instructions and drawings are courtesy of Pat and Dave Cunningham, owners of Ryas Doberman Pinschers, Vinemount, Ontario, Canada. They were originally done by Pat Cunningham, who is a talented artist as well as a knowledgeable and experienced breeder of Dobermans, as part of an information booklet the Cunninghams have prepared and provide for the purchasers of their puppies. We were delighted when Pat agreed that we might use them here, as we feel that they will be helpful to many of our readers with puppies at this stage of their development.

Taping Cropped Ears

Approximately one week after cropping, when the cut edges of the ear have healed, begin to train the hardening cartilage in the ears into an erect position. You will require a roll of 1″ wide adhesive tape (Zonas or ZO brand by Johnsons is a good choice), and popsicle sticks. Sensitive skin tape is not sticky enough to hold an active puppy's ears. Masking or other non-breathing tapes do not allow for adequate ventilation. Tongue depressors are too wide, but may be split length-wise if care is taken to shave off any sharp corners.

Begin by cutting two 11″ lengths of tape, one 14″ length and two 1½″ tapes. Cover two sticks as indicated in the diagrams below.

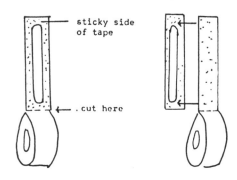

Pull a length of tape from the roll, with the sticky side facing you, and place the stick in the center of the tape about 1½″ from the top. Cut the tape ½″ below the stick. Cut another piece of tape the same length and attach the NON-ADHESIVE side of the second tape over top of the stick onto the adhesive side of the first tape.

Have all of these components handy, and sit the pup on a helper's knee, seated directly in front of you. Have him steady the pup's head by holding behind the head and around the muzzle, as is shown in the diagram below.

Stretching the ear upwards, press one of the tape-covered sticks to the inside of the ear. See diagram below.

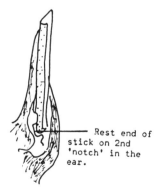

Rest end of stick on 2nd 'notch' in the ear.

Take care that you do not release the upward stretch on the ear as you reach for the next piece of tape.

Attach one of the 11″ lengths of tape to the 'flap' of ear at the front base of the ear. Follow the direction of the 'flap' with the tape (refer to the directional arrows in the diagram below). Be sure to pull the tape fairly snug, as it will loosen as the puppy plays.

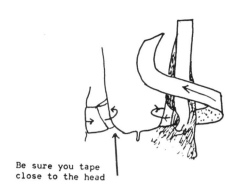

Be sure you tape close to the head

Prevent the tips of the ears from curling. Use the 1½″ tapes to secure the ear tips to the tape-covered sticks.

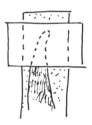

Use the 14″ length of tape as a bridge between the ears. Begin by attaching the tape to the ear on YOUR left, bring it to the ear on your right, checking to be sure the ears are parallel to each other. Attach the tape to the second ear. Bring the tape around the second ear and UP TO the first half of the bridge. Follow the diagram below for the other ear.

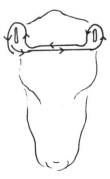

Once in place, lift the bridge and stick the two cross bars together, so that they will not stick to the top of the pup's head. Be sure that the tape is not too high on the ear, as is demonstrated on the right ear in the diagram below or the ears may begin to tilt inward. (see dotted line).

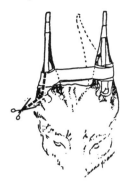

Tapes may remain on, as long as they remain in the parallel position, for up to one week. Remove them by cutting through all layers as indicated above, loosening the 1½ tapes on the ear tips, and briskly remove. Repeat the entire procedure as often as is necessary, giving a day's breathing time between.

The second set of instructions for after-cropping care of ears is the "no tape" ear taping method, about which we have been hearing good things. We bring you these instructions courtesy of Leslie Hall, Chairman of the Doberman Pinscher Club of America's Top Twenty Committee, who notes, "This is an incredibly safe, easy, PAINLESS method. I did not think it up (wish I did). It was handed to me third person. No one seems to know where the idea originated, but it is SUPER." This method was called to my attention by Ross Petruzzo, who says that he and Carol use it extensively and feel that it is very successful. So we bring it to you as a choice if you prefer it to the more traditional taping method.

The "No Tape" Ear Taping Method

All but the two that are staying are gone—from a flood of nine puppies down to a trickle—from a thundering herd, to a pitter patter. It's been twelve weeks since their birth, and six weeks since they were cropped. Their ears have been posted for the last five weeks—no crimps, no crinkles—and when you talk silly to them they wrinkle their brows—ears straight up, without a speck of tape—a bridge—or a rack.

They've been together—all nine at the beginning—without a stay coming down due to

the other pups. When they bump into something (usually another brother; there were eight males, one bitch—whew!) their ears bend, then spring right back.

We used this "no tape" method five days after the litter was cropped. The ears were cared for while they were up, resulting in no crimps or curling from scar tissue on cut edges. Of course, you must be extremely careful while putting them up, but the cropped edge was easily accessible.

If the puppies are newly cropped, it's easier to do this with two people, but it can be done with one. Two people can do a litter of nine in less than an hour and a half—including preparation!

Sound incredible? It is—this is the miracle method; the "recipe" follows:

INGREDIENTS:
One (1) Puppy (more if you're so lucky...)
One (1) square Dr. Scholl's MOLEFOAM (NOT Moleskin) per TWO (2) pups. Available at any drugstore or discount store.
SURGICAL GLUE—Skin Bond is excellent.
Scissors
A ruler and pen

Here's the How-To's:
1) Clean all the ears well, with peroxide for newly cut ears, alcohol for healed ears. 2) Take as many squares of MOLEFOAM as needed—two pups per square—and prepare as follows: Do all of one step before proceeding to the next (i.e., cut six squares in half, then do next step on each stay). It goes faster. Note: LEAVE PLASTIC BACKING ON MOLEFOAM UNTIL ALL CUTTING IS DONE.

Using the ruler, measure halfway—vertically from backing edge to backing edge (see illustration). Now, take the ruler and draw a line DIAGONALLY from corner to corner, leaving a half inch at top. Cut following lines.

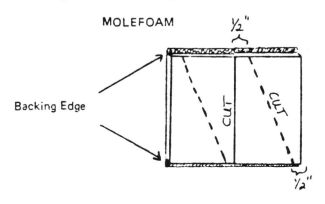

Cut off bottom in a slight arc; this removes the "points," rounding the portion to go in the bell.

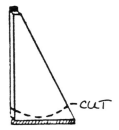

Peel off plastic backing on all stays to be used. There is adhesive on the foam, but it is not sticky enough to stay put.

Place an ample amount of surgical glue on the white, sticky side, starting from about ¾ of an inch up from the bottom. Glue ALL stays to be used and set aside.

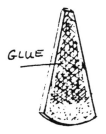

Now place an ample amount of glue, being sure to completely cover the ear—evenly—starting from the little knob just above the canal (see illustration). Wait a minute or so, NOT the four or five minutes as instructed on the glue, being careful not to let the pup shake its head, or you'll glue the ear to the side of the head.

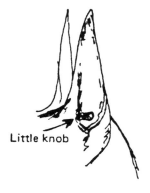

NOW, roll the base of the stay.

Be careful not to let the stay stick to the ear before you have positioned it well into the canal (as far down as you would place any other method of posting). Holding the ear in the position you want it to stand, attach the stay—from the bottom up—straightening edges on healing ears. Rub stay to ear to make sure it's well adhered.

Don't worry about taking stays out; they fall out by themselves in about ten days, from the oil on the pup's ear. They seem to be virtually "puppyproof," as the others chew on them, etc., but they don't come out prematurely. There's no problem AT ALL with infection or glop inside the ear canal, because air can get in freely. There's no danger of taping too tightly or cuts and gouges from tape at the base. It is an incredibly safe, easy, painless method.

A popular method with many people is that which employs a foam rubber "crown" placed between the ears on the top of the puppy's head, supporting the ears which are taped to it. For this, one needs upholsterer's foam rubber, some one-inch-wide toupee tape (the sort available to hold men's hairpieces in place), and cloth tape in both one-inch and one-half-inch widths. Cut the foam into a wedge-shaped piece of a size that will fit on top of the puppy's head between the ears. The widest side should be sightly rounded to

1. Ch. Srigo's Kase Kuchen, C.D., Best of Breed under judge Bob Salomon at Bronx County, 1968. Owned by Kay Martin, Brooklyn, New York. Handled by her breeder, Felicia Luberich of "Srigo" fame.
2. Carlos Rojas winning Best in Show with Ch. Marienburg's Lone Eagle for Dr. and Mrs. Anthony DiNardo, East Hartford, Connecticut, October 1978.
3. Livie de la Morliere winning Best in Show. Annie and Daniel Mulero, owners, Dompierre/Mer, France.

1▲   ▼2

fit in place; the entire wedge should be slightly taller than the puppy's ears will be when stretched upright. Wrap the foam completely in the toupee tape, which is sticky on both sides with paper covering on one, removing the paper covering as you go. The foam should be covered on the sides, across the bottom and over the top. Place the wedge on top of the puppy's head, pressing carefully to be sure that is is securely "anchored" (the toupee tape to the head). You will need an extra pair of hands helping you for this job, as it is important that it be done with care. The ears should be even with one another, up straight, the cut edges being carefully placed. With someone holding the ears firmly in place for you, run a strip of half-inch tape to the inside of one ear, across the top of the foam where it should adhere firmly to the toupee tape, and down the inside of the other ear. Be sure that you do not pull in on, or shorten, either ear in the process. Then a strip of the one-inch tape should be placed, about halfway between the top of the head and the ear tip, from the inside of one ear across the front of the foam and inside the other ear.

Whatever method you use, do be sure that the puppy's ears are not permitted to become overly sore or sensitive. Keep watching to see that all seems to be progressing well, and if this is your first puppy, or your first litter, do seek the opinion of an experienced breeder or your veterinarian if you feel that all is not well.

It is very foolish to purchase a puppy until after the ear cropping has been attended to and the ears have had the opportunity to completely heal. The aftercare is no job for a novice owner, although handled quite easily by an experienced breeder. So until you start breeding puppies of your own, do not take on any which do not have the cropping behind them.

Unlike the cropping of ears, tails are cropped when the puppies are just a few days old. Here again, consult someone who has raised Doberman puppies regarding the length and manner in which this should be done until you become proficient.

Dewclaws are also removed at the same time the tails are done. Both procedures are quite simple when one has learned how.

Ch. Hotai Copper Tattoo, owned by Dee Chiantella and David M. Polk, is the winner of 150 times Best of Breed, 100 Group placements, and numerous other records and awards.

CHAPTER EIGHTEEN

Showing Your Doberman Pinscher

The groundwork for showing your Doberman has been accomplished with your careful selection and purchase of your future show prospect. If it is a puppy, we assume that you have gone through all the proper preliminaries of good care, which actually should be the same whether the puppy is a pet or a future show dog, with a few extra precautions in the case of the latter.

General Considerations

Remember that a winning dog must be kept in trim, top condition. You want him neither too fat nor too thin, so do not spoil his figure and his appearance, or his appetite for proper nourishing food, by allowing family members or guests to be constantly feeding him "goodies." The best "treat" of all is a small wad of ground raw beef or one of the packaged dog "goodies." To be avoided are ice cream, potato chips, cookies, cake, candy, and other fattening items which will cause the dog to gain weight. A dog in show condition must never be fat, nor must he be painfully thin to the point of his ribs fairly sticking through the skin.

The importance of temperament and showman ship cannot possibly be overemphasized. These two qualities have put many a mediocre dog across, while lack of them can ruin

the career of an otherwise outstanding specimen. So, from the day your dog or puppy arrives home, socialize him. Keep him accustomed to being with people and to being handled by people. Encourage your friends and relatives to "go over" him as the judges will in the ring, so that at the shows this will not be a strange, upsetting experience. Practice showing his "bite" (the manner in which his teeth meet) deftly and quickly. It is quite simple to spread the lips apart with your fingers, and the puppy should be accustomed and willing to accept this from you or from the judge, without struggle. The puppy should also be accustomed to having his jaws opened wide in order for his teeth to be counted, since missing teeth, if other than premolars, is a serious fault. Some judges ask the exhibitors to handle the mouths, showing them bite and jaws, rather than doing it themselves. These are the considerate judges who prefer not to risk spreading any possible virus infections by taking their hands from one dog's mouth to another's; but the old-fashioned judges still persist in doing the latter, so the dog should be prepared for either.

Take you future show dog with you in the car, so that he will love riding and not become carsick when he travels. He should associate going in the car with pleasure and attention. Take him where it is crowded: downtown, shopping malls, or, in fact, anywhere you go where dogs are permitted. Make the expeditions fun for him by frequent petting and words of praise; do not just ignore him as you go about your errands or other business.

Do not overly shelter your future show dog. Instinctively you may want to keep him at home, especially while a young puppy, where he is safe from germs or danger; but this can be foolish on two counts. To begin with, a dog kept away from other dogs or other environments builds up no natural immunity against all the things with which he will come in contact at the dog shows. Actually it is wiser to keep him well up-to-date on all protective "shots" and then allow him to become accustomed to being among other dogs and dog owners. Also, a dog who never goes among people, to strange places, or among strange dogs, may grow up with a timidity of spirit that will cause you deep problems when his show career gets underway.

Keep you Doberman's coat in immaculate condition with daily grooming (which takes only a few minutes) and baths when the latter are necessary. For the latter, use a shampoo designed and sold for use on dogs or whatever the person who bred your puppy may suggest. Several of the "brand name" products do an excellent job, and there are several which are beneficial toward keeping the dog free of fleas. Look for them at your pet supplier's. Be sure to rinse the dog thoroughly, leaving no traces of soap which may cause itching or skin irritation. It is a wise precaution to put a drop of castor oil in each eye to ensure no soap irritation. Use warm water (be sure it is not uncomfortably hot or chillingly cold) and a good spray. An electric hair dryer is a great convenience; use it after first blotting off the excess moisture with a turkish towel. Do not let water find its way into the ear cavity. A wad of cotton in each ear guards against this possibility. Toenails also should be watched and trimmed every few weeks. It is important not to let nails grow too long, as they can become painful and ruin the appearance of foot and pastern.

Assuming that you will be handling the dog personally, or even if he will be professionally handled, it is important that a few moments of each day be spent practicing dog-show routine. Practice "stacking," or "setting him up," as you have seen the exhibitors do at the shows you've attended, and teach him to hold this position once you have him stacked to your satisfaction. Make the learning pleasant by being firm but lavish in your praise when he behaves correctly. Work in front of a mirror for setting up practice; this enables you to see the dog as the judge does and to learn what corrections need to be made by looking at the dog from that angle.

Teach your Doberman to gait at your side on a loose lead. When you have mastered the basic essentials at home, then look for and join a training class for future work and polishing up your technique. Training classes are sponsored by show-giving clubs in many areas, and their popularity is steadily increasing. If you have no other way of locating one, perhaps your veterinarian may know of one through some of his clients; but if you are sufficiently aware of the dog-show world to

want a show dog, you will probably be personally acquainted with other fanciers who will share information of this sort with you.

Accustom your show dog to being in a crate (which you should be doing, even if the dog is to be only a pet). He should be kept in the crate "between times" for his own well-being and safety.

A show dog's teeth must be kept clean and free of tartar. Hard dog biscuits can help toward this end. If tartar does accumulate, see that it is removed promptly by your veterinarian. Bones are not suitable for show dogs once they have their second teeth as they tend to damage and wear down the tooth enamel (bones are all right for puppies, as they help with the teething process).

Beyond these special considerations, your show-prospect Doberman will thrive under the same treatment as accorded any well-cared-for family pet. In fact, most of the foregoing is applicable to a pet Doberman as well as to a show Doberman, for what it boils down to is simply keeping the dog at his best.

Match Shows

Your Doberman's first experience in show-ring procedure should be at match show competition. There are several reasons for this. First of all, this type of event is intended as a learning experience for both the puppies and for the exhibitors; thus you will feel no embarrassment if your puppy misbehaves or if your own handling technique is obviously inept. There will be many others in that same position. So take the puppy and go, and the two of you can learn together what it is like to actually complete against other dogs for the approval of the judge.

Another reason for beginning a show career at match shows is the matter of cost. Entries at the point shows nowadays cost well over ten dollars. True, there are many clubs who reduce this fee by a few dollars for the Puppy Classes (but by no means do all of them), but even so it is silly to throw this amount away when you know full well your puppy will not yet have the ring presence to hold his own. For the match shows, on the other hand, the entry fee is usually less than five dollars, so using those shows as a learning ground for you and your puppy certainly makes better sense. Another advantage of match shows is that advance entries for them are seldom necessary, and even those clubs having them usually will accept additional entries the morning of the show. If you wake up feeling like taking the puppy for an outing, you can go right ahead. The entries at point shows, however, close about two-and-a-half weeks in advance.

You will find the judges more willing to discuss your puppy with you at a match show than during the day of a full and hectic point show; one of their functions, when officiating at a match, is to help new exhibitors with comments and suggestions. We might wish that we could do so at the point shows; but, generally speaking, our schedules do not permit this time to be taken. Unless you stay until the judge's working day has ended, it is often difficult to get even a few words with him. The informality of match shows makes it far easier to get a judge's verbal opinion there; and since judges at these events are usually professional handlers or already licensed judges who are working toward applying for additional breeds, the opinions should be knowledgeable and helpful.

As with training classes, information regarding match shows can be obtained from breeders in your area, your local kennel club if there is one, your veterinarian, or, of course, the person in charge of your training class, if you belong to one. The A.K.C. can also furnish this information; and if your local newspaper carries a pet column, announcements of such coming events will almost certainly appear there.

Point Shows

Entries for American Kennel Club licensed or member point shows must be made in advance. This must be done on an official entry blank of the show-giving club and then filed either in person or by mail with the show superintendent (or show secretary) in time to reach the latter's office prior to the published closing date and hour or the filling of the advertised quota. These entries should be written out clearly and carefully, signed by the owner of the dog or his agent (your professional handler), and must be accompanied by the entry fee; otherwise they will not be accepted. Remember, it is not when the entry blank leaves your hands or is postmarked that counts but the time that the entry arrives at its destination. If you are relying on the postal system, bear in mind that it is not always reliable, and waiting until the last moment may cause your entry to arrive too late for acceptance. Leave yourself a bit of leeway by mailing *early*.

A dog must be entered at a dog show in the name of the actual owner at the time of entry closing date for that specific show. If a registered dog has been acquired by a new owner, the dog must be entered in the name of that new owner at any show for which entries close following the date of purchase, regardless of whether or not the new owner has actually received the registration certificate indicating that the dog is registered in the new owner's name. State on the entry form whether or not the transfer application has been mailed to the American Kennel Club, and it goes without saying that the latter should be promptly attended to when you purchase a registered dog.

When you fill out your entry blank, be sure to type, print, or write legibly, paying particular attention to the spelling of names, correct registration numbers, and so on. Sign your name as owner *exactly*—not one time as Jane Doe, another as Jane C. Doe, and another as Mrs. John Doe.

Puppy Classes are for dogs or bitches that are six months of age and under twelve months, were whelped in the United States, and are not champions. The age of a puppy is calculated up to and inclusive of the first day of a show you are entering. For example, the first day a dog whelped on January 1st is eligible to compete in a Puppy Class at a show is July 1st of the same year; and he may continue competing in Puppy Classes up to and including a show on December 31st of the same year, but he is *not* eligible to compete in a Puppy Class at a show held on or after January 1st of the following year.

The Puppy Class is the first one in which you should enter your puppy, for several reasons. To begin with, a certain allowance for behavior is made in recognition of the fact that they *are* puppies and lack show experience; a puppy who is immature or displays less than perfect ring manners will not be penalized so heavily as would be the case in an adult class such as Open. It is also quite likely that others in the Puppy Class will be suffering from the same puppy problems as your own; all of the puppies will be pretty much on equal footing where age and ring assurance are concerned. A puppy shown in the same class with fully matured Dobermans who are experienced in the show ring looks all the more young and inexperienced and thus is far less likely to gain the judge's admiration than in a class where the puppy does not seem out of place. There are many good judges who will take a smashing good puppy right from the Puppy Class on through to Winners, but more often than not, this puppy started the day and was "discovered" by the judge right where it belonged, in the Puppy Class. Another bonus of using Puppy Class is the fact that numerous clubs offer a reduced entry fee to those competing in it; this certainly is beneficial because showing dogs is becoming increasingly expensive.

One word of caution on entering the Puppy Class: carefully check the classification, as in some cases it is divided into a 6-9 months old section and a 9-12 months old section; if this is the case you will have to ascertain that your puppy is entered in the correct section for the age he will be on the day of the show.

The Novice Class is for dogs six months of age and over, whelped in the United States or in Canada, who *prior to* the official closing date for entries have *not* won three first prizes in the Novice Class, any first prize at all in the Bred-by-Exhibitor, American-bred, or Open Classes, or one or more points toward championship. The provisions for this class are confusing to many people, which is probably the reason it is so infrequently used. A dog may win any number of first prizes in the Puppy Class and still retain his eligibility for Novice. He may place second, third, or fourth not only in Novice on an unlimited number of occasions but also in Bred-by-Exhibitor, American-bred, or Open and still remain eligible for Novice. But he may no longer be shown in Novice when he has won three blue ribbons in that class, when he has won even one blue ribbon in either Bred-by-Exhibitor, American-bred, or Open, or even a single championship point.

In determining whether or not a dog is eligible for the Novice Class, keep in mind the fact that previous wins are calculated according to the official published date for closing of entries, not by the date on which you may actually have made the entry. So if, in the interim, between the time you made the entry and the official closing date, your dog makes a win causing it to become ineligible for Novice, change your class *immediately* to another for which your Doberman will be eligible. The Novice Class always seems to have the fewest entries of any class, and therefore it is a splendid "practice ground" for you and your young Doberman while you both are getting the "feel" of being in the ring.

Bred-by-Exhibitor Class is for dogs whelped in the United States or, if individually registered in the American Kennel Club Stud Book, for dogs whelped in Canada that are six months of age and over, are not champions, and are owned wholly or in part by the person or the spouse of the person who was the breeder or one of the breeders of record. Dogs entered in this class must be handled *in this class* by an owner or by a member of the immediate family of the owner. Members of an immediate family for this purpose are husband, wife, father, mother, son, daughter, brother, or sister. This is the class which is really the "breeder's showcase," the one which breeders should enter with special pride, to show off their achievements. It is *not necessary* for the winner of Bred-by-Exhibitor to be handled by an owner or a member of the owner's family in the Winners Class, where the dog or bitch *may be handled by whomsoever the exhibitor may choose*, including a professional handler.

The American-bred Class is for all dogs excepting champions, six months of age or older, who were whelped in the United States by reason of a mating which took place in the United States.

The Open Class is for any dog six months of age or older (this is the only restriction for this class). Dogs with championship points compete in it; dogs who are already champions can do so; dogs who are imported can be entered; and, of course, American-bred dogs compete in it. They rush to enter their pointed dogs in it, under the false impression that by so doing they assure themselves of greater attention from the judges. This really is not so; and it is my feeling that to enter in one of the less competitive classes, with a better chance of winning it and then getting a second crack at gaining the judge's approval

1. Am. and Can. Ch. Laurenwald's Never Delay, owned by Fred and Lucille Sherman and handled by Jeffrey Lynn Brucker. Judge, Ted Wurmser. This splendid dog is a Best in Show winner.
2. Ch. Weichardt's Rosen Cavalier, C.D., owned by Terry and Denyse Lee, Concord, California. By Ch. Alnwick's Black Fury Bismarck, C.D. (sire of 28 champions) ex Weichardt's Princess Athena, C.D. (dam of two champions). Photo courtesy of Marjorie Brooks, Santa Rosa, California. Pictured taking Best in Show, 1973, at the Golden Gate Kennel Club.

1▲   ▼2

Feb. 3 & 4 1973
Golden Gate Kennel Club
Best in Show

1▲   ▼2

1. Ch. Ansa vom Riedstern, a German import, taking Winners Bitch at Westchester in 1971. Handled by J. Monroe Stebbins.
2. The Quaker City Doberman Pinscher Club Specialty, December 1967. Mrs. Augustus Riggs selects as Best of Breed the magnificent Ch. Gra-Lemor Demetrius v. d. Elbe, handled by J. Monroe Stebbins for Mrs. Grace Moore, Gra-Lemor Kennels. Photo courtesy of the Stebbinses.

by returning to the ring in the Winners Class, can often be a more effective strategy.

One does not enter for the Winners Class. One earns the right to compete in it by winning first prize in Puppy, Novice, Bred-by-Exhibitor, American-bred, or Open. No dog or bitch who has been defeated on the same day in one of these classes is eligible to compete in Winners, and every dog or bitch who has been a blue-ribbon winner in one of them and not defeated in any of the others *must* do so. Following the selection of the Winners Dog or the Winners Bitch, the dog or bitch receiving that award leaves the ring. Then the dog or bitch who placed second in the class, unless previously defeated by another dog or bitch at the same show, re-enters the ring to compete against the remaining first-prize winners for Reserve. The latter award means that the dog or bitch receiving it is standing by "in reserve" should the one that received Winners be disallowed through any technicality when the awards are checked at the American Kennel Club. In that case, the one that placed Reserve is moved up to Winners, at the same time receiving the appropriate championship points.

Winners Dog and Winners Bitch are the awards which carry points toward championship with them. The points are based on the number of dogs or bitches actually in competition; and the points are scaled one through five, the latter being the greatest number available to any dog or bitch at any one show. Three-, four-, or five-point wins are considered majors. In order to become a champion, a dog or bitch must win two majors under two different judges, plus at least one point from a third judge, and the additional points necessary to bring the total to fifteen. When your dog has gained fifteen points as described above, a certificate of championship will be issued to you, and your Doberman's name will be published in the list of new champions which appears monthly in *Pure-Bred Dogs/American Kennel Gazette*, the official publication of the American Kennel Club.

The scale of championship points for each breed is worked out by the American Kennel Club and reviewed annually, at which time the number required in competition may be either changed (raised or lowered) or remain the same. The scale of points for all breeds is published annually in the May issue of the *Gazette*, and the current ratings for each breed within that area are published in every dog-show catalog.

When a dog or a bitch is adjudged Best of Winners, its championship points are, for that show, compiled on the basis of which sex had the greater number of points. If there are two points in dogs and four in bitches and the dog goes Best of Winners, then *both* the dog and the bitch are awarded an equal number of points, in this case four. Should the Winners Dog or the Winners Bitch go on to win Best of Breed, additional points are accorded for the additional Dobermans defeated by so doing, provided, of course, that there were entries specifically for Best of Breed competition, or Specials, as these specific entries are generally called. If your dog or bitch takes Best of Opposite Sex after going Winners, points are credited according to the number of the same sex defeated in both the regular classes and Specials competition. Many a one- or two-point class win has grown into a major in this manner.

Moving further along, should your Doberman win the Working Group from the classes (in other words, if it has taken either Winners Dog or Winners Bitch, Best of Winners, and Best of Breed), you then receive points based on the greatest number of points awarded to any breed included within that Group during that show's competition. Should the dog's winning streak also include Best in Show, the same rule of thumb applies, and your Doberman receives points equal to the highest number of points awarded to any other dog of any breed at that event.

Best of Breed competition consists of the Winners Dog and the Winners Bitch, who automatically compete on the strength of those awards, in addition to whatever dogs and bitches have been entered specifically for this class for which champions of record are eligible. Dobermans who, according to their owner's records, have completed the required number of points for a championship after closing of entries for the show but whose championships are unconfirmed, may be transferred from one of the regular classes to the Best of Breed competition, provided this transfer is made by the show superintendent or show secretary *prior to the start of judging at the show.*

This has proven an extremely popular new rule, as under it a dog can finish on Saturday and then be transferred and compete as a Special on Sunday. It must be emphasized that the change *must* be made a half hour *prior* to the start of the day's judging, which means to the start of *any* judging at the show, not your individual breed.

In the United States, Best of Breed winners are entitled to compete in the Variety Group which includes them. This competition is not mandatory; it is a privilege which Doberman exhibitors should value. The dogs winning *first* in each Variety Group *must* compete for Best in Show.

Non-regular classes are sometimes included at the all-breed shows, and they are almost invariably included at Specialty shows. These include Stud Dog Class and Brood Bitch Class, which are judged on the quality of the offspring (usually two) accompanying the sire or dam. The quality of the latter two is beside the point; it is the youngsters that count, and the qualities of *both* are averaged to decide which sire or dam is the best and most consistent producer. Then there is the Brace Class (which, at all-breed shows, moves along to Best Brace in Show), which is judged on the similarity and evenness of appearance of the two members of the brace. In other words, the Dobermans should look like identical twins in size, color, and conformation and should move together almost as a single dog, one person handling with precision and ease. The same applies to the Team competition except that four dogs are involved and, if necessary, two handlers.

The Veterans Class is for the older dog, the minimum age of whom is usually seven years. This class is judged on the quality of the dogs, as the winner competes for Best of Breed, and, on a number of occasions, has been known to win it. So the point is *not* to pick the oldest looking dog, as some seem to think, but the best specimen of the breed, exactly as throughout the regular classes.

Then there are Sweepstakes and Futurity Stakes, sponsored by many Specialty clubs, sometimes as part of their shows and sometimes as separate events. The difference between the two is that Sweepstakes entries usually include dogs and bitches from six to eighteen months of age, and entries are made at the usual time as others for the show, while for a Futurity the entries are bitches nominated when bred and the individual puppies entered at or shortly following their birth.

Junior Showmanship

If there is a youngster in your family between the ages of ten and seventeen, I can suggest no better or more rewarding a hobby than having a Doberman to show in Junior Showmanship competition. This is a marvelous activity for young people. It teaches responsibility, good sportsmanship, the fun of competition where one's own skills are the deciding factor of success, proper care of a pet, and how to socialize with other young folks. Any youngster may experience the thrill of emerging from the ring a winner and the satisfaction of a good job done well.

Through the years, the Doberman has always seemed especially popular with Junior Showmanship-minded youngsters. Being of such superb intelligence and being easily trainable, they are agreeable dogs for the youngsters to work with; and judging by the success of Dobermans with their young handlers which we have noted, the breed seems well suited for this type of competition.

Entry in Junior Showmanship is open to any boy or girl who is at least ten years old and under seventeen years old on the day of the show. The Novice Junior Showmanship Class is open to youngsters who have not already won, at the time the entries close, three firsts in this class. Youngsters who have won three firsts in Novice may compete in the Open Junior Showmanship Class. Any junior handler who wins his third first-place award in Novice may participate in the Open Class at the same show, provided that the Open Class has at least one other junior handler entered in it. The Novice and Open Classes may be divided into Junior and Senior Classes. Youngsters between the ages of ten and twelve, inclusively, are eligible for the Junior division; and youngsters between thirteen and seventeen, inclusively, are eligible for the Senior division. Any of the foregoing classes may be separated into individual classes for boys and for girls. If such a division is made, it must be indicated on the premium list. The premium list also indicates the prize for Best

1. Colby Homer with her noted brace, Warjo's Melodee v. Scudamore and Warjo's Cantata of Homer Hill. These full sisters have two all-breed Best Brace in Show Awards (one of which is pictured) to their credit, plus multiple Best Brace in Group awards. Patrick and Colby Homer, owners, Wheeling, West Virginia.

2. Am. and Can. Ch. Biggin Hill's Becket, bred and owned by Phyllis and Norman Biggin, West Kingston, Rhode Island. By Am. and Can. Ch. Biggin Hill's Alarich ex Am. and Can. Ch. Biggin Hill's Adele. Shown taking best of Breed with Tess Henseler, he then went on to Best in Show under Anne Rogers Clark.

Junior Handler, if such a prize is being offered at the show. Any youngster who wins a first in any of the regular classes may enter the competition for this prize, provided the youngster has been undefeated in any class at that show.

The high point of each year's Junior Showmanship competition is when those talented juniors who qualify compete in these classes at the Westminster Kennel Club Dog Show in Madison Square Garden in New York City each February. The privilege of doing so is gained by the number of classes won during the preceding year, and the qualifications are explained in detail on the Westminster premium list and entry blank.

Junior Showmanship Classes, unlike regular conformation classes in which the dog's ability is judged, are judged entirely on the skill and ability of the junior handling the dog. Which dog is best is not the point—it is which youngster does the best job with the dog that is under consideration. Eligibility requirements for the dog being shown and other detailed information can be found in *Regulations for Junior Showmanship*, issued by the American Kennel Club.

A junior who has a dog that he or she can enter in both Junior Showmanship and conformation classes has twice the opportunity for success and twice the opportunity to get into the ring and work with the dog. Dobermans and juniors work well together, and this combination has often wound up in the winner's circle. There are no age restrictions on a child showing in breed competition, and a youngster may start at any age his parents think suitable. Of course, much depends upon the individual child, and I hardly need point out the irresponsbility of turning too young a child, or one not yet able to control it, loose at a dog show with one of *any* of the large, powerful breeds. Too many totally unexpected things could happen.

Pre-show Preparation

Preparation of the things you will need as a Doberman exhibitor should not be left until the last moment. They should be planned and arranged for at least several days before the show in order for you to relax and be calm as the countdown starts.

The importance of the crate has already been discussed, and we assume it is already in use. Of equal importance is the grooming table, which we are sure you have already acquired for use at home. You should take it along with you, as your dog will need final touches before entering the ring. If you do not have one yet, a folding table with a rubber top is made specifically for this purpose and can be purchased from the concession booths found at most dog shows. Then you will need a sturdy tack box (also available at the show's concessions) in which to carry your dog's brush, comb, scissors, nail clippers, whatever you use for last minute clean-up jobs, cotton swabs, first-aid equipment, and anything else you are in the habit of using on the dog, such as a leash or two of the type you prefer, some well-cooked and dried-out liver or any of the small packaged "dog treats" your dog likes for use as "bait" in the ring, and a turkish towel.

Take a large thermos or cooler of ice, the biggest one you can accommodate in your vehicle, for use by "man and beast." Take a jug of water (there are lightweight, inexpensive ones available at all sporting goods shops) and a water dish. If you plan to feed the dog at the show, or if you and the dog will be away from home more than one day, bring food from home so that he will have the type to which he is accustomed.

You may or may not have an exercise pen. Personally, I think that one is a *must*, even if you have only one dog. While the shows do provide areas for exercise of the dogs, these are among the best places to come into contact with any illnesses that may be going around, and I feel that having a pen of your own for your dog's use is excellent protection. Such a pen can be used in other ways, too, such as a place other than the crate in which to put the dog to relax and a place in which the dog can exercise at rest areas or motels during your travels. A word of caution: never tie a dog to an exercise pen or leave him unattended in it while you wander of, as the pens are not sufficiently secure to keep the dog there should he decide to leave, at least not in most cases. Exercise pens are also available at the dog-show concession booths should you not already have yours when you reach the dog's first show. They come in a variety of heights and sizes.

Bring along folding chairs for the members of your party, unless all of you are fond of

1. Corky Vroom as a Junior Handler, already displaying the talent and expertise which have made him one of the most admired and successful of professionals.
2. Best in Show, Old Dominion Kennel Club, October 1968. Judge, Keith Browne; handler, Jane Kay. The winner, Ch. Zorohaven's Camilla.

BEST DOG IN SHOW

1. A correctly "stacked" Doberman rear, the way you want the hindquarters when viewed from the rear. The puppy should learn to be "set up" in all sorts of weather and all sorts of conditions as will be met with at the dog shows. Photo courtesy of Ann Lanier, Sierra Dobermans, Pacifica, California.

2. Set the puppy up on concrete, as well as on grass, carpet, rubber mats, etc. Ch. Wynterwynds Sierra Shadow, at seven months, practicing.

3. The judge will examine the puppy's mouth (or ask you, the exhibitor, to show it for examination). The puppy must be trained to tolerate this, as the "bite," down sides of jaw, and finally the open jaws are carefully checked for missing teeth. *P.S.* And the teeth should be CLEAN! Here the judge, famous Dobe breeder Jane Kay, is making the examination as Gene Haupt handles Wynterwynd's Sierra Shadow.

4. Teresa Nail with Ch. Tolivar's Aristotle of Azteca winning the Top Junior Handler Award at Westminster Kennel Club in 1977. Teresa is the daughter of Mrs. Edd Bivin.

standing, as these are almost never provided by the show-giving clubs. Have your name stamped on the chairs so there will be no doubt as to whom the chairs belong. Bring whatever you and your family enjoy for drinks or snacks in a picnic basket or cooler, as show food, in general, is expensive and usually not great. You should always have a pair of boots, a raincoat, and a rain hat with you (they should remain permanently in your vehicle if you plan to attend shows regularly), as well as a sweater, a warm coat, and a change of shoes. A smock or big cover-up apron will assure that you remain tidy as you prepare the dog for the ring. Your overnight case should include a small sewing kit for emergency repairs, headache and indigestion remedies, and any personal products or medications you normally use.

In your car you should always carry maps of the area where you are headed and an assortment of motel directories. Generally speaking, we have found that Holiday Inns are the friendliest about taking dogs. Some Ramadas and some Howard Johnsons do so cheerfully (the Ramadas indicate on each listing in their directory whether or not pets are welcome). Best Western usually frowns on pets (not all of them but enough to make it necessary to find out which do). Some of the smaller chains welcome pets. The majority of privately owned motels do not.

Have everything prepared the night before the show to expedite your departure. Be sure that the dog's identification and your judging program and other show information are in your purse or briefcase. If you are taking sandwiches, have them ready. Anything that goes into the car the night before will be one thing less to be concerned with in the morning. Decide upon what you will wear and have it out and ready. If there is any question in your mind about what to wear, try on the possibilities before the day of the show; don't risk feeling you may want to change when you see yourself dressed a few moments prior to departure time! In planning your outfit, wear something simple that will make an attractive background for your Doberman, providing contrast to his color, calling attention to the *dog* rather than to yourself. Sports clothes always seem to look best at a dog show. What you wear on your feet is important, as many types of flooring are slippery, and wet grass, too, can present a hazard as you move the dog. Make it a rule to wear rubber soles and low or flat heels in the ring, so that you can move along smartly.

Your final step in pre-show preparation is to leave yourself plenty of time to reach the show that morning. Traffic can get extremely heavy as one nears the immediate vicinity of the show, finding a parking place can be difficult, and other delays may occur. You'll be in better humor if you can take it all in your stride without the pressure of watching every second because you figured the time too closely.

Day of the Show

From the moment of your arrival at the dog show until after your Doberman has been judged, keep foremost in your mind the fact that he is your purpose for being there. You will need to arrive in advance of the judging in order to give him a chance to exercise after the trip to the show and take care of personal matters. A dog arriving in the ring and immediately using it for an exercise pen hardly makes a favorable impression on the judge. You will also need time to put the final touches on your dog, making certain that he goes into the ring looking his very best.

When you reach ringside, ask the steward for your arm-card with your Doberman's entry number on it and anchor it firmly into place on your arm with the elastic provided. Make sure that you are where you should be when your class is called. The fact that you have picked up your arm-card does not guarantee, as some seem to think, that the judge will wait for you more than a minute or two. Judges are expected to keep on schedule, which precludes delaying for the arrival of exhibitors who are tardy.

Even though you may be nervous, assume an air of cool, collected calm. Remember that this is a hobby to be enjoyed, so approach it in that state of mind. The dog will do better, too, as he will be quick to reflect your attitude.

If you make a mistake while presenting the dog, don't worry about it—next time you'll do better. Do not be intimidated by the more expert or experienced exhibitors. After all, they, too, were once newcomers.

Always show you Doberman with an air of pride. An apologetic attitude on the part of the exhibitor does little to help the dog win, so try to appear self-confident as you gait and set up the dog.

The judging routine usually starts when the judge asks that the dogs be gaited in a circle around the ring. During this period the judge is watching each dog as it moves along, noting style, topline, reach and drive, head and tail carriage, and general balance. This is the time to keep your mind and your eye on your dog, moving him at his most becoming gait and keeping your place in line without coming too close to the dog ahead of you. Always keep your dog on the inside of the circle, between yourself and the judge, so that the judge's view of the dog is unobstructed.

Calmly pose the dog when requested to set up for examination. If you are at the head of the line and many dogs are in the class, do not stop halfway down the end of the ring and begin stacking the dog. Go forward enough so that sufficient space is left for the other dogs. Simple courtesy demands that we be considerate and give others a chance to follow the judge's instructions, too.

Space your Doberman so that on all sides of the dog the judge will have room in which to make his examination; this means that there must be sufficient room between each of the dogs for the judge to move around. Time is important when you are setting up your Doberman, so practice in front of a full-length mirror at home, trying to accustom yourself to "getting it all together" correctly in the shortest possible time. When you set up your Doberman, you want his forelegs well under the dog, feet directly below the elbows, toes pointing straight ahead, and hindquarters extended *correctly*. Hold the dog's head up with your hand at the back inner corner of the lips, your left hand extending the tail to its proper position. You want the dog to look "all of a piece," head carried proudly on a strong neck, correct topline, hindquarters nicely angulated, the front straight and true, and the dog standing firmly on his feet.

Listen carefully as the judge instructs the manner in which the dog is to be gaited, whether it is straight down and straight back; down the ring, across, and back; or in a triangle. The latter has become the most popular pattern with the majority of judges. "In a triangle" means down the outer side of the ring to the first corner, across that end of the ring to the second corner, and then back to the judge from the second corner, using the center of the ring in a diagonal line. Please learn to do this pattern without breaking at each corner to twirl the dog around you, a senseless maneuver we sometimes have noted. Judges like to see the dog move in an *uninterrupted* triangle, as they get a better idea of the dog's gait.

It is impossible to overemphasize that the gait at which you move your Doberman is tremendously important, and considerable thought and study should be given to the matter. At home, have someone move the dog for you at different speeds so that you can tell which shows him off to best advantage.

Do not allow your Doberman to sidetrack, flop, or weave as you gait him, and do not let him pull so that he appears to lean on the lead as you are gaiting him. He should move in a straight line, proudly, smoothly, and firmly. That is your goal as you work with him on a lead in preparation for his show career. Movement is an important feature of a Doberman; thus, it is essential that yours displays his movement to full advantage.

Baiting your dog should be done in a manner which does not upset the other Dobermans in the ring or cause problems for their handlers. A tasty morsel of well-cooked and dried-out liver is fine for keeping your own dog interested, but discarded on the ground or floor, it can throw off the behavior of someone else's dog who may attempt to get it. So please, if you drop liver on the ground, pick it up and take it with you when you have finished.

When the awards have been made, accept yours courteously, no matter how you may actually feel about it. To argue with a judge is unthinkable, and it will certainly not change the decision. Be gracious, congratulate the winners if your dog has been defeated, and try not to show your disappointment. By the same token, please be a gracious winner; this, surprisingly, sometimes seems to be even more difficult.

1. The great Ch. Dolph von Tannenwald in November 1971. Truly an immortal in the Doberman breed, Dolph here is winning one of his Bests in Show. The judge is L. E. Piper and Jeffrey Lynn Brucker is handling as usual. Dolph is owned by George and Sheila West. Photo courtesy of Mr. Brucker.

2. Ch. Moraga's Hills High Fashion, a Black Rites daughter. Currently the dam of nine champions, she was many times presented with Awards of Merit from the Specialties. Photo courtesy of Donald V. Simmons, Silver Spring, Maryland.

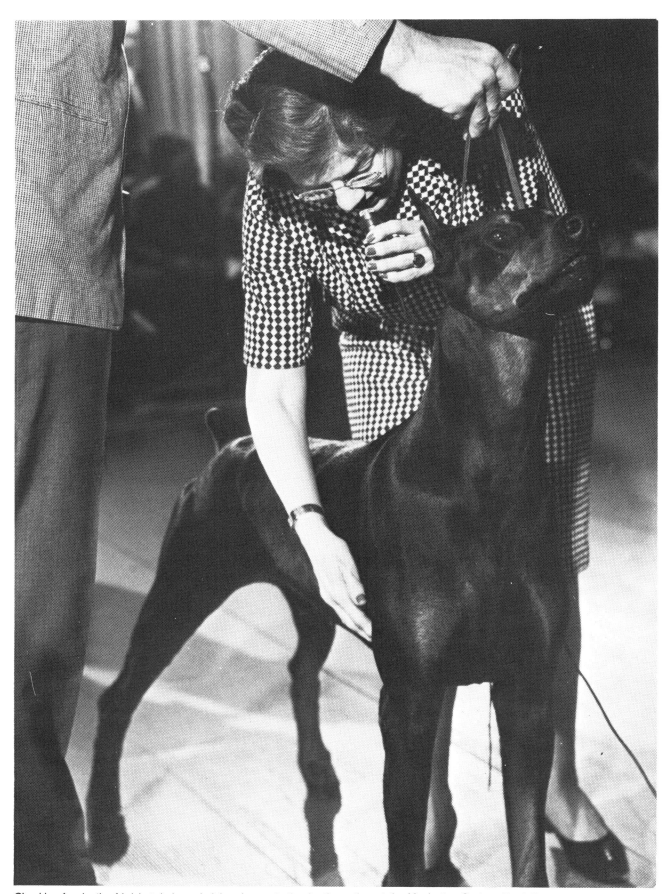

Checking for depth of brisket during a judging demonstration by the author at the Manhattan Savings Bank Dog Exhibit in New York City.

CHAPTER NINETEEN

Judging the Doberman Pinscher

The author of this book is a person who feels very strongly the importance of the quality of judging within a breed. It is quite true that future trends in breeding programs take shape from the decisions reached in our rings and that, therefore, every tool towards complete and thorough understanding of the Doberman and of the task at hand should receive very special attention.

In a breed so popular as the Doberman, this is particularly a challenge. Few breeds have ever attained, consistently, entries so high numerically. Nor are the judges of the majority of others required to make correct decisions involving so many cases of truly keen competition. To judge Dobermans well, a person must possess complete knowledge of the breed and understand the art of applying this knowledge to comparisons and evaluations made in the ring. No breed of dog is more fortunate in the quality of its breeders than this one, which means that literally hundreds of worthy Dobermans appear for our consideration each year. To be sure, opinions vary. With quality as high as it is in this breed, decisions very often come down to very fine points, to appearance and behavior "on the day," and to the judge's personal interpretation of the standard. Half a dozen Dobermans can be placed half a dozen different

ways without too many gross errors being made. Quite truly, "beauty *is* in the eye of the beholder," and each judge has his own set of values and interpretation of the standard's message.

Considering all this, and also considering the circulation this book will have in all parts of the world, we feel very strongly that our chapter on judging must be one of great strength and helpfulness, putting truly authentic, accurate and helpful information into the hands of our readers. So where do we turn? Our first thought was to Mrs. Margaret Kilburn, whom we know to be an outstanding judge and a breeder of quality Dobes. How great it would be if she would take on the assignment!

Mrs. Kilburn graciously consented to do so when she received our request. But then she had an even *better* idea, for she is a member of the DPCA Judges' Educational Committee, the purpose of which is to "help persons who judge Dobermans, and persons who are preparing to judge Dobermans, learn to apply the standard of the Doberman in the show ring." To do this, the committee offers materials and seminars and carries on special projects. This committee has spent many hours in the preparation of a manual to be used in conjunction with their program and at the symposiums. It was Mrs. Kilburn's thought that the subject could in no way be better or more thoroughly and competently covered than in this manner. Thus she contacted Frank Grover, chairman of the committee, and asked him for approval of our using this material, in condensed version and with a few additional personal comments by Mrs. Kilburn, as the chapter on judging Dobermans in this book. Mrs. Kilburn received Mr. Grover's permission and approval, as well as that of Peggy Adamson, who is a dedicated member of the committee and very much involved with the preparation of the manual.

We are honored, grateful and delighted at the privilege of featuring what I sincerely believe to be the finest and most helpful treatise on judging Dobermans I have ever read. What an honor to bring this to our readers! And what a tremendous additional service to Doberman judges, present and future, that the Judges' Educational Committee is willing to allow us to bring it to so many of them the world over. But then, that is the Doberman

Pinscher Club of America. A truly remarkable *dedicated* parent specialty club always ready and willing to support more thorough and wide understanding of its beloved breed.

Excerpts from the DPCA
Judges' Educational Committee
Manual

One who aspires to judge Doberman Pinschers should first study two excellent books about judging: *The Nicholas Guide To Dog Judging* by Anna Katherine Nicholas and the *Dog Judges Handbook* by Sari Brewster Tietjen. The latter contains as the frontispiece an excellent visualization of basic Doberman structure. Each book is valuable in its own way and both should be studied; therefore, I shall make but one or two suggestions on ring procedure.

Doberman entries are frequently very large, and these suggestions may help manage large entries. Have the dogs enter the ring in catalog order. Have the steward ask that no bait be fed before the judge has examined mouths. Check arm-card numbers and teeth and testicles as the dogs enter the ring. You should have a small note pad and mark each number as it enters the ring; also mark any missing teeth or mouth problems at this time. This saves quite a bit of time because the judge can check absentees and need not wait for the exhibit to be restacked after these examinations.

By dividing classes, all exhibits receive equal treatment under like conditions. There is enough room for each dog to be evaluated and you will not become confused and lost in a vast maze of dogs. (For a full discussion of this subject, please read pages 126 to 128 in *The Dog Judges Handbook* and pages 92 to 93 in *The Nicholas Guide To Dog Judging*.) The purpose of judging is to assess each dog individually against the Standard and to arrive at a rating of some sort and gradually sort down to the ones most closely approximating the Standard. The Standard of the Doberman Pinscher is designed to guide evaluation of each dog as a whole. The Standard assumes the judges know and accept that the breed is a short-backed galloper as distinct from a natural trotter. The Standard also assumes the judges know and accept that the Doberman is

bred to be a constant loyal companion and guard of his master and his or her possessions. The basis of the Standard is not to specify faults in words, i.e., downface or dishface or eweneck, but to specify the ideal and to consider any deviation from the ideal as a fault to the degree of its deviation. The location of a fault does not determine its importance; the degree of deviation does. You judge the *whole* dog when you judge by the Standard.

Under general appearance in the Standard we stress key breed characteristics: size, proportions, attributes, and behavior. These set the basics. Size has two aspects—the appearance of medium size, and height specification. A dog that does not appear medium-sized but meets the height specifications, still does not fit the Standard, and the opposite is also true. The key proportions are height to length, height to width, elbow to ground, and elbow to withers; that is to say, parts to whole. Key attributes are: compact, elegant, and powerful with great endurance and speed. Behavior: must act and react as a Doberman should. If we apply these guidelines carefully and rigorously, we can do a tolerable job of selecting in most situations.

Judges, in evaluating Dobermans, assess them on these primary characteristics before evaluating the worth of the parts: a) be sure each specimen is of acceptable size; b) be sure each specimen is of acceptable general proportions; c) be sure each speciment has the attributes of elegance, compactness, and nobility, built for the impressions of power, endurance, and speed; and d) be sure each specimen behaves as a Doberman should.

Size
Size in a dog is a generalized term referring to a combination of height and bone and substance, or bulk. To judge Dobermans well, you need a clear mental picture of the ideal bone and substance needed for correct breed balance. It is always in relation to the dog's height. The taller the dog, the more bone and substance are required to keep the dog in balance. Thus the only reference for how much bone and substance is the dog under study.

You also need considerable skill in estimating height at the withers of individual Dobermans. The Standard specifies height of the breed, and it is interesting that many who are able to see one-fourth of an inch excess on a Sheltie are not able to estimate Dobermans within two inches. You need to practice estimating height of individual specimens (both dogs and bitches), and you will need to devise a system for checking your estimates while in the ring.

Remember, the Doberman *must appear of medium size* and be within certain height specifications. Size is a fundamental breed characteristic.

In the year following the approval of the current Doberman Standard, a letter from the DPCA was sent to all Doberman judges cautioning them to give careful consideration to the height limits in the Standard.

Perhaps it also should be noted that on two occasions the DPCA membership has voted to disqualify heights more than an inch over the Standard. Up to the present, such a disqualification has not been added, but historically the conviction is strong that the Doberman should remain a medium-sized breed.

Proportions

Proportions required in a Doberman are: a dog that is square with the distance from elbow to the ground about the same as from the elbow to the withers and with a broad chest. The square Doberman is measured from the withers to the ground which equals from the front of the forechest to the rear projection of the upper thigh. No exact proportion is given for the widths of the Doberman, but after one measures several, a minimum of thirty percent of the height seems essential and more nearly thirty-three percent.

These are the general proportions; in addition, the head, neck, legs and so forth are in proportion to the body depth and length. The parts of the whole dog must be in proportion and that includes enough bone and substance.

Attributes

1. That the dog be structurally compact and powerful.

2. That it give the impression of an animal capable of both speed and endurance.

3. Yet this strong, robust dog must also be elegant in appearance and carry itself proudly. Its lines must be trim, its movements graceful.

These attributes are not separate. They arise from the dog as a whole, including the correct proportions and size.

To be powerful and compactly built, a dog must have adequate bone and substance; but to have speed also, it must not be heavy or cumbersome. Fine-boned, spindly animals or ponderous plodders would be equally unacceptable. The Standard requires a combination of endurance and speed that could only be achieved in a medium-sized dog. Hence the height limitations; thirty-inch animals in the range of giant breeds might have the power, but they could not combine it with the lightning reactions and action that are the very essence of the Doberman.

What does "elegant in appearance" mean? Certainly the dog must appear to be "all in one piece." The superbly arched neck flows into the smooth shoulders. The strong topline has no bumps or dips, and the tail seems to be a continuation of the spine. The hair must be hard, short, and shiny-clean; there is no excess of flesh, and so perfectly does the coat fit the body that the dog seems to have been poured into it.

The ears are erect, whether the dog is moving or posing free, and the posture is upstanding. There can be no head-hanging, slumping or crouching. To be elegant and noble in appearance, a Doberman must be able to stand on its own, four-square, without benefit of molding by human hands.

Temperament and Behavior

Breeders of the American Doberman have come to prize dogs with steady, sure reactions rather than dogs ready to attack anything unusual. Steadiness and judgment are the characteristics treasured by American owners and breeders. The assessment of temperament begins with "reading" the dog's eyes. The desired look is that of an interested, confident, curious animal—even with a twinkle of fun. The dog is ready for anything and sure that he can handle whatever occurs. This ideal is not found regularly, but when it is, it should be recognized.

Puppies present the greatest challenge, for ones with good temperament often behave very poorly. Poor behavior is ample reason to drop a very good one well down the line. In the more mature dogs, no special excuses seem adequate for placing high a poorly be-having Doberman. In a specials class, any sign of unsteadiness will be very severely penalized.

If you have any questions about a dog's temperament, before making a final judg-ment, have the dog stand on a loose leash. Walk around the dog. Note his reactions. Do-bermans should be steady, confident, "fearl-ess" dogs.

Behavior of Dobermans in the show ring is specified by the Standard in two ways: first, it describes a Doberman's ideal *reactions* to things and people; second, it states the posi-tive *actions* which require the judge to dismiss the dog from the ring. Reactions of the Do-berman should exemplify the following:

1. The Doberman should appear *energetic*. This is a breed characteristic. A dog that plods, or one that is drooping, listless or lack-ing in energy does not act like a Doberman. A good specimen appears to be filled with controlled energy.

2. The Doberman should be *watchful*. The dog must be keenly aware of what is going on all around. This does not mean he should ap-pear wary or cautious—unless the situation calls for these reactions. For example, a Do-berman after meeting the judge seems to pay no attention to him or her; but the watchful dog will remain aware of the judge's ap-proach, flicking an ear or tossing his head or glancing at the judge. The dog that just looks at liver may not be demonstrating this characteristic.

3. The Doberman is *determined*. This must be distinguished from stubbornness, sullen-ness or singlemindedness. The determination may be shown in subtle ways. While gaiting, the dog may see something on the floor and seize an opportunity the next time when mov-ing near to investigate. The dog may refuse to stand in a certain manner or place. It is a breed of contrasts and contradictions—a tractable, strong-minded dog.

4. The Doberman is *fearless*. By this we mean that the Doberman's reaction to some-thing new or unusual is not to back away but

to stand ready. The dog that exhibits a ten-dency to "move away" from possible danger is not demonstrating excellent Doberman re-actions. Approaching an otherwise excellent specimen when it is standing on a free leash, as mentioned, is one way to check the dog's reactions. To accomplish this, the judge may have the handler loosen the leash and step back away from the dog, preferably toward the dog's rear. The judge then approaches. Does the dog back off at the approach? Does the dog come forward and greet the judge? Does the dog study the judge, standing stead-ily but ready? Does the dog seek support of the handler? Each of these reactions tells you how the dog's reactions should be rated that day.

5. The Doberman is *loyal*. This, the trait that to many fanciers is the hallmark of the breed, seems almost impossible to assess in the show ring. It can be inferred only that a Doberman with excellent expression, atti-tudes, and behavior will form the deep attach-ments to persons that typify the breed.

6. The Doberman is *obedient*. In the show ring, we expect the Doberman to respond im-mediately to the handler's commands, both leash commands and verbal orders. The dog that is unruly or unresponsive is not demon-strating this breed characteristic.

Study these reactions and let them form a picture in your mind of ideal behavior. It is a peculiar, special behavior. We should look for it in the ring, just as we look for proportions and size.

If a Doberman behaves so poorly that he is clearly shy or vicious, the Standard requires the judge to dismiss him from the ring. This simply means that the dog is not counted at that show. The Standard does not leave to the judge the definition of shyness or viciousness; it defines them, and the definitions are in terms of *positive reactions*.

Judging the Head

Judging Doberman heads requires exami-nation from fairly close with two views; full front looking down on the head, and full pro-file. It also requires a longer view from the

1. Hoss von Klosterholz on the way to the title. Saw Mill
River Kennel Club, March 1968.
2. Ch. Ericka v Tannenwald, by Ch. Cassio vom Ahrtal ex
Ch. Kay Hill's Witch Soubrette, with her handler, Jane
Kay, winning under Alva Rosenberg at Lancaster Kennel
Club in 1968.

1▲ ▼2

The great Demetrius. Ch. Gra-Lemor Demetrius v. d. Elbe taking Winners Dog on the way to his title during the mid-1960's. By Ch. Damasyn Derringer ex Jerry Run's Boo Sprite, he was bred and owned by Grace Moore. He was campaigned in the East by J. Monroe Stebbins, then in California by Mike Shea. More than 40 champions to date are to his credit, plus he is himself a Best in Show and Group winner. Photo courtesy of Mr. and Mrs. J. Monroe Stebbins.

side and one-half front to assess the proportion of head to body.

Looking down on an excellent Doberman head, one sees that the width of the skull will be about twice the width of the muzzle. The muzzle will not be too narrow for that dog as a whole. From the muzzle back to the ears as you look down there will be an almost unbroken line. Place your hands on the side of the head, flat. They will fit with no bulges or big bumps.

From the side or profile, the skull will appear flat, and the line of the skull will be parallel to the line of the muzzle. The muzzle line will also be essentially flat or straight. Again, a simple check on this is to place our hand flat on the skull and note the extension of the plane. You will see immediately the "downface" on many otherwise pleasing heads. (In a "downface," the plane of the muzzle descends from the top, and the planes of the head are not parallel.) The wedge of the head looking down from above and the profile wedge should be approximately the same.

The head should be correctly proportioned for the body. A currently increasing problem is that of the head being too small for the body. Occasionally we still see a head too large. Judgment can be sharpened by forming a good frame of reference with a careful study of Dobermans, particularly from the front.

The skull width should be about one-half the width of the dog at the shoulders. Narrower becomes an almost Collie-sized head.

The whole head is dry...no loose skin. "Clean" and "smooth" are adjectives more commonly used, which are effects of dryness and the very tight, short coat typical on the head.

Eyes are almond shaped, rather deeply set, and the darker the better. A simple rule in judging is that any prominence of eye is a fault. Light eyes, round eyes, pop eyes, poor expression...all give prominence to the eyes.

The desired expression is vigorous and energetic. It is interested, confident, curious and kind. Some Dobes have a decidedly sinister expression. This is a very unpleasant fault and is to be penalized even if the expression is vigorous and alert.

There are several reasons for a sinister expression. Contributing factors may be: too

dark a muzzle (lacking large enough markings), too light a color of the eyes, and eyes that are set too close together or are set in a slanted position. Eyes which are too small and slit-like contribute to this impression also.

One must judge the heads on our Dobermans by the Standard, not by personal preference. And one must evaluate them along with the rest of the dog, giving head type full consideration and neither neglecting to take it into account or overemphasizing its importance in the overall picture of the dog.

Tips on Teeth for Judges and Exhibitors

Beware of counting the *gaps* and assuming that these indicate missing teeth. Sometimes they do, but many times they don't. The Doberman often has spacing between the teeth which can be confused with missing teeth. The teeth are not as close together as in shorter-headed breeds, principally in the case of the premolars. For the same reason, it is easy to make the mistake of thinking a dog has two missing teeth, when in reality it has only one but the spacing is not quite right. This occurs most frequently between the third and fourth premolars in the lower jaw if the fourth premolar is very close to the big molar. When in doubt, count the teeth, not the gaps.

The reason for the great emphasis put on dentition in the Standard is the change in a very short period of time from the original short-headed dog to a long-headed one. In accomplishing this, the Germans were aware of the ever-present danger of weak jaws and incomplete dentition. The mouths of the early Dobermans were more like those of the Rottweiler—large teeth close together. With the lengthening of head, this became difficult to attain though still highly desirable.

Another frequent mistake is counting the lower big molar as two teeth. In some Dobermans, the back part of this tooth is of such size as to make it appear to be two teeth, though close inspection will show that it is only one.

What is the most frequent disqualification site? This is usually at the far back of the mouth, and it is the easiest place to overlook it. There can be two, four, or even six small molars missing in the far back of the mouth, a fact which cannot be determined without opening the jaws. Lifting the lip or running the finger along the gum with the jaws closed will not reveal the absent small molars as many judges have learned, to their embarrassment, when they overlooked a disqualification.

The next most common site is the lower front jaw where one or two incisors may be missing with no discernible gap. (If a puppy has 6 baby incisors, there is an almost-certainty that it will have 6 permanent; in the case of 5, a fair chance that it will have 6 permanent; and in the case of 4, only a small chance that there will be a full set. In the latter case, the incisors will probably be crowded.)

The fourth premolar in the lower jaw is one of the last permanent teeth to cut (just before five months) and if the deciduous tooth does not become loose at about that time, there is an unhappy chance that there is no permanent tooth underneath. When a dog loses this tooth at a later date, it is losing the deciduous tooth and never did have the permanent tooth. The first premolar is very small, often a bud, and very easy to lose.

The Doberman occasionally has extra teeth, but the Standard does not require that these be penalized. There is a possibility that there may be a relationship between extra and missing teeth but it has never been proven, nor do we know the exact mode of transmission of missing teeth.

How to check teeth easily and quickly: The Doberman Standard has two disqualifications which involve the mouth. With a little practice, the bite and the teeth can be thoroughly checked in 30 seconds, or 15-20 if the dog is cooperative.

Show Dobermans are accustomed to this procedure, since the breeders make frequent checks on puppies during the teething period, which lasts from about three-and-a-half months to five or six months, by which time the permanent teeth should all be visible. In a few cases, the small molars at the far back may not be cut until eight or nine months, but at an AKC show, the judge cannot make allowances for this.

Bites which are overshot or undershot are rarely seen, but bites which meet evenly are not uncommon and wear down the front teeth. Since the Standard requires a scissors bite, even (level) bites are rather serious since

one-eighth of an inch undershot is a disqualification. In a mature adult, the bite will usually improve and an undershot bite will often get worse. In the case of an even bite, there is a possibility that it may gradually become slightly undershot.

The judge does not count the total number of teeth that are *present*; he counts the number that are *missing*. ONE tooth missing is a minor fault; TWO teeth missing is a rather serious one; THREE teeth missing is very serious; and FOUR or more is a disqualification. The Standard requires 42 teeth *correctly placed*. If a dog has extra teeth, he may have 42 teeth yet still have missing teeth, since an extra tooth in one part of the mouth will not cancel out a missing tooth in another.

The distribution of teeth in a Doberman's mouth is logically divided into groups. If each is memorized, the judge can develop a technique of rapidly observing groups at a glance, finding it necessary only in rare instances to do actual teeth counting in any group.

Between the four canines or fangs (long pointed teeth), two of which are in the lower jaw and two in the upper, there should be six incisors in each jaw. Behind the canine on each side of the lower jaw there are *four* smallish pointed teeth of increasing size (premolars), then one very large tooth, and behind it are two quite small teeth. (These are called molars.) Behind the canine on each side of the upper jaw, there should be *three* (not four as in the lower jaw) smallish teeth of increasing size, then *two* large teeth, and behind them one quite small tooth. (These two large teeth are not quite the same in shape but are noticeably bigger than the others.)

Judging the Forequarters
Following are the specifications made by the Standard:

1. Equal lengths of shoulder and upper arm.
2. Shoulder lay at 45 degree angle to the ground line; shoulder and upper arm meeting at an angle of 90 degrees.
3. Distance from elbow to ground about equal to the distance from elbow to withers.
4. Straight legs; good bone; well muscled.
5. Broad chest.
6. Pronounced forechest.

7. Firm pasterns, almost perpendicular to the ground.
8. Feet cat-like, compact, turning neither in nor out.

To assess these, you may find the following procedure is helpful. At the side of the dog, lift the foreleg about four inches off the ground. This clearly exposes the shoulder and upper arm, and lengths can be compared. Drop the leg, letting it fall naturally. Approximate angulation will be more evident, and will be even more clearly observed, if you find the high point of the shoulder and drop an imaginary vertical line to the ground. This line should go through the middle of the elbow, the center of the leg bone, and intersect the ground just behind the foot. This indicates general balance in forequarters. If the line does not follow this course, the forequarters are out of balance. The line also helps you see angulation.

Step back from the dog and to the side. Check leg length, straightness, body depth, pasterns, and feet. Step to the front (for persons of average height, about eight feet away) and check breadth of chest; brisket line at elbows; legs for bone, straightness, and musculature; elbows; pasterns; and feet. Have the dog take a step forward if you wish an additional check.

Some additional items from Gruenig* and tradition:

The line at the elbows on a properly built Doberman is one where the brisket line appears flat and straight across *at the elbow* when viewed from the front. At each leg, the line descends.

After lifting the leg from the side, reach in front. Find the front end of the sternum. Find the joints of shoulder and upper arms. These three points should be in an exact horizontal line, if the leg assembly is properly placed on the ribs as far as vertical positioning is concerned.

Conceptual Problems: The Standard specifies angles in regard to shoulder lay and upper arm to shoulder. These have become a tremendous judging problem to many persons, as they do not find such angles on Dobermans. It is important to remember that bone lengths and balance of weight are basic in the forequarters. Look for them. Also look for a

"well-laid-back shoulder." Straightness of pastern is also a problem to some judges, who think an absolutely straight pastern *appears* almost straight; it is slightly forward of the upright leg bone. This gives enough cushioning for the dog in jumping and galloping. Remember, a vertical line dropped from the high point of the shoulder goes through the middle of the elbow, the middle of the leg bone, and lands *just behind the heel* of the foot.

*Note that Gruenig does not call for the same front assembly the American Standard demands. This should be noted carefully, in checking reading references.

Judging the Body

In the Standard all measurements are proportional to height at the withers; all parts are in proportion to the body. To judge the body, you must see the dog from the side, front, rear, and above.

From the side: Check backline, underline, forechest.
From the front: Check width and fullness of chest.
From the rear and above: Check width at shoulders, ribs, loin, and hips.

The implication of the Standard's specification of topline is that the neck descends into the pronounced withers (the highest point of the body) and then descends to a short, firm, straight back which ends in a slightly rounding croup and continues to a tail that seems a continuation of the spine and is *carried out rather than up*.

The ideal backline so implied is not the "ski-slope" (hyena) topline sometimes seen and even sought by a few Doberman fanciers. The correct topline fits a dog whose legs are under him, ready to move in any direction. The dog's major weight is balanced on his front feet; his rear legs are squarely set, ready to move forward or to the side. The extremely sloping topline fits a dog in pose but not ready for movement.

The underline is formed by a brisket deep to the elbow, flowing back through well-developed ribs that extend far back in the body, gradually shortening to give a marked tuck-up and flowing into a short loin. The depth of the brisket, the length of the extension of ribs, the shortness of loin, as well as the marked tuck-up, are all important to a correct body and the feeling of power and endurance. Underlines have as many or more faults as toplines. A close assessment is necessary to see such problems as: the brisket may be properly deep to the elbow, but if the ribs don't entend back far enough and the tuck-up is extreme, the dog has a weak or "whippety" look. A reverse problem can be too little tuck or no tuck, giving the appearance of power but not the appearance of speed. Desirable is a marked but moderate tuck-up and good, long rib extension.

When one looks down on the dog, the shoulders, ribs, and muscles of the hips should all be about the same width. The loin should be wide and strong. So, looking down, you see a solid dog—quite a contrast to the sighthound, for example. The loin comes in slightly from the width of the rib and flows back to full width again in the hindquarters.

The body from the front has been discussed at some length in previous sections.

Croup angle (specified in the Standard) is very difficult to assess when the dogs are posed. Handlers distort rears even more than fronts. The angle of a croup is best judged when the dog is standing free or while moving.

Tail carriage is a relatively minor problem, but it should be stressed that the correct Doberman carriage is out, and only slightly above horizontal.

Handlers frequently push the tail upright in the misguided idea that this is correct, making it appear that the dog has a flat croup and a terrier tail. This is building a fault into the breed picture.

Judging the Hindquarters

Hindquarters are judged from the side and from the rear.

The Standard specifies:

1. A 30-degree fall away from the spinal column of the hip bone.
2. Upper shank at right angle to hip bone—long, wide, well-muscled on both sides of thigh.
3. Clearly defined stifle.
4. Upper and lower shanks of equal length.
5. Hock to heel perpendicular to the ground when dog is "at rest."
6. Straight legs, parallel to each other and wide enough for body.
7. Cat feet turning neither in nor out.

To check manually the angle of hip bone to spinal column, lay the index finger along the spine line and extend the middle finger as far away as possible. If it centers on the hip bone, the angle is about right.

Equal lengths of upper and lower shanks can be assessed more readily if you lift the dog's rear foot off the ground. A further check is to lift the leg until the upper shank lies in a horizontal line and the lower shank is against it. If the lower shank extends well beyond the hip, the lower shank is substantially longer than the upper shank.

Two or three aspects of the Standard in regard to hindquarters cause many judges difficulty. First, rear angulation is specified as *"in balance with the front."* This assessment must be made, rather than faulting the rear "to itself." Second, the Standard calls for equal length of upper and lower shanks. This is a distinctly different rear from the one we look for in many terriers and poodles. Third, the Standard calls for a "clearly defined stifle," but does not call for a "well-turned" stifle.

The reasons for these requirements are partly in the function of the dog and partly in the genetic problems of the breed. In the early mixtures, many Dobermans appeared with longer rear legs than front legs. Getting balance between them has been a plaguing problem through the history of the breed. The judge that "prefers" the longer-legged rear end may be augmenting the problem.

Traditionally, if you drop a line from the end of the hip of a Doberman at rest, the vertical goes through the hock joint and ends just behind the rear paw. One inch or two inches beyond this is not unusual in our good specimen. You will see many that exhibit much more than that.

The musculature on the upper and lower shanks is very important. It is easiest checked from the rear. Often, the inside musculature of the lower shank is somewhat less than ideal. Real weaknesses will be quickly noted as the dog steps forward.

Cat feet are best viewed from the side.

Coat Color in the Doberman

The Standard lists the four coat colors as black, red, blue, and fawn (Isabella), but red is really reddish brown, blue is bluish gray, and fawn is silvery beige. The easiest way to understand these color divisions is to think of them as black, brown, gray, and beige, gray being the dilute of black and beige the dilute of brown. Of course they all have characteristic markings which ideally should be rust-red, though they vary in color from shades of wine, mahogany, apricot, tan, and yellow to an almost straw color!

At some point in the past, Americans started referring to the brown Doberman as "red." Of course it is not red; it is brown with a reddish cast. The Germans, who originated Dobermans, called them "browns" and reserved the word "red" for their markings (which they certainly were not but which the Germans hoped eventually to achieve). In our previous Standard and earlier ones, and in the German, English, and all Doberman Standards, the color has been brown. Other adjectives have been used such as liver, coffee, chestnut, chocolate, and cocoa, but the most beautiful is the rich brown with the reddish glow. There is a very dark brown with no red in either the coat or the markings, which are often almost yellow, and there is a light brown which is almost orange.

In the artificial light of indoor shows, the coat color of the black Doberman shows to better advantage than any of the other three colors. The black shines, whereas the brown gleams. Except in rare instances, the blues and Isabellas do not have the sheen of the other two colors because of the coat texture. The real beauty of a colored Doberman can never be truly appreciated until it is seen in a natural setting in sunlight at an outdoor show.

In Little's book on the inheritance of coat color, he points out that, except for the tan-point pattern, the fawn Doberman and the Weimaraner have the same genetic formula. American Doberman breeders tend to avoid the word "fawn," preferring "Isabella," lest it be confused with the color of the fawn Boxer or Dane, which, curiously, are classified as "gold" (yellow) by the Germans. The German word for "fawn" is "biesterbraun," which would probably be translated into English as "beige." In coloring, the fawn Doberman is closer to the Weimaraner, described in its Standard as mouse-gray to silver-gray, though the Doberman has a slightly beige tone.

The Isabella Doberman has been variously described as silvery beige, sandy, camel's hair, palomino, ash-blond, cafe au lait, chocmalt, mouse-gray, mauve-beige, driftwood, and Weimaraner-colored.

Just as the Isabella is the dilute of brown, the blue Doberman is the dilute of black. It is actually a medium-to-dark shade of gray, and ideally it has a definitely bluish cast. It has been described as slate-gray, steel-gray, blue-gray, gun-metal, and the color of a blue Great Dane.

The Doberman is a solid-colored dog with the typical "tan-point" pattern of markings. While there is a considerable range of shades in each coat color, as previously noted, if its basic coat is not one of the four allowed colors, it must be disqualified. The situation calling for disqualification is highly unlikely, and if it ever should occur, it would probably be with an animal that was white, parti-colored or brindle.

A solid-colored Doberman with no markings at all is not subject to disqualification (as in the Rottweiler Standard). This is not because it is any more acceptable in the Doberman than in the Rottweiler, but because such animals have not been seen in the Doberman show ring for more than 50 years and would be highly suspect as to the purity of their breeding. The judge would penalize heavily or withhold a ribbon for lack of merit in such cases.

In coat texture, length, and quantity, you look for a short, hard, thick coat that seems to cling to the skin. Run your fingers forward through the coat. You feel the hard texture, the length is evident, and the tight feel can be detected. A good coat will return immediately to position with scarcely a hair out of place. A thin coat is evident, for the skin shows through.

In markings, rust ones are specified. Deep color, rich color, and cleanly defined markings are desired. A careful study of photographs will develop an eye for perfection in markings.

Of all the lessons in learning to judge Dobermans, recognition of excellence in markings is probably the task to work at last. Generally, imperfections in markings are faulted only to the degree that they affect the total picture of the dog.

Judging Gait

The Standard asks for free, balanced, and vigorous movement. There should be good reach in front and good driving power behind. Doberman gait is usually judged from three views: the dog going straight away, the dog coming straight into the judge, and the dog moving in profile to the judge.

Going away and coming toward the judge, the Doberman should be "straight"; that is, he should move so his rear leg on the right is moving in line with the front leg on the right. True straight movement is rare in Dobermans and is usually a combination of structure, training, and handling. You are also watching joints. Does the dog move with efficiency or is there extra movement of joints or lack of movement? "Free, balanced, and vigorous" are the Standard's requirements.

Going away and coming in, you will also note the dog's tendency to "single track." Note the Standard's requirement: "a properly built Doberman will single track at a fast trot." Speeds have been measured on different dogs. Some single track within the first few steps. Others do not single track until at speeds beyond that practical in a show ring. The speed at which the dog moves in will be governed generally by the total conformation of the animal. Thus, *how the dog moves in* toward a centerline may be more important than whether it does.

From the side, you will be judging many aspects of the Doberman: his backline and croup, his reach in front (which ideally will be as far as his nose), his drive behind (which is a reaching under and propelling forward but not kicking out and up behind). You will also note his balance of reach in front and drive behind.

The gait requirements of the Standard are fairly simple. We use a dog "in action" or "in movement" to see many different things—to make any observations that go beyond the simple requirements of gait. We note problems in moving that confirm problems we had

noted when the dog was standing. We use it as an additional check, as a guard against over-posing.

But we also need to be aware that a Doberman, probably more than most breeds, moves each foot according to his own mind. His control of foot placement and action is remarkable, even at very high speeds. This ability can explain some of the odd movements you may observe in a Doberman one day but not find when you see the dog again.

Problems in judging gait:

1. Our literature and talk are filled with theories of gait; while none of us can clear our minds of these theories, from time to time we should review the exact requirements of the Standard to be sure we are applying them—not our own theories.

2. "Gait as a whole" can be a real problem for certain dogs. The dog may look very good going away but move with very short steps when viewed from the side. Putting the discordant views together into one concept of how the dog moves can be very difficult.

3. Trying to assess how much of a dog's gaiting problems come from the way the dog is handled is a constant difficulty. Many dogs will side-wind simply to watch for bait from the handler.

4. Assessing not only whether the Doberman is coming toward a centerline but whether it is coming in reasonably soundly is a constant problem.

5. Using the trot as a clue to the Doberman's ability at its natural gait—the gallop—is a problem to the judge.

6. Poor handling and inexperienced dogs are usually even more of a problem to judge when moving than when standing still. The inexperienced or inept handler can make a good moving dog move very poorly; and the inexperienced dog may react to so many things in so many different directions that it is almost impossible to tell whether or not the dog can handle itself well. These make overall evaluations very difficult.

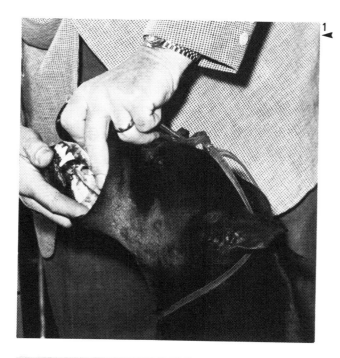

1. Mouth examination during Doberman judging starts with the bite.
2. Hotai Sweet Fantasy, who needs just one point to finish, is an inbred granddaughter of Ch. Hotai Sweet William. By his son, Ch. Hotai Willson, from his daughter, Hotai Airara. She is owned by Virginia Markley and Linda Zeesler.

Special Notes on Judging This Noble Breed

You should remember the Doberman responds to individuals—not to people.

A Doberman expects respect.

If an occasional dog does not trust you to approach from the rear, drop the dog from consideration, if possible, in the class.

When approaching, avoid intense, direct eye contact. If the dog seeks to "look you in the eye" (some of them do), you will know it.

Avoid lifting and dropping hindquarters as is done on terriers. A Doberman doesn't think that sort of thing fits his dignity.

Avoid trying to lift a Doberman's tail; again, this is not respectful.

Avoid reaching over and around a Doberman's neck. Some find this particularly objectionable.

Before making a final decision in any class, ask yourself the fundamental questions:

1. Is the dog of acceptable size?
2. Is the dog of acceptable general proportions?
3. Does the dog exhibit the attributes that make him seem a Doberman?
4. Has the dog behaved in the ring as a Doberman should?

We wish to acknowledge excerpts which were taken from *Learning to Judge The Doberman Pinscher*, the manual of The Judges Education Committee of the Doberman Pinscher Club of America. Chairman, Frank Grover; Supervisors, Mrs. Bob Adamson, Pat Doniere, Mrs. Jane Kay, Mrs. Margaret Kilburn, and Dr. Wilfrid E. Shute (deceased); and General Adviser, Charles A. T. O'Neill.

Macho, Carol Chavez's first Doberman, going through his paces on the way to earning his U.D. and WAC. Camino Real Dobermans, Leavenworth, Kansas.

CHAPTER TWENTY

Obedience and Working Doberman Pinschers

Dobermans have a well-deserved reputation for great intelligence, loyalty, and service. Properly trained and managed, Dobermans have distinguished themselves not only in the show ring but also in other endeavors. Many, many Dobermans who are show champions also have earned one or more obedience titles; and many Dobermans have achieved success in various fields of specialized work, only one of which is described in detail here.

Obedience

For its own protection and safety, every dog should be taught, at the very least, to recognize and respond promptly and correctly to the basic commands "Come," "Heel," "Down," "Sit," and "Stay." Doing so might at sometime save the dog's life and, in less extreme circumstances, will certainly make him a better citizen, more well-behaved and far more pleasant as a companion.

It you are patient and enjoy working with your dog, study some of the excellent books available on the subject of obedience and start at an early age to teach your Doberman puppy these basic manners. If you need the stimulus of working in a group, find out where obedience training classes are available (usually your veterinarian, your dog's breeder, or a dog-owning friend can tell you) and you and your dog can join up. If you have difficulty locating such a class, the American Kennel Club will, upon request, provide you with this information.

As an alternative, you could, of course, let someone else do the training by sending your dog to class, but this is far less rewarding as you then lose the opportunity of working with the dog, developing the rapport and closeness which the two of you can enjoy by working together. Since there could hardly be found a more intelligent, easily trainable breed of dog than a Doberman, it certainly should prove worth your while to attempt the task yourself.

If the latter has been your decision, there are some basic rules which you should follow. You must remain calm and confident in attitude at all times. You must never lose your temper and frighten your dog or punish him unjustly. Never, ever, resort to cruelty. Be quick and lavish with your praise each time a command is correctly followed. Make it fun for the dog and he will be eager to please you by responding correctly. Repetition is the keynote, but it should not be continued without recess to the point of tedium. Limit the training sessions to ten- or fifteen-minute periods each time.

Formal obedience training can be followed, and very frequently is, by entering the dog in obedience competition to work toward an obedience degree, or several of them, depending on the dog's aptitude and your own enjoyment. Obedience trials are held in conjunction with the majority of conformation dog shows, both all-breed and specialty, and as separate events as well. If you are working alone with your dog, you will need to obtain information on these from someone local, from a Doberman club to which you may belong, or from the American Kennel Club. If you have been working with a training class, you will find information readily available regarding dates and locations of trials.

The goals for which one works in the formal American Kennel Club member or licensed obedience trials are the following titles: C.D. (Companion Dog), C.D.X. (Companion Dog Excellent), and U.D. (Utility Dog). These degrees are earned by receiving three qualifying scores, or "legs," at each level of competition. The degrees must be earned in order, with one completed prior to starting work on the next. For example, a dog must have earned a C.D. prior to starting work on C.D.X. Then C.D.X. must be completed before U.D. work begins. The ultimate title possible to attain in obedience work is that of Obedience Trial Champion (O.T.Ch.). In order to qualify for this one, a dog must have received the required number of points by placing first or second in Open or Utility after having earned the Utility Dog rating. There is also a Tracking Dog title (T.D.) to be earned at tracking trials and a new, more difficult-to-attain degree, Tracking Dog Excellent (T.D.X.).

When you see the letters C.D. following a dog's name, you will know that the dog has satisfactorily completed the following exercises: heel on leash and figure eight, heel free, stand for examination, recall, long sit, and long down. C.D.X. means that tests have been passed in all of the exercises for Companion Dog plus heel free and figure eight, drop on recall, retrieve on flat, retrieve over high jump, broad jump, long sit, and long down. U.D. indicates that the dog has additionally passes tests in scent discrimination (leather article), scent discrimination (metal article), signal exercises, directed retrieve, directed jumping, and group stand for examination.

The letters T.D. indicate that the dog has been trained for and passed the test to follow the trail of a stranger along a path on which the trail was laid between thirty minutes and two hours previously. Along this track there must be more than two right-angle turns, at least two of which are well out in the open where no fences or other boundaries exist for guidance of the dog or handler. The dog wears a harness and is connected to the handler by a lead twenty to forty feet in length. Inconspicuously dropped at the end of the track is an article to be retrieved, usually a glove or wallet, which the dog is expected to locate and the handler to pick up. The letters T.D.X. indicate that the dog has passed a more difficult version of the Tracking Dog test, with a longer track and more turns to be successfully worked through.

The owner of a dog holding the U.D. title and the T.D. title may then use the letters U.D.T. following the dog's name. If the dog

has gained his U.D. title and his T.D.X. title, then the letters U.D.T.X. may follow his name, indicating that he is a Utility Dog and Tracker Excellent.

American and Canadian Obedience Trial Champion Duchess Danielle, II, WAC

Richard Simmet of Eden Prairie, Minnesota is the owner of a very talented and admired Doberman bitch who has truly scaled the performance heights in bringing home honors in this field. Dana, as she is known, was born June 2, 1976. Her career in obedience started at age six-and-a-half months and never stopped until her retirement at age seven years.

From the very first, Dana obviously loved her work in obedience, taking to the shows with ease. Her first time in the ring was at a fun match where she took first place with a score of 197. By her owner's count, Dana has been High in Trial on 36 occasions, has won 165 first place awards, and has been in second place 58 times. Numerous "High Combineds" have been hers, plus the very impressive distinction of being the only Dobe to take the first three Top Twenty obedience competitions consecutively, which she swept through with ease.

Dana's achievements include belonging to the "200 Club," being the No. 1 Obedience Dobe in the Nation for four years in a row, gaining her above mentioned victories at the first three Top Twenty obedience competitions, and winning her multiple High in Trials. She passed her Working Aptitude Test with flying colors, and she has won approximately 500 trophies in a span of four-and-a-half years.

It is interesting that Dana's background stems from one of the finest, oldest and most successful show kennels for Dobermans in America. This is vom Ahrtal, and her sire was Priam v Ahrtal;, her dam, Mystic Lady. Thus Dana is a granddaughter of the famed Cassio vom Ahrtal.

Her Obedience Trial Championship was completed by Dana in Houston, Texas. Going there needing 34 more points, she garnered a total of 99 points over that one weekend to become one of the most famous Dobermans in obedience history.

1. Dobermans used for police work in the Fiji Islands. Pictured are Faith, Baron, Trudi, Fenella, and Falcon. Photo courtesy of Peggy Adamson.
2. Damasyn The Redstone with Art O'Keefe, his partner. "Rocky" is by Damasyn Commander ex Damasyn The Christmas Holly. Bred by Melinda Aron and one of the first Dobermans used by the San Francisco Police Department. He performed brilliantly, but he was killed by a bullet in the line of duty shortly after this photo was taken.
3. Gayamon The Midnight Moon, C.D., WAC, showing his obedience talents as he takes the broad jump. Jo Ann James, owner, Brykris Dobermans, Miami, Florida.

1. Am. and Can. O.T. Ch. Vanessa Von Heink, Am. and Can. U.D., WAC, by Ch. Mikadobe's Cupid ex Ch. Moluch's Sacha Sue, was born in November 1980. This talented Doberman bitch has 15 High in Trial Awards within a one-year period, all from Open "B" and Utility competition. In 1979 she was awarded the most High in Trials received by an individual Doberman, and the Most Blue Ribbons received by an individual Doberman. Owned by Judith A. Goldman, Venture Kennels, Gaithersburg, Maryland.
2. Coming over the high jump is Gayamon The Midnight Moon, C.D., WAC. Owned and handled by Jo Ann James, Brykris Dobermans, Miami, Florida. Photo by Bill James.
3. This Doberman earned a perfect score of 200 in Open B at the 1972 Doberman Pinscher Club of America Specialty under judge Carl Spitz. Leon K. Mathews, owner-handler. By the famous combination which produced so many champions, Ch. Schauffelein's Troll Arabasque ex Ch. Lowenbrau Aloha Schauffelein. Photo courtesy of Peggy Adamson.
4. Garry von Hagenstern at three months old; a son of Juon. Annie and Daniel Mulero, Dompierre/Mer, France.

The Simmets keep their kennel small, breeding only when they need a pup themselves or when they have a minimum of five people who have deposited money to reserve a pup.

As we write this book, Danielle II's granddaughter is showing extremely good potential and aptitude in about fifteen fun matches, usually winding up first in her class with scores of 196-199, several first placements, and a High in Match. May she carry on in her grandmother's tradition!

Venture

Venture Dobermans began in the early 1980's with the breeding of Judith Goldman's noted obedience bitch, American and Canadian Obedience Trial Champion Vanessa Von Heink, American and Canadian U.D., WAC, to Champion Lujac's Daniel. To date the kennel, at Gaithersburg, Maryland, contains only the products of this breeding: Canadian Champion Venture's Solar Coronation, C.D., known as "Cory," co-owned by Dr. Kyle Sibinovic and Mrs. Goldman, and who has both "majors" in the United States and several points; Venture's Starburst Anthem, C.D.X., WAC, with two points; Venture's Solar Eclipse, C.D.X. and Venture's Andromeda, C.D.X. are the other two. Anthem and Solar Eclipse belong to Mrs. Goldman. The fourth to have been shown from this litter of eight, Venture's Andromeda, C.D.X., was placed in the Top Twenty Novice Dogs in Obedience by *Doberman World* in 1983. This bitch is spayed and owned by Ann Deihm. All four of the above hold Canadian C.D. degrees.

Venture Kennels' other brood bitch has been a disappointment, produced no puppies, and will not be used again.

The young Solar Eclipse is the sire of a promising litter being watched with interest from a tightly linebred Satan's Image granddaughter. A male and two of the bitches look promising.

American and Canadian Obedience Trial Champion Vanessa Von Heink, American and Canadian U.D., WAC, has made a very distinguished and exciting record in obedience competition. Starting her career at seventeen months of age, all three of her U.S. degrees were earned within eleven months; all three Canadian degrees were earned within thirteen

months, each requiring only one trip to Canada. She earned the *Dog World* Award with the completion of her Canadian C.D. title, and she was an American U.D. and Canadian Obedience Trial Champion at two years four months of age.

"Ember," as she is known, was shown only sparingly in the spring of 1980, then retired through the summer in anticipation of her puppies. She was brought back out briefly in the fall for three shows, then retired at the end of that season. Thus her entire obedience career actually was earned in approximately two years from the beginning of her degrees to the end of her Obedience Trial Championship.

Vanessa Von Heink, or Ember, was obtained at four-and-a-half months of age from Jean and William Heinkal with the warning that "this is the only puppy from the litter that had not been successfully lead trained." She was completely trained, and owner-handled, to all of her obedience triumphs by Judy Goldman.

We are pleased to salute Ember and tell her story in this book. Her obedience record has contributed to putting Dobermans back on the Obedience Top Ten of All Breeds as true obedience contenders.

Bishop's Adora's Rocker, C.D.X., WAC, Sch.H. I, TT giving a demonstration of Schutzhund training. Owned by Kay Martin, Brooklyn, New York.

CHAPTER TWENTY-ONE

Schutzhund Work With Dobermans

The Doberman is a particularly apt and suitable dog to be trained for Schutzhund work, and the interest in this phase of Dobe ownership is increasing steadily in the United States and other countries, in keeping with the original German tradition. A number of Dobe owners in the U.S. are adding a Schutzhund degree or two or even three to the credits of their Dobermans, taking pride and satisfaction in the results.

For the uninitiated, following is a resume of what is covered by the various Schutzhund procedures and scoring, with points and ratings in each category. For this we extend thanks to Mr. and Mrs. Robert Dear of Vero Beach, Florida, who are very active these days in Schutzhund work, and successfully, we might add. Schutzhund training and titles are not recognized by the American Kennel Club. There are, however, Schutzhund clubs and Schutzhund groups carrying on the work, and the number of people and dogs so involved is growing at a steady speed.

In reply to my inquiry regarding her Schutzhund dogs, Mrs. Dear has written as follows:

"Our primary interest over the past eighteen months has been in the sport of Schutzhund. For those unfamiliar with this sport, I would like to take this opportunity to briefly explain.

"Schutzhund was originally intended to serve as an all-around temperament test for the working breed dogs for the purpose of selecting those dogs which would be most suitable to use for breeding. It has developed into a highly competitive sport on an international basis with a total membership of the DVG, (Deutscher Verband der Gebrauchshund sportvereine), which is based in Germany, of approximately 84,000 members. There are currently 666 members in active competition in the United States who belong to this particular organization. The DVG is an all-breed club and any dog who is able to perform all of the required exercises is eligible to compete. The sport is basically geared to the temperament of the German Shepherd Dog, but there are some other working breeds out there performing, among them the Doberman Pinscher.

"Schutzhund consists of three phases and in order for a dog to receive his title he must successfully complete all three of these phases in one day. There are three levels of training with three titles given.

Schutzhund I (SchH. I)	Basic
Schutzhund II (SchH. II)	Intermediate
Schutzhund III (SchH. III)	Advanced

"The three phases consist of Tracking, Obedience and Protection Work. The purpose is to have an all-around reliable animal who is self-confident, dependable, and in full control by the handler at all times. These animals are asked to think for themselves and work away from their handlers while still aware of and willing to obey their every command. They make exceptionally good family dogs who are well adjusted, loving animals, sound in both mind and body."

Following are copies of Pointing and Rating schedules along with a summary of each level.

Points and Ratings of SchH. I, II, III

In each category a maximum of 100 points can be made, making a total of 300 points for all three categories.

Category A Tracking	100 points
Category B Obedience	100 points
Category C Protection	100 points

A minimum score of 70 points in categories A and B and a minimum of 80 points in category C is required to obtain a title or degree.

To qualify for a SchH. degree (I, II, III) all dogs entered must pass a temperament test. Dogs not passing this test shall be disqualified from the trial.

RATING OF EXCELLENCE

0 to 109 points	unsatisfactory
110 to 219 points	insufficient
220 to 239 points	satisfactory
240 to 269 points	good
270 to 285 points	very good
286 to 300 points	excellent

Summary of Schutzhund I — Procedure and Scoring

Tracking: 400-500 paces long, 2 articles, minimum 20 minutes old, handler lays the track. Dog is scored on his accuracy and attitude. **100 points.**

Obedience: Heeling on leash — The dog and handler are judged as a team at a normal pace, fast, slow, two right turns, two left turns and two halts with automatic sits. Heeling into a group of moving people and cannot exhibit shyness or aggressiveness. 15 points. Heeling off leash — Dog is heeled back into the group and procedure is repeated. Heeled out of group and two shots fired. Dog must not exhibit gunshyness. 20 points. Sitting from motion — Dog will be told to sit while heeling and the handler continues to walk away. Dog must sit and stay until handler returns. 10 points. Retrieve on flat — An article belonging to the handler will be thrown and the dog must retrieve it promptly. 10 points. Down in motion with recall—Dog will be commanded to down while handler continues walking away. Dog will then be called to handler. 10 points. Retrieve over high jump — Article is thrown over the jump and the dog must jump the hurdle and retrieve. The jump must be made in both directions. 15 points. Go ahead and down — Dog is sent out ahead of the handler and commanded to down. Minimum 40 paces for full points. 10 points. Long down under distraction — During another dog's performance of obedience, the dog must remain down; his handler is about 40 paces away with his back to the dog. If he

exhibits gunshyness, during gunfire, he is disqualified. 10 points. **TOTAL 100 points.**

Protection: Upon command from the handler, the dog must locate the Agitator and HOLD AT BAY AND BARK, remain guarding until the handler picks him up. GUARD: 3 points, BARK: 2 points. Next the handler will heel his dog towards a designated blind where the Agitator is hidden. Heel on Lead: 5 points, Heel off the Lead: 5 points; this is a control exercise. ATTACK ON THE HANDLER: The dog will attack and hold firm under two hits from the switch, release on command. 25 points. PURSUIT AND COURAGE TEST: The dog is scored on the "attitude" of his pursuit to attack the agitator. 20 points. The attack on the Courage Test must show strength and conviction by the dog; he must release on command and remain guarding until the handler comes to him. 40 points. **TOTAL 100 points.**

The dogs are also graded: A, B, or C. A — Courage, strongly pronounced. B — Courage, average. C — Courage, insufficient.

Summary of Schutzhund II — Procedure and Scoring

Tracking: 600-700 paces long, 2 articles, minimum 30 minutes old, stranger lays the track. The dog is scored on his accuracy and attitude. **100 points.**

Obedience: (See Schutzhund I for details)

Heeling on Leash	10 points
Heeling off Leash	15 points
Sitting from motion	5 points
Down in motion/ Recall	10 points
Retrieve on flat (2 lb. dumbbell)	10 points
Retrieve over high jump (1½ lb. dumbbell)	15 points
Retrieve over 5 ft. wall (article or dumbbell)	15 points
Go ahead and down	10 points
Long down/ Distraction	10 points
TOTAL	**100 points**

Protection: Searching for agitator — while agitator is hiding, handler sends dog to search to the left and right five to six times. 5 points. Finding and Barking — Dog finds agitator and barks until commanded to heel by handler. Handler then searches agitator. 5 plus 5 points. Escape and defense — Agitator tries to escape from dog. Dog prevents this by biting hard. Dog releases when agitator freezes. Agitator then threatens dog with switch. Dog should bite hard again. Handler then searches agitator while dog is watching. 40 points. Transport — Handler has dog heel and tells agitator to walk ahead. 5 points. Attack, Courage Test, Fighting Instinct — During transport agitator attacks handler. After firm bite the attack is stopped and the handler calls the dog off. Agitator walks away, after 50 paces makes threatening motion and runs. Handler sends dog. Agitator turns towards dog. Dog must bite hard immediately. Agitator is transported back to judge. 40 points. Full points for fighting instinct can only be given to dogs who demonstrate exceptional courage and hardness. **TOTAL 100 points.**

Summary of Schutzhund III — Procedure and Scoring

Tracking: 1200-1400 paces long, 50 minutes old, laid by stranger, 3 articles, four turns. **100 points.**

Obedience: (See Schutzhund I for details)

Heeling off Leash	10 points
Sitting from motion	5 points
Down in motion/ recall	10 points
Stand in motion	5 points
Running stand/recall	10 points
Retrieve on flat (4 lb. dumbbell)	10 points
Retrieve over high jump (1½ lb. dumbbell)	15 points
Retrieve over 6 ft. wall (article or dumbbell)	15 points
Go ahead and down	10 points
Long down/ distraction	10 points
TOTAL	**100 points**

Protection: (See Schutzhund II for details)

Search	5 points
Find and bark	5 + 5 points
Escape and Defense	35 points
Transport	5 points
Attack and Courage Test	45 points
TOTAL	**100 points**

The Schutzhund III performance should be with more control and accuracy than I or II and will be judged accordingly.

Summary of the VB (Traffic Secure Companion Dog)

All breeds and sizes eligible. Minimum age is 12 months old. No points. Dog either passes or fails. Heeling pattern off and on lead. Gunfire. Must show mangeability and behavior in street traffic, even under difficult conditions and towards people and other animals. Also when turned loose in a park, must show attachment to its master and return to him when called.

Summary of the WH (Watch Dog)

All breeds and sizes eligible. Minimum age 12 months old. No points given. The dog either passes or fails. The dog is required to heel on and off lead; through a group with gunfire; walking sit; walking down with recall; fetch an object. The dog must be attached enough to its master to want to find him in a group of people. He must guard an article; guard (simulated) property, like a home or car. Show watchfulness on a running line with an agitator coming at him from either direction.

Summary of Fahrtenhund (FH) (Procedure and Scoring)

This is considered the "Master in Tracking." The dog must have at least a SchH. I degree or a VB title. The track is approximately 1,500 paces long; 3 hours old; 6 angles; 4 articles; 3 misleading tracks. Perfect score is 100 points. Minimum score is 70 points.

Some Notable Schutzhund Dobermans

Nanci Little of Miami, Florida remarks, "They say that there is only one outstanding dog in each person's lifetime. If that is true, then mine was Shady Acres Persuasion, UDT, WAC, SchH.III, FH, VB, WH, AD, known to friends as Shady."

Shady was born July 23, 1973 and died on December 16, 1982. Her breeder was Anita Chandler, Lazy Acres Dobermans, also in Miami, and she was by Amerbrit's Valient ex Chandler's Second Chance, C.D. Her sire, owned by a close friend of the Chandlers' veterinarian, was a large-boned gentle Doberman who herded horses and cows for his owner. Mrs. Chandler describes him as having had "the look of eagles," so elegant was his carriage and demeanor.

A friend of Anita Chandler's was Nanci Little, and the puppy called Shady was given to her as a gift. No one at that time had the remotest conception of the heights this talented bitch would reach, nor the multitude of titles which would be earned by her during her lifetime! Nanci trained and handled Shady herself every inch of the way, thrilling to each and every one of her successes.

Shady received her Schutzhund II and Schutzhund III titles in three shows within the year between June 1975 and June 1976. She was titled eighteen times in DVG, NASA, and United States competition and competed in five National Championships, placing third in 1980 under Herr Rubel. Her highest single score in Schutzhund III was 292 points; her average total score from March 1980 through May 1982 was 286. Her average protection score was 97.5 points.

In 1981, Shady and her son Caine (Shady Acres Hurrah Caine, SchH.III, FH, AD) were on the winning team at the National Championship in Boston, Massachusetts. In 1983 her son, daughter and granddaughter won the team championship at Dallas, Texas. At the Doberman National Specialty Schutzhund Trial in New Orleans, Louisiana, held under FCI rules in 1983, Shady's son Bliss (Shady Acres Destiny Bliss, SchH.III, C.D., VB) placed first; Shady's daughter Caprice and granddaughter, also named Shady, placed second and third.

The original Shady was once bred to Champion Dorr's Reward of Maestro, C.D.X., SchH.II, ROM, a litter which produced two Schutzhund II dogs and a Schutzhund III, C.D.X., TD bitch.

The protection scores on Shady's titled progeny, which Nanci Little personally trained and handled, were in the 96-100 points range. Caine, owned and handled by Ken Rowe of Ft. Lauderdale, Florida, scored 100 points in his first Schutzhund III protection. Caprice, handled by Shareen Conn of Garland, Texas scored 98 points at the Dallas Team Championship event in 1983.

Starting 1984 off in good manner, Bliss, handled by Nanci Little, scored 100 points in both Tracking and Protection for his first Schutzhund III title at Miami during February.

Shady Acres Persuasion, UDT, WAC, SchH.III, FH, VB, WH, AD has six titled grandchildren to date, all having attained their Schutzhund III degrees. Numerous other of Shady's descendants also are in training, and there are some who have already obtained their obedience titles under American Kennel Club rules.

As for this remarkable bitch's own accomplishments, she started out by receiving her C.D. and C.D.X. in three shows each, accompanied by a galaxy of trophies, and her U.D. in seven shows with three first place trophies. She had her UDT and Schutzhund III in June 1986 at less than three years old.

Shady's son, Caine, already mentioned above, was bred by Nanci Little, owned/trained/handled by Ken Rowe. He and his dam, Shady, were in the top five of all Schutzhund III dogs (all breeds) in the United States for the year in 1981. Before his death he was worked in fourteen Schutzhund III trials, earning V rating in five of them, SG rating in seven, and failing only twice.

Anita Chandler, Shady's breeder, acting on Nanci Little's suggestion, later took Shady's dam, Chandler's Second Chance, for breeding to Champion Fuego's Lucky Copper to help fill the demand for puppies of breeding similar to Shady's as Shady became famous. At least one of the bitches from this litter was shown and pointed in conformation. Following several years of being around Nanci and Shady at the Schutzhund trials, Anita Chandler fell in love with a bitch puppy bred by Nanci, and so she purchased Shady Acres Endless Summer and began attending matches with her. There Anita was told that due to a white patch on Summer's chest, this bitch would never do well in the breed ring. So the Chandlers started training her for

1. Ch. Charmaron's Rockette, WAC, by Indigo Rock, during a Doberman Pinscher Club of America WAC test. Owned by Bob Bishop; photo courtesy of Kay Martin.
2. Glenayr Jamison, by Ch. Glenayr Dufferinand of Tedell ex Tara's Harp, doing Schutzhund work. An all-around dog, owned by Jay-Mee's Dobbies in Puerto Rico.
3. Glenayr Jamison doing Schutzhund work with trainer Luis Solis. Owned by Jay-Mee's Dobbies.
4. Here is the great European winner, Danica Stamm's Juon, champion in many countries, giving an example of his working abilities. Owned by the Muleros, who are noted French fanciers of Dobermans.

1. This distinguished Doberman is Shady Acres Endless Summer, C.D., Sch.H. III, VB, WH, AD. By Sandy's Derringer Dirk, U.D.T., Sch.H. II ex Shady Acres Foxfire, C.D. Bred by Nanci Little. Owned by Anita Chandler, Miami, Florida.
2. Shady Acres Hurrahcaine, Sch.H. III, FH, AD, owned and trained by Ken Howe, Ft. Lauderdale, Florida.
3. Schutzhund Seminar in Puerto Rico, August 1983. Mr. Ken Howe observes Jay-Mee's Latin Dandy, a Glenayr Jamison and Taina Red Poison offspring. Dandy was bred by Jay-Mee's Dobbies and is owned by Tony and Hilda Morales. Trainer, Luis Solis. Dandy has been a highly successful show dog and Schutzhund worker.
4. Ch. Knox's Carbon Copy, C.D.X., T.D., ROM, Sch.H. III, FH, AD demonstrates proper tracking procedure for his T.D. title. Owned by Bill and Susan Knox, Cookeville, Tennessee.
5. Ch. Carosel Musical Light, C.D., ROM, demonstrating how a Schutzhund Doberman is trained. Carol Selzle Petruzzo, owner, Carosel Kennels, Freehold, New Jersey.

Schutzhund, with the result that as we go to press she has attained her Schutzhund III title along with her C.D., VB, WH, AD, and is now working towards her C.D.X. and U.D.T. as well.

The latest news from Shady Acres is that Summer was bred to a Shady son and excitement is high over at least three of the puppies who show great promise for Schutzhund work, most particularly a little bitch who has been named Chandler's Firecracker.

The lady who provided much of our Schutzhund information, Jonni Dear of Vero Beach, Florida has, with her husband Bob, become a very enthusiastic follower of this sport. The first Doberman owned by the Dears was a black and rust female, Santos Santana, C.D., born in November 1978. At present the Dears have six Dobes, three of which are in active competition. One of them is the bitch, American and Canadian Champion Wenfrey's Annie Oakley, which Evelyn (Jonni) Dear co-owns with her breeder Wendy Serra who is written up elsewhere in this book. But their prime interest over the past eighteen months or so has been in the Schutzhund field where two of their dogs have been highly successful.

Nero v. Stoberhai, C.D., SchH.III, a black and rust male, was born December 3, 1979. He gained his Schutzhund II title on February 9, 1984 in Miami, Florida and his owners have great hopes for his future. He has been used at stud just once to date and has passed on not only his ideal temperament but his very good conformation and bone structure as well. Schutzhund training is not accomplished overnight, but the Dears feel that Nero will be a top competing dog in the sport in the very near future. Nero is the son of a German import who carries the Schutzhund III title, and FH title, and is from the Forrell and Furstenfeld bloodlines. His dam is heavily Ahrtal bred with a touch of Damasyn.

Santos Santana, C.D., the Dears' own bitch, is the one who was bred to Nero for his first litter. This produced a red male, Ziegfried v. Stoberhai, whom the Dears also own and are enjoying in Schutzhund training. He was born February 9, 1981 and is close to his Schutzhund II at this time. Once he has attained Schutzhund III, the Dears are seriously considering starting him out in conformation, and in obedience for his C.D.

When "Ziggy" gained Schutzhund I, he became the seventh generation in his line of Schutzhund titled dogs, according to Mrs. Dear's records as stated in his pedigree, which points out the importance of good breeding principles. Both Nero and Ziggy have been trained by Mr. and Mrs. Dear and handled exclusively by the former.

The Dears' first bitch, Santos Santana, C.D., is not yet involved with Schutzhund work but finished her C.D. with some nice honors, including High in Trial with a score of 193 the day she gained the second leg towards it at the Greater Miami Training Club trial. She represents Damasyn and Tarrado bloodlines.

3

4

5

Kaukauna's Hi-Mark, Ch. Jagermeister's Blackmail (at 12 weeks), and Tanya's Cassandra. Owned by Joe and Janet Lobb, Dobenhaus Kennels, Brucefield, Ontario, Canada.

CHAPTER TWENTY-TWO

Breeding Doberman Pinschers

Breeding good dogs requires a lot of hard work. It is not easy to produce dogs who conform as closely as possible to the Standard, and it takes years to develop a strain of good and successful dogs. A lot of time and effort must go into choosing the stud dog and brood bitch, and then more time must be spent with the litter once it arrives.

The Stud Dog

Choosing the best stud dog to complement your bitch is not an easy task. The principal factors to be considered are the stud's quality and conformation and his pedigree. The pedigree lists the various bloodlines involved with the ancestry of the dog. If you are a novice in the breed, I would suggest that you seek advice from some of the more experienced breeders who are old-timers in the fancy and thus would be able to discuss with you some of the various dogs behind the one to which you are planning to breed your bitch. Many times such people accurately recall in minute detail the dogs you need to know about, perhaps even having access to photos of them. And do be sure to carefully study the photos in this book, as they show representatives of important Doberman bloodlines.

It is extremely important that the stud's pedigree be harmonious with that of your bitch. Do not just rush out and breed to a current winner with no regard for whether or not he can reproduce his quality. Take time to check out the progeny being sired by the dog, or dogs, under your consideration. A dog that has sired nothing of quality for others probably will do no better for you, unless, of course, it is a young stud just starting out; such a stud may not have had the opportunity to produce much of anything, good or bad, thus far. Do you want to waste your bitch's time on an unknown quantity? Wouldn't you prefer to use a dog with a good producing record? You may get a little-known or unproven dog for a less expensive stud fee, but is that really sensible?

Breeding dogs is not a moneymaking proposition. By the time you pay a stud fee, take care of the bitch during gestation, whelp the litter, and raise and care for the puppies (including shots, and food, among other things) until they reach selling age, you will be fortunate if you break even on the cost of the litter. Therefore, it is foolish to skimp on the stud fee. Let nothing influence your selection except that the dog be best suited to your bitch in background and conformation, with the best producing record, regardless of the cost. It is just as expensive to raise mediocre puppies as good ones, and you will certainly fare better financially if you have show-prospect puppies to sell than if you come up with nothing but pets, which you will probably wind up selling for far less than you had intended or you'll end up giving away to get them good homes. Remember, the only excuse for breeding and bringing puppies into the world is an honest effort to improve the breed. So in choosing the stud you use, remember that the best, most suitable one you can find with an impressive producing record will almost certainly be by far the greatest bargain in the long run.

You will have to decide on one of three courses to follow in planning the breeding of your bitch: inbreeding, linebreeding, or outcrossing. Inbreeding is normally considered to be mating father to daughter, mother to son, or sister to brother. Linebreeding is combining two dogs belonging originally to the same strain or family of Dobermans, descended from the same ancestors, such as half-brother to half-sister, niece to uncle, granddaughter to grandsire, and so on. Outcross breeding is using a dog and a bitch of

585

completely different bloodlines with no mutual ancestors, or only a few, and these far back, if at all.

Each of these methods has advantages and disadvantages; each has supporters and detractors. I would say that linebreeding is probably the safest, the most generally approved, and the most frequently used with the desired results. Thus, I would say, it is perfect for the novice breeder because it is the easiest to figure out, especially until one has acquired considerable experience with the breed and the various bloodlines of which it consists.

Inbreeding should be left for the experienced, very sophisticated breeder who knows the line extremely well and thus is in a position to evaluate the probable results. Outcrossing is normally done when you are trying to bring in a specific feature or trait, such as better movement, better head type, superior bone or substance, or better personality or temperament.

Everyone sincerely interested in breeding dogs wants to develop a line of their own, but this is not accomplished overnight. It takes at least several generations before you can claim to have done so, and during this time the close study of bloodlines and the observation of individual dogs are essential. Getting to know and truthfully evaluate the dogs with which you are working will go a long way in helping you preserve the best in what you have while at the same time remove weaknesses.

As a novice breeder, your wisest bet is to start by acquiring one or two bitches of the finest quality and background you can buy. In the beginning, it is really foolish to own your own stud dog; you will make out better and have a wider range of dogs with which to work if you pay a stud fee to one of the outstanding producing Dobermans available to service your bitch. In order to be attractive to breeders a stud dog must be well known, must have sired at least one champion (and usually one that has attracted considerable attention in specials competition), and must have winning progeny in the ring; this represents a large expenditure of time and money before the dog begins to bring in returns on your investment. So start out by paying a stud fee a few times to use such a dog, or

dogs, retaining the best bitch out of each of your first few litters and breeding those once or twice before you seriously think of owning your own stud dog. By that time, you will have gained the experience to recognize exactly what sort of dog you need for this purpose.

A future stud dog should be selected with the utmost care and consideration. He must be of very high standard as he may be responsible for siring many puppies each year, and he should not be used unless he clearly has something to contribute to the breed and carries no hereditary disease. Ideally, he should come from a line of excellent Dobermans on both sides of his pedigree, the latter containing not only *good* dogs but also ones which are *proven successful producers of quality*. The dog himself should be of sufficient quality to hold his own in competition in his breed. He should be robust and virile, a keen stud dog who has proved that he is able to transmit his best qualities to his progeny. Do not use an unsound dog or a dog with a major or outstanding fault such as missing teeth. Not all champions seem able to pass along their individual splendid quality and, by the same token, occasionally one finds a dog who never finished but who does sire puppies better than himself *provided that his pedigree is star-studded with top-producing dogs and bitches*. Remember too, that the stud dog cannot do it alone; the bitch must have what it takes too, although I must admit that some stud dogs, the truly dominant ones, can consistently produce type and quality regardless of the bitch or her background. Great studs like this, however, are few and far between.

If you are the proud owner of a promising young stud dog, one that you have either bred from one of your own bitches or that you have purchased after much serious thought and deliberation, do not permit him to be used for the first time until he is about a year old. The initial breeding should be to a proven matron, experienced in what is expected of her and thus not likely to give the stud a bad time. His first encounter should be pleasant and easy, as he could be put off breeding forever by a maiden bitch who fights and resents his advances. His first breeding should help him develop confidence and assurance. It should be done in quiet surroundings, with only you and one other person (to hold the bitch) present. Do not make a circus of it, as the first time will determine your stud's attitude and feeling about future breedings.

Your young stud dog must allow you to help with the breeding, as later there will be bitches who will not be cooperative and he will need to develop the habit of accepting assistance. If, right from the beginning, you are there helping and praising him, he will expect and accept this as a matter of course whenever it may be necessary.

Before you introduce the dogs, be sure to have some K-Y Jelly at hand (this is the only lubricant that should be used) and either a stocking or a length of gauze with which to muzzle the bitch should it seem necessary, as you do not want either yourself or your stud dog bitten. Once they are "tied," you will be able to remove the muzzle, but, for the preliminaries, it is best to play it safe by muzzling her.

The stud fee is paid at the time of the breeding. Normally a return service is offered should the bitch fail to produce. Usually one live puppy is considered to be a litter. In order to avoid any misunderstanding regarding the terms of the breeding, it is wise to have a breeding certificate which both the owner of the stud and the owner of the bitch should sign. This should spell out quite specifically all the conditions of the breeding, along with listing the dates of the matings (usually the bitch is bred twice with one day in between, especially if she is a maiden bitch). The owner of the stud should also, at this time, provide the owner of the bitch with a copy of the stud dog's pedigree, if this has not previously been done.

Sometimes a pick-of-the-litter puppy is taken instead of a stud fee, and this should be noted in the breeding certificate along with such terms as at what age the owner of the stud dog is to select the puppy and whether it is to be a dog puppy, a bitch puppy, or just the "pick" puppy. All of this should be clearly stated to avoid any misunderstandings later on.

In almost every case, the bitch must come to the stud dog for breeding. Once the owner of the bitch decides to what stud dog she will preferably be bred, it is important that the owner of the stud be contacted immediately to discuss the stud fee, terms, approximate time the bitch is due in season, and whether she will be shipped in or brought to the stud owner. Then, as soon as the bitch shows signs of coming into season, another phone call to the stud owner must follow to finalize the arrangements. I have experienced times when the bitch's owner has waited until a day or two before the bitch should be bred to contact me, only to meet with disappointment owing to the dog's absence from home.

It is essential that the stud owner have proper facilities for housing the bitch while she is there. Nothing can be more disheartening than to have a bitch misbred, or still worse, to have her get away and become lost. Unless you can provide safe and proper care for visiting bitches, do not offer your dog at public stud.

Owning a stud dog is no easy road to riches, as some who have not experienced it seem to think; making the dog sufficiently well known is expensive and time-consuming. Be selective in the bitches you permit this dog to service. It takes two to make the puppies; and while some stud dogs do seem almost to achieve miracles, it is a general rule that an inferior bitch from a mediocre background will probably never produce well no matter how dominant and splendid may be the stud to whom she is bred. Remember that these puppies will be advertised and perhaps shown as sired by your dog. You do not want them to be an embarrassment to yourself or to him, so do not accept just any bitch who comes along in order to get the stud fee. It may prove far too expensive in the long run.

A stud fee is generally based on the going price of one show-type puppy and on the sire's record as a producer of winners. Obviously, a stud throwing champions in every litter is worth a greater price than a dog that sires mediocre puppies. Thus a young stud, just starting his career as a sire, is less expensive before proven than a dog with, say, forty or fifty champions already on the record. And a dog that has been used more than a few times but has no winning progeny should, it goes without saying, be avoided no matter how small the fee; he will amost certainly be a waste of your bitch's time.

I do not feel that we need to go into the actual breeding procedure here, as the experienced fancier already knows how it should be

1A

▼2

1. Ch. Steb's Top Skipper, owned by Natalie and Monroe Stebbins, was one of the most important dogs Doberman history has ever known. Top Sire of the Year three times consecutively, he had an imposing list of great ones to his credit, including the famous "football" litter, adding up to the amazing total of 50 champions.

2. Am., Can., and Col. Ch. Belita von Tamara, C.D., owned and shown by Mrs. Ellen Hoffman, Elfred Kennels, Harriman, New York.

handled and the novice should not attempt it for the first time by reading instructions in a book. Plan to have a breeder or handler friend help you until you have become accustomed to handling such matters or, if this is not practical for you, it is very likely your veterianian can arrange to do it for you or get someone from his staff to preside.

If a complete "tie" is made, that breeding should be all that is actually necessary. However, with a maiden bitch, a bitch who has "missed" (failed to conceive) in the past, or one who has come a long distance, most people like to give a second breeding, allowing one day to lapse in between the two. The second service gives additional insurance that a litter will result; and if the bitch is one with a past record for misses, sometimes even a third mating takes place in an effort to take every precaution.

Once the "tie" has been completed, be sure that the stud's penis goes back completely into its sheath. The dog should be offered a drink of water and a short walk, and then he should be put in his crate or kennel somewhere alone to settle down. Do not permit him to mingle with the other males for a while, as he will carry the odor of the bitch about him and this could result in a fight.

The bitch should not be allowed to urinate for at least an hour. In fact, many people feel that she should be "upended" (held with her rear end above her front) for several minutes following the "tie" in order to permit the sperm to travel deeper. She should then be offered water, crated, and kept quiet.

There are no set rules governing the conditions of a stud service. They are whatever the owner of the stud dog chooses to make them. The stud fee is paid for the act, not for the litter; and if a bitch fails to conceive, this does not automatically call for a return service unless the owner of the stud sees it that way. A return service is a courtesy, not something that can be regarded as a right, particularly as in many cases the failure has been on the part of the bitch, not the stud dog. Owners of a stud in whom they take pride and whom they are anxious to have make records as the sire of numerous champions, however, are usually most generous in this respect; and I do not know of any instances where this courtesy has been refused when no puppies resulted from the breeding. Some stud owners insist on the return service being given to the same bitch only, while others will accept a different bitch in her place if the owner wishes, particularly if the original one has a previous record for missing.

When a bitch has been given one return breeding and misses again, the stud owner's responsibility has ended. If the stud dog is one who consistently sires puppies, then obviously the bitch is at fault; and she will quite likely never conceive, no matter how often or to how many different studs she is bred. It is unreasonable for the owner of a bitch to expect a stud's owner to give more than one return service.

The Brood Bitch

One of the most important purchases you will make in dogs is the selection of your foundation brood bitch, or bitches, on whom you plan to base your breeding program. You want marvelous blood lines representing top-producing strains; you want sound bitches of basic quality, free of any hereditary problems. There is no such thing as a "bargain" brood bitch. If you are offered one, be wary and bear in mind that you need the *best* and that the price will be correctly in ratio to the quality.

Conscientious Doberman breeders feel quite strongly that the only possible reason for producing puppies is the desire to improve and uphold quality and temperament within the breed, certainly not because one hopes to make a quick cash profit on a mediocre litter, which never works out that way in the long run and can very well wind up adding to the nation's shocking number of unwanted canine waifs. The only reason for breeding a litter is the ambition to produce high-quality puppies of intelligence, show potential, and sound temperament. That is the thought to be kept in mind right from the moment you begin to yearn for puppies.

Your Doberman bitch should not be bred until her second period in season; but if she starts her season at an extra early age, say, barely over six months of age, and then for the second time just past one year of age, you would be wise to wait until her third heat. Many breeders prefer to wait and finish their bitch's championship and then breed her, as pregnancy can be disastrous to a show coat and getting it back in shape again takes time. The waiting period can be profitably spent carefully watching for the ideal stud to complement her own qualities and be compatible with her background. Keeping this in mind, attend dog shows and watch the males who are winning and, even more important, siring the winners. Subscribe to Doberman magazines and some of the all-breed magazines and study the pictures and stories accompanying them to familiarize yourself with dogs in other areas of which you may not have been aware. Be sure to keep in mind that the stud should be strong in the bitch's weak points; carefully note his progeny to see if he passes along the features you want and admire. Make special note of any offspring from bitches with backgrounds similar to your bitch's; then you can get an idea of how well the background fits with his. When you see a stud dog that interests you, discuss your bitch with the owner and request a copy of his dog's pedigree for your study and perusal. You can also discuss the stud dog with other knowledgeable breeders, including the one from whom your bitch was purchased. You may not always get an unbiased opinion (particularly if the person giving it also has an available stud dog), but discussion is a fine teacher. Listen to what they say and consider the value of their comments. As a result, you will be better qualified to reach a knowledgeable and intelligent decision on your own.

When you have made a tentative choice, contact the stud's owner to make the preliminary arrangements regarding the stud fee (whether it will be in cash or a puppy), approximate time the bitch should be ready, and so on. Find out, too, the requirements (such as a copy of your bitch's pedigree, health certificates, and tests) the stud owner has regarding bitches accepted for breeding. If you will be shipping the bitch, find out which airport and airline should be used.

The airlines will probably have special requirements, too, regarding conditions under which they will or will not take dogs. These requirements, which change from time to time, include such things as crate size and type they will accept. Most airlines have their own crates available for sale which may be purchased at a nominal cost, if you do not already have one that they consider suitable. These are made of fiberglass and are the safest type in which to ship a dog. Most airlines also require that the dog be at the airport two hours before the flight is scheduled to depart and that the dog is accompanied by a health certificate from your veterinarian, including information about rabies inoculation. If the airline does not wish to accept the bitch because of extreme temperature changes in the weather but will do so if you sign a waiver stating that she is accustomed to them and should have no problem, think it over carefully before doing so, as you are thus relieving them of any responsibility should the bitch not reach her destination alive or in good condition. And always insure the bitch when you can.

Normally the airline must be notified several days in advance for the bitch's reservation, as only a limited number of dogs can be accommodated on each flight. Plan on shipping the bitch on her eighth or ninth day, but if at all possible arrange it so that she avoids travelling on the weekend when schedules are not always the same and freight offices are likely to be closed.

It is important that, whenever possible, you ship your bitch on a flight that goes directly to the airport which is her destination. It is not at all unusual, when stopovers are made along the way, for a dog to be removed from the plane with other cargo and either incorrectly loaded for the next leg of the flight or left behind. Take every precaution that you can against human error!

It is simpler if you can plan to bring the bitch to the stud dog. Some people feel that the trauma of the plane trip may cause the bitch not to conceive; others just plain prefer not sending them that way. If you have a choice, you might do better to take the bitch in your own car where she will feel more relaxed and at ease. If you are doing it this way, be sure to allow sufficient time for the drive to get her to her destination at the correct time for the breeding. This usually is any time from the eighth to the fourteenth day, depending on the individual bitch and her cycle. Remember that if you want the bitch bred twice, you must allow a day in between the two services. Do not expect the stud's owner to put you up during your stay. Find a

590

1. A litter containing all four colors, sired by Stevemor's Bannerman of Bellmarsh out of Thumbles Jinny Wriglette. Bred by Mrs. Pat Bolton. Photo courtesy of Mrs. B. Rowland, Dorking, Surrey, England.

2. The sensational winning bitch of the late 1960's—early 1970's; Ch. Aventina's Tamiko, owned by Frank and Ellie D'Amico, winning the Working Group under the late Alva Rosenberg at Newton Kennel Club in August 1970. Jane Forsyth handling.

1▲

▼2

WORKING GROUP 1 ST.

good, nearby motel that accepts dogs, and make a reservation for yourself there.

Just prior to your bitch's season, you should make a visit to your veterinarian with her. Have her checked for worms, make sure that she is up-to-date on all her shots, and attend to any other tests the stud owner may have requested. The bitch may act and be perfectly normal up until her third or fourth week of pregnancy, but it is better for her to have a clean bill of health before the breeding than to bother her after it. If she is overweight, right now is when you should start getting the fat off her; she should be in good hard condition, neither fat nor thin, when bred.

The day you've been waiting for finally arrives, and you notice the swelling of her vulva, followed within a day or two by the appearance of a colored discharge. Immediately call the stud's owner to finalize arrangements, advising whether you will ship her or bring her, the exact day she will arrive, and so on. Then, if she is going by plane, as soon as you know the details, advise the stud owner of the flight number, the time of arrival, and any other pertinent information. If you are shipping the bitch, the check for the stud fee should be mailed now. If the owner of the stud dog charges for his trips to the airport, for picking the bitch up and then returning her, reimbursement for this should either be included with the stud fee or sent as soon as you know the amount of the charge.

If you are going to ship your bith, do not feed her on the day of the flight; the stud's owner will do so when she arrives. Be sure that she has had access to a drink of water just before you leave her and that she has been exercised prior to being put in her crate. Place several layers of newspapers, topped with some shredded papers, on the bottom of the crate for a good bed. The papers can be discarded and replaced when she reaches her destination prior to the trip home. Rugs and towels are not suitable for bedding material as they may become soiled, necessitating laundering when she reaches her destination. A small towel may be included to make her feel more at home if you wish. Remember to have her at the airport two hours ahead of flight time.

If you are driving, be sure to arrive at a reasonable time of day. If you are coming from a distance and get in late, have a good night's sleep before contacting the stud's owner first thing in the morning. If possible, leave the children and relatives at home; they will not only be in the way, but, also, most stud owners definitely object to too many people around during the actual breeding.

Once the breeding has been completed, if you wish to sit and visit for a while, that is fine; but do not leave the bitch at loose ends. Take her to her crate in the car where she can be quiet (you should first, of course, ascertain that the temperature is comfortable for her there and that she has proper ventilation). Remember that she should not urinate for at least an hour following the breeding.

If you have not already done so, pay the stud fee now, and be sure that you receive your breeding certificate and a copy of the dog's pedigree if you do not have one.

Now you are all set to await, with happy anticipation, the arrival of the puppies.

Pedigrees

To anyone interested in the breeding of dogs, pedigrees are the basic component with which this is best accomplished. It is not sufficient to just breed two nice-looking dogs to one another and then sit back and await outstanding results. Chances are they will be disappointing, as there is no equal to a scientific approach to the breeding of dogs if quality results are the ultimate goal.

We have selected for you pedigrees of Doberman dogs and bitches who either are great producers or have come from consistently outstanding producing lines. Some of these dogs are so dominant that they have seemed to "click" with almost every strain or bloodline. Others, for best results, need to be carefully linebred. The study of pedigrees and breeding is both a challenge and an exciting occupation.

Even if you have no plans to involve yourself in breeding and just anticipate owning and loving a dog or two, it is fun to trace back the pedigree of your dog, or dogs, to earlier generations and thus learn the sort of ancestors behind your own. Throughout this book you will find a great many pictures of dogs and bitches whose names appear in these pedigrees, enabling you not only to trace the names in the background of your Doberman but also to see what the forebears look like.

CH. GLENAYR DUFFERINAND

PARENTS	GRANDPARENTS	GREAT GRANDPARENTS	GREAT GREAT GRANDPARENTS
CH. Gra-Lemor Demetrius vd Victor *SIRE*	CH. Damasyn Derringer	Duke of Lombardi	CH. Dictator von Glenhugel CH. Damasyn the Sultry Sister
		Stark's Black Beauty	Blitzen of Valhalla Wanda von Trausnitz
		CH. Steb's Captain Treble	CH. Dortmund Delly's Colonel Jet Damasyn the Easter Bonnett
	Damasyn the Tcheska	Damasyn the Royal Flush	CH. Damasyn the Solitaire Eldorado Rowena
	CH. Steb's Top Skipper	CH. Dortmund Delly's Colonel Jet	CH. Delegate v.d. Elbe Tauzieher Lady Amber Crest
	Jerry Run's Boo Sprite	Damasyn the Easter Bonnett	CH. Rancho Dobe's Storm Damasyn Sikhandi
		CH. Rebel of Jerry Run	Westphalia's Damon Joan of Jerry Run
	Venture's Blue Waltz	CH. Venture of Jerry Run	CH. Axel von Gotenburg Quickly of Jerry Run
CH. Tedell Barcarolle *DAM*	CH. Gra-Lemor Demetrius vd Victor	CH. Damasyn Derringer	Duke of Lombardi CH. Damasyn the Solitaire Stark's Black Beauty
		Damasyn the Tcheska	CH. Steb's Captain Treble Damasyn the Royal Flush
		CH. Steb's Top Skipper	CH. Dortmund Delly's Colonel Jet Damasyn the Easter Bonnett
	Jerry Run's Boo Sprite	Venture's Blue Waltz	CH. Rebel of Jerry Run CH. Venture of Jerry Run
	CH. Tedell Eleventh Hour	CH. Cassio vom Ahrtal	Xandu vom Ahrtal CH. Juno vom Ahrtal
	CH. Triadel's Honey B	CH. Highbriar Valencia	CH. Felix vom Ahrtal CH. Highbriar Halla, CD
		CH. Thane vom Ahrtal	CH. Felix vom Ahrtal Iduna vom Ahrtal
	CH. Peniwil's Kelly, CD	Samantha vom Ahrtal	CH. Florian vom Ahrtal CH. Zessica vom Ahrtal

BREEDER-OWNER: Barbara & Richard Duklis, R.D. 1, Box 420C, Barto, Pa. 19504 (215) 679-7681

CH. FANFARE'S RINGMASTER

PARENTS	GRANDPARENTS	GREAT GRANDPARENTS	GREAT GREAT GRANDPARENTS
CH. Laudor Fanfare *SIRE*	CH. Steb's Renegade	CH. Steb's Top Skipper	CH. Dortmund Delly's Colonel Jet
		CH. Delegate vd Elbe Tauzler Lady Ambercrest	
		Damasyn The Easter Bonnett	CH. Rancho Dobes Storm Damasyn Sikhandi
	Ebonaire Joyeuse Noel	Ebonaire's Russett Riff	Damasyn The Captain Sabre Damasyn The Flash
		Candleglow of Ebonaire	Damasyn The Fabulous Forge Damasyn The Wild Wing
	Elblac's Zatumo	CH. Delegate vd Elbe	CH. Kama of Westphalia CH. Belydia vd Elbe
	Elblac's Doria	Elblac's Oriana	CH. Elblac's Blitz C.D. CH. Elblac's Dorcas
		CH. Courtier of Irisland	CH. Delegate vd Elbe Zita of Norfleet Road
	Laudor's Quarta	CH. Beowulf's Gaiety	CH. Beowulf vd Ravensburg CH. Elblac's Electra C.D.X.
Heidi's Kriss *DAM*	Damasyn The Troubleshooter	Damasyn The Commodore	CH. Storm's Donner
		CH. Rancho Dobes Storm Storm's Tempesta	
		Damasyn The L'il Red Sailboat	CH. Damasyn The Solataire Damasyn The Little Red Sandel
	Damasyn Dorie	Duke of Lombardi	CH. Damasyn The Solataire Stark's Black Beauty
		Damasyn The Tcheska	CH. Steb's Captain Treble Damasyn The Royal Flush
	Kriss of K-Ree	CH. Falco of Bronxville	Tri Int. CH. Duke vd Ravensburg Damasyn The Huntress
	Wilmar's Heidi	Brandendorf's Cressida	Int. CH. Beltane of Tamarack CH. Rancho Dobes Libra
		CH. Storm's Donner	CH. Rancho Dobes Storm Storm's Tempesta
	Laudor's Xclusive	Laudor's Quadrille	CH. Courtier of Irisland CH. Beowulf's Gaiety

OWNERS: Theresa Lazzaro & Patricia Laurans, Kent Road, Wassaic, New York 12592 Tel: 914-373-8380 HANDLER: J.M. Stebbins, Jr.

Ch. Stebs Top Skipper
Ch. Stebs Gunga Din
Ebonaires Flashing Star
Ch. Tarrados D'Artagnon
Ch. Alnwicks Black Fury Bismarck CD
Ch. Tarras Adelina
Ch. Highbriar Jasmine
Ch. Van Majers Elijahs Red Sun
Ch. Damasyn Derringer
Ch. Gra-Lemor Demetrius vd Victor
Jerry Runs Boo Sprite
Van Majers Hi Hope of Gra-Lemor (maj. ptd.)
Ch. Marks-Tey Shawn
Gra-Lemor Fascination Fling
Gra-Lemor Eve of Destiny

CH. RED SUN'S NOTORIOUS

Ch. Felix v Ahrtal
Ch. Tarrados Corry
Ch. Highbriar Jasmine
Ch. Tarrados Flair
Ch. Ravensburgs Falsta
Ch. Highbriar Piping Rock
Ch. Highbriar Rock Sand
Van Majers Get Up And Go (ptd.)
Ch. Stebs Top Skipper
Ch. Egothells All American
Doner The Wind Storm
Van Majers Black Pepper (Maj. ptd.)
Ch. Siggier v Ahrtal
Bagatelles Prima Donna
Bagatelles Nancy of the Hills

Ch. Dortmund Dellys Colonel Je
Damasyn the Easter Bonnet
Damasyn the Captain Saber
Damasyn the Flash
Ch. Felix v Ahrtal
Mikadobes Flambeau
Ch. Florian v Ahrtal
Ch. Highbriar Tea For Two
Duke of Lombardi
Damasyn the Tcheska
Ch. Stebs Top Skipper
Ventures Blue Waltz
Ch. Derek of Marks-Tey
Ch. Marks-Tey Melanie
Ch. Damasyn Derringer
Jerry Runs Boo Sprite
Ch. Lakecrest Thunderstorm
Ch. Willa v Ahrtal
Ch. Florian v Ahrtal
Ch. Highbriar Tea For Two
Ch. Florian v Ahrtal
Ch. Ravensburgs Bitzen
Ch. Florian v Ahrtal
Ch. Highbriar Blackbird CD
Ch. Dortmunds Delly Colonel Je
Damasyn the Easter Bonnet
Rancho Dobes Storm
Ch. Mikadobes Redwing
Ch. Florian v Ahrtal
Ch. Zessica v Ahrtal
Ch. Kriss of Rheingold
Stebs Hot Ticket

CH. ELFRED'S THE PRESIDENT
Elfred's Rock And Rye
CH. ELFRED'S NIKKI
CH. ROCKELLE'S SPARKLIN' BURGANDY
CH. DAMASYN THE TROYCEN
CH. HIGH TOR'S ARABELLA
CH. EBONAIRE'S LAUREL
CH. ROCKELLE'S BUTCH CASSIDY, WAC
Red & Rust
Am.Can. CH. TRANELL'S MAXWELL SMART
CH. TAMAREK'S RAMPAGE V FLORES
CH. TAMAREHL'S TASMINE V REHLI
CH. ROCKELLE'S COUNTRY BUMPKIN
CH. DAMASYN THE TROYCEN
CH. HIGH TOR'S ARABELLA
CH. EBONAIRE'S LAUREL
CH. PAJANT'S ENCORE V. ROCKELLE, WAC
CH. PAJANT CURTIN CALL V ROCKELLE
CH. PAJANT CENTIR STAGE V. ROCKELLE
CH. FANFARE'S RINGMASTER
Am. Can.CH. TRANELL'S MAXWELL SMART
CH. TRANELL'S MINNALITE
CH. MARWOOD ANUBIS DE SCUDAMORE, CD, ROM
CH. FANFARE'S RINGMASTER
Shel-Macht's Holly Golitely
Damasyn The Captivator
CH. KOCOT PAJANT DE SCUDAMORE, CD, ROM
Red & Rust
Am.Can.CH. DAMASYN THE TARTIAN
CH. DAMASYN THE TROYCEN
Damasyn Bo-Tassi of Ardon
Honeybucket's Mandy Love
Honeybucket's Brutus
Honeybucket's Regal Natasha
Sarabee's Regal Enchantress

Elfred's Telestar
Bremon Bittersweet
CH' JO'S BRANDY ALEXANDER
CH. ELFRED'S ENCHANTING ELAINA, CD
Am.Can.CH. DAMASYN THE TARTIAN
Damasyn Bo-Tassi of Ardon
CH. DAMASYN BO-TAIRIC OF ARDON
Ebonaire's Betsy Ross, CD
CH. FANFARE'S RINGMASTER
CH. TRANELL'S MINNALITE
Rehli's Robert Merrill
Dobe Den's Tracy Patrick
Am.Can. CH. DAMASYN THE TARTIAN
Damasyn Bo-Tassi of Ardon
CH. DAMASYN BO-TAIRIC OF ARDON
Ebonaire's Betsy Ross, CD
CH. STEB'S RENEGADE
Elblac's Doria
Damasyn The Troubleshooter
Tranell's Ember
CH. LAUDOR FANFARE
Heidi's Kriss
Damasyn The Syndharr
Damasyn The Timken, CD
CH. STEB'S TOP SKIPPER
Damasyn The Strawberry Tart, CD
CH. DAMASYN THE BOATSWAIN
CH. BROWN'S WENDY, CD
Diamond Jim of Muse
Barbary's Paprika
Centre Moby of Carly
Gillespie's Tania Maria

594

"DABNEY"

LINDA & JOHN KRUKAR
3281 GLENDON ROAD
BETHLEHEM, PENNSYLVANIA
18017
215-866-5693

Pedigree Certificate

Name: CH. AMULET'S LUKA OF SNO-GLENN, C.D.

Breed_____ Sex:_____ Breeder:_____

Color:_____ Whelped:_____

SIRE CH. ELEXA'S FINAL FLAIR OF SELENA

- SIRE CH. TARRADO'S FLAIR
  - SIRE CH. TARRADO'S CORRY
    - SIRE CH. FELIX VOM AHRTAL
      - SIRE CH. LAKECREST THUNDERSTORM
      - DAM CH. WILLA VOM AHRTAL
    - DAM CH. HIGHBRIAR JASMINE
      - SIRE CH. FLORIAN VOM AHRTAL CD
      - DAM CH. HIGHBRIAR TEA FOR TWO uD
  - DAM CH. HIGHBRIAR PIPING ROCK
    - SIRE CH. RAVENBURG'S FALSTA
      - SIRE CH. FLORIAN VOM AHRTAL CD
      - DAM CH. RAVENSBURG BITZEN
    - DAM CH. HIGHBRIAR ROCK SAND
      - SIRE CH. FLORIAN VOM AHRTAL CD
      - DAM CH. HIGHBRIAR BLACKBIRD CD

- DAM AM./CAN. CH. VIVIAN'S SELENA
  - SIRE CH. CZARR BRUTUS THE BLUE OF BRU-GART
    - SIRE HOTAI EXODUS
      - SIRE CH. HIGHBRIAR BANDANA
      - DAM HOTAI SIBYL SELENE
    - DAM LISITZA'S ELITA VOM CASSIO
      - SIRE CH. CASSIO VOM AHRTAL
      - DAM CH. TARRADO'S ELITA
  - DAM VIVIAN'S TISH OF EXODUS
    - SIRE CH. MATTAPPANY THE ARGONAUT
      - SIRE CH. HIGHBRIAR BANDANA
      - DAM CH. MARKS TEY SHAY
    - DAM CH. HOTAI REBEKAH
      - SIRE CH. HIGHBRIAR BANDANA
      - DAM HOTAI SIBYL SELENE

DAM AMULET'S AMANDA OF SNO-GLENN

- SIRE CH. AMULET'S FORTUNE HUNTER
  - SIRE CH. TARRADO'S FLAIR
    - SIRE CH. TARRADO'S CORRY
      - SIRE CH. FELIX VOM AHRTAL
      - DAM CH. HIGHBRIAR JASMINE
    - DAM CH. HIGHBRIAR PIPING ROCK
      - SIRE CH. RAVENSBURG FALSTA
      - DAM CH. HIGHBRIAR ROCK SAND
  - DAM CH. AMULET'S STAR ATTRACTION
    - SIRE CH. TARRADO'S FLAIR
      - SIRE CH. TARRADO'S CORRY
      - DAM CH. HIGHBRIAR PIPING ROCK
    - DAM CHANCE RUN'S ENCHANTED STAR, CD.
      - SIRE CH. STORMSON JET GALLANT THANE, CD.
      - DAM WILSON'S RAVEN JET

- DAM VEGA'S KOOL KELLY OF EDELHALL
  - SIRE CH. EDELHALL GRANDEE OF AMULET
    - SIRE CH. TARRADO'S FLAIR
      - SIRE CH. TARRADO'S CORRY
      - DAM CH. HIGHBRIAR PIPING ROCK
    - DAM AMULET'S CARELESS HEART
      - SIRE CH. ROCKLAND'S J.E.T.
      - DAM AMULET'S ANTIGO
  - DAM NEL-VON'S VEGA CD.
    - SIRE CH. TARRADO'S CORRY
      - SIRE CH. FELIX VOM AHRTAL
      - DAM CH. HIGHBRIAR JASMINE
    - DAM TEDELL'S FLOWER SONG
      - SIRE CH. TEDELL ELEVENTH HOUR
      - DAM CH. CHECKMATES FLOWER GIRL

THIS PEDIGREE IS CERTIFIED TO BE CORRECT TO THE BEST OF MY KNOWLEDGE AND BELIEF.

Signed_____ Date_____

CH. ALISATON TOUCHDOWN V. D'MASCUS
CH. ALISATON QB SNEAK V. D'MASCUS

- CH. ALISATON'S KINSMAN
  - Am Can CH. DAMASYN THE TARTIAN
    - CH. STEB'S TOP SKIPPER
      - CH. DORTMUND DELLY'S COLONEL JET
      - DAMASYN THE EASTER BONNETT
    - DAMASYN THE STRAWBERRY TART, CD
      - CH. DAMASYN THE SOLITAIRE, CDX
      - DAMASYN THE TCHESKA
  - CH. DAMASYN THE TROYCEN
  - DAMASYN BO-TASSI OF ARDON
    - CH. DAMASYN THE BOATSWAIN
      - CH. DAMASYN DERRINGER
      - DAMASYN THE LI'L RED LAMBCHOP
    - CH. BROWN'S WENDY, CD
      - CH. BROWN'S DION
      - CH. BROWN'S SAMANTHA OF DAMERIC
  - CH. ARABAR'S IMPERTINENCE
    - CH. DAMASYN BO-TAIRIC OF ARDON
      - CH. DAMASYN THE BOATSWAIN
        - CH. DAMASYN DERRINGER
        - DAMASYN THE LI'L RED LAMBCHOP
      - CH. BROWN'S WENDY, CD
        - CH. BROWN'S DION
        - CH. BROWN'S SAMANTHA OF DAMERIC
    - KANDY'S MARIA
      - CH. STEB'S KANDA v.d. ELBE
        - CH. STEB'S TOP SKIPPER
        - FLAME OF LOVE
      - SHATZIE OF NIEDERBAYERN
        - CH. WESTERHOLZ KAMA
        - GINGER OF THE CLOVER LEAF

- AmCan CH. SCHAUFFELEIN'S TROLL ARABESQUE
  - Can CH. SCHAUFFELEIN'S EXTRA SPECIAL
    - Can CH. SCHAUFFELEIN'S BLACKBERRY BRANDY
    - SCHAUFFELEIN'S SPECIALLY FANCY
  - Can CH. MIDNIGHT GLOW OF ARABESQUE
    - Can CH. KURTHAUS THUNDER
    - QUINESTAS TWILIGHT FANTASY
  - AmCan CH. SCHAUFFELEIN'S VINTAGE YEAR
    - Can CH. SCHAUFFELEIN'S EXTRA SPECIAL
      - Can CH. SCHAUFFELEIN'S BLACKBERRY BRANDY
      - SCHAUFFELEIN'S SPECIALLY FANCY
    - Can CH. LOWENBRAU ALOHA SCHAUFFELEIN
      - Can CH. KONIGSHANSEN HONOR
        - Can CH. SABRE v. MANNARHEIM
        - Can CH. KONIGSHANSEN DEDICATION

- CH. ALISATON KINDER ROSE
  - am Can CH. DAMASYN THE TARTIAN
    - CH. STEB'S TOP SKIPPER
    - DAMASYN THE STRAWBERRY TART, CD
  - CH. DAMASYN THE TROYCEN
  - DAMASYN BO-TASSI OF ARDON
    - CH. DAMASYN THE BOATSWAIN
    - CH. BROWN'S WENDY, CD
  - CH. ALISATON'S KINDERWICKE, WAC
    - CH. DAMASYN BO-TAIRIC OF ARDON
      - CH. DAMASYN THE BOATSWAIN
      - CH. BROWN'S WENDY, CD
    - CH. ARABAR'S IMPERTINENCE
      - CH. STEB'S KANDA v.d. ELBE
    - KANDY'S MARIA
      - SHATZIE OF NIEDERBAYERN

CH. CAROSEL B IN A HURRY CD ROM

			Xandu Vom Ahrtal
		Ch. Cassio Vom Ahrtal	
	Ch. Tevrac's Top of the Mark CD		Ch. Juno V Ahrtal
			Ch. Fortuna's Maestro
		Ch. Jessamyn II Vom Ahrtal	
Ch. Brown's B - Brian			Ch. Zessica V Ahrtal
			Ch. Brown's Eric
		Ch. Brown's Dion	
	Ch. Brown's Gi Gi of Arbel		West Begins Dagmar
			Ch. Brown's Eric
		Ch. Brown's Bridget	
			West Begins Dagmar
			Ch. Stebs Top Skipper
		Ch. Damasyn the Tartian	
	Ch. Damasyn the Troycen		Damasyn the Strawberry Tart CD
			Ch. Damasyn the Boatswain
		Damasyn Bo-Tassi of Ardon	
Ch. Damasyn The Limelight			Ch. Brown's Wenoy CD
			Ch. Storm's Donner
		Damasyn the Commodore	
	Damasyn the Legacy CD		Damasyn the Lil Red Sailboat CD
			Duke of Lombardi
		Damasyn the Classy Hassi CD	
			Silkey

CERTIFIED PEDIGREE

Name of Dog __CH TOLIVAR'S BOO RADLEY DOB MANN__ Sex __MALE__ Reg. No. __WE223649__

Breed _____DOBERMAN PINSCHER_____ Color __BLACK & RUST__

Date Whelped __AUGUST 27, 1978__ Breeder __ANNA M PLATT__

		[7] CH RU-MAR'S MORGANSONNE CD WA264849 9-63
	[3] CH AZTECA'S BEACON WA715011 12-68	
		DEBONAIRES PRINCESS ALLURE [8] WA338341 5-66
CH TOLIVAR'S ARISTOTLE OF AZTECA WB536982 ˙5-71		[9] CH AZTECA'S TIMMERMAN WA381688 2-66
Sire-1	COUNTESS SAMANTHA VON DEAR [4] WA718920 12-69	
		BLACK TAMBRA DEAR [10] WA185192 4-66
		[11] CH AXEL VON TANNENWALD WA320104 1-65
	[5] CH VON MAC'S MANOC WA987413 6-70	
		CH BRITTA VON TANNENWALD [12] WA472586 2-67
Dam-2	VON MAC'S OMEGA TU WC477402 11-75	
		[13] CH HOLLYHIGH'S ADMIRAL WA553513 7-66
	CH VON MAC'S MACHEN MITTSU [6] WB606951 10-73	
		CH BRITTA VON TANNENWALD [14] WA472586 2-67

The Seal of The American Kennel Club affixed hereto certifies that
this pedigree has been compiled from official Stud Book records.

Date Issued __06/17/82__

596

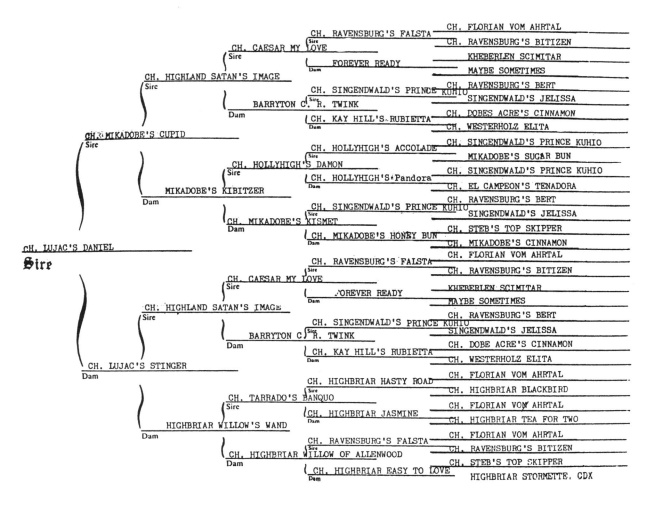

CH. LUJAC'S DANIEL — Sire

- Sire: CH. MIKADOBE'S CUPID
  - Sire: CH. HIGHLAND SATAN'S IMAGE
    - Sire: CH. CAESAR MY LOVE
      - Sire: CH. RAVENSBURG'S FALSTA
        - CH. FLORIAN VOM AHRTAL
        - CH. RAVENSBURG'S BITIZEN
      - Dam: FOREVER READY
        - KHEBERLEN SCIMITAR
        - MAYBE SOMETIMES
    - Dam: BARRYTON C. R. TWINK
      - Sire: CH. SINGENDWALD'S PRINCE KUHIO
        - CH. RAVENSBURG'S BERT
        - SINGENDWALD'S JELISSA
      - Dam: CH. KAY HILL'S RUBIETTA
        - CH. DOBES ACRE'S CINNAMON
        - CH. WESTERHOLZ ELITA
  - Dam: MIKADOBE'S KIBITZER
    - Sire: CH. HOLLYHIGH'S DAMON
      - Sire: CH. HOLLYHIGH'S ACCOLADE
        - CH. SINGENDWALD'S PRINCE KUHIO
        - MIKADOBE'S SUGAR BUN
      - Dam: CH. HOLLYHIGH'S Pandora
        - CH. SINGENDWALD'S PRINCE KUHIO
        - CH. EL CAMPEON'S TENADORA
    - Dam: CH. MIKADOBE'S KISMET
      - Sire: CH. SINGENDWALD'S PRINCE KUHIO
        - CH. RAVENSBURG'S BERT
        - SINGENDWALD'S JELISSA
      - Dam: CH. MIKADOBE'S HONEY BUN
        - CH. STEB'S TOP SKIPPER
        - CH. MIKADOBE'S CINNAMON
- Dam: CH. LUJAC'S STINGER
  - Sire: CH. HIGHLAND SATAN'S IMAGE
    - Sire: CH. CAESAR MY LOVE
      - Sire: CH. RAVENSBURG'S FALSTA
        - CH. FLORIAN VOM AHRTAL
        - CH. RAVENSBURG'S BITIZEN
      - Dam: FOREVER READY
        - KHEBERLEN SCIMITAR
        - MAYBE SOMETIMES
    - Dam: BARRYTON C. R. TWINK
      - Sire: CH. SINGENDWALD'S PRINCE KUHIO
        - CH. RAVENSBURG'S BERT
        - SINGENDWALD'S JELISSA
      - Dam: CH. KAY HILL'S RUBIETTA
        - CH. DOBE ACRE'S CINNAMON
        - CH. WESTERHOLZ ELITA
  - Dam: HIGHBRIAR WILLOW'S WAND
    - Sire: CH. TARRADO'S BANQUO
      - Sire: CH. HIGHBRIAR HASTY ROAD
        - CH. FLORIAN VOM AHRTAL
        - CH. HIGHBRIAR BLACKBIRD
      - Dam: CH. HIGHBRIAR JASMINE
        - CH. FLORIAN VOM AHRTAL
        - CH. HIGHBRIAR TEA FOR TWO
    - Dam: CH. HIGHBRIAR WILLOW OF ALLENWOOD
      - Sire: CH. RAVENSBURG'S FALSTA
        - CH. FLORIAN VOM AHRTAL
        - CH. RAVENSBURG'S BITIZEN
      - Dam: CH. HIGHBRIAR EASY TO LOVE
        - CH. STEB'S TOP SKIPPER
        - HIGHBRIAR STORMETTE, CDX

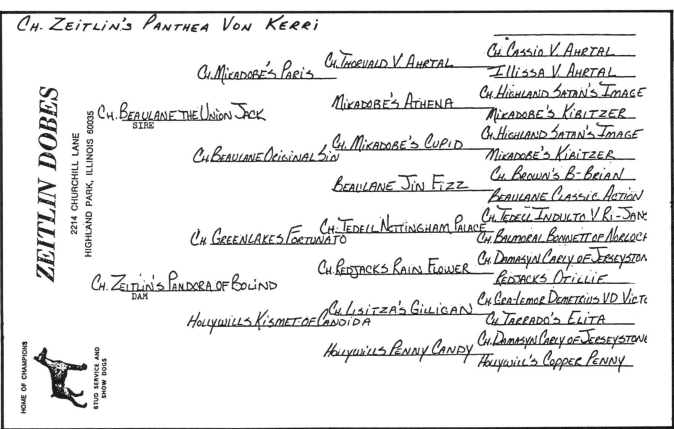

CH. ZEITLIN'S PANTHEA VON KERRI

ZEITLIN DOBES
2214 CHURCHILL LANE
HIGHLAND PARK, ILLINOIS 60035

HOME OF CHAMPIONS

STUD SERVICE AND SHOW DOGS

- SIRE: CH. BEAULANE THE UNION JACK
  - CH. MIKADOBE'S PARIS
    - CH. THORVALD V. AHRTAL
      - CH. CASSIO V. AHRTAL
      - ILLISSA V. AHRTAL
    - MIKADOBE'S ATHENA
      - CH. HIGHLAND SATAN'S IMAGE
      - MIKADOBE'S KIBITZER
  - CH. BEAULANE ORIGINAL SIN
    - CH. MIKADOBE'S CUPID
      - CH. HIGHLAND SATAN'S IMAGE
      - MIKADOBE'S KIBITZER
    - BEAULANE JIN FIZZ
      - CH. BROWN'S B-BRIAN
      - BEAULANE CLASSIC ACTION
- DAM: CH. ZEITLIN'S PANDORA OF BOLIND
  - CH. GREENLAKES FORTUNATO
    - CH. TEDELL NOTTINGHAM PALACE
      - CH. TEDELL INDULTO V RI-JAN
      - CH. BALMORAL BONNETT OF NORLOCH
    - CH. REDJACKS RAIN FLOWER
      - CH. DAMASYN CARLY OF JERSEYSTON
      - REDJACKS OTILLIE
  - HOLLYWILLS KISMET OF CANDIDA
    - CH. LISITZA'S GILLIGAN
      - CH. GRA-LEMOR DEMETRIUS VD VICTO
      - CH. TARRADO'S ELITA
    - HOLLYWILLS PENNY CANDY
      - CH. DAMASYN CARLY OF JERSEYSTONE
      - HOLLYWILL'S COPPER PENNY

Certificate of Pedigree

Registered Name	Ch. Zigeuner's Fiesta
Sex	Female
Breed	
A.K.C.S.B. No.	
A.K.C. Litter No.	
Date of Birth	10/21/60
Birthplace	
Breeder	Mr. & Mrs. C.E. Mozley
Address	
City	

GENERAL DESCRIPTION

Color and Markings: Blk./Rust.

Marienburg Kennels, Reg.

Sire: (1) Ch. Rancho Dobe's Bach
Owner: Marienburg Kennels

- Ch. Rancho Dobe's Riff (3)
  - Ch. Roxanna's Emperor Von Reemon (7)
    - Ch. Emperor of Marienland (15)
    - Ch. Westphalia's Roxanna (16)
  - Rhumba of Rancho Dobe (8)
    - Ch. Ames v. Sidlo (17)
    - Juno of Moorpark (18)
- Ch. Rancho Dobe's Roulette (4)
  - Ch. Rancho Dobe's Presto (9)
    - Ch. Alcor v. Millsdod (19)
    - Ch. Rancho Dobe's Kashmir (20)
  - Ch. Maedel v. Randahof (10)
    - Mr. Butch V. Rittenhouse (21)
    - Ch. Indra v. Lindenhof

Dam: (2) Ch. Zigeuner's Conga

- Ch. Rancho Dobe's Primo (5)
  - Ch. Alcor v. Millsdod (11)
    - Ch. Westphalia's Uranus (23)
    - Ch. Maida v. Coldod (24)
  - Ch. Rancho Dobe's Kashmir (12)
    - Ch. Roxanna's Emperor v. Reemon (25)
    - Rhumba of Rancho Dobe (26)
- Vernhof's Valkyrie II (6)
  - Ch. Kilburn Conquery (13)
    - Ch. Alcor v. Millsdod (27)
    - Ch. Kilburn Audacity (28)
  - Erica of Vernhof (14)
    - Ch. Eric IV v. Palanka (29)
    - Elica v. Troll (30)

Sire (31)–Dam (62): (blank)

I Hereby Certify that to the best of my knowledge and belief the above Pedigree is true and that all ancestors named above are of the same breed.

Signed this _____ day of _____, 19__

Address _____

Pedigree of "Bellmarsh Grace" (C. Jade)

BREED	Dobermann
SEX	Bitch
COLOUR & MARKINGS	Bk. & Tan
DATE OF BIRTH	6 August 1983
BREEDER	Mrs. B.A. Rowland
REGISTRATION No.	G. H4507801 H11
DATE OF REGISTRATION	
OWNER	Mrs. Lesley Wright
ADDRESS	"Club Caprice", Cliff Terrace, Cliftonville, Margate, Kent.

PARENTS	GRAND-PARENTS	GREAT GRAND-PARENTS	G.G. GRAND-PARENTS	G.G.G. GRAND-PARENTS
SIRE Stevemors Bannerman of Bellmarsh (Kennel Club No. E08 E3258803 E08) Owner: Mrs B.A. Rowland, "Woodmancote" Springwell Rd, Boare Green, Nr. Dorking, Surrey	SIRE Champion Olderhill Sheboygan	SIRE Phileens Duty Free of Tavey	SIRE Am. Champion Tarrados Corry	SIRE Ina Felix v. Ahrtal / DAM Ina Whirlwind Jasmina
			DAM Kay Hills Outrigger	SIRE Arc Dolph v. Tannewald / DAM Kay Hills Kat-a-mara
		DAM Olderhill Dhobi	SIRE Champion Iceburg of Tavey	SIRE Ch Barramation of Tavey / DAM Juno of Colorgate
			DAM Charmer of Triogen	SIRE Triogen Texas Cowboy / DAM Yogni of Kilmicheal
	DAM Treasurequest Pearl	SIRE Champion Davelogs Crusader	SIRE Champion Tumlow Satan	SIRE Ch Tumlow Impeccable / DAM Tumlow Odette
			DAM Edwina Vivacious	SIRE Naytilla Gay Crusader / DAM Tumlow Vivacious
		DAM Findjans Armetis	SIRE Phileens D.F. of Tavey	SIRE Am Ch Tarrados Corry / DAM Kay Hills Outrigger
			DAM Ch. Mitrasandra Gay Lady of Findjans	SIRE Ch Tumlow Satan / DAM Findjans Gay Allure
DAM Simrons Black Diamond (Kennel Club No. E07 E2424608 E07) Owner: Mrs B.A. Rowland	SIRE Champion Studbriar the Red	SIRE Phileens Duty Free of Tavey	SIRE Am. Champion Tarrados Corry	SIRE Ina Felix v. Ahrtal / DAM Ina Whirlwind Jasmina
			DAM Kay Hills Outrigger	SIRE Arc Dolph v. Tannewald / DAM Kay Hills Kat-a-mara (U.S.A. import)
		DAM Taveys Renaissance	SIRE Bayard of Tavey	SIRE Dictator v. Glenhugel (U.S.A. import) / DAM Taveys Wachwinde Quid (German import)
			DAM Yogi of Tavey	SIRE Ch Iceburg of Tavey / DAM Niobe of Tavey
	DAM Ikos Technika at Simron	SIRE Champions Arkturus Valans Choice	SIRE Winhoff the Pagan	SIRE Wilm v. Forell / DAM Winhoff Triogen Tosca
			DAM Findjans Princess Pleasurama	SIRE Ch Tuvalu Trouble Spot / DAM Boogie Sunset Shell
		DAM Ikos Gloriosa	SIRE Knight of Romancastle of Ikos	SIRE Helmy High Jump / DAM Coppertan of Heolylan
			DAM Couch Harness Brown Bess of Ikos	SIRE Winhoff Moonshiner / DAM Couch Harness Simba

598

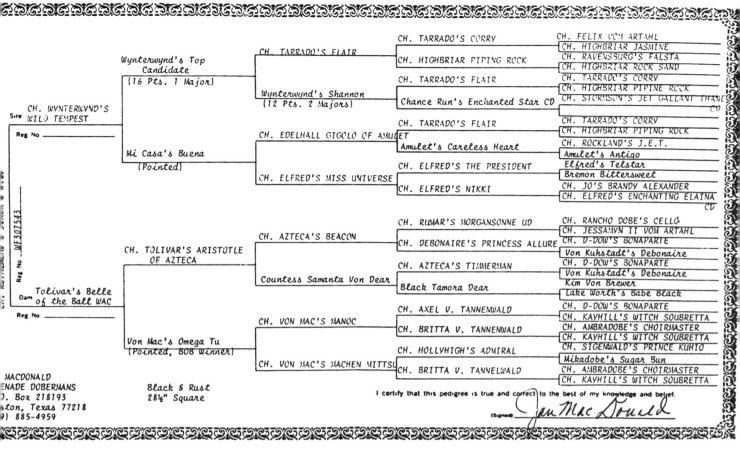

CH. WYNTERWYND'S WILD TEMPEST
Sire
Reg No _____
Reg No. WE307543
Dam
Reg No _____

Tolivar's Belle of the Ball WAC

MACDONALD
...NADE DOBERMANS
...). Box 218193
...ston, Texas 77218
...9) 885-4959

Black & Rust
28½" Square

- CH. WYNTERWYND'S WILD TEMPEST
  - Wynterwynd's Top Candidate (16 Pts. 1 Major)
    - CH. TARRADO'S FLAIR
      - CH. TARRADO'S CORRY
        - CH. FELIX VOM ARTAHL
        - CH. HIGHBRIAR JASMINE
      - CH. HIGHBRIAR PIPING ROCK
        - CH. RAVENSBURG'S FALSTA
        - CH. HIGHBRIAR ROCK SAND
    - Wynterwynd's Shannon (12 Pts. 2 Majors)
      - CH. TARRADO'S FLAIR
        - CH. TARRADO'S CORRY
        - CH. HIGHBRIAR PIPING ROCK
      - Chance Run's Enchanted Star CD
        - CH. STORMSON'S JET GALLANT THANE CD
  - Mi Casa's Buena (Pointed)
    - CH. EDELHALL GIGOLO OF AMULET
      - CH. TARRADO'S FLAIR
        - CH. TARRADO'S CORRY
        - CH. HIGHBRIAR PIPING ROCK
      - Amulet's Careless Heart
        - CH. ROCKLAND'S J.E.T.
        - Amulet's Antigo
    - CH. ELFRED'S MISS UNIVERSE
      - CH. ELFRED'S THE PRESIDENT
        - Elfred's Telstar
        - Bremon Bittersweet
      - CH. ELFRED'S NIKKI
        - CH. JO'S BRANDY ALEXANDER
        - CH. ELFRED'S ENCHANTING ELAINA CD

- Tolivar's Belle of the Ball WAC
  - CH. TOLIVAR'S ARISTOTLE OF AZTECA
    - CH. AZTECA'S BEACON
      - CH. RUMAR'S MORGANSONNE UD
        - CH. RANCHO DOBE'S CELLO
        - CH. JESSAMYN II VOM ARTAHL
      - CH. DEBONAIRE'S PRINCESS ALLURE
        - CH. D-DOW'S BONAPARTE
        - Von Kuhstadt's Debonaire
    - Countess Samanta Von Dear
      - CH. AZTECA'S TIMMERMAN
        - CH. D-DOW'S BONAPARTE
        - Von Kuhstadt's Debonaire
      - Black Tamora Dear
        - Kim Von Brewer
        - Lake Worth's Babe Black
  - Von Mac's Omega Tu (Pointed, BOB Winner)
    - CH. VON MAC'S MANOC
      - CH. AXEL V. TANNENWALD
        - CH. D-DOW'S BONAPARTE
        - CH. KAYHILL'S WITCH SOUBRETTA
      - CH. BRITTA V. TANNENWALD
        - CH. AMBRADOBE'S CHOIRMASTER
        - CH. KAYHILL'S WITCH SOUBRETTA
    - CH. VON MAC'S MACHEN MITTSU
      - CH. HOLLYHIGH'S ADMIRAL
        - CH. SIGENWALD'S PRINCE KUHIO
        - Mikadobe's Sugar Bun
      - CH. BRITTA V. TANNELWALD
        - CH. AMBRADOBE'S CHOIRMASTER
        - CH. KAYHILL'S WITCH SOUBRETTA

I certify that this pedigree is true and correct to the best of my knowledge and belief.

(Signed) Jan Mac Donald

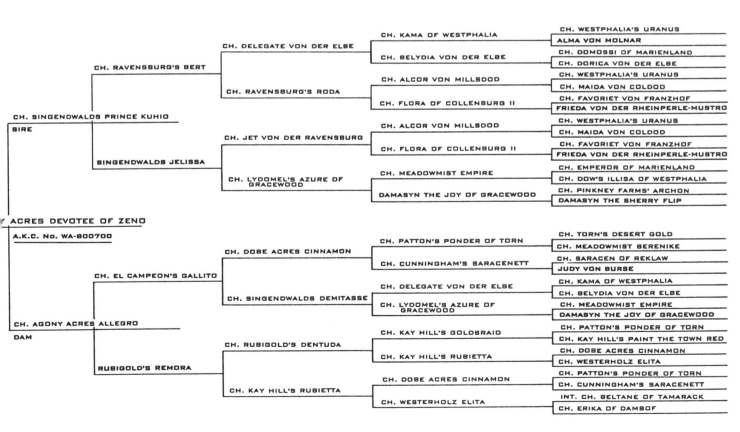

- ... ACRES DEVOTEE OF ZENO
  A.K.C. No. WA-800700

- CH. SINGENDWALDS PRINCE KUHIO
  SIRE
  - CH. RAVENSBURG'S BERT
    - CH. DELEGATE VON DER ELBE
      - CH. KAMA OF WESTPHALIA
        - CH. WESTPHALIA'S URANUS
        - ALMA VON MOLNAR
      - CH. BELYDIA VON DER ELBE
        - CH. DOMOSSI OF MARIENLAND
        - CH. DORICA VON DER ELBE
    - CH. RAVENSBURG'S RODA
      - CH. ALCOR VON MILLSDOD
        - CH. WESTPHALIA'S URANUS
        - CH. MAIDA VON COLDOD
      - CH. FLORA OF COLLENBURG II
        - CH. FAVORIET VON FRANZHOF
        - FRIEDA VON DER RHEINPERLE-MUSTRO
  - SINGENDWALDS JELISSA
    - CH. JET VON DER RAVENSBURG
      - CH. ALCOR VON MILLSDOD
        - CH. WESTPHALIA'S URANUS
        - CH. MAIDA VON COLDOD
      - CH. FLORA OF COLLENBURG II
        - CH. FAVORIET VON FRANZHOF
        - FRIEDA VON DER RHEINPERLE-MUSTRO
    - CH. LYDOMEL'S AZURE OF GRACEWOOD
      - CH. MEADOWMIST EMPIRE
        - CH. EMPEROR OF MARIENLAND
        - CH. DOW'S ILLISA OF WESTPHALIA
      - DAMASYN THE JOY OF GRACEWOOD
        - CH. PINKNEY FARMS' ARCHON
        - DAMASYN THE SHERRY FLIP

- CH. AGONY ACRES ALLEGRO
  DAM
  - CH. EL CAMPEON'S GALLITO
    - CH. DOBE ACRES CINNAMON
      - CH. PATTON'S PONDER OF TORN
        - CH. TORN'S DESERT GOLD
        - CH. MEADOWMIST BERENIKE
      - CH. CUNNINGHAM'S SARACENETT
        - CH. SARACEN OF REKLAW
        - JUDY VON BURSE
    - CH. SINGENDWALDS DEMITASSE
      - CH. DELEGATE VON DER ELBE
        - CH. KAMA OF WESTPHALIA
        - CH. BELYDIA VON DER ELBE
      - CH. LYDOMEL'S AZURE OF GRACEWOOD
        - CH. MEADOWMIST EMPIRE
        - DAMASYN THE JOY OF GRACEWOOD
  - RUBIGOLD'S REMORA
    - CH. RUBIGOLD'S DENTUDA
      - CH. KAY HILL'S GOLDBRAID
        - CH. PATTON'S PONDER OF TORN
        - CH. KAY HILL'S PAINT THE TOWN RED
      - CH. KAY HILL'S RUBIETTA
        - CH. DOBE ACRES CINNAMON
        - CH. WESTERHOLZ ELITA
    - CH. KAY HILL'S RUBIETTA
      - CH. DOBE ACRES CINNAMON
        - CH. PATTON'S PONDER OF TORN
        - CH. CUNNINGHAM'S SARACENETT
      - CH. WESTERHOLZ ELITA
        - INT. CH. BELTANE OF TAMARACK
        - CH. ERIKA OF DAMBOF

599

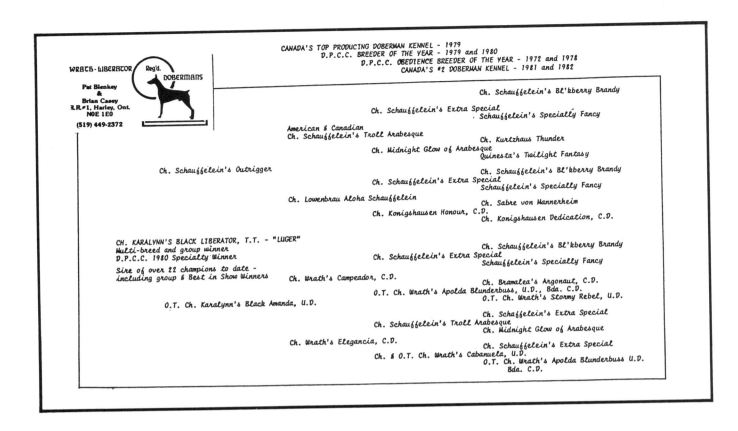

WRATH-LIBERATOR Reg'd. DOBERMANS

Pat Blenkey & Brian Casey
R.R.#1, Harley, Ont.
N0E 1E0
(519) 449-2372

CANADA'S TOP PRODUCING DOBERMAN KENNEL - 1979
D.P.C.C. BREEDER OF THE YEAR - 1979 and 1980
D.P.C.C. OBEDIENCE BREEDER OF THE YEAR - 1972 and 1978
CANADA'S #2 DOBERMAN KENNEL - 1981 and 1982

American & Canadian
Ch. Schauffelein's Troll Arabesque

Ch. Schauffelein's Extra Special
Ch. Schauffelein's Bl'kberry Brandy
Schauffelein's Specially Fancy

Ch. Midnight Glow of Arabesque
Ch. Kurtzhaus Thunder
Quinesta's Twilight Fantasy

Ch. Schauffelein's Outrigger

Ch. Lowenbrau Aloha Schauffelein

Ch. Schauffelein's Extra Special
Ch. Schauffelein's Bl'kberry Brandy
Schauffelein's Specially Fancy

Ch. Konigshausen Honour, C.D.
Ch. Sabre von Mannerheim
Ch. Konigshausen Dedication, C.D.

CH. KARALYNN'S BLACK LIBERATOR, T.T. - "LUGER"
Multi-breed and group winner
D.P.C.C. 1980 Specialty Winner
Sire of over 22 champions to date -
including group & Best in Show Winners

Ch. Wrath's Campeador, C.D.

Ch. Schauffelein's Extra Special
Ch. Schauffelein's Bl'kberry Brandy
Schauffelein's Specially Fancy

O.T. Ch. Wrath's Apolda Blunderbuss, U.D., Bda. C.D.
Ch. Bramalea's Argonaut, C.D.
O.T. Ch. Wrath's Stormy Rebel, U.D.

O.T. Ch. Karalynn's Black Amanda, U.D.

Ch. Wrath's Elegancia, C.D.

Ch. Schauffelein's Troll Arabesque
Ch. Schauffelein's Extra Special
Ch. Midnight Glow of Arabesque

Ch. & O.T. Ch. Wrath's Cabanuela, U.D.
Ch. Schauffelein's Extra Special
O.T. Ch. Wrath's Apolda Blunderbuss U.D. Bda. C.D.

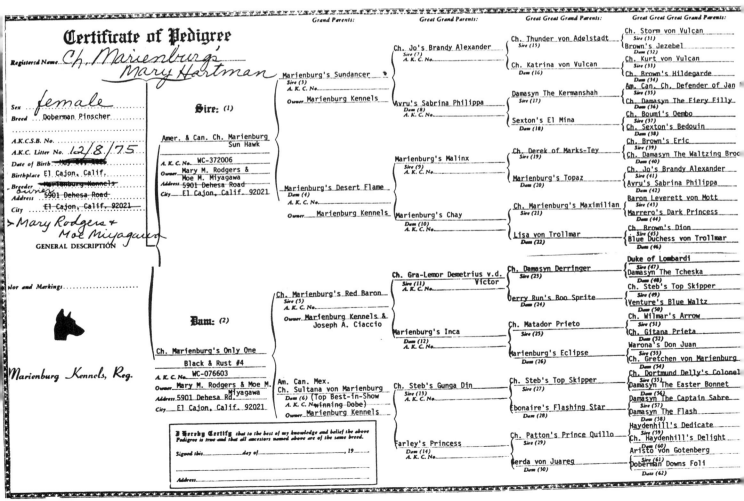

Certificate of Pedigree

Registered Name: Ch. Marienburg's Mary Hartman

Sex: female
Breed: Doberman Pinscher
A.K.C.S.B. No. _____
A.K.C. Litter No. 12/8/75
Date of Birth: _____
Birthplace: El Cajon, Calif.
Breeder: Marienburg Kennels
Address: 5901 Dehesa Road
City: El Cajon, Calif. 92021

Mary Rodgers & Moe Miyagawa
GENERAL DESCRIPTION

Color and Markings: _____

Marienburg Kennels, Reg.

Sire: (1)
Amer. & Can. Ch. Marienburg Sun Hawk
A.K.C. No. WC-372006
Owner: Mary M. Rodgers & Moe M. Miyagawa
Address: 5901 Dehesa Road
City: El Cajon, Calif. 92021

Dam: (2)
Ch. Marienburg's Only One
Black & Rust #4
A.K.C. No. WC-076603
Owner: Mary M. Rodgers & Moe M. Miyagawa
Address: 5901 Dehesa Rd.
City: El Cajon, Calif. 92021

I Hereby Certify that to the best of my knowledge and belief the above Pedigree is true and that all ancestors named above are of the same breed.

Signed this _____ Day of _____, 19___

Address: _____

	Grand Parents:	Great Grand Parents:	Great Great Grand Parents:	Great Great Great Grand Parents:
	Marienburg's Sundancer Sire (3) A.K.C. No. Owner Marienburg Kennels	Ch. Jo's Brandy Alexander Sire (7) A.K.C. No.	Ch. Thunder von Adelstadt Sire (15)	Ch. Storm von Vulcan Sire (31) Brown's Jezebel Dam (32)
			Ch. Katrina von Vulcan Dam (16)	Ch. Kurt von Vulcan Sire (33) Ch. Brown's Hildegarde Dam (34)
		Avru's Sabrina Philippa Dam (8) A.K.C. No.	Damasyn The Kermanshah Sire (17)	Am. Can. Ch. Defender of Jan Sire (35) Ch. Damasyn The Fiery Filly Dam (36)
			Sexton's El Mina Dam (18)	Ch. Boumi's Qembo Sire (37) Ch. Sexton's Bedouin Dam (38)
	Marienburg's Desert Flame Dam (4) A.K.C. No. Owner Marienburg Kennels	Marienburg's Malinx Sire (9) A.K.C. No.	Ch. Derek of Marks-Tey Sire (19)	Ch. Brown's Eric Sire (39) Ch. Damasyn The Waltzing Broo Dam (40)
			Marienburg's Topaz Dam (20)	Ch. Jo's Brandy Alexander Sire (41) Avru's Sabrina Philippa Dam (42)
		Marienburg's Chay Dam (10) A.K.C. No.	Ch. Marienburg's Maximilian Sire (21)	Baron Leverett von Mott Sire (43) Marrero's Dark Princess Dam (44)
			Lisa von Trollmar Dam (22)	Ch. Brown's Dion Sire (45) Blue Duchess von Trollmar Dam (46)
	Ch. Marienburg's Red Baron Sire (5) A.K.C. No. Owner Marienburg Kennels & Joseph A. Ciaccio	Ch. Gra-Lemor Demetrius v.d. Victor Sire (11) A.K.C. No.	Ch. Damasyn Derringer Sire (23)	Duke of Lombardi Sire (47) Damasyn The Tcheska Dam (48)
			Jerry Run's Boo Sprite Dam (24)	Ch. Steb's Top Skipper Sire (49) Venture's Blue Waltz Dam (50)
		Marienburg's Inca Dam (12) A.K.C. No.	Ch. Matador Prieto Sire (25)	Ch. Wilmar's Arrow Sire (51) Ch. Gitana Prieta Dam (52)
			Marienburg's Eclipse Dam (26)	Warona's Don Juan Sire (53) Ch. Gretchen von Marienburg Dam (54)
	Am. Can. Mex. Ch. Sultana von Marienburg Dam (6) (Top Best-in-Show winning Dobe) A.K.C. No. Owner Marienburg Kennels	Ch. Steb's Gunga Din Sire (13) A.K.C. No.	Ch. Steb's Top Skipper Sire (27)	Ch. Dortmund Delly's Colonel Sire (55) Damasyn The Easter Bonnet Dam (56)
			Ebonaire's Flashing Star Dam (28)	Damasyn The Captain Sabre Sire (57) Damasyn The Flash Dam (58)
		Farley's Princess Dam (14) A.K.C. No.	Ch. Patton's Prince Quillo Sire (29)	Haydenhill's Dedicate Sire (59) Ch. Haydenhill's Delight Dam (60)
			Gerda von Juareg Dam (30)	Aristo von Gotenberg Sire (61) Doberman Downs Foli Dam (62)

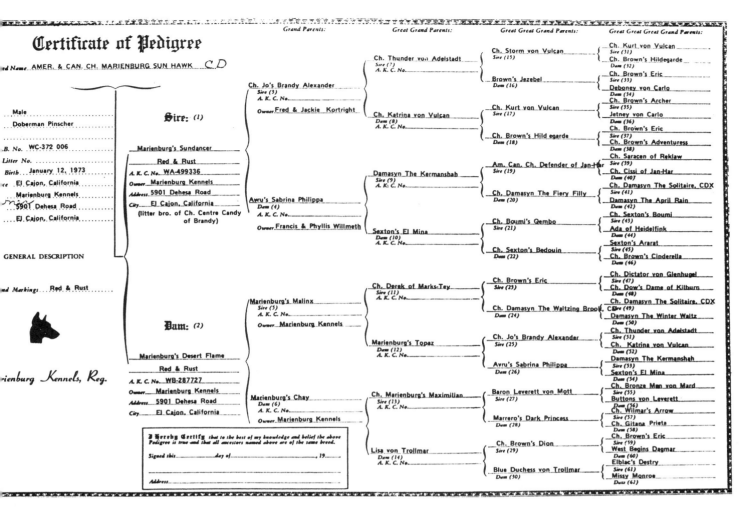

Certificate of Pedigree

Breed Name: AMER. & CAN. CH. MARIENBURG SUN HAWK C.D.

Male
Doberman Pinscher
Reg. No. WC-372 006
Litter No.
Birth: January 12, 1973
Place: El Cajon, California
Breeder: Marienburg Kennels
Address: 5901 Dehesa Road
City: El Cajon, California

GENERAL DESCRIPTION

Color and Markings: Red & Rust

Marienburg Kennels, Reg.

Sire: (1)
Marienburg's Sundancer
Red & Rust
A. K. C. No. WA-499336
Owner: Marienburg Kennels
Address: 5901 Dehesa Road
City: El Cajon, California
(litter bro. of Ch. Centre Candy of Brandy)

Dam: (2)
Marienburg's Desert Flame
Red & Rust
A. K. C. No. WB-287727
Owner: Marienburg Kennels
Address: 5901 Dehesa Road
City: El Cajon, California

I Hereby Certify that to the best of my knowledge and belief the above Pedigree is true and that all ancestors named above are of the same breed.

Signed this _____ day of _____ 19__

Address: _____

Grand Parents	Great Grand Parents	Great Great Grand Parents	Great Great Great Grand Parents
Ch. Jo's Brandy Alexander — Sire (3) — A.K.C. No. — Owner Fred & Jackie Kortright	Ch. Thunder von Adelstadt — Sire (7) — A.K.C. No.	Ch. Storm von Vulcan — Sire (15)	Ch. Kurt von Vulcan — Sire (31)
			Ch. Brown's Hildegarde — Dam (32)
		Brown's Jezebel — Dam (16)	Ch. Brown's Eric — Sire (33)
			Deboney von Carlo — Dam (34)
	Ch. Katrina von Vulcan — Dam (8) — A.K.C. No.	Ch. Kurt von Vulcan — Sire (17)	Ch. Brown's Archer — Sire (35)
			Jetney von Carlo — Dam (36)
		Ch. Brown's Hildegarde — Dam (18)	Ch. Brown's Eric — Sire (37)
			Ch. Brown's Adventuress — Dam (38)
Avru's Sabrina Philippa — Dam (4) — A.K.C. No. — Owner Francis & Phyllis Willmeth	Damasyn The Kermanshah — Sire (9) — A.K.C. No.	Am. Can. Ch. Defender of Jan-Har — Sire (19)	Ch. Saracen of Reklaw — Sire (39)
			Ch. Cissi of Jan-Har — Dam (40)
		Ch. Damasyn The Fiery Filly — Dam (20)	Ch. Damasyn The Solitaire, CDX — Sire (41)
			Damasyn The April Rain — Dam (42)
	Sexton's El Mina — Dam (10) — A.K.C. No.	Ch. Boumi's Qembo — Sire (21)	Ch. Sexton's Boumi — Sire (43)
			Ada of Heidelfink — Dam (44)
		Ch. Sexton's Bedouin — Dam (22)	Sexton's Ararat — Sire (45)
			Ch. Brown's Cinderella — Dam (46)
Marienburg's Malinx — Sire (5) — A.K.C. No. — Owner Marienburg Kennels	Ch. Derek of Marks-Tey — Sire (11) — A.K.C. No.	Ch. Brown's Eric — Sire (23)	Ch. Dictator von Glenhugel — Sire (47)
			Ch. Dow's Dame of Kilburn — Dam (48)
		Ch. Damasyn The Waltzing Brook, CDX — Dam (24)	Ch. Damasyn The Solitaire, CDX — Sire (49)
			Damasyn The Winter Waltz — Dam (50)
	Marienburg's Topaz — Dam (12) — A.K.C. No.	Ch. Jo's Brandy Alexander — Sire (25)	Ch. Thunder von Adelstadt — Sire (51)
			Ch. Katrina von Vulcan — Dam (52)
		Avru's Sabrina Philippa — Dam (26)	Damasyn The Kermanshah — Sire (53)
			Sexton's El Mina — Dam (54)
Marienburg's Chay — Dam (6) — A.K.C. No. — Owner Marienburg Kennels	Ch. Marienburg's Maximilian — Sire (13) — A.K.C. No.	Baron Leverett von Mott — Sire (27)	Ch. Bronze Man von Mard — Sire (55)
			Buttons von Leverett — Dam (56)
		Marrero's Dark Princess — Dam (28)	Ch. Wilmar's Arrow — Sire (57)
			Ch. Gitana Prieta — Dam (58)
	Lisa von Trollmar — Dam (14) — A.K.C. No.	Ch. Brown's Dion — Sire (29)	Ch. Brown's Eric — Sire (59)
			West Begins Dagmar — Dam (60)
		Blue Duchess von Trollmar — Dam (30)	Elblac's Destry — Sire (61)
			Missy Monroe — Dam (62)

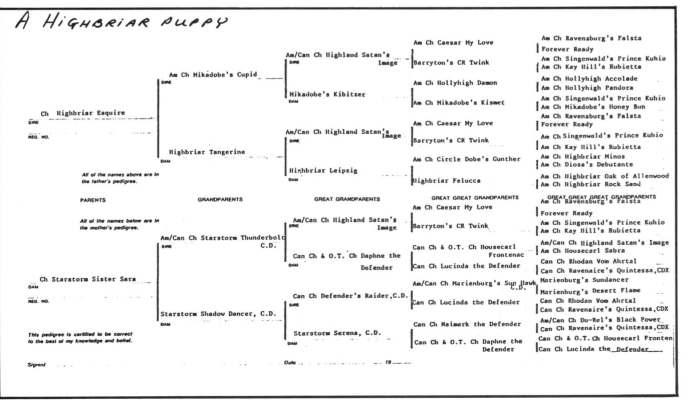

A HIGHBRIAR PUPPY

PARENTS	GRANDPARENTS	GREAT GRANDPARENTS	GREAT GREAT GRANDPARENTS	GREAT GREAT GREAT GRANDPARENTS
Ch Highbriar Esquire (SIRE) REG. NO.	Am Ch Mikadobe's Cupid (SIRE)	Am/Can Ch Highland Satan's Image (SIRE)	Am Ch Caesar My Love	Am Ch Ravensburg's Falsta / Forever Ready
			Barryton's CR Twink	Am Ch Singenwald's Prince Kuhio / Am Ch Kay Hill's Rubietta
		Mikadobe's Kibitzer (DAM)	Am Ch Hollyhigh Damon	Am Ch Hollyhigh Accolade / Am Ch Hollyhigh Pandora
			Am Ch Mikadobe's Kismet	Am Ch Singenwald's Prince Kuhio / Am Ch Mikadobe's Honey Bun
	Highbriar Tangerine (DAM)	Am/Can Ch Highland Satan's Image (SIRE)	Am Ch Caesar My Love	Am Ch Ravensburg's Falsta / Forever Ready
			Barryton's CR Twink	Am Ch Singenwald's Prince Kuhio / Am Ch Kay Hill's Rubietta
		Highbriar Leipzig (DAM)	Am Ch Circle Dobe's Gunther	Am Ch Highbriar Minos / Am Ch Diosa's Debutante
			Highbriar Felucca	Am Ch Highbriar Oak of Allenwood / Am Ch Highbriar Rock Sand
Ch Starstorm Sister Sara (DAM) REG. NO.	Am/Can Ch Starstorm Thunderbolt C.D. (SIRE)	Am/Can Ch Highland Satan's Image (SIRE)	Am Ch Caesar My Love	Am Ch Ravensburg's Falsta / Forever Ready
			Barryton's CR Twink	Am Ch Singenwald's Prince Kuhio / Am Ch Kay Hill's Rubietta
		Can Ch & O.T. Ch Daphne the Defender (DAM)	Can Ch & O.T. Ch Housecarl Frontenac	Am/Can Ch Highland Satan's Image / Am Ch Housecarl Sabra
			Can Ch Lucinda the Defender	Can Ch Rhodan Vom Ahrtal / Can Ch Ravenaire's Quintessa, CDX
	Starstorm Shadow Dancer, C.D. (DAM)	Can Ch Defender's Raider, C.D. (SIRE)	Am/Can Ch Marienburg's Sun Hawk C.D.	Marienburg's Sundancer / Marienburg's Desert Flame
			Can Ch Lucinda the Defender	Can Ch Rhodan Vom Ahrtal / Can Ch Ravenaire's Quintessa, CDX
		Starstorm Serena, C.D. (DAM)	Can Ch Naimark the Defender	Am/Can Ch Du-Rel's Black Power / Can Ch Ravenaire's Quintessa, CDX
			Can Ch & O.T. Ch Daphne the Defender	Can Ch & O.T. Ch Housecarl Fronten / Can Ch Lucinda the Defender

All of the names above are in the father's pedigree.

All of the names below are in the mother's pedigree.

This pedigree is certified to be correct to the best of my knowledge and belief.

Signed _____ Date _____ 19__

Ch. Ru-Mar's Morgansonne, C.D.

		Ch. Rancho Dobe's Riff	Int.Ch. Roxanna's Emperor v. Reemon
	Ch. Rancho Dobe's Bach	W-17378	Rumba of Rancho Dobe
	W-524658	Ch. Rancho Dobe's Roulette	Int.Ch.Rancho Dobe's Presto
Ch. Rancho Dobe's Cello		W-97492	Ch. Maedel v Randahof
WA-966208		Ch. Rancho Dobe's Primo	Ch. Alcor von Millsdod
	Hannah of Adobe Hill	W-57334	Ch. Rancho Dobe's Kashmir
	W-772867	Christina of Adobe Hill	Ch. Zigeuner's Calypso C.D.
		W-67674	Maha Jet of Flickerville
		Ch. Berger's Blue Beard	Int.Ch. Roxanna's Emperor v. Reemon
	Cn. Fortuna's Maestro	W-167687	Ch. Brown's Adventuress
	W-451828	Ch. Anona von Tamara	Ch. Oberon of Jerry Run
Ch. Jessamyn II vom Ahrtal		W-276673	Ch. Kitchawan's Tamara
W-977868		*Alaric v. Ahrtal C.D.X., T.D.	Ch. Delegate v.d. Elbe
	Ch. Zessica vom Ahrtal	W-208214	Kriemhild vom Ahrtal C.D.
	W-760299	Ch. Friederun vom Ahrtal	Ch. Delegate v.d. Elbe
		W-303611	Meadowmist Isis of Ahrtal

All dogs in this pedigree are black & rust except where indicated by an * which are red & rust!

Owners
Address

MRS. RUTH M. EDWARDS
P. O. Box 622
Monterey, CA 93942-0622
(408) 649-4280

Phone

	Grand Parents:	Great Grand Parents:	Great Great Grand Parents:
			Ch. Iago v. Ahrtal
		Ch. Schauffelein's Blackberry Brandy	Ch. Schauffelein's Silhouette
	Ch. Schauffelein's Extra Special		Ch. Bramaleas Argonaut
		Schauffelein's Specially Fancy	Schauffelein's Starfire
Sire: Ch. Schauffelein's Troli Arabesque			Ch. Storm's Donner
		Ch. Kurtzhaus Thunder	Ch. Schauffelein's Soliloquoy
	Ch. Midnight Glow of Arabesque		Ch. Bar-Jac's Ceasar
		Quinestas Twilight Fantasy	Jessica
CH. SCHAUFFELEIN'S VINTAGE YEAR			
		Ch. Schauffelein's Blackberry Brandy	Ch. Iago v. Ahrtal
	Ch. Schauffelein's Extra Special		Ch. Schauffelein's Silhouette
		Schauffelein's Specially Fancy	Ch. Bramaleas Argonaut
Dam. Ch. Lowenbrau Aloha Schauffelein			Schauffelein's Starfire
		Ch. Sabre v. Mannerheim	Ch. Brown's Dion
	Ch. Konigshansen Honor		Ch. Kaukana's Gold Braide
		Ch. Konigshansen Dedication	Ch. Dobe Acre's Cinnamon
			Ch. Kay Hill's Ebonetta

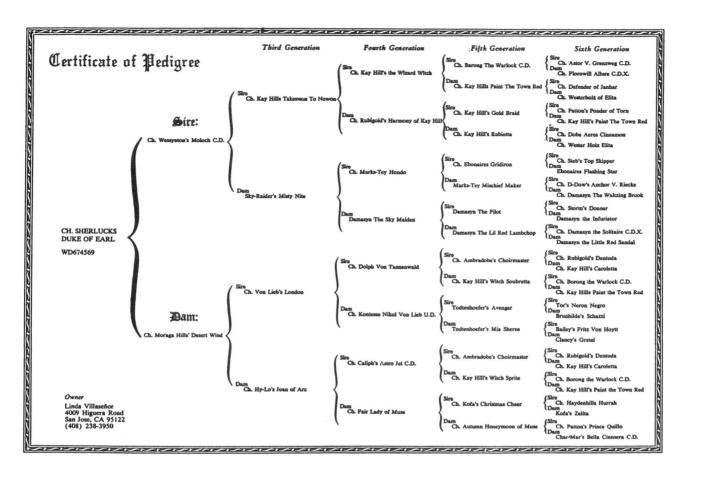

Certificate of Pedigree

| | Third Generation | Fourth Generation | Fifth Generation | Sixth Generation |

Sire: Ch. Wessynton's Moloch C.D.

Dam: Ch. Moraga Hills' Desert Wind

CH. SHERLUCKS DUKE OF EARL
WD674569

Sire: Ch. Wessynton's Moloch C.D.
- Sire: Ch. Kay Hills Takeswon To Nowon
  - Sire: Ch. Kay Hill's the Wizard Witch
    - Sire: Ch. Barong The Warlock C.D.
      - Sire: Ch. Astor V. Grenzweg C.D.
      - Dam: Ch. Florowill Allure C.D.X.
    - Dam: Ch. Kay Hills Paint The Town Red
      - Sire: Ch. Defender of Janhar
      - Dam: Westerholz of Elita
  - Dam: Ch. Rubigold's Harmony of Kay Hill
    - Sire: Ch. Kay Hill's Gold Braid
      - Sire: Ch. Patton's Ponder of Torn
      - Dam: Ch. Kay Hill's Paint The Town Red
    - Dam: Ch. Kay Hill's Rubietta
      - Sire: Ch. Dobe Acres Cinnamon
      - Dam: Ch. Wester Holz Elita
- Dam: Sky-Raider's Misty Nite
  - Sire: Ch. Marks-Tey Hondo
    - Sire: Ch. Ebonaires Gridiron
      - Sire: Ch. Steb's Top Skipper
      - Dam: Ebonaires Flashing Star
    - Dam: Marks-Tey Mischief Maker
      - Sire: D-Dow's Anchor V. Riecks
      - Dam: Ch. Damasyn The Waltzing Brook
  - Dam: Damasyn The Sky Maiden
    - Sire: Damasyn The Pilot
      - Sire: Storm's Donner
      - Dam: Damasyn the Infuriator
    - Dam: Damasyn The Lil Red Lambchop
      - Sire: Ch. Damasyn the Solitaire C.D.X.
      - Dam: Damasyn the Little Red Sandal

Dam: Ch. Moraga Hills' Desert Wind
- Sire: Ch. Von Lieb's London
  - Sire: Ch. Dolph Von Tannenwald
    - Sire: Ch. Ambradobe's Choirmaster
      - Sire: Ch. Rubigold's Dentuda
      - Dam: Ch. Kay Hill's Caroletta
    - Dam: Ch. Kay Hill's Witch Soubretta
      - Sire: Ch. Borong the Warlock C.D.
      - Dam: Ch. Kay Hills Paint the Town Red
  - Dam: Ch. Kontesse Nikol Von Lieb U.D.
    - Sire: Todtenhoefer's Avenger
      - Sire: Tor's Neron Negro
      - Dam: Brunhilde's Schazzi
    - Dam: Todtenhoefer's Mia Sheree
      - Sire: Bailey's Fritz Von Hoytt
      - Dam: Clancy's Gretel
- Dam: Hy-Lo's Joan of Arc
  - Sire: Ch. Caliph's Astro Jet C.D.
    - Sire: Ch. Ambradobe's Choirmaster
      - Sire: Ch. Rubigold's Dentuda
      - Dam: Ch. Kay Hill's Caroletta
    - Dam: Ch. Kay Hill's Witch Sprite
      - Sire: Ch. Borong the Warlock C.D.
      - Dam: Ch. Kay Hill's Paint The Town Red
  - Dam: Ch. Fair Lady of Muse
    - Sire: Ch. Kofa's Christmas Cheer
      - Sire: Ch. Haydenhills Hurrah
      - Dam: Kofa's Zelita
    - Dam: Ch. Autumn Honeymoon of Muse
      - Sire: Ch. Patton's Prince Quillo
      - Dam: Char-Mar's Bella Cinnsera C.D.

Owner
Linda Villaseñor
4009 Higuera Road
San Jose, CA 95122
(408) 238-3950

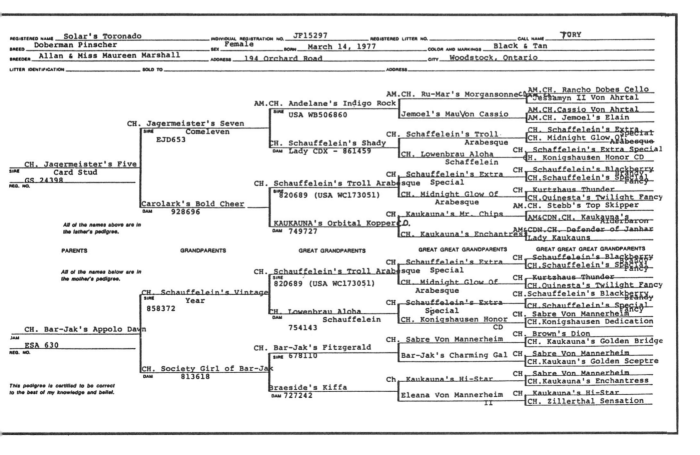

| REGISTERED NAME | Solar's Toronado | INDIVIDUAL REGISTRATION NO. | JF15297 | REGISTERED LITTER NO. | | CALL NAME | TORY |

BREED: Doberman Pinscher SEX: Female BORN: March 14, 1977 COLOR AND MARKINGS: Black & Tan

BREEDER: Allan & Miss Maureen Marshall ADDRESS: 194 Orchard Road CITY: Woodstock, Ontario

LITTER IDENTIFICATION _____ SOLD TO _____ ADDRESS _____

SIRE: CH. Jagermeister's Five Card Stud GS 24398
- CH. Jagermeister's Seven Comeleven EJD653
  - AM.CH. Andelane's Indigo Rock USA WB506860
    - AM.CH. Ru-Mar's MorgansonneC.D.
      - AM.CH. Rancho Dobes Cello
      - Jessamyn II Von Ahrtal
    - Jemoel's MauVon Cassio
      - AM.CH. Cassio Von Ahrtal
      - AM.CH. Jemoel's Elain
  - CH. Schauffelein's Shady Lady CDX - 861459
    - CH. Schaffelein's Troll Arabesque
      - CH. Schaffelein's Extra Special
      - CH. Midnight Glow Of Arabesque
    - CH. Lowenbrau Aloha Schaffelein
      - CH. Schauffelein's Extra Special
      - H. Konigshausen Honor CD
- Carolark's Bold Cheer 928696
  - CH. Schauffelein's Troll Arabesque 820689 (USA WC173051)
    - CH. Schauffelein's Extra Special
      - CH. Schauffelein's Blackberry Brandy
      - CH. Schauffelein's Special Fancy
    - CH. Midnight Glow Of Arabesque
      - CH. Kurtzhaus Thunder
      - CH. Quinesta's Twilight Fancy
  - KAUKAUNA's Orbital Kopper C.D. 749727
    - CH. Kaukauna's Mr. Chips
      - AM.CH. Stebb's Top Skipper
      - AM&CDN.CH. Kaukauna's Alderbaron
    - CH. Kaukauna's Enchantress
      - AM&CDN.CH. Defender of Janhar
      - Lady Kaukauns

DAM: CH. Bar-Jak's Appolo Dawn ESA 630
- CH. Schauffelein's Vintage Year 858372
  - CH. Schauffelein's Troll Arabesque 820689 (USA WC173051)
    - CH. Schauffelein's Extra Special
      - CH. Schauffelein's Blackberry Brandy
      - CH. Schauffelein's Special Fancy
    - CH. Midnight Glow Of Arabesque
      - CH. Kurtzhaus Thunder
      - CH. Quinesta's Twilight Fancy
  - CH. Lowenbrau Aloha Schauffelein 754143
    - CH. Schauffelein's Extra Special
      - CH. Schauffelein's Blackberry Brandy
      - CH. Schauffelein's Special Fancy
    - CH. Konigshausen Honor CD
      - Sabre Von Mannerheim
      - CH. Konigshausen Dedication
- CH. Society Girl of Bar-Jak 813618
  - CH. Bar-Jak's Fitzgerald 678110
    - CH. Sabre Von Mannerheim
      - Brown's Dion
      - CH. Kaukauna's Golden Bridge
    - Bar-Jak's Charming Gal
      - Sabre Von Mannerheim
      - CH. Kaukaun's Golden Sceptre
  - Braeside's Kiffa 727242
    - Ch. Kaukauna's Hi-Star
      - Sabre Von Mannerheim
      - CH. Kaukauna's Enchantress
    - Eleana Von Mannerheim
      - CH. Kaukauna's Hi-Star
      - CH. Zillerthal Sensation

PARENTS GRANDPARENTS GREAT GRANDPARENTS GREAT GREAT GRANDPARENTS GREAT GREAT GREAT GRANDPARENTS

All of the names above are in the father's pedigree.

All of the names below are in the mother's pedigree.

This pedigree is certified to be correct to the best of my knowledge and belief.

AMERICAN, CANADIAN, DOMINICAN, MEXICAN & INTERNATIONAL (F.C.I.)
CH. LIQUORISH THE RON RICO
AMERICAN, CANADIAN & MEXICAN C.D. R.O.M.

CH. FLORIAN VOM AHRTAL

CH. RAVENSBURG'S FALSTA

CH. RAVENSBURG'S BITZEN

CH. HIGHBRIAR OAK OF ALLENWOOD

CH. STEB'S TOP SKIPPER

CH. HIGHBRIAR EASY TO LOVE

HIGHBRIAR STORMETTE C.D.X.

CH. HIGHBRIAR OSIRIS

CH. LAKECREST'S THUNDERSTORM

CH. FLORIAN VOM AHRTAL C.D.

CH. WILLA VOM AHRTAL

CH. HIGHBRIAR ROCKSAND

CH. JET VON DER RAVENSBURG

CH. HIGHBRIAR BLACKBIRD C.D.

HIGHBRIAR STORMETTE C.D.X.

"RICO"

CH. RUBIGOLD'S DENTUDA

CH. AMBERDOBE'S CHOIRMASTER

CH. KAY HILL'S CAROLETTA

CH. DOLPH VON TANNENWALD

CH. BORONG THE WARLOCK C.D.

CH. KAY HILL WITCH SOUBRETTA

CH. KAY HILL'S PAINT THE TOWN RED

GAYAMON THE BRANDY ALEXANDRA C.D.X.
(POINTED — U.S. & CAN.)

CH. STEB'S TOP SKIPPER

CH. EGOTHEL'S ALL AMERICAN

DONAR THE WINDSTORM

CH. ARJEAN'S THE FORTUNE COOKIE

CH. EBONAIRE'S TOUCHDOWN

CH. ARJEAN'S EXTRA POINT C.D.

ERIC'S DUCHESS VON MITCHELL

Black/Rust
28" Tall - 85 lbs.

"Rico's" elegance is surpassed
only by his temperament
and pedigree.

OFA Certified
Brucellosis Free

Owners/Breeders
Liquorish Dobes
Grace & Jeff Joffe
6920 SW 182 Way
Ft. Lauderdale, Fla. 33331
305 - 434-0064

Bitches are required to have
current Brucellosis free certificate
when shipped to
Miami International Airport
or
Fort Lauderdale

MEMBERS: D.P.C.F.; D.P.C.A.; M.O.C.; A.D.O.A.

604

Gestation, Whelping, and the Litter

When your bitch has been bred and is back at home, remain ever watchful that no other male gets to her until at least the twenty-second day of her season has passed. Prior to that time, it will still be possible for an undesired breeding to take place, which, at this point, would be catastrophic. Remember, she actually can have two separate litters by two different dogs, so *be alert and take care*.

In all other ways, the bitch should be treated quite normally. It is not necessary for her to have any additives to her diet until she is at least four to five weeks pregnant. It is also unnecessary for her to have additional food. It is better to underfeed the bitch this early in her pregnancy than to overfeed her. A fat bitch is not an easy whelper, so by "feeding her up" during the first few weeks, you may be creating problems for her.

Controlled exercise is good, and necessary, for your pregnant bitch. She should not be permitted to just lie around. At about seven weeks, the exercise should be slowed down to several sedate walks daily, not too long and preferably on the leash.

In the fourth or fifth week of pregnancy, calcium may be added to the diet; and at seven weeks, the one meal a day may be increased to two meals with some nutritional additives in each. Canned milk may be added to her meals at this time.

A week before she is due to whelp, your Doberman bitch should be introduced to her whelping box, so that she will have accustomed herself to it and feel at home there by the time the puppies arrive. She should be encouraged to sleep there and be permitted to come and go as she pleases. The box should be roomy enough for her to lie down and stretch out in; but it should not be too large or the pups will have too much room in which to roam, and they may get chilled if they move too far away from the warmth of their mother. Be sure that there is a "pig rail" for the box, which will prevent the puppies from being crushed against the side of the box. The box should be lined with newspapers, which can easily be changed as they become soiled.

The room where the whelping box is placed, either in the home or in the kennel, should be free from drafts and should be kept at about eighty degrees Fahrenheit. It may be necessary during the cold months to install an infrared lamp in order to maintain sufficient warmth, in which case guard against the lamp being placed too low or too close to the puppies.

Keep a big pile of newspapers near the box. You'll find that you never have enough of these when there is a litter, so start accumulating them ahead of time. A pile of clean towels, a pair of scissors, and a bottle of alcohol should also be close at hand. Have all of these things ready at least a week before the bitch is due to whelp, as you never know exactly when she may start.

The day or night before she is due, the bitch will become restless; she'll be in and out of her box and in and out of the door. She may refuse food, and at this point her temperature will start to drop. She will start to dig and tear up the newspapers in her box, shiver, and generally look uncomfortable. You alone should be with her at this time (or one other person who is an experienced breeder, to give you confidence if this is one of your first litters). The bitch does not need an audience or any extra people around. This is not a sideshow, and several people hovering over the bitch may upset her to the point where she may hurt the puppies. Stay nearby, but do not fuss too much over her. Keep a calm attitude; this will give her confidence. Eventually she will settle down in her box and begin to pant; shortly thereafter she will start to have contractions and soon a puppy will begin to emerge, sliding out with one of the contractions. The mother immediately should open the sac and bite the cord and clean up the puppy. She will also eat the placenta, which you should permit. Once the puppy is cleaned, it should be placed next to the bitch, unless she is showing signs of having another one immediately. The puppy should start looking for a nipple on which to nurse, and you should make certain that it is able to latch on and start doing so at once.

If a puppy is a breech birth (*i.e.*, born feet first), then you must watch carefully that it is delivered as quickly as possible and the sac removed very quickly so that the puppy does not drown. Sometimes even a normally positioned birth will seem extremely slow in coming. Should either of these events occur, you might take a clean towel and, as the bitch contracts, pull the puppy out, doing so gently and with utmost care. If the bitch does not open the sac and cut the cord, you will have to do so. If the puppy shows little signs of life, make sure the mouth is free of liquid and then, using a turkish towel or terry cloth, massage the puppy's chest, rubbing back and forth quite briskly. Continue this for about fifteen minutes. It may be necessary to try mouth-to-mouth breathing. Open the puppy's jaws and, using a finger, depress the tongue which may be stuck to the roof of the puppy's mouth. Then blow hard down the puppy's throat. Bubbles may pop out of its nose, but keep on blowing. Rub with the towel again across the chest, and try artificial respiration, pressing the sides of the chest together, slowly and rhythmically, in and out, in and out. Keep trying one method or the other for at least fifteen minutes (actual time—not how long it seems to you) before giving up. You may be rewarded with a live puppy who otherwise would not have made it.

If you are able to revive the puppy, it should not be put with the mother immediately, as it should be kept extra warm for a while. Put it in a cardboard box near a stove, on an electric heating pad, or, if it is the time of year when your heat is running, near a radiator until the rest of the litter has been born. Then it can be put in with the others.

The bitch may go for an hour or more between puppies, which is fine as long as she seems comfortable and is not straining or contracting. She should not be allowed to remain unassisted for more than an hour if she does continue to contract. This is when you should call your veterinarian, whom you should have alerted ahead of time of the possibility so that he will be somewhere within easy reach. He may want the bitch brought in so that he can examine her and perhaps give her a shot of Pituitrin. In some cases, the veterinarian may find that a Caesarean operation is necessary, because a puppy may be lodged in some manner that makes normal delivery impossible. This can occur due to the size of a puppy or may be due to the fact that the puppy is turned wrong. If any of the foregoing occurs, the puppies already born must be kept warm in their cardboard box, which should have been lined with shredded newspapers in advance and which should have a heating pad beneath it.

Assuming that there have been no problems, and the bitch has whelped normally, you should insist that she go outside to exercise, staying just long enough to make herself comfortable. She can be offered a bowl of milk and a biscuit, but then she should settle down with her family. Be sure to clean out the whelping box and change the newspapers so that she will have a fresh bed.

If the mother lacks milk at this point, the puppies will need to be fed by hand, kept very warm, and held against the mother's teats several times a day in order to stimulate and encourage the secretion of her milk, which will probably start shortly.

Unless some problem arises, there is little you need do about the puppies until they become three to four weeks old. Keep the box clean with fresh papers. When the puppies are a couple of days old, the papers should be removed and turkish towels should be tacked down to the bottom of the box so that the puppies will have traction when they move. This is important.

If the bitch has difficulties with her milk supply, or if you should be so unfortunate as to lose the bitch, then you must be prepared to either hand-feed or tube-feed the puppies if they are to survive. We prefer the tube method as it is so much faster and easier. If the bitch is available, it is better that she continue to clean and care for the puppies in the normal manner, except for the food supplements you will provide. If she is unable to do this, then after every feeding, you must gently rub each puppy's abdomen with wet cotton to induce urination, and the rectum should be gently rubbed to open the bowels.

Newborn puppies must be fed every three or four hours around the clock. The puppies must be kept warm during that time. Have your veterinarian show you how to tube-feed. Once learned it is really quite simple, fast, and efficient.

After a normal whelping, the bitch will require additional food to enable her to produce sufficient milk. She should be fed twice daily now, and some canned milk should be available to her several times during the day.

When the puppies are two weeks old, you should clip their nails, as they are needle-sharp at this point and can hurt or damage the mother's teats and stomach as the pups hold on to nurse.

Between three and four weeks of age, the puppies should begin to be weaned. Scraped beef (prepared by scraping it off slices of raw beef with a spoon, so that none of the muscle or gristle is included) may be offered in very small quantities a couple times daily for the first few days. If the puppy is reluctant to try it, put a little on your finger and rub it on the puppy's lips; this should get things going. By the third day, you can mix in ground puppy chow with warm water as directed on the package, offering it four times daily. By now the mother should be kept out of the box and away from the puppies for several hours at a time. After the puppies reach five weeks of age, she should be left in with them only overnight. By the time they are six weeks old, the puppies should be entirely weaned and the mother should only check on them with occasional visits.

Most veterinarians recommend a temporary DHL (distemper, hepatitis, leptospirosis) shot when the puppies are six weeks old. This remains effective for about two weeks. Then, at eight weeks, the series of permanent shots begins for the DHL protection. It is a good idea to discuss with your vet the advisability of having your puppies inoculated against the dreaded parvovirus at the same time. Each time the pups go to the vet for shots, you should bring stool samples so that they can be examined for worms. Worms go through various stages of development and may be present in a stool sample even though the sample does not test positive. So do not neglect to keep careful watch on this.

The puppies should be fed four times daily until they are three months old. Then you can cut back to three feedings daily. By the time the puppies are six months old, two meals daily are sufficient. Some people feed their dogs twice daily throughout their lifetime, while others cut back to one meal daily when the puppy reaches one year of age.

The ideal time for Doberman puppies to go to their new homes is when they are between eight and twelve weeks old, although some puppies successfully adjust to a new home when they are six weeks of age. Be certain that they go to their future owners accompanied by a description of the diet you've been feeding them and a schedule of the shots they have received and those they still need. These should be included with a registration application and a copy of the pedigree.

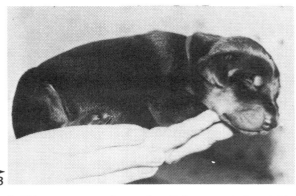

1. This gorgeous, and appealing, Dobe puppy is the mighty Ch. Dictator v Glenhugel at six months of age. Peggy Adamson, owner, Roslyn Heights, New York.
2. Gwen Satalino DeMilta in the whelping box feeding the first litter of Ch. Alisaton Bewitched. Photo courtesy of Kay Harrison.
3. A two-week-old male future champion, by Ch. Royalmead's Joker's Wild ex Wynterwynd's Lady O'The Nite. Owned by Serenade Dobermans, Jan MacDonald, Houston, Texas.

A typical Maestro pup in the 1970's, "weighing in" at age four weeks. Karen Vroom Parkhurst, owner, Chino, California.

608

CHAPTER TWENTY-THREE

The Veterinarian's Corner

Joseph P. Sayres, DVM
Buffalo, New York

By way of introduction to this chapter concerning the medical aspects of the care of the Doberman Pinscher, I think we should devote a few paragraphs to how to choose your veterinarian.

Until recent years, there has been a lot of misunderstanding and even animosity between veterinarians and breeders. Some distrust arose on the breeder's part because most veterinarians were not familiar with, nor even interested in learning about, purebred dogs. Some of the problems encountered were peculiar to certain breeds and some would crop up at inconvenient times. Veterinarians were then beset by breeders who thought that they knew more about the medical problems of their dogs than the vets did. The veterinarians very often were only called for emergencies, or when it was too late to save a sick dog that had been treated too long by people in the kennel. Another problem was that many breeders had never included veterinary fees in their budgets and were slow to pay their bills, if indeed they paid them at all. Fortunately, these problems have been, to a large extent, solved. Education and better communication between breeders and veterinarians have eliminated most areas of friction.

Today, veterinary education and training have advanced to a point paralleling that of human standards. This resulted from advances in the field of Veterinary Science in the last two decades. Sophisticated diagnostic procedures, new and advanced surgical techniques, and modern well-equipped hospitals all make for improved medical care for our dogs.

Educated breeders now realize that while they may know more about the general husbandry of their dogs, and the unique traits of the Doberman Pinscher, they should not attempt to diagnose and treat their dogs' ailments.

In choosing your veterinarian, be selective. He or she should be friendly, should be interested in your dogs, and, in the case of breeders, should be interested in your breeding programs. Veterinarians should be willing to talk freely with you. Such things as fees, availability for emergencies, what services are and are not available, should be discussed and understood before a lasting relationship with your veterinarian can be established.

You can expect your veterinarian's office, clinic, or hospital to be clean, free of undesirable odors, well equipped, and staffed by sincere, friendly personnel who willingly serve you at all times. All employees should be clean, neat in appearance, and conversant with whatever services you require. You should also expect your dog to be treated carefully and kindly at all times by the doctor and his staff.

Your veterinarian should participate in continuing education programs in order to keep up with changes and improvements in his field. He should also be aware of his limitations. If he doesn't feel confident in doing certain procedures, he should say so and refer you to qualified individuals to take care of the problem. Seeking second opinions and consultation with specialists on difficult cases are more the rule than the exception nowadays. That is as it should be.

You will know that if your veterinarian is a member of the American Animal Hospital Association, he and his facility have had to measure up to high standards of quality and are subjected to inspections every two years. Many excellent veterinarians and veterinary hospitals by choice do not belong to the

American Animal Hospital Association. You can satisfy your curiosity about these places by taking guided tours of the facilities, and by learning word of mouth about the quality of medicine practiced at these hospitals.

So far we have discussed only what you should expect from your veterinarian. Now, let's discuss what the veterinarian expects from his clients. Most of all, he expects his clients to be open and frank in their relations with him. He doesn't like to be double-checked and second-guessed behind his back. He also wants you to handle your pet so that he, in turn, can examine him. He expects you to leash your dog, to control him, and to keep him from bothering other pets in the room. He expects to be paid a fair fee and to be paid promptly for services rendered. Fees in a given area tend to be consistent, and variations are due only to complications or unforeseen problems. Medicine is not an exact science; therefore, things unpredictable can happen. If you are dissatisfied with the services or fees, then ask to discuss these things in a friendly manner with the doctor. If his explanations are not satisfactory or he refuses to talk to you about the problem, then you are justified in seeking another doctor.

The veterinarian expects to provide his services for your animals during regular hours whenever possible. But he also realizes that in a kennel or breeding operation that emergencies can occur at any time and that his services will be needed at "off" hours. You should find out how these emergencies will be handled, and then be satisfied with the procedures.

No veterinarian can be on duty twenty-four hours of every day. Today cooperative veterinarians group together to take turns covering each other's emergency calls. Some cities have emergency clinics that operate solely to take care of those catastrophies that seem usually to happen in the middle of the night or on weekends.

My conclusion, after thirty years of practice, is that most disagreements and hard feelings between clients and veterinarians are a result of a breakdown in communication. Find a veterinarian to whom you can talk and with whom you can be comfortable and you'll make a valuable friend.

In using veterinary services to their best advantage, I believe that you will find that prevention of diseases and problems is more important than trying to cure these things after they occur. In other words, "an ounce of prevention is worth a pound of cure."

Congenital Defects

Doberman Pinschers have their share of congenital defects. From publications, such as "Current Veterinary Therapy VIII" by Kirk and "Medical and Genetic Aspects of Pure Bred Dogs" edited by Clark and Stainer, the following conditions are listed as congenital defects in Doberman Pinschers.

A. Bundle of His Degeneration — a heart defect that can cause sudden death.

B. Cervical Vertebral Instability ("Wobbler Syndrome") — Hindquarter incoordination to complete paralysis; usually occurs in middle age.

C. Color Mutant Alopecia — hair loss, dandruff, and excessively dry skin. Most commonly found in blue Dobermans.

D. Congenital Renal Hypoplasia — defective kidney development.

E. Cranio Mandibular Osteopathy — boney proliferation of the jaw bones.

F. Cryptorchidism — failure of testicles to descend.

G. Flank Sucking — usually a temporary condition.

H. Hip Dysplasia — degeneration of hip joints.

I. Immune Complex Disorders — manifested by bacterial skin infections. Demodectic mange, hair loss, itchiness.

J. Narcolepsy — sudden attacks of sleep.

K. Polystatic Fibrous Dysplasia — bone defect of forearm.

L. Von Willebrand's Disease — prolonged and frequent bleeding episodes.

Vaccines

By proper and vigilant vaccination programs, the following contagious diseases can be eliminated: distemper, rabies, hepatitis,

610

parainfluenza, leptospirosis, and parvovirus enteritis.

The following "shot" schedule should be set up and strictly followed to prevent infectious diseases:

Disease	Age to vaccinate
distemper	Six to eight weeks old. Second inoculation to be given at ten to twelve weeks of age. When given in combination with parvo vaccine, a third inoculation given at fourteen to sixteen weeks of age is advisable. Revaccinate annually.
hepatitis (adenovirus)	Same as distemper.
parainfluenza (kennel cough)	Same as distemper
leptospirosis	Give first vaccine at nine weeks old. Revaccinate with second DHLP (distemper, hepatitis, leptospirosis, parainfluenza) at twelve to sixteen weeks of age. Revaccinate annually.
parvovirus	Give first vaccine at seven to eight weeks old. Second vaccine four weeks later. Third vaccine four weeks later. Duration of immunity from three injections established at one year at the time of this writing. See explanation below. Revaccinate annually.
rabies	First inoculation at three to four months old, then revaccinate when one year old, and at least every three years thereafter. If dog is over four months old at the time of the first vaccination, then revaccinate in one year and then once every three years thereafter.

Vaccines used are all modified live virus vaccines except the one for leptospirosis, which is a killed bacterium. New and improved vaccines to immunize against parvovirus have appeared recently. The long-awaited modified live virus vaccine of canine origin was made available. It is safe and should produce immunity lasting one year. Currently there are questions arising concerning the efficacy of combination vaccines as opposed to using single entity vaccines, *i.e.*, giving plain parvo vaccine instead of including it in the one for distemper, hepatitis, parainfluenza, and leptospirosis. Some experts think that there may be a suppression of immunity when combination vaccines are used. Consult your own veterinarian, and be guided by his advice.

Other communicable diseases for which no vaccine has been perfected as yet are: canine brucellosis, canine coronavirus, and canine rotavirus.

Infectious and Contagious Diseases

Distemper — Caused by a highly contagious, airborne virus. The symptoms are varied and may involve all of the dogs' systems. A pneumonic form is common with heavy eye and nose discharges, coughing, and lung congestion. The digestive system may be involved as evidenced by vomiting, diarrhea, and weight loss. The skin may show a pustular type of rash on the abdomen. Nervous system involvement is common with convulsions, chorea, and paralysis as persistent symptoms. This virus may have an affinity for nerve tissue and cause encephalitis and degeneration of the spinal cord. These changes for the most part are irreversible and death or severe crippling ensues.

We have no specific remedy or cure for distemper, and recoveries when they occur can only be attributed to the natural resistance of the patient, good nursing care, and control of secondary infections with antibiotics.

That's the bad news about distemper. The good news is that we rarely see a case of distemper in most areas today because of the efficiency of the vaccination program. This is proof that prevention by vaccination has been effective in almost eradicating this dreaded disease.

Hepatitis — Another contagious viral disease affecting the liver. This is not an airborne virus and can only be spread by contact. Although rarely seen today because of good prevention by vaccination programs, this virus is capable of producing a very acute, fulminating, severe infection and can cause death in a very short time. Symptoms of high temperature, lethargy, anorexia, and vomiting are the same as for other diseases. Careful evaluation by a veterinarian is necessary to confirm the diagnosis of this disease.

The old canine infectious hepatitis vaccine has been replaced by a canine adenovirus type 2 strain vaccine which is safer and superior. The new vaccine seems to be free of post-vaccination complications such as blue eye, shedding of the virus in the urine, and some kidney problems.

Leptospirosis — This is a disease that seriously affects the kidneys of dogs, most domestic animals, and man. For this reason, it can become a public health hazard. In urban and slum areas, the disease is carried by rats and mice in their urine. It is caused by a spirochete organism which is very resistant to treatment. Symptoms include fever, depression, dehydration, excess thirst, persistent vomiting, occasional diarrhea, and jaundice in the latter stages. Again, it is not always easy to diagnose so your veterinarian will have to do some laboratory work to confirm it.

We see very few cases of leptospirosis in dogs and then only in the un-vaccinated ones. The vaccine is generally given concurrently with the distemper and hepatitis vaccinations. Preventive inoculations have resulted in the almost complete demise of this dreaded disease.

Parainfluenza — This is commonly called kennel cough. It is caused by a throat-inhabiting virus that causes an inflammation of the trachea (windpipe) and larynx (voice box). Coughing is the main symptom and fortunately it rarely causes any other systemic problems. The virus is airborne, highly contagious, and is the scourge of boarding kennels. A vaccine is available that will protect against this contagious respiratory disease and should be given as part of your vaccination program, along with the distemper, hepatitis, leptospirosis and parvovirus shots. Pregnant bitches should not be vaccinated against parainfluenza because of the possibility of infecting the unborn puppies. As there may be more than one infectious agent involved in contagious upper respiratory disease of dogs, vaccination against parainfluenza is not a complete guarantee to protect against all of them.

Rabies — This is a well-known virus-caused disease that is almost always fatal and is transmissible to man and other warm-blooded animals. The virus causes very severe brain damage. Sources of the infection include foxes, skunks, and raccoons, as well as domesticated dogs and cats. Transmission is by introduction of the virus by saliva into bite wounds. Incubation in certain animals may be from three to eight weeks. In a dog, clinical signs will appear within five days. Symptoms fall into two categories depending on what stage the disease is in when seen. We have the dumb form and the furious form. There is a change of personality in the furious form; individuals become hypersensitive and overreact to noise and stimuli. They will bite any object that moves. In dumb rabies, the typical picture of the loosely hanging jaw and tongue presents itself. Diagnosis is confirmed only by a laboratory finding the virus and characteristic lesions in the brain. All tissues and fluids from rabid animals should be considered infectious and you should be careful not to come in contact with them. Prevention by vaccination is a *must* because there is no treatment for rabid dogs.

Canine Coronavirus (CCV) — This is a highly contagious virus that spreads rapidly to susceptible dogs. The source of infection is through infectious feces. The incubation period is one to four days, and the virus will be found in feces for as long as two weeks. It is hard to tell the difference sometimes between cases of diarrhea caused by coronavirus and parvovirus. Coronavirus generally is less severe or causes a more chronic or sporadic type of diarrhea. The fecal material may be orange in color and have a very bad odor; occasionally, it will also contain blood. Vomitting sometimes precedes the diarrhea, but loss of appetite and listlessness are consistent signs of the disease. Fever may or may not be present. Recovery is the rule after eight to ten days, but treatment with fluids, antibiotics, intestinal protectants, and good nursing care are necessary in the more severe watery diarrhea

612

cases. Dogs that survive these infections become immune but for an unknown length of time.

To control an outbreak of this virus in a kennel, very stringent hygienic measures must be taken. Proper and quick disposal of feces, isolation of affected animals, and disinfection with a 1 to 30 dilution of Clorox are all effective means of controlling an outbreak in the kennel.

There is no vaccine yet available for prevention of canine coronavirus. Human infections by this virus have not been reported.

Canine Parvovirus (CPV) — This is the newest and most highly publicized member of the intestinal virus family. Cat distemper virus is a member of the same family but differs from canine parvovirus biologically, and it has been impossible to produce this disease in dogs using cat virus as the inducing agent; and conversely canine parvovirus will not produce the disease in a cat. However, vaccines for both species will produce immunity in the dog. The origin of CPV is still unknown.

Canine parvovirus is very contagious and acts rapidly. The main source of infection is contaminated feces. Direct contact between dogs is not necessary, and carriers such as people, fleas, and medical instruments may carry and transmit the virus.

The incubation period is five to fourteen days. The symptoms are fever, severe vomiting and diarrhea, often with blood, depression, and dehydration. Feces may appear yellowish gray streaked with blood. Young animals are more severely affected, and a shock-like death may occur in two days. In animals less than six weeks old, the virus will cause an inflammation of the heart muscle, causing heart failure and death. These pups may not have diarrhea. A reduction in the number of while blood cells is a common finding early in the disease.

The virus is passed in the feces for one to two weeks and may possibly be shed in the saliva and urine also. This virus has also been found in the coats of dogs. The mortality rate is unknown.

Dogs that recover from the disease develop an immunity to it. Again, the duration of this immunity is unknown.

Control measures include disinfection of the kennels, animals, and equipment with a 1

to 30 dilution of Clorox and isolation of sick individuals.

Treatment is very similar to that for coronavirus; namely, intravenous fluid therapy, administration of broad spectrum antibiotics, intestinal protectants, and good nursing care.

Transmission to humans has not been proven.

Clinical studies have proven that vaccination with three injections of the new modified live virus vaccine of canine origin with four weeks between injections will be over ninety percent effective. Recent work at the James A. Baker Institute for Animal Health at Cornell University has shown that maternally derived antibodies can interfere with the immunizing properties of our vaccines for as long as fifteen to sixteen weeks. This means that some of our puppies, especially those from dams with good immunity, will not become susceptible to successful vaccination until they are sixteen weeks old. It is also known that the maternal protection afforded these puppies, while enough to prevent successful vaccination, may not be enough to protect them from an exposure to the virus. The best advice is to give our puppies three inoculations of a canine origin modified live virus vaccine four weeks apart, starting when they are eight weeks old. Then, hope for the best and revaccinate annually.

Canine Rotavirus (CRV) — This virus has been demonstrated in dogs with a mild diarrhea but again with more severe cases in very young puppies. Very little is known about this virus.

A milder type of diarrhea is present for eight to ten days. The puppies do not run a temperature and continue to eat. Dogs usually recover naturally from this infection. There is no vaccine available for this virus.

Canine Brucellosis — This is a disease of dogs that causes both abortions and sterility. It is caused by a small bacterium closely related to the agent that causes undulant fever in man and abortion in cows. It occurs worldwide.

Symptoms of brucellosis sometimes are difficult to determine, and some individuals with the disease may appear healthy. Vague symptoms such as lethargy, swollen glands, poor hair coat, and stiffness in the back legs may be present. This organism does not cause death and may stay in the dog's system for months and even years. The latter animals, of course, have breeding problems and infect other dogs.

Poor results in your breeding program may be the only indication that brucellosis is in your kennel. Apparently, normal bitches abort without warning. This usually occurs forty-five to fifty-five days after mating. Successive litters will also be aborted. In males, signs of the disease are inflammation of the skin of the scrotum, shrunken testicles, and swollen tender testicles. Fertility declines and chronically infected males become sterile.

The disease is transmitted to both sexes at the time of mating.

Other sources of infection are aborted puppies and birth membrane and discharge from the womb at the time of abortions.

Humans can be infected, but such infections are rare and mild. Unlike in the dog, the disease in humans responds readily to antibiotics.

Diagnosis is done by blood testing which should be done carefully. None of the current tests are infallible and false positives may occur. The only certain way that canine brucellosis can be diagnosed is by isolating the *B. canis* organism from blood or aborted material and for this, special techniques are required.

Treatment of infected individuals has proven ineffective in most cases. Sterility in males is permanent. Spaying or castrating infected pets should be considered as this will halt the spread of the disease and is an alternative to euthanasia.

At present, there is no vaccine against this important disease.

Our best hope in dealing with canine brucellosis is prevention. The following suggestions are made in order to prevent the occurrence of this malady in your dogs.

1. Test breeding stock annually and by all means breed only uninfected animals.
2. Test bitches several weeks before their heat periods.
3. Do not bring any new dogs into your kennel unless they have two negative tests taken a month apart.
4. If a bitch aborts, isolate her, wear gloves when handling soiled bedding, and disinfect the premises with Roccal.

5. If a male loses interest in breeding or fails to produce after several matings, have him checked.
6. Consult your veterinarian for further information about this disease; alert other breeders; and support the research that is going on at the James A. Baker Institute for Animal Health at Cornell University.

External Parasites

The control and eradication of external parasites depends on the repeated use of good quality insecticide sprays or powders during the warm months. Make a routine practice of using these products at seven-day intervals throughout the season. It is also imperative that sleeping quarters and wherever the animal habitates be treated also.

Fleas — These are brown, wingless insects with laterally compressed bodies and strong legs, and they are bloodsuckers. Their life cycle comprises eighteen to twenty-one days from egg to adult flea. They can live without food for one year in high humidity but die in a few days in low humidity. They multiply rapidly and are more prevalent in the warm months. They can cause a severe skin inflammation in those individuals that are allergic or sensitive to the flea bite or saliva of the flea. They can act as a vector for many diseases and do carry tapeworms. Control measures must include persistent, continual use of flea collars or flea medallions, or sprays or powders. The dog's bedding and premises must also be treated because the eggs are there. Foggers, vacuuming, or professional exterminators may have to be used. All dogs and cats in the same household must be treated at the same time.

Ticks — There are hard and soft species of ticks. Both species are bloodsuckers and at times cause severe skin inflammations on their host. They act as a vector for Rocky Mountain Spotted Fever, as well as other diseases. Hibernation through an entire winter is not uncommon. The female tick lays as many as 1000 to 5000 eggs in crevices and cracks in walls. These eggs will hatch in about three weeks and then a month later become adult ticks. Ticks generally locate around the host's neck and ears and between the toes. They can cause anemia and serious blood loss if allowed to grow and multiply. It is not a good idea to pick ticks off the dogs because of the danger of a reaction in the skin. Just apply a tick spray directly on the ticks which then die and fall off eventually. Heavily affected dogs should be dipped every two weeks in an anti-parasitic bath. The premises, kennels, and yards should be treated every two weeks during the summer months, being sure to apply the insecticide to walls and in all cracks and crevices. Frequent or daily grooming is effective in finding and removing ticks.

Lice — There are two kinds of lice, namely the sucking louse and the biting louse. They spend their entire life on their host but can be spread by direct contact or through contaminated combs and brushes. Their life cycle is twenty-one days, and their eggs, known as nits, attach to the hairs of the dog. The neck and shoulder region, as well as the ear flaps, are the most common areas to be inhabited by these pesky parasites. They cause itchiness, some blood loss, and inflammation of the skin. Eradication will result from dipping or dusting with methyl carbonate or Thuron once a week for three to four weeks. It is a good idea to fine-comb the dogs after each dip to remove the dead lice and nits. Ask your veterinarian to provide the insecticides and advice or control measures for all of these external parasites.

Mites — Less commonly occurring parasitic diseases such as demodectic and sarcoptic mange, caused by mites, should be diagnosed and treated by your veterinarian. You are wise to consult your doctor whenever any unusual condition occurs and persists in your dog's coat and skin. These conditions are difficult to diagnose and treat at best, so that the earlier a diagnosis is obtained, the better the chances are for successful treatment. Other skin conditions such as ringworm, flea bite allergy, bacterial infections, eczemas, hormonal problems, among others, all have to be considered.

Internal Parasites

The eradication and control of internal parasites in dogs will occupy a good deal of your time and energy.

Puppies should be tested for worms at four weeks of age and then six weeks later. It is also wise to test them again six weeks following their last worm treatment to be sure the treatments have been successful. Annual fecal tests are advisable throughout your dog's life. All worming procedures should be done only with the advice and supervision of your veterinarian. The medicants used to kill the parasites are, to a certain extent, toxic, so they should be used with care.

Ascarids — These include roundworms, puppy worms, stomach worms, milk worms. Puppies become infected shortly after birth and occasionally even before birth. Ascarids can be difficult to eradicate. When passed in the stool or thrown up, they look somewhat like cooked spaghetti when fresh or like rubber bands when they are dried up.

Two treatments at least two weeks apart will eliminate ascarids from most puppies. An occasional individual may need more wormings according to the status in its system of the life cycle of the worm at the time of worming. Good sanitary conditions must prevail and immediate disposal of feces is necessary to keep down the worm population.

Hookworms — These are bloodsuckers and also cause bleeding from the site of their attachment to the lining of the intestine when they move from one site to another. They can cause a blood-loss type of anemia and serious consequences, particularly in young puppies. Their life cycle is direct and their eggs may be ingested or passed through the skin of its host. Treatment of yards and runs with products available from your veterinarian is said to kill the eggs in the soil where the dogs defecate. Two or three worm treatments three to four weeks apart may be necessary to get rid of hookworms. New injectible products administered by your veterinarian have proven more effective than remedies used in the past. Repeated fecal examinations may be necessary to detect the eggs in the feces. These eggs pass out of the body only sporadically or in showers, so that it is easy to miss finding them unless repeated stool testing is done. As is true with any parasite, good sanitary conditions in the kennel and outside runs will help eradicate this worm.

Whipworms — These are a prevalent parasite in some kennels and in some individual dogs. They cause an intermittant mucus-type diarrhea. As they live only in the dog's appendix, it is extremely difficult to reach them with any worm medicine given by mouth. Injections seem to be the most effective treatment, and these have to be repeated several times over a long period of time to be effective. Here again, repeated fresh stool samples must be examined by your veterinarian to be sure that this pest has been eradicated. Appendectomies are indicated in only the most severe chronic cases. The fact that cleanliness is next to godliness cannot be emphasized too often; it is most important in getting rid of this parasite.

Tapeworms — They are another common internal parasite of dogs. They differ in their mode of transmission as they have an indirect life cycle. This means that part of their cycle must be spent in an intermediate host. Fleas, fish, rabbits, and field mice all may act as an intermediate host for the tapeworm. Fleas are the most common source of tapeworms in dogs, although dogs that live near water may eat raw fish and hunting dogs that eat the entrails of rabbits may get them from those sources. Another distinguishing feature of the tapeworm is the suction apparatus which is part of the head and which enables the tapeworm to attach itself to the lining of the intestine. If, after worming, just the head remains, it has the capability of regenerating into another worm. This is one reason why tapeworms are so difficult to get rid of. It will require several treatments to get the entire parasite out of a dog's system. These worms are easily recognized by the appearance of their segments which break off and appear on top of a dog's feces or stuck to the hair around the rectal area. These segments may appear alive and mobile at times, but most often they are dead and dried up when found. They look like flat pieces of rice and may be white or brown when detected. Elimination of the intermediate host is an integral part of any plan to rid our dogs of this worm. Repeated wormings may be necessary to kill all the adult tapeworms in the intestine. An injection to rid dogs of tapeworms is now available.

Heartworms — Heartworm disease is caused by an actual worm that goes through its life cycle in the bloodstream of its victims. Ultimately it makes its home in the right chambers of the heart and in the large vessels that transport the blood to the lungs. They vary in size from 2.3 inches to 16 inches. Adult worms can survive up to five years in the heart.

By its nature, this is a very serious disease and can cause irreversible damage to the lungs and heart of its host. Heart defect and lung pathology soon result in serious problems for the dog.

The disease is transmitted and carried by female mosquitoes that have infected themselves after biting an infected dog; they then pass it on to the next dog with which they come in contact.

The disease has been reported wherever mosquitoes are found, and cases have been reported in most of the United States. Rare cases have been reported in man and cats. It is most prevalent in warmer climates where the mosquito population is the greatest, but hotbeds of infection exist in the more temperate parts of the United States and Canada also.

Concerted effect and vigorous measures must be taken to control and prevent this serious threat to our dog population. The most effective means of eradication I believe will come through annual blood testing for early detection, by the use of preventive medicine during mosquito exposure times, and also by ridding our dogs' environment of mosquitoes.

Annual blood testing is necessary to detect cases that haven't started to show symptoms yet and thus can be treated effectively. It also enables your veterinarian to prescribe safely the preventive medicine to those individuals that test negative. There is a ten to fifteen percent margin of error in the test, which may lead to some false negative tests. Individuals that test negative but are showing classical symptoms of the disease such as loss of stamina, coughing, loss of weight, and heart disease should be further evaluated with chest X-rays, blood tests, and electrocardiograms. Newer, more accurate tests have recently been approved for use by veterinarians.

Serious consequences may result when the preventive medication is given to a dog that already has heartworms in his system. That is why it is so important to have your dog tested annually before starting the preventive medicine.

In order to be most effective, the preventive drug diethylcarbamazine should be given in daily doses of 2.5 mg. to 3 mg. per pound of body weight or 5 mg. per kilogram of body weight of your dog. This routine should be started fifteen days prior to exposure to mosquitoes and be continued until sixty days after exposure. Common and trade names for this drug are Caricide, Styrid-Caricide, and D.E.C. It comes in liquid and tablet forms.

This drug has come under criticism by some breeders and individuals who claim that it affects fertility and causes some serious reactions. Controlled studies have shown no evidence that this drug produces sterility or abnormal sperm count or quality. Long-term studies on reproduction, when the drug was given at the rate of 4.9 mg. per pound of body weight (two times the preventive dose level) for two years, showed no signs of toxic effects on body weight maintenance, growth rate of pups, feed consumption, conception rate, numbers of healthy pups whelped, ratio of male to female pups, blood counts, and liver function tests. It is reported as a well-tolerated medication, and many thousands of dogs have benefitted from its use. From personal experience, I find only an occasional dog who will vomit the medicine or get an upset stomach from it. The new enteric coated pills have eliminated this small problem.

However, if you still don't want to give the preventive, especially to your breeding stock, an alternative procedure would be to test your dogs every six months for early detection of the disease, so that it can be treated as soon as possible.

Heartworm infestation can be treated successfully. There is a one to five percent mortality rate from the treatment. It can be expected that treatment may be completed without side effects if the disease hasn't already caused irreversible problems in the heart, lungs, liver, kidneys, or other organs. Careful testing, monitoring, and supervision are essential to success in treatment. Treatment is far from hopeless these days, and if the disease is detected early enough, a successful outcome is more the rule than the exception.

In conclusion, remember that one case of heartworm disease in your area is one too many, especially if that one case is your dog. By following the steps mentioned here, we can go a long way in ridding ourselves of this serious threat to our dogs.

Home Remedies and First Aid

You have repeatedly read here of my instructions to call your veterinarian when your animals are sick. This the best advice I can give you. There are a few home remedies, however, that may get you over some rough spots while trying to get professional help.

I think it is a good idea to keep some medical supplies in a first aid kit. The kit should contain the following items: a roll of cotton, gauze bandages, cotton applicator swabs, adhesive tape, hydrogen peroxide, tincture of metaphen, BFI powder, boric acid ointment and crystals, a jar of petroleum jelly, tweezers, and a rectal thermometer.

A word here on how to take a dog's temperature may be in order. Always lubricate the thermometer with petroleum jelly and carefully insert it well into the rectum. Hold it in place for two to three minutes and then read it. The thermometer should be held firmly so that it doesn't get sucked up into the rectum.

To administer liquid medicines to dogs, simply pull the lips away from the side of the mouth, making a pocket for depositing the liquid. Slightly tilt the dog's head upward and he will be able to swallow the liquid properly. Giving liquids by opening the mouth and pouring them directly on the tongue is an invitation to disaster because inhalation pneumonia can result. Putting it in the side of the mouth gives the dog time to hold it in his mouth and then swallow it properly.

Tablets are best administered by forcing the dog's mouth open and pushing the pill down over the middle of the tongue into the back of his mouth. If put in the right place, a reflex tongue reaction will force the pill down the throat and thus be swallowed. There is no objection to giving the pills in favorite foods as long as you carefully determine that the medicine is surely swallowed with the food.

Vomiting — To stop vomiting, mix one tablespoon of table salt to one pint of water and dissolve the salt thoroughly; then give one tablespoonful of the mixture to the patient. After waiting one hour, repeat the procedure and skip the next meal. The dog may vomit a little after the first dose, but the second dose works to settle the stomach. This mixture not only provides chlorides but also acts as a mild astringent and many times in mild digestive upsets will work to stop the vomiting.

Diarrhea — In the case of adult Dobermans, give three or four tablespoons of Kaopectate or Milk of Bismuth every four hours. Use one-third of this dosage for puppies. Skip the next meal, and if diarrhea persists, then start a bland diet of boiled ground lean beef and boiled rice in the proportions of half and half. Three or four doses of this medicine should suffice. If the diarrhea persists and, particularly, if accompanied by depression, lethargy, and loss of appetite, your veterinarian should be consulted immediately. With all these new viral-caused diarrheas floating around, time is of essence in securing treatment.

Mild Stimulant — Dilute brandy half and half with water, add a little sugar, and give a tablespoonful of the mixture every four to five hours. For puppies over three months old, reduce the dosage to a teaspoonful of the mixture every four to five hours.

Mild Sedative — Dilute brandy half and half with water, add a little sugar and give a tablespoon of the mixture every twenty to thirty minutes until the desired effect is attained. For puppies over three months old, reduce the dosage to a teaspoonful of the mixture every twenty to thirty minutes.

Using brandy for both sedation and stimulation is possible by varying the time interval between doses. Given every four to five hours, it's a stimulant; but given every twenty to thirty minutes, it acts as a sedative.

Minor Cuts and Wounds — Cleanse them first with soap and water, preferably tincture of green soap. Apply mild antiseptic such as Bactine or tincture of metaphen two or three times daily until healed. If the cut is deep, and fairly long and bleeding, then a bandage should be applied until professional help can be obtained.

Whenever attempting to bandage wounds, first apply a layer or two of gauze over the cleaned and treated wound. Then apply a layer of cotton and then another layer or two of gauze. The bandage must be snug enough to stay on but not so tight as to impair the circulation to the body part. Adhesive tape should be applied over the second layer of gauze to keep the bandage as clean and dry as possible until you can get your dog to the doctor.

Tourniquets should be applied only in cases of profusely bleeding wounds. They are applied tightly between the wound and the heart, in addition to the pressure bandage that should be applied directly to the wound. The tourniquet must be released and reapplied at fifteen-minute intervals.

Burns — Application of ice or very cold water and compresses is the way to treat a skin burn. Apply cold packs as soon as possible and take the dog immediately to your vet.

Frostbite — Frostbite is a rarely occurring problem. The secret in treating this condition is to gradually restore normal body temperature to the affected parts. In other words, use cold water, then tepid water, to thaw out the area slowly and restore circulation. In cases of severe freezing or shock due to bitter cold temperature, take the animal to the veterinarian as soon as possible.

Abscesses and Infected Cysts — Obvious abscesses and infected cysts that occur between the toes may be encouraged to drain by using hot boric acid packs and saturated dressings every few hours until professional aid can be secured. The boric acid solution is made by dissolving one tablespoon of crystals to one pint of hot water. Apply frequently to the swollen area. Further treatment by a veterinarian may involve lancing and thoroughly draining and cleaning out the abscess cavity. As most abscesses are badly infected, systemic antibiotics are generally indicated.

Heatstroke or Heat Exhaustion — A word about the serious effects of heat on a dog is timely. It never ceases to amaze me how many people at dog shows have to be warned and advised not to leave their dogs in cars or vans on a warm day.

A dog's heat-regulating mechanism is not nearly as efficient as ours. Consequently, dogs feel the heat more than we do. Keep them as cool and as well ventilated as possible in hot weather. Another inducement for shock is taking your dog out of a cool air-conditioned vehicle and exposing him immediately to the hot outdoors. Make that change as gradual as you can because a rapid change can cause a shock-like reaction.

In cases of suspected heatstroke, which manifests itself with very high body temperatures (as high as 106-108 F. sometimes), severe panting, weakness, shaking and collapse, act quickly to get your dog into a cold bath or shower or put ice cold compresses on his head. Then, again without delay, rush him to the nearest veterinarian for further treatment. Prevention is the key here and with a little common sense, heatstroke and heat exhaustion can be avoided.

Poisons — Many dogs are poisoned annually by unscrupulous people who hate dogs. Many others are victims of poisoning due simply to the careless use of rat and ant poisons, insecticides, herbicides, anti-freeze solutions, drugs, and so forth. Dogs also frequently insist on eating poisonous plants, either in the house or outdoors, which can lead to serious consequences. Common sources of these toxic products are named below.

Plants that can be a source of poison for dogs include the following (this list contains only the most common ones): daffodils, oleanders, poinsettias, mistletoe, philodendron, delphiniums, monkshood, foxglove, iris, lillies of the valley, rhubarb, spinach, tomato vines, sunburned potatoes, rhododendron, cherry, peach, oak, elderberry, black locust, jack-in-the-pulpit, Dutchman's-breeches, water hemlock, mushrooms, buttercups, poison hemlock, nightshade, jimsonweed, marijuana, locoweed and lupine. Also, grain contaminants can exist in dog food. The most common ones are ergot, corn cockle, and grotolaria.

Poisonous animals include such snakes as vipers, rattlesnakes, copperheads, water moccasins, and the coral snake. Lizards like the Gila monster and Mexican beaded lizard are bad. Some toads, spiders, insects, and fish also are potential sources of trouble.

Chemicals comprise perhaps the largest and most common source of poisoning in our environment. These are hazards that our dogs may be exposed to every day. Careful handling and awareness of these products are essential. Toxic materials are found in arts and crafts supplies, photographic supplies; and automotive and machinery products, which include such things as antifreeze and de-icers, rust inhibitors, brake fluids, engine and carburetor cleaners, lubricants, gasoline, kerosene, radiator cleaners, and windshield washers. Cleaners, bleaches and polishes, disinfectants, and sanitizers all contain products that potentially are dangerous. Even

health and beauty aids may contain toxic materials if ingested in large enough quantities: some bath oils, perfumes, corn removers, deodorants, anti-perspirants, athlete's foot remedies, eye makeup, hair dyes and preparations, diet pills, headache remedies, laxatives, liniments, fingernail polish and polish removers, sleeping pills, suntan lotions, amphetamines, shaving lotions, colognes, shampoos, and certain ointments. Paints and related products also can be dangerous. Caulking compounds, driers, thinners, paints, paint brush cleaners, paint and varnish removers, preservatives, and floor and wood cleaners all fit into this category. Pest poisons for the control of birds, fungi, rats, mice, ants, and snails all can be toxic and sometimes fatal to dogs. Miscellaneous items like fire extinguishers and non-skid products for slippery floors can be unsafe. Almost all solvents like carbon tetrachloride, benzene, toluene, acetone, mineral spirits, kerosene, and turpentine are bad. Just look at the number of products in our everyday environment which can be hazardous or fatal to our dogs!

In cases of suspected poisoning, be aware of what to do until professional help can be obtained:

1. Keep the animal protected, quiet, and warm.

2. If a contact is on the skin, eye, or body surface, cleanse and flush the area with copious amounts of water. If the dog gets something in this eye, do this also. Protect him from further exposure.

3. Inducing vomiting may be dangerous and should be done only on the advice of a veterinarian. Giving peroxide may induce vomiting in some cases. It is better to allow the animal to drink as much water as he wants. This will dilute the poison. Giving milk or raw egg whites is helpful many times to delay absorption of the toxic products.

Do not attempt to give anything by mouth if the patient is convulsing, depressed, or unconscious.

Do not waste time in getting veterinary service. Take any vomited material, and suspected causative agents with their containers, with you to the vet. When the suspected product is known, valuable time can be saved in administering specific treatment.

A word to the wise should be sufficient. Keep away from your dog all products that can harm him in any way.

Whelping

We cannot leave the subject of emergencies without considering the subject of whelping. Most bitches whelp without any problems. It is wise, however, to watch them closely during this time. I feel that no bitch should go more than two hours in actual labor without producing a puppy. This includes the time before the first one as well as between puppies. If more than two hours elapse, then the dam should be examined by a veterinarian. It will then be determined if she is indeed in trouble or is just a slow whelper. This rule of thumb gives us time to find out if there is a problem and what it may be, and it gives us time to save both dam and puppies in most cases.

It is good practice to have your bitches examined for pregnancy three-and-a-half weeks after mating, as well as at term around the fifty-eighth or fifty-ninth day. These procedures will enable the veterinarian to discover any troubles that may occur during pregnancy, as well as alert him as to when the whelping is going to take place. Knowing this, he can plan to provide service, if needed, during off hours.

Bitches that are difficult to breed, miss pregnancies, or have irregular reproductive cycles should have physical exams including laboratory tests to determine the cause of the trouble. These tests may be expensive, but a lot of breeding and sterility problems due to sub-par physical condition, hormonal imbalances, or hypo-thyroidism can be corrected. If a valuable bitch is restored to her normal reproductive capacity, the reward more than offsets the medical costs.

Another important thing to remember about whelping and raising puppies is to keep them warm enough. This means a room temperature of 80-85°F. for the first ten days to two weeks until the puppies are able to generate their own body heat. Be sure the dam keeps them close to her; leave a light burning at night for the first week so she won't lose track of any of them or accidentally lie on one of them. Chilling remains the biggest cause of

death for newborn puppies. Other causes are malnutrition, toxic milk, hemorrhage, and viral and bacterial infections. Blood type incompatibilities have been understood lately as causes of trouble.

Consultation with your veterinarian concerning these and any other breeding problems you've had in the past may result in the solution of these problems. This may result in larger litters with a higher survival rate.

Care of the Older Dog

Providing medical services from cradle to grave is the slogan of many veterinarians, and rightly so. The average life expectancy for our dogs these days is about thirteen years. Sad to say, this is a short time compared to our life span. Larger breeds historically do not live as long as the medium-sized or smaller breeds. However, I think that with proper care your Dobes should be able to reach this expectancy.

This, then, is a good time to speak about approaching old age and some of the problems we can expect during that time. Arthritis, kidney disease, heart failure, and cataracts are probably the most common ailments in older dogs.

When your pet has trouble getting up in the morning, jumping up, or going upstairs, you can bet that some form of joint problem is starting. Giving two enteric coated aspirin tablets three times a day for five days very often will help these individuals. This dosage is for adult dogs. This is relatively free of side effects and as long as nothing else is wrong, your dog will get a bit of relief.

Signs of kidney weakness are excessive drinking, inability to hold urine through the night, loss of weight, lack of appetite, and more than occasional bouts of vomiting and diarrhea. If any of these signs present themselves, it would be worthwhile to have a checkup. Very often corrective measures in diet and administering some medicine will prolong your dog's life.

Some form and degree of heart failure exists in a lot of older animals. Symptoms of chronic congestive heart failure consist of a chronic cough, especially after exercise, lack of stamina, lethargy, abdominal enlargement, and labored breathing at times. If diagnosed and treated early in the disease, many canine heart patients live to a ripe old age.

Cataracts form in the lenses of most, if not all, old dogs. They are a part of the normal aging process. Total blindness from cataracts generally does not result for a long time. Distant and peripheral vision remain satisfactory for the expected life span of the dog. Rarely is total blindness produced by these aging cataracts before the dog's life expectancy is reached. There is no effective treatment for cataracts other than their surgical removal, which is not recommended in the older patient that has any vision left at all.

Hip dysplasia occurs in Doberman Pinschers. Signs of this condition vary from one dog to another but some of the more common ones are difficulty in getting up after lying for awhile, a rabbit-like gait with both rear legs moving forward at the same time when running, lethargy, and walking with a swaying gait in the rear legs. In many cases, a period of pain and discomfort at nine months to one year old will resolve itself; and even though the dysplasia is still there, most of the symptoms may disappear.

It is recommended that dysplastic individuals not be bred, that they not be allowed to become overweight, and that they have moderate exercise.

The selection of dysplastic-free individuals for breeding stock eventually will result in the production of sounder hip joints in affected Doberman strains and lines. This factor, of course, is only one consideration in the breeding and production of an overall better Dobe.

Canine Nutrition

It is generally agreed that great strides have been made in canine nutrition in the past few years, and that most of our well-known commercial dog foods provide all the essential ingredients of a well-balanced diet for our dogs. Probably the greatest problem is providing good quality protein in proper proportions. It behooves us to read dog food labels and to know what we are feeding, and how much is necessary to provide the requirements for a lean healthy individual. The tendencies in our society today are to overfeed and under exercise both our dogs and ourselves.

We must know the energy content or caloric value of the foods we are feeding. Then we must determine the energy requirements of our dogs. These will vary with time and circumstances. Your adult Doberman Pinscher requires about twenty-five to thirty calories per pound of body weight daily for maintenance.

Generally speaking, for the average adult Doberman house dog, a diet consisting of 16% high quality protein, 10% fat, and 44% carbohydrates is a good mix. For working dogs, dogs being shown, or pregnant bitches, increase the protein and fat percentages by about 25% and decrease the carbohydrate proportion by 25%. To meet the needs of the increased stress of growth in young puppies and nursing bitches, the protein and fat components should be increased yet another 10 to 15% and the percentage of carbohydrates should be decreased by the same amount. Any stress situation means a rise in caloric requirement. For example, in the case of pregnancy, it is advisable to increase the amount of food intake by 20% after four weeks of gestation and by 75% after six weeks of gestation, and so forth.

We are assuming that the vitamins and minerals in the foods used are complete and balanced.

You may have to combine, mix, and juggle various types and brands of food to attain the desired diet, but don't despair; it can be done. Prescription and special diet foods are available through your veterinarian. These probably cost more initially but may pay off in the long run.

As to exactly how much to feed each individual dog, no one can give you a magic formula that works in all cases. My best advice is to use common sense and a scale. The guidelines on dog food containers have a tendency to be over-inflated. It is better to err on the low side than to overfeed. Remember, keep you dog slim and fit with proper diet and plenty of exercise. That's not a bad idea for your own well being also.

621

Appendix A

Appendix B

Appendix C

Highest Scoring Dog in Trial
(Doberman Pinscher Club of America Specialty Shows)

		Class	Score
1937	Ducat v d Rheinaperle Owner: Frank L. Grant	Open A	249
1938	Duke of Schroth Valley Owner: Henry G. Schmitt	Novice A	98
1939	Princess B. Wilhelmina Owner: H. E. Crebs	Utility	198
1940	King IV, C.D.X. Owner: Harry Carson	Utility	199½
1941	Tiger of Pontchartrain Owner: Willy Necker	Utility	199.7
1942	No event		
1943	Ch. Danny V. Neckerheim Owner: Lester Erhardt	Novice A	96.1
1944	Princess B. Wilhelmina Owner: Hugh E. Crebs	Utility	199½
1945	No event		
1946	Ines Gozo De Feliz Owner: Dorothy H. Pagel	Novice A	93
1947	Fritz V Darburg Owner: Gilbert F. Berger	Utility	197½
1948	Ch. Assault V Aleck, C.D.X. Owner: Clarence C. Alexander	Open B	199½
1949	Von Ritter Owner: Anthony Wilkas	Utility	199
1950	Abbenoir Owner: Mr. & Mrs. Frank H. Grover	Novice B	199
1951	No event		
1952	Teresa V. Mac, C.D.X. Owners: Mr. & Mrs. Joseph McKann	Utility	199
1953	Beechursts Ajax The Great Owners: Beechurst Kennels	Open B	197

1954	Creb's Betty Girl Owner: Hugh. E. Crebs	Open B	197
1955	Readington's Dynamite, U.D. Owner: Barflerdobes Kennel	Open B	196
1956	No event		
1957	Guiding Eye's Magdolin Owners: Lewis and Bessie Fowler	Novice A	195
1958	No event		
1959	Titan of Ashworth Owners: Mr. & Mrs. Luke Reilly	Novice A	197
1960	Rad's Friendly Jest of Summer Owner: Velma Janek	Open B	199½
1961	No event		
1962	No event		
1963	Ch. Commando's Silver Sandal Owners: Melvin and Virginia Spafford	Utility	198½
1964	Valjan's Amber Owner: Robert T. Self	Open B	197
1965	Ch. Commando's Silver Sandal, U.D.T. Owners: Melvin and Virginia Spafford	OB-Ut.	198
1966	Ch. Commando's Silver Sandal, U.D.T. Owners: Melvin and Virginia Spafford	Utility	198
1967	Little Mist V Frederick, U.D.T. Owners: Rosalie and Fred Simpson	Open B	198
1968	Azteca's Bellona, C.D. Owner: Teresa Nail	Open A	199½
1969	Countess Misty of Manistee, C.D.X. Owners: Robert and Patricia Schultz	Open B	197½
1970	Ava Danica Hartman, U.D. Owner: Genevieve C. McMillen	Open B	197
1971	Ronsu's Clipper Blue Jacket Owner: Wayne Boyd	Utility	198
1972	Schauffelein's Dilemma Owner: Leon K. Matthews	Open B	200
1973	April Acres Black Magic Owner: Rickie L. Brooks	Open A	198
1974	April Acres Black Magic, C.D.X. Owner: Rickie L. Brooks	Open B	197½
1975	Frederick's Trimbrel, U.D. Owners: R. G. and L. G. Simpson	Open B	197
1976	Hahn's Fawn Von Hoytt, C.D. Owner: Donald F. Hahn	Open A	197½
1977	Fiesta Tushee Twister, C.D.X. Owner: Nancy Defiesla	Open B	197
1978	Larwyck's Czarina, C.D.X. Owners: Dr. & Mrs. John Abercrombie	Open B	198
1979	Shatara's Blackbird V Shadin Owners: Paula K. and John R. Weaver	Novice B	195½
1980	Thor Warrick Engelbert, U.D. Owner: Rodney Williams	Open B	198
1981	Shatara's Blackbird V. Shadlin Owner: Paula K. Weaver	Novice B	197½
1982	Acadia's Black Swan, U.D. Owner: Rodney P. Mack	Open B	199
1983	Tucari's Racime Razzmatazz, C.D.X. Owners: R. H. and G. Chambers		
1984	Heelalong's PMGS Free Spirit, C.D.X. Owner: Pat Geske	Open B	198
1985	O.T. Ch. Heelalong's PMGS Free Spirit, C.D.X. Owner: Pat Geske	Open B	197½

Appendix D

Best of Breed Winners — 1924 to 1985
(Doberman Pinscher Club of America Specialty Shows)

1924	Red Roof Hilda Owner: George H. Earle, III
1925	Apollo V Schuetzeneck Owner: Dr. R. C. Bauman
1926	Hella of Pontchartrain Owner: Glenn S. Staines
1927	Claus B Sigalsburg Owner: E. J. Robinson
1928	Ch. Claus V Sigalsburg Owner: E. J. Robinson
1929	Alphabet of Dawn Owner: Kettle Kove Kennels
1930	Modern V Simmenau Rhinegold Owner: J. C. Zimmerman
1931	Ch. Hamlet V Herthasse Owner: M. V. Reynolds
1932	Ch. Hamlet V Herthasse Owner: M. V. Reynolds

1933 Dash of Bardo
Owner: Joseph A. Stoffel

1934 Ch. Muck V Brunia
Owner: Owen A. West

1935 Jockel V Burgund
Owner: Owen A. West

1936 Ch. Jockel V Burgund
Owner: Owen A. West

1937 Ch. Jessy v d Sonnenhohe
Owner: F. F. H. Fleitmann

1938 Ch. Rigo V Lindehof
Owner: Ray Soldwell

1939 Ora V Sandburg-Lindenhof
Owner: A. D. Nast, Jr.

1940 Ellie V Granzhof
Owner: Miss Charlotte V. Bergen

1941 Cerita of Marienland
Owner: Marienland Kennels,
   R. C. Webster

1942 No event

1943 Ch. Dow's Dodie V Kienlesburg
Owner: Bert T. Dow

1944 Ch. Dictator V Glenhugel
Owner: Captain and Mrs. Bob
   Adamson

1945 No event

1946 Ch. Alcor V Millsdod
Owner: Mrs. A. Ernest Mills

1947 Ch. Quo Shmerk V Marienland
Owner: Rupprechthelm Kennels

1948 Ch. Alcor V Millsdod
Owner: Mrs. A. Ernest Mills

1949 Ch. Jet v d Ravensburg
Owner: Mr. and Mrs. Walter A.
   Dencker

1950 Ch. Jet v d Ravensburg
Owner: Mr. and Mrs. Walter A.
   Dencker

1951 Ch. Kitchawan's Caramia
Owner: Kitchawan Kennels

1952 Ch. Meadowmist Elegy
Owner: Mrs. Wilheim F. Knauer

1953 Ch. Rontyelee Lady Alleyne
Owner: Bishop C. C. Alleyne

1954 Ch. Dortmund Delly's Colonel Jet
Owner: Boxdob Kennels

1955 Ch. Dortmund Delly's Colonel Jet
Owner: Boxdob Kennels

1956 Ch. Borong The Warlock, C.D.
Owners: Henry G. and Theodosia
   Frampton

1957 Ch. Borong The Warlock, C.D.
Owners: Henry G. and Theodosia
   Frampton

1958 Ch. El Campeon's Diosa
Owners: Mr. and Mrs. George S.
   Forbes

1959 Ch. Haydenhill's Diana
Owner: Mr. and Mrs. Robert Sikes

1960 Ch. Borong The Warlock, C.D.
Owners: Henry G. and Theodosia
   Frampton

1961 Ch. Brown's Bridget
Owners: Colonel R. B. Hoover and
   Hazel C. Samara

1962 Ch. Singenwald's Prince Kuhio
Owner: Singenwald Kennels

1963 Ch. Singenwald's Prince Kuhio
Owner: Singenwald Kennels

1964 Ch. Jem's Amythest V Warlock
Owners: Henry G. and Theodosia
   Frampton

1965	Ch. Ru Mar's Tsushima, C.D. Owner: Margaret Carveth
1966	Ch. Toledobes Linebacker Owner: Loren D. Nickols
1967	Ch. Sultana Von Marienburg Owner: Mary M. Rodgers
1968	Ch. Sultana Von Marienburg Owner: Mary M. Rodgers
1969	Ch. Rosevale's Little Nip of Loron Owners: Ronald and Loretta Batacao
1970	Ch. Checkmate's Nite Cap Owner: Jim Roe
1971	Ch. Brown's A-Amanda Owner: Eleanor Brown
1972	Ch. Lujac's Stinger Owners: Jack and Louise Strutt
1973	Ch. Brown's B-Brian Owner: Eleanor Brown
1974	Ch. Loran's Aviator Owners: Helen F. Kamerer and Nancy Hogans
1975	Ch. Brown's B-Brian Owner: Eleanor Brown
1976	Ch. Marienburg's Sun Hawk Owners: Mary M. Rodgers and Moe Miyagawa
1977	Ch. Welchardis A Go-Go, C.D. Owner: Joan Barrett
1978	Ch. Marienburg's Sun Hawk Owners: Mary M. Rodgers and Moe Miyagawa
1979	Ch. Marienburg's Mary Hartman Owners: Mary M. Rodgers and Moe Miyagawa
1980	Ch. Mi Gar's Jenne Owners: David Staddon, Gary Martin, and M. A. Vatardi, III

1981	Ch. Star Dobe's Irish Fantasy Owners: Don and Nora Gau
1982	Ch. Redyn's Touch of Class Owner: Paul Hotz
1983	Ch. Marienburg's Mary Hartman Owners: Mary and Moe Miyagawa
1984	Ch. Eagle's Devil "D" Owners: Dr. and Mrs. Anthony DiNardo
1985	Ch. Tereden's Crystal Gayle Owners: Denisye and Jennifer Lee

Ch. Barchet Fiddler On The Roof made a big winning record for Mrs. Alan Robson, handled by Terry Lazzaro, during the early 1980's. An excellent dog of tremendous quality.

Glossary

To the uninitiated, it must seem that fanciers of purebred dogs speak a special language all their own, which in a way we do. The following is a list of terms, abbreviations, and titles which you will run across through our pages which may be unfamiliar to you. We hope that this list will lead to fuller understanding and that it will additionally assist you as you meet and converse with others of similar interests in the world of purebred dogs.

A.K.C. The commonly used abbreviation of American Kennel Club.

Albino. A deficiency of pigmentation causing the nose leather, eye rims, and lips to be pink.

Almond eye. The shape of the tissue surrounding the eye, which creates the almond-shaped appearance required by some breed standards.

American Kennel Club. The official registry for purebred dogs in the United States. Publishes and maintains the Stud Book and handles all litter and individual registrations, transfers of ownership, and so on. Keeps all United States dog show, field trial, and obedience trial records; issues championships and other titles in these areas as they are earned; approves and licenses dog show, obedience trial, and field trial judges; licenses or issues approval to all championship shows, obedience trials, and recognized match shows. Creates and enforces the rules, regulations, and policies by which the breeding, raising, exhibiting, handling, and judging of purebred dogs in the United States are governed. Clubs, not individuals, are members of the American Kennel Club, each of which is represented by a delegate selected from the club's own membership for the purpose of attending the quarterly American Kennel Club meetings as the representative of the member club, to vote on matters discussed at each meeting and to bring back a report to the individual club of any decisions or developments which took place there.

Angulation. The angles formed by the meeting of the bones, generally referring to the shoulder and upper arm in the forequarters and the stifle and hock in the hindquarters.

Apple head. An exaggerated roundness of the top-skull.

Apron. Frill, or longer hair, below the neck.

Bad bite. Can refer to a wryness or malformation of the jaw, or to incorrect dentition.

Bad mouth. One in which the teeth do not meet correctly according to the specifications of the breed standard.

Balance. Symmetry and proportion. A wellbalanced dog is one in which all of the parts appear in correct ratio to one another: height to length, head to body, skull to foreface, and neck to head and body.

Beefy. Overmusculation or overdevelopment of the shoulders or hindquarters or both.

Benched Show. Dog show at which the dogs are kept on benches while not being shown in competition.

Best in Show. The dog or bitch chosen as the most representative of any dog in any breed from among the group winners at an all-breed dog show. (The dog or bitch that has won Best of Breed next competes in the group of which its breed is a part. Then the first-prize winner of each group meets in an additional competition from which one is selected the Best in Show.)

Best of Breed. The dog that is adjudged best of any competing in its breed at a dog show.

Best of Opposite Sex. The dog or bitch that is selected as the best of the opposite sex to the Best of Breed when the latter award has been made.

Best of Winners. The dog or bitch selected as the better of the two between Winners Dog and Winners Bitch.

Bitch. A female dog.

Bite. The manner in which the upper and lower jaws meet.

Bloom. The sheen of a coat in healthy, lustrous condition.

Blue-ribbon winner. A dog that has won first prize in the class for which it is entered at a dog show.

Bone. Refers to the girth of a dog's leg bones. A dog called "good in bone" has legs that are correct in girth for its breed and for its own general conformation. Well-rounded bone is round in appearance, flat bone rather flattish. Light bone is very fine and small in diameter, almost spindle-like in appearance; legs are extremely slender. Heavy bone refers to legs that are thick and sturdy.

Brace. Two dogs, or a dog and a bitch, closely similar in size, markings, color, and general appearance, moving together in unison.

Breed. Purebred dogs descended from mutual ancestors refined and developed by man.

Breeder. A person who breeds dogs.

Breeding particulars. Name of the sire and dam, date of breeding, date of birth, number of puppies in the litter, their sex, and name of the breeder and of the owner of the sire.

Brisket. The forepart of the body between the forelegs and beneath the chest.

Brood bitch. A female dog used primarily for breeding.

CACIB. A Challenge Certificate offered by the Federation Cynologique Internationale towards a dog's championship.

Canine teeth. The four sharp pointed teeth at the front of the jaws, two upper and two lower, flanking the incisors; often referred to as fangs.

Canines. Dogs, jackals, wolves, and foxes as a group.

Carpals. Pastern joint bones.

Castrate. To neuter a dog by removal of the testicles.

Cat foot. The short-toed, round tight foot similar to that of a cat.

C.D. An abbreviation of the Companion Dog title.

C.D.X. An abbreviation of the Companion Dog Excellent title.

Ch. Commonly used abbreviation of champion.

Challenge Certificate. A card awarded at dog shows in Great Britain by which championship there is gained. Comparable to our Winners Dog and Winners Bitch awards. To become a British champion a dog must win three of these Challenge Certificates at designated championship dog shows.

Champion. A dog or bitch that has won a total of fifteen points, including two majors, the total number under not less than three judges, two of whom must have awarded the majors at A.K.C. point shows.

Character. Appearance, behavior, and temperament considered correct in an individual breed of dog.

Cheeky. Cheeks which bulge out or are rounded in appearance.

Chest. The part of the body enclosed by the ribs.

Chiseled. Clean-cut below the eyes.

Choke collar. A chain or leather collar that gives maximum control over the dog. Tightened or relaxed by the pressure on the lead caused by either pulling of the dog or tautness with which it is held by the handler.

Chops. Pendulous, loose skin creating jowls.

Cloddy. Thickset or overly heavy or low in build.

Close-coupled. Compact in appearance. Short in the loin.

Coarse. Lacking in refinement or elegance.

Coat. The hair which covers the dog.

Companion Dog. The first obedience degree obtainable.

Companion Dog Excellent. The second obedience degree obtainable.

Condition. General health. A dog said to be in good condition is one carrying exactly the right amount of weight, whose coat looks alive and glossy, and that exhibits a general appearance and demeanor of well-being.

Conformation. The framework of the dog, its form and structure.

Coupling. The section of the body known as the loin. A short-coupled dog is one in which the loin is short.

Cow-hocked. Hocks turned inward at the joint, causing the hock joints to approach one another with the result that the feet toe outward instead of straight ahead.

Crabbing. A dog moving with its body at an angle rather than coming straight at you;

otherwise referred to as side-wheeling or side-winding.

Crest. The arched portion of the back of the neck.

Crop. Cut the ear leather, usually to cause the ear to stand erect.

Crossing action. A fault in the forequarters caused by loose or poorly knit shoulders.

Croup. The portion of the back directly above the hind legs.

Cryptorchid. An adult dog with testicles not normally descended. A dog with this condition cannot be shown and is subject to disqualification by the judge.

Cynology. A study of canines.

Dam. Female parent of a dog or bitch.

Dentition. Arrangement of the teeth.

Dewclaws. Extra claws on the inside of the legs. Should generally be removed several days following the puppy's birth. Required in some breeds, unimportant in others, and sometimes a disqualification—all according to the individual breed standard.

Dewlap. Excess loose and pendulous skin at the throat.

Diagonals. The right front and left rear leg make up the right diagonal; the left front and right rear leg the left diagonal. The diagonals correctly move in unison as the dog trots.

Dish-faced. The tip of the nose is placed higher than the stop.

Disqualification. A fault or condition which renders a dog ineligible to compete in organized shows, designated by the breed standard or by the American Kennel Club. Judges must withhold all awards at dog shows from dogs having disqualifying faults, noting in the Judges Book the reason for having done so. The owner may appeal this decision, but a disqualified dog cannot again be shown until it has officially been examined and reinstated by the American Kennel Club.

Distemper teeth. Discolored, badly stained, or pitted teeth. A condition so-called due to its early association with dogs having suffered from this disease.

Divergent hocks. Hock joints turn outward, creating the condition directly opposite to cow-hocks. Frequently referred to as bandy legs or barrel hocks.

Dock. Shorten the tail by cutting it.

Dog. A male of the species. Also used to describe male and female canines collectively.

Dog show. A competition in which dogs have been entered for the purpose of evaluation and to receive the opinion of a judge.

Dog show, all-breeds. A dog show in which classification may be provided, and usually is, for every breed of dog recognized by the American Kennel Club.

Dog show, specialty. A dog show featuring only one breed. Specialty shows are generally considered to be the showcases of a breed, and to win at one is a particularly valued honor and achievement, owing to the high type of competition usually encountered at these events.

Domed. A top-skull that is rounded rather than flat.

Double coat. A coat consisting of a hard, weather-resistant, protective outer covering over a soft, short, close underlayer which provides warmth.

Down-faced. A downward inclination of the muzzle toward the tip of the nose.

Down in pastern. A softness or weakness of the pastern causing a pronounced deviation from the vertical.

Drag. A trail having been prepared by dragging a bag, generally bearing the strong scent of an animal, along the ground.

Drive. The powerful action of the hindquarters which should equal the degree of reach of the forequarters.

Drop ear. Ears carried drooping or folded forward.

Dry head. One exhibiting no excess wrinkle.

Dry neck. A clean, firm neckline free of throatiness or excess skin.

Dual champion. A dog having gained both bench show and field trial championships.

Dudley nose. Flesh-colored nose.

Elbow. The joint of the forearm and upper arm.

Elbow, out at. Elbow pointing away from the body rather than being held close.

Even bite. Exact meeting of the front teeth, tip to tip with no overlap of the uppers or lowers. Generally considered to be less serviceable than the scissors bite, although equally permissible or preferred in some breeds. Also known as level bite.

Ewe neck. An unattractive, concave curvature of the top area of the neckline.

Expression. The typical expression of the breed as one studies the head. Determined largely by the shape of the eye and its placement.

Eyeteeth. The upper canine teeth.

Faking. The altering of the natural appearance of a dog. A highly frowned upon and unethical practice which must lead, upon recognition by the judge, to instant dismissal from the show ring with a notation in the Judges Book stating the reason.

Fancier. A person actively involved in the sport of purebred dogs.

Fancy. The enthusiasts of a sport or hobby. Dog breeders, exhibitors, judges, and others actively involved with purebred dogs as a group comprise the dog fancy.

Fangs. The canine teeth.

F.C.I. Abbreviation of the Federation Cynologique Internationale.

Feathering. The longer fringes of hair that appear on the ears, tail, chest, and legs.

Federation Cynologique Internationale. A canine authority representing numerous countries, principally European, all of which consent to and agree on certain practices and breed identifications.

Feet east and west. An expression used to describe toes on the forefeet turning outward rather than directly forward.

Fetch. Retrieving of game by a dog, or the command for the dog to do so.

Fiddle front. Caused by elbows protruding from the desired closeness to the body, with the result that the pasterns approach one another too closely and the feet toe outward. Thus, resembling the shape of a violin.

Field champion. A dog that has gained the title field champion has defeated a specified number of dogs in specified competition at a series of American Kennel Club licensed or member field trials.

Field trial. A competition for specified Hound or Sporting breeds where dogs are judged according to their ability and style on following a game trail or on finding and retrieving game.

Finishing a dog. Refers to completing a dog's championship, obedience title, or field trial title.

Flank. The side of the body through the loin area.

Flat bone. Bones of the leg which are not round.

Flat-sided. Ribs that are flat down the side rather than slightly rounded.

Fld. Ch. Abbreviation of field champion, used as a prefix before the dog's name.

Flews. A pendulous condition of the inner corners of the mouth.

Flush. To drive birds from cover. To spring at them. To force them to take flight.

Flyer. An especially exciting or promising young dog.

Flying ears. Ears correctly carried dropped or folded that stand up or tend to "fly" upon occasion.

Flying trot. The speed at which you should *never* move your dog in the show ring. All four feet actually briefly leave the ground during each half stride, making correct evaluation of the dog's normal gait virtually impossible.

Forearm. The front leg from elbow to pastern.

Foreface. The muzzle of the dog.

Front. The forepart of the body viewed head-on. Includes the head, forelegs, shoulders, chest, and feet.

Futurity Stakes. A competition at shows or field trials for dogs who are less than twelve months of age and for which puppies are nominated at or prior to birth. Highly competitive among breeders, usually with a fairly good purse for the winners.

Gait. The manner in which a dog walks or trots.

Gallop. The fastest gait. Never to be used in the show ring.

Game. The animals or wild birds which are hunted.

Gay tail. Tail carried high.

Get. Puppies.

Goose rump. Too sloping (steep) in croup.

Groom. To bathe, brush, comb, and trim your dog.

Groups. Refers to the variety groups in which all breeds of dogs are divided.

Gun dog. One that has been specifically trained to work with man in the field for retrieving game that has been shot and for locating live game.

Guns. The persons who do the shooting during field trials.

Gun-shy. Describes a dog that cringes or shows other signs of fear at the sound or sight of a gun.

Hackney action. High lifting of the forefeet in the manner of a hackney pony.

Ham. Muscular development of the upper hind leg. Also used to describe a dog that loves applause while being shown, really going all out when it occurs.

Handler. A person who shows dogs in competition, either as an amateur (without pay) or as a professional (receiving a fee in payment for the service).

Hard-mouthed. A dog that grasps the game too firmly in retrieving, causing bites and tooth marks.

Hare foot. An elongated paw, like the foot of a hare.

Haw. A third eyelid or excess membrane at the corner of the eye.

Heat. The period during which a bitch can be bred. Also referred to as being "in season."

Heel. A command ordering the dog to follow close to the handler.

Hindquarters. Rear assemblage of the dog.

Hie on. A command used in hunting or field trials, urging the dog to go further.

Hock. The joint between the second thigh and the metatarsus.

Hocks well let down. Expression denoting that the hock joint should be placed quite low to the ground.

Honorable scars. Those incurred as a result of working injuries.

In season. *See* **Heat.**

Incisors. The front teeth between the canines.

Int. Ch. An abbreviation of international champion.

International champion. A dog awarded four CACIB cards at F.C.I. dog shows.

Jowls. Flesh of lips and jaws.

Judge. Person making the decisions at a dog show, obedience trial, or field trial. Judges residing in the United States must be approved and licensed by the A.K.C. in order to officiate at events where points toward championship titles are awarded; residents of another country whose governing body is recognized by the A.K.C. may be granted special permits to officiate in the United States.

Kennel. The building in which dogs are housed. Also used when referring to a person's collective dogs.

Knee joint. Stifle joint.

Knitting and purling. Crossing and throw- ing of forefeet as dog moves.

Knuckling over. A double-jointed wrist, or pastern, sometimes accompanied by enlarged bone development in the area, causing the joints to double over under the dog's weight.

Layback. 1) Describes correctly angulated shoulders. 2) Describes a short-faced dog whose pushed-in nose placement is accompanied by undershot jaw.

Leather. The ear flap. Also the skin of the actual nose.

Level bite. Another way of describing an even bite, as teeth of both jaws meet exactly.

Level gait. A dog moving smoothly, topline carried level as he does so, is said to be moving in this manner.

Lippy. Lips that are pendulous or do not fit tightly.

Loaded shoulders. Those overburdened with excessive muscular development.

Loin. Area of the sides between the lower ribs and hindquarters.

Lumber. Superfluous flesh.

Lumbering. A clumsy, awkward gait.

Major. A win of either Winners Dog or Winners Bitch carrying with it three, four, or five points toward championship.

Mane. The long hair growing on the top and upper sides of the neck.

Match show. An informal dog show where no championship points are awarded and entries can usually be made upon arrival, although some require pre-entry. Excellent practice area for future show dogs and for novice exhibitors as the entire atmosphere is relaxed and congenial.

Mate. To breed a dog and a bitch to one another. Littermates are dogs which are born in the same litter.

Maturity Stakes. For members of a particular breed who the previous year had been entered in the Futurity Stakes.

Milk teeth. The first baby teeth.

Miscellaneous Class. A class provided at A.K.C. point shows in which specified breeds may compete in the absence of their own breed classification. Dogs of breeds in the process of becoming recognized by A.K.C. may compete in this class prior to the eventual provision of their own individual breed classification.

Molars. Four premolars are located at either side of the upper and lower jaws. Two molars exist on either side of the upper jaw, three on either side below. Lower molars have two roots; upper molars have three roots.

Monorchid. A dog with only one properly descended testicle. This condition disqualifies a dog from competition at A.K.C. dog shows.

Muzzle. 1) The part of the head in front of the eyes. 2) To fasten something over the mouth, usually to prevent biting.

Nick. A successful breeding that results in puppies of excellent quality.

Non-slip retriever. A dog not expected to flush or to find game; one that merely walks at heel, marks the fall, then retrieves upon command.

Nose. Describes the dog's organ of smell, but also refers to his talent at scenting. A dog with a "good nose" is one adept at picking up and following a scent trail.

Obedience trial. A licensed obedience trial is one held under A.K.C. rules at which it is possible to gain a "leg" towards a dog's obedience title or titles.

Obedience trial champion. Denotes that a dog has attained obedience trial championship under A.K.C. regulations by having gained a specified number of points and first place awards.

Oblique shoulders. Shoulders angulated so as to be well laid back.

Occiput. Upper back point of skull.

Occipital protuberance. A prominent occiput noted in some of the Sporting breeds.

O.F.A. Commonly used abbreviation for Orthopedic Foundation for Animals.

Orthopedic Foundation for Animals. This organization is ready to read the hip radiographs of dogs and certify the existence of or freedom from hip dysplasia. Board-certified radiologists read vast numbers of these files each year.

O.T. Ch. An abbreviation of the obedience trial champion title.

Out at elbow. Elbows are held away from the body rather than in close.

Out at shoulder. Shoulder blades set in such a manner that joints are too wide and jut out from body.

Oval chest. Deep with only moderate width.

Overshot. Upper incisors overlap the lower incisors.

Pacing. A gait in which both right legs and both left legs move concurrently, causing a rolling action.

Paddling. Faulty gait in which the front legs swing forward in a stiff upward motion.

Pad. Thick protective covering of the bottom of the foot. Serves as a shock absorber.

Paper foot. Thin pads accompanying a flat foot.

Pastern. The area of the foreleg between the wrist and the foot.

Pedigree. Written record of dog's lineage.

Pigeon chest. A protruding, short breastbone.

Pigeon-toed. Toes point inward, as those of a pigeon.

Pile. Soft hair making a dense undercoat.

Plume. A long fringe of hair on the tail.

Poach. To trespass on private property when hunting.

Pointed. A dog that has won points toward its championship is referred to as "pointed."

Police dog. Any dog that has been trained to do police work.

Put down. To groom and otherwise prepare a dog for the show ring.

Quality. Excellence of type and conformation.

Racy. Lightly built, appearing overly long in leg and lacking substance.

Rangy. Excessive length of body combined with shallowness through the ribs and chest.

Reach. The distance to which the forelegs reach out in gaiting, which should correspond with the strength and drive of the hindquarters.

Register. To record your dog with the American Kennel Club.

Registration Certificate. The paper you receive denoting that your dog's registration has been recorded with the A.K.C., giving the breed, assigned names, names of sire and dam, date of birth, breeder and owner, along with the assigned Stud Book number of the dog.

Reserve Winners Bitch or **Reserve Winners Dog.** After the judging of Winners Bitch and Winners Dog, the remaining first prize dogs (bitches or dogs) remain in the ring where they are joined by the bitch or dog that placed second in the class to the one awarded Winners Bitch or Winners Dog, provided she or he was defeated only by that one bitch or dog. From these a Reserve Winner is selected. Should the Winners Bitch or Winners Dog subsequently be disallowed due to any error or technicality, the Reserve Winner is then moved up automatically to Winners in the A.K.C. records, and the points awarded to the Winners Bitch or Winners Dog then transfer to the one which placed Reserve. This is a safeguard award, for although it seldom happens, should the winner of the championship points be found to have been ineligible to receive them, the Reserve dog keeps the Winners points.

Roach back. A convex curvature of the top- line of the dog.

Rocking horse. An expression used to describe a dog that has been overly extended in forequarters and hindquarters by the handler, *i.e.,* forefeet placed too far forward, hind feet pulled overly far behind, making the dog resemble a child's rocking horse. To be avoided in presenting your dog for judging.

Rolling gait. An aimless, ambling type of action correct in some breeds but to be faulted in others.

Saddle back. Of excessive length with a dip behind the withers.

Scissors bite. The outer tips of the lower incisors touch the inner tips of the upper incisors. Generally considered to be the most serviceable type of jaw formation.

Second thigh. The area of the hindquarters between the hock and the stifle.

Septum. The vertical line between the nostrils.

Set up. To pose your dog in position for examination by the judge. Same as "stack."

Shelly. A body lacking in substance.

Shoulder height. The height of the dog from the ground to the highest point of the withers.

Sire. The male parent.

Skully. An expression used to describe a coarse or overly massive skull.

Slab sides. Flat sides with little spring of rib.

Soundness. Mental and physical stability. Sometimes used as well to denote the manner in which the dog gaits.

Spay. To neuter a bitch by surgery. Once this operation has been performed, the bitch is no longer eligible for entry in regular classes or in the Veterans Class at A.K.C. shows.

Special. A dog or bitch entered only for Best of Breed competition at a dog show.

Specialty club. An organization devoted to sponsoring an individual breed of dog.

Specialty dog show. *See* **Dog show, specialty.**

Stack. *See* **Set up.**

Stake. A class in field trial competition.

Stance. The natural position a dog assumes in standing.

Standard. The official description of the ideal specimen of a breed. The Standard of Perfection is drawn up by the parent specialty club (usually by a special committee to whom the task is assigned), is approved by the membership and by the American Kennel Club, and then serves as a guide to breeders and to judges in decisions regarding the merit, or lack of it, in evaluating individual dogs.

Stifle. The joint of the hind leg corresponding to a person's knee.

Stilted. The somewhat choppy gait of a dog lacking correct angulation.

Stop. The step-up from nose to skull; the indentation at the juncture of the skull and foreface.

Straight behind. Lacking angulation in the hindquarters.

Straight-shouldered. Lacking angulation of the shoulder blades.

Stud. A male dog that is used for breeding.

Stud book. The official record kept on the breeding particulars of recognized breeds of dogs.

Substance. Degree of bone size.

Swayback. Weakness, or downward curvature, in the topline between the withers and the hipbones.

Sweepstakes. Competition at shows for young dogs, usually up to twelve or eighteen months of age; unlike Futurity, no advance nomination is required.

Tail set. Manner in which the tail is placed on the rump.

T.D. An abbreviation of the Tracking Dog. title.

T.D.X. An abbreviation of the Tracking Dog Excellent title.

Team. Generally consists of four dogs.

Thigh. Hindquarters from the stifle to the hip.

Throatiness. Excessive loose skin at the throat.

Topline. The dog's back from withers to tail set.

Tracking Dog. A title awarded dogs who have fulfilled the A.K.C. requirements at licensed or member club tracking tests.

Tracking Dog Excellent. An advanced tracking degree.

Trail. Hunt by following a trail scent.

Trot. The gait at which the dog moves in a rhythmic two-beat action, right front and left hind foot and left front and right hind foot each striking the ground together.

Tuck-up. A natural shallowness of the body at the loin creating a small-waisted appearance.

Type. The combination of features which makes a breed unique, distinguishing it from all others.

U.D. An abbreviation of the Utility Dog title.

U.D.T. An abbreviation of the Utility Dog Tracker title.

U.D.T.X. An abbreviation of the Utility Dog and Tracker Excellent titles.

Unbenched show. Dog show at which dogs must arrive in time for judging and may leave anytime thereafter.

Undershot. The front teeth of the lower jaw reach beyond the front teeth of the upper jaw.

Upper arm. The foreleg between the forearm and the shoulder blade.

Utility Dog. Another level of obedience degree awarded after the completion of the C.D. and C.D.X. titles.

Utility Dog and Tracker. A double title indicating a dog that has gained both utility and tracking degrees. Also known as Utility Dog Tracking.

Utility Dog and Tracker Excellent. A double title indicating a dog that has gained both utility and advanced tracking degrees.

Walk. The gait in which three feet support the body, each lifting in regular sequence, one at a time, off the ground.

Walleye. A blue eye, fish eye, or pearl eye caused by a whitish appearance of the iris.

W.C. An abbreviation of Working Certificate.

Weedy. Lacking in sufficient bone and substance.

Well let down. Short hocks, hock joint placed low to the ground.

Wet neck. Dewlap, or superfluous skin.

Wheel back. Roached back with topline considerably arched over the loin.

Winners Bitch or Winners Dog. The awards which are accompanied by championship points, based on the number of dogs defeated, at A.K.C. member or licensed dog shows.

Withers. The highest point of the shoulders, right behind the neck.

Working Certificate. An award earned by dogs who have proven their hunting ability and who are not gun-shy.

Wry mouth. Lower jaw is twisted and does not correctly align with the upper jaw.

General Index

Index of People

Index of Kennels